BAJA

NIKKI GOTH ITOI

D1021731

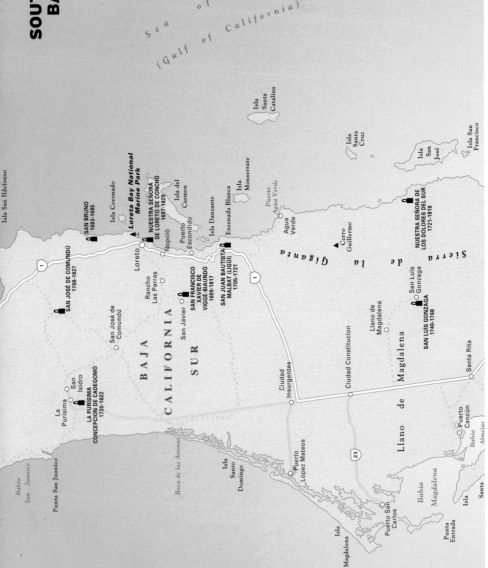

SOUTHERN BAJA

Sea of Cortez
(Gulf of California)

Isla Santa Catalina

Isla Santa Cruz

Isla San José

Isla San Francisco

Isla San Ildefonso

SAN BRUNO 1683-1685

Isla Coronado

Loreta Bay National Marine Park

NUESTRA SEÑORA DE LORETO DE CONCHÓ 1697-1829

Nopoló

Isla del Carmen

Puerto Escondido

Isla Danzante

Ensenada Blanca

Isla Monserrate

Puerto Agua Verde

Agua Verde

NUESTRA SEÑORA DE LOS DOLORES DEL SUR 1721-1818

SAN JOSÉ DE COMUNDÚ 1708-1827

Rancho Las Parras

SAN FRANCISCO XAVIER DE VIGGE-BIAUNDO 1699-1817

San Javier

SAN JUAN BAUTISTA MALBAT (LIGÜÍ) 1705-1721

Loreto

San José de Comundú

▲ Cerro Guillermo

Sierra de la Giganta

San Luis Gonzaga

SAN LUIS GONZAGA 1740-1768

La Purísima

San Isidro

LA PURÍSIMA CONCEPCIÓN DE CADEGOMÓ 1720-1822

BAJA CALIFORNIA SUR

Llano de Magdalena

Ciudad Insurgentes

Ciudad Constitucion

Santa Rita

Llano de Magdalena

Bahía San Juanico

Punta San Juanico

Boca de las Ánimas

Isla Santo Domingo

Puerto López Mateos

Puerto San Carlos

Isla Magdalena

Bahía Magdalena

Isla Santa

Puerto Cancún

Bahía Almejas

Punta Entrada

1

1

23

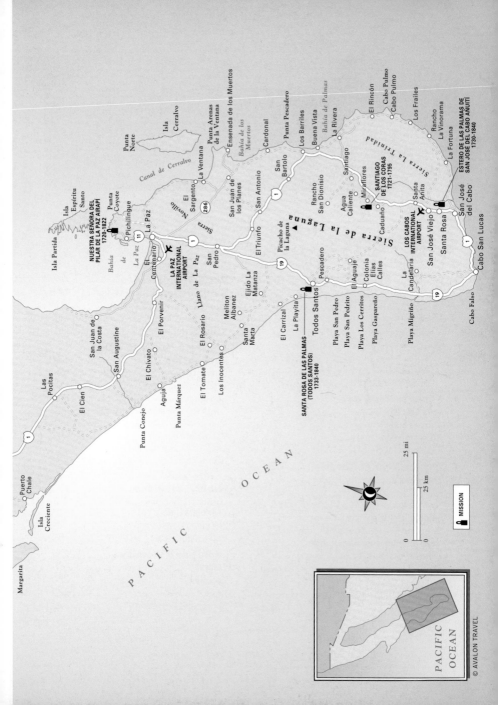

PACIFIC OCEAN

Isla Creciente

Margarita

Puerto Chale

Las Pocitas

San Juan de la Costa

El Cien

San Augustine

El Chivato

El Porvenir

Aguaje

Punta Conejo

Punta Márquez

El Tomate

Los Inocentes

El Rosario

Melitón Albañez

Santa Marta

Ejido La Matanza

San Pedro

Llano de La Paz

Sierra

La Novilla

El Centenario

LA PAZ INTERNATIONAL AIRPORT

La Paz

Bahía de La Paz

Pichilingue

Punta Coyote

NUESTRA SEÑORA DEL PILAR DE LA PAZ AIRAPÍ 1720-1822

Isla Partida

Isla Espíritu Santo

Isla Cerralvo

Punta Norte

Canal de Cerralvo

El Sargento

La Ventana

Punta Arenas de la Ventana

Ensenada de los Muertos

Bahía de los Muertos

(286)

San Juan de los Planes

San Antonio

San Bartolo

San

El Triunfo

Picacho de la Laguna

El Carrizal

La Playita

Todos Santos

SANTA ROSA DE LAS PALMAS (TODOS SANTOS) 1733-1840

Playa San Pedro

Playa San Pedrito

Playa Los Cerritos

Playa Gaspareño

Playa Migriño

El Pescadero

Pescadero

El Aguaje

Colonia Elías Calles

La Candelaria

Sierra de la Laguna

Caduaño

Agua Caliente

Rancho San Dionisio

Santiago

Miraflores

SANTIAGO DE LOS CORAS 1721-1795

Cardonal

Punta Pescadero

Los Barriles

Buena Vista

La Rivera

Bahía de Palmas

El Rincón

Cabo Pulmo

Cabo Pulmo

Los Frailes

Rancho La Vinorama

La Fortuna

ESTERO DE LAS PALMAS DE SAN JOSÉ DEL CABO AÑUITÍ 1730-1840

Sierra La Trinidad

Santa Anita

San José del Cabo

Santa Rosa

San José Viejo

LOS CABOS INTERNATIONAL AIRPORT

Cabo San Lucas

Cabo Falso

19

19

1

1

1

1

11

PACIFIC OCEAN

25 mi

25 km

MISSION

© AVALON TRAVEL

PACIFIC OCEAN

Contents

► **Discover Baja**. 10
  Planning Your Trip 12
  Explore Baja. 16
  • Best of Baja Road Trip. 16
  • Island Hopping. 20
  • Around the Cape in Seven Days . . 21
  • Scuba Diving Tips. 22
  • Four-Day Getaways 24
  • Seaside Romance. 27

► **Tijuana, Rosarito,
  and Tecate**. **29**
  Tijuana and Vicinity 32
  Rosarito and Vicinity 45
  Tecate and Vicinity 52

► **Ensenada to El Rosario** **63**
  Ensenada and Vicinity 66
  Valle de Guadalupe. 81
  Sierra de Juárez 86
  Maneadero to Vicente Guerrero . . . 87
  Sierra de San Pedro Mártir 92
  Valle and Bahía de San Quintín 95
  El Rosario. 99

► **Mexicali to San Felipe**. **100**
  Mexicali 103
  Mexicali to Tecate 112
  San Felipe and Vicinity 114

► **Desierto Central to
  Bahía de los Angeles**. **125**
  Into the Interior. 128
  Bahía de los Angeles. 130
  South of Punta Prieta. 136

► **Guerrero Negro to Bahía
  Concepción** **138**
  Guerrero Negro and Vicinity 141
  Vizcaíno Peninsula 147
  San Ignacio and Vicinity. 155
  Santa Rosalía and Vicinity 163
  Mulegé and Vicinity 169
  Bahía Concepción 176
  La Purísma, Comondú,
    and Vicinity 180

► **Loreto and
  Bahía Magdalena**. **183**
  Loreto and Vicinity 186
  Ensenada Blanca to
    Ciudad Constitución 204
  Bahía Magdalena. 206

► **La Paz and Vicinity** **211**
  Sights 217
  Beaches 220
  Islands 222
  Sports and Recreation 225

Entertainment and Events 235
Shopping 236
Accommodations 238
Food 243
Information and Services 248
Getting There and Around 249
Southeast of La Paz 252

▶ **The East Cape and the**
  Sierra de la Laguna **261**
  Bahía de las Palmas 264
  El Camino Rural Costero 280
  Sierra de la Laguna and Vicinity . . . 289

▶ **Los Cabos** **301**
  San José del Cabo 309
  The Corridor 332
  Cabo San Lucas 340

▶ **The West Cape**
  and Todos Santos **373**
  The West Cape 377
  Todos Santos 385

▶ **Background** **405**
  The Land 405
  Flora 408
  Fauna 411

History 414
Government and Economy 420
People and Culture 421

▶ **Essentials** **424**
  Getting There 424
  Getting Around 429
  Visas and Officialdom 437
  Sports and Recreation 439
  Accommodations and Camping 445
  Food and Drink 447
  Conduct and Customs 450
  Tips for Travelers 451
  Health and Safety 453
  Information and Services 457
  Communications and Media 459

▶ **Resources** **462**
  Glossary 462
  Spanish Phrasebook 463
  Suggested Reading 469
  Internet Resources 472

▶ **Index** **474**

▶ **List of Maps** **483**

Discover Baja

All travelers who make the journey to the tip of the Baja California peninsula remember their first taste of the "real" Baja: The first night spent sleeping in a hammock under a palm shelter by the sea. That chance encounter of a baby sea turtle release. A plunge into a sparkling freshwater pool high in the mountains. The farmer who helped fix a flat tire. Hooking a red snapper from a line cast into the surf.

The typical pattern of discovery goes something like this: Fly to Los Cabos for a short trip to see if Baja is for you. Return for a longer vacation a year later with family or friends in tow. Then plan a sabbatical, take a leave of absence, retire early, or volunteer to shuttle supplies to a local charity – any excuse to spend the first of many seasons exploring every beach and town from Ensenada to Cabo San Lucas.

The Baja California that appeals to these travelers is a land of extremes: a few cities and large towns mixed in with dozens of tiny settlements; desert, tropical, coastal, and mountain environments; communities made up of native Baja California families, mainland Mexican immigrants, and foreign expatriates; historic missions and contemporary art galleries; luxury resorts and rustic fishing camps; *panga* boats and fishing cruisers and 100-foot yachts.

The earliest Spanish explorers believed Baja to be an island. They were wrong about the geography, but their maps captured the spirit of the place. Though we know better now, much of the 800-mile-long peninsula that was once known as Antigua California continues to exist happily outside the mainstream — even as paved highways, international airports, and information technology keep trying to link it to the outside world.

From the multicultural border zone to the heavily visited Los Cabos Corridor, the peninsula's two states, Baja California (Norte) and Baja California Sur, offer contrasting visitor experiences. Wherever you go, you'll find plenty of opportunity for outdoor recreation and environmental education. Indeed, Baja California was an eco-destination long before travel industry marketers invented the term. Kayaking, snorkeling, scuba diving, surfing, stand-up paddle boarding, kiteboarding, sailing, and sportfishing rank among the most popular coastal activities. The interior offers terrain suitable for mountain biking, horseback riding, and wilderness hiking. And when you've worn yourself out in the water or on land, you can shift your focus to cultural experiences and culinary adventure. For those who want to make a difference, there are sea turtle conservation programs, whale-shark research, gray-whale encounters, and numerous other ways to support a worthy cause.

Traveling around Baja is about collecting moments — and forming friendships — that will stay with you forever.

Planning Your Trip

▶ WHERE TO GO

Tijuana, Rosarito, and Tecate

As the peninsula's largest city, Tijuana is a high-risk, high-reward place. Outstanding cuisine, trendsetting nightclubs, and bargain shopping attract loyal weekenders from Southern California. But the stories you hear of drug and sex trafficking, corrupt cops, rip-off artists, and predatory cab drivers are not urban legend. On the Pacific coast to the south, Rosarito draws surfers and college students on spring break. East of Tijuana, Tecate offers a more relaxed border crossing and pleasant town plaza, and serves as a gateway to the Valle de Guadalupe wine country along Mexico 3.

Ensenada to El Rosario

South of the border region, Ensenada has hopping clubs and bars at its north end and a quiet and more upscale *malecón* (waterfront promenade) downtown. Nearby are boutique wineries and empty beaches along Bahía

boulders near the border at Tecate

IF YOU HAVE . . .

- **FOUR DAYS:** Plan a weekend getaway in Valle de Guadalupe wine country, Loreto, La Paz, or San José del Cabo. These destinations are all close to major international airports.

- **SEVEN DAYS:** With a full week, you can complete the Los Cabos–East Cape–La Paz–West Cape loop, book a liveaboard diving or sailing trip, or explore part of the Spanish mission trail.

- **THREE WEEKS:** Three weeks is ample time for driving down the peninsula and back, making stops at all the key towns along the way. It's also enough time to get to know one place really well, so you might opt to rent a condo in Loreto, Todos Santos, La Paz, or Los Cabos and spend your days exploring the immediate vicinity.

- **THREE MONTHS:** Travelers with time on their hands can manage to visit just about every out-of-the-way place, including the peaks of the sierras, Bahía de Los Angeles, the Vizcaíno Peninsula, Laguna San Ignacio, and El Candelaria, plus many of the lesser-known islands, such as Isla Cedros, Isla San Marcos, and Isla Cerralvo.

de San Quintín. El Rosario marks the gateway to the Desierto Central that makes up the peninsula's interior.

Mexicali to San Felipe

Mexicali is the state capital of Baja California (Norte), a regional center of agricultural commerce, and a supply depot for travelers passing through to points south. Its Chinesca district offers a Mexican twist on Chinese cuisine. Nearby are hot springs in the Cañon de Guadalupe and a sizable expat community in San Felipe on the Sea of Cortez. You can hike among towering cacti in the Valle de los Gigantes or camp on secluded beaches near Puertecitos and Bahía San Luis Gonzaga.

Desierto Central to Bahía de los Angeles
Here begins the quintessential Baja. You'll drive through miles of undisturbed desert terrain. Stop to stretch your legs in Cataviña and walk among the boulders. Head west to find waves at The Wall or east to explore the timeless fishing outpost of Bahía de los Angeles on the Sea of Cortez.

Guerrero Negro to Bahía Concepción
Guerrero Negro marks the state line between Baja California (Norte) and Baja California Sur. From mission towns to mining towns and prehistoric rock art sites, this region is rich with opportunities for cultural exploration. On the Pacific coast are two lagoons where gray whales come to bear their calves. On the Gulf coast, the shallow bays of Bahía Concepción are ideal for paddling, snorkeling, and cruising.

Loreto and Bahía Magdalena
The site of the first permanent Jesuit mission, Loreto has a deep-rooted history. Today it is becoming a government-sponsored tourist corridor that entertains visitors with full-service resorts, sportfishing charters, and a national marine park. Nearby, San Javier gives a taste of life in the isolated interior. Across the peninsula, on the Pacific, gray whales congregate in Bahía Magdalena during the winter months.

La Paz and Vicinity

Known for its beautiful sunsets and lively *malecón scene,* La Paz is an authentic Mexican city with a strong mainland influence. White-sand beaches along the Pichilingue Peninsula invite relaxation, while Isla Espíritu Santo and other protected islands offshore support a rare and fragile ecosystem.

The East Cape and the Sierra de la Laguna

Travelers with a passion for water sports and a willingness to rough it will find paradise along the Gulf coast. This is a place of solar power, dirt roads, *panga* boats, and *palapa* restaurants. The Sea of Cortez offers secluded beaches, steady winter winds, abundant game fish, a living coral reef, and 30-meter visibility underwater in summer. Inland, the Sierra de la Laguna attracts hikers and horseback riders with cascading waterfalls and 2,100-meter peaks.

Los Cabos

Los Cabos (The Capes) refers to the towns of San José del Cabo and Cabo San Lucas at the tip of the Baja Peninsula. One entertains

sunrise boat ride on the Sea of Cortez

the young and young at heart, while the other offers a more sophisticated scene of gourmet restaurants and fine art.

The West Cape and Todos Santos

Along the Pacific coast, a rugged shoreline extends from Cabo San Lucas north to the growing artist community of Todos Santos. The West Cape remains the least-developed stretch of coastline on either side of the peninsula south of La Paz.

► WHEN TO GO

Northwestern Baja

Northwestern Baja enjoys a mild Pacific climate, which makes it comfortable year-round. High season is May-October, when the sun shines the brightest and beaches are warmest. To get away from the crowds and enjoy low-season prices, visit October-April. December–February can be chilly and cloudy.

Mountains

Summer is the season to hike in the Sierras, as temperatures stay comfortably cool above 1,500 meters (5,000 ft.). Expect a winter-like climate at higher elevations October–April.

Deserts

The desert is prettiest after the rainy season, usually in November, when flowering cacti fill the landscape with splashes of color. Daytime temperatures are dangerously hot May–October, but the rest of the year is fine for exploration. Remember that nights in the desert can be cold at any time of year.

Sea of Cortez Coast

Along Baja's Gulf coast, moderate temperatures prevail October–mid-June. In summer and early fall, the weather can be uncomfortably hot and many businesses close while their owners flee to cooler temperatures in the north. The busiest tourist season is November–March, even though for most visitors the northern stretch of coastline is too cold for swimming at this time. You can pursue a variety of water sports year-round from Loreto to Cabo, even in the winter. Fishing and diving are best in summer.

Los Cabos

The tip of the Baja Peninsula, from San José del Cabo to Cabo San Lucas, is pleasantly warm throughout the year. The best travel season for Los Cabos depends on your activity of choice. Anglers and scuba divers prefer summer, when the game fish are running and the Sea of Cortez reaches its warmest temperatures. The air on land can be intolerably hot this time of year. Head to the Pacific coast if you need to cool off. Surfers flock to beaches on the Pacific in winter to catch the north swell, and they choose the Corridor or the East Cape when the summer swell rolls in from the south. Winter brings gray whales to the shallow birthing lagoons along the Pacific. It's also the windy season for kiteboarders and windsurfers.

► BEFORE YOU GO

Passports and Other Documents

Passports are now required for U.S. citizens. If you are driving your own vehicle, bring two copies of your Mexican auto liability insurance policy, plus road maps and at least a basic auto repair kit.

Transportation

Buy round-trip airfare to San Diego, Tijuana, Loreto, La Paz, or Los Cabos. Reserve a rental car for pickup at the airport, or plan to take a shuttle or taxi into town and use public transportation to get around.

agave growing in Tecate

Explore Baja

▶ BEST OF BAJA ROAD TRIP

The road may be paved now and fuel much easier to come by than in the early days of peninsular travel, but Baja California remains a classic route for travelers who enjoy the thrill of a long road trip. All you need is ample time, a reliable vehicle, and an ability to cope with unpredictable situations. This itinerary follows Mexico 1 from the border crossing in Tecate to the Los Cabos tourist corridor at the southern tip of the peninsula, 1,600 kilometers away, with a few options for side trips and off-highway scenic drives along the way.

Day 1

Cross the U.S.-Mexico border at Tecate early in the day and pick up some *pan dulce* at El Mejor Pan de Tecate or tour the Tecate brewery before you head southwest along Mexico 3. Visit a couple of wineries in the Valle de Guadalupe on the way to Ensenada. Explore the downtown promenade, order fish tacos of the Mercado de Mariscos, and spend the night at one of the modest hotels in town.

Day 2

Head south on Mexico 1 and take the turn-off to La Bufadora to watch seawater explode out of a blowhole in the rocks. Return to the highway and head south toward San Quintín. At low tide, dig for clams along Playa Santa María. Then continue on to El Rosario and book a room at the Baja Cactus Motel. Try the famous lobster roll at Mama Espinoza's. If you're in a hurry to reach destinations farther south and have the stamina for a long day of driving, you can skip some of these northern attractions and overnight at Guerrero Negro instead.

A crowd gathers at La Bufadora.

Day 3

Buy fresh tortillas and stock up on water and groceries in El Rosario. Then prepare to make the four-hour trip across the desert. A wonderland of cacti—some of them 13 meters tall and hundreds of years old—extends from highway to horizon in all directions. Giant boulder piles, roadside shrines, and jagged peaks of the Sierra de la Asamblea complete the picture. Fill up on gas in Cataviña if the station is open, and stay overnight if daylight is waning; otherwise, continue to Guerrero Negro.

Day 4

Walk along the salt flats in the morning, and if it's winter, consider a half-day trip to Laguna Ojo de Liebre to encounter pairs of newborn gray whales and their mothers. A 145-kilometer drive from Guerrero Negro leads to the palm oasis of San Ignacio. Tour the historic mission, arrange a guided trip to nearby cave paintings, or in winter head west to Laguna San Ignacio to see the gray whales.

Days 5-6

Today's journey brings the first glimpse of the Sea of Cortez as you descend into the historic silver mining town of Santa Rosalía (74 km from San Ignacio). Walk the busy streets, visit the hilltop museum, and note the French influence that lingers from its days as a company town. In the afternoon, follow Mexico 1 to Mulegé, 134 kilometers farther south. Spend a couple nights at a bed-and-breakfast along the river, or camp on a beach along Bahía Concepción. Spend the next two days wandering the town; book a day of diving through Cortez Explorers; snorkel the beaches along Bahía Concepción; or arrange a guided tour of the nearby cave paintings.

Days 7-9

Pack up for the 135-kilometer (2.5-hr.) drive south to Loreto. Settle in for a few days to

balcony at an inn in La Paz

enjoy the opportunities for outdoor recreation in the national marine park. Stroll around the plaza, tour the small museum, and enjoy fresh seafood in open-air restaurants.

SIDE TRIP
Visit one of the best-preserved Jesuit missions on the peninsula in the tiny village of San Javier, a 36-kilometer drive southwest of Loreto.

Day 10
This is a travel day to La Paz, 367 kilometers south on Mexico 1. Allow six hours for the trip, including a brief stop for gas and food in the agricultural supply center of Ciudad Constitución. Book a room near the *malecón* in La Paz and head out by foot in time to catch the sunset.

SIDE TRIP
During whale-watching season (Nov.–Mar.), Puerto San Carlos on Bahía Magdalena is worth a side trip west from Ciudad Insurgentes (57 km).

Day 11
Spend at least one day at the beach or in the water. Explore the pristine beaches along

Bahía de La Paz, finishing the day at breezy Playa El Tecolote, 30 minutes from downtown. Or book a day of diving or kayaking and snorkeling at Isla Espíritu Santo.

Day 12
Shop for souvenirs, supplies, and gifts in the morning; then stock up on groceries and prepare to begin the loop around the southernmost part of Baja. Next up: the East Cape. It's a 90-minute drive through the mountains and mining-turned-farming towns of El Triunfo,

off-road excursion along the East Cape

San Antonio, and San Bartolo. Los Barriles has several modest hotels, RV campgrounds, a kiteboarding/windsurfing camp, and some private vacation rentals; a half-hour farther south, Cabo Pulmo has more primitive lodging in solar-powered *casitas* and three dive operators. In between are a handful of fishing lodges and private vacation rentals.

SIDE TRIP

During the windy season (Nov.–Mar.), add one day of travel and drive 40 kilometers southeast from La Paz along BCS 286 to Bahía de La Ventana and the neighboring villages of La Ventana and El Sargento. Watch the colorful sails of kiteboarders and windsurfers gliding through the chop; or pile into a *panga* for a day of diving at Isla Cerralvo across the channel. Return to Mexico 1 via the newly paved road that connects San Juan de los Planes to San Antonio.

Day 13

Spend today playing on, in, or near the Sea of Cortez; then continue the cape loop to the southernmost tip of the peninsula. Prepare for culture shock as you enter the scenic Los Cabos Corridor. After two weeks of relative isolation, the mega-resorts and developed tourist infrastructure of San José del Cabo and Cabo San Lucas may come as a surprise.

Wander the streets surrounding the plaza and Boulevard Mijares to get a feel for San José del Cabo. Browse the galleries and splurge on a late lunch or early dinner in the Historic Art District. Continue along the Transpeninsular Highway to Cabo San Lucas if you're in the mood for late-night entertainment.

Day 14

Snorkel at Playa Chileno or Playa Santa María on the Corridor. Book a massage at one of the five-star resorts if the mood strikes and budget allows. Tour the marina and downtown area of Cabo San Lucas, and take a water taxi to Playa del Amor and El Arco at Land's End. Stay the night to enjoy the lively bar and disco scene around town.

Day 15

Now it's time to point the GPS north and explore the West Cape and Todos Santos. Follow Mexico 19 out of Cabo San Lucas. Look for surf, or just have a picnic at one of the rugged beaches west of the highway. Continue north to Km. 64 and Playa Los Cerritos. Swim, boogie board, or surf at one of the only sheltered beaches along the West Cape. Then make your way to accommodations on the beach in El Pescadero (Km. 62) or in the town of Todos Santos a few kilometers farther north.

beachfront surf shop at Playa Los Cerritos

ISLAND HOPPING

Whether you are already a pro or are picking up a paddle for the very first time, kayaks are a perfect way to experience Sea of Cortez marinelife up close. Whales, flying mantas, and sea turtles are just some of the creatures you might see from the surface. Throw on a mask and fins, and an entire world becomes visible below. Beach camping on uninhabited islands completes the experience. Overnight trips can take a couple of days, a full week, or more; organized trips are an appealing option, especially for novices.

WHERE TO GO

Mulegé to Loreto

Many kayakers begin their Baja expedition paddling the islands of **Carmen** and **Danzante,** offshore from Loreto, for a week or more. Protected by land on three sides, 14-mile-long **Bahía Concepción** between Mulegé and Loreto is a good choice for novice kayakers who want to try a multiday paddle. It takes 5-7 days to complete the coastal trip from Mulegé to Loreto.

Loreto to La Paz

A more ambitious coastal route begins in Loreto and ends in La Paz, taking in the nearby island of **Espíritu Santo** at the finish. This 65-mile paddle usually takes 8-10 days. For a shorter trip, make La Paz your home base and spend two or three days camping on the islands offshore.

Bahía de los Angeles

With its many islets and islands, Bahía de los Angeles appeals to kayakers of all levels, though the strong channel currents require some caution.

Pacific Coast

Conditions are much rougher on the Pacific, even in the most protected parts of the coast. Experienced kayakers head to **Punta Banda,** an inlet-scalloped cape near Ensenada. **Bahía Magdalena,** a large, protected bay in southern Baja, attracts many kayakers during the winter whale-watching season.

WHEN TO GO

Temperatures are hottest July-September, and winds are strongest November-February, making March-May the best months for a long-distance paddle. Whale-watching trips take place on the Pacific coast November-March.

Day 16

Head northwest across the *huerta* to *el otro lado,* the other side of Todos Santos, where you can catch waves, cast a fishing line in the surf, or simply stroll the beach at Playa La Pastora. In winter, watch for flying mantas and whales breaching just offshore. Around 3 P.M., drive south to Punta Lobos to watch local fishermen unload their fresh catch, and buy some dorado (mahimahi) or *huachinango* (red snapper) for dinner.

Days 17-18

Complete the cape loop along Mexico 19 by returning to La Paz, where you'll pick up Mexico 1 again. Now it's time to begin retracing your steps, filling in any missed sights or optional side trips along the way. Spend the first night in Loreto after a seven-hour drive, and the next in San Ignacio (5 hrs.) or Guerrero Negro (7 hrs.).

Days 19-20

Leave the state of Baja California Sur early in the morning and head back across the desert to El Rosario (5 hrs.) or San Quintín (6 hrs.).

Day 21

Follow Mexico 1 north to the last military checkpoint at Maneadero. At El Sauzal, north of Ensenada, choose between the toll road north to Tijuana or Mexico 3, which heads northeast to Tecate (105 km). Savor one last meal of tacos and cerveza. Then cross the border and leave Baja behind, for now.

► AROUND THE CAPE IN SEVEN DAYS

Travelers with a week or more can experience the many dimensions of the lower Baja Peninsula by making a circular route around the region via paved highways Mexico 1 and Mexico 19. Extending a total distance of approximately 564 kilometers, this route takes visitors along the lower slopes of the Sierra de la Laguna, through the sierra's former mining towns, across the plains of La Paz, and along the coastlines of the East and West Capes as well as the Corridor between San José del Cabo and Cabo San Lucas.

It's possible to complete the loop by bus, but expect to do a fair amount of walking to get from the stops along the highway to the scenic coastal areas. A rental car affords more flexibility and convenience, and you can park easily in all the towns along the route.

This loop can be driven in two or three days, but since there are many towns worth exploring and activities to enjoy at each stop, most travelers prefer to allow a week or longer. For more of an adventure, consider widening the loop by taking the sandy Camino Rural Costero (Rural Coastal Road) from San José del Cabo to La Ribera.

Day 1

Arrive at Los Cabos International Airport (SJD); transfer to a hotel in downtown San José del Cabo and spend the evening around town. Browse galleries in the Historic Art District and Mexican fire opal stores downtown before sitting down to a leisurely dinner of contemporary Mexican cuisine.

Day 2

Drive to Cabo Pulmo via Mexico 1 (1–1.5 hrs.), exiting at La Ribera and heading east to pick up the coastal road. The last few miles will be on dirt road. Head straight for the beach and spend the rest of the day snorkeling the live coral reef that comes all the way into shore. Order fish tacos and an icy *michelada* at one of several outdoor eateries. Book your activity of choice, such as fishing, kayaking, snorkeling, or diving, for the next morning.

shopping for *artesanía* in San José del Cabo's Historic Art District

SCUBA DIVING TIPS

Certified divers have some difficult choices to make when planning a trip to the Sea of Cortez. Wherever you go, you'll encounter one of the world's richest marine ecosystems, with sea lions, sea turtles, whale sharks, manta rays, amberjacks, and schooling hammerheads all living among the islands, seamounts, and bays in the sea. Water temperatures are comfortable most of the year; visibility rarely falls below 6 meters and can exceed 30 meters on the best of days.

For those divers who are seriously dedicated to the sport, liveaboard trips are another option to consider while visiting Baja.

WHERE TO DIVE
Cabo San Lucas

If you choose to stay close to the lively scene in Cabo San Lucas, short boat rides are an advantage to diving here; crowds and noise from harbor traffic are the main deterrents.

A **deep submarine canyon** just 45 meters offshore offers exciting underwater topography for experienced divers. The canyon is known for its **"sand falls,"** streams of falling sand channeled between rocks along the canyon walls. But even when the rivers aren't running, the dive offers varied marine life, large and small.

Another popular dive from Cabo San Lucas begins in the surge under a sea lion colony on the Sea of Cortez side of **Land's End** and concludes with an underwater swim around to the Pacific side.

Cabo Pulmo

Alternatively, you can sacrifice nightlife and amenities to explore the **living coral reef** and national marine park offshore from Cabo Pulmo in the East Cape region. The coral attracts a wide variety of fish of all sizes and colors; other smaller reefs, as well as shipwrecks, lie in the general vicinity. Drift dives are common here, and boat rides are short. Several sites, including a **sea lion colony,** are ideal for novices.

La Paz

The islands and seamounts offshore from La Paz harbor some of the most exciting underwater topography and the largest marine creatures in the sea. Boat rides are long – an hour or more – and currents tend to be strong at these sites. The reward is the chance to experience the deep blue and to spot some of the largest pelagics in the sea. An advanced dive site called **El Bajo** is famous for its summer population of giant manta rays and, in summer, schooling hammerhead sharks. Beginners will enjoy dives in the bays around **Isla Espíritu Santo** and the sea lion colony at **Los Islotes.**

WHEN TO DIVE

From La Paz south, onshore water temperatures are around 21°C (70°F) in winter and 29°C (85°F) in summer and early fall. Water visibility is best July–October, when it exceeds 30 meters; this is also when the air temperature is warmest, often reaching well over 32°C (90°F).

Dive shops are a common sight along the Sea of Cortez.

EXCURSION

At Santiago, head west to reach the Cañon de la Zorra and a 10-meter waterfall, just a 10-minute walk from the parking lot.

ALTERNATE ROUTE

To avoid the off-road driving and relatively primitive accommodations, skip Cabo Pulmo and stay on Mexico 1 until Los Barriles, popular with anglers, kiteboarders, and stand-up paddlers.

Day 3

Spend the morning out at sea, and in the afternoon continue north along Mexico 1 to La Paz (1.5–2 hrs.), stopping to explore the ghost towns of San Antonio and El Triunfo along the way. Check into a downtown hotel and walk the *malecón* at sunset. Enjoy seafood *cocteles* at Mariscos Moyeyo's or *arranchera* at Rancho Viejo; then head out for drinks at Tailhunter Bar & FUBAR Cantina or Bar Salipuedes on the *malecón,* or catch a music performance at one of many cultural venues around town.

Day 4

Take a *panga* shuttle to Isla Espíritu Santo for a day of kayaking and snorkeling, or book a day of diving. Alternatively, paddle or drive to a few of the beaches along the Pichilingue Peninsula. Enjoy the views from one of the waterfront seafood restaurants at Playa El Tecolote. Spend the next morning exploring the Museo Regional de Antropología e Historia in downtown La Paz and shopping for pottery and other crafts.

Depart La Paz in the afternoon, heading south on Mexico 1 to Mexico 19, which leads to Todos Santos (45 minutes). Check into a boutique hotel in town, such as the Todos Santos Inn or Casa Bentley, or choose a vacation rental near the beach. For dinner, savor tacos *al pastor* at El Pastorcito, tapas and made-in-Baja wines at La Casita, or homemade Italian fare at Tres Galline.

EXCURSION

In winter, travelers with extra time can add a day for a gray-whale encounter in Bahía Magdalena, approximately 3.5 hours by car from La Paz.

Day 5

Walk the historic district in Todos Santos, with brick buildings and colorful facades that date back to the late 19th century, when the

silver mine ruins in the ghost town of El Triunfo

town was Baja's sugarcane capital. Admire the artwork in a few of the town's dozen galleries. Drive north along the coast to Playa La Pastora or south along Mexico 19 to Playa Los Cerritos, at Km. 64, to stroll the beach in the afternoon. Continue south along Mexico 19 to reach Cabo San Lucas before dark (1 hr.). Check into a hotel in downtown Cabo San Lucas or a resort along the Corridor, such as the Sirena del Mar Welk Resort. For dinner, make a reservation at Patagonia steakhouse or Romeo and Juliet for an Italian meal.

Day 6

Hire a water taxi, paddle a kayak, or rent a WaveRunner to visit Playa del Amor, or plan a day of fishing or diving out of Cabo San Lucas. Wander the shops and enjoy afternoon cocktails at The Nowhere Bar or the Giggling Marlin along the marina. Take a nap so you can rally for the nightlife at Cabo Wabo or El Squid Roe after dark.

Rent watercraft to visit Playa del Amor.

Day 7

Schedule a massage for your last morning in paradise. Take a dip in the pool, hit the shops, and return to the airport with sand in your shoes.

▶ FOUR-DAY GETAWAYS

Winter blues got you down? Looking to escape muggy summer days at home? A long weekend in the dry Baja sun may be just the answer. Travelers based in the western United States can reach San Diego, Ensenada, Loreto, La Paz, or Los Cabos by air in a matter of hours. From these international airports, a variety of weekend itineraries are possible. Here are just three of the options.

Wine Country
DAY 1

Cross the U.S.–Mexico border at San Ysidro after the morning rush hour and head south through Tijuana and onto the toll road. Stop in Rosarito for lunch at El Nido. Sit in the shaded back patio if it's not too hot and try the locally raised quail and venison dishes. Walk off lunch by cutting through the Rosarito Beach Hotel and onto the pier that runs 600 yards out over the Pacific.

The total driving time from Tijuana to Ensenada will be less than two hours on the Cuota (toll road) and around 2.5 hours on the Libre (free road), depending on traffic. When you arrive in Ensenada, check into the Corona Hotel. Hit the downtown area for dinner, and then head north to Hussong's Cantina for a beer. If the spirit moves you, walk to the corner and join the party at Papas and Beer until the wee hours of the morning.

DAY 2

If you weren't out too late and you've called

ahead, hop on a chartered fishing boat with Sergio's Sportfishing Center. Back on the docks, take your catch to vendors in the Mercado de Mariscos to have them cook up a custom batch of fish tacos.

Spend the afternoon strolling the shops along López Mateos and visit La Esquina de Bodegas for some preliminary wine tasting. In the late afternoon make your way north out of Ensenada to Route 3. A green overhead sign will welcome you to the Ruta del Vino. Check into the Tuscan-style La Villa del Valle for the next two nights, and grab a casual dinner at La Casa Vieja.

DAY 3

After breakfast at the Villa, hang out by the pool until you are ready to explore some of the surrounding wineries. Enjoy tastings at Baron Balché, Monte Xanic, and Chateau Camou. Carefully choose the single bottle you're allowed to take back home.

Retreat to the Villa del Valle for some much-earned rest. For dinner, get directions to Restaurant Laja.

DAY 4

An after-breakfast massage at the hotel will prepare you for the drive home. If you have

time, grab a lobster roll in Puerto Nuevo on your way north. Get to the border crossing before 3 P.M. on a weekday. If you're crossing on a Sunday, you'll have plenty of time to reflect on your trip as you crawl through traffic back into the United States.

Loreto
DAY 1

Arrive midday at Loreto International Airport and check in to Las Cabañas de Loreto, Coco Cabañas, or La Damiana. Stroll Plaza Salvatierra and follow the paseo to the *malecón* as the sun sinks into the Sierra de la Giganta behind you. Mingle with local expats over dinner at 1697 or Papagayo Cantando, or sample the legendary fish tacos at El Rey del Taco.

DAY 2

Rise early to spend the day fishing, kayaking, diving, or touring the islands in the Loreto Bay National Marine Park directly offshore. Then reward yourself with a traditional Mexican meal at La Picazón and drinks at the second-story, open-air Bar Eclipse.

DAY 3

Visit one of the best-preserved Jesuit missions on the peninsula in the tiny village of

courtyard at Las Cabañas de Loreto

San Javier, a 36-kilometer drive southwest of Loreto. Finish the day with a meal at Del Borracho Saloon and Grill.

DAY 4

Take an early morning walk along the waterfront. Browse the shops near the plaza for souvenirs. Take one last dip in the pool, and then it's time to say goodbye.

San José del Cabo

DAY 1

Arrive at Los Cabos International Airport (SJD); transfer to a hotel in downtown San José or a resort along the Corridor. Consider the Yuca Inn for a budget room, El Encanto Suites for modest accommodations, or Casa Natalia for an upscale experience. If it's Thursday, browse open galleries on the weekly evening Art Walk in downtown San José. Order a homemade tamale from Tamales Doña Nina on the plaza. Savor the tastes of *alta cocina mexicana* at one of San José's stylish restaurants, such as La Panga Antigua, Tequila Restaurant, or Don Emiliano.

DAY 2

Grab a pastry for breakfast at the French Riviera or drive to The Container at the Puerto Los Cabos Marina for brunch. Later, snorkel the rock reefs at Playa Chileno or

An egret keeps watch over a *panga* fishing marina.

Playa Santa María, looking for green moray eels, spotted eagle rays, and schools of tropical fish; or catch some waves at Playa Costa Azul. Book a sunset horseback-riding tour along Playa California, the beach that fronts the hotel zone in San José del Cabo. In the evening, enjoy a seafood dinner at an oceanview restaurant along the Corridor, such as Puerta Vieja or Sunset da Mona Lisa. Finish the night with music at Morgan's Restaurant and Cellar or a pint of Baja Blond at the Baja Brew Pub near the plaza in San José.

DAY 3

Head out for a day of fishing from La Playita or surfing at Playa Costa Azul. Alternatively, you could travel to Cabo San Lucas to go diving. Or browse the many interior design shops in San José, dreaming of ways to decorate your own vacation home. Better yet, sign up for a massage at one of the luxurious spas at the Westin Los Cabos, Marquis Los Cabos, or Esperanza Resort.

Head to El Chilar for contemporary Mexican food centered around the chile or Pier 19 Seafood Bar for raw oysters. Afterward, head to the Tropicana Bar and Grill on Boulevard Mijares for regional Mexican music or Shooters rooftop bar for a livelier scene.

Excursion

To see a more remote side of Baja, drive to La Playita (15 min.) and head north along the Camino Costero Rural (Rural Coastal Road). Stop for lunch or dinner at Buzzard's Bar and Grill in Laguna Hills.

DAY 4

Last chance to work on a tan by the pool. Stroll Boulevard Mijares one last time to pick up gifts and souvenirs at Sol Dorado or Antigua Los Cabos. Pack your bags and leave in time for lunch at Mariscos Mazatlán II on your way to the airport.

Cabo San Lucas

DAY 1

Arrive at Los Cabos International Airport (SJD); transfer to accommodations in downtown Cabo San Lucas or a resort along the Corridor. Consider Casa Bella for a central location or the Hotel Solmar for a quieter setting. Head to Playa El Médano to dip your feet in the bay. Order a cocktail at Nikki Beach or the Mango Deck and watch the sun sink behind the arch at Land's End.

After dark, explore downtown Cabo San

SEASIDE ROMANCE

Weddings, honeymoons, and anniversaries often inspire romance. Here are just a few of the ways to celebrate the occasion.

MOST ROMANTIC RESORTS

- The luxury suites at **Dreams Los Cabos** are a favorite for celebrating special occasions.

- Select linens for your bed from a menu when you check in at **Las Ventanas al Paraíso.** Then enjoy a private movie showing on the beach at night.

- The remote setting on the Pacific coast and no-kids policy of **Pueblo Bonito Pacifica** appeals to those in search of a quieter Los Cabos experience. Oceanview rooms have private plunge pools at **Capella Pedregal.**

MOST INTIMATE BOUTIQUE HOTELS

- Watch stunning sunsets from the pool or bar at **Posada de las Flores,** on the *malecón* in La Paz or enjoy the historic setting at **El Ángel Azul** bed and breakfast.

- Relax in European surroundings at **Casa Natalia,** in the heart of downtown San José del Cabo, or retreat from the bustle of Cabo San Lucas at the beautifully restored **Casa Bella.**

BEST CANDLELIGHT DINNERS

- In the heart of downtown La Paz, sample creative *bajacaliforniano* cuisine at **Las Tres Vírgenes** or choose Italian ambience at **Caffé Milano.**

- Try the six-course tasting menu at **Don Emiliano** in San José.

- Reserve a private booth at **Don Manuel's,** the signature restaurant inside the Capella Pedregal resort.

- Head to **Café Santa Fe** in Todos Santos or bring a picnic to **Playa Palmilla** and watch the sun set into the Pacific.

BEST BEACHES TO WALK AT SUNSET

- Watch surfers catch their last waves of the day at **Playa Costa Azul,** just outside San José del Cabo.

- See the sun melt into the Pacific from **Playa Solmar,** which runs along the southwestern edge of the Cape.

- Observe the birds in action along the **Estero San José,** just outside San José del Cabo, or at **Playa Las Pocitas,** near Todos Santos.

BEST SPAS

- Enjoy treatment rooms with a view at the **Marquis Los Cabos.**

- Heavenly body wraps and oceanside massages set the mood at the **Westin Los Cabos,** near San José del Cabo.

- Soak in the indoor steam caves and waterfalls at **Esperanza,** close to Cabo San Lucas.

SHOPAHOLICS, REJOICE

- Browse **contemporary fine art** on display in the galleries of Todos Santos and San José

- Find a **Mexican fire opal** in one of San José's jewelry shops.

- Watch artisans making ceramics at **Ibarra's Pottery** in La Paz. Admire the designer furnishings at Casa Paulina in downtown San José.

Lucas by foot, taking in the shops and clubs along Boulevard Marina. Savor the seafood at Mocambo de Los Cabos. Then head to Cabo Wabo for live music. Finish the evening with a Cuban cigar at Hemingway's.

DAY 2

Pack a beach bag and hire a water taxi to take you to Playa del Amor, or rent a kayak and paddle there yourself before the wind kicks up. Sunbathe on the beach and snorkel around Pelican Rock before catching a boat ride back to town. Head to Las Gardenias or La Fonda for an authentic Mexican lunch. Spend the afternoon browsing the shops in Plaza Bonita and the Puerto Paraíso mall, and head to the rooftop Baja Brew Pub at Cabo Villas for drinks and a sunset view. In the evening, enjoy Argentinian-style grilled steak at Patagonia or shellfish at Maro's Shrimp House, followed by live jazz at Edith's.

DAY 3

Grab a latte at Theory Café in Plaza Bonita or a full breakfast at Mama's Royal Café before you head out for a day at sea. Bring lunch, and spend most of the day on a guided fishing, kayaking, diving, or snorkeling tour. Don't forget the sunblock; and divers, remember to allow 24 hours before your return flight. When you return, take a nap or lounge by the pool before another night out on the town. Head to DOC Wine Bar for a glass of made-in-Baja wine. For dinner, try Desperado's for Tex-Mex, Cabo Wabo for tequila shrimp, or Nick-San for a blowout sushi experience.

Start the night's festivities at the Giggling Marlin or The Nowhere Bar on the waterfront. Then move to Barometro or one of Cabo's notorious late-night discos, such as El Squid Roe. If it's a Saturday, check out the Latin rock music at Desperado's.

Excursion

The bohemian town of Todos Santos, with art galleries, organic markets, and a small historic district, is just an hour away by car.

DAY 4

Browse the traditional Mexican handicrafts at the Marina Mercado or the silver jewelry at Taxco or Joyería Albert. Admire ceramic sculptures at the Sergio Bustamante gallery and professional photographs of Baja California in the Tomas Spangler gallery. Take one last chance to fill your shoes with sand at Playa El Médano. Then off to the airport you go.

artesanía for sale on Playa El Médano

TIJUANA, ROSARITO, AND TECATE

Whether you end up loving it or hating it, Northwestern Baja makes a vivid first impression. As a dynamic border zone between Mexico and the United States, the region encompassing Tijuana, Rosarito, and Tecate has a complex, multicultural identity shaped by rapid economic growth, immigration, and the harsh reality of sharing a border with a much wealthier country. The change in scenery as you cross from Alta to Baja California is shocking and depressing. The lush green lawns and newly paved streets of San Diego become dusty roads and shantytowns on the outskirts of Tijuana, with signs of industrial pollution all around. Downtown Tijuana has modern skyscrapers, glitzy shopping malls, and wealthy residential neighborhoods, but you have to walk or drive through the less attractive parts of the city to get to them.

As the gateway to Baja California, Tijuana marked its 121st birthday in July 2010. But the event was not the celebration it might have been a few years ago. This one-of-a-kind city once lured hundreds of thousands of visitors a day to cross the border and spend their dollars. They came to shop, eat, and party. Some went home that day, others stayed the weekend, and a few simply passed through on their way to coastal attractions farther south. Caesar salad, Tecate beer, Nortec music, and trendsetting nightclubs all were part of the experience. In recent years, headlines of gruesome narco-crimes have scared all but the hardiest gringos away; European and Mexican visitors have taken over the cafés and bars along Avenida Revolución. And the city is struggling to cope with the dramatic loss in

HIGHLIGHTS

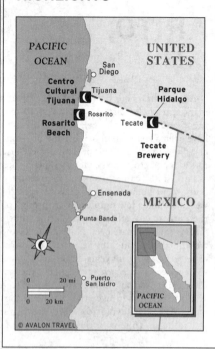

◖ Centro Cultural Tijuana: Experience the art, history, and culture of Baja California at this complex covering eight acres in downtown Tijuana (page 34).

◖ Rosarito Beach: A string of mega-clubs along Rosarito Beach provide 24/7 entertainment for college students from the United States during the annual spring break holiday (page 46).

◖ Parque Hidalgo: Food and festivities center around Tecate's shady plaza, making it a suitable launch point for a Northern Baja adventure (page 53).

◖ Tecate Brewery: Tour the plant that produces Baja's most popular brew. Located on the site of the original keg brewery, today's operation uses modern, high-tech equipment to produce 40 million liters per month (page 54).

LOOK FOR ◖ TO FIND RECOMMENDED SIGHTS, ACTIVITIES, DINING, AND LODGING.

tourist revenue. Good things sometimes come out of adversity, however, and downtown Tijuana appears to be experiencing the beginnings of a transformation. Creative types are taking over empty buildings and turning them into new shops and eateries that cater to local residents. The result is a low-key and authentic community, as opposed to the hyped-up tourist scene that once prevailed.

Less than 80 kilometers east of the metropolis of Tijuana, laid-back Tecate is the oldest border town in Baja and maintains the feel of an authentic Mexican community, although it is growing at an alarming rate as people from southern Mexico move north to work in the surrounding factories.

South along the coast, beachside Rosarito has long been a favored getaway for San Diego and Los Angeles residents—especially surfers—except in March and April, when spring breakers come from across the western United States come to town.

As Mexico's drug war rages on, the news of murders, kidnappings, and military interventions continues to deter many would-be travelers from visiting the border region. Faced with extremely low demand, many outfitters have had to change or cancel longstanding trips to the region. Even as the global economy begins to recover, it's a cycle that's going to be difficult to reverse.

But for every traveler who has decided

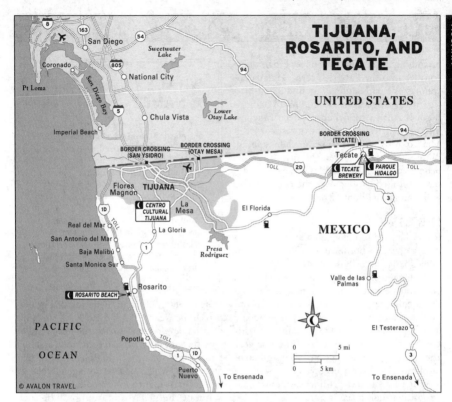

Northern Baja is too risky, there are others who are following through on their plans. And most of them are getting through the border region trouble-free. The violence is real, and it's scary, but it's not the whole story.

PLANNING YOUR TIME

Many travelers prefer to limit time in the border region in order to maximize time at Southern Baja destinations; however, Tijuana, Rosarito, and Tecate each have their own appeal. You might spend a day, a weekend, or, in the case of Rosarito, a whole week enjoying the culture and adjusting to the change of pace.

A popular weekend itinerary involves crossing from San Diego into Tijuana, heading south to Rosarito and Ensenada and then northeast via Mexico 3 and the Ruta del Vino (Wine Route) to exit at Tecate.

If you're heading all the way to Baja California Sur, you can cover the length of Baja California (Norte) from Tijuana to Guerrero Negro in one long day, or, more comfortably, with a stopover in San Quintín or El Rosario.

Northwestern Baja enjoys a dry and comfortable climate year-round, much like Southern California. The beaches between Rosarito and Ensenada are warmest and most crowded July–September. Winter months tend to be cold and cloudy.

Tijuana and Vicinity

Straddling the Río Tijuana, now a canal, which empties into the Pacific Ocean, Tijuana encompasses a population of around 2.5 million (estimates range from 1.6 million to 3.5 million). Its urban sprawl covers deep canyons, hills, and plateaus in the northwest corner of Mexico. Most visitors come for the shopping, dining, and clubbing, but the city also draws people who want to drink underage, buy prescription medications over the counter, and visit its legal red-light district.

HISTORY

It may be hard to imagine today, but Tijuana wasn't always a border town. The Treaty of Hidalgo, signed in 1848, ceded Alta California to the United States and commenced Tijuana's rapid transformation from an insignificant cattle ranching settlement to a center of tourism, industry, and immigration. It was officially founded as Tijuana in 1889. Many U.S. citizens first heard of the city in 1911, one year after the Mexican Revolution, when a group of revolutionaries briefly occupied the town.

When the Panama-California International Exposition took place in San Diego in 1916, Tijuana put itself on the global tourism map, drawing a number of attendees over to the border for a concurrent traditional Mexican fair. With its lineup of arts and crafts, local foods, hot springs, horse racing, and boxing matches, the city made a lasting impression.

The U.S. Prohibition era brought foreigners over the border in greater numbers to drink and gamble. In 1928 the historic Agua Caliente hotel, casino, and spa opened to entertain elite Hollywood types, and the resort quickly became an icon of the growing city. The party lasted until 1935, when then-president Cárdenas outlawed gambling and closed Mexico's casinos, causing a severe recession.

By this point, however, the city was primed for growth through tourism and domestic immigration, and from 1940 to 1950 its population tripled from approximately 20,000 to

WHAT'S IN A NAME?

The origin of the name Tijuana is a matter of some dispute. In pre-Hispanic times, the Yumano tribes that lived here called the valley Ti-wan (Near the Sea), a name that the Spanish later changed to Tijuan on their early maps of the peninsula. A local ranch that dates back to the early 19th century called itself Rancho Tia Juana (Aunt Jane), which sounded similar but was easier to pronounce. Americans living in California adopted this pronunciation and stuck to it, long after the city's name was officially decided as Tijuana.

more than 60,000, and then exploded by 600 percent between 1950 and 1970. An era of industrial development fueled the next wave of growth, with international companies opening hundreds of manufacturing plants called maquiladoras, which take advantage of cheaper labor costs to produce goods for export. Without the infrastructure to handle such explosive growth, Tijuana faced severe housing shortages and pollution. Collaboration between the United States and Mexico led to improvements through the end of the 20th century, and today the standard of living is much improved—to the point where tens of thousands of U.S. nationals have made Tijuana their permanent residence.

Present-day Tijuana is a multicultural, cosmopolitan city facing a host of socioeconomic challenges. Its 16 universities draw students from all over the country as well as overseas. As the fourth-largest city in Mexico (after Mexico City, Guadalajara, and Monterrey), it also has the busiest international border crossing in the world, through which 70 million people pass each year. Tijuana has one of the highest income per capita of any city in the country, but as a border zone, it also must cope with a

TIJUANA

UNITED STATES

To San Diego

CALIFORNIA
BAJA CALIFORNIA

CARRETERA AEROPUERTO

To Abelardo L. Rodriguez International Airport

To Terminal de Autobuses

To Hotel la Mesa Inn, Tecate, and Mexicali

BLVD DIAZ ORDAZ

ESTADIO CALIENTE

TAPACHULA

U.S. CONSULATE

SHUTTLE BUSES TO TIJUANA
TIJUANA TROLLEY

MEXICAN CUSTOMS

RAILROAD STATION

PUEBLO AMIGO INN

PLAZA PUEBLO AMIGO

MONUMENTO A DIANA LA CAZADORA

MONUMENTO A PADRE MIGUEL HIDALGO

PASEO DE TIJUANA

P KINO

DEPORTIVAS

PEDESTRIAN BRIDGE

PEDESTRIAN BRIDGE

PALACIO MUNICIPAL

PLAZA RIO TIJUANA

HOTEL CAMINO REAL

MARISCOS LOS ARCOS

HOTEL REAL DEL RIO

BABYROCK

HOTEL LUCERNA

MONUMENTO A GENERAL IGNACIO ZARAGOZA

HOTEL HACIENDA DEL RIO

LA DIFERENCIA

FIESTA INN

RODRIGUEZ

BLVD AGUA CALIENTE

GRAND HOTEL TIJUANA

TIJUANA COUNTRY CLUB

AV G. SALINAS

TANGALOO

RIVIERA

TABOADA

AV SANTA MARIA

AV 16 DE SEPTIEMBRE

BANCOMER

BANAMEX

MEXICANA AIRLINES

MONUMENTO A CUAUHTEMOC

CALIMAX

MONUMENTO A ABRAHAM LINCOLN

PLAZA FIESTA

MONUMENTO A LA RAZA

CALLE 16

VIA ORIENTE

VIA PONIENTE

INDEPENDENCIA

CENTRO CULTURAL TIJUANA

PASEO DE LOS HEROES

ZONA RIO

AV OCAMPO

AV NEGRETE

AV QUINTANA ROO

PIO PICO

AV

CALLE 9

CALLE 10

CALLE 11

PE CALLES

BLVD AGUA CALIENTE

CUAUHTEMOC

HOTEL PALACIO AZTECA

AV B. JUAREZ

To Rosarito and Ensenada via free road

POST OFFICE

CERVEZA TIJUANA

BLVD FUNDADORES

SEE "AVENIDA REVOLUCIÓN" MAP

TOURIST INFORMATION

PEDESTRIAN BRIDGE

PEDESTRIAN BRIDGE

U.S. CUSTOMS

Trolley

Tijuana

Rio

MERCADO DE ARTESANIAS

TIJUANA ARCH

REVOLUCION

CONSTITUCION

NIÑOS HEROES

MARTINEZ

MUTUALISMO

CATEDRAL GUADALUPE

Parque Guerrero

INTERNACIONAL

AV

AV

AV

AV

AV

AV

AV

AV

AV

AV F

AV G

AV H

CALLE 1 (ARTICULO 123)

CALLE 2 (B. JUAREZ)

CALLE 3

CALLE 4 (D. MIRON)

CALLE 5

CALLE 6

CALLE 7

To Rosarito, Ensenada, and Playas de Tijuana via toll road

0.5 mi

0.5 km

0

0

© AVALON TRAVEL

sizable immigrant population (legal and illegal, foreign and national), widespread poverty, and deep-rooted organized crime.

At its heart, multicultural, cosmopolitan Tijuana remains a young city searching to find its place in the world. Even as it struggles to cope with systemic crime and poverty, this urban community finds itself at the forefront of global trends in music and art. If it can find a way to harness and nurture that creative, edgy spirit while restoring law and order, Tijuana could reemerge as an economic and cultural leader in the region.

SIGHTS
Zona Río
Officially called the Zona Urbana Río Tijuana, this part of the city borders the Tijuana River/Canal across from the *palacio municipal.* The heart of the district is the **Plaza Río Tijuana** (Paseo de los Héroes btw Independencia/Cuauhtémoc), with dozens of shops and restaurants, several hotels, and some of the city's hottest dance clubs. In fact, the Zona Río boasts some of the largest and liveliest clubs in the world. A day trip here might encompass bargain shopping, a gourmet dinner, a musical performance, and a night of drinking and dancing until the wee hours of the morning.

🄲 Centro Cultural Tijuana
A block away from the Plaza Río, across Avenida Independencia, is the Tijuana Cultural Center, with more than 60 works of art by the famous Mexican painter Raul Anguiano.

Well-known Mexican architects Pedro Ramírez Vásquez and Manuel Rosen Morrison designed Tijuana's industrial-looking landmark, the Centro Cultural Tijuana (Héroes and Independencia, tel. 664/687-9600, www.cecut.gob.mx), with a giant, white spherical planetarium (now an IMAX theater). The government-sponsored complex covering 8.6 acres opened in 1982 with the goals of strengthening national identity in Northern Baja and promoting cultural tourism. Today its 1,000-seat performing-arts theater hosts the Baja California Orchestra (OBC) and other performances (with

the Centro Cultural Tijuana at night

COURTESY OF WWW.TIJUANAONLINE.ORG

some outdoor events in summer). Some 1.5 million visitors tour the center each year, many of them children. The **Museo de las Californias,** with historical, anthropological, and archaeological exhibits (10 A.M.–6:30 P.M. Tues.–Fri., 10 A.M.–4 P.M. Sat.–Sun., US$2). The center also has a café, bookstore, and shops. Tickets are sold 10 A.M.–6 P.M. daily. In 2008 CECUT expanded with the opening of El Cubo, a large space for art exhibitions that took three years and US$9 million to build.

Avenida Revolución
More shopping, dining, and nightlife are to be found along an eight-block stretch of Avenida Revolución (La Revo, in San Diego-speak), where the remaining clubs are oriented toward an increasingly local Southern California crowd.

Tijuana Arch and Monumental Clock
This controversial addition to the skyline is located at Avenida Revolución and Primera, but

AVENIDA REVOLUCIÓN

ZONA NORTE

TIJUANA ARCH

CANACO OFFICE

CALLE 1 (ARTICULO 123)

TOURIST INFORMATION

TIJUANA WAX MUSEUM

CENTRAL DE AUTOBUSES

HARD ROCK CAFÉ

BITAL

CALLE 2 (B. JUÁREZ)

BANAMEX

CALLE 3 (CARRILLO PUERTO)

IGUANAS RANAS

SANBORNS CAFÉ

CALLE 4 (D. MIRON)

BAR SAN MARCOS

CAESAR'S SPORTS BAR & GRILL

HOTEL CAESAR

REVOLUCIÓN

CONSTITUCIÓN

MADERO

CALLE 5 (E. ZAPATA)

TILLY'S 5TH AVE

CALLE 6 (F. MAGON)

TERMINAL TURÍSTICA TIJUANA

MARGARITA VILLAGE

CALLE 7 (GALEANA)

TIA JUANA TILLY'S

HOTEL LA VILLA DE ZARAGOZA

CALLE 8 (HIDALGO)

POLICE STATION

SANBORNS RESTAURANT/ DEPARTMENT STORE

FIRE STATION

BANCOMER

CALLE 9 (ZARAGOZA)

SCALE NOT AVAILABLE

CALIMAX

CALLE 10 (SARABIA)

© AVALON TRAVEL

it is visible from most of the city. To its backers, it's the symbolic gateway to Baja, but to most locals it's a visual hangover from the Y2K celebration. Either way, it's a good landmark to meet your friends after a long night in TJ.

Playas de Tijuana

A boardwalk and seawall along the beach have given Playas de Tijuana a facelift and are intended to help keep erosion in check, but problems with water quality and police corruption persist. Although many foreign residents live here, tourists are few and far between. Reports of parking scams in which police direct drivers to illegal lots and then tow their cars or allow the homeless to break into them are enough to keep visitors away. It's best to park at the border and take a taxi. At the north end of the beach, the U.S.-Mexico border fence extends across the sand and out into the ocean, dividing Tijuana from the neighboring community of Imperial Beach, California.

At the north end of the district stands the historic Plaza Monumental Bullring by the Sea. Two universities are located near the toll road: Universidad Iberoamericana del Noroeste and the Colegio de la Frontera Norte.

South of Playas de Tijuana, the **Real del Mar** (Km. 19.5, Mexico 1-D, tel. 664/631-3401, US$70–100) resort has comfortable accommodations and a golf course. **Hacienda del Mar** (Paseo Playas 116, Playas de Tijuana, tel. 664/630-8603, US$50–60) is a more central and less expensive option.

On the boardwalk, **Café Latitud 32** (Malecón de Playas de Tijuana 50, no tel., mains US$5–10) serves coffee drinks and sandwiches and hosts occasional live music.

SPORTS AND RECREATION
Spectator Sports
BASEBALL

In 2010 the Cimarrones de Tijuana, or Big Horn Sheep (formerly Los Potros), played in the Golden Baseball League at the 18,000-seat **Estadio Béisbol Calimax** (formerly the Estadio Nacional de Tijuana), which is located off Boulevard Los Insurgentes near the Otay-Mesa border crossing. The team was inactive at last check due to financial troubles.

SOCCER

Tijuana has a 33,000-seat state-of-the-art fútbol stadium that has been open since 2007. **Estadio Caliente** is part of the Hipódromo Agua Caliente complex (Blvd. Agua Caliente 12027, tel. 664/682-3110, www.caliente.com.mx, US$20), where the local Club Tijuana team plays.

Golf

Founded in 1927 as part of the Agua Caliente Club complex, the **Club Campestre Tijuana,** or Tijuana Country Club (tel. 664/681-7855, toll-free U.S. tel. 888/217-1165, www.tijuanacountryclub.com), off Boulevard Agua Caliente has a 6,800-yard, par-72, 18-hole course. The Mexican Open is played here on occasion. Greens fees are US$18–45. The club has a driving range and pro shop and offers golf lessons.

Swimming and Running

Unidad Deportiva CREA (Cañon Aviacíon at Via Rápida Oriente s/n, tel. 664/215-9000, 7 A.M.–9 P.M. Mon.–Sat.) is a public sports complex in the Zona Río with a six-lane, 25-meter pool and diving pool. Athletes from around the world come to practice for marathons.

Organized Tours

Turista Libre (www.turistalibre.com) offers a refreshing alternative to the usual Tijuana tourist scene. Day trips focusing on the "overlooked and underrated" visit local museums, parks, dive bars, and the occasional pro soccer games at the Estadio Caliente.

ENTERTAINMENT AND EVENTS

There are myriad ways to spend an evening out in Tijuana, from professional sporting events and cultural performances to a night of drinking and clubbing.

Dance Clubs

Tijuana's once-vibrant nightclub scene is a shadow of its former self. A few mainstays have survived, but most others have closed or evolved into something different. In the meantime, a new and trendy bar scene has emerged along Calle 6 with more than 30 bars thriving in roughly a six-block area. Most of Tijuana's top dance clubs enforce a dress code of no jeans or sneakers, and some insist on even more formal attire. The clubs begin to fill up around midnight and often stay open until dawn. The later the hour, the louder the music. Here are a few of the mainstays on the circuit. For current information online, search Facebook or MySpace, as few of the clubs maintain their own websites these days.

In business since 1988, **Las Pulgas Disco Club** (Revolución 1127, tel. 664/685-9574, www.laspulgas.info) consists of five different dance halls. **Salon Rojo** (10 A.M.–5 A.M. daily) plays rock music from the 1970s to pop hits. **Salon Cachanilla** (9 P.M.–6 A.M. Mon.–Tues. and Thurs.–Sun.) plays *banda, norteña,* and ranchero tunes. Larger **Salon Vaquero** holds 1,500 people and is open 9 P.M.–6 A.M. Wednesday and Friday–Sunday. The other two dance halls, **Salon Teatro** and **Salon Palomar** are open for special events.

Pyramid-like **Club Balak** (Plaza Pueblo Amigo, Vía Oriente, tel. 664/682-9222, from 9 P.M. Thurs.–Sat.) is an upscale venue with attentive service and a dress code.

Run by a global entertainment group and located inside a seven-story "cave" **Babyrock** (Diego Rivera 1482, tel. 664/622-3800, www.clubbabyrock.com, until dawn daily) has been a favorite for more than 20 years. A million-dollar sound system and state-of-the-art light shows bring a European club experience to TJ. Internationally recognized DJs play a range of techno and house music.

Mike's Disco (tel. 664/685-3534, till 5 A.M. nightly), on the east side of Avenida Revolución at Calle 6, is a gay and lesbian dance club with drag shows on weekends.

Bars

Calle 6 is the epicenter of Tijuana's new and

ultra-hip bar scene. Check out **Indie Go** (Calle 6 at Revolución), **La Mezcalera** (Calle 6 btw Revolución/Madero, 5 P.M.–2 A.M. daily), and **Zebra Mexican Pub** (Héroes 10001 Local 21-A, Plaza Fiesta, noon–midnight Mon–Wed., noon–2 A.M., Thurs.–Sat.) which serves dozens of beers from around the world in a cozy setting. Order pub fare for under US$5. Made in Mexico is the theme at bohemian **Santa Leyenda Bar Tijuana** (Av. 6 1942), which serves wines from the Valle de Guadalupe as well as martinis and national beers.

Avenida Revolución also features a multitude of bars—some historic, some divey, some fancy. Mariachi bands do their rounds, and the scene is usually a mix of locals, expats, and out-of-towners. **Bar San Marcos** (Calle 5 at Revolución, tel. 664/688-2794), adjoining Caesar's Sports Bar & Grill, has survived since its heyday in the 1950s. The Nortec Collective has composed a song about **El Dandy Del Sur** (Calle 6 and Revolución, tel. 664/688-0052), where the drinks keep flowing until dawn. Near El Dandy del Sur, tiny **Don Loope Cantina** (Calle 6 btw Revolución/Madero, 7 P.M.–3 A.M. Wed.–Sat.) could be set in New York with its velvet and red neon decor, except for the Nortec music that often plays.

Large and loud, **La Cantina de los Remedios** (Diego Riviera 2476, tel. 664/634-3087, 1 P.M.–midnight Mon.–Sat., 1–10 P.M. Sun.), in the Zona Río, is a chain with similar restaurant/bars in several cities on the mainland. It serves *botanas* and daily *menudo* (lunch), too. Complimentary valet parking is a plus.

Tijuana's **Zona Norte,** from Calle 1 downtown north almost to the border, is the city's red-light district; it's best to avoid this area, especially at night.

At **Cervecería Tijuana** (Fundadores 2951, tel. 664/638-8662, www.tjbeer.com, 1 P.M.–midnight Mon.–Wed., 1 P.M.–2 A.M. Thurs.–Sat.), you can try six different brews in an Old World atmosphere with a modern twist: sports on the big screen and karaoke.

The largest Baja California winery, L.A. Cetto, operates a wine store and tasting room, **Cava Tijuana** (Cañón Johnson 2108,

tel. 664/685-3031, www.cettowines.com, 10 A.M.–5 P.M. Mon.–Sat.), in the Zona Río. Tastes are US$2 for most wines, US$5 for reserve wines.

Performances
Centro Cultural Tijuana (Héroes and Independencia, tel. 664/687-9600, www.cecut.gob.mx) has a 1,000-seat performing-arts theater where the Baja California Symphonic Orchestra plays.

Events
Visit the family-friendly **Tijuana Fair** (La Feria de Tijuana, mid-August–mid-September, US$5) in August or September, a traditional fair that celebrates Mexico's independence with music, amusement rides, and arts and crafts. Concerts start at 8 P.M. Events take place at the Parque Morelos and Museo del Trompo.

The **Tijuana Tequila Expo** (Revolución at Calle 7, tel. 664/255-7692, www.expo-tequila.com, US$5) takes place in mid-October with more than 300 brands of tequila. Festivities include Mexican food, folk dancing, and *norteña* music. Transportation is provided from San Diego and Los Angeles via Five Start Tours (U.S. tel. 619/232-5040).

SHOPPING
The majority of Tijuana visitors come to shop in the free-trade zone (up to US$400). You'll find a long list of goods for sale, from arts and crafts souvenirs and hand-embroidered dresses to name-brand apparel and discount prescription drugs. You can pay with U.S. dollars anywhere in the city; some stores will also accept credit cards. Most of the stores along Avenida Revolución have someone who speaks English on staff.

Avenida Revolución between Calle 2 and Calle 9 has a concentration of upscale boutiques selling leather goods, Talavera pottery, silver jewelry, and more. **Tolan** (Revolución 1111 at Calle 7, tel. 664/688-3637) carries a nice selection of glassware, pottery, and other high-end arts and crafts. For a wider selection of pottery at lower prices than the boutiques,

TIJUANA

COURTESY OF WWW.TIJUANAONLINE.ORG

a festive scene at the Tijuana Fair

head to the **Mercado de Artesanías** (Ocampo and Calle 2, no tel.). Across from the Tijuana Cultural Center at Paseo de los Héroes and Avenida Independencia, **Mercado Hidalgo** is a more traditional farmers market with fresh produce and other foods as well as *artesanía*.

Plaza Río Tijuana (Paseo de los Héroes btw Via Poniente/Cuauhtémoc, www.plazarioti-juana.com.mx), in the Zona Río, is a modern shopping mall with more than 100 businesses. The main department stores here include Comercial Mexicana, Dax, Solo Un Precio, and Dorian's. You can buy everything from a pair of glasses to jewelry and fine art. The **Metropoli Alternative Shop** is a collection of several boutiques located at Calle 6 and Revolución, where you can find clothing by local designers, vintage apparel, skateboards, and sombreros.

A number of tile and furniture stores line Boulevard Agua Caliente between Avenida Revolución and the Caliente complex. You can buy high-quality pieces made of wood or wrought iron at much lower prices than you'd pay in the United States or Canada. Just be

sure to check the latest U.S. Customs regulations before filling up your car.

La Caja Galería (Callejon de las Moras 118-B, tel. 664/686-3056, www.lacajagaleria.com) represents contemporary Mexican artists, many of them from Tijuana itself.

San Diego residents frequent **Sanborns** department store (Revolución 1102 at Calle 8, tel. 664/688-1433, www.sanborns.com.mx) for English-language books, arts and crafts, medications, and liquor.

Tijuanenses buy their shoes, liquor, medications, and other day-to-day items on Avenida Constitución, one block west of Avenida Revolución. Prices are accordingly lower. For last-minute souvenirs or to pass the time at the border, browse the kitschy crafts in the indoor/outdoor **Plaza Viva Tijuana** (Frontera and Av. de la Amistad), just before the border gate).

On the first Friday evening of the month, artists open studios along **Pasaje Rodriguez Arte y Diseño (PRAD)** (Av. Revolución 721 btw Calles 3–4, pradtj.webs.com) to celebrate local art and culture.

ACCOMMODATIONS

The hotel business in Tijuana is not well developed for a city of its size because the vast majority of visitors do not spend the night. The nicer places cater to business travelers from elsewhere in Mexico and overseas. Safe and clean budget hotels are hard to find in downtown Tijuana. Budget travelers are better off continuing south to Ensenada.

US$50-100

Hotel Palacio Azteca (16 de Septiembre/ Cuauhtémoc Sur 213, off Agua Caliente, tel. 664/681-8100, toll-free U.S. tel. 888/901-3720, www.hotelpalacioazteca.com, US$60) provides above-average accommodations with large TVs as well as heat and air-conditioning. Guests may use laundry facilities as well as a swimming pool and parking lot.

Renovated in 2008, **Hotel Real del Río** (J. M. Velazco 1409, tel. 664/634-3100, www.realdelrio.com, US$70) is a good value for business travelers, though street noise can be a nuisance.

◖ **Hotel Hacienda del Río** (Sánchez Taboada 10606, tel. 664/684-8644, toll-free U.S. tel. 800/303-2684, www.bajainn.com, US$55–80) is a reliable and modern business-oriented establishment with its own restaurant/bar, heated pool, fitness center, and business center. Choose from 130 large rooms and suites, which feature satellite TV, Internet access, and climate control. Ask for rooms at the back of the hotel facing the pool, since the front rooms are at ground level and face the road. The same company also runs the slightly lower priced **Hotel La Mesa Inn** (Díaz Ordaz at Gardenias, tel. 664/681-5622, www.bajainn.com, US$50–60).

If you're driving and want to stay within walking distance of La Revolución, try the **Hotel La Villa de Zaragoza** (Madero 1120 btw Calles 7/8, tel. 664/685-1832, www.hotellavilla.biz, US$55–70). Rooms are hit or miss, but your best bet is to ask for one of the garden rooms. Amenities include heat/air-conditioning, TVs, phones, parking, and laundry. Nonsmoking and accessible rooms are available. The security guards do a good job, but the front desk staff can be surly.

Relative newcomer ◖ **Hotel Ticuán** (Calle 8 btw Constitución/Revolución, tel. 664/685-8069, toll-free US tel. 877/730-8308, www.hotelticuan.com, US$65–85) has well maintained single and double rooms as well as suites in a central location. Rooms have plasma TVs, phones, and Wi-Fi. Its **Restaurant Albahca** serves casual fare including salads, sandwiches, and burgers.

US$100-150

Your best choice in this price range is located in the Zona Río: ◖ **Hotel Lucerna** (Paseo de los Héroes 10902, tel. 664/633-3900, U.S./ Canada tel. 800/582-3762, www.hoteleslucerna.com/tijuana, US$90–110) has all the amenities one would expect from a large, international business hotel: restaurants, pools, gardens, fitness center, and car rental desk. Ask for a room in the annex if one is available.

The **Grand Hotel Tijuana** (Agua Caliente 4500, tel. 664/681-7000, U.S./Canada tel. 800/472-6385, www.grandhoteltij.com.mx, US$85–115) was one of Tijuana's first skyscrapers. With 22 floors and more than 400 rooms, it is a full-service resort, but the walls are thin and you can easily hear what your neighbor is watching on TV. The shopping area here has a ghost-town feel.

In addition to these options, the **Marriott** (Tijuana Marriott Hotel, Agua Caliente 11553, tel. 664/622-6600, www.marriott.com, US$90–120) and **Fiesta** (Fiesta Inn Otay at the airport, tel. 664/979-1900, www.fiestainn.com, US$100) chains also have a presence in the city.

US$150-250

Business travelers and well-off weekenders like the **Hotel Camino Real** (Paseo de los Héroes 10305 and Cuauhtémoc, tel. 664/633-4000, toll-free U.S. tel. 800/722-6466, www.caminoreal.com, US$130) chain for its luxury amenities, such as marble baths and high-end toiletries; however, experiences at this property have been inconsistent in recent years. The rooms are underwhelming, but the staff generally makes up for it with top-tier service. Its Maria Bonita restaurant is open 1 P.M.–1 A.M. Monday–Saturday and 1–5 P.M. Sunday.

FOOD

Aside from its shopping, bars, and nightlife, Tijuana is a culinary destination in its own right, with everything from mouthwatering street food to serious haute cuisine.

Avenida Revolución and Vicinity

Caesar salad was invented in Tijuana by Italian-Mexican brothers Alex and Caesar Cardini in 1924. 《 **Caesar's Sports Bar & Grill** (Calle 5 at Revolución, tel. 664/685-1664, lunch and dinner daily, mains US$10–15), located next to the Caesar Hotel, still carries on the tradition. A server prepares the salad at your table, and the key ingredient is coddled eggs instead of raw.

The **Sanborns** department store chain has several of its popular *cafeterías* around town (Revolución at Calle 8, Revolución btw Calles 3/4, Revolución 737, and Plaza Río, tel. 664/668-1462, breakfast, lunch, and dinner daily, mains US$10–15). The food is good enough (think Denny's) and so are the prices.

In business since 1947 under a couple of different names, **Tia Juana Tilly's** (Calle 7 at Revolución, tel. 664/685-6024, reservations tel. 664/685-1213, www.tiajuanatillys.com. mx, noon–midnight daily, until 3 A.M. Fri. and Sat., mains US$15 and up) is popular with locals and San Diego folks for Mexican dinners as well as steaks and seafood. The friendly staff makes visitors feel welcome.

Zona Río

If you only have time for one "nice" meal in Tijuana, call 《 **La Diferencia** (Sánchez Taboada 10521, Río Tijuana, tel. 664/634-3346, www.ladiferencia.com.mx, 8 A.M.–10 P.M. Mon.–Sat., 8 A.M.–6 P.M. Sun., US$10–20) for a reservation. The seasonally available *chile en nogada* or the duck with *jamaica* (hibiscus flower) sauce are standouts on

an all-around excellent menu. Attentive service and a contemporary setting make the meal.

For truly authentic Mexican cuisine, 《 **La Casa de Mole Poblano** (Paseo de los Héroes 1501, tel. 664/634-6920, 10 A.M.–11 P.M. daily, mains under US$10) matches its chili-chocolate, chili-almond, and sesame-seed sauces with a variety of meat and poultry. The high ceilings, ivy, and mariachi bands create an upbeat and family-friendly environment popular with locals.

A highlight on the menu at **Mariscos Los Arcos** (Salinas 1000, tel. 664/686-4757, 8 A.M.–10 P.M. Sun.–Wed., 8 A.M.–midnight Thurs.–Sat.) is Mazatlán-style *pescado zarandeado*—a whole fish rubbed in herbs and spices and then seared and broiled. This restaurant is part of a well-regarded chain with several locations in Mexico.

Vips Restaurant Cafetería (Sánchez Taboada 10750, tel. 664/634-6196, 7 A.M.–10 P.M. daily, mains under US$10) is part of a large coffee-shop chain, and it offers a long list of breakfast and lunch fare, including Mexican plates. The locals like it, and it's affordable.

Casa de la 9 blends coffee with independent films, art, and concerts (Calle 9 btw Quintana Roo/Pío Pico, tel. 664/688-0113, http://lacasadelanueve.blogspot.com). *Chilaquiles* are a popular breakfast order at **La Espadaña** (Sánchez Taboada 10813, tel. 664/634-1489).

Also in the Zona Río, **Villa Saverios** (Sánchez Taboada at Escuadron 201, tel. 664/686-6442, ext. 104, www.villasaverios. com, mains US$20) is a Mediterranean/Baja fusion restaurant with a 20-year history of serving creative cuisine. Start with a plate of local cheeses or yellow fin tostadas and then move on to heartier fare such as the twice-cooked pork belly served with *huitlacoche* polenta and sautéed kale. Internationally celebrated chef Javier Plascencia is a member of Slow Food International and the mastermind behind seven Tijuana restaurants, including the famous Caesar's. He recently opened another trend-setting eatery, **Misión 19** (Misión de San Javier 10643, tel. 664/634-2493, www. mision19.com, mains US$20).

COURTESY OF WWW.TIJUANAONLINE.ORG

in the kitchen at Villa Saverios

Agua Caliente

Check the specials menu on the blackboard on your way in at **La Querencia** (Escuadron 201 No. 3110, Sánchez Taboada at Salinas, tel. 664/972-9940, www.laquerenciatj.com, mains US$10–25). It's easy to get distracted by the strange combination of safari decor and industrial chic. The lamb chops are well prepared and not oversauced. Just make sure your cab driver doesn't mistake it for the well-known La Diferencia.

Carnitas Uruapán (Díaz Ordaz 12650, opposite Plaza Patria, tel. 664/681-6087, 7 A.M.–5 A.M. daily, mains US$10–15, cash only) sells house-made carnitas by the kilo for family-style dining. Sides include rice, beans, salsa, and guacamole.

Food becomes art at **Restaurant Uno** (Av. de las Ferias 5202, tel. 664/681-3203), and Baja California wines play a central role in the performance.

Groceries

Calimax has dozens of grocery stores around the city, including one at 791 Avenida Constitución (tel. 664/688-0737) in the Zona Centro and another at Boulevard Agua Caliente 11988 (tel. 664/681-2511).

INFORMATION AND SERVICES
Tourist Assistance

The **Tourist Information Booth** (Revolución at Calle 1, tel. 664/688-0555, 8 A.M.–8 P.M. Mon.–Fri., 10 A.M.–3 P.M. Sat.–Sun.) has a bilingual staff and the usual collection of maps and brochures covering Northern Baja. Additional booths are at the border crossing and the airport. The **Tijuana Convention and Visitors Bureau** (COTUCO, main office Paseo de los Héroes 9365-201, Zona Río, tel. 664/684-0537 or 664/684-0538, www. tijuanaonline.org, 9 A.M.–6 P.M. daily) has Visitor Information Centers set up at the pedestrian border crossing, the airport, and on Avenida Revolución between Calles 3/4. The privately run **Tijuana Tourism Board** (Agua Caliente 4558-1108, tel. 664/686-1103, toll-free U.S./Canada tel. 888/775-2417, www.seetijuana.com) represents a group of local businesses.

TIJUANA PHONE NUMBERS

- Tijuana Area Code: 664
- Fire Department: 068
- General Hospital: 684-0922
- Green Angels: 624-3479
- Highway Patrol: 682-5285
- Immigration: 682-3439
- Police: 060
- Red Cross: 066
- State Police: 685-4444
- State Tourism Office: 688-0555
- Tourist Assistance: 078

The **Cámara Nacional de Comercio, Servicios y Turismo de Tijuana** (CANACO, Revolución at Calle 1, tel. 664/684-0537, www.canacotijuana.com, 9 A.M.–7 P.M. Mon.–Fri.) has tourist information, mailing supplies, restrooms, and a public telephone.

For any questions that these organizations cannot answer or for legal assistance, contact the **State Secretary of Tourism** (SECTUR, Plaza Patria, 3rd floor, Díaz Ordaz, tel. 664/688-0555).

Money
You can use U.S. dollars just about everywhere in Tijuana, except for bus fare. The city has numerous ATMs, including a Banamex southeast of Plaza Fiesta and Plaza Zapato on Paseo de los Héroes.

Post and Telephone
Tijuana's main post office (Calle 11 at Negrete) is open 8 A.M.–7 P.M. Monday–Friday.

Internet Access
Most hotels and coffee shops now have wireless Internet service for their patrons. Look along the northern end of Avenida Revolución if you need an Internet café.

Immigration and Customs
The Tijuana-San Ysidro border crossing processes all immigration and customs paperwork (daily 24/7).

Foreign Consulates
Visit the **U.S. Consulate** (Tapachula 96, Col. Hipódromo, tel. 664/622-7400, 8 A.M.–5 P.M. Mon.–Fri., closed U.S. and Mexican holidays) for help with lost or expired U.S. passports or visa issues. Other consulates in town include **Canada** (Germán Gedovius 10411-101, Condominio del Parque, Zona Río, tel. 664/684-0461, 9 A.M.–1 P.M. Mon.–Fri.); **France** (Revolución 1651, 3rd floor, tel. 664/681-3133, btdmex@telnor.net); **Germany** (Cantera 400, Building 304, tel. 664/680-2512); and **United Kingdom** (Salinas 1500, Col. Aviación, La Mesa, tel. 664/686-5320, fax 664/681-8402).

Green Angels
Mexico's Green Angels automotive emergency assistance service maintains headquarters at the Otay Mesa border crossing (Edificio Federal Garita, tel. 664/624-3479).

GETTING THERE
By Air
Tijuana has an international airport in Mesa de Otay, about 10 kilometers northeast of downtown: **Abelardo L. Rodríguez International Airport** (TIJ, tel. 664/607-8200, http://tijuana.aeropuertosgap.com.mx). Several international and discount airlines offer service to and from Tijuana, including:

- **Aeroméxico** (Plaza Río Tijuana 12-A1, Paseo de los Héroes, tel. 664/638-8444 or 800/021-4010, toll-free U.S. tel. 800/237-6639, www.aeromexico.com)
- **Mexicana** (Edificio Fontana, Diego Rivera 1511 at Paseo de los Héroes, tel. 664/634-6566, airport tel. 664/682-4184 or

UNITED STATES-MEXICO BORDER CROSSINGS

Crossing	Hours
Calexico (Mexicali) East	6 A.M.-midnight
Calexico (Mexicali) West	24 hrs./day
Los Algodones	6 A.M.-10 P.M.
Otay Mesa (Tijuana)	24 hrs./day
San Ysidro (Tijuana)	24 hrs./day
Tecate	5 A.M.-11 P.M.

Visit the U.S. Customs Border Protection website at http://apps.cbp.gov/bwt/index.asp to check border wait times before you cross.

800/509-8960, toll-free U.S./Canada tel. 800/531-7921)

- **Aero California** (Plaza Río Tijuana C-20, Paseo de los Héroes, tel. 664/684-2876, toll-free U.S. tel. 800/237-6225)

- **Aviacsa** (Sánchez Taboada 4499, Plaza Guadalupe 6, tel. 664/622-5024, airport tel. 664/683-8202 or 800/711-6733, toll-free U.S. tel. 888/528-4227, www.aviacsa.com), based out of Monterrey

- **Volaris** (www.volaris.com.mx) is one of a handful of low-cost carriers that fly in and out of Tijuana—an increasingly appealing way to mitigate the rising cost of airfare from LAX. It opened for business in 2006, and the best part about flying with this airline is that it runs a shuttle from the San Diego train station to the Tijuana airport (US$15), so travelers don't have to deal with driving themselves through the busy streets of Tijuana. From the shuttle pickup, it's a 30-minute drive to the airport, including a short stop at the border. The planes

are new, and most of your fellow passengers will be gringos in the know. This is a great way to get to La Paz and Los Cabos in Baja California Sur.

The airport has food, books, and gift shops, plus an ATM and parking garage. TIJ is an official port of entry for foreign pilots. Check with **Bush Pilots International** (www.bajabushpilots.com) for current information.

Airport Transportation: Taxi service between the airport and any destination within the city limits costs US$12 for up to five passengers and slightly less to the Central de Autobuses. Public buses signed "Centro" offer frequent connections to the downtown area (US$0.60 pp).

By Bus

Tijuana's **Central de Autobuses de Tijuana** is located five kilometers east of the city on Lázaro Cárdenas at Boulevard Arroyo Alamar (tel. 664/621-2982). It has a restaurant, *lonchería,* telephone service, immigration office, and currency exchange. **Transportes Norte de Sonora** (TNS) and **Autotransportes de Baja California** (ABC, tel. 664/621-2668, www.abc.com.mx) offer connections east to Mexicali (US$9–12, nine buses/day) and the Mexican mainland. **Transportes de Pacífico** and **Chihuahuenses** offer more frequent connections to destinations on the mainland.

ABC's *ejecutivo* buses depart for Ensenada every half hour 6 A.M.–midnight from the second Central de Autobuses (Madero and Calle 1). Regular buses (no air-conditioning) leave for Ensenada from **Plaza Viva** at the border. ABC offers both *ejecutivo* and regular bus service to San Felipe as well.

Autotransportes Aguila offers intercity service to points south, including El Rosario, Santa Rosalía, and La Paz.

Greyhound (toll-free U.S. tel. 800/231-2222) buses from San Diego and Los Angeles arrive at the Tres Estrellas de Oro terminal (México and Madero, tel. 664/688-0082), which also has frequent ABC buses to Tecate.

Mexicoach out of San Ysidro has its own station at the Terminal Turística Tijuana (Revolución btw Calles 6/7).

By Taxi

Taxi service from the border to downtown is about US$5 (flat rate); to Rosarito US$35 (one-way); and to Ensenada US$100.

By Car

Most visitors heading to Tijuana by car cross at San Ysidro. You don't need a permit for your vehicle unless you plan to continue on to the mainland. You do need a validated tourist permit if you plan to go south of Maneadero or stay longer than 72 hours anywhere on the peninsula. A Mexican auto insurance policy is essential.

On Foot

A popular way to get to Tijuana from Southern California is to park at San Ysidro and walk across the border. The route is well marked and it takes about 15–20 minutes to get to Avenida Revolución this way. If you don't want to drive to the border, you can take the **Tijuana Trolley** (www.sdmts.com, 5 A.M.–12:40 A.M. daily, US$2.50) from San Diego instead.

GETTING AROUND
By Bus

Tijuana has a complex bus system that can be useful for budget travelers or anyone who'd rather not have to negotiate with a taxi driver. As with other cities in Baja, the end destination of the bus is displayed in the windshield. You need pesos for the fare (around US$0.50). Walk along Avenida Constitución to find buses arriving and departing from the downtown area.

By Taxi

Taxi rides within the downtown area should cost less than US$5, and under US$15 to the airport or Central de Autobuses. You can pay in U.S. dollars. The yellow taxis that shuttle pedestrians from the border to downtown are a special breed. Drivers often ask more than the going rate of US$8, and they often get kickbacks from certain businesses downtown, so they may try to discourage you from going to the place you request. To avoid this hassle, consider taking a shuttle bus from the Blue Line

Trolley terminal in San Ysidro to Avenida Revolución (US$1 pp).

Route taxis *(taxis de ruta)* are similar to buses, except the vehicles are station wagons that can hold up to 12 passengers and they stop wherever someone flags them down, which makes for more flexible transportation. Rates are slightly higher than the going bus fare.

By Car
RENTAL CARS

You can rent from any of several international chains, including Avis, Budget, Central, Dollar, Hertz, and National. Rates are lower here than in neighboring Ensenada or Mexicali. Reserve ahead, since fleets are small. When you arrive at the counter, you'll need to give a major credit card (not a debit card) as a deposit on the rental.

DRIVING

Traffic in Tijuana is heavy, though not insurmountable. Parking is another challenge. If you're used to navigating urban environments in the United States, you can probably figure it out here. Street parking is difficult along Avenida Revolución, but there are several pay lots open 24/7 for US$5 per day.

LEAVING TIJUANA
To the United States

To return to San Ysidro and Southern California, head north on Avenida Revolución and follow signs to San Diego. Avenida Padre Kino, north of the downtown area, is an alternative when traffic is heaviest. It connects you to the east lanes of the border crossing, which tend to be less crowded.

South to Rosarito and Ensenada

The 100-kilometer route from Tijuana to Ensenada is easy to follow. Most travelers these days take the four-lane toll road *(Cuota)*, Mexico 1-D, south, but you can also choose the two-lane *Libre* (free road), which is the original Mexico 1. The toll road hugs the coast more closely but offers fewer opportunities for stops.

To get on the toll road from downtown

Tijuana, get on Calle 3 heading west and look for signs to Ensenada; traffic may crawl until the toll-road entrance near Playas de Tijuana. There are three tolls (*casetas de cobro,* US$2–3 each for regular passenger vehicles) along the way. You can pay in dollars or pesos, and your change may come in either currency depending on what the toll collector has on hand.

If you can manage to find it from downtown Tijuana, the *Libre* follows an inland route at first and meets the coast at Rosarito. It then parallels the shore until La Misíon, where it heads into the mountains again. Access to the free road is not well marked downtown. Drive south along Avenida Revolución until it joins Boulevard Agua Caliente and watch for a sign that says A Rosarito (To Rosarito) and points right. Pass the Calimax store on the right and take the next right turn onto Boulevard Cuauhtémoc, which leads eventually to Mexico 1.

East to Tecate and Mexicali

If you want to travel east on the *Libre,* take Boulevard Agua Caliente southeast. It will turn into Boulevard Díaz Ordaz and then Mexico 2. If you want to take the toll road to Tecate, follow the signs for the airport, not the signs for Tecate, which direct you toward the free road.

ISLAS LOS CORONADOS

A group of islands called Los Coronados lie within sight of shore 11 kilometers west of San Antonio de Mar, which is 12 kilometers

south of Tijuana. The islands have a colorful past that includes pirates, rum-running, and a Prohibition-era casino known as the Coronado Islands Yacht Club. Steep terrain makes the islands impractical for habitation, but the Mexican navy maintains an outpost on one of them.

The islands are the peaks of a submerged mountain range. The southernmost island is the largest at three kilometers long and 204 meters high. The northern island, Coronado del Norte, is one kilometer long and 142 meters high. The two islands in the middle are little more than rocky outcroppings. Since no one is allowed to land on the islands, they are popular nesting sites for brown pelicans and more 160 other species of birds. There is a large sea lion colony on the west side of Coronado del Norte.

Fishing and Diving

From April–October, yellowtail fishing is excellent around the islands. There are rock cod, bonito, calicos, and halibut.

Los Coronados offers good visibility for diving and playful sea lions. There aren't many large fish, but there are plentiful moray eels and schooling small fish. The main sites are the Lobster Shack, off the northeastern coast of Coronado del Norte, and the Keyhole archway at the south end of the same island. No regular dive boats frequent the islands, but San Diego-based **Horizon Charters** (U.S. tel. 858/277-7823, www.horizoncharters.com) will run a charter trip.

Rosarito and Vicinity

Once a quiet ranching community, Rosarito (pop. 130,000) became something of a mini Las Vegas, only without the casinos, but fell on hard times in the wake of drug wars and an ongoing global recession. Development began in the 1920s with the opening of El Rosario Resort and Country Club and reached a feverish pitch in the 1990s, when Fox Studios came to town. Located just 30 miles south of

San Diego, Rosarito's fate as a party town was sealed when the Hotel Festival Plaza built a huge entertainment complex right on the waterfront. The town's greatest appeal today—as then—is its long, sandy beach, which the high-rise hotels and luxury condos are slowly crowding out.

Until 1995 Rosarito belonged to the *municipio* (county) of Tijuana, and played a major

TIJUANA

ROSARITO

To Tijuana

SECTUR

Free road

0   0.25 mi

0   0.25 km

LA FLOR DE MICHOACÁN

PACIFIC OCEAN

EJIDO MAZATLÁN SHOPPING PLAZA

QUINTA DEL MAR RESORT
QUINTA PLAZA

AV MIRAMAR
LAUREL
COSTA AZUL
BLVD JUÁREZ
AV MAR DEL NORTE
EBANO
AV MAR MEDITERRANEO
HOTEL & RESTAURANT LOS PELICANOS
CEDRO
ROSARITO BEACH
ABETO
ALAMO
SPAZIO CAFFE & CREPES
TOURIST OFFICE
RESTAURANT LA TIA
POLICE
LA CAZUELA DEL MOLE
ACACIAS
ROBLE
MERCADO DE ARTESANIAS
ORTEGA'S
EL NIDO
PAPAS & BEER
TACQUERÍA LOS POBLANOS
ANIMALE
HOTEL FESTIVAL PLAZA
PALMA
IGGY'S
AV MOSSEAU
PINO
ROSARITO BEACH HOTEL
TAXIS TO TIJUANA
TOURIST INFORMATION
RENE'S SPORTS BAR RESTAURANT
TOLL PLAZA
To Ensenada
BAJA STUDIOS
© AVALON TRAVEL

TOLL

role in funding the larger city's annual budget. Rosarito residents lobbied for 15 years to create their own *municipio*, so they could use the city's relatively high income to develop its own infrastructure and services rather than supporting Tijuana's.

Tourism drives Rosarito's economy today, but like Tijuana and Tecate, the town has been severely affected by the wave of drug-related violence sweeping through Northwestern Baja. To their credit, local authorities have taken steps to improve security, and they have results to show for it. Crime in the town declined 21 percent in 2009 to a five-year low, thanks to the efforts of former mayor Hugo Torres, who served his second three-year term 2007–2010. By replacing corrupt officers and training a dedicated tourist police force, Mr. Torres has begun to win back the confidence of expats and travelers; however, hotels and beaches remain almost empty.

Many first-time visitors to Rosarito return home disappointed in the overall scene and the quality of their accommodations. This is a party town; on weekends and any day in the summer, the clubs rock until dawn. Chances are you will hear the music from your room, especially if you stay anywhere close to the main strip. March and April bring groups of college kids on spring break, while an older crowd from Mexico and the United States visits during the peak summer months. If you know what you're in for, it can be a fun time, but if you're looking for a quiet escape in a boutique hotel, this isn't the place.

Between Rosarito and Ensenada are a few beaches, coves, surf spots, and residential communities, collectively dubbed the Gold Coast by marketing-minded real estate developers.

SIGHTS
◖ Rosarito Beach

The action in Rosarito centers around the beach—an eight-kilometer-long stretch of sand. You can swim, snorkel, or surf here, but most people just come to relax on the beach and party at the clubs. North of the pier are several mega-clubs that provide beach chairs and drinks by day and DJ music at night. During the annual spring break holiday, college students from the United States invade the town and take full advantage of the 18-year-old drinking age. You can rent ATVs, fish from the pier, or just people-watch as you sunbathe.

Rosarito Beach Hotel

There are a few truly iconic hotels in Baja, and the Rosarito Beach Hotel (south end of Juárez, tel. 661/612-1111, toll-free U.S. tel. 800/343-8582, www.rosaritobeachhotel.com) is one of them. It started as the only place to stay in Rosarito in the 1920s. During the 1940s and '50s, it became popular with the Hollywood crowd, counting Mickey Rooney, Lana Turner, and Orson Welles among its regulars. In 2010 the hotel celebrated its 85th anniversary with a series of promotions and events that featured local art and music.

The founder's nephew, Hugo Torres, was a recent mayor of the town, and he became the owner of the hotel in 1974. It has grown from 12 to 280 rooms, and its dramatic ocean pier anchors the Rosarito Beach vista. The 500-meter **Rosarito Pier** (daily 10 A.M.–6 P.M.) is popular for sportfishing, but the height makes landing fish from the surface far below a challenge and the activity can be sporadic. Admission to the pier is US$1 for adults, free for children under 12. Fishing from the pier costs US$5 for the public.

SPORTS AND RECREATION
Surfing

There are at least 25 named surf breaks between Rosarito and Ensenada—far too many to cover in detail here. Some are overhyped and packed with boards; others are consistent yet never crowded. Whether you are a beginner or an advanced surfer, you can probably find a spot that works for your skill level. For info break by break, pick up a copy of *The Surfer's Guide to Baja*.

Spas

Spas are a relatively new addition to the Rosarito activity list. In part of the original

A surfer catches a wave near the Rosarito Pier.

mansion of the Rosarito Beach Hotel, **Casa Playa Spa** (south end of Juárez, tel. 661/614-4410, U.S. tel. 619/946-2987, ext. 1364, spa@rosaritobeachhotel.com, 8 A.M.–6 P.M. Sun.–Fri.) offers massage, facials, body wraps, and scrubs. Treatments range US$40–100.

ENTERTAINMENT AND EVENTS
Bars and Nightclubs
The best-known mega-club in town is **Papas and Beer** (Eucalipto 400 at Coronado, tel. 661/612-0444, www.papasandbeer.com), a huge entertainment center and nightclub covering about 4,600 square meters of sand with multiple bars, dance areas, and beach volleyball; the low cover charge keeps it packed on warm summer nights, but it's empty in winter. Papas and Beer celebrated its 27th anniversary in 2010. It has satellite locations in Ensenada and La Paz.

The open-bar policy at **Iggy's,** next to the Rosarito Beach Hotel, for the price of the cover (negotiable), can seem like a deal, but the drinks are often watered down. You can overcome that problem by working with the same bartender and tipping well. The crowds seem to pass by Señor Frog's located on Boulevard Juárez and head straight for the beachside clubs.

Rene's Sports Bar (Km. 28, Mexico 1, tel. 661/612-1061), next to Paraíso Ortiz at the south end of town, has pool tables and TVs for watching the game.

Festivals and Events
Aside from spring break, the best-known event in Rosarito is the **Rosarito-Ensenada 50-Mile Bicycle Ride,** which takes places twice a year, in April and September, and attracts thousands of cyclists. For more information, contact **Bicycling West** in San Diego (U.S. tel. 619/424-6084, www.rosaritoensenada.com). Even if you can't beat the course record of 2 hours and 13 minutes, you'll still have a great time.

SHOPPING
Rosarito offers much of the same shopping you'll find in Tijuana, just on a smaller scale.

There are handicrafts, furniture stores, leather shops, and art galleries.

For souvenirs, head to the **Mercado de Artesanías** (9 A.M.–6 P.M. daily), on the west side of Boulevard Juárez, about midway between the Quinta del Mar and Rosarito Beach Hotel. This crafts market has hundreds of vendors selling all kinds of Mexican-made arts and crafts. Shop around and bargain to get a fair price for any items you buy. For beachwear and boutique shops, browse the many shopping plazas around town.

ACCOMMODATIONS
Most of Rosarito's hotels line busy Boulevard Juárez, which runs parallel to the beach. Condos and vacation homes are another option for travelers who want to cook some of their own meals. Contact the tourist office at the north end of town (Juárez, tel./fax 661/612-0200, www.sectur.gob.mx, 9 A.M.–7 P.M. Mon.–Fri., 10 A.M.–4 P.M. weekends).

US$50-100
Originally built by the same family that established the Rosarito Beach Hotel and Rene's Sports Bar, **Motel Paraíso Ortiz** (Km. 28, Carr. Libre a Ensenada, tel. 661/612-1020, US$45–65) consists of simple beach cottages close to but not on the beach, behind the Rosarito Beach Hotel. Comfortably removed from the noise of the main strip (and therefore hard for some first-time visitors to find), **Hotel Los Pelicanos** (Ebano 113, tel. 661/612-0445, US$60–85) has 39 large rooms, all with heat and TV. Call ahead for directions.

On the north side of town, **Hotel Quinta Terranova** (Juárez 25500, tel./fax 661/612-1650, www.hotelquintaterranova.iwarp.com, US$65–109) is pet friendly, as long as your pooch is well-behaved and you bring proof of current vaccinations. Midweek rates drop to US$34 for standard rooms.

US$100-150
The best part about a stay at the **Rosarito Beach Hotel** (south end of Juárez, tel. 661/612-1111, toll-free U.S. tel. 800/343-8582,

www.rosaritobeachhotel.com, US$90–150) is the beachfront location. This property has evolved into an enormous complex over the years. Given the piecemeal construction of the hotel, the rooms can vary in age and decor. The newly opened Pacifico Tower has the most up-to-date rooms. Visitors continue to report their disappointment with the basic nature of the accommodations. At any given time, some rooms will need a fresh coat of paint, and hot water may or may not work. Some rooms have kitchenettes, a great way to save on restaurant tabs.

North of the Rosarito Beach Hotel, the **Hotel Festival Plaza** (Juárez 1207, tel. 661/612-2950, toll-free U.S. tel. 888/295-9669, www.festival-plazahotel.com, US$100–160) is still the party epicenter in Rosarito for summer and spring break. Its proximity to the beach clubs keeps drawing the crowds, but in recent years readers have reported thefts, incidences of bedbugs, and general disrepair at the hotel. The valet parking system is of particular concern, since you have to leave your keys with the staff. The hotel/entertainment complex includes a Ferris wheel and tequila bar, plus restaurants, clubs, and a heated swimming pool. The 114-room hotel section has basic rooms that have been frat-partied nearly to death. Suites, condos, and *casitas* are better, though pricier, options. Service tends to be a little better in the off-season. Wristbands are required to enter the hotel, so you won't be able to invite guests back to your room unless they are staying at the hotel already.

FOOD

Most of Rosarito's many dining options are crowded along Boulevard Juárez. You can find everything from tacos to steak and seafood. Much of the food is adapted to gringo tastes. The larger hotels have their own restaurants as well.

El Nido (Juárez 67, tel. 661/612-1430, http://elnidorosarito.net, 8 A.M.–midnight daily, US$6–23), has great atmosphere and the food to back it up. The beef is grilled over an open fire. For breakfast, try the quail eggs and venison *machaca*. The restaurant's owner raises his own quail and red deer.

La Cazuela del Mole (Juárez at Calle René Ortiz, tel. 661/612-2910, noon–8 P.M. Wed.–Mon., mains US$5), specializes in authentic sauces called moles as well as house-made tamales.

La Flor de Michoacán (Juárez 291, tel. 661/612-1858, 8 A.M.–10 P.M. daily, mains US$5–10) still makes outstanding carnitas, and you can order them by the kilo (US$20 includes the usual sides of beans, guacamole, salsa, and tortillas).

Ortega's Place (Juárez 200, tel. 661/612-0022, breakfast, lunch, and dinner daily, mains US$15) is one of the original Puerto Nuevo lobster places, now with a restaurant in Rosarito. It still offers the lobster, but the buffet is more popular. Champagne brunch is a Sunday tradition.

Tacquería Los Poblanos (11 A.M.–1 A.M. daily), on Boulevard Juárez, across from the Festival Plaza, serves up spicy but good *tacos al pastor* for US$1. **Restaurant La Tia** (8 A.M.–3:30 P.M. daily) sits across from the Pemex on the southwest side of Calle Ciprés, packed with locals and not a tourist in sight. It serves *birria,* chicken, or beef in chipotle sauce. Plates start at US$5.

For espresso drinks, **Café Spazio** (Paseo de los Héroes 10958, tel. 664/631-3131, 7 A.M.–10 P.M. Mon.–Fri., 9 A.M.–10 P.M. Sat., noon–10 P.M. Sun., US$4–6), in the Zona Río is a good option.

INFORMATION AND SERVICES
Tourist Assistance

The national **Secretaría de Turismo** (Secretary of Tourism or SECTUR, Calle Juan Ruiz de Alarcón 1572, Zona Río, tel. 664/682-3367, www.discoverbajacalifornia.com, 9 A.M.–7 P.M. Mon.–Fri., 10 A.M.–4 P.M. weekends) distributes information about local sights, accommodations, and restaurants.

Money

Rosarito has plenty of ATMs these days. For example, Banamex and Serfín have branches on Boulevard Juárez, near the Hotel Festival Plaza.

GETTING THERE AND AROUND

Taxis de ruta make the 40-minute trip between Tijuana and Rosarito for about US$35 per person. You can hail one on Boulevard Juárez. These taxis can also provide service to the coastal towns south of Rosarito. The white-and-red taxis you see around town offer local service only.

Mexicoach (tel. 664/685-1470, U.S. tel. 619/428-9517, www.mexicoach.com) also runs shuttles between Tijuana and Rosarito (US$15 pp).

You can take the toll road (Mexico 1-D) or the free road (Mexico 1) from Tijuana to Rosarito. The distance is about the same, but the toll road is faster and easier to find.

If you're driving north out of Rosarito, follow the sign toward San Diego; the one for Tijuana puts you on the highway heading south to Ensenada.

Small shuttles called *calafias* are another way to get around locally on Boulevard Juárez. The fare is only a few pesos.

POPOTLA

Fifteen minutes south of Rosarito (6.5 km), around Km. 33, a concrete arch in need of a paint job marks the entrance to Popotla, known for its collection of seafood vendors and other food stands. Menus are based on the catch of the day, which lands right there at the beach. It doesn't get much fresher than this, and prices are a little lower than what you'll pay in Rosarito or Puerto Nuevo. The stands begin serving around 11 A.M. daily.

Accommodations

Near Popotla, **Las Rocas Resort and Spa** (Km. 37.5, Mexico 1, tel. 661/614-0354, toll-free U.S./Canada tel. 888/527-7622, www.lasrocas.com, US$70–110) has a rustic feel with views of a popular surf break, fireplaces, and kitchenettes in its rooms. The rooms can be hit or miss, so ask to see one before you commit. Amenities include secured parking, cable TV, a restaurant, swimming pool, and hot tub. The hotel's on-site spa provides a full menu of treatments, such as massage and facials, and a steam room.

PUERTO NUEVO

Foodie alert: Baja's self-proclaimed lobster capital awaits in Puerto Nuevo at Km. 44 at the north end of Bahía Descanso. Harvests have dwindled since the first in-home restaurants opened in the 1940s and '50s, and the scene is too touristy for some (mediocre food), but the village's lobster tradition is still going strong. Choose from dozens of seafood restaurants steps from the ocean (most listed at www.puertonuevolobster.com), which feature the signature lobster platter, with rice, beans, and tortillas on the side. There are a few different styles of presentation, including deep fried and grilled, *ranchera* style with tomatoes and chili, or just plain boiled.

If you happen to be traveling in mid-October, stop by for the **Festival del Vino y la Langosta** (Festival of Wine and Lobster, US$25 pp), which takes place in Puerto Nuevo's restaurant zone. Call the local restaurant association, Cámara Nacional de la Industria Restaurantera (CANIRAC, tel. 661/612-0700), for information.

It's easy to find your way around the village, as it consists of only three blocks. Four streets run parallel to the ocean, and they are bound by the Avenida Rentaria (one-way toward the beach) to the north and Calle Barracuda (one-way toward the highway) to the south.

Misión El Descanso

Misión El Descanso (1817–1834) is one of the least-visited mission sites on the peninsula. It was founded by Dominican padre Tomás de Ahumada in 1817, after the flood that washed away the crops at Misión San Miguel, just 13 kilometers to the south. The two missions were closely linked for the short time that El Descanso was in operation. A modern church is built on top of the original mission foundation.

Accommodations

The **Grand Baja Resort** (Km. 44.5, Mexico 1, tel. 661/614-1493, toll-free U.S. tel. 877/315-

1002, www.grandbaja.com, US$75–150), just south of Puerto Nuevo, overlooks the Pacific Ocean. The views are great; the rest is not. Most units are in need of repairs, and the beds and linens are old. This is not the place for neat freaks.

A better bet is a rental home or condo in the 【 **Las Gaviotas** (one-bedroom US$100–175) gated community, located eight miles south of Rosarito. Several property managers offer rentals in this development. Visit www.las-gaviotas.com or www.golasgaviotas.com for current listings.

Food

Prices are the same at most of the lobster houses, ranging US$15–30 for main dishes, and you'll need to pay in cash. Hours are generally 10 A.M.–8 P.M. weekdays, with later hours on Friday and Saturday nights. **Puerto Nuevo I** (s/n Rentaria, no tel.) is the original Puerto Nuevo restaurant and still a perennial favorite. Next door, **Puerto Nuevo II** (Rentaria 2, tel. 661/614-1454) is more upscale. These family-run places have been serving lobster for many years: **Chela's** (Arpon 15, tel. 661/614-1058), **La Escondida** (Anzuelo/Paseo del Mar, no tel.), **El Galeón** (Anzuelo, no tel.), and **La Perlita** (Barracuda, just west of the highway, tel. 661/614-1276).

LA FONDA AND LA MISIÓN

Mexico 1 *(Libre)* and Mexico 1-D (toll road) diverge between La Fonda (a.k.a. K-58 or La Salina), on the coast at the southern end of Bahía Descanso, and La Misión, to the southeast (and not to be confused with Playa La Misión, which is a little south of La Fonda on Bahía Descanso). La Fonda offers the best beaches in the area, several of which have surfable waves. Take the exit for La Misión–Alisitos from the toll road at Km. 59.

Misión San Miguel Arcángel de la Frontera

East of the highway, historic Misión San Miguel Arcángel de la Frontera (1788–1833) is part of the Spanish mission trail in Baja. Dominican Padre Luis Salles came here from

Misión Santo Tomás to the south in search of a strategic point of connection between the Baja California missions and the newer Alta California missions that were under construction. Relatively little is known about the mission today, but it did grow corn and wheat and had around 400 indigenous people at its peak. A flood in 1816 destroyed much of the mission, and it was abandoned in 1833, at which point the population had declined to only 25. The scant remains of its adobe compound—just two walls in a present-day schoolyard—are now protected by the Instituto Nacional de Antropología e Historia (INAH).

Accommodations and Food

La Fonda Hotel (Km. 59.5, Mexico 1-D Rosarito–Ensenada Toll Road, tel. 646/155-0307, www.lafondamexico.com, US$55–85) is a quirky area classic. There are standard rooms as well as multiroom apartments with fireplaces and kitchenettes (US$100–150). Movement around the cliff-side hotel involves numerous steep staircases, so if mobility is an issue, make sure to ask the front desk for an accessible room. The restaurant serves reliably tasty seafood and steaks (mains US$12–25). Make sure to get a good seat on the terrace for the sunset, and if it gets chilly, the waiters bring small blankets and turn on the patio heaters.

Alisitos K-58 Surf Camp (Km. 58, Mexico 1-D Rosarito–Ensenada Toll Road, tel. 646/155-0120, U.S. tel. 949/313-7059, www.alisitosk58.com, US$16) is a board shop and campground that can accommodate RVs. Amenities are few (flush toilets and cold showers), but the beach is a good one, and you can't complain about the price.

The **Poco Cielo Bed and Breakfast** (Km. 59, Mexico 1-D, tel. 646/155-0606, U.S. tel. 760/670-3336, www.pococielo.com, US$65–150) has four well-appointed rooms that are true to their themes down to the construction of the walls, murals, sinks, and sculpted entry rooms. A private stairwell leads down to the beach, and a new restaurant serves margaritas for US$7. It's a little Disneyland, but the good service and friendly owner make it a fine choice for those looking to escape the bustle of Ensenada and Rosarito.

Baja Seasons (Mexico 1-D, Km. 72, tel. 646/155-4015, toll-free U.S. tel. 800/754-4190, www.baja-seasons.com) is a full-service resort with villas (US$140–320), motel rooms (US$90), and campsites suitable for tents or RVs (US$80 oceanfront or US$55 interior). You can only get to the park from the southbound toll road. Make a U-turn if you're driving north from the Ensenada area.

SAN MIGUEL AND EL SAUZAL

San Miguel and El Sauzal are neighboring communities on the Pacific coast, known primarily these days for good surf. In fact, San Miguel might be Baja's most consistent point break. It's located just south of the third toll booth on Mexico 1. Parking is US$5, and the crowds will be on it if the surf is good. Get there early to catch it before the onshores start up in the late morning.

Accommodations

(**Hostel Sauzal** (Av. L 344, tel. 646/174-6381, http://hostelsauzal.tripod.com, US$15 pp) has been the starting point for many a Baja backpacking trip. It offers rare oceanview hostel accommodations in dorm room bunks. Rates include bed linens, storage lockers, hot showers, continental breakfast, and bike/surfboard storage. The hostel's four rooms have desks for writing letters and updating travel journals; plus there is a small library containing books, maps, and magazines. To find the hostel from the toll road southbound, go through the tollbooth at San Miguel and continue on the highway for about three more kilometers, passing under the footbridge. Next, turn left at a stoplight after the Pemex. Go two blocks and turn right; then go one block more and turn left up a dirt road. The hostel is the third house on the right.

Several of the beaches along this stretch allow tent and RV camping for less than US$15 per night.

Tecate and Vicinity

Mountainous Tecate (pop. 120,000) sits at an elevation of 514 meters (1,690 ft.) in the Sierra de Juárez, which makes for a pleasant climate year-round. The highest peak nearby is Mount Cuchumá, which straddles the U.S.-Mexico border. Protected by its geography from its industrial neighbors of Tijuana and Mexicali—and from the extreme climates of the Pacific coast and San Felipe Desert—Tecate is an oasis of sorts along the international border zone. Fresh air and clean spring water led to the establishment of Tecate's two most famous enterprises: the Tecate Brewery and Rancho La Puerta health spa. High literacy and employment rates allow many people to live in relative comfort here; however, a mass migration from states in southern mainland Mexico toward the maquiladoras in the border region poses serious growth challenges. The population of the town has risen from 77,000 in 2000 to more than 120,000 today and is on track to reach 153,000 by 2020. By some estimates, 70 percent of the current Tecate residents were not born in the town. It is difficult to provide adequate infrastructure and public services for so many new people and even more difficult to build a sense of community and togetherness that will prevent crime. The river that flows through town is badly polluted.

Beyond the city limits, around 100 rancho resorts and numerous aquatic recreation parks offer accommodations and entertainment.

Mexican American writer Daniel Reveles (www.danielreveles.com) has written several books of short stories that take place in Tecate and poke fun at cultural differences between the Mexican and American ways of thinking. They can be an enjoyable way to get acquainted with the town.

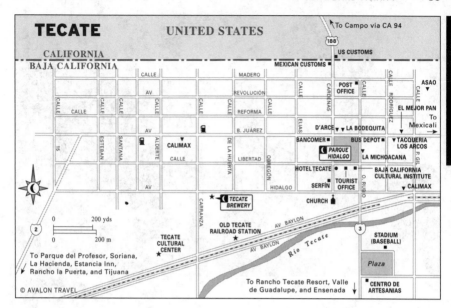

HISTORY

In its earliest history, the fertile valley and abundant water supply here supported a group of Yuma, who called the area Zacate (the most likely origin of the name Tecate). They believed the 1,520-meter Cerro Cuchumá (also spelled Kuchumaa) had important spiritual significance.

In the early 19th century, Mexicans began cultivating the land, and in the 1830s, a Peruvian named Juan Bandini founded the town with a land grant from the Mexican government. Later in the century, the government built a railroad to connect the three emerging border towns of Tijuana, Tecate, and Mexicali, and Tecate became the capital of its own Mexican municipality in 1892.

In 1914 the San Diego-Arizona Railroad reached Tecate. Construction of the original plaza began in 1919.

The most significant development in the city's history took place in 1943, when the Tecate Brewery opened for business. As the border zone industrialized later in the century, Tecate gained a number of maquiladoras east of the city on Mexico 2. The economy today is mainly driven by manufacturing, with farming and tourism playing smaller roles.

SIGHTS
【 Parque Hidalgo

Tecate has five main parks within its limits, and the most popular is shady Parque Hidalgo (Juárez and Calle Lázaro Cárdenas, Zona Centro). Built in 1952, this small park and plaza are the center of town life and give the visitor a good sense of the place. A pretty gazebo and wrought-iron benches invite quiet contemplation. A small cactus garden has labels so you can learn to tell a yucca from a *cholla*. Eat ice cream, get a shoe shine, and watch the locals play a game of dominoes. Note the statue of Miguel Hidalgo, the Dolores priest who issued the call for Mexican independence in 1810, in the southeast corner of the park. There is a large map of the area on a sign near the cactus garden and free Wi-Fi. Surrounding the park are local government offices, restaurants, taco stands, and a few shops selling *artesania*. One block away, on

TIJUANA

© NIKKI GOTH ITOI

gazebo in Tecate's Parque Hidalgo

Hidalgo, stands the 1941 Iglesia de Nuestra Señora de Guadalupe.

🄲 Tecate Brewery

Entrepreneur Alberto Aldrete came up with the idea for a brewery to complement his malt-making business. He ran out of money 10 years after creating Tecate beer, but a Monterrey businessman, Eugenio Garza Sada, bought the label and added it to the lineup offered by Cervecería Cuauhtémoc.

Canned Tecate is brewed in Monterrey, but bottles and kegs are made only in its namesake Tecate. If you've tried Tecate beer only in the United States, chances are you haven't experienced the real thing. Exported Tecate does not use the pure spring water of Tecate, and has a lower alcohol content than domestically consumed Tecate (3.2 percent compared to 3.6 percent).

The brewery today (Dr. Arturo Guerra 70, tel. 665/654-9478, www.tecate.com.mx, 10 A.M.–noon and 3–4:30 P.M. Mon.–Fri., 9–10:30 A.M. Sat.) occupies the same site as

the original keg brewery, right in the middle of town. High-tech German equipment is used to produce 40 million liters per month and ship to 100 countries around the world. Group tours are available by appointment. Your first beer is included after the tour.

Old Tecate Railroad Station

Built in 1915, the Old Tecate Railroad Station was part of a line that connected San Diego to Yuma, Arizona, and played an important role in the industrial development of the area. In its time, the station held a waiting room, office, and small warehouse on its ground floor, and a residence for the station master above. The station is now part of a small historic district, which includes the Tecate Brewery and is protected by the city.

The **Pacific Southwest Railway Museum** (State Hwy. 94 and Forest Gate Rd., Campo, U.S. weekday tel. 619/465-7776, U.S. weekend tel. 619/478-9937, www.sdrm.org, US$43) offers occasional Saturday rail trips from its Campo depot (80 minutes by car from downtown San Diego) to Tecate—a 75-minute ride. Trains leave Campo at 10:30 A.M. and return at 4:30 P.M. In summer, twilight trips depart Campo at 3 P.M. and return at 9 P.M. At press time, this route was temporarily closed due to the need for repairs in one of the tunnels following a fire. Reservations are required. Credit cards and PayPal are accepted. An alternative is the Turistic Train that rides from Tijuana to Tecate.

Tecate Cultural Center

For travelers interested in Baja California history and culture as well as sustainable tourism, the new Tecate Cultural Center (CECUTEC, Calle Tláloc 400, tel. 665/655-6419, hours vary) will delight. The center is a joint effort led by a nonprofit civil association called CAREM with collaboration from many organizations, including San Diego State University, the Secretaría de Turismo del Estado de Baja California, Fundación La Puerta, Rancho La Puerta, and the Municipio de Tecate. Walk through the **Museo Kumiai** (scheduled to open in 2011) to learn the history of native peoples in the valley—from living descendants of the tribe. Its gift shop sells handicrafts that have been sourced according to fair-trade principles. A well-known sustainable design architect from San Diego, James Hubble, helped design the museum building.

Next door, browse the collection of 2,000 Baja books in the **Cuchuma Library** (tel. 665/521-3970, 9 A.M.–1 P.M. and 2:30–6:30 P.M. Mon.–Fri.). A community auditorium hosts workshops, seminars, concerts, author readings, and other programs. An oral history project seeks to capture the voices of Tecate residents for the Cuchuma Library archives. In addition to these programs, CAREM is involved in the restoration of Baja California missions and other historical sites and offers multiday guided tours to them.

Parque del Profesor

This 24-acre park set against a hillside on the outskirts of the town center is a memorial to Profesor Edmond Szekely, the founder of

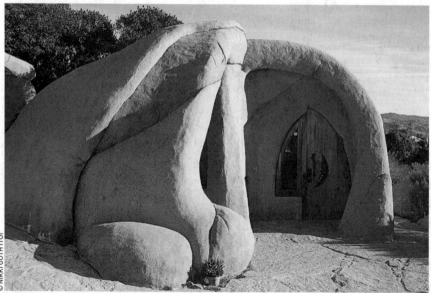

environmental education center at the Parque del Profesor

Rancho La Puerta. Designed by his daughter, an architect, and set in the midst of a 2,000-acre conservation easement, the park contains a soccer stadium that's used by local teams every day of the week, and above it, a beautiful plaza with views of the mountains. A small **environmental education center** runs programs for school-age children.

Rancho La Puerta

Aside from its beer, Tecate is known the world over for its pioneering fitness resort and spa, Rancho La Puerta (U.S. tel. 760/744-4222 or toll-free U.S. tel. 800/443-7565, www.rancholapuerta.com), which sits on 3,000 acres at the base of Mt. Cuchumá (or Kuchumaa). Something of a summer camp for grown-ups, this resort has a sense of history and place that is rarely experienced in modern times. In the 1940s, founders Deborah and Edmond Szekely advocated a simple and health-oriented retreat in a beautiful natural setting as an antidote to the busy modern lifestyle. Their first visitors paid US$17 for a week and brought their own tents. A small museum on the property contains memorabilia from the early days of the ranch and historic photos of the founders at work in Tecate and on the road meeting with a long list of foreign leaders. The ranch library has a large collection of books on Baja California, including many of the "Profesor's" own works. Today Rancho La Puerta employs hundreds of local residents, many of whom begin their tour in entry-level jobs and ascend the ranks to management positions. At age 89, founder Deborah Szekeley remains actively involved in the operations of the business and an inspiration to loyal guests. The only way to visit is to sign up as a guest for a week or book a one-day trip out of San Diego.

SPORTS AND RECREATION

Outdoor recreation in the Tecate area centers around dozens of family-oriented rancho resorts located east of Tecate on the way to Mexicali. Activities include hiking, swimming, hot springs, water slides, bird-watching, and rock climbing.

Hiking

Guests of **Rancho La Puerta** (U.S. tel. 760/744-4222 or toll-free U.S. tel. 800/443-7565, www.rancholapuerta.com) enjoy daily hikes along 25 miles of trails at the base of Mt. Cuchumá, but locals advise against independent exploration here because of the proximity to the international border and possibility of encountering illegal immigration activity.

Organized Tours

The addition of the popular **Saturdays at the Ranch** (tel. 665/654-9155, toll-free U.S. tel. 877/440-7778, 8 A.M.–8 P.M., US$215 pp, spa treatments cost extra) has opened Rancho La Puerta up to a wider audience. These one-day visits include fitness, spa, and culinary components, all packed into a single 12-hour day that begins and ends in San Diego.

CAREM, the nonprofit civil association behind the Tecate Cultural Center (CECUTEC, Calle Tláloc 400, tel. 665/655-6419, www.carem.org) offers multiday guided tours of Baja California's mission sites and other historic buildings, such as Campo Alaska.

ENTERTAINMENT AND EVENTS

The state-funded **Baja California Cultural Institute** (ICBC, Av. Ortiz Rubio and Callejón Libertad s/n, Zona Centro, tel. 665/654-1483, www.icbc.gob.mx/tecate, 8 A.M.–7 P.M. Mon.–Fri., 9 A.M.–1 P.M. Sat.) holds concerts, lectures, and art exhibitions in the Galería de la Ciudad. The Tecate Cultural Center also hosts performances, workshops, classes, and other cultural activities.

A tour of the **Tecate Brewery** (Dr. Arturo Guerra 70, tel. 665/654-9478, www.tecate.com.mx, 10 A.M.–noon and 3–4:30 P.M. Mon.–Fri., 9–10:30 A.M. Sat.) is a popular way to experience a bit of Tecate history. Reservations are required.

Nightlife is virtually nonexistent in Tecate, although a few of the nicer restaurants such as **El Mezquite** (Juárez 1450, tel. 665/521-3066) also have bars. Guests from Rancho La Puerta in search of a real Mexico experience often head here for a margarita or two.

In the daytime, off-road races provide a popular pastime for locals and visitors alike. The Santa Veronica Offroad Park and Roadway (www.ranchosantaveronica.com), at Rancho Santa Veronica, 30 kilometers east of Tecate off Mexico 2, produces a few such events each year, including the **Gran Carrera de Tecate,** a three-day festival held in late May. The **Gran Carrera de Caballos** is more popular among locals. It takes place on the last weekend in March.

The **SCORE Tecate Baja 500** occurs in June and early November (U.S. tel. 818/225-8402).

During the second week of October, the city celebrates the **Fiesta de la Fundación de Tecate,** which commemorates Tecate's founding in a multiday festival of parades, live music, and (rare in Baja) fireworks.

SHOPPING

There are a few shops near the plaza, but the best place to browse for souvenirs is the **Centro de Artesanias de Tecate** (Calzada Universidad, near Parque Adolfo López Mateos, no tel., 8:30 A.M.–6 P.M. Mon.–Fri., 10 A.M.–3 P.M. Sat.). Originally a workshop for glassblowing, the center sells a full range of pottery, jewelry, and other crafts.

To bring home a bottle of Baja California wine (one is the limit, per U.S. customs), go to **La Bodeguita** on the plaza (Juárez 346, tel. 665/101-7652, 1–9 P.M. Tues.–Sun.) and enjoy a free tasting.

The **Mercado** (9 A.M.–5 P.M. daily) at Rancho La Puerta stocks high quality souvenirs, ceramics, T-shirts, hats, and several beautiful cookbooks—including *Cooking with the Seasons with Rancho La Puerta,* by Deborah Szekely and Deborah M. Schneider. You can also buy DVDs of exercise programs developed by the resort's fitness instructors. At press time the **Museo Kumiai** at the Tecate Cultural Center was planning to open a small gift shop with handicrafts from fair-trade sources.

COURTESY OF DISCOVER BAJACALIFORNIA.COM/JULIO RODRIGUEZ

an artisan at work

ACCOMMODATIONS
Under US$50

A mainstay on the plaza for decades, **Hotel Tecate** (Cárdenas y Callejón Libertad No. 20, tel. 665/654-1116, US$35) has 12 simple rooms, some of which overlook the plaza. The hotel is above a sushi restaurant and Subway chain. Centrally located **El Paraíso** (Aldrete 83 at Juárez, tel. 665/654-1716, US$25 pp) has 38 clean rooms with air-conditioning and hot showers. The management also provides space heaters for chilly winter nights. There is secure parking in an underground garage.

La Hacienda (Juárez 861, tel. 665/654-1250, US$40) offers clean and safe accommodations on the outskirts of town. Rooms have air-conditioning and cable TV, and there is secure parking. It has a restaurant that's open 8 A.M.–4 P.M. daily, except for Monday, when it closes at noon. A cab ride to the town center costs about US$5.

US$50-100

If you need modern accommodations in a central location for an overnight stop on your way through town, **(Estancia Inn** (Juárez 1450, Col. Encanto, tel. 665/521-3066, www.estanciainn.com.mx, US$60–75) will do. It caters to business travelers with an adjoining restaurant, El Mezquite Restaurante. Its 80 rooms and 9 suites come with cable TV, phones, and air-conditioning. Other amenities include a swimming pool, gym, parking, 24-hour security, and high-speed Internet.

On the road to Ensenada, just outside of town, the **Hotel Rosita Resort Inn** (Km. 3.6, Carr. Tecate-Ensenada, tel. 665/103-0093, hotelrositainn@live.com.mx, US$50–100) has 52 rooms and suites with air-conditioning, phone, cable TV, and high-speed Internet. Its restaurant serves Mexican specialties (7 A.M.–10 P.M. Mon.–Sat.), and the recreation area has a swimming pool. Secure parking is another feature.

Ranch Resorts

Popular with the ATV and motorcycle crowds, **Hacienda Santa Verónica** (Km. 95, Carr. Tijuana-Mexicali Cuota/Mexico 2-D, tel. 665/521-0017 or -0018, toll-free U.S. tel. 888/556-6288, www.ranchosantaveronica.com, US$70) is located about 30 kilometers east of Tecate. Mission-style accommodations (52 rooms and 8 suites) have fireplaces and patios, and meal plans are an option. Activities include tennis, off-road riding (quad rentals US$40/hr), horseback riding, swimming, volleyball, and basketball, and you can come for just the day (8 A.M.–10:30 P.M.) Its campground/RV park is open to the public. To find the resort, exit at Km. 106 from the free road and follow the signs; there is no exit for the ranch from the toll road. An unusual beer bath was recently added to the menu of treatments at the on-site **El Descanso Spa.** Massages here are US$50 for 50 minutes.

(Rancho Los Chabacanos (Km. 118, Carr. Mexicali-Tecate, tel. 665/655-1624, U.S. tel. 619/565-1183, www.rancholoschabacanos.com, US$80–285) has a distinct colonial feel in both its hacienda-style architecture and the surrounding eco-preserve. There are no TVs or phones in its 17 *casitas,* though Wi-Fi is an option. Guests enjoy black mud treatments and steam treatments at the on-site spa.

Stays at the historic **(Rancho La Puerta** (U.S. tel. 760/744-4222 or toll-free U.S. tel. 800/443-7565, www.rancholapuerta.com) are a full week and include all meals. Guests stay in modern cottages or suites—most with fireplaces and each with its own private garden—and the resort can hold 150 guests at a time. All-inclusive prices range from US$3,780 per week for a studio with bath to US$4,715 for a two-bedroom villa suite. Summer rates (late June–early September) are lower.

Before making a reservation, be sure you have a good idea of what a stay here will entail. It's quite different from the typical spa experience. The mantra here is healthy living (not just relaxation), which means taking care of mind, body, and the environment. Gray water systems, alternative energy, organic farming, conservation programs, and community involvement are some of the ways in which the resort gives back.

Upon arrival, guests receive a program of activities offered each hour of the day

© NIKKI GOTH ITOI

porch of a villa at Rancho La Puerta

6 A.M.–8 P.M. and a blank calendar on which to note the classes they want to take. The typical day begins with a sunrise hike and ends with healthy-living lectures. In between are classes in yoga, meditation, group cycling, pilates, and more. When not in an exercise class or eating a family-style meal in the dining hall, guests make appointments at the spa, walk the labyrinth, or relax in a poolside hammock.

A genuine and attentive staff tends to guests' needs. Rancho La Puerta employees stay for decades, beginning as bellboys and eventually graduating into management positions.

There is friendly competition among repeat visitors. At the start of each week, the staff posts a list of returning guests with the number of previous visits, and it's not uncommon to see 20, 25, or 30 visits at the top. (The record is around 100 visits—people with a lot of vacation time on their hands!) A very energetic and engaged 89-year-old Deborah Szekely continues to run the business today, along with her daughter.

Accommodations are pleasantly rustic—mostly studio *casitas* made of brick with some high-end touches inside, such as luxury linens, iPod players, filtered water, a hot-water dispenser for herbal tea, and nightly turndown service. If you have a fireplace, the staff will build a fire for you each night. Bathrooms are simply tiled and could use an update in some of the units, but chances are you'll spend most of your time at the spa anyway.

If you're used to a diet of burgers and soda, the spa cuisine may come as a shock to the system. Rice and beans play heavily in the daily menu, with some fish and seafood mixed in. There are bowls of flax and chia seeds on the condiment table and honey and agave syrup for sweeteners. Ingredients are fresh and seasonal, often picked the same day from the ranch's own vegetable farm nearby. Portions are small to help prevent overeating, but you can always go back for seconds or request a yam or potato as a side.

A morning garden tour or evening cooking class at Rancho La Puerta's cooking school adds another opportunity for enrichment during the week. **La Cocina que Canta** is set amid fields of organic vegetables, flowers, and fruit and olive trees about two miles from the ranch property. The school hosts visiting chefs who are skilled in a wide variety of cuisines.

You might find fancier accommodations and more pampering closer to home for the same amount of money, but this is a one-of-a-kind place that has found a way to stay true to its mission while embracing the trends of the time.

Camping and RV Parks

Rancho Ojai (Km. 112, Carr. Libre Mexicali-Tecate, tel. 665/655-3014, www.rancho-ojai.com, reservaciones@campinginbaja.com) offers tent sites, RV sites with full hookups, and cabins on a working ranch. This is a family-friendly place that is popular with upscale Tijuana and Tecate residents, who come for the immaculate cabins, pool, and miniature golf. Rancho Ojai is part of the KOA network, and has been voted one of top KOA campgrounds in the world. Cabins with shared bath are US$69–83, US$92–107 with private bath, and US$138 with private bath and kitchenette. Tent sites cost US$12 and RV sites are US$31. The ranch is 21 kilometers east of Tecate on Mexico 2. Exit the toll road at El Hongo and drive west on Mexico 2 for eight kilometers to the Rancho Ojai gates.

Rancho Santa Verónica (30 km east of Tecate at Km. 98, Mexico 2, toll-free U.S. tel. 888/556-6288, www.ranchosantaveronica.com, US$20) also has full-hookup slots and tent spaces. Guests may use any of the ranch's recreational facilities.

FOOD

There is no better place in Baja to try your first real tacos than the stands near Tecate's Hidalgo Park. Each one does this Mexican standard a little differently; Mexicans tend to eat tacos for their evening meal, but the taquerias are usually open from late morning until late in the evening.

Taquería Los Arcos on Avenida Juárez near the famous Tecate bakery (on the opposite side

of the street) is a good place to try simple carne asada or the more adventurous *tacos de cabeza*. Several popular stands are set up along Juárez heading west from the plaza. Look for the longest line and join the crowd.

With a history dating back to 1969, **El Mejor Pan de Tecate** (Juárez 331, btw Rodríguez/Portes Gil, tel. 665/654-0040, www.elmejorpandetecate.com, 24 hours daily) has impressed many a visitor with its handmade brick-oven breads. Tray upon tray of *pan dulce*, empanadas, pies, cakes, muffins, rolls, and more come out of the kitchen piping hot and get placed on racks that stretch from floor to ceiling. Grab a tray and some tongs and load up for the day. These truly are among the best sweets you'll find anywhere on the peninsula.

La Bodeguita on the plaza (Juárez 346, tel. 665/101-7652, 1–9 P.M. Tues.–Sun.) serves wines from Baja California and local cheeses to go with them. Next door, **D'Arce Restaurant** (Juárez at Cárdenas, tel. 665/654-1616) makes a pleasant stop for guacamole and a *limonada*. It also has a full menu of Mexican staples. La Michoacana on the plaza has cold treats, including *paletas*.

For upscale fusion food presented with a creative flare, head to **Asao** (Lerma, north of Juárez, three blocks east of the plaza, tel. 665/654-4777, www.santuariodiegueno.com, noon–11 P.M. Thurs.–Sat., noon–8 P.M. Sun., mains US$10–25) on a hilltop overlooking the valley and international border. Plans call for development of a boutique hotel called Santuario Diegueño (tel. 665/654-4777, www.santuariodiegueno.com), but for now it's just the restaurant.

El Mezquíte Restaurante at the Estancia Inn serves dependable Mexican fare. Closer to Rancho La Puerta, on the south side of Boulevard Juárez, **La Misión** grills juicy steaks and pours strong margaritas, and **El Faro,** a little farther west on Avenida Juárez, is the place for fresh seafood.

Groceries

Several *tiendas* on Avenida Juárez and Avenida Hidalgo stock the basics; a **Calimax supermarket** (Juárez/Carranza, tel. 665/654-

0039), has a larger selection, and there are two additional locations around town. Big-box stores Soriana and Super Ley are located in a modern shopping center west of the town center.

INFORMATION AND SERVICES
Tourist Assistance

The **Secretaría de Turismo** (Secretary of Tourism, or SECTUR, tel. 665/654-1095, 8 A.M.–8 P.M. Mon.–Fri., 9 A.M.–1 P.M. Sat., 10 A.M.–2 P.M. Sun.) is located on the south side of Parque Hidalgo, next door to the police station. Or stop by the smaller booth at the border crossing (Lázaro Cárdenas and Madero).

Money

Most places in Tecate accept U.S. currency. There's a money exchange in Tecate, California, in the same plaza as the U.S. post office and Western Union.

The Banamex on Avenida Juárez and Serfín on Calle Cárdenas both have ATMs and currency exchange services.

Post

Tecate's post office is on the corner of Calles Madero and Ortiz Rubio.

Immigration and Customs

The immigration and customs offices at the border crossing are open 5 A.M.–1 A.M. daily.

GETTING THERE
By Bus

Tecate's bus depot is on Avenida Juárez at Calle Rodríguez; it has a snack bar and long-distance telephone service. **Autotransportes de Baja California** (ABC, tel. 664/621-2668, www.abc.com.mx) has regular connections to Mexicali, Tijuana, and Ensenada.

By Car

From San Diego, take I-805 to CA 94 and follow this highway southeast for 66 kilometers to the exit for Tecate. From Arizona, pick up CA 94 from I-8 west. Plan to arrive between 5 A.M. and 1 A.M., when the border gate is open.

Be sure to buy a Mexican auto insurance policy online or at the border before you cross into Mexico. Temporary vehicle import permits (required for driving on the mainland but not in Baja), are issued 8 A.M.–4 P.M. Monday–Saturday at the customs office.

Two Baja California (Norte) state highways pass through Tecate: Mexico 2 (to Tijuana or Mexicali) and Mexico 3 (to Ensenada). The toll road (US$10) between Tijuana and Tecate, Mexico 2-D, parallels the border.

By Rail

The **Pacific Southwest Railway Museum** (State Hwy. 94 and Forest Gate Rd., Campo, CA, U.S. weekend tel. 619/478-9937, U.S. weekday tel. 619/465-7776, www.sdrm.org, US$43) offers a periodic rail tour to the Old Tecate Railroad Station (one-day or twilight).

By Foot

For a day trip, you can park in any number of lots on the U.S. side of the border and walk over to Tecate. A recommended strategy is to park under a street light in the Payless parking lot right across from the U.S. immigration office. The cost is US$5 per day.

MEXICO 3 TO ENSENADA

Mexico 3 is a two-lane state highway that begins in Tecate, follows the foothills of the Sierra de Juárez to the Valle del Guadalupe Wine Country, and ends near Ensenada. This route makes a longer but pleasant alternative to the coastal road from Tijuana.

MEXICO 2 TO MEXICALI

East of Tecate, Mexico 2 heads toward the Sierra de Juárez, where several palm canyons named Tajo, El Carrizo, Guadalupe, and El Palomar offer prime hiking, off-roading, and wilderness camping. Tajo also is known among rock climbers. Spring-fed streams run year-round, but the time to go is between November and April. From May to October, the temperatures can get above 38°C. Next, you'll reach the northern edge of **Laguna Salada,** a 100-kilometer-long dry salt lake. The Pemex station near Km. 24 is the only option for fuel until La Rumorosa (53 km farther west). If you take the Cuota, Mexico 2-D, between Tecate and Mexicali, you'll pass through two toll booths, each of which costs approximately US$2.50.

After Laguna Salada, the highway ascends the northern foothills of the Sierra de los Cucapá and eventually arrives in Mexicali.

Laguna Hanson

At Km. 73, west of La Rumorosa, there is a graded dirt road that leads 63 kilometers to Laguna Hanson (elev. 5,000 feet) in the Parque Nacional Constitución de 1857. The second half of the road is for high-clearance vehicles only; four-wheel drive is recommended. The park is more easily approached via Mexico 3, southeast of Ensenada.

Cañon de Guadalupe

Of the four larger canyons in this part of the Sierra de Juárez, 400-hectare Cañon de Guadalupe is the most popular among hikers and campers because of its healing hot springs. In this high-elevation oasis, granite peaks tower over a sea of blue fan palms. Waterfalls, prehistoric rock art, and solar power all are part of the experience. Rock climbers find challenging pitches at Canon Tajo.

Campsites at **Guadalupe Canyon Hot Springs and Campground** (U.S. tel. 949/673-2670, www.guadalupe-canyon.com, US$50–75) are arranged to afford some privacy. Each of the eight campsites features its own private hot tub made of river rock and concrete, and you can adjust the temperature between 26–41°C. The sites can accommodate multiple vehicles, and there is a two-night minimum on weekends and a three-night minimum on holiday weekends. Pets are welcome, with proof of vaccinations.

Facilities for campers include outhouses, showers, and a market that sells the basics. Refrigeration is provided by 45-kilogram blocks of ice. The owners do not want you to collect firewood or disturb any of the natural surroundings, but firewood is for sale. The canyon is popular on the holidays and the weekends, so book early.

For tours of the Cañon de Guadalupe, contact **Rupestres** (cell tel. 686/158-9921, explorandobajacalifornia@hotmail.com, US$70).

La Rumorosa and Vicinity

Near Km. 44, the highway climbs the steep Juárez escarpment to the town of La Rumorosa. Named for the whispering winds that blow by the 1,275-meter pass, the village is populated with the summer homes of Mexicali and Tijuana residents. The old highway was infamous for the number of fatal accidents. After the old road was closed, it was used in the filming of a James Bond movie. La Rumorosa's most famous resident might be El Diablito (Little Devil). He is a small red figure painted in a cave in the nearby El Vallecito. Only on December 21, the winter solstice, a ray of sunlight illuminates the figure. For tours of El Vallecito and La Rumorosa, contact **Rupestres** (cell tel. 686/158-9921, explorandobajacalifornia@hotmail.com, US$60).

MUSEO CAMPO ALASKA

With the completion of the paved highway between Tijuana and Mexicali in 1916, Mexicali became instantly connected to the rest of the state of Baja California. In 1923–1929 then governor Abelardo L. Rodriguez built a massive stone garrison at Campo Alaska along the highway, which served as summer offices for the state government in the town of Campo Alaska. Today the former federal quarters hold Museo Campo Alaska (tel. 686/552-8279, www.inah.gob.mx, 10 A.M.–4 P.M. Wed.–Sun.), a small museum that documents the history of the indigenous people of the area.

MUSEO DE SITIO EL VALLECITO

At Km. 72, stop at the Museo de Sitio El Vallecito (tel. 686/552-8279, 10 A.M.–4 P.M. Wed.–Sun.) to view some of the most accessible cave paintings on the peninsula. Other sites require multiple days of hiking into the backcountry with burros for a chance to glimpse the mysterious work of an ancient people; this one requires only a stop on the toll road.

ENSENADA TO EL ROSARIO

Whether they are on a cruise from Los Angeles, driving from San Diego, or passing through on the way to points south, many travelers find themselves in Ensenada for an afternoon or longer. Those who venture away from the commercial port and busy tourist zone into the town center find a surprisingly pleasant Mexican town to explore.

Beyond the border region but still within easy reach of San Diego, Ensenada has an identity all its own. Cruise ships bring tourists who roam the *malecón* by day and return to their ships at night, leaving the town to the locals and visitors who've driven themselves from the other side of the border for an overnight getaway.

Accordingly, the commercial district along the busy waterfront is crowded with tourist shops and services. But a few blocks inland, Ensenada transforms into a regional center of commerce with a much more local—and inviting—feel. Ranches, fisheries, and wineries all conduct their business here. Students come to study at several universities. And travelers from mainland Mexico come to explore the wine country in the nearby Valle de Guadalupe. A Dominican mission, Russian colony, and beautiful coastline add to Ensenada's appeal.

South of Ensenada, Mexico 1 meanders through a series of farming communities, including the rolling hills and vineyards of the Valle de Santo Tomás. Legendary sportfishing

© NIKKI GOTH ITOI

HIGHLIGHTS

Riviera del Pacífico: For a slice of Ensenada history, walk the grounds of the former Playa Ensenada Hotel and Casino, once run by American boxer Jack Dempsey and now the city's cultural center (page 66).

La Bufadora: One of the more touristy attractions in Northern Baja, this blowhole is an easy excursion from Ensenada. Visitors congregate around the top of a cavern to watch spumes shoot 30 meters in the air (page 80).

Ruta del Vino: Taste Mexico's world-class vintages at the growing number of boutique wineries in the rural Valle de Guadalupe along Mexico 3 between Ensenada and Tecate (page 81).

Valle de Santo Tomás: Mexico 1 passes rolling hills carpeted in green, a historic winery, and mission ruins in this grape- and olive-growing region (page 88).

Parque Nacional Sierra San Pedro Mártir: The tallest peaks on the peninsula offer a refreshing contrast to Baja's desert scenery (page 92).

LOOK FOR [TO FIND RECOMMENDED SIGHTS, ACTIVITIES, DINING, AND LODGING.

Ensenada coastline

and surfable waves await all the way south to San Quintín. El Rosario, at the southern end of this region, marks the gateway to the vast central desert and the Valle de los Cirios.

Away from the Pacific coast, hikers and backpackers can explore two mountain ranges, the Sierra de Juárez and the Sierra de San Pedro Mártir, which has the tallest peak on the Baja Peninsula, an internationally known observatory, and nearly 69,000 hectares of untouched wilderness.

PLANNING YOUR TIME

Half a day is plenty of time to get a feel for Ensenada. If you have a car, you might spend a few hours or an entire day visiting wineries along the Ruta del Vino. Anglers will be content to spend a week or more plying the waters of Bahía San Quintín.

For sierra-bound visitors, the best hiking seasons are mid-April–mid-June (good for wildflowers) and late September–early November (when quaking aspens put on a show).

Ensenada and Vicinity

Although it hosts a high volume of visitors, Ensenada is not a purpose-built resort destination. Thanks to the commercial fishing, aquaculture, and agriculture industries, Ensenada has grown to become the third-largest city in Baja. Farms in the area grow olives and grapes on land and yellowtail and halibut in the water. Ensenada's port does more business than any other on the peninsula.

Most first-time visitors begin their tour of Ensenada with a stroll along Avenida López Mateos near the waterfront. But if you walk a few blocks away from the harbor, across Avenida Juárez, you'll find yourself in a much quieter, residential part of town with more local-style shops and restaurants.

HISTORY

Spanish explorers Juan Cabrillo (1542) and Sebastián Vizcaíno (1602) were the first Europeans to land at Ensenada, and the first ranches were established through a land grant from Spain in the early 1800s. One of these ranches, Rancho Ensenada, became the inspiration for the town's name. Ensenada experienced dramatic growth when gold was discovered in 1870 and the town transformed into a mining center.

From 1882 to 1915, Ensenada served as the capital city of the Territory of Baja California. U.S. Prohibition fueled another boom in the 1920s, which saw the opening of the historic Ensenada Hotel and Casino, but this time the prosperity was short-lived due to the repeal of Prohibition and the onset of the Great Depression.

In the 1950s travelers from the United States began visiting Ensenada to take advantage of the sportfishing opportunities, and the city became known as the Yellowtail Capital of the World.

Today Ensenada is the capital city of the *municipio* (county) of Ensenada, which extends south to the border with Baja California Sur. Around 40,000 expats are permanent residents in the area. The economy is driven by fishing and aquaculture, fish processing, farming, and the import/export trade. The addition of a cruise ship pier and village, plus a scenic *malecón* further enhanced the city's appeal to visitors. As with other once-popular destinations in Baja, tourism is significantly down here, due to the drug wars in the border zone and the global slowdown in travel. This means Ensenada today is a quieter town than you may have experienced in the recent past, and there are deals to be found.

SIGHTS
◖ Riviera del Pacífico

During the U.S. Prohibition era, heavyweight boxing celebrity Jack Dempsey built a massive resort on the Ensenada waterfront called the Playa Ensenada Hotel and Casino. On opening night in 1929, Bing Crosby and the Xavier Cugat Orchestra entertained the crowd. A local singer named Margarita Carmen Cansino joined the orchestra—and later changed her name to Rita Hayworth. A symbol of Ensenada's newfound prosperity, the resort thrived for a few years until the repeal of Prohibition and the onset of the Great Depression sent most of the gamblers home. Management tried reopening the hotel as the Riviera del Pacífico, but by 1938, the doors had closed for good.

Forty years later, the Mexican government intervened and restored the legendary building as the city's **Centro Social Cívico y Cultural Riviera** (Social, Civic, and Cultural Center, corner of Costero and Riviera, tel. 646/176-4310). It contains government offices and a public library as well as a small museum, the **Museo de Historia de Ensenada** (tel. 646/177-0594, 9:30 A.M.–2 P.M. and 3–5 P.M. Mon.–Sat., 10 A.M.–5 P.M. Sun., by donation), with historical exhibits that represent the indigenous people of Baja California, the era of European exploration, and the Dominican missions.

The **Galería de la Cuidad** (tel. 646/177-3130, 9 A.M.–6 P.M. Mon.–Fri.), at the north end of the building, showcases the works of Baja California artists.

Throughout the building, much of the original tile and paintings have been preserved. The street-level **Bar Andaluz** features a mural by Alfredo Ramos Martínez (1871–1946), who established Mexico City's Las Escuelas de Pintura al Aire Libre (Schools of Painting in the Open Air).

Museo Histórico Regional

Ensenada's Museum of Regional History (Gastelum near López Mateos, tel. 646/178-

2531, 10 a.m.–5 p.m. Tues.–Sun., by donation) occupies a former 1886 military garrison that housed the Ensenada jail until 1986. The permanent collection consists of native artifacts.

Museo Ex-Aduana Marítima de Ensenada

This historic building downtown was built by the U.S.-based International Land Company of Mexico, which acquired much of the coastline from the Mexican government in the 19th century. Mexico's Aduana Marítima (Maritime

DOWNTOWN ENSENADA

SEMARNAT

GUADALUPE

2A

3A

FLORESTA

AV

CALLE

CALLE

ESPINOZA

AV

DESERT INN

POST OFFICE

AV

LAS DUNAS

LAS ROCAS

STATE TOURISM OFFICE

ROTARIO

AV

CORONA HOTEL

COSTA BAJA INN

MATEOS

RIVIERA DEL PACÍFICO

HOTEL MISIÓN SANTA ISABEL

CASTILLO

LOPEZ

POSADA EL REY SOL

HOTEL CORTEZ

2A

CASA DEL SOL

AV

CENTRO ARTESANAL

COSTERO

BOAT RAMP

BLANCARTE

3A

RESTAURANT EL REY SOL

CALLE

AV

MARINA

CRUISEPORT TERMINAL

ALVARADO

HERTZ

AV

MONUMENTAL FLAG

HOTEL HACIENDA

RIVEROLL

AV

M A L E C Ó N

CALLE

BOULEVARD

MACHEROS

AV

P u e r t o   d e   E n s e n a d a

MIRAMAR

AV

PLAZA MARINA

BAJA INN HOTEL SANTO TOMÁS

CALLE

Plaza Cívica

ENSENADA SPORTFISHING TERMINAL

SANBORNS

GASTELUM

CAFÉ CAFÉ

COTUCO OFFICE

MUELLE TRES

MERCADO DE MARISCOS

AV RUIZ

PAPAS & BEER

MUSEO HISTÓRICO REGIONAL

AV

OBREGÓN

HUSSONG'S CANTINA

LA COCHINITA

MANZANILLA

CUSTOMS OFFICE

PLAZA HUSSONG/ LAS CONCHAS OYSTER BAR AND RESTAURANT

MUSEO EX-ADUANA MARÍTIMA DE ENSENADA

PORT OFFICE

AZUELA

RYERSON

IMMIGRATION OFFICE

BOULEVARD

© AVALON TRAVEL

200 yds

200 m

0

0

Customs) took over in 1922. Then the Instituto Nacional de Antropología e Historia (INAH) stepped in to restore the building and convert it into a museum (Ryerson and Calle Uribe, tel. 646/178-2531, 9 A.M.–4 P.M. Tues.–Sun., by donation). Temporary exhibits cover various Mexican cultural themes.

Malecón

Ensenada's *malecón,* built in the 1990s, is a relatively new fixture on the waterfront. With its giant Mexican flag and bay views, the promenade is a good place to get your bearings before a walk around town. At the north end of the *malecón* are the sportfishing terminal and *mercado de mariscos* (seafood market). Near here, **Plaza Cívica** features statues of three pivotal figures in Mexican history: Benito Juárez (Mexico's first president), Padre Miguel Hidalgo (initiator of the Mexican Revolution), and Venustiano Carranza (first president after the revolution). At the south end, across the narrow Bahía Ensenada, is the cruise ship pier and the Riviera del Pacífico.

Wineries

Ensenada has a long history in the grape-growing/winemaking business and a growing reputation for bottling world-class vintages. Most of the vineyards are located in the nearby Valle de Guadalupe, but several operations have offices and/or tasting rooms in downtown Ensenada.

Part of **Bodegas de Santo Tomás** (Miramar 666, tel. 646/178-3333, www.santo-tomas. com, 10 A.M.–9 P.M. Mon.–Sat., 10 A.M.–6 P.M. Sun.), Tienda Miramar is a good place to get acquainted with the local varietals. As Mexico's oldest winery, its roots go back to the Dominican mission in the Valle de Santo Tomás. The winery offered its first wine to the public in 1888 and moved its winemaking headquarters to Ensenada in 1934. Today most of the action centers around its vineyard in the Valle de Santo Tomás. The winery also runs a restaurant, shop, and tours at Km. 95 on Mexico 3 in the valley of San Antonio de las Minas.

SPORTS AND RECREATION
Fishing

Commercial fishing has taken its toll since Ensenada's heyday as a sportfishing getaway in the 1950s and '60s. But a day on a *panga* or cruiser can still yield a decent catch in the peak summer season. Lingcod, rockfish, and bonito are among the most common species.

For an old-school fishing experience, hire a *panga* at the Ensenada Sportfishing Terminal near the north end of the harbor or at Punta Banda, south of Ensenada. **Sergio's Sportfishing Center** (tel./fax 646/178-2185, toll-free U.S. tel. 800/336-5454, www.sergiosfishing.com, US$62 pp, including your Mexican fishing license) is a good choice if you're looking for a six-pack boat. **Gordo's Sportfishing** (tel. 646/178-3515 or 646/178-2377, www.gordossportfishing.com) has larger open party boats and offshore tuna rigs. Be prepared to be badgered by sportfishing salesmen as you walk along the marina to book with any of the outfitters.

Note: By law, anyone who goes out on a fishing boat needs to buy a license, even if you don't plan to fish.

Boating

Marina Coral (radio VHF 71, tel. 646/175-0000, toll-free U.S. tel. 800/862-9020, www.hotelcoral.com), has 500 yacht slips to 135 feet and a floating fuel dock. The marina has a full suite of shore services, including hookups, lockers, restrooms, telephones, and wireless Internet. Use of the boat launch ramp is US$35/day and about half that for guests of the hotel.

Ensenada Cruiseport Village Marina (tel. 646/173-4141, fax 646/173-4151, toll-free U.S. tel. 877/219-5822, www.ecpvmarina.com) has 198 slips (US$1.50 per foot per day) and a 350-foot pier for mega-yachts (US$2.25 per foot per day) and a complete list of shore facilities.

As Ensenada is an official Mexican port of entry, arriving boaters must check in with the port captain on Boulevard Azueta. Ensenada's Marina Coral offers the *Ventanilla Unica* (Single Window) service. Boaters can get their tourist cards and TIP (Temporary Import Permits) and pay at the adjoining bank machine. It's open 8 A.M.–5 P.M. Monday–Friday.

Surfing

By the time you've reached the surf spots around Ensenada, you've distanced yourself beyond the reach of most weekend warriors from San Diego. Ensenada has several surf shops located on the north end of town. Try the **Baja Board Shop** (Loc. 720-4 Costero, Plaza Bocarelli, tel. 646/175-7218. chimbosurfer@hotmail.com) for boards, board shorts, ding repair, and other surfing needs. The shop has Internet and a café on-site.

San Miguel might be Baja's most consistent point break. It's located just south of the toll booth on Mexico 1. Parking is US$5 and the crowds will be on it if the surf is good. Get there early to catch it before the onshores start up in the late morning. There are several spots as you drive south that are less consistent.

Isla Todos Santos is located 20 kilometers offshore of Ensenada. Killers is located on the northwest side of the island and breaks on winter swells coming from the northwest. Because of its direct exposure to the north and a deep water canyon that channels the long period swell, Killers can get huge. It is not for the uninitiated. You can hire a boat from the Ensenada harbor for a ride to the island for around US$100.

Diving

There is little shore diving around Ensenada, but boat trips take divers to explore several underwater pinnacles.

Almar Dive Shop (Macheros 149, tel. 646/178-3013, almardive@hotmail.com) offers rental gear and lessons. **Dale's La Bufadora Dive Shop** (Rancho La Bufadora, tel. 646/154-2092, www.labufadoradive.com, open weekends or by appointment) rents gear and does boat trips to the pinnacles just offshore.

Whale-Watching

Sergio's Sportfishing Center (tel./fax 646/178-2185, toll-free U.S. tel. 800/336-5454,

www.sergiosfishing.com) and **Gordo's** (tel. 646/178-3515 or 646/178-2377, fax 646/174-04810, www.gordossportfishing.com) offer whale-watching boat tours late December–late March. You won't get as close to the gray whales here as you can in the birthing lagoons farther south, but it's still a pleasant way to get out on the water if you're not interested in fishing or diving. Both outfitters are located on the Ensenada Sportfishing Pier on the *malecón*.

Cruises

You can visit Ensenada as part of a four-day cruise along the Pacific coast with Royal Caribbean's **Monarch of the Seas** (toll-free U.S. tel. 800/327-6700, www.royalcaribbean. com, US$219–379). The ship departs from Los Angeles. Carnival (www.carnival.com) offers three- and four-day Baja trips aboard the **Paradise** at comparable prices.

Spa Services

Choose from a variety of treatments and service packages at the spa at **Hotel Coral & Marina** (Km. 103, Carr. Tijuana-Ensenada #3421, Zona Playitas, tel. 646/175-0000, toll-free U.S. tel. 800/862-9020, www.hotelcoral. com, 8 A.M.–8 P.M. Mon.–Sat., 8 A.M.–6 P.M. Sun.). Services include Swedish massage, body wraps, and facials.

ENTERTAINMENT AND EVENTS
Nightlife

Most of the evening entertainment takes place along Avenida López Mateos and Boulevard Costero between Calle Sanginés and Avenida Macheros. Some of the hotels and bars host live music, and there are a few discos, but it's nothing compared to what you'll find in Tijuana. Many places have closed in recent years due to the drop in tourism.

Ensenada's best-known bar has been serving patrons since 1892. Opened by German immigrant Johan Hussong, **Hussong's Cantina** (Ruiz 113, tel. 646/178-3210, www.cantinahussongs. com, 10 A.M.–1 A.M. daily) has been a gathering place for expats and locals ever since, and many veteran Baja travelers kick off each road trip down the peninsula with a Tecate, Bohemia, or Dos Equis (XX) beer here. Late afternoon is the best time to beat the rowdy crowds. Weekly specials include two-for-one beers on Tuesdays, two-for-one *micheladas* on Thursdays, and two-for-one margaritas on Saturdays.

Two-story **Papas and Beer** (Ruiz and López Mateos, tel. 646/174-0145, www.papasandbeer. com, noon–3 A.M. daily), across the street, has less character but is also a little mellower.

A few wine bar/restaurants offer an appealing alternative to the usual bar scene. Wine comes first at **La Contra** (Moctezuma 623 at Calle 6, tel. 646/178-8213, www.lacontravinos.com, mains US$7–15) which represents most of the best local labels and offers a menu of fresh salads, pizzas, and pasta. **La Casa del Arte** (Moctezuma 479 btw Calles 4/5, tel. 646/175-7035, www.lacasadelarte.com.mx, 2 P.M.–midnight Mon.–Sat.) features jazz on Fridays starting at 8 P.M. The restaurant has indoor and outdoor seating and a broad menu ranging from Serrano ham to spaghetti and meatballs and rib-eye steak.

Festivals and Events
FEBRUARY
Ensenada puts on a good show for **Carnaval,** during the six days before Ash Wednesday. The festivities include parades, amusement rides, live music, costumes, and lots of food and drink.

APRIL
Thousands of cyclists ride in the **Rosarito-Ensenada 50-Mile Fun Bicycle Ride** (tel. 619/424-6084, www.rosaritoensenada.com) each April. Register online in advance (US$35) or on the day of the event (US$40).

The **Tommy Bahama Newport-Ensenada Race** (www.nosa.org) is a regatta in which hundreds of yachts sail from Southern California to Ensenada.

JUNE
SCORE International and Tecate beer sponsor the annual **Baja 500** (U.S. tel. 818/225-8402,

www.score-international.com) off-road race, which starts in Ensenada.

JULY
Beach volleyball players from all over the world compete for sizable cash prizes in the **Baja Volleyball Open** (www.bajaopen.com) held at Playa Hermosa.

AUGUST
The wine country celebrates the **Fiesta de la Vendimia Bajacaliforniana** (Baja California Wine Harvest Festival, tel. 646/174-0170, www.caniracensenada.com or www.fiestas-delavendimia.com) with 10 days of wine-tasting, winery tours, and gourmet cooking at the wineries around town and in the Valle de Guadalupe. Admission prices vary by location.

SEPTEMBER
J. D. Hussong Baja International Chili Cookoff & Salsa Contest (tel. 646/174-4575, www.hussongs.com/chilicookoff.html, US$10) takes place on a Saturday afternoon at the Quintas Papagayo Resort. Chili connoisseurs battle for the opportunity to attend the annual International Chili Society's World Championship in Omaha, Nebraska. This is one of the most popular events in Ensenada each year.

OCTOBER
The local restaurant association CANIRAC organizes the popular **Feria Internacional del Pescado y el Marisco** (International Seafood Fair, tel. 646/174-0448 or 646/174-0435, www.caniracensenada.com), featuring restaurants from Ensenada and as far away as Tijuana and Southern California.

Pro surfers compete in a two-day **Mexican Surf Fiesta** at Playa de San Miguel (tel. 858/586-9173).

NOVEMBER
The **SCORE-Tecate Baja 1000** (U.S. tel. 818/225-8402, www.score-international. com) off-road race takes over much of the Baja

Peninsula for a week each November. On alternate years, the course goes all the way to La Paz. If you happen to be driving on Mexico 1 during the week of the race (or the two weeks leading up to it), you'll see clouds of dust following the motorcycles, trucks, and dune buggies that are on the dirt course. And they'll probably be traveling much faster than traffic on the paved highway.

SHOPPING

Ensenada shopping is more international and upscale than what you'll find in Tijuana, a reflection of the sorts of things that cruise ship passengers like to buy. The stores along Avenida López Mateos and Boulevard Costero have an assortment of souvenirs and beachwear. Some of the most popular purchases are silver jewelry, leather goods, pottery, fine art, and accessories for the beach. In general, prices drop the farther you get from the waterfront.

The **Centro Artesanal** (Costero 1094 at the end of Castillo, no tel.) has arts and crafts from all over Mexico. Ensenada also has several large shopping plazas, including **Centro Comercial Misión** (Calle 11 and Reforma), with a Gigante supermarket, Banamex ATM, Lavamática Express, Smart and Final, and Cinema Gemelos.

Open since 1988, **Galería de Pérez Meillón** (Centro Artesanal, Loc. 40, Costero 1094 and Castillo, tel. 646/175-7848, adalbertopm@hotmail.com, 9 A.M.–5 P.M. daily) specializes in Mata Ortiz pottery made by Native Americans from a small village in the mainland state of Chihuahua. Owner Adalberto Pérez Meillón selects each piece directly from the artists. He also carries a variety of other Native American handicrafts as well as works by contemporary artists living in Baja California and mainland Mexico.

The wide variety of *artesanías* and friendly English-speaking staff create a pleasant shopping experience at **Bazar Casa Ramírez** (López Mateos 496-3, tel. 646/178-8209, bramirez717@hotmail.com). This large family-

Handmade blankets are a popular souvenir.

run shop contains high-quality crafts from all over Mexico, including Talavera pottery, wrought-iron sculptures, decorative mirrors, and works of carved wood and blown glass. For silver jewelry from Taxco, try **Arriaga de Taxco** (two locations: López Matéos 821 and 865, tel. 646/174-0704, sterling@telnor.net, 10 A.M.–7 P.M. Mon.–Fri., until 8 P.M. Sat., until 6 P.M. Sun.).

Los Globos (Calle 9, three blocks east of Reforma, 9 A.M.–6 P.M. daily) is a flea market with vendors selling housewares, furniture, apparel, and more. Weekends are best.

For leather goods, try **Nuevo México Lindo** (López Mateos 688, tel. 646/178-1381). It specializes in saddles and related gear but also has handbags.

A few fine-art galleries have sprung up around town, including **Galería La Esquina de Bodegas** (Miramar and Calle 6, tel. 646/178-3557, 8 A.M.–10 P.M. Sun.–Fri.), which is located across from Bodegas de Santo Tomás and shows the works of Mexican and international artists.

ACCOMMODATIONS
Downtown

Ensenada's hotels are concentrated along Avenida López Mateos and Boulevard Costero. Late-night noise is a concern here, especially if you end up in a room that faces the street. Also, many of the longtime favorite establishments have let standards slip in recent years to the point where we can no longer recommend them. Aside from peak travel times of July–August, Carnaval (February), and U.S. college spring break (March), hotels are rarely full and rates are negotiable.

The high season in Ensenada is May–September, and weekdays are generally slower than weekends year-round. Rates listed here do not include 12 percent tax, unless specified. Some places also add a 10 percent service charge to the nightly rate.

UNDER US$50

Hotel Hacienda (Calle 2 #211 at Alvarado, tel. 646/178-2344, US$40) has a good location just one full block from the main drag. Traffic noise is an issue for the rooms that face Calle 2, but all the rooms are well maintained and clean.

Three blocks north of Hussong's Cantina, **Hotel Ritz** (Ruiz 379 at Calle 4, tel. 646/174-0501, fax 646/178-3262, US$32) appeals to travelers who don't need off-street parking and who prefer to stay a comfortable distance from the main tourist drag (but still within the downtown area). Rooms on the lower level are dark; balconies on the more expensive second and third stories are a nice feature.

US$50-100

The northernmost property in the small **Desert Inn** (Floresta at Bucaneros, tel. 646/176-2601, toll-free U.S. tel. 800/346-3942, www.desertinns.com, US$75–130) chain of hotels in Baja has 50 rooms in a three-story building. Rooms come with air-conditioning, heat, TV, and phone. There are a restaurant and pool on-site but no off-street parking. It's adequate enough for a place to crash but certainly nothing special.

◖ **Hotel Misión Santa Isabel** (Costero 1119 btw Castillo/López Mateos, tel. 646/178-3616, fax 646/178-3345, US$39–139) is a large, mission-style building with clean rooms and friendly service—something that seems increasingly hard to find in Ensenada accommodations. Its 57 guestrooms have colonial-style wood furnishings, with modern amenities such as air-conditioning, heat, satellite TV, and direct-dial phones. The welcoming grounds include a restaurant/bar, gift shop, and one of the cleaner swimming pools in town; secure parking is another plus.

Rooms in the mission-style **Casa del Sol Hotel** (López Mateos 1001, tel. 646/178-1570, toll-free U.S. tel. 877/316-1684, www.casadelsolmexico.net, US$56–100) come with tiled baths, air-conditioning, TV, phone, and Wi-Fi. Services include secure parking and the on-site Bistro Café Sutaza and Essence Spa, with a full menu of treatments. Your morning coffee is on the house.

Suites are a good value at the **Baja Inn Hotel**

Santo Tomás (Costero 609 at Miramar, tel. 646/178-1503 or 800/026-6999, toll-free U.S. tel. 800/303-2684, US$80), which is part of the same group of Baja Inn hotels. Its 80 clean rooms have air-conditioning, heat, and satellite TV, and there's secure parking and a restaurant.

The well-run **Hotel Cortez** (López Mateos 1089, tel. 646/178-2307 or 800/026-6999, toll-free U.S. tel. 800/303-2684, www.bajainn. com, US$55) has 75 rooms in a two-story colonial-style building with an attractive lobby. Amenities include air-conditioning, heat, direct-dial phones, and cable TV. Nonsmoking rooms are available. The hotel also has a heated pool, restaurant/bar, and secure parking.

The five-story, 93-room (**Corona Hotel** (Costero 1442, tel. 646/176-0901, www.hotel-corona.com.mx, US$64–83) gives you an in-town location that's removed from the worst of the noise. Rooms feature bay views, balconies, satellite TV, air-conditioning, and heat. The spa is well appointed and clean. The bar has the feel of a hip ski bar in Switzerland. The secure parking out front can handle any size rig. You can even back your car up to the ground-floor rooms at the front of the hotel.

US$150-250

Popular with the yachting crowd, the (**Hotel Coral & Marina** (Km. 103, exit Mexico 1 at Ensenada Centro, tel. 646/175-0000, toll-free U.S. tel. 800/862-9020, www.hotelcoral.com, US$130–170) has a full-service marina in addition to clean and contemporary accommodations. Its suites have balconies overlooking the marina. There is a restaurant serving *alta cocina mexicana*, plus a long list of guest services such as a nightclub, heated indoor and outdoor pools, hot tub, sauna, lighted tennis courts, and parking garage. The place is kid friendly to boot.

Posada El Rey Sol (Blancarte 130, tel. 646/178-1601, toll-free U.S. tel. 888/311-6871, US$80–200) is part of the Americas Best Value chain. It has 52 good-sized rooms and a heated pool, spa, restaurant, bar, and enclosed parking. It's a block from the waterfront, with a friendly and helpful staff.

Outside Ensenada

US$150-250

Overlooking the Pacific Ocean five kilometers north of town, **Punta Morro Hotel and Suites** (Km. 106, Mexico 1, tel. 646/178-3507, toll-free U.S. tel. 800/526-6676, www.punta-morro.com, US$160–185) has clean and quiet suites, from studios to three-bedroom units. Highlights include well-equipped kitchens, fireplaces, and terraces. The food and spa aren't at the same level as the accommodations, however.

Ocean views are the best part about a night's stay at **Las Rosas Hotel and Spa** (Km. 105.5, Ensenada Road, tel. 646/174-4595 or 866/447-6727, fax 646/175-9031, www.lasrosas.com, US$160–170), which is located six kilometers north of town on Mexico 1. The tradeoffs are small baths and no air-conditioning. Amenities include a restaurant with somewhat pricey food, pool, hot tub, sauna, exercise center, and tennis court.

OVER US$250

Once worth the high price, **Casa Natalie** (Km. 103.3, tel. 646/174-7373, toll-free U.S. tel. 800/562-8254, www.casanatalie.com, US$220 and up), located near the Hotel Coral & Marina, is under new ownership, and prices have climbed even higher. Its suites are furnished to a level rarely seen in Baja. If money is not a factor, this would still be a convenient home base for a weekend of wine-tasting in the Guadalupe Valley.

FOOD

Fish tacos and seafood cocktails top the list of foods to try in Ensenada (or anywhere in coastal Baja, for that matter). One of the best places to try these local delights is the (**Mercado de Mariscos** (Seafood Market, Costero at Miramar, late morning–early evening daily), behind the Plaza Marina on the waterfront. You can also buy fresh fish here to cook yourself.

Mexican

(**Manzanilla** (Teniente Azueta 139, tel. 646/175-7073, www.rmanzanilla.com, noon–midnight Wed.–Sat., US$10–30) remains one of Ensenada's top restaurants. Guests are greeted by the co-owner, and the restaurant is known for its rib eye, raw fish, and local wines. The restaurant uses local organic ingredients and seafood.

Rinconcito Oaxaqueño (no tel., 9 A.M.–5 P.M. daily), off Diamante and a block south of Reforma, serves authentic Oaxacan cuisine. You can order nopales, *chicharron,* or carne asada in a taco or plate (US$1–5). If they are in season, and you're an adventurous eater, try the grasshoppers *(chapulines)* washed down with an ice-cold Dos Equis.

Acambaro (El Refugio Ensenadense) (Iturbide 528, off Juárez btw Calles 5/6, tel. 646/176-5235, breakfast, lunch, and dinner daily, mains US$10–15) serves tasty Mexican dishes in a rustic wood and brick setting. Plates arrive with the works: limes, oregano, and salsa.

A group of restaurants along Avenida López Mateos specializes in roast chickens: **Hacienda del Charro** (López Mateos 454, tel. 646/178-2114, lunch and dinner till 11:30 P.M. daily) is the best one along this strip, also offering chicken tamales and *pollo pipián* (chicken cooked in a pumpkin-seed mole). The tangy flavor of homemade *agua de jamaica* (hibiscus) balances the savory chicken.

Las Cazuelas Restaurant Bar (Sanginés 6, near Costero, tel. 646/176-1044, 7 A.M.–11 P.M. daily, mains US$10–25) is an old standby serving border-style cuisine, including *codorniz* (quail), seafood, steaks, ribs, and hearty Mexican breakfasts.

The most unique food experience in Ensenada is still offered at (**El Taco de Huitzilopochtli** (Av. de las Rosas 5, Col. Valle Verde, tel. 646/174-2381, 9 A.M.–5 P.M. Sat.–Sun., mains under US$10). The house specialty is *mixiote,* which is lamb wrapped in maguey leaves and then baked for 16 hours in a wood-fired oven. They start the process on Friday, and the food isn't ready until Saturday morning. The menu is limited only by your sense of adventure. You can order *huitlacoche* (corn fungus tacos) or *huanzontle,* a reedy vegetable. The

MEXICAN-STYLE EGGS

Mexican-style egg-and-beans plates come in many different styles. They typically are served as a late breakfast or brunch on weekends and holidays. Here are some of the preparations you may see on the menu:

- *huevos revueltos:* scrambled eggs
- *huevos duros:* hard-boiled eggs
- *huevos escafaldos:* soft-boiled eggs
- *huevos estrellados:* eggs fried sunny-side up
- *huevos a la Mexicana/huevos mexicanos:* eggs scrambled with chopped tomato, onion, and chilies
- *huevos rancheros:* fried eggs served on a tortilla
- *huevos divorciados:* two *huevos estrellados* separated by beans, each egg usually topped with a different salsa
- *con chorizo:* with ground sausage
- *con machaca:* with dried, shredded meat
- *con tocino:* with bacon
- *con jamón:* with ham

easiest way to get there is to take a taxi from downtown, and you'll appreciate not having to drive if you're there when the owner breaks out the "house" tequila.

On the corner of Espinoza and Juárez, **Tacos Fénix** (7 A.M.–8 P.M. daily) serves up some of the town's best seafood tacos out of a stand across from the Calimax. Shrimp tacos are light and crispy, and they cost US$1–1.50 each. **La Cochinita** (Paseo Hidalgo next to Maritime Customs, tel. 646/178-5445, www.lacochinita.com.mx, lunch and dinner daily) is a Baja chain that specializes in Mexican-style Japanese food. There are a dozen locations in Ensenada and more in major cities throughout the peninsula.

For a quick, though not necessarily healthy, bite to eat, **Icarus Wings** (Calle Ambar at 29 de Noviembre, tel. 646/178-6055, www.icarus-go.com, 1–9 P.M. Tues.–Thurs., till 11 P.M. Fri.–Sat., till 7 P.M. Sun.) grills chicken, burgers, fries, and, of course, wings.

Seafood

Las Conchas Oyster Bar and Restaurant (tel. 646/175-7375, lunch and dinner daily, mains US$15 and up), in Plaza Hussong, draws a crowd for oysters (*ostiones*) and other seafood specialties. It's a popular place, so expect to wait for a table.

In San Miguel, **Boules** (San Miguel, tel. 646/175-9769, from 1 P.M. Thurs.–Mon.) is a hotspot for seafood paired with Valle de Guadalupe wines.

On the *malecón,* across from the Mercado Negro, casual 🄲 **Muelle Tres** (Teniente Azueta 187-A, tel. 646/189-7608, muelletres@gmail.com, 1–6 P.M. Wed.–Sun., till 8 P.M. in summer) serves some of the freshest *mariscos* around, including local oysters on the half shell, steamed mussels, and clam ceviche. It is run by celebrated chef Benito Molina, of Manzanilla fame. Nearby, **La Cocedora de Langosta** (tel. 646/178-3742, lacocedoradelangosta@gmail.com, 8 A.M.–9 P.M. daily) makes an outstanding *aguachile* with local scallops, an unusual abalone sandwich, and, of course, the namesake lobster.

Near the Puente Zona Centro, a bridge that crosses over the arroyo, **Barra Azul** (Calle 11 at Espinoza, www.barrazul.com, from 1:30 P.M. Wed.–Mon., mains US$5–10) has a seafood bar that makes tempura oysters and oyster shooters, among other delights. There are several kinds of ceviche and sashimi plates as well.

European

El Rey Sol (López Mateos 1000 at Blancarte, tel. 646/178-1733, www.elreysol.com, 7:30 A.M.–10:30 P.M. daily, mains US$20 and up) is an Ensenada institution for fine French cuisine. The restaurant was founded in 1947 by a native of Santa Rosalía (a town in southern Baja that was built by a French mining company) named Doña Pepita, who studied at the Cordon Bleu cooking school in France. Whether you choose a seafood, poultry, or meat entrée, it will arrive with fresh herbs and vegetables from the family's ranch in the Valle de Santo Tomás, south of Ensenada.

In the Bodegas de Santo Tomás building, **La Embotelladora Vieja** (Miramar 666 at Calle 7, tel. 646/174-0807, noon–11 P.M. Mon. and Wed., noon–11 P.M. Thurs.–Sat., noon–5 P.M. Sun., mains US$20 and up), has a Mediterranean menu and an international wine list.

At Km. 104, a chef from Chihuahua has mastered the art of Mediterranean cooking at **Belio Restaurant** (Km. 104, Carr. Ensenada-Tijuana, El Sauzal, tel. 646/175-8810, restaurantbelio@gmail.com, mains US$15–40). Patio dining on the waterfront setting adds to the charm of this decidedly upscale venue.

Cafés

Stop in for a quick bite at **El Faro Café** (no tel., mains under US$10) before a day of sportfishing. Located next to Gordo's Sportfishing, behind Plaza Marina on the waterfront, the café opens early at 4:30 A.M. and serves breakfast only.

Pueblo Café Deli (Ruiz 96, tel. 646/178-8055, 8 A.M.–midnight daily) serves espresso drinks, plus breakfast foods, Mexican fare, salads, pastries, wine, and beer.

Dependable **Sanborns Café** (Plaza Marina, Costero, tel. 646/174-0971, 7:30 A.M.–10 P.M. daily, mains US$10–15) always has a number of soups, salads, sandwiches, breakfasts, and Mexican dishes on the menu.

Café Café (López Mateos 496, tel. 646/178-8209, from 9 A.M. daily) is a combination coffee house/art gallery that also hosts occasional cultural events and performances.

Wine Bars

Wine comes first at **La Contra** (Moctezuma 623 at Calle 6, tel. 646/178-8213, www.

lacontravinos.com, mains US$7–15) which represents most of the best local labels and offers a menu of fresh salads, pizzas, and pasta. **La Casa del Arte** (Moctezuma 479 btw Calles 4/5, tel. 646/175-7035, www.lacasadelarte. com.mx, 2 P.M.–midnight Mon.–Sat.) features jazz on Fridays starting at 8 P.M. The restaurant has indoor and outdoor seating, and a broad menu ranging from Serrano ham to spaghetti and meatballs to rib-eye steak.

Groceries

The **Gigante** at Avenidas Reforma and Delante is the largest supermarket in town and the easiest to find on your way through. Stop here to pick up just about anything you left behind at home.

Avenida Diamante has a string of local *panaderías, tortillerías,* and *dulcerías.* Vendors along the highway south of town sell fresh tamales as well as local olives, chilies, and honey.

INFORMATION AND SERVICES
Tourist Assistance

The **Baja California State Tourism Secretariat** (Costero and Las Rocas, tel. 646/172-3022, 8 A.M.–5 P.M. Mon.–Fri., 10 A.M.–3 P.M. Sat.–Sun.) has a wealth of information regarding local events, restaurants, and accommodations as well as for the entire state. The staff speaks English and is happy to help.

The **Ensenada Tourism Trust** (Lázaro Cárdenas 609-5, tel. 646/178-8578 or 800/025-3991, toll-free U.S. tel. 800/310-9687, www. enjoyensenada.com) has much of the same information.

Money

There are several ATMs in town, including a Banamex at Avenidas Juárez and Riveroll and a Banca Serfín at Avenida Ruiz 290. Most banks in Ensenada refer visitors to a *casa de cambio* for foreign-exchange services. Several shopping centers along Avenida Juárez and Avenida Reforma feature money-changing booths or storefronts.

Post and Telephone

There is a **post office** (8 A.M.–6 P.M. Mon.–Fri., 9 A.M.–1 P.M. Sat.) at the corner of Avenidas López Mateos and Rotario (Riviera), across from the Desert Inn. Public telephones are a better deal for local and long-distance calls than hotel phones.

Immigration

If you plan to travel south of Maneadero and haven't validated your tourist card yet (US$25), you'll need to pay a visit to the Ensenada immigration office (tel. 646/174-0164, 9 A.M.–5 P.M. daily), next to the port captain's office (COTP) on Avenida Azueta. Look for the turnoff near the waterfront at the northern entrance into town. Parking here can be a challenge, since there is no public lot for the office, and most of the curbs nearby are painted red. Consider parking farther away and walking in.

If you run into any problems getting your tourist permit here, go to the state tourism office (Costero and Calle Las Rocas, tel. 646/172-3022) and ask for help from the SECTUR *delegado.*

Language Schools

Colegio de Idiomas de Baja California (Baja California Language College, Av. Riveroll 1287, tel. 646/174-1741, U.S. tel. 619/758-9711 or toll-free U.S. tel. 877/444-2252, www.baja-cal.com) teaches 30-hour Spanish classes for US$279. Classes are small groups and courses take one week to complete.

The **Center of Languages and Latin American Studies** (Calle Felipe Angeles #15, tel. 646/178-7600, www.spanishschoolbaja.com) also has a one-week program (US$270), with discounts for four or more weeks. Materials, homestays, meals, and registration cost extra.

Emergencies

The **Clínica Hospital ISSSTE** (Sanginés and Pedro Loyola, tel. 646/176-5276) offers 24/7 emergency medical services. For ambulance service, call **Cruz Roja** (tel. 066). If you need emergency treatment at San Diego medical facilities, contact **TransMedic Ambulance**

(842-3 Av. Ruiz, tel. 646/178-1400), a 24/7 emergency service that offers air and land transportation to San Diego.

GETTING THERE
By Air
Ensenada's **Aeropuerto El Ciprés** (tel. 646/177-4503) is located three kilometers south of town off Mexico 1. It is a military base and an official Mexican airport of entry with a paved airstrip; however, only two regional airlines currently offer regular service. If you aren't flying your own plane or travel to and from Guerrero Negro or Isla Cedros, this airport isn't going to be of much use.

By Bus
Autotransportes de Baja California (ABC, tel. 800/025-0222, www.abc.com.mx) offers intercity connections on air-conditioned buses, departing from the Central de Autobuses terminal at Avenida Riveroll and Calle 11 (tel. 646/178-6680). Buses leave this terminal twice a day for points south, including San Quintín (4 hrs.), Guerrero Negro (8 hrs.), Santa Rosalía (12 hrs.), Loreto (15 hrs.), and La Paz (20 hrs.).

Buses without air-conditioning leave from the smaller terminal at Avenida Riveroll and Calle 8 (tel. 646/177-0909, to Tijuana 5 A.M.–9:30 P.M. every hour).

The **Transportes Norte de Sonora** (TNS, Tijuana tel. 664/688-1979) and **Estrellas de Oro** (Tijuana, tel. 664/683-5022) companies all offer connection to Guaymas, Los Mochis, Mazatlán, Guadalajara, and Mexico City on the mainland.

By Car
Ensenada marks the end of the toll road, Mexico 1-D, from Tijuana. From here until Los Cabos, Mexico 1 is a paved, two-lane highway that's narrow and without a shoulder for much of its length.

Mexico 3 from Tecate also passes through Ensenada on its way to the Sierra de Juárez and the intersection with Mexico 5 near San Felipe. Here's how to pick up Mexico 3 heading east out of Ensenada: Take Avenida Juárez

© NIKKI GOTH ITOI

Explore Ensenada by bike.

to Avenida Reforma at the Benito Juárez statue. Cross Avenida Reforma and follow the street called Calzada Cortés until it turns left and becomes Mexico 3.

GETTING AROUND
By Bus
Ensenada's compact tourism zone can be managed by foot, but a number of public buses do run along the main streets (US$0.50). The route is usually given as a street name posted in the window.

By Taxi
Taxis can be found along Avenidas López Mateos or Juárez, and at the bus depot on Calle 11 at Avenida Riveroll. Trips within the city should cost under US$10. Negotiate the fare before you get in. A taxi ride to La Bufadora costs US$10–15.

By Car and Motor Scooter
RENTAL CARS AND MOTOR SCOOTERS
Since it doesn't have an international airport, Ensenada has less demand for rental cars, and fewer agencies means higher prices. Most visitors either drive their own car, take the bus, or rent a car in San Diego. Only a few of the major chains still allow cars to be driven into Mexico (Avis and Hertz are two that do; you'll have to buy Mexican auto insurance when you pick up the vehicle at the San Diego airport). **Fiesta Rent-A-Car** (Costero 1442, in the lobby of Hotel Corona, tel. 646/176-3344) is one local option. If you don't mind prepaying and not knowing which company you will rent from, you can also book a car through a discount service like HotWire.com. Rates at press time started at US$35 per day (without Mexican auto insurance).

DRIVING
Ensenada is a big city with busy streets, but it's not impossible to navigate. Just take your time, watch for signs, and stop at every intersection, whether you see a stop sign or not. Absolutely do not speed or drink while driving.

ESTERO BEACH
Twelve kilometers south of Ensenada, the Río San Carlos meets Bahía de Todos Santos to form an estuary environment. The beach here isn't the prettiest that Baja has to offer (unless you're into tidal flats), but it tends not to be too crowded, except in the middle of the summer. Turn off Mexico 1 7.5 kilometers south of the Gigante at Avenidas Reforma and Delante.

Accommodations
There are a few motels near the beach, but the Estero Beach Resort or its attached RV park are the best options if you want to spend the night. The well-worn and family-oriented **Estero Beach Resort Hotel** (Km. 14, Carretera Transpeninsular, tel. 646/176-6225 or 646/176-6230, U.S. tel. 619/335-1145, www.hotelesterobeach.com, US$80–150) has 100 rooms and suites, most of which have views of the beach and are set amidst landscaped grounds of grass and palms. This is a full-service resort, but think Super 8 more than Crowne Plaza, and you'll be pleasantly surprised. Families who fall in love with the place tend to return every year until their kids are grown. Guest services include tennis courts, boat rentals, horseback riding, a swimming pool, playground, restaurant/bar, general store, and small historical museum. The adjoining RV park has 60 spaces with full hookups and grassy campsites (US$35–45). This place is popular with caravans, so book early. Campers are allowed to use the hotel facilities. There are several less expensive campgrounds and trailer parks along the beach.

Getting There
City buses signed for the Chapultepec neighborhood run between downtown Ensenada and the estuary.

PUNTA BANDA
The estuary at the south end of Bahía Todos Santos is protected by a sharp, rocky peninsula that extends northwest and ends at a cape called Cabo Banda. The name Punta Banda is

ENSENADA TO EL ROSARIO

used to reference the peninsula, the cape, and a settlement on the bay.

A large-scale real estate development, including a golf course designed by Tiger Woods, has been in the works for several years but has made little progress to date.

◖ La Bufadora

If you miss the chance to see gray whales spouting offshore Punta Banda, this blowhole on the south side of the peninsula is not a bad substitute. A frequent stop on the tour bus circuit—and popular with locals as well—La Bufadora (The Snorter) creates a spectacular display as incoming swells push seawater into an underground canyon and out through a hole in the rocks. The resulting explosion of water and spray reaches heights of 25–30 meters. The sight has been developed with a small visitor center and restrooms. A number of food vendors line the road to the parking area.

Recreation

Dale's La Bufadora Dive Shop (Rancho La Bufadora, tel. 646/154-2092, www.labufadora-dive.com, open weekends or by appointment) is a multisport operation on tiny Bahía Papalote that offers *panga* fishing (US$35 pp, min. two people), unguided dive trips (US$35 pp, min. two people), and kayak rentals (US$20 per half day, US$30 per full day).

La Bufadora is an excellent place to begin a scuba-diving tour of the Baja Peninsula if you don't mind cold water. Its pinnacles, kelp beds, and giant green anemones make for memorable dives. Conditions in the bay are best for intermediate to advanced divers, as there is a good amount of surge except on the calmest of days. Currents keep the water here a few degrees colder than temperatures in San Diego. You'll need lots of neoprene or, preferably, a dry suit to be comfortable. You can rent gear and reserve a boat from Dale's,

or through the **Almar dive shop** (Macheros 149, tel. 646/178-3013, almardive@hotmail.com) in Ensenada.

Another option for fishing is **Vonny's Fleet** (tel. 646/154-2046, www.vonnysfleet.com, US$139/boat up to three people), which launches *pangas* from the beach at Punta Banda.

Camping and RV Parks

La Jolla Beach Camp (Km. 12.5, BCN 23, La Jolla, tel. 646/154-2005, US$15) is a large, basic park that faces Bahía de Todos Santos. Its 200 sites come with access to hot showers, boat ramp, tennis court, and dump station (no hookups, except for a few sites with electricity). The park also has its own market and restaurant.

Next door, smaller **Villarino RV Park** (Km. 13, BCN 23, La Jolla, Ensenada, tel. 646/154-2004, US$22–28) has a little more character, plus some of its sites have full hookups. The park has clean restrooms, hot showers, picnic tables, a boat ramp, boat rentals, restaurant, and market. The office is open daily 9 A.M.–noon and 1–5 P.M.

Three *ejido*-run campgrounds on the peninsula have restrooms and water but no other facilities (US$5).

You can walk to Dale's La Bufadora Dive Shop from **Rancho La Bufadora** (tel. 646/178-7172, US$15), which overlooks Bahía Papalote. It has primitive campsites, and there are flush toilets and 24/7 security.

Getting There

To get to Punta Banda from Ensenada by car, follow Mexico 1 about 25 kilometers south to BCN 23, a right turn that comes before Maneadero. Take this road west through the retirement community of La Jolla and along the peninsula. The road will climb over the rocks and around to south-facing La Bufadora. A taxi ride from Ensenada to La Bufadora runs about US$15–20.

Valle de Guadalupe

The scenic Guadalupe Valley follows the Río Guadalupe between Ensenada and Tecate on Mexico 3, with a small town at Km. 77.

SIGHTS
Misión Nuestra Señora de Guadalupe del Norte

Padre Félix Caballero established the last of nine Dominican missions (1834–1840) in Baja in 1834, 24 kilometers east of the next closest mission (San Miguel), above the Río Guadalupe. The missions were already on the decline at this point, but the new settlement became a successful farm and ranch with 400 indigenous people under its tutelage, if only for a few short years. The mission ruins are not recognizable today.

Colonia Rusa

After the Mexican government secularized the mission properties, a group of Russian pacifists called the Molokans (milk drinkers, who abstained from drinking alcohol) fled the Russian Orthodox Church and purchased the land surrounding this settlement to start a new colony in 1905.

The original families planted crops and vineyards, raised livestock, built adobe houses, and went about their simple way of life.

In 1938 then president Cárdenas seized all foreign-owned property in the country, and 3,000 Mexicans arrived to take over the colony, renaming it Francisco Zarco. Only a few of the original Russian families stayed in the area, but the area retains a Russian look and feel. Some of the Molokan homes have survived the years, and tombstones in the town cemetery have Russian inscriptions.

The neighboring **Museo Comunitario del Valle de Guadalupe** (10 A.M.–6 P.M. Tues.–Sun., by donation) and **Museo Histórico del Valle de Guadalupe** (10 A.M.–5 P.M. Tues.–Sun., by donation) display historical artifacts such as clothing, photos, and tools. To find the cemetery (across from the Monte Xanic winery)

and museums, turn off the highway at Francisco Zarco and follow the paved road to its end. Turn right and go another 150 meters.

◖ RUTA DEL VINO

The Valle de Guadalupe is an internationally recognized winemaking region that has been gaining attention from Southern California residents and the U.S. travel press in recent years. Baja California wines are shipped all over Mexico and Western Europe, but because of U.S. and Canadian trade policies, they weren't exported north of the border until recent years. They're still difficult to find in Canada and the United States.

Wineries

The highest concentration of wineries—more than two dozen at last count—are located in the 23-kilometer-long Valle de Guadalupe, located off Mexico 3, northeast of Ensenada. The introduction of stainless steel tanks and temperature-controlled barrels at many of these vineyards have helped put Baja wines on the map. But you can still enjoy personal service and, often, time with the winemakers themselves as you make your way through the valley. Spring and summer are the most popular time to visit, though Mexican holiday weekends also draw a crowd.

You might start your tour at the west end of Guadalupe Valley in the village of San Antonio de las Minas. At **Vinisterra** (Km. 94.5, tel. 646/178-3350, www.vinisterra.com, 11 A.M.–4:30 P.M. Sat., 11 A.M.–3 P.M. Sun.), Abelardo and Patricia Macouzet Rodriguez offer a cabernet sauvignon-merlot blend, *tempranillo,* and other award-winning wines.

Inquire about the award-winning merlot at family-owned **Viña de Liceaga** (Km. 93.5, tel. 646/155-3091, www.vinosliceaga.com, 8 A.M.–3 P.M. Mon.–Fri., 11 A.M.–3 P.M. Sat.–Sun.). Choose from several tasting options for US$3–5. Reservations are recommended. Nearby, contemporary **Casa de Piedra** (Km.

VALLE DE GUADALUPE AND THE RUTA DEL VINO

San José de la Zorra
Progreso
Sin Arroyo
Batequí
To Ignacio Zaragoza
Agua Escondida

Cañada El Golpe

Cañada Guadalupe

Valle Guadalupe

CASA PEDRO DOMECQ
L. A. CETTO

CHATEAU CAMOU

LA CASA DE DOÑA LUPE

MUSEO COMUNITARIO DEL VALLE DE GUADALUPE

MONTE XANIC

MUSEO HISTÓRICO DEL VALLE DE GUADALUPE

Francisco Zarco

Encinal

BARÓN BALCH'É

Cañada San Felipe

VIÑOS SUEÑOS

Miramontes

ADOBE GUADALUPE B&B

MISIÓN GUADALUPE

LA ESCUELITA

Chapingo

La Ampliación (El Porvenir)

Loza

Cañada El Colgado

3

Sierra Blanca

BIBAYOFF

Aguaje Escondido

Cañón Matajanal

MONTEFIORI

LAJA

San Miguel

HACIENDA LA LOMITA

Milagros

El Mogor

Cubillas

LA VILLA DEL VALLE

MOGOR BADÁN

Santa Rosa

Chivato

San Marcos

Barre

Cañón Borreguero

RUTA DEL VINO

1

RESTAURANTE LA CABAÑA DE LAS LOMAS

Encinos

Bakarta

El Olvido

RESTAURANTE MUSTAFA

Buenavista

VIÑA DE LICEAGA

LA CASA VIEJA

CASA DE PIEDRA

San Antonio de las Minas

VINISTERRA

El Junco

Rinconada

El Tigre

1-D

Las Pinales

Las Delicias

San Felipe

3

San Fernando

Ruiz Cortines

El Sauzal

1

Bahía de Todos Santos

To Ensenada

0   2 mi
0   2 km

© AVALON TRAVEL

BAJA CALIFORNIA'S WINE TIMELINE

Though it's a relatively new phenomenon to many foreign wine connoisseurs, Baja California's wine history dates back several centuries.

- **Early 1500s:** Hernán Cortés introduces Spanish vines to Mexico.

- **1597:** The Jesuits set up a winery in the present-day state of Coahuila.

- **1697:** Padre Juan Ugarte transplants the cuttings to Misión San Javier.

- **1791:** Dominican Padre José Lorieto establishes Misión Santo Tomás de Aquino, introducing the first vines of Spanish origin to the Valle de Santo Tomás, 45 kilometers south of Ensenada.

- **1888:** Italian miner Francisco Andronequi assumes control of the former mission vineyard and renames it Bodegas de Santo Tomás.

- **1906:** A Russian Christian sect acquires a tract of land in the Valle de Guadalupe and plants more vineyards, which prove to grow exceptionally well in the hot, dry Baja climate.

- **1939:** A former general from the Mexican Revolution, Abelardo Lujan Rodríguez, buys Bodegas de Santo Tomás and moves its headquarters north to Ensenada.

- **Early 1960s:** Rodríguez hires a winemaker from the internationally renowned school for viticulture and enology at the University of California at Davis, who introduces new varietals as well as modern winemaking technology.

- **1972:** Pedro Domecq, a maker of brandy from Spain, establishes a wine-making operation in the Valle de Guadalupe, creating a buzz for Baja wines within the international wine community.

- **1990s:** Boutique wineries, including Monte Xanic and Chateau de Camou (Viñas de Camou), raise the bar even higher, establishing credibility and visibility for the emerging wine region.

- **2007:** Baja California wineries account for approximately 90 percent of all wine made in the country.

- **2010:** The annual Fiesta de la Vendimia Bajacaliforniana attracts 50,000 food and wine connoisseurs for a 10-day celebration.

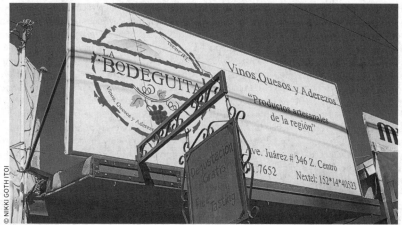

© NIKKI GOTH ITOI

Wine bars are increasingly popular in Baja California.

93.5, tel. 646/155-3097, www.vinoscasadepiedra.com) offers tastings in a farmhouse setting. Reservations are required. Once a year it offers a four-weekend winemaking seminar. **La Casa Vieja** (Km. 93.5, tel. 646/155-3153, lacasavieja.baja@hotmail.com) opens at 9 A.M. daily and closes at sunset, or whenever the crowd disperses. In addition to offering tastings, this winery has a deli, arts and crafts store, and information center on-site.

Chateau Camou (tel. 646/177-2221 or 646/177-3303, www.chateau-camou.com.mx, 8 A.M.–3 P.M. Mon.–Sat., 9 A.M.–2 P.M. Sun.) specializes in expensive Bordeaux-style reds. It offers three tasting/tour options: Try four wines and a tour for US$5, six tastings and a tour for US$10, or a tour with the winemaker and a complete tasting, including a barrel sample, for US$40.

Next up, **Mogor Badán** (Km. 86.5, tel. 646/177-1484, abadan@cicese.mx) is a combination organic produce farm, vineyard, and winery with tours, tastings, and shopping. Reservations are required. Baja's most acclaimed winery, **Monte Xanic** (tel. 646/174-7055, www.montexanic.com, 9 A.M.–4 P.M. Mon.–Fri., 8 A.M.–noon Sat.), produces 50,000 cases of wine per year, and many of its labels have won awards in the United States, Canada, and Mexico. The winery charges US$4 for tasting whites and an additional US$4 for reds. Reservations are required.

Housed in an adobe brick building, **Barón Balch'é** (El Porvenir, tel. 646/183-9501, www.baronbalche.com, 10 A.M.–4 P.M. daily) is another boutique winery using the latest technology to make wine—10,000 cases a year.

The largest winery in the region—and in all of Latin America—Italian-owned **L. A. Cetto** (Km. 73.5, tel. 646/155-2179, www.cettowines.com or www.lacetto.com, 10 A.M.–3 P.M. daily) has gardens and a picnic area as well as an inviting tasting room. You can tour the winery without reservations, and there are no tasting or tour fees. Past L. A. Cetto, **La Casa de Doña Lupe** (Rancho La Gotita, Francisco Zarco, tel. 646/155-2323, www.donalupe.com, 9 A.M.–7 P.M. daily) tempts visitors with home-baked goods as well as farm-fresh cheese, honey, and produce and organically grown wines. In the same vicinity, you'll pay US$2.50 to taste the *tempranillo, graciano,* and *mazuelo* varietals at **Casa Pedro Domecq** (Km. 73.5, tel. 646/155-2333, www.vinosdomecq.com.mx, 10 A.M.–4 P.M. Mon.–Fri., 10 A.M.–5 P.M. Sat.). The fee includes a cellar tour, plus use of a picnic area on the grounds.

Also at Domecq, **GaleríAH** (Km. 73, tel. 646/175-3132) represents contemporary artists from Mexico along with artists from around the world.

In San Antonio de las Minas, **Hacienda La Lomita** (tel. 646/156-8459, www.haciendalalomita.com.mx) opened in 2009 with 8 hectares of merlot, *tempranillo,* Shiraz, and chardonnay vines. Italian-run **Villa Montefiori** (www.villamontefiori.com.mx) is another one of the newer wineries, located in El Porvenir. Also in El Porvenir, a former olive oil factory has been converted into the **Estación de Oficios El Porvenir,** known locally as La Escuelita (Km. 3.5, Carr. Tecate-Ensenada, tel. 646/175-0000). This wine school runs a popular four-week class each summer for aspiring winemakers.

Baja Wine Country Tours

Local resident Steve Dryden (U.S. tel. 619/300-4976, www.mexicowinetours.com) offers wine-tasting tours by private van or motor coach. Day-long bus tours depart from San Diego and include tastings at three wineries and lunch at Mustafa's Moroccan Restaurant. Steve is a former Napa Valley winery manager with extensive knowledge of the Mexican wine industry as well as the Kumiai people, Russian (Molokan) history, and the culture and history of Baja California. To follow the action in Baja's wine country, read his *Baja Times* column online (www.bajatimes.com/bajawine.asp).

Fiesta de la Vendimía Bajacaliforniana

Each August, the Valle de Guadalupe wineries celebrate a 10-day winemaking festival with tastings, food/wine pairings, vineyard tours, and the requisite music and dancing, in the valley and in downtown Ensenada. For information on upcoming festivals, call 646/174-0170 or Bodegas de Santo Tomás in Ensenada (tel. 646/178-3333) or contact CANIRAC, the Ensenada restaurant association (www.caniracensenada.com).

ACCOMMODATIONS
Under US$50
Budget travelers can rent a cottage for US$35 a night at **Viños Sueños** (tel. 646/179-4763, 9 A.M.–5 P.M. daily), a winery in Francisco Zarco.

US$50-100
Warm colors set the tone in affordable rooms at **El Mezon del Vino** (tel. 664/162-9010, www.hotelmezondelvino.com, US$80). The hotel has a restaurant (8 A.M.–7 P.M. weekends) for wine-tasting as well as breakfast and lunch.

US$100-250
Tuscan-style (**La Villa del Valle** (6 km west of Mexico 3 from Km. 88, btw San Antonio de las Minas/Ejido El Porvenirtel. 646/183-9249, U.S. tel. 818/207-7130, www.lavilladelvalle.com, US$175–195) stands atop a hill on 28 hectares with sweeping views of surrounding vineyards, orchards, and gardens. Four of its six rooms have private balconies; all have luxury linens and many more elegant touches. In between tastings, guests relax by the pool or soak in the hot tub, book a massage on-site, or play a game of bocce ball. Rates include full breakfast, an afternoon glass of wine and *botanas,* and Wi-Fi access. There is a two-night minimum on weekends.

Near the Monte Xanic and Chateau Camou wineries, the **Adobe Guadalupe B&B** (Francisco Zarco, tel. 646/155-2094, www.adobeguadalupe.com, US$190) was the first winery to offer accommodations in the valley. The 24-hectare winery offers six guestrooms in a rambling adobe-walled, hacienda-style complex. Rates include a complete breakfast served at a common table in the huge kitchen. Other meals may be arranged at additional cost.

Camping
You can camp on a 32-hectare farm at **Bibayoff-Bodegas Valle de Guadalupe** (tel. 646/177-2722, bibayoff@telnor.net), run by a Russian family in San Antonio de las Minas. Exit Mexico 3 at El Tigre and follow the dirt road to Rancho Bibayoff. The Kumiai have opened a campground just north of L. A. Cetto Winery. Some say it resembles a California state park at the turn of the 20th century. Sites cost US$5, and services include firewood, water, showers, and a general store. Guided hikes, horseback riding, cultural displays, and crafts are also available. Reservations are required. Contact Horacio Moncada at tel. 646/178-8093 or 646/118-9113.

FOOD
The valley now has a few well-known restaurants to go with its boutique wineries: Around 22 kilometers northeast of Ensenada, perched on a hill just north of the small community of San Antonio de las Minas, **Restaurant Mustafa** (Km. 93, Carr. Tecate-Ensenada, tel. 646/155-3185, 8 A.M.–7 P.M. Wed.–Mon., mains US$7–12) serves Moroccan-influenced dishes, including lamb shish kebab and chicken breast stuffed with spinach and cheese, along with a menu of Mexican specialties. In San Antonio itself, **El Mesón** (Km. 93, Carr. Tecate-Ensenada, tel. 646/155-3185) is popular for breakfast and lunch; it's closed on Thursday. The owner is an admirer of British aviation artist Robert Taylor and displays Taylor's work on the restaurant walls.

Visiting gourmands praise (**Restaurant Laja** (Km. 83, Carr. Tecate-Ensenada, tel. 646/155-2556, www.lajamexico.com, 1:30–5 P.M. Wed., 1:30–8:30 P.M. Thurs–Sat., prix fixe menu US$60 for eight courses or US$45 for four courses) for farm-fresh cuisine on par with California's celebrated Chez Panisse and French Laundry restaurants. The brainchild of former Four Seasons chef Jair Téllez, the restaurant is located about 50 meters off Mexico 3 via a washboard road, in a private home with white walls and a red tile roof.

In Francisco Zarco, **Doña Chuy's** (Km. 83, Mexico 3, Francisco Zarco, no tel., mains under US$10) has reasonably priced Mexican plates, and **La Cabaña de las Lomas** (Km. 91.5, Cajeme St., tel. 646/155-3033, 8 A.M.–5 P.M. Fri.–Sun.) prepares northern Mexican specialties such as fresh quail.

Mercado La Chica and **Abarrotes C. R.,** both in Francisco Zarco, can meet basic needs for food and supplies.

GETTING THERE

The Valle de Guadalupe is less than a two-hour drive (113 km) south of San Diego on the toll road from Tijuana to Ensenada. After paying the last toll, watch for a sign to Tecate via Mexico 3 and the Ruta del Vino. Travel east on Mexico 3 for 11 kilometers until you drop down into the Baja wine country at San Antonio de las Minas. This is the western end of the Guadalupe Valley wine region, which extends 22 kilometers east toward Tecate, ending near Km. 73.5 at L. A. Cetto and Domecq wineries.

Sierra de Juárez

The least-traveled highway on the Baja Peninsula, Mexico 3, connects Ensenada to Mexico 5 and San Felipe on the Sea of Cortez. Along the way, it passes a Dominican mission site, provides access to a small national park, Constitución de 1857, and crosses the Sierra de Juárez via the San Matías Pass.

There are four places to buy gas along the route: Ojos Negros (Km. 39), Independencia (Km. 94), and Lázaro Cárdenas and Francisco R. Serrano, closer to the east end of the highway.

PARQUE NACIONAL CONSTITUCIÓN DE 1857

This 5,000-hectare park covers a sub-alpine plateau in the center of the Sierra de Juárez range. Granite boulders and Ponderosa pines ring its two natural lakes, Laguna La Chica and Laguna Juárez (Laguna Hanson). The latter has campsites (US$5) with fire pits and grills, but there are no marked hiking trails in the park.

The park is generally deserted except during Semana Santa (the week before Easter), when off-roaders invade. Be prepared for snow in winter.

Getting There

The easiest access road to the park heads northeast off Mexico 3 at Km. 55 near Ojos Negros. This route is mostly paved now, and is passable for most vehicles, except after winter storms.

If you don't want to retrace your steps to Mexico 3, you can continue on the access road heading northeast to the other side of the park, and meet Mexico 2 60 kilometers from Laguna Hanson, near La Rumorosa.

MISIÓN SANTA CATALINA VIRGEN Y MÁRTIR

Padre José Loriente founded this mission (1797–1840) to the west of a strategic mountain pass that led to the San Felipe desert and the Colorado River beyond. At 1,067 meters, the mission was built to serve as a fort, protecting the coastal missions against raids from indigenous people to the east. At one time, it claimed the most converts of any Dominican mission on the peninsula, but it was destroyed in 1840 in a rebel attack. Only traces of the mission walls remain in the present-day village of Santa Catarina, which is eight kilometers east of Independencia (Km. 94) along a graded dirt road.

Maneadero to Vicente Guerrero

Between Ensenada and San Quintín, Mexico 1 meanders inland along low mesas, through the fertile valley of Santo Tomás, and on south past a series of ranchos and agricultural supply towns. Four Dominican mission sites dot the highway along the way.

MANEADERO

Once you pass into the farming town of Maneadero, 20 kilometers south of Ensenada, you've reached the end of the "free zone" and will need immigration papers (tourist card or visa) to proceed farther south. The military often has a checkpoint set up here, and the *topes* (speed bumps) are plentiful, so take it slow.

Camping

Las Cañadas Campamento (Km. 31–32, tel. 646/153-1055, toll-free U.S. tel. 800/027-3828, www.lascanadas.com, US$16 pp) originally opened as a day-use swimming complex in the summer, but it also has a few campsites with full hookups and lakeside tent camping, both of which are open year-round. Basic cabins rent for US$65 per night; bring your own linens.

LA BOCANA AND PUERTO SANTO TOMÁS

The first opportunity for off-road exploration south of Ensenada comes at Km. 46–47, where a gravel road heads west, following the Cañon Santo Tomás to the coast. Sheltered by Punta Santo Tomás to the north, the fishing settlements of La Bocana and Puerto Santo Tomás have free camping on the beach and cabins for rent. *Panga* fishing and kayak fishing are popular activities, with rock cod and snapper among the common catches. There is a boat launch for small watercraft, and the kelp beds in the bay could make for an interesting dive if you have your own equipment.

There are a couple of *tiendas,* but don't count on much. You're off the grid here, so phones and other power-intensive amenities aren't going to be available. Cell phones don't get much of a

signal either. It takes about an hour and a half to get to Puerto Santo Tomás by car.

Surfing

Surfers find occasional reef and point breaks in Bahía Santo Tomás and at Punta China to the south (turn left when you reach the coastal road and La Bocana). But the waves are more consistent and the rides often longer at the next point south, Punta San José. Popular with surfers from San Diego, the point has free cliffside camping above the surf, with outhouses but no services. There are two ways to reach San José. The best road leaves the highway just south of the Pemex in Santo Tomás. Go about 23 kilometers and bear right at the fork; continue another 16 kilometers to the lighthouse and camping area. Alternatively, if you have a high-clearance vehicle you might attempt an ungraded road that branches south from the Cañon Puerto Santo Tomás road, about 20.5 kilometers west of Mexico 1. From the turnoff, it's about 11 kilometers of rough driving to the break. Inquire in town about the road conditions before you choose this route.

Accommodations

The **Puerto Santo Tomás Resort** (Ensenada message tel. 646/154-9415, www.puertosanto-tomas.com) has rustic cabins (US$40–50) and larger houses (US$100–150) for rent as well as campsites (US$14, includes showers and toilets) and a cantina serving Mexican and seafood dishes. You need to book ahead to eat here, so the management can get the supplies it needs in time for your arrival. *Panga* fishing rates are US$130–160 per day. To find the resort, look for a road sign for Puerto Santo Tomás between Km. 46 and 47 and turn right about 45 meters after the sign. (If you reach the village of Santo Tomás on Mexico 1, you've passed the turn.) Follow this road 29 kilometers west, staying right each time the road forks. The road meets the coast at La Bocana (The Mouth). Turn right (north) and follow the road over a small hill and along the coast for about five kilometers to Puerto Santo Tomás.

◧ VALLE DE SANTO TOMÁS

You know you've entered the agricultural valley of Santo Tomás (pop. 400) when you start to see rolling hills covered in a carpet of brilliant green, rows of grapevines, olive groves, and fields of wildflowers.

Misión Santo Tomás de Aquino

Dominican Padre José Loriente established this mission (1791–1849) midway between Misión San Miguel to the north and San Vicente to the south. He planted to raise livestock and planted the first mission crops, including olives and grapes. The mission's wine became known all over the peninsula, and the Bodegas de Santo Tomás continues the tradition today.

The mission had a prosperous but turbulent history. Indigenous people here were less receptive to missionary efforts than those the Jesuits had first encountered in Southern Baja, and two of the resident priests would be murdered before the mission was secularized in 1849.

There are two places to see what little remains of the mission ruins (a few adobe mounds, barely recognizable). The Dominicans built the original buildings west of Mexico 1, on a low mesa off the gravel road that parallels the Cañon Santo Tomás. Later, the community moved to the present-day village of Santo Tomás, east of the highway and north of the Palomar Trailer Park.

Bodegas de Santo Tomás

Founded in 1888, this winery (Rancho los Dolores, Km. 49, Mexico 1, Ensenada office tel. 646/178-3333, 11 A.M.–3 P.M. daily) owns the majority of the vineyards in the Valle de Santo Tomás and has an office in Ensenada. It makes a highly regarded wine called Duetto through a partnership with Wente Vineyard of California. The winery offers group tours by reservation only.

Accommodations and Food

A mainstay on the Northern Baja travel circuit for more than a half century, **El Palomar** (Km. 51–52, Mexico 1, Santo Tomás, tel. 646/153-8002, www.elpalomar.ws) consists of a restaurant (7 A.M.–10 P.M. daily, mains start at US$7), motel (US$18 pp), campground with two swimming pools, and Pemex station. The campsites and pool are in an olive grove on the east side of the highway (and you have to descend a steep driveway to get there), but the office, restaurant, motel, and Pemex are on the west side at the base of a hill as you come around a bend in the road. RV camping costs US$16.50 per night for two people (full hookups) and includes two free margaritas.

ERÉNDIRA AND PUERTO SAN ISIDRO

For another side trip to the coast, turn west from Mexico 1 at Km. 78 on the paved road that leads out to the Ejido Eréndira. There is a sign for Coyote Cal's at the turn. The road winds 24 kilometers through a canyon to the nondescript village of Eréndira (pop. 1,500). Head north along the dirt road five kilometers to Coyote Cal's hostel, at the end of the power lines.

Three more kilometers north along the coast will bring you to Punta Cabras. South of this point, Half Moon Bay is protected from the prevailing northwest winds and catches the summertime south swells. Long Beach, to the north of the point, catches most swells and offers plenty of peaks, unless the onshore winds are killing it. There have been numerous reports of thefts in the area around River's Mouth, but you can leave valuables at Coyote Cal's for safekeeping.

Fishing

About 1.5 kilometers north of Eréndira, you'll find San Isidro Cove. The buildings on the cliff on the north side above the boat ramp are **Castro's Place** (tel. 646/176-2897). Vicente Castro starting fishing the area in 1949, and now his kids run the operation. They use a rusty tractor to tow their *pangas* in and out of the cove. With experienced captains, the bottom fishing in this area is a no-brainer and a *panga*-load of four anglers can fill a 100-quart cooler in a day. Surface fishing for yellowtail and dorado is possible, but the best opportunities are on the bottom. Castro's provides bait, licenses, and gear, but you can use your own if you prefer. There are also clean cabins with bunks for US$25–30 per night, and you can camp for a nominal fee.

Accommodations

Coyote Cal's Mexico Hostels (Ejido Eréndira, tel. 646/154-4080, www.coyotecals. com) is a classic Baja meeting place for surfers, European backpackers, and touring motorcyclists. One of the reasons for its popularity is that there is a room for every budget. You can camp out front on the "beach" (a sandy front yard) for US$10, plus US$3 for breakfast (midsized RVs okay if self-contained). On the other end of the spectrum, there's the top-floor Crow's Nest room for US$60 per night (three-night minimum, reserve online) with panoramic views of the surrounding cliffs and ocean. Bunks go for a reasonable US$15–18 per person and private rooms are US$45–50 per couple. The hostel also rents surfboards, mountain bikes, and snorkeling gear. Its new Barefoot Cantina serves XX lager, Sol, and Tecate beer as well as a menu of mixed drinks. The cantina does not serve meals, however, so plan to buy your own supplies in Ensenada on the way down.

Getting There

Many budget travelers reach Coyote Cal's without their own transportation. Bus fare from Ensenada costs about US$11 and drops you off at Km. 78. From here, you need to hitch a ride (easy to do, according to those who've done it). Catch the bus before 2 P.M. to reach the hostel before dark. Alternatively, stay on the bus until San Vicente. When you depart, look across the street and to the left of the Pemex for Mimi Hotel. Inquire here about taxi service (tel. 646/165-6747, available 24/7 for US$25–30) to the hostel. You'll need to speak Spanish to arrange the ride.

A third option is to hire a station wagon taxi

from Ensenada (US$75 flat fee; to avoid extra costs negotiate before you get in and tell the driver the trip will include about five kilometers of dirt road driving). The taxi can stop at the Calimax store, where you can buy food, and then take you directly to the hostel.

SAN VICENTE

The next valley south of Santo Tomás is almost as picturesque, with more agricultural crops and the Llano Colorado (Reddish Plain) beyond it. The town itself (pop. 3,500) is a small-sized commercial center, with a few restaurants and stores as well as an ABC bus terminal—all right along the highway. The only real point of interest here is the historic Dominican mission of San Vicente Ferrer, located one kilometer north of town at Km. 88.

Misión San Vicente Ferrer

Founded by Padres Miguel Hidalgo and Joaquín Valero in 1780, this mission (1780–1833) and military outpost played an important role in connecting the Baja California missions to the newer settlements in Alta California. It also had one of the largest building complexes of any Dominican mission. In 1997 Mexico's Instituto Nacional de Antropología e Historia (INAH) began an archeological dig to uncover, reinforce, and protect the remaining mission ruins. Today the site is lined with gravel paths and the adobe walls are covered in a waterproof layer. To find the mission site, look for a dirt road heading west off Mexico 1, just south of Km. 88.

COLONET AND SAN ANTONIO DEL MAR

The farming town of Colonet has a Pemex and handful of places to eat and shop. Use it as a supply station for trips to the coast or into the sierra. There aren't any sights of interest in the town proper.

Almost due west of Colonet, San Antonio del Mar is a remote beach camp on an estuary with a few homes and trailers. The exposed, sandy beach faces west, and there are good shore fishing and decent beach breaks in

vineyards near San Vicente

both directions. This is a good bet to escape the crowds. Stock up on supplies and fill your tank with gas in Colonet. Primitive camping with no facilities costs US$5 per night. Turn off Mexico 1 at Km. 126, a little north of town and just before the bridge. From here, it's 12.5 kilometers to the coast.

Bahía Colonet (14 km southwest) is supposedly a target for development as part of the Escalera Nautica project, but nothing has materialized to date. The north point of this bay, Cabo Colonet, breaks on northwest swells. On the bay itself, **Cuatro Casas** is one of the more crowded longboarding breaks along this stretch of coastline. It is also a fickle spot that doesn't break consistently.

Crime warning: An armed robbery of a surf instructor and longtime Baja traveler was widely reported in the San Diego press in 2007. He was camping with his girlfriend in a deserted spot along the coast after getting lost on the road to Cuatro Casas after dark. Take precautions when exploring this area. Leave your valuables behind, travel in groups, camp at the hostel, and don't be conspicuous.

Accommodations

On an exposed bluff overlooking the break, **Cuatro Casas Hostel Surf** (U.S. tel. 619/756-0639, www.myspace.com/cuatrocasas) has a variety of clean rooms starting at US$15 in a large house and camping for US$5. The parking area is fenced, and the owner has a bright spotlight on the roof to ward off would-be intruders. In recent years, we've seen shortsighted fishermen out front using bleach to ferret out octopuses from their holes in the tide pools.

To find Cuatro Casas coming from the north on Mexico 1, drive 13.8 kilometers south of Colonet to a Pemex on the left and then another kilometer and a half on the highway after that toward the intersection with the paved road to San Telmo. After you pass a yellow auto parts store, turn right onto a dirt road that leads to the coast (12.9 km). Call or text the owner, Richard, for reservations.

PUNTA SAN JACINTO

Nine kilometers west of Camalú on Mexico 1 via a wide, graded dirt road, Punta San Jacinto offers surfing and primitive camping on a sandy but exposed beach. The turnoff to Punta San Jacinto comes between Km. 149 and 150 on Mexico 1.

The town of Camalú, beginning at Km. 157, can meet most basic- traveler needs with its several markets, pharmacies, and eateries. There is also an auto mechanic and Pemex station with diesel fuel. Directly west of town (turn right at the stoplight north of the Pemex and drive straight out to the beach), Punta Camalú is a worthwhile right point break, reportedly more consistent than Cuatro Casas to the north.

Surfing

The surf is found at the site of a huge freighter, *Isla del Carmen,* that is beached on the sand. It's a soft wave but a good choice for days when the northwest swell is huge. **Baja Surf Adventures** (toll-free U.S. tel. 800/428-7873, www.bajasurfadventures.com) runs a solar-powered resort here, providing lessons and basic accommodations for up to 16 guests.

Camping

You can camp for free on the sand dunes behind the beach, but it's not recommended, since crime in this area is a real concern.

VICENTE GUERRERO

As a regional hub for agricultural commerce, Colonia Vicente Guerrero (pop. 10,600) has a post office, police station, and medical clinic as well as a grocery store, ATMs, and several places to eat. The Pemex is open around the clock. ABC buses stop here, and there are three RV parks in town.

Migrant workers from mainland Mexico tend to crops of tomatoes and strawberries in the surrounding fields. On the coast, surf-casting is a popular pastime for locals and visitors alike.

Misión Santo Domingo de la Frontera

Padres Miguel Hidalgo and Manuel García founded the second Dominican mission (1775–1839) in Baja near the Arroyo Santo Domingo, northeast of Vicente Guerrero. Although it occupied a strategic location, with ample freshwater and easy coastal access, the mission grew slowly at first. It produced large quantities of corn and wheat and traded otter furs with ships that came to nearby San Quintín. But the indigenous people suffered from disease, and the mission was abandoned in 1839.

During its life, the mission occupied three sites in the Vicente Guerrero area. Ruins at the third and final site are among the most recognizable of all the ruins on the peninsula. Mexico's INAH agency has protected the site by reinforcing the crumbling adobe walls, putting a fence around the mission quadrangle, and adding an entry kiosk. A building on-site now contains a small collection of items from the mission era.

Accommodations

The San Quintín Valley has a new property offering outstanding quality and value in accommodations: The 32 rooms at the **Mission Inn** (tel. 616/166-4400, U.S. tel. 877/560-7666, www.hotelmissioninn.com, US$50, tax included) have parquet floors, comfortable beds, good lighting, a desk and chair for computer work, and fluffy towels. Other features include flat-screen high-definition TVs, remote-control air-conditioning, Wi-Fi, plenty of parking, and 24-hour security. Two of the rooms are wheelchair accessible. The attached **La Misión Restaurant** serves regional Mexican food 7 A.M.–10 A.M. daily.

RV caravans often spend the night at **Posada Don Diego RV Park and Restaurant** (Km. 174, Mexico 1, tel. 616/166-2181, www.posadadondiego.com, 8 A.M.–9 P.M. daily). Under its current ownership since 1979, this park has 100 campsites (50 with full hookups for US$11, the rest with electricity and water only for US$10), plus four motel-style rooms for US$35. There are also a three-bedroom house and four trailers for rent. On-site activities include basketball and volleyball. Its restaurant serves Mexican plates, a full lineup of steaks, baby back ribs, and seafood dishes, all at reasonable prices. Breakfast mains cost US$3.50–9 and dinners are US$7–14.

To find Posada Don Diego, go about a kilometer and a half south of the only stoplight in town and turn right (west) just before the propane plant.

Sierra de San Pedro Mártir

For true wilderness seekers, the highest mountain range on the Baja Peninsula offers a dramatic change from the desert and coastal scenery below. Lodgepole pines, quaking aspens, and the endemic San Pedro Mártir cypress are just a few of the unusual trees that have attached themselves to the slopes and canyons of the Sierra de San Pedro Mártir. The rare *borregón* (bighorn sheep) lives on the range, and the California condor was recently reintroduced.

At 3,095 meters, the tallest peak in the range, Picacho del Diablo (Devil's Peak), also goes by the names Cerro de la Encantada (Enchanted Mountain) and La Providencia (Providence). Its two granite peaks are often capped with snow in winter. Experienced backpackers typically approach the summit from the eastern side on a three-day trip.

SIGHTS
◖ Parque Nacional Sierra San Pedro Mártir

Founded by a presidential decree in 1974, the 68,796-hectare (170,000-acre) Parque Nacional Sierra San Pedro Mártir (7 A.M.–7 P.M. daily, US$7.50 per vehicle) centers around the San Pedro Mártir Plateau (elev. 1,800 m), which covers approximately 70 kilometers by 15 kilometers at the north end of the range. Given its remote location, it is one of the least visited national parks in all of Mexico, which can make a trip here all the more enjoyable.

Backcountry hikes and self-contained camping are permitted within the park, but infrastructure and services are limited. Few trails are marked, so you'll need to bring a GPS and topo maps (*San Rafael H11B45* and *Santa Cruz H11B55*), which Santa Barbara, California-based **Mexico Maps** (U.S. tel. 805/687-1011, www.mexicomaps.com) sells for US$15.95 per map. The easiest trails to follow are located along the northeastern edge of the park, near the observatory. If you're not confident that you can navigate the wilderness environment on your own, you can hire a guide through Meling Ranch (tel. 646/179-4106, www.melingguestranch.com) or EcoTur (www.mexonline.com/baja/ecotur3.htm).

© AVALON TRAVEL

MAJOR BAJA CALIFORNIA MOUNTAIN RANGES

Range	Highest Peak	Summit Elevation
Sierra de San Pedro Mártir	Picacho del Diablo	3,095 meters (10,154 ft.)
Sierra de la Laguna	Picacho de la Laguna	2,161 meters (7,090 ft.)
Sierra de San Francisco	Pico Santa Monica	2,104 meters (6,904 ft.)
Sierra San Borja	Pico Echeverría	1,907 meters (6,258 ft.)
Sierra de Juárez	Cerro Torre Blanco	1,800 meters (5,904 ft.)
Sierra de la Giganta	Cerro La Giganta	1,765 meters (5,792 ft.)
Sierra de la Asamblea	Cerro Dos Picachos	1,658 meters (5,438 ft.)
Sierra de Guadalupe	Monte Thetis	1,640 meters (5,380 ft.)

Hunting and the possession of firearms (even with a Mexican permit) are prohibited, as is off-road driving. You can build campfires in fire rings at a few sites in the park. As with any wilderness environment, let the local rangers know the details of your trip before you head off on the trail.

Summer temps hover around 26°C during the day, dropping to 4.5°C at night. July and August also bring heavy rains and afternoon thunderstorms to the sierra. In winter temperatures range 4.5°C–12°C, and snowfall is common above 2,000 meters. Days are pleasantly warm in spring and fall, but night can dip below freezing. Accordingly, the best hiking seasons are mid-April–mid-June, when the wildflowers are in bloom and freshwater is plentiful, and late September–early November, before the snows begin.

The park entrance is located 78 kilometers from Mexico 1 via a paved road that heads west from Mexico 1 at San Telmo; follow signs marked Observatorio. Another way to access the Sierra de San Pedro Mártir is via a rough dirt road (high clearance required) through the farming town of Valle de la Trinidad, off Mexico 3 (Km. 121). This route is 48-kilometers long and takes you to the northern boundary of the national park.

Observatorio Astronómico Nacional

Clear air and nonexistent light pollution led the Mexican government to choose Cerro de la Cúpula (elev. 2,830 m) as the location for a world-class observatory, called the Observatorio Astronómico Nacional (Ensenada tel. 646/174-4580, www.astrosen.unam.mx, 11 A.M.–1 P.M. Sat., by reservation). Built in 1975, its three telescopes (2.1 meters, 1.5 meters, and 84 centimeters) assess the brightness of the sky, the state of the atmosphere, and a long list of meteorological data. This facility is regarded as one of the best places on the planet to observe the stars and planets above. It's open to the public, but hours are limited and vary by season.

The observatory is located at the end of the park access road, also called the San Telmo de Abajo road (20 km past the park entrance). Park before the locked gate and walk the final two kilometers to the buildings.

Misión San Pedro Mártir de Verona

Dominican Padre José Loriente established a mountain mission (1794–1824) high in the Sierra San Pedro Mártir to serve a small population of indigenous people, but the rugged terrain and cold winter climate made for a challenging mission environment. Its 20-hectare orchard grew wheat, corn, and beans primarily. Only the faint ruins of a few walls survive today, and access is difficult: from the observatory, it's a two-day guided horseback ride to reach the site.

ACCOMMODATIONS
Rancho Meling
Between Km. 140 and 141, a newly paved road goes east to the settlement of San Telmo and then climbs into the Sierra San Pedro Mártir. Along the way, 50 kilometers from the highway, the historic Rancho Meling has been entertaining and feeding adventurous guests since the turn of the 20th century.

Owned and operated by the Johnson/Meling families since 1910, Rancho Meling (also known as Rancho San José, tel. 646/179-4106, www. ranchomeling.com, US$50 pp) was born as a base for gold-mining operations and then destroyed by bandits in the Mexican Revolution. It was rebuilt as a 4,000-hectare cattle ranch, and today it is a haven for motorcyclists, eco-tourists, fly-in guests, and anyone seeking the solitude of a rustic getaway in the mountains.

The working cattle ranch sits at an elevation of 670 meters in a stand of pines at the base of the sierra. Its 12 rooms all have private baths, hot water, and a fireplace or wood stove for heat. For larger groups or families, there is a four-bedroom/three-bath cabin. Hearty meals (US$6 breakfast, US$8 lunch, US$11 dinner) are cooked over a wood-fired stove and served at a long wooden table beside a large stone fireplace in the main house. The generator goes off at 10 P.M., but you can read by the light of a kerosene lamp after that.

The road to San Telmo comes 13.9

kilometers south of Colonet, just past a Pemex on the left. (Fill up before you head into the sierra.) Alternatively, you can fly your own plane and land on the ranch's dirt landing strip. Baja Bush Pilots members receive 10 percent off daily rates.

Mike's Sky Ranch
Just beyond Km. 138 on Mexico 3, a dirt road heads 35.5 kilometers south to Mike's Sky Ranch (tel. 664/681-5514), a rustic resort in the sierra foothills (elev. 1,200 m) at the northwestern edge of the national park. Popular with off-road bikers, the ranch has been a checkpoint on the Baja 500 and Baja 1000 races for many years. Accommodations are in 27 basic cabins (US$60 pp), and the rates include family-style meals and use of the swimming pool. Campsites cost US$5 per vehicle per night (water and shower use only). Campers can pay US$12 additional for dinner and US$7 for breakfast (served 6–10 A.M.) and lunch.

The road to Mike's is rough in spots and can change drastically with recent rains. Beyond the ranch, this road continues southwestward to join the newly paved road between Mexico 1 and the national park.

GETTING AROUND
Guided Trips
Ensenada native Francisco Detrell has been organizing sierra tours since the 1980s through his company **EcoTur** (Costero 1094, Local 14, Ensenada, www.mexonline.com/baja/ecotur3. htm, ecoturbc@ens.com.mx, tours US$12–150). Guided trips include waterfall hikes, Picacho del Diablo summits, and observatory tours. Francisco speaks English and Spanish.

Rancho Meling also offers guided hikes into the sierra.

Valle and Bahía de San Quintín

South of Vicente Guerrero on Mexico 1, the wide, flat coastal plain of San Quintín begins. Two rivers, Río San Miguel and Río Santa María, provide water that fuels the local agricultural economy. Workers' camps on the outskirts of town house farm workers from mainland Mexico who come to work the fields.

Visitors who stop here—mainly the sportfishing set—enjoy a unique coastal environment that consists of three connected bays:

narrow Bahía San Quintín and Bahía Falsa and the larger Bahía Santa María. In between are tidal zones and marshes filled with marine life.

The town of San Quintín itself (pop. 20,000) offers some practical services for travelers (clinic, banks, Internet) but is primarily another agricultural hub. Five kilometers south of San Quintín, Lázaro Cárdenas has Mexico's 67th Infantry battalion camp, an intercity bus terminal, and some shops and restaurants.

ENSENADA TO EL ROSARIO

HISTORY

Named by Sebastián Vizcaíno, San Quintín caught the attention of foreign investors as early as the 1880s as a potentially lucrative wheat-growing area; however, early colonists, first from the United States and later from England, failed to realize the vision. Before giving up, they dredged the harbor, dug wells, laid train tracks, and set up gristmill machinery—the remains of which you can still see along the inner bay shoreline today.

In the 1950s and '60s, San Quintín captured the imagination of some pioneering anglers from the United States, and the first few resorts opened for business. Among them, the Old Mill Motel became a legend in its time.

Today a small community of expats lives on the bayfront in a neighborhood called Pedregal, and a few fishing lodges cater to the sportfishing crowd.

SPORTS AND RECREATION
Beach and Bay Access

Follow signs to the Old Mill Motel from Mexico 1 to reach the bay. You can launch small boats here or from the Pedregal area on the west shore of the bay. Follow a gravel road from Mexico 1 (btw the Pemex and military camp) west of Lázaro Cárdenas 14 kilometers to Bahía Falsa. When the road forks, take the left (south) branch to reach Pedregal.

Alternatively, continue west at the fork another few hundred meters to Ostiones Guerrero, where you may be able to buy fresh oysters by the dozen. The road ends at a fish camp on the ocean.

To reach Bahía Santa María, drive 16 kilometers south of Lázaro Cárdenas and turn right (west) on the paved road to Santa María. Follow signs to the Desert Inn Hotel; local clam diggers frequent Playa Santa María at low tide. It's a long, sandy beach, located just past the hotel.

Fishing and Hunting

The unique marine environment here, with the shallow bay system and several rocky seamounts just offshore in the Pacific, creates fantastic opportunities for both surf casting and deep-sea fishing. Rock cod, yellowtail, and lingcod are common, and that's just the beginning of the list. Experienced anglers say they are able to catch upwards of 20 different species in one day of fishing.

The presence of several large-scale oyster farms along the inner bays shows just how clean the marine environment is. (They need pristine conditions to thrive.)

San Quintín Sportfishing (Rancho Cielito Lindo, tel. 616/165-6046, book4fish@aol. com), **Tiburon's Pangas Sportfishing** (near the Old Mill, U.S. tel. 619/428-2779), **Don Eddie's Landing** (tel. 616/165-6061), and **Campo Lorenzo** (tel. 616/165-6022 or Skype tel. 909/581-4140) can arrange guided fishing trips for around US$200–300 per *panga*, depending on the season.

San Quintín offers hunters the opportunity to pursue ducks and valley quail, but it's best known for the brandt hunting. Contact Lorenzo at Campo Lorenzo to arrange quail hunting. **Sporting Field International** (www. sportingfield.com) brokers pricey brandt hunts using local guides. The cost will end up being US$2,000 or so for a three-day hunt (Thurs.–Sun. only). The season for brandt is January–February.

Surfing

The beach breaks along Playa San Ramón, which runs between Vicente Guerrero and San Quintín (access at Km. 172), are nothing special, but they don't get crowded either. The better-known but still uncrowded breaks are at Cabo San Quintín, with more consistent surf and longer rides. Access is difficult, via the road to Bahía Falsa and then a coastal road heading south to the point. Conditions are typically cold and super windy.

ACCOMMODATIONS
Under US$50

Motel Chávez (San Quintín, tel. 616/165-2005, motelchavez@hotmail.com, US$20–30, cash only), next to a highway bridge toward the south end of town, has been a mainstay on the budget travel circuit for years. Its clean rooms have fans. Also on the highway, the **Hotel Real de Cora** (San Quintín, tel. 616/166-8576, US$32) has secure parking.

A relatively new option in town is the **Villa de San Quintín** (Av. A #5 btw 8th/9th, San Quintín, tel. 616/165-1800, www.hotellavilla. biz, US$35), an offshoot of a Tijuana hotel that was built in 2005. It has 32 nonsmoking, carpeted rooms with private baths, and air-conditioning, TV, phone, and free high-speed Internet. Secure parking is designed for trailers and boats, and an on-site restaurant is open 6:30 A.M.–9:30 P.M. daily.

At the northeast end of Bahía San Quintín, **Don Eddie's Landing** (tel. 616/165-6061, www.doneddies.com, US$45) has older rooms with lots of beds and sagging mattresses. Fishing packages are available and include lodging, boat, and food.

South of Don Eddie's Landing and next to the public boat launch, the **Old Mill Motel** (tel. 800/208-2154, U.S. tel. 619/428-2779, US$40–50) occupies the former gristmill site. A regular crowd of hunters and anglers frequents the place, and they like to party at night. Accommodations are in cabins arranged around a courtyard, with an attached campground (US$10). Rates often include two cold beers. No heat or air-conditioning. The road out to these two places can get extremely muddy after a heavy rain; high clearance is recommended.

Next to Bahía Santa María, **Rancho Cielito Lindo** (U.S. tel. 619/593-2252, cielitolindo@bajasi.com, US$10) is a restaurant and bar with a few rooms and a campground on the premises.

US$50-100

On Bahía Santa María, the **Desert Inn** (tel. 616/165-9008, toll-free U.S. tel. 800/800-9632, www.desertinns.com/sanquintin, US$75) was about to change hands at press time. Spacious rooms have remote-control heat and air-conditioning units, plus sea views and terraces. Modern tiled baths have glass shower doors; full-size bath towels are a treat. A palm-

lined walkway leads to the beach. If you find yourself in the area at sundown and you don't want to shack up in a sportfishing lodge, this hotel is a good bet for a quiet night's sleep.

The newly renovated **(Hotel Jardines Baja** (U.S. tel. 619/591-8922, www.hotel-jardinesbaja.com, US$50–75) has raised the bar considerably for accommodations in the San Quintín area. It has several rooms, including a suite with its own deck and separate living room; some of the rooms have working wood-burning fireplaces. Its new restaurant opened in 2008 to rave reviews. Beds are comfortable, the grounds are beautiful, and the coffee is strong. Watch for the Jardines sign on Mexico 1, south of Lázaro Cárdenas, at the sign that points the way to Bahía San Quintín. Turn right and follow this road for about 1.5 kilometers to the sign for Hotel Baja Jardines. Turn left here, and the hotel will be a few hundred meters down on the right.

Camping and RV Parks

One of the newcomers on the San Quintín scene for RV camping is **Los Olivos Family Park** (tel. 616/165-6123, US$15), popular because it is close to the highway, so you don't have to drive your big rig down a long bumpy dirt road just to crash for the night. This secure park has full hookups and a swimming pool, and hot showers were under construction at press time. It is located on the road to the Jardines Hotel and Restaurant.

Rancho Cielito Lindo (U.S. tel. 619/593-2252, cielitolindo@bajasi.com, US$12 RV, US$10 tent) has 15 campsites—some with *palapas*—for tents or RVs.

A favorite among repeat Baja campers, **El Pabellón RV Campground** (Km. 16, Mexico 1, US$5–10) is comfortably removed from the towns of San Quintín and Lázaro Cárdenas and set back from the highway. It has campsites in a large open lot fronting the beach, with water and sewer hookups but no electricity. Restrooms are clean and have hot water. A fellow camper here once shared a delicious Peruvian-style ceviche made of Pismo clams dug that day at the beach.

Beach camping is permitted but not recommended in the San Quintín area due to a persistent problem with theft.

FOOD

Take your pick of taco and *mariscos* stands that line the highway in both Lázaro Cárdenas and San Quintín. Clam cocktails are a local treat. **La Pasadita** (no tel., 9 A.M.–4 P.M. daily, mains US$5) does reliable *tacos de pescado* on the plaza in Lázaro Cárdenas.

Pollos Lalos (10 A.M.–10 P.M. daily, US$5–10), on the west side of the highway in San Quintín, makes tasty *pollos al carbon*. Nearby **Tuco's Pizza** (3–10 P.M. daily, mains US$10) will satisfy your pizza cravings.

The best Mexican dining experience in the area awaits at **Restaurant Viejo San Quintín**, open for breakfast, lunch, and dinner daily (US$5–10). This friendly establishment is located between two pharmacies and across from the post office in Lázaro Cárdenas. Order the *machaca*, chiles rellenos, carne asada, or enchiladas, and your beer will arrive in a frosted mug.

Gaston's Cannery (5:30 A.M.–9:30 P.M. daily, mains US$10–28) is part of the Old Mill complex. It serves Mexican food and seafood dinners at relatively high prices for the area. If you're driving to the Old Mill Motel in the afternoon, make sure to pay attention to each turn along the way so you can find your way back when you drive out that evening. It's easy to get lost in the maze of sandy roads at night.

The **Hotel Jardines Baja** (U.S. tel. 619/591-8922, www.hotel-jardinesbaja.com, 8 A.M.–10 P.M. Tues.–Thurs., 8 A.M.–2 A.M. Fri.–Sun., mains US$10–15) opened its new restaurant in 2008 with a menu that features seafood, wings, and desserts.

Rancho Cielito Lindo (tel. 616/165-6046, U.S. reservations 619/593-2252, cielitolindo@bajasi.com, mains US$10) serves fresh seafood dishes at good prices (dinner only).

Both San Quintín and Lázaro Cárdenas have *abarrotes* stores if you need to replenish food supplies.

INFORMATION AND SERVICES

There is a state tourism office between Vicente Guerrero and San Quintín at Km. 178 on the west side of the highway. The office is officially open 8 A.M.–5 P.M. weekdays and 10 A.M.–3 P.M. weekends, but hours tend to change with the seasons.

For medical emergencies, go to Clínica Santa María (tel. 616/165-2653, open 24 hours) in San Quintín.

GETTING THERE

San Quintín and Lázaro Cárdenas each have a Pemex station. There is an intercity bus depot in Lázaro Cárdenas, on the west side of Mexico 1; however, this area is not ideal for travelers without their own transportation, as the beaches are far from the highway.

Campo Lorenzo has a 760-meter unpaved licensed airstrip, air park, and trailer park for permanent residents. It is a private airstrip but available to pilots who call ahead to Skype 909/581-4140 or the Mexican landline at 616/165-6022. The camp can make arrangements for transportation, and there is only a US$25 fee to land and park if you are staying at Don Eddie's.

El Rosario

Baja road-trippers tend to remember their first time passing through the commercial center of El Rosario (pop. 3,500) because it's the last chance to gas up before the long haul across the desert. As if to emphasize the point, the town has one of the largest Pemex stations in the area, and it's open 24/7. There are two other reasons to hang around a while: If it's late in the day and you need a place to crash for the night, the Baja Cactus Motel has great rooms at unbelievably low prices. And if you just need a bite to eat on your way through, recently re-modeled Ed's Baja's Best is a good bet.

MISIÓN NUESTRA SEÑORA DEL ROSARIO DE VIÑADACO

The Dominicans established Misíon Nuestra Señora del Rosario De Viñadaco (1774–1832), the first of their nine Baja California missions, in present day El Rosario in 1774, led by Padres Vicente Mora and Francisco Galisteo. Adobe ruins of its second site are visible just off the west side of the highway at the sharp bend in the road. (Turn right at the grocery store and then left at the first road. Cross the arroyo and look for the ruins on the right.)

The standard mission crops of barley, corn, and beans grew especially well here, and the mission was able to convert hundreds of indigenous people before European illnesses began to take their toll on the population. By 1832 the mission was turned over to the local people.

ACCOMMODATIONS AND FOOD

Between the Pemex station and Mama Espinosa's restaurant, the **Baja Cactus Motel** (Km. 55, tel. 616/165-8850, www.bajacactus.com) has caused quite a stir among

Transpeninsular insiders in recent years. Where else in the world can you enjoy all the amenities of a four-star establishment—immaculate tiled baths, granite counters, four-poster king-size beds, luxury linens, gorgeous woodwork, 29-inch satellite TVs, purified water, air-conditioning—for US$35 a night? The story goes that the son of the motel owners wanted to help his parents fix the place up. All 22 rooms are wired with Ethernet cables, so that when high-speed Internet comes to El Rosario, Baja Cactus patrons will be among the first to enjoy it. You probably won't escape the sound of trucks decelerating through town, but you'll enjoy some of the finest accommodations anywhere on the peninsula.

The dining experience at historic **Mama Espinosa's** (east side of Mexico 1, just past the large Pemex as you enter the town from the north, no tel., breakfast, lunch, and dinner daily) has slipped of late, with higher prices (US$13–20) and disappointing meals. Stop in if you want to see all of the Baja 1000 memorabilia and learn a bit about the town's matriarch, Doña Anita, but lower your expectations for a memorable meal.

On the south side of town, recently remodeled **Baja's Best Café** (no tel., 7 A.M.–7 P.M. daily, mains US$7–15) serves a mean breakfast with real sausage and dependable coffee. It also runs a bed-and-breakfast on the premises. Rooms have comfortable beds and rain showers (US$50).

El Rosario has several grocery stores that carry produce, bread, and basic household supplies. **Mercado Hermanos Jaramillo** (Mexico 1, no tel.), near Mama Espinosa's, is the best of the bunch.

MEXICALI TO SAN FELIPE

Among Baja's international border towns, agricultural Mexicali strikes a balance between bustling Tijuana and quiet Tecate. Its palm-lined boulevards are cleaner and less touristy than other Baja California cities of its size (pop. 1 million). In addition to farming, state government drives much of the local economy, as Mexicali is the capital of Baja California (Norte).

Across the border from Mexicali, smaller Calexico is in every way a symbiotic community—equally dependent on agriculture and related businesses. The whimsical names of the Mexicali and Calexico border towns reflect the laid-back tone in these sister cities. Outside of the immediate border-crossing area, the focus on tourism that colors the visitor's experience in Tijuana and Ensenada is largely absent. Among other Baja cities, Mexicali is most similar to

La Paz in its mixed population of mainland Mexicans and foreign immigrants and the presence of a thriving local middle class. The city welcomes visitors, but its businesses do not cater to their every need. If you've had your fill of Americanized beach resorts with their activity booths and timeshare reps, Mexicali offers independent travelers a refreshing view of life in an ordinary Mexican city.

For California and Arizona residents, Mexicali is a gateway to both the Baja Peninsula and mainland Mexico. San Felipe and the northern beaches along the Sea of Cortez are just a couple of hours away by car. Southwest of Mexicali there are plenty of opportunities for desert hiking, soaking in natural hot springs, and off-road racing, as well as some of the best fishing and hunting in the country.

© NIKKI GOTH ITOI

HIGHLIGHTS

☾ La Chinesca: Born of a lack of essential ingredients, Mexicali-style Chinese food has become a fusion cuisine all its own. Try it here, in the only true Chinatown in all of Mexico (page 106).

☾ Cañon de Guadalupe: Hot springs in the Sierra de Juárez above the San Felipe desert reward backcountry explorers willing to drive the washboard access road (page 112).

☾ San Felipe *Malecón:* At night, the action in San Felipe takes place in discos and clubs along the waterfront. Start the evening off right with a seafood dinner in one of the town's open-air restaurants (page 116).

☾ Valle de los Gigantes: Between San Felipe and Puertecitos, the Valle de los Gigantes is an ideal place to snap postcard-perfect images of the world's tallest cactus species, some of which live to be hundreds of years old (page 122).

☾ Bahía San Luis Gonzaga: Popular with pilots and seasoned Baja travelers, this remote, gray-sand beach on the Gulf coast offers a slice of the old Baja (page 123).

LOOK FOR ☾ TO FIND RECOMMENDED SIGHTS, ACTIVITIES, DINING, AND LODGING.

PLANNING YOUR TIME

It takes about two hours to drive to Mexicali from the San Diego airport. Once you've arrived, you could spend just an afternoon and evening getting oriented and preparing for a trip to San Felipe, or a couple of days to explore the city's few attractions.

The most popular weekend itinerary in this area is a trip from Mexicali to San Felipe and back (two hours by car each way).

With a week or more, you could add a side trip to the Cañon de Guadalupe, and continue south of San Felipe to Puertecitos. With a four-wheel-drive vehicle, you could turn this trip into a loop, following the coastal road all the way to Gonzaga Bay and heading inland to meet the Transpeninsular Highway at Chapala. From there, you can head south to Bahía de los Angeles or turn north to Ensenada and Mexico 3, which returns to Mexicali.

MEXICALI TO SAN FELIPE

To San Diego
CALIFORNIA
Yuma
Calexico
UNITED STATES
MEXICO
BORDER CROSSINGS
Algodones
To Tucson
Cuidad Morelos
Río Colorado
LA CHINESCA
Benito Juárez
MEXICALI
TOLL
To Tecate
San Luis Río Colorado
ARIZONA
CAÑON DE GUADALUPE
Cañon de Guadalupe
To Nogales
Colonia La Puerta
Delta
Sierra
Laguna Salada
Guadalupe Vitória
de
Campo Sonora
Guardines de la Patria
Río Colorado
Desierto del Altar
Juárez
BAJA CALIFORNIA
SONORA
La Ventana
Isla Montague
Isla Pelicano
Golfo de Santa Clara
To Tecate
Boca La Bahía
Héroes de Independencia
Bahía Ometepec
Valle La Trinidad
Lázaro Cárenas
El Michoacano
Salinas Ometepec
San Matias
El Crucero la Trinidad
Sierra
Esteros La Ramada
RANCHO VILLA DEL SOL
San
0   10 mi
0   10 km
Sierra San Pedro Mártir National Park
RANCHO SANTA CLARA
Felipe
Sea of Cortez (Gulf of California)
NATIONAL OBSERVATORY
SAN FELIPE MALECÓN
San Felipe
Picacho del Diablo
To BAHÍA SAN LUIS GONZAGA
© AVALON TRAVEL
VALLE DE LOS GIGANTES
Punta Estrella

Mexicali

Founded March 14, 1903, Mexicali has little resemblance to its border cousins, Tecate and Tijuana. As the capital of the state of Baja California (Norte) and a major agricultural hub, most of the city's one million people are too busy to take much notice of the steady stream of tourists that make their way through Mexicali to San Felipe and points south. What the city lacks in painted donkeys and street vendors it makes up for with efficient business hotels and fine restaurants that depend on local repeat customers. The *zona hotelera* and the area along Calle Benito Juárez offer adequate nightlife with several clubs and bars.

As a visitor to Mexicali, you can choose to blend in with the locals by catching an Aguilas baseball game, watching a bullfight, or sampling *Bajanese* cuisines in La Chinesca, Mexico's only true Chinatown. If your vacation destination is beyond the city's borders, there are several hotels that cater to the guests who view Mexicali as a border staging area with secure parking and low rates.

The nicest times to visit Mexicali are any month except the peak of summer, when temperatures regularly top 38°C.

HISTORY

The Spanish first came to the Valle de Mexicali along the Camino del Diablo (Devil's Road) in the Sonora Desert. The Yumano tribes that inhabited the area grew squash, peas, melon, and corn. They also had advanced uses for medicinal herbs and used the desert flora and fauna in a variety of ways.

The Cucapá (People of the River) was a major Yumano group that traveled the Río Colorado in reed rafts. The arrival of the Spanish reduced the numbers of Cucapás to the point that today the descendents live in a small corner of the delta. Very few indigenous customs remain.

© NEIL KRAFT

Mexicali barber shop

Mexicali's emergence as an agricultural center followed irrigation of the Imperial Valley on the U.S. side of the border at the turn of the 20th century. *Los Angeles Times* publisher Harry Chandler was a key figure behind the irrigation of the Valle de Mexicali on the Mexico side of the border. With Chinese immigrant laborers imported to dig its canal, Mexicali became green virtually overnight. However, a 1905 storm rerouted the entire flow of the river into the valley, flooding Mexicali and filling the Salton Sea once again.

The Southern Pacific Railroad worked for several years to route the river back into the Sea of Cortez, leaving only the original channel off the main canal.

In 1911 the Magonista faction of revolutionaries briefly took control of Mexicali. To protect the border, the Mexican government moved the capital of the Territory of Baja California to Mexicali from Ensenada. With the passage of Prohibition in the United States, Mexicali experienced an influx of tourism that was made famous by the song "Mexicali Rose." Jack Tenney wrote the lyrics, originally called "The Waltz" and claimed it wasn't about a dancing girl but was written for an elderly bar patron. Bing Crosby recorded it before Gene Autry starred in a movie by that name. Tenney went to law school and was elected to the California State Legislature. Chinese workers who had helped build the irrigation canals opened many of the area's Prohibition-era businesses.

Baja California (Norte) became a Mexican state in 1952. Cotton was initially the cash crop in the valley, but with the invention of synthetic fibers, asparagus, green onions, and other crops became more important to the economy. The Agrobaja convention (www.agrobaja.com), held in March each year, brings 50,000 U.S. and Mexican agricultural and fishery interests to town.

With the addition of a manufacturing base in the form of in-bond plants and maquiladoras, the population of Mexicali began to rise, and it has doubled since the 1970s.

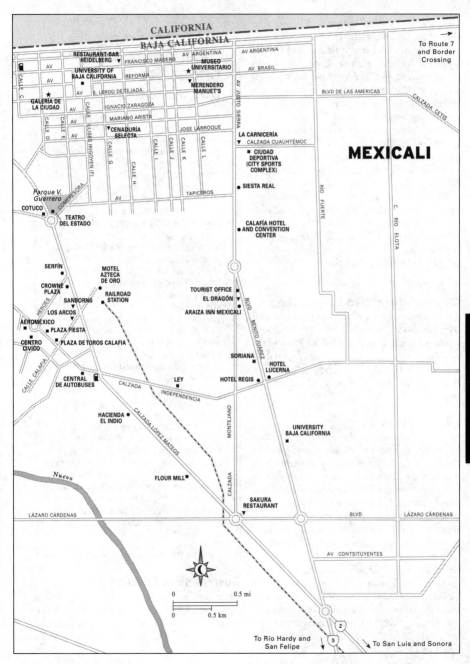

Mexicali's economy remains closely tied to that of the United States, and the current economic downturn has resulted in widespread layoffs at the maquiladoras. Some forays into clean-tech industry may help the city through the cycle: Silicon Border is a company that is trying to build out a science park and manufacturing complex located to the west of Mexicali along the international border. The groundbreaking ceremony took place in 2005, but the park was without a tenant until 2008, when a solar-power manufacturer committed to moving in.

The Cerro Prieto geothermal power plant opened south of Mexicali in 1973. Today it is one of the largest producers of geothermal power in the world. In early 2009 the company signed a deal with the City of Los Angeles to sell power from its plant.

SIGHTS
Centro Interactivo Sol del Niño
This children's museum (López Mateos and Alfonso Esquer, tel. 686/554-9595 or -9696, www.sol.org.mx, 9 A.M.–7 P.M. Mon.–Fri., 10 A.M.–2 P.M., Sat.–Sun., free), located in a former cotton seed warehouse, has more than 250 interactive science and technology exhibits.

◖ La Chinesca
Mexicali is home to Mexico's only distinct Chinatown. The intersection at the heart of the district is Calle Benito Juárez and Calle Altamirano, close to the border crossing. The city itself boasts 100 Chinese restaurants, mostly serving Cantonese-style cuisine. Earlier in the 20th century, the percentage of Chinese residents in the city was much higher, and the only two cinemas in the city played movies in Chinese. Today relatively few Chinese families remain, but Chinese culture and traditions live on. The signature monument to the Chinese presence in Mexicali is the pagoda on Plaza de Amistad (just outside the district). It was made entirely by Chinese craftsmen using materials shipped from China and was dedicated in 1994.

ALTO GOLFO DE CALIFORNIA AND DELTA DEL RÍO COLORADO

Mexicali and Calexico occupy the same valley bordered by the Colorado River delta to the east and the Sierra de Cucapá to the west. Developers renamed the valley north of the border the Imperial Valley. It's also known as the Salton Sink. South of the border, it's simply called Valle de Mexicali. The entire valley was once part of the Gulf of California, before silt from the flooding of the river pushed the shoreline to the south.

The Colorado River is the deciding geographical factor in this area. For millennia, the river flowed directly to the Gulf, bounded by its own natural levees, which were built up by silt. The valley itself lay underwater. Periodically, the river would break its banks and flood the Salton Sink. Over time, the break would fill back up with silt, and the temporary Salton Sea would evaporate.

In 1905 developers lost control of an irrigation project and accidentally diverted virtually the entire flow of the Colorado River into the Salton Sink. It took a railroad company's crews several years to repair the breach and correct the river's flow.

Today the irrigation system leftover from the early 20th-century developers continues to support a vibrant agricultural economy. But 90 percent of the Colorado River is diverted prior to reaching the border. And the All-American Canal north of the border might be paved, which would prevent further seepage flows south of the border.

Bosque de la Ciudad
Visit Bosque de la Ciudad in southwest Mexicali (Ocotlán and Alvarado, 9 A.M.–5 P.M. Tues.–Sun.) when you need a break from the dusty downtown. This large city park has its own lake and zoo.

RECREATION AND ENTERTAINMENT

Baseball

Mexicali's professional baseball team, **Las Aquilas** (The Eagles), is part of the Mexican Pacific League and plays at El Nido de las Aguilas (Eagles' Nest) stadium, located in the **Cuidad Deportiva** (City Sports Complex, Calz. Justo Sierra, tel. 686/567-5129, www.aguilas-demexicali.com.mx, Nov.–Jan.). General admission tickets start at US$40.

Nightlife

Antrojo (Calz. Juárez 1807, tel. 686/568-2129) plays house music for a younger crowd. It's open until 2 A.M. Wednesday, Friday, and Saturday. **La Capilla** is a music and dance club inside the Hotel Lucerna (Calz. Juárez 2151, tel. 686/564-7000, until 2 A.M. nightly). Bars at the Hotel Crowne Plaza, Araiza Inn Mexicali, and Araiza Inn Calafía often have live music in the evening.

Theater

Baja California's state theater, the **Teatro del Estado,** (tel. 686/554-6419, icbcteatrode-lestado@hotmail.com) occupies a 1,100-seat venue at Calzado López Mateos and Avenida Castellanos. The city tourist office also has performance schedules (tel. 888/268-8262).

Festivals and Events

Baja Prog (www.bajaprog.org) takes place in March, with four days of progressive rock band performances. Most of the festival takes place at the Hotel Araiza, but the finale is held at the Teatro Del Estado (State Theatre) on Boulevard López Mateos.

In March or April, the **Mexicali 500** (www.codeoffroad.com.mx) off-road race starts in Mexicali and ends in San Felipe. The course follows the Laguna Salada dry lakebed.

In September–October, the **Fiesta del Sol** (Parque Vicente Guerrero, www.fiestasdelsol.com.mx) draws some 500,000 people over the course of 21 days to commemorate the founding of Mexicali in 1904. During the event, a festival queen is named and a number of cultural performances and art shows provide entertainment.

In November the local chamber of restaurants, CANIRAC, holds **Muestra Gastronómica,** a food fair featuring Mexican, seafood, and Chinese cuisines (tel. 686/554-3285, www.canirac.org.mx).

On Sunday afternoons, mariachi groups often play at **Parque Constitución,** a park at Avenida Hidalgo and Calle Aldama.

SHOPPING

Unless you're buying agricultural supplies or prescription medication, the visitor-oriented shopping is limited in Mexicali. The border zone along Calle Melgar has the usual shops selling kitschy souvenirs. **Plaza Cataviña** (Calz. Cetys 1800, Col. Cataviña, tel. 686/567-2896) caters to the young, upscale crowd with a modern health club and a variety of electronics, clothing, and jewelry stores.

El Armario (Calz. Justo Sierra 1700 at Blvd. Juárez, Plaza Azteca, tel. 686/568-1906) has rustic Mexican furniture, glassware, and handicrafts.

handicraft for sale in Mexicali

© NIKKI GOTH ITOI

MEXICALI TO SAN FELIPE

Plaza Cachanilla (Calz. López Mateos, northwest of Parque Vicente Guerrero, tel. 686/553-4177 or -4108) is a huge mall located just a few minutes away from the international border. In the summer, when the weather is hot, local families will spend the day inside the cool shopping mall.

ACCOMMODATIONS

Mexicali accommodations cost less than their counterparts in Tijuana and Ensenada. If you shop around when you arrive, you can often get much lower rates than if you make reservations ahead of time. The higher-end hotels cater to Mexican business travelers with meeting rooms and business centers. On the less-expensive end of the spectrum, there are a number of hotels that supply visitors with functional rooms, off-street parking, and air-conditioning.

Under US$50

Motel Reforma (Reforma 625, tel. 686/533-6831, US$30) caters to budget travelers looking for accommodations near the border. It's slightly better than the **Hotel San Juan Capistrano** (Reforma 646, tel. 686/552-4104, US$30) a few doors down. As you head west of Boulevard López Mateos, the motels get cheaper, but they are real dives.

Motel Azteca de Oro (Calle de la Industria 600, tel. 686/557-1433, www.hotelaztecadeoro.com, US$42–60) is a typical two-story motel with air-conditioned rooms, but six rooms are combined with a private enclosed one-car garage. The rooms are standard for the price range, with older beds and shabby bathrooms. Two-story **Hotel Hacienda del Indio** (López Mateos 101 at Fresnillo, tel. 686/557-2277, US$45) has 50 recently renovated rooms that surround an enclosed courtyard. **Hotel Regis** (Calz. Juárez 2150, tel. 686/566-8801, www.hotel-regis.com.mx, US$45) is another good choice for clean, basic rooms.

US$50-100

If you're simply stopping over on your way south or looking for a base from which to launch a fishing or hunting trip, the **Hotel Siesta Real** (Calz. Justo Sierra 899, tel. 686/568-2001, toll-free U.S. tel. 800/426-5093, www.hotelsiesta-real.com, US$48–80) is a convenient option. Its 90 rooms have air-conditioning, TVs, and phones. Guests may also use a swimming pool, restaurant, and off-street parking lot.

Hotel Posada Inn (Blvd. López Mateos 939 at Calle Torneros, tel. 686/558-6100, www.hotelposadainn.com.mx, US$60) has wireless Internet, air-conditioned rooms, off-street parking in a courtyard, and a nice sitting area on the upper walkway. It's situated on the east side of a partitioned road, so it can be difficult to get in and out by car.

The **Calafía Hotel and Convention Center** (Calz. Justo Sierra 1495, tel. 686/568-3311 or 800/026-5444, toll-free U.S. tel. 877/727-2492, www.araizainn.com.mx, US$80) houses the Calafía Steakhouse and a separate sports bar. Part of the Araiza chain, it is a clean, four-story motel with 170 rooms. The hotel caters to traveling families with a pool and secure parking. It is located next to a police station.

US$100-150

South of the Calafía along the same boulevard (which changes names en route), the **Araiza Inn Mexicali** (Calz. Juárez 2220, tel. 686/564-1100 or 800/686-5444, U.S. tel. toll-free 877/727-2492, www.araizainn.com.mx, US$70–120) has 190 rooms. The Fonda restaurant is often packed. Some of the suites have been renovated and are very nice, with flat-screen TVs, shoe-buffing machines, and spinning cycles. This hotel also has a swimming pool, coffee shop, bar, and disco.

Hotel Lucerna (Calz. Juárez 2151, tel. 686/564-7000, US$130) has 176 rooms, each with air-conditioning, minibar, satellite TV, and phone. There are two pools, a fitness center, and the Restaurant Mezzosole. The tower you see when you turn left out of the reception office is worn out. For the best accommodations, ask for a bungalow. They were newly renovated and have the feel of a W Hotel room. The family suite has a separate bedroom, spinning cycle, bathrobes, and two flat-screen TVs. Also note, this hotel has limited secured parking.

The **Fiesta Inn Mexicali** (Calz. López Mateos 1029, tel. 686/837-3300, www.fiestainn.com, US$83–135) is a newly built hotel with more than 150 rooms in a multistory white building. It's located a few minutes from the border, across from the city's bullfighting arena and within striking distance of several shopping malls.

The **Crowne Plaza** (Blvd. López Mateos at Av. de los Héroes, tel. 686/557-3600, toll-free U.S. tel. 800/227-6963, www.crowneplaza.com, US$100–150) has most of the same amenities as the Araiza and Fiesta chains. A sports bar features pool tables and a wide-screen TV. Nonsmoking rooms are available.

FOOD

Mexicali has a less-developed food scene than Tijuana or Ensenada, but it does have its own signature cuisine, Mexicali-Chinese, and plenty of places to find an enjoyable meal.

Chinese

At last count, there were just under 100 Chinese restaurants in Mexicali. The cooking is mostly Cantonese, but Mexicali-Chinese has evolved into a unique cuisine. For example, a bowl of ketchup-like sauce is commonly served as a condiment. You may also be served a bowl of jalapeños with soy sauce, limes, and salt.

Dragón (Libertad 990, tel. 686/557-4425, lunch and dinner daily, mains US$10) is an upscale Cantonese restaurant that can hold several hundred diners. The signature dish here is duck with mushrooms. Another good choice is **Fortune House** (Lázaro Cárdenas 1153, tel. 686/555-8848, 11 A.M.–11 P.M. daily, mains US$10), near the exit to Mexico 2 and Tijuana.

Other International

Close to downtown, **Restaurant-Bar Heidelberg** (Madero at Calle H, tel. 686/554-2022, http://restauranteheidelberg.com/, noon–1 A.M. Mon.–Sat., mains US$15–25) offers German and Continental fare. The atmosphere is pleasant, but prices are high. With an attached piano bar, **Restaurant Italiano**

Mandolino (Reforma 1070, tel. 686/552-9544, lunch and dinner daily, mains US$10–15) has long been popular for Italian cuisine.

Mexicali has a good option for sushi as well: **Sakura Restaurant** (Lázaro Cárdenas 2004 at Montejano, tel. 686/566-0514 or -4848, 8 A.M.–midnight Tues.–Sun., mains US$10–15) serves teppanyaki and sushi with the **Karaoke Video Bar** upstairs. **Tatoro** (Calle D 126, Col. Nueva, tel. 686/552-4590) brings a taste of Spain to Baja California. Popular dishes include paella and roast pork.

Mexican

In a former American-style drive-in, **Merendero Manuet's** (Calle L at Pino Suárez, tel. 686/552-5694, 10 A.M.–1 A.M. daily, mains US$5–10) has a full menu of *antojitos* and a full bar occupied by local ranchers and farmers in cowboy hats. The waitresses waited on the parents of some of the younger patrons who drink beer and smoke in the parking lots on weekends.

Another option for *antojitos* was brand-new at press time: **Mr. Choby's** (Juárez 1199 at Carranza, no tel., noon–10 P.M. Sun.–Thurs., 10 A.M.–1 A.M. Fri.–Sat.), in the Las Villas food court. Full *botana* platters go for US$22, while individual mains start at US$5.

Fonda de Mexicali (Juárez 2220, tel. 686/564-1100, ext. 721, mains US$15 and up) in the Hotel Araiza does a huge brunch buffet on Sundays for US$15. The food is a notch above the typical hotel restaurant fare.

In business since 1945, **La Cenaduría Selecta** (Arista 1510 at Calle G, Col. Nueva, tel. 686/552-4047, 7 A.M.–5 P.M. Mon., 8 A.M.–11 P.M. Tues.–Sun., mains US$12 and up) is best known for its mole dishes.

La Carnicería (Panamá 190 at Justo Sierra, Col. Cuauhtémoc, tel. 686/568-1011, lunch and dinner daily, mains US$18) is an elegant steakhouse that features an indoor grill and brick oven behind glass. Try the mini *al pastor* tacos to start and the very good *Queso Fondido* (fondue platter). There is a bar attached to the restaurant with modern decor and live music occasionally on the weekends.

Seafood

☖ Los Arcos Restaurant/Bar (Calafía 454, tel. 686/556-0903, www.restaurantlosarcos.com.mx, 11 A.M.–10 P.M. Mon.–Thurs., 11 A.M.–11 P.M. Fri.–Sun., mains US$10–15) is part of a chain of 14 restaurants scattered throughout Mexico. Located in the Centro Cívico district, it is the best place in town for fresh seafood.

Groceries

The warehouse-style **Soriana** (three locations, López Mateos 1100, tel. 686/557-2428, Calzada Anáhuac 1301, tel. 686/838-2239, Universidad 1700, tel. 686/556-2203), and 24-hour **Ley,** at Plaza Fiesta on Calzada López Mateos (tel. 686/561-6282), are your best options for stocking up on food and supplies. There is a **Costco** (Km. 7.5, Carr. San Luis-Río Colorado, tel. 686/580-4530, 9 A.M.–9 P.M. daily) on the road out of town as you drive on Mexico 5 toward San Felipe.

INFORMATION AND SERVICES
Tourist Assistance

The Mexicali Tourism and Convention Bureau (COTUCO) has offices on Boulevard López Mateos at Calle Camelias (tel. 686/552-4401 or 888/342-7323, www.mexicaliturismo.com, 8 A.M.–7 P.M. Mon.–Fri.). The information counter has a friendly and helpful staff that speaks English.

The state tourism department, SECTUR, also has an office in town, at Boulevard Benito Juárez 1 and Calzada Montejano (tel. 686/566-1161 or 686/558-1000, 8 A.M.–5 P.M. Mon.–Fri., 10 A.M.–3 P.M. Sat.–Sun.). The state's legal assistance department (Attorney for Tourist Protection, tel./fax 686/566-1116) is based here as well.

Money

Banks are numerous in Mexicali. Banamex, Bancomer, and Serfín each have multiple branches, most with ATMs. If you need to exchange currency, the banks offer this service only until about noon each day. Numerous *casas de cambio* on both sides of the border are another option.

Post and Telephone

Mexicali's main post and a Western Union office are located at Calzada Independencia and Calle Pioneros (8 A.M.–3 P.M. Mon.–Fri., 9 A.M.–1 P.M. Sat.). But it's probably better to mail your postcards across the border in Calexico on Birch Street and George Avenue, four blocks west of Imperial Avenue.

Long-distance Ladatel phones can be found throughout Mexicali. Check the rates before you dial an international number. Many U.S. mobile phones continue to pick up a signal across the border into Mexicali. Beyond this zone, you'll need to set yourself up for international roaming (call your service provider before you go). Mobile phones that use the international GSM standard are the only ones that can connect reliably throughout Baja California.

Visas and Officialdom

For information about immigration paperwork for traveling into Mexico, including vehicle import permits for driving on the mainland, visit the **Mexican consulate** on the U.S. side of the border in Calexico (331 W. Second St., U.S. tel. 760/357-3863, fax 760/357-6284, 8 A.M.–3 P.M. Mon.–Fri.).

Border Crossing

The main (west) Mexicali border crossing stays open around the clock every day. The crowds here will be considerably thinner than the crossing at Tijuana, but lines do back up during the morning and afternoon commutes. East of the main crossing, a second gateway joins Calexico East with Mexicali's industrial zone (6 A.M.–10 P.M. daily). Wait times here are typically less half the time at the main crossing; however, if your ultimate destination is San Diego or other points west, you'll spend a good amount of time circling east and back around to the west.

If you are a hunter coming back to the United States with game to declare, use the east crossing;

the border officials at the main crossing may not know how to handle the paperwork.

If you're traveling south of Mexicali, you'll need a tourist permit, which you can pick up at the Oficina de Federal building that's marked *Migracion* or *Aduana,* located to the left of the border gates as you pass through from the U.S. side.

GETTING THERE
By Air
Mexicali has an international airport, **Aeropuerto Internacional General Rodolfo Sánchez Taboada** (MXL), 20 kilometers east of the city via Boulevard de las Américas. No U.S. airlines currently serve the airport, but **Aeroméxico** (Pasaje Alamos 1008-D, Centro Cívico Comercial, tel. 686/557-2551) and **Mexicana** (Obregón, tel. 686/553-5401) offer connections from Hermosillo, Sonora, on the mainland. Mexicana also flies to and from Guadalajara, Monterrey, and Mexico City.

A taxi from the airport to downtown Mexicali runs about US$15.

By Car
From the San Diego airport, take I-5 north to I-8 past El Centro, and take Route 111 south to the border. This route takes about two hours. There is parking on the Calexico side of the border at **Double AA Parking** (201 W. Second St., U.S. tel. 760/357-3213) or **Calexico Parking & Storage** (465 W. Second St., tel. 760/357-2477, 6 A.M.–6 P.M. Mon.–Fri.), where you can also store your vehicle (US$1.50/day) or trailer (US$3/day).

After passing through the border patrol, you'll reach a Y in the road. Stay right. The toll crossing is in the middle of town itself, with the usual insurance companies, fast-food restaurants, and money exchangers lining the last few blocks on the U.S. side.

To reach the east crossing, take I-8 to Route 7 south. For current border wait times, visit http://apps.cbp.gov/bwt/.

Mexicali's main north–south roads are well marked. The smaller streets running north–south are named by letters in the alphabet, starting with A near Route 111 and descending as you head east.

By Bus
Mexicali's **Central de Autobuses** (on the south side of Independencia btw Calz. López Mateos/Centro Cívico, tel. 686/557-2410 or -2450) offers intercity connections to Baja and the mainland. **Autotransportes de Baja California** (ABC, Tijuana tel. 664/683-5681, www.abc.com.mx) offers connections to Mexicali from Ensenada and Tijuana. **Estrellas del Pacífico** (Tijuana tel. 664/683-5022 or -6789) also runs buses to and from Mexicali and Ensenada. **Transportes Norte de Sonora** (TNS), **Transportes del Pacífico** (Independencia 1244, tel. 686/556-1418) and **Elite** (tel. 800/025-0220, www.abc.com.mx) provide connections to the mainland.

To reach the bus terminal via public transportation, catch a local Calle 6 bus from one of the stops along Calzada López Mateos.

The small ABC terminal on López Mateos (btw Azueta/Madero) offers frequent service to Tecate, Tijuana, and Ensenada.

The **Greyhound** station in Calexico (123 First St., U.S. tel. 760/357-1895), right at the pedestrian border crossing, runs direct connections to San Diego and Los Angeles. From the Calexico depot, you walk across through the border gate and take a taxi to the Mexicali bus depot (under US$10).

GETTING AROUND
By Bus
Mexicali's city buses are signed for their final destination (e.g., Centro Cívico, Justo Sierra). Many of these bus routes originate on Calle Altamirano downtown, close to the border crossing. Fares are less than US$1.

By Taxi
Taxis de ruta (route taxis) cover many of the same routes for a slightly higher fare. Private taxi fare runs about US$5 downtown, US$6–8 to or from the border to the Centro Cívico area or the Boulevard Juárez hotel zone. Aside from the pedestrian border crossing, the larger

hotels are good places to find an available taxi. To order a taxi, call **Radio Taxis Cervantes** (tel. 686/568-3718) or **Ecotaxi** (tel. 686/562-6565).

By Car

Aside from its many traffic circles, called *glorietas,* Mexicali is a fairly easy city to navigate by car. Street parking is readily available.

Follow Calle Juárez to find Mexico 5 south to San Felipe. There are several ways to get to Mexico 2, which goes east to Sonora and west to Tecate and Tijuana.

Pemex stations are easy to find, and these days, most offer Premium fuel.

MEXICO 5 SOUTH TO SAN FELIPE

If you want to proceed directly to Mexico 5 south toward San Felipe from the main border crossing (Route 111), keep right as you approach the border booths. Stop for the border light, which will flash either green or red. If it's green, you can continue. If it's red, you will need to pull over for further inspection. If you need to get a tourist visa or have an FM3 stamped, the immigration office is on the immediate right.

As you cross the border, bear right to get onto Boulevard López Mateos. Continue past the first traffic circle with the statue of Ignacio Allende. Get into the right-hand lane and follow the signs to San Felipe as the road forks to the right and you cross the railroad tracks. At the next traffic circle, follow the signs to San Felipe, and then take a left at the next light. This road will turn into Mexico 5 and will take you all the way into San Felipe.

Coming from the new border crossing to the east, the road will end in a T a few hundred meters from the border. Go right at the T and then take a left onto Boulevard Gomez Morin. This will take you straight to Mexico 5. Stay in the middle of the three lanes to avoid most of the abrupt stops.

The drive is mostly flat, but you'll have plenty to look at as you go from farmland to lakebed to desert. About an hour and a half into the drive you can often see the Gulf of California in the distance. As you get closer to San Felipe, you'll encounter construction crews that are widening the road from two lanes to four. Eventually, the entire stretch from Mexicali to San Felipe will have four lanes.

The total drive time from the border to San Felipe is around two hours. For the return trip north, add at least one hour to make sure you have enough time to cross the border. During rush hour or on holidays the border wait can be several hours.

Mexicali to Tecate

West of Mexicali, Mexico 2 follows the northern foothills of the Sierra de los Cucapá and the top of **Laguna Salada,** a 100-kilometer-long dry salt lake. The Pemex station near Km. 24 is the only option for fuel until La Rumorosa (53 km farther west). If you drive along Mexico 2-D between Mexicali and Tecate, you'll pass through two toll booths, each of which costs approximately US$2.50.

After Laguna Salada, the highway ascends the Sierra de Juárez, where several palm canyons named Tajo, El Carrizo, Guadalupe, and El Palomar offer prime hiking, off-roading, and wilderness camping. Tajo also is known among rock climbers. Spring-fed streams run year-round, but the time to go is between November and April. From May to October, the temperatures can get above 38°C.

◖ CAÑON DE GUADALUPE

Of the four larger canyons in this part of the Sierra de Juárez, 400-hectare Cañon de Guadalupe is the most popular among hikers and campers because of its healing hot springs. In this high-elevation oasis, granite peaks tower over a sea of blue fan palms. Waterfalls,

COURTESY OF WWW.DISCOVERBAJACALIFORNIA.COM

ceramics made by a native Mexicali tribe

prehistoric rock art, and solar power all are part of the experience. Rock climbers will find challenging pitches at Cañon Tajo.

Camping

Campsites at **Guadalupe Canyon Hot Springs and Campground** (U.S. tel. 949/673-2670, www.guadalupe-canyon.com, US$50–75) are arranged to afford some privacy. Each of the eight campsites features its own private hot tub made of river rock and concrete, and you can adjust the temperature between 26 and 41°C. The sites can accommodate multiple vehicles, and there is a two-night minimum on weekends and a three-night minimum on holiday weekends. Pets are welcome, with proof of vaccinations.

Facilities for campers include outhouses, showers, and a market that sells the basics. Refrigeration is provided by 45-kilogram blocks of ice. The owners do not want you to collect firewood or disturb any of the natural surroundings, but firewood is for sale. The canyon is popular on the holidays and the weekends, so book early.

Guided Hikes

For tours of the Cañon de Guadalupe, contact **Rupestres** (cell tel. 686/158-9921, explorandobajacalifornia@hotmail.com, US$70).

Getting There

From Mexicali, take Calle Guadalajara about eight kilometers south to Mexico 2 West and follow the highway for 32 kilometers. The first turn is labeled Cañon de Guadalupe and Laguna Salada. The road is available only from the eastbound lanes, so you'll need to pass the intersection and double back at the next U-turn opportunity. This first turn is faster and more direct, but because it uses the dry lakebed of the Laguna Salada for 40 kilometers, it will be muddy and impassable following any rain. When you drive across the lakebed, don't worry if there are multiple tracks. Follow the most worn route, keep heading south/southwest, and look for the occasional sign to the canyon. If you're not comfortable navigating the lakebed, you can take the second turnoff, which is 4.3 kilometers farther west and also labeled Cañon de Guadalupe. This road has a higher elevation, so it's less vulnerable to rain, but it takes longer (about 45 minutes to go 43 km) and is a less comfortable ride. Both roads merge at the opening of the canyon. The rest of the drive is increasingly winding and rocky and recommended only for high-clearance vehicles.

Eleven kilometers from the main road, a very rocky few hundred meters will bring you to the entrance.

LA RUMOROSA AND VICINITY

Heading west from Mexicali, at around Km. 44, the highway climbs the steep Juárez escarpment to the town of La Rumorosa. Named for the whispering winds that blow by the 1,275-meter pass, the village is populated with the summer homes of Mexicali and Tijuana residents. The old highway was infamous for the number of fatal accidents. After the old road was closed, it was used in the filming of a James Bond movie. La Rumorosa's most famous resident might be El Diablito (Little Devil). He is a small red figure painted in a cave in the nearby El Vallecito. Only on December 21, the winter solstice, a ray of sunlight illuminates the figure. For tours of El Vallecito and

La Rumorosa, contact **Rupestres** (cell tel. 686/158-9921, explorandobajacalifornia@hotmail.com, US$60).

Museo Campo Alaska

With the completion of the paved highway between Tijuana and Mexicali in the 1916, Mexicali became instantly connected to the rest of the state of Baja California. In 1923–1929, then-governor Abelardo L. Rodriguez built a massive stone garrison at Campo Alaska along the highway, to serve as summer offices for the state government in the town of Campo Alaska. Today the former federal quarters hold Museo Campo Alaska (tel. 686/552-8279, www.inah.gob.mx, 10 A.M.–4 P.M. Wed.–Sun.), a small museum that documents the history of the indigenous people of the area.

Laguna Hanson

At Km. 73, west of La Rumorsa, there is a graded dirt road that leads 63 kilometers to Laguna Hanson (elev. 5,000 feet) in the Parque Nacional Constitución de 1857. The second half of the road is for high-clearance vehicles only; four-wheel drive is recommended. The park is more easily approached via Mexico 3, southeast of Ensenada.

San Felipe and Vicinity

San Felipe (pop. 25,000) is a small coastal town on the Sea of Cortez, about two hours' drive south of the U.S.-Mexico border. California and Arizona residents flock here for weekend RV and fishing trips. Punta San Felipe protects the bay from north winds. To get oriented, begin your trip by climbing the stairs to the top of the 240-meter **Cerro El Machorro** located on the point. You'll see a shrine to the Virgin of Guadalupe and panoramic views of the bay.

In the 1940s and '50s, American fishermen came down to catch the abundant *totuava,* a sporting croaker that could reach up to 115 kilograms. The tasty fish proved to be too

popular and it's now on the endangered species list and off limits for any fishing. San Felipe faces a similar clash of supply and demand today. Recent fishing and shrimping practices have endangered a rare breed of small porpoise called the *vaquita.* The Zoological Society of London has designated it as one of the 100 EDGE species (Evolutionarily Distinct, Globally Endangered), which makes it a top priority for conservationists. There is a monument to the *vaquita* at the center of the *malecón* in San Felipe.

The populated area around San Felipe stretches for quite a few kilometers of coastline to the north and south. Besides fishing, there

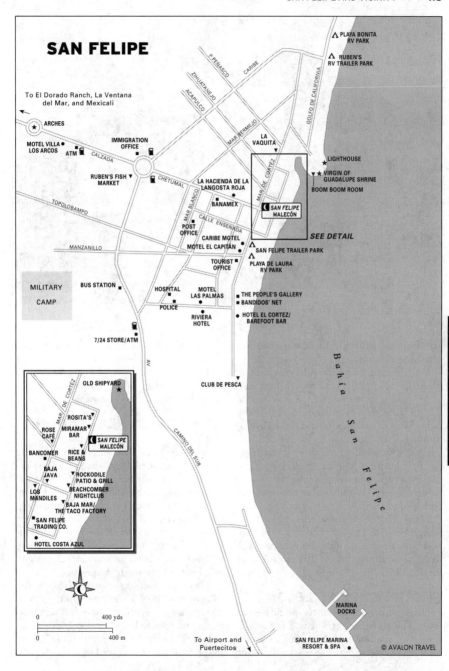

SAN FELIPE

PLAYA BONITA RV PARK

RUBEN'S RV TRAILER PARK

To El Dorado Ranch, La Ventana del Mar, and Mexicali

ARCHES

LIGHTHOUSE

MOTEL VILLA LOS ARCOS

ATM

IMMIGRATION OFFICE

LA VAQUITA

VIRGIN OF GUADALUPE SHRINE

BOOM BOOM ROOM

RUBEN'S FISH MARKET

LA HACIENDA DE LA LANGOSTA ROJA

BANAMEX

SAN FELIPE MALECÓN

CHETUMAL

SEE DETAIL

POST OFFICE

CALLE ENSENADA

CARIBE MOTEL

MOTEL EL CAPITÁN

SAN FELIPE TRAILER PARK

TOURIST OFFICE

PLAYA DE LAURA RV PARK

MILITARY CAMP

BUS STATION

HOSPITAL

MOTEL LAS PALMAS

THE PEOPLE'S GALLERY

BANDIDOS' NET

POLICE

RIVIERA HOTEL

HOTEL EL CORTEZ/ BAREFOOT BAR

7/24 STORE/ATM

CLUB DE PESCA

OLD SHIPYARD

ROSITA'S

ROSE CAFÉ

MIRAMAR BAR

SAN FELIPE MALECÓN

BANCOMER

RICE & BEANS

BAJA JAVA

ROCKODILE PATIO & GRILL

BEACHCOMBER NIGHTCLUB

LOS MANDILES

BAJA MAR/ THE TACO FACTORY

SAN FELIPE TRADING CO.

HOTEL COSTA AZUL

Bahía San Felipe

MARINA DOCKS

0   400 yds
0   400 m

To Airport and Puertecitos

SAN FELIPE MARINA RESORT & SPA

© AVALON TRAVEL

MEXICALI TO SAN FELIPE

lighthouse on Playa San Felipe

are sand dunes for ATVs and dune buggies, which are a common site around town.

Until recently, the town has a splash of nightlife along the *malecón* with several clubs, bars, and the periodic S.W.A.T invasion. S.W.A.T is a tour company that brings in busloads of college students during spring break and throughout the year for all-inclusive party weekends. The partying has pretty much come to a halt as of 2011 with the decline in tourism overall. The city has repainted the parking lines along the *malecón*, perhaps in anticipation of more visitors.

Most visitors choose the months of November–April to visit the area. The temperatures are generally milder than Mexicali in the summer months, but they can still often break 38°C.

🄲 SAN FELIPE *MALECÓN*

Public life in San Felipe centers around the *malecón*. This waterfront promenade is a smaller version of the one in La Paz and similar to Loreto's in size. There are several bars and

nightclubs that offer a scaled-down version of the Rosarito beach scene. Several restaurants and shops also line the strip. **Playa San Felipe** stretches the length of the *malecón* and is popular with sunbathers and *pangueros* for hire.

SPORTS AND RECREATION
Fishing

Even though you'll hear seasoned area anglers pine for the good old days, the San Felipe fishing scene is still the big draw—for visitors and retirees alike. Croakers can be found year-round, but the peak months for cabrilla, yellowtail, sierra, and grouper are May–October. Head north above Punta San Felipe for the best onshore fishing. You can still fish from shore without a license, so all you need are a shore rod, food and water, and some lures.

There are multiday trips available to the Midriff islands 400 kilometers to the south. These trips are usually six-day fishing marathons and involve large 100-foot-plus fishing vessels. The term "mothership fishing" refers to the 6–10 *pangas* that the larger vessels carry a windless day on the northern Sea of Cortez

with them. It takes around 24 hours to reach the fishing grounds from San Felipe. From there, the *pangas* typically head out with three anglers each for a morning and afternoon run. Everyone pitches in to make bait during the night.

Tony Reyes Fishing Tours (Mar Bermejo 130, tel. 686/577-1120, www.tonyreyes.com) and **Baja Sportfishing** (tel. 800/770-2341, bajasportfishinginc.net) operate these long-range trips. Prices for the week run US$1,000–1,350 and include everything but tip, drinks, and tackle.

Boating

You can launch your own boat at the Motel El Cortez, Ruben's Trailer Park, or the San Felipe Marina. **Baja Directions** (www.bajadirections.com) has an updated and detailed atlas for the Baja sportfishing areas, including boat ramps, bathymetry, and gas stations.

Golf

Las Caras de Mexico Golf Course (tel. 686/576-0517, www.lascarasdemexico.com) is an 18-hole, 7,200-yard course that opened in 2005. It's part of the El Dorado Ranch and La Ventana del Mar developments. Greens fee are US$25–50 and carts are complimentary. No need to pack your clubs; you can rent a pro bag of TaylorMades (US$30/18 holes, US$15/9 holes). The turn for La Ventana del Mar is 11 kilometers north of San Felipe at Km. 176.5. A mountain course on the other side of highway is under construction.

ENTERTAINMENT AND EVENTS
Nightlife

The enormous **Boom Boom Room** (Guaymas, northern end of the *malecón,* across the footbridge that leads to the Shrine of Guadalupe, no tel., noon–3 A.M. daily) features a high-tech sound system and stunning views.

For a less caffeinated experience, grab a drink at the relatively quiet **Club Miramar** (Av. Mar de Cortés, tel. 686/577-1192, 10 A.M.–3 A.M. daily), a San Felipe classic at the north end of the *malecón*. To get away from the crowds, head south of the *malecón* to the Hotel El Cortez's **Barefoot Bar** (tel. 686/577-1055) and enjoy the tranquil view of the sea over a cold margarita.

Festivals and Events

February and March are busy months on the San Felipe events calendar. Like Ensenada and La Paz, San Felipe celebrates **Carnaval,** usually in late February or early March. The **Tecate SCORE San Felipe 250** off-road race take place in March. U.S. college students take over the town during the latter part of March for **spring break.** Steer clear unless you want to partake in the madness.

June 1 brings the national **Navy Day** (Día de la Marina Nacional); the celebration includes a street festival with live music and dancing.

SHOPPING

Run by Steve and Linda Sullivan, **The People's Gallery** (Av. Mar de Cortés Sur 381, tel. 686/577-2898, 10 A.M.–5 P.M. daily), sells the works of local artists, including handmade furniture, jewelry, masks, paintings, and other crafts. The owners also publish the informative *San Felipe Newsletter* (sfnewsster@gmail.com).

For new and used books, try the **San Felipe Trading Company** (Av. Mar de Cortés, across from the IMSS clinic and a half block north of the Costa Azul, no tel.), or a new bookstore called **The New Bookstore** (Calzada Chetumal, no tel.), one block west of the Chinese restaurant.

ACCOMMODATIONS

Given its proximity to the U.S. border, San Felipe has historically had pricier accommodations than similar Baja fishing towns. Outside of the peak months (Nov.–Apr.), though, prices may be as much as 30 percent lower. Rates shown here do not include 12 percent hotel tax or 10 percent service charge, unless specified.

US$50-100

Repeat guests continue to report satisfactory stays with the clean, friendly, and safe **Chapala**

(Av. Mar de Cortés 142, tel. 686/577-1240, US$60). It's a no-frills place, but you can't beat the price. A short walk from the beach, **Motel El Capitán** (Av. Mar de Cortés 298, tel./fax 686/577-1303, toll-free U.S. tel. 866/540-7370, www.motelcapitan.com, US$50–60) has 45 clean rooms on two levels surrounding a parking lot and pool. Amenities include air-conditioning and TV.

Two blocks from the beach, **La Hacienda de la Langosta Roja** (Red Lobster, Calz. Chetumal 125, tel. 686/577-0483 or 800/967-0005, www.sanfelipelodging.com, US$50–60) is now managed by the El Dorado Ranch. The 39 rooms in this pink two-story building were recently refurnished, but they still feel a little Motel 6. Amenities include air-conditioning and satellite TV with 15 channels. Ask for a room in the front building.

Next to Bandodos' Net, **Hotel El Cortez** (Av. Mar de Cortés, tel. 686/577-1055 or 686/577-1056, hotelcortez1@prodigy.net.mx, US$85) has 112 basic rooms facing the beach. Take a look at one before you commit. The facilities here are in much better shape than the rooms themselves, which need an overhaul and more thorough day-to-day maintenance. The hotel has a swimming pool, boat launch, laundry facilities, *palapas,* and the Barefoot Bar. Its 112 rustic rooms come with air-conditioning, TVs, and phones.

The **Caribe Motel** (Av. Mar de Cortés at Calle Ensenada, across from the Costa Azul, US$40–80) opened in 2008 with 15 rooms. Those on the front side have decks and cost more. The motel is designed in a courtyard style, with two levels. Guestrooms are upstairs and off-street, plus there is secure parking below (each spot gets its own light). Vinyl curtains and tile floors make for harsh acoustics, but the rooms are large and come with cable TV and air-conditioning. Hot-water issues were still being worked out when we visited.

US$100-150

San Felipe Marina Resort and Spa (Km. 4.5, Carr. San Felipe-Puertecitos, tel. 686/577-1569 or 800/025-6925, toll-free U.S. tel. 800/291-

5397, www.sanfelipemarina.net, US$130–150), has been renovated with new paint and fixtures. It's located farther south off Avenida Camino del Sur and has rooms with kitchenettes decorated in bright colors and simple furnishings, but it's not a resort in the five-star sense. Rooms are well worn, and amenities include only TV with limited channels and phones. Wi-Fi, for an extra charge, works from the lobby only. On the premises are two swimming pools (indoor and outdoor, not heated in winter), tennis courts, a restaurant/bar, and spa that still doesn't seem to offer any treatments. Service is inconsistent—sometimes attentive and others times sorely lacking. The beach is the best part about a stay here.

Overlooking the sea on the road to Puertecitos, **Las Casitas Beach and Tennis Resort** (Km. 1.6, Carr. San Felipe-Puertecitos, tel. 686/577-1195 or 686/187-9422, toll-free U.S. tel. 877/270-2272, www.lascasitas.com.mx, US$110–130) has air-conditioned bungalows and studios with king-size beds and private decks.

New in 2009, **Playa del Paraíso** (Misión de Loreto 130, tel. 686/577 0822, toll-free U.S. tel. 888/647-5292, www.playadelparaiso.com, studio US$90–140, one-bedroom US$195) offers high-end condo-style accommodations in a new real estate development on the beach north of town. The property has an infinity pool and 200 units (some privately owned, others offered as hotel rooms) ranging from US$90 for a studio to US$400 for a three-bedroom condo.

Vacation Rentals

Condominiums Playa Bonita (U.S. tel. 626/967-8977, www.sanfelipebeachcondos.com, US$60–125) has eight one-bedroom units on the beach and an adjoining RV park.

North of town, the gated **El Dorado Ranch** (tel. 686/576-0402, toll-free U.S. tel. 877/787-2624, www.eldoradoranch.com) development often has vacation rentals available in different sizes and at varying price points. Residents and guests may use community's tennis club, restaurant/bar, *palapas,* heated pool, and hot

tub. The new **La Ventana del Mar** (toll-free U.S. tel. 877/787-2624, www.laventanadelmar.com, US$130–230 per night) has several two- and three-bedroom units complete and available for rent.

Camping and RV Parks

Condo developments have taken over some of San Felipe's largest campgrounds in recent years. More than 20 campgrounds remain, but of these, few, if any, are designed with big rigs in mind. Amenities are often lacking, and you'll have to battle the permanent and monthly renters to get a spot. In summer the parks that are located along the beach north of Punta San Felipe tend to stay cooler than those on Bahía San Felipe. A signature feature of the nicer San Felipe campgrounds are the *palapa* structures that provide a shady kitchen area underneath and a lookout deck on top. You can park your small RV under the structure or larger ones beside it. **Playa Bonita RV Park** (tel. 686/577-1215, U.S. tel. 626/967-8977, www.playabonitaresort.com/rv/index.html, US$22–40 for full hookups) and **Ruben's RV Trailer Park** (Av. Golfo de California 703, tel. 686/577-1442, US$20, full hookups only) both offer this type of *palapa* for their guests.

North of town, past the El Dorado resort, **Big RV's Camp** (Km. 174–175, Mexico 5, U.S. tel. 760/427-6469, US$10–15 per night) can accommodate big rigs with full hookups. **Pete's Camp** (Km. 178, Mexico 5, U.S. tel. 951/694-6704, www.petescamp.com) has 79 sites, but no hookups, for US$15. **Playa del Sol** (Km. 182.5, Mexico 5, tel. 686/576-0292, US$10–15) has *palapa*-shaded tents and RV sites that overlook the beach. Limited amenities include the proximity to **El Sol restaurant** (Playa del Sol, Km 182.5, Mexico 5, tel. 686/576-0292, Wed.–Sun., mains US$5–10), which serves Mexican staples for lunch and dinner.

Budget camping options nearby include **Marco's** (Av. Golfo de California 788, off Av. Mar de Caribe, tel. 686/577-1875 or -1842) and **Vista del Mar** (Av. Mar de Cortés 601, tel. 686/577-1252) at US$10–15 per vehicle. The tradeoff is you won't be on the beach.

South of town, long-favored **Campo San Felipe** (Av. Mar de Cortés 301, tel. 686/577-1012, www.camposanfelipe.com, US$15–20) has 34 full-hookup sites, and Internet access, too. **Playa de Laura RV Park** (Av. Mar de Cortés 333, tel. 686/577-1128) offers just the basics, but it's still a popular place. Rates are about US$10 for tents, US$16–30 for RVs, depending on how close you are to the beach. At the far south end of town, **Club de Pesca RV and Trailer Park** (Av. Mar de Cortés, tel. 686/577-1180, fax 686/577-1888, clubdepescasf@yahoo.com, US$15–20) is removed from much of the action in San Felipe but close enough that you can walk to the shops and restaurants. It has 54 spots, many of them reserved for permanent residents. Call ahead.

FOOD
Seafood
Fish tacos, cold *cockteles,* and seafood platters anchor just about every San Felipe menu. **La Vaquita Restaurant & Bar** (Puerta Peñasco and Av. Mar de Cortés North, tel. 686/577-2837, 11 A.M.–10 P.M. Wed.–Mon.) serves breakfast, lunch, and dinner in an open-air setting. Seafood cocktails (US$6) are its specialty, but the menu also features fish plates (US$6–10) and tacos (US$4 per order). Close to the *malecón,* ◖ **La Hacienda de la Langosta Roja** (Chetumal 121, tel. 686/577-0484, www.sanfelipelodging.com, 7 A.M.–11 P.M. daily, dinner mains US$14–28) serves Italian-style seafood (*piccata,* Florentine, scampi, etc.) at reasonable prices. Its sunny patio is a plus on winter afternoons.

At **Chuy's Place** (Av. Mar de Cortés, no tel., dinner daily, mains US$15) owner Jesus Davis does an amazing shrimp entrée with oyster sauce and ginger, as well as lamb chops with mango sauce.

Mexican
On the *malecón,* **Rice and Beans** (tel. 686/577-1770, riceybeans@hotmail.com, 7 A.M.–11 P.M. Mon.–Fri., breakfast mains US$2–6, lunch/dinner mains US$14–16) serves breakfast, lunch, and dinner with tables inside (air-conditioned) and on a street-side terrace. Fresh fish and carne asada anchor a menu of Mexican fare.

Rosita's Restaurant (Av. Mar de Cortés 381, tel. 686/540-6218, www.rositarest.com, 9 A.M.–10 P.M. daily, US$6–13) is a friendly, if touristy, place with decent Mexican food, including shrimp tacos.

Also on the *malecón,* two-story **Licoraria** (no tel.) is first and foremost a place to try fish tacos, but it also serves *machaca, chilaquiles,* and other types of tacos for US$1.50 apiece.

If you're on the hunt for an authentic Mexican meal, head to **La Fonda Los Portales** (Manzanillo, one block west of the tourist office, no tel., mains US$7–12), open daily for breakfast, lunch, and dinner. It's known for its rich chicken mole and other Mexican classics of Aztec origin. Traditional tortilla soup and refreshing *agua de jamaica* round out the menu. The restaurant does not serve alcoholic beverages, but you can bring your own.

International
At the golf course of La Ventana del Mar Resort, **Pavilion** (toll-free U.S. tel. 877/629-2852 or 619/299-5990, 8 A.M.–7 P.M. Mon.–Fri., 8 A.M.–9 P.M. Sat., 10 A.M.–9 P.M. Sun., mains US$10–18) offers a gourmet menu with entrées such as fricassee of veal, walnut-encrusted rack of lamb, and champagne-poached scallops.

Perched high above the town, the **Lighthouse Lounge** (Guaymas 152, tel. 686/577-2540, lighthouselounge1@prodigy.net.mx, 8 A.M.–10 P.M. Tues.–Sun., mains US$10–15) has the most unique view around and cheerful and festive decor. On the menu are omelets, burgers, sandwiches, and salads, plus steaks and Mexican plates for dinner.

South of the Caribe Motel, **The George** (Av. Mar de Cortés, tel. 686/577-1057, 6 A.M.–10 P.M. daily, US$12–22) is a cross between a steakhouse and a diner, with leather booths and bright lighting. The menu includes Mexican fare, as well as steaks.

El Nido Steakhouse (Av. Mar de Cortés 348, tel. 686/577-1028, 2–10 P.M. Thurs.–Tues., mains US$18–25) is a Baja chain known for its Western decor and steaks grilled over a mesquite wood fire. Guests sit in tall leatherback chairs at heavy wood tables, under the dim light of red lamps.

Baja Mar/The Taco Factory (on the *malecón* near Chetumal, tel. 686/577-2648) specializes in shrimp dishes, and the guacamole is a standout. Tacos cost US$1–1.50 each. Entrées run US$8–20, and the seafood combo (US$48) is large enough for two. There is an enclosed dining room, but the larger dining area is outside on a large deck with a bar in the middle.

Try **Baja Burger** (Av. Mar de Cortés 162, no tel., breakfast and lunch daily, mains US$3–9) for a quick bite, such as *chilaquiles* for breakfast or a burger with fries for lunch.

Cafés

Behind the Beachcomber Bar and on the second story of the building, **Baja Java** (Av. Mar de Cortés and Chetumal, no tel., baja_java@highes.net, breakfast and lunch daily) is the place for espresso drinks. Enjoy the sea views from its sunny patio. Downstairs is the **Smoke Signals** (no tel.) cigar shop and lounge.

Groceries

Many of the stores you'll need for groceries and supplies are located along Calzada Chetumal on the way into town. At the entrance to town is **Ruben's Fish Market** (Mar Caribe Sur 158, tel. 686/577-1442). Avenida Mar de Caribe also has several bakeries. Near the north end of the *malecón*, **La Vaquita Dos** (Puerto Peñasco 292, tel. 686/577-1710, until 11 P.M. daily) has meat and produce counters, as well as fresh tortillas made on-site. On the weekends, they'll barbecue your meat, free of charge. You can also pick up a variety of household supplies. Special orders are welcome.

INFORMATION AND SERVICES
Tourist Assistance

The Secretary of Tourism for San Felipe (Manzanillo 300 at Av. Mar de Cortés, tel. 686/577-1155 or -1865, www.sanfelipe.com.

mx, 8 A.M.–7 P.M. Mon.–Fri., 9 A.M.–3 P.M. Sat., 10 A.M.–1 P.M. Sun.) distributes maps, brochures, and other visitor information.

Money

There are a half dozen ATMs around town, including a machine at the 7-Eleven/Pemex station as you enter town, a Bancomer on Avenida Mar de Cortés, and a Banamex on Calzada Chetumal. There is a *casa de cambio* on Calzada Chetumal, across from the Beachcomber.

Post and Telephone

You'll find San Felipe's post office (8 A.M.–1 P.M. and 2–6 P.M. Mon.–Fri.) on Mar Blanco, one block south of Calzada Chetumal. For other mail and business services, try Yet Mail Etc. (Av. Mar de Cortés 75, tel. 686/577-1255).

Internet Access

The Net (Av. Mar de Cortés, Plaza Canela 1, tel. 686/577-1600, www.sanfelipe.com.mx/business/internet.html, 8 A.M.–4 P.M. Mon.–Fri., 9 A.M.–1 P.M. Sat., closed Sat. in summer), next to the El Cortez motel, charges US$4 per hour for high-speed wired or wireless access.

Emergencies

The **Abasolo Medical Clinic** (Calz. Chetumal, near the Pemex, tel. 686/577-1706, 9 A.M.–2 P.M. and 4–8 P.M. Mon.–Fri., emergencies anytime) is run by the former head of the local hospital. He speaks excellent English and has been in the San Felipe area for two decades. He can also arrange for emergency ground or air transportation to San Diego if needed. **Hospital San Felipe** (Mar Negro Sur 1285, tel. 686/577-0117 or -2849) and the **police station** (Mar Negro Sur, tel. 686/577-1134 or dial 060) are located next to each other on the south side of town. The Red Cross is on Puerto Peñasco.

GETTING THERE AND AROUND
By Air

San Felipe has an international airport (SFE, Mar Caribe Sur/Airport Road, tel. 686/577-

1368 or -1568, danielpg60@hotmail.com, winter 7 A.M.–5 P.M. daily in winter, 8 A.M.–6 P.M. daily in summer), but it isn't served by any commercial airlines. The closest major airport is Mexicali. **Grey Eagle Aviation** (U.S. tel. 760/804-8680 or toll-free 888/280-8802, www.greyeagleaviation.com/sanfelipeinfo.htm) advertises an air taxi service from Long Beach or San Diego, California, to San Felipe on Tuesday, Friday, and Sunday. Services for private pilots include aviation gas and customs clearing. The trip to town is 9.2 kilometers and costs US$15 by taxi.

By Bus

San Felipe has a bus depot (tel. 686/577-1516) on Avenida Mar Caribe Sur, south of Calzada Chetumal and near the Pemex. It's open daily 5 A.M.–11 P.M. (when the last bus from Mexicali arrives). **Autotransportes de Baja California** (ABC, www.abc.com.mx) offers connections to Mexicali, Ensenada, and Tijuana. You can buy your ticket an hour before the bus departs. To reach the Tijuana office, call 664/683-5681. **Estrellas del Pacífico** (Tijuana tel. 664/683-5022 or -6789) also runs buses to San Felipe from Mexicali and Ensenada.

By Taxi

Taxis congregate on Calzada Chetumal near Los Mandiles, or you can call 686/577-1293 to order one. Local trips around town should cost under US$5.

SAN FELIPE TO PUERTECITOS

South of San Felipe, the coastal road deteriorates, though it is paved as far as Puertecitos (85 km south of San Felipe). Construction had commenced in early 2009 to pave the road beyond Puertecitos; however, only the first few kilometers were under way at press time, and in the meantime, the old dirt road was in terrible shape. There is no gas until Punta Willard/Alfonsina, so fill up your tank before leaving town, and bring some fuel to spare. Watch for *vados* (drainage dips) and potholes along the way. Accommodations are primitive camps, and supplies are few and far between.

Estero Percebú

About 16 kilometers south of San Felipe, a dirt road turn-off leads one kilometer east to a lagoon and white-sand beach with a small community of gringo homes. You can swim or kayak here, as long as you bring your own gear. The area is also known as Shell Island, which refers to a spit of land that's only accessible at low tide. Beachcombers will delight in the possibilities for collecting shells.

Rancho Percebú (Km. 16, Carr. San Felipe-Puertecitos, tel. 686/577-1259, open year-round, US$10) has campsites, *palapas,* restrooms, and hot showers. There is also a restaurant/bar at the camp. The friendly Lopez family has run the ranch for several decades and counting. The campground is four kilometers east of the highway.

◖ Valle de los Gigantes

Fifteen kilometers south of San Felipe, on the way to Puertecitos, photographers and naturalists will enjoy the chance to view the world's tallest cactus species up close. The *Pachycereus,* or *cardón,* grows to heights of more than 18 meters and can weigh up to 12 tons. Many live to be hundreds of years old.

Besides the namesake giants, the park holds ocotillo, paloverde, cholla, and many other cacti. Desert fauna includes mountain quail, eagles, owls, coyotes, roadrunners, and buzzards. Daytime temperatures will climb above 100°F in summer and to about 50°F in winter. Bring your own water for hiking the trails.

Look for a turnoff near Km. 14 on the west side of the highway and follow the unpaved road about 200 meters to the park entrance. The closest place to camp is Playa Punta Estrella (Km 13., Carr. San Felipe-Puertecitos, tel. 686/565-2784, US$10), with *palapas,* flush toilets, and hot showers but no hookups. Soft sand could pose a problem for RVs here. The campground is 1.6 kilometers east of the highway.

For guided hikes in the Valle de los Gigantes, contact **Rupestres** (cell tel. 686/158-9921, explorandobajacalifornia@hotmail.com).

Camping

Continuing south, the coastline presents a series of beaches, most with primitive *campos* that charge US$5–10 a night, depending on the season and the facilities they offer. **Playa Destiny** (Km. 71–72, Carr. San Felipe-Puertecitos, no tel., US$15) has toilets, cold showers, grills, and picnic tables. **Playa Escondida** (Km. 85–86, Carr. San Felipe-Puertecitos, no tel., US$10) occupies a white-sand cove. Outhouses and cold showers are about it for amenities, but there are fishing *pangas* for hire.

PUERTECITOS

Civilization, such as it is, appears again at Puertecitos, but don't get too excited. This fishing village has weather-worn homes and trailers, *panga* fishing boats, and natural hot springs (US$5) to offer weary travelers. The beach is small, and the only businesses are a restaurant (6 A.M.–10 P.M. daily Oct.–Apr.) and a grocery store *(tienda de abarrotes)*.

Accommodations

The beach camp, **Campo Puertecitos** (Km. 89, Carr. San Felipe-Puertecitos, tel. 686/577-1155 or -1865) has 14 sites for primitive camping (US$20) and four barebones rooms for rent. The property has *palapas* for shade and grills for cooking your fresh catch.

PUNTA BUFEO TO PUNTA FINAL

You need high clearance, sturdy tires, good shocks, and a lot of driving patience to continue south of Puertecitos. Plan on 5–6 hours of driving to make the 72.5-kilometer trip to Alfonsina's on Bahía Willard.

Punta Bufeo

Fishing fanatics enjoy the onshore catch off Punta Bufeo and around the **Islas Encantadas** just offshore. This group of islands provides the ideal habitat for yellowtail, croaker, corvina, and sierra.

The next settlement to the south,

Alfonsina's (Tijuana tel. 664/648-1951) has supplies, including gas (but not diesel). **Rancho Grande** (no tel.) also may have gas if Alfonsina's is out.

ACCOMMODATIONS AND FOOD

Campo Punta Bufeo (56 km south of Puertecitos along the dirt road that parallels the coast) has campsites (US$5–10) on the beach, as well as a restaurant, toilets, showers, and simple motel rooms (US$20).

Punta Willard, the next point south, about 12 kilometers south of Punta Bufeo, has a legendary settlement called **Papa Fernández** (www.papafernandez.com). This campground on the beach has *palapa* shelters (US$5), outhouses (but no showers), a boat ramp, and *panga* fishing. The best part about Papa Fernández is its restaurant (no tel., dawn–dusk, and often later, daily, mains US$6–14), which serves homemade tortillas and chile rellenos and will cook your catch.

Papa Fernández does not have its own telephone; however, in an emergency, you can dial the mini-mart at Rancho Grande on a satellite phone (tel. 555/151-4065). Leave a call-back number, as well as your name and the name of the person you are trying to contact. It's also a good idea to describe the vehicle that your contact is driving in Baja. On the message, ask Rancho Grande to contact Papa Fernández on the marine radio.

☾ Bahía San Luis Gonzaga

Popular with private pilots and experienced Baja adventurers, the flat, gray-sand beach along remote Bahía San Luis Gonzaga is reminiscent of an earlier time. A few dozen rustic beach homes line the shore—each with its private plane, boat, or dune buggy parked outside. **Rancho Grande** (tel. 555/151-4065) offers beach camping for US$5 a night. Facilities include outhouses, showers, and a minimarket.

Punta Final is a small cape with several points and a small lagoon. It marks the south end of Gonzaga Bay and offers good views of the bay from above.

CEVICHE, GONZAGA-BAY STYLE

Ann Hazard's Baja cookbooks have become a peninsular favorite, with recipes collected from many famous restaurants and devised from the author's own travels and culinary adventures. Whether you want to prepare a few of your own meals on the road or bring the flavors of Baja back to your own home, this basic ceviche recipe is a keeper. The acid from the lime juice "cooks" the fish, so there's no need for a heat source to prepare the meal.

INGREDIENTS

- 2 lbs. cubed white fish or bay scallops, raw
- 2 cups juice from *limónes* (Mexican limes)
- 5-10 fresh Serrano or jalapeño chiles, diced (remove seeds if you prefer it less spicy)
- 1 red bell pepper, diced
- 1 green bell pepper, diced
- 1 onion, diced
- 3 ripe tomatoes, diced
- 2 cloves garlic, minced
- 1 bunch cilantro, with stems removed, finely chopped
- 1 tsp. brown sugar
- Salt and pepper to taste
- 2 avocados, diced
- Tortilla chips or saltine crackers

INSTRUCTIONS

In a bowl, cover the cubed fish with lime juice. Cover and refrigerate for 2-3 hours, stirring occasionally. Fish should become quite white and scallops will lose their translucent appearance. (Once this happens, you will know the lime juice has "cooked" them and they are okay to eat.)

Transfer to a larger bowl and mix with all other ingredients except avocado. Immediately prior to serving, add diced avocados and remaining cilantro. Serve in a bowl surrounded with chips or saltine crackers.

– Reprinted with permission from *Cooking with Baja Magic Dos*, by Ann Hazard (www.bajamagic.com)

TO MEXICO 1

From Bahía San Luis Gonzaga, it's 64.5 kilometers (approximately 90 min.) of graded dirt-road driving to the Transpeninsular Highway. The road intersects Mexico 1 at Km. 229–230 in the town of Chapala.

About halfway from the coast to the highway, you'll come across **Coco's Corner,** a café that's famous for its beer-can decor (and desert plants, too). Stop here for cold beer, soda, and burritos. Camping costs US$5 a night if you've run out of daylight. Owner Coco moved to the desert from Ensenada in 1990, following an accident in which he lost one leg. He speaks some English and knows the area extremely well. When you sign his guestbook, he will draw a picture of your vehicle next to the entry.

DESIERTO CENTRAL TO BAHÍA DE LOS ANGELES

In an age of satellite TV, mobile phones, and wireless Internet, one part of Baja California continues to offer true desert solitude. This is the central peninsula, which lies between El Rosario in the north and La Paz in the south. With an average population density of just one inhabitant per 10,000 square kilometers, cirio cacti outnumber people here by a very wide margin. New government-sponsored ecotourism projects promise to protect this diverse and fragile ecosystem. Informative signs now lead travelers along historic trails, while training and education programs are helping local residents become knowledgeable guides and preserve their homes and natural resources rather than exploit them.

Compared to the northern and southern tips of the peninsula, Central Baja has experienced relatively little external influence to date. However, that most certainly will change as commercial development and technological progress continue their forward march. Already, power lines have been installed throughout the entire area, putting once isolated towns on the grid. Phones and even Internet access are now widely available, and newly paved roads connect many outlying areas to the Transpeninsular Highway. For the adventure traveler who wants to experience a taste of the frontier, now is the time to visit.

In the vicinity of the Valle de los Cirios, the Velicatá Mission is the only church built by Franciscan missionaries in Baja. On the Gulf coast, Bahía de los Angeles offers a protected channel for water activities such

© NIKKI GOTH ITOI

HIGHLIGHTS

🌙 **Misión San Fernando Velicatá:** Baja's only Franciscan mission settlement was active from 1769 to 1818, and remnants of the original buildings can be found in a scenic arroyo located midway between the Pacific and Gulf coasts (page 128).

🌙 **Valle de los Cirios:** In an unprecedented effort to save a fragile desert ecosystem, Mexico has designated this large area between Cataviña and Guerrero Negro for ecotourism development (page 128).

🌙 **Canal de las Ballenas:** If you've come to Baja for a chance to swim with a whale shark, this waterway offshore from Bahía de los Angeles has them, along with a wide variety of the largest creatures in the sea (page 131).

🌙 **Sea Turtle Research Station:** In Bahía de los Angeles, a marine biologist has transformed a former turtle fishing operation into an engine of conservation (page 131).

🌙 **San Borja:** Head to the village of San Borja for an off-road adventure along the Spanish mission trail (page 136).

LOOK FOR 🌙 TO FIND RECOMMENDED SIGHTS, ACTIVITIES, DINING, AND LODGING.

as snorkeling/scuba diving, sportfishing, windsurfing/kiteboarding, and kayaking—and a chance to view the majestic whale shark during its summer migration. High in the Sierra San Borja are a Spanish mission settlement and a series of prehistoric cave paintings.

PLANNING YOUR TIME

It takes about 15 hours to drive the 1,124 kilometers from El Rosario to La Paz. The stretch from El Rosario to Parador Punta Prieta is 240 kilometers, and this marks the turnoff to Bahía de los Angeles. From there, it's another 68 kilometers (about an hour of driving time) to the coast.

It's a good idea to stock up on supplies in El Rosario before making the trek across the desert, but after Km. 115, a number of ranchos along the highway operate small restaurants, where you can sample a plate of basic Mexican fare.

Mission Velicatá is an easy excursion off Mexico 1. Allow a couple of days to explore the Valle de los Cirios and three or four days for Bahía de los Angeles—longer if you are going there to dive, fish, or windsurf/kiteboard. Add another day for a side trip to San Borja.

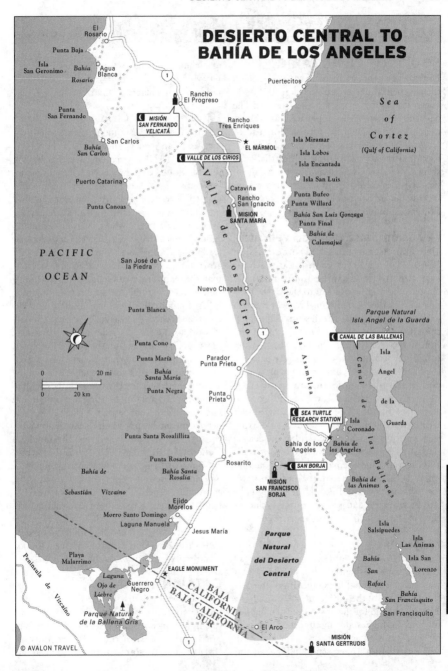

DESIERTO CENTRAL TO BAHÍA DE LOS ANGELES

El Rosario
Punta Baja
Isla San Geronimo
Bahía Rosario
Agua Blanca
Puertecitos
Rancho El Progreso
MISIÓN SAN FERNANDO VELICATÁ
Rancho Tres Enriques
Punta San Fernando
Bahía San Carlos
San Carlos
EL MÁRMOL
VALLE DE LOS CIRIOS
Isla Miramar
Isla Lobos
Isla Encantada
Isla San Luis
Puerto Catarina
Cataviña
Rancho San Ignacito
MISIÓN SANTA MARÍA
Punta Bufeo
Punta Willard
Bahía San Luis Gonzaga
Punta Final
Bahía de Calamajué
Punta Canoas

Sea of Cortez
(Gulf of California)

PACIFIC OCEAN

San José de la Piedra
Nuevo Chapala
Punta Blanca
Punta Cono
Punta María
Bahía Santa María
Punta Negra
Parador Punta Prieta
Punta Prieta

Parque Natural Isla Angel de la Guarda

Valle de los Cirios
Sierra de la Asamblea

CANAL DE LAS BALLENAS
Isla Angel de la Guarda
Canal de las Ballenas

0   20 mi
0   20 km

Punta Santa Rosalillita
Punta Rosarito
Bahía de Sebastián Vizcaíno
Bahía Santa Rosalia
Rosarito
SEA TURTLE RESEARCH STATION
Isla Coronado
Bahía de los Angeles
Bahía de los Angeles
SAN BORJA
MISIÓN SAN FRANCISCO BORJA
Bahía de las Animas

Ejido Morelos
Morro Santo Domingo
Laguna Manuela
Jesus María
Parque Natural del Desierto Central
Isla Salsipuedes
Isla Las Animas
Bahía San Rafael
Isla San Lorenzo

Playa Malarrimo
Península de Vizcaíno
Laguna Ojo de Liebre
Guerrero Negro
EAGLE MONUMENT
BAJA CALIFORNIA
BAJA CALIFORNIA SUR
Bahía San Franciscito
San Franciscito

Parque Natural de la Ballena Gris
El Arco
MISIÓN SANTA GERTRUDIS

© AVALON TRAVEL

DESIERTO CENTRAL

Into the Interior

SOUTH OF EL ROSARIO

For travelers who are making their way down the Baja peninsula, the terrain below El Rosario marks the beginning of the real adventure. The next sizable town lies a couple of hundred kilometers away; meanwhile, pristine desert scenery unfolds with every turn. Around Km. 62, cirio and *cardón* cacti begin to dot the landscape. This drive is particularly spectacular if you arrive toward the end of the rainy season in October or November, when all the desert flowers are in bloom.

◖ Misión San Fernando Velicatá

The Franciscans built only one mission (1769–1818) in lower California; the little that remains of it can be found relatively close to the highway (8 km to the west), off a dirt road that begins at Km. 121 near Rancho Progresso. Although the Jesuits discovered the site in 1766, it was Franciscan Father Junípero Serra who established the mission in 1769. A strategic location halfway between the Pacific and Gulf coasts ensured an important, if short-lived, role. In time, some 1,500 indigenous people came to live and worship at San Fernando. The mission came under Dominican control in 1772 but would experience a rapid decline by the end of the decade due to an epidemic. Only some bits of walls and the foundation remain; the real attraction today is the arroyo setting. You'll find two *ranchitos* near the site. Look for petroglyphs and pictographs dating back to the 17th century in the rock cliffs above the arroyo.

El Mármol

At Km. 149, a 15-kilometer graded dirt road heads east to an abandoned onyx quarry that was run by a San Diego mining company from the turn of the 20th century through the 1950s. Demand for the brown-and-tan banded mineral was highest during the art deco period, when it was used as a substitute for marble in American homes. Today you'll find the remains of a schoolhouse made entirely of onyx, a cemetery with onyx-covered gravestones, and a scattering of onyx blocks around the site.

◖ Valle de los Cirios

Mexico's largest sustainable development effort, led by an agency called the Areas Naturales Protegidas (ANP) covers an area that begins just north of Cataviña and reaches almost to Guerrero Negro. According to desert plant specialist Robert R. Humphrey, the area contains one of the most interesting and varied types of desert flora in the world. This government-funded project has resulted in chain of ecologically sound cabanas throughout the area; all are rustic, solar-powered, constructed from local materials, and built to blend as much as possible with the natural surroundings. Each locale is based on proximity to longstanding ranches, and the ranchers themselves have been trained to work as hosts and guides to the surrounding area. The idea behind the project is to preserve the fragile ecosystem by empowering its few inhabitants to live off of the natural beauty around them, while providing tourists with a low-impact way of experiencing this unique environment. The average price is US$120 for two people; reasonably priced meals can be arranged through the families operating the ranches. Concepción Recoder (tel. 615/157-2849, cell tel. 646/161-8149, crecoder@conanp.gob.mx) will put interested visitors in touch with the appropriate ranch. The Valle de los Cirios office is attached to the Comisión Nacional de Areas Naturales Protegidas (CONANP) office in Guerrero Negro (Profesor Domingo Carballo Félix s/n at Ruiz Cortinez, Col. Marcelo Rubio, Guerrero Negro, www.conanp.gob.mx).

CATAVIÑA

After a morning of driving the 123 hot and dry kilometers between El Rosario and Cataviña, this desert outpost emerges as a pleasant surprise in the midst of the protected **Parque Natural del Desierto Central**. The town itself offers a few places to stay and limited options for food and supplies. All around are giant boulders and a most impressive collection of picture-perfect desert plants. This is the place to open your field guide and learn to identify *cardón* cacti, elephant trees, cirios, and the rest of the flora that makes the region one of a kind.

Cave Paintings
For travelers making their way down the Transpenisular Highway, the first convenient opportunity to view a cave painting (the origins of which are unknown) comes at Km. 176, where a large arroyo crosses the road. Park near the INAH sign on the east side of the road. Before beginning your hike, look up at the bluffs in front of you for a white wooden sign that marks the cave. Keep the sign as your directional guide and you will find a trail up the rocks once you get to the bottom of the bluffs, or you can scamper up several different ways. Once you reach the sign, you must go into the overhang behind it to see the paintings. Unfortunately, graffiti on the rocks leading up to the cave detracts somewhat from the experience.

Misión Santa María de los Angeles
Whether you're following the Baja California mission trail or simply want to enjoy the spectacular desert scenery, be forewarned that the 23 kilometers track that leads to the adobe ruins of the Misión Santa María de los Angeles (1767–1769) is about as rough as they come in Baja. A dirt bike or ATV may be the only motorized vehicles able to pass, and even then you'll likely have to walk the last mile or so. A better plan would be to hire a guide and mules from Rancho Santo Inés. Though there is little to see today, the mission is significant because it was the last one the Jesuits established before their expulsion from the peninsula in 1767. The Cochimí called the site Cabujakaamung.

Accommodations
Cabañas Linda (Cataviña village, east side of the highway, no tel.), a pink, single-story motel

on the east side of Mexico 1, offers basic rooms for US$35. The proprietor, Lucy, also serves lunch or dinner daily for US$5 and coffee for US$1. A kilometer south of Cataviña, Lucy's mother, Matilde, offers meals, hot showers, and hostel-style rooms at **Rancho Santa Inés** (Km. 181, no tel.). A room for 6–8 people runs US$35. Campers and self-contained RVers can choose a spot under any of the widely spaced mesquite trees in the dirt lot for US$6 a night. The area around the camping lot makes for incredible hiking. And the family at Rancho Santa Inés will guide hikers in the area for US$10 per group.

Until recently, this **Desert Inn** (tel. 200/124-9123, toll-free U.S. tel. 800/800-9632, www.desertinns.com, US$80) property was part of a Baja chain, but it was sold in 2011. Future plans for the property are unknown at this time.

Cirio cacti dot the grounds of the **Parque Natural Desierto Central de BC RV Park,** which has 66 spaces for US$6. Look for the sign on the west side of Mexico 1 before the Desert Inn.

Food
🄲 **Café La Enramada** (no tel., daily, mains US$5–9), in front of the old highway Pemex station across from the Desert Inn, is a reliable place to fill up on large portions of inexpensive Mexican food, including its own specialties, such as Chicken a La Enramada and Chicken al Mármol. The Desert Inn has a full-service restaurant open daily for breakfast, lunch, and dinner. Rancho Santa Inés now offers *antojitos* (traditional Mexican snacks) at the ranch instead of at a former location on Highway 1.

At any given time, there may be another taco and/or burger stand open in Cataviña. The same applies for a couple of small markets with basic groceries. It's better to come prepared to camp, if that is your plan, rather than expecting to find essential supplies in town.

Information and Services
Across from the Desert Inn, the old Pemex

DESIERTO CENTRAL

station appears to be under renovation. In the meantime, there is usually someone selling gas from a barrel here or across the street. If you've filled your tank in El Rosario before the long drive across the desert, you shouldn't need fuel in Cataviña, but it never hurts to top off whenever you have the opportunity, since it's a long way between Pemex stations in this part of the peninsula. The next closest stations are at Villa Jesús María, about 60 kilometers to the south, and Bahía de los Angeles, 170 kilometers to the southeast. Several towns—including Punta Prieta, El Nuevo Rosarito, and Chapala—do sell gas from drums along Highway 1.

SOUTH TO PARADOR PUNTA PRIETA

About 30 kilometers south of Cataviña, off the west side of the highway between Km. 209 and 210, the boulders that make up the hill of **El Pedregoso** stretch 610 meters into the sky. Though they appear to be a massive man-made art installation, the rocks are actually a natural formation that has resulted from thousands of years of erosion.

Between Km. 229 and 230, at Chapala Junction, you can take a graded road northeast to Bahía San Luis Gonzaga and Bahía de Calamajué on the Gulf coast. Keep an eye out for cirio, *cardón,* yucca, and cholla along the way.

At Km. 280, **Parador Punta Prieta,** an abandoned rest stop, marks the turnoff to Bahía de los Angeles. Follow the east fork southeast 68 kilometers to reach the Sea of Cortez. At this junction, the basic **Lonchería Ramirez** (no tel.) serves coffee and *antojitos.* Gas is sometimes available from a drum.

Bahía de los Angeles

Shortly after veering southeast from Highway 1, the road to Bahía de los Angeles (called the east branch of Highway 1) crosses through the Sierra de la Asamblea. The drive is especially scenic in summer, when abundant *copalquín* (elephant trees) are in bloom. At Km. 44, travelers with high-clearance vehicles can take the turnoff southwest 35 kilometers to the restored Misión San Borja. Alternatively, a better road connects San Borja to Rosarito from the west branch of Highway 1. As you descend out of the mountains to the bay and village below, the Sea of Cortez presents itself, a carpet of blue dotted with islands big and small.

Spanish explorer Francisco de Ulloa discovered the bay in 1539 during the last expedition financed by Hernán Cortés. It later became an important access point for exporting gold and silver from mines in the Sierra San Borja.

Today watersports are the main draw at this still-remote seaside village. Adventurous anglers discovered the spot in the 1940s when thatched-roof huts were the only structures to be found. Today kayaking, kiteboarding, and windsurfing bring tourists. A new sailboat monument on the main boulevard through town harbors the arrival of visiting yachters, though they have yet to appear in any great number.

In November 2007 power lines made their way to the bay, ending decades of reliance on a generator that shut down at night. As of spring 2009, most of the town had been connected to the new power lines, but some businesses were still awaiting the fulfillment of their promised connections, as were those along the bay just out of town.

You can pick up postcards or books on Baja at the **Museo de Naturaleza y Cultura** (on a dirt road south of the main commercial strip and west of the town plaza, no tel., 9 A.M.– noon and 2–4 P.M. daily) while you soak up some local history and culture. Inside are mining exhibits, a collection of shells and fossils, and Native American artifacts.

Like La Paz and Loreto, Bahía de los Angeles is an access point to a string of 16 protected desert islands. Sixty-eight-kilometer-long **Isla**

To **☾SEA TURTLE RESEARCH
STATION,** Airstrip, Campo
Archelón, Los Vientos Spa
and Resort, and Daggett's

To Mexico 1

BAHÍA DE
LOS ANGELES

Bahía de los Angeles

LA PALAPA
RESTAURANT

TELNOR

RESTAURANT LAS HAMACAS
MOTEL LAS HAMACAS

MARKET/
RESTAURANT ISLA/
HOTEL ISLA (UC)

MARKET

LA PLAYA RV PARK/
VILLA VITTA RV PARK

COSTA DEL SOL

VILLA VITTA

GCC FIELD
STUDIES CENTER

GUILLERMO'S
RV PARK AND
RESTAURANT

Plaza

MUSEUM

To **☾CANAL DE
LAS BALLENAS**

SUPER XITLALI

CASA DÍAZ
RV PARK

0   200 yds
0   200 m

To
Camp Gecko,
Mines, and Bahía
San Francisco

© AVALON TRAVEL

Angel de la Guarda is the second-largest island in the Sea of Cortez (after Isla Tiburón), with cirios, sea lions, and beaches suitable for camping. Stop by the office of the **Islas del Golfo de California** (9 A.M.–2 P.M. and 4–6 P.M. Mon.–Fri., 9 A.M.–2 P.M. Sat., permits US$4 pp per day), located in town between the Hotel Villa Vitta and the Delegacion building, to obtain a permit.

☾ CANAL DE LAS BALLENAS

The canal that runs parallel to shore in the shelter of Isla Angel de la Guarda teems with marine life, especially of the larger variety: Bryde's, minke, blue, sperm, humpback, and pilot whales, finbacks, orcas, and the occasional gray whale as well as common and bottlenose dolphins, all pass through at various times throughout the year. The best season for spotting these pelagics is July–October, when the water is warmest (26–32°C). Visit in August for the best chance to swim with a juvenile whale shark.

California sea lions live along island shores, and northern elephant seals are sometimes seen in the spring.

☾ SEA TURTLE
RESEARCH STATION

Until populations dwindled in the 1960s and 1970s, Bahía de los Angeles was a busy center for turtle fishing; today it has evolved into a more sustainable center for turtle conservation because of its strategic role as a nesting ground. At the north end of the bay, marine biologist Antonio Resendiz has run a sea turtle research station since 1979, called the Centro Regional de Investigacion Pesquera (CRIP) Sea Turtle Research Station (no tel., 9 A.M.–2 P.M. Mon.–Tues. and Thurs.–Fri., 9 A.M.–1 P.M. Sat., US$2). Visitors are welcome to stop by to see the loggerheads and greens that are contained in their tank for tagging and observation or to hear an occasional lecture on turtle behavior and conservation efforts.

Antonio's work received worldwide recognition in 1995 when a 97-kilogram loggerhead named Rosita, who had been released from the Pacific coast of Baja in 1994, was picked up by a fisherman in Japan. Antonio also owns the adjacent Campo Archelón.

SPORTS AND RECREATION
Hiking

From the bay, a number of arroyos lead inland to the Sierra San Borja; following one of these out and back makes for a pleasant day hike in the desert. Just be sure to keep the bay in sight so you don't get lost. Two abandoned mines are also within walking distance from the town. A trail to **Mina Santa Marta** begins

BAHÍA DE LOS ANGELES AND VICINITY

Isla Coronado

Canal de las Ballenas

Punta la Gringa

LOS VIENTOS SPA AND RESORT

Ensenada la Gringa

Isla El Piojo

☾ CANAL DE LAS BALLENAS

Isla Pata

Isla La Ventana

VILLA BAHÍA

AIRSTRIP ✕

△ DAGGETT'S

△ CAMPO ARCHELÓN

☾ SEA TURTLE RESEARCH STATION ★ PROGRAMA TORTUGA MARINA

△ BRISA MARINA

Isla Cabeza de Caballo

Puerto don Juan

0   1.5 mi

0   1.5 km

POSADA CERRITO ●

Bahía de los Angeles ○

Punta Arena

Punta La Herradura

SUPER XITLATI

CAMP GECKO △

Bahía de los Angeles

Ensenada El Quemado

Isla El Pescador

Ensenada El Pescador

To Mina Santa Marta

Ensenada El Alacrán

✕ AIRSTRIP

To Mina San Juan and Bahía San Francisco ▼

© AVALON TRAVEL

at the town dump, about 3.5 kilometers south of Casa Díaz. From here, walk west until you reach the remains of a railway grade that was used to transport the gold and silver from the mines. Then continue west to the sight of the mine. One day is enough time for the round-trip hike, but you can also camp overnight at the mine.

To reach **Mina San Juan,** follow the same railway grade 17.5 kilometers southwest of the bay to Valle Las Flores. If you continue past the second mine, you can get to several cave painting sites in the Sierra San Borja. The graded road meanders through the mountains all the way to **Bahía San Francisquito,** approximately 132 kilometers south of Bahía de los Angeles.

Fishing

Onshore anglers catch sand bass, guitarfish, and triggerfish here; in spring, there are croaker and halibut at Punta la Gringa. In summer, nearby islands offer opportunities for yellowtail, white and black sea bass, dorado, tuna, and grouper. Yellowtail also sometimes run January–March.

You can rent a *panga* for a fishing or scuba diving trip through any hotel or campground in town. **Daggett's** (about 2.5 km north of town, along the coastal road, tel. 200/124-9101, www.campdaggetts.com), **Guillermo's** (tel. 200/124-9104, www.guillermos.net), **Villa Bahía** (no tel., www.villabahia.com), **Ricardo's Dive Center** (tel. 200/124-9262), and **Casa Díaz** (tel. 200/124-9112) arrange guided fishing trips for US$250–300 a day.

Boating and Kayaking

A number of businesses, including **Guillermo's** (tel. 200/124-9104), **Villa Vitta** (tel. 200/124-9103, U.S. tel. 619/454-6108, www.villavitta.com), and **Casa Díaz** (tel. 200/124-9112), provide boat launches (US$5–10) and rent *pangas*. **Isla Angel de la Guarda** protects the channel from most high winds, except when the winter *El Norte* blows. Ask the locals for advice on the conditions before heading out to sea on your own.

When the winds subside May–October, kayakers arrive en masse to explore the islands offshore. Popular itineraries include a paddle to **Isla Coronado** (also known as Isla Smith), three kilometers northeast of Punta la Gringa, or to the southern tip of Isla Angel de la Guarda, 19 kilometers away.

Kiteboarding and Windsurfing

Bahía de los Angeles is a good choice for beginning windsurfers and kiteboarders because the islands offshore protect it from large swells. Head to the northern parts of the bay for the strongest winds. A 10- to 12-kilometer downwind run begins at Punta la Gringa, passes the small islands west of Isla La Ventana, and goes right in to the shore at the town's edge. Bring your own gear.

Diving

Ricardo's Diving Tours (tel. 200/124-9262) is run by ex-commercial diver Ricardo Arce. The center is located off the right side of the main road as you head into town. It is equipped to take groups or individuals out to the various dive sites within the bay and onto the islands as well. Prices start at US$65 for a two-tank dive to the closer destinations and go up according to distance; the longest trips take divers out to Isla Angel de la Guarda. Ricardo's also offers wildlife and fishing tours, as well as guided snorkeling (often with whale sharks in peak season) and overnight expeditions.

Another option for a dive boat charter is to contact Jean and Roger at **Villa Bahía** (no tel., www.villabahia.com), who will rent out their cabin cruiser to a group of five or six divers for US$225 or their *panga* (which accommodates three people) for US$150; they do not have gear or tanks, but they do have a compressor.

Bird-Watching

The ecosystem around Bahía de los Angeles supports a thriving population of marine birds, among them terns, pelicans, gulls, egrets, herons, cormorants, petrels, boobies, and ospreys. Bird-watchers will find the best opportunities for observation at **Isla Partida** and **Isla Raza.** **Casa Díaz** (tel. 200/124-9112) and **Ricardo's Dive Tours** (tel. 200/124-9262) offer bird-watching tours on request.

ACCOMMODATIONS

Some longtime Baja travelers remember the days of generators and the electricity turning off at night, but mainstream power has arrived at last. Most of the town's hotels now offer 24-hour power, and around-the-clock Internet access is likely not far behind.

Under US$50

At the south end of town, near one of the town's two Pemex stations, family-run **Casa Díaz** (tel. 200/124-9112, US$30) offers large rooms fronting the bay. You can book fishing and bird-watching trips out to the islands and stock up on supplies at the on-site market.

Centrally located with 30 rooms, **Villa Vitta** (tel. 200/124-9103, U.S. tel. 619/454-6108, www.villavitta.com, $45–75) is a single-story motel with a pool, restaurant/bar, boat ramp, and parking. Hot water does not run on electricity here, so it is always available. Fishing packages are available. An adjoining RV park and campground (US$10/night) has 25 spaces

DESIERTO CENTRAL

with electrical hookups and 11 without, a dump station, and bathrooms/showers.

Mauro's Posada (www.bahiadelosangeles.info/mauros-posada.htm, US$20) introduces the first ecologically sound accommodations in Bahía de los Angeles. Owned and run by an Italian-U.S. couple, Mauro and Patty, the posada offers a low-impact stopover (composting toilet and all-natural construction and decoration) for nature-minded travelers. Beds are arranged dormitory style with six bunks in two rooms. The hostel offers a huge communal kitchen, Internet service, an Italian-style café and restaurant, plenty of local knowledge, and, above all, the most spectacular view of the bay anywhere in town. The hostel is located on a hill on the road into town from Highway 1, about a minute before the Pemex and along a hand-cut and graded road.

US$50-100

North of Villa Vitta, **Costa del Sol** (tel. 200/124-19110, cell tel. 646/178-8167, costadelsolhotel@hotmail.com, US$65, credit cards accepted), has a half dozen large, clean rooms. Amenities include hot showers, air-conditioning, and 24-hour electricity. You can dine in the hotel's small restaurant/bar for breakfast, lunch, or dinner. Or rent a kayak for a paddle around the bay.

The rooms at **Guillermo's RV Park and Restaurant** (tel. 200/124-9104, www.guillermos.net, US$45–65) each have two king-size beds and one double bed, as well as air-conditioning 24/7. Its restaurant serves seafood entrées for US$12–24 and fish tacos for US$6. You can camp on the beach here for about US$5 per person; RV hookups run US$17.

On the way to La Gringa, 🔊 **Villa Bahía** (no tel., www.villabahia.com, $60–95), is an interesting complex consisting of different-sized buildings on the waterfront. Each unit holds at least six people, comes with a full kitchen, and includes the use of an outdoor communal kitchen with grills. A three-bedroom, two-bath upstairs unit is great for a group stay, and features an especially intricate metal sculpture of a coral reef wall, complete

with fish, by an Ensenada artist whose works can be found all over the property. Satellite Internet is offered free to guests in the office area, and pedal boats are available for use on calm days. The Villa runs on wind and solar power, with a generator for backup when occupancy is high. Owners Jean and Roger also charter fishing, diving, and sightseeing trips on their cabin cruiser and *panga.*

US$100-150

Three miles north of town, on the way to Punta la Gringa, **Los Vientos Spa and Resort** (Ensenada tel. 646/178-1440, www.losvientosspaandresort.com, US$96–156) has a large stone fireplace in the lobby and 13 rooms and suites with air-conditioning and power 24/7. At last check, the resort was building four new rooms and a new outdoor bar. The hotel also allows each room to select four DirecTV channels. The management needs advanced notice to arrange a massage, since there hasn't yet been much demand. Although the property is well maintained, prices seem a bit high.

Camping and RV Parks

Across the street from its motel, **Villa Vitta** (tel. 200/124-9103, U.S. tel. 619/454-6108, www.villavitta.com) maintains 25 campsites with electrical hookups and 11 more without, plus a dump station and bathrooms with hot showers for US$10 per night.

Just south of Villa Vitta and close to the plaza, **Guillermo's** (tel. 200/124-9104, www.guillermos.net), is a longtime trailer park, motel, and restaurant with *palapas,* tent sites at US$5 per person, and full hookups for US$17 per night. Guests can use the boat launch free of charge, as well showers and toilets. There is also a small market and gift shop on the premises.

Casa Díaz (tel. 200/124-9112) has nine RV sites with full hookups for US$8.50 a night.

Just past the sea turtle station, on the way to La Gringa, **Campo Archelón** (no tel.) has several *palapa*-roofed rock shelters for bayside camping (US$8 pp).

Another longstanding Bahía de los Angeles business, **Daggett's** (about 2.5 km north of town, along the coastal road, tel. 200/124-9101, www.campdaggetts.com) has sites with wooden ramadas and grills, as well as showers and outhouses, for US$10. You can book fishing and diving trips through Daggett's as long as you come fully equipped.

Even without hot water, **Camp La Ventana** (just south of Los Vientos, no tel.) is one of the best choices for campers. The 10 lattice-wood structures have their own grills, bathrooms are clean, and the grounds are well kept by the camp's owner, Marina, who lives just beside the property. For US$5 a person, the solitude and access to the beautiful beachfront area seem like a steal.

You can still find some sites for free camping along the graded road to **Punta la Gringa,** which marks the north end of the bay. Along the way are a number of open campsites where camping is free. East and south of the town, several sandy coves have camping areas, including **Puerto Don Juan, Ensenada del Quemado,** and **Ensenada del Pescador.**

FOOD

Given the small size of the town and relatively isolated location, food options are somewhat limited—and pricey—in Bahía de los Angeles. One alternative is to stock up on groceries and supplies in Guerrero Negro before making the journey east to the bay.

You might begin a visit to Bahía de los Angeles with a margarita under a *palapa* at **Guillermo's** (tel. 200/124-9104, 6 A.M.–10 P.M. daily, mains US$5–10). Its menu features a number of seafood specialties. At the other end of town, **Restaurant Las Hamacas** (tel. 200/124-9114, 6 A.M.–9 P.M. daily, mains US$5–15) offers seafood and ranchero dishes.

Reyna's Place (tel. 200/124-9148, 6 A.M.–10 P.M. daily, US$5–14) is the bright orange building right at the town's entrance, with the U.S., Canadian, and Mexican flags flying overhead. Owners Reyna and Salino (of Reyna's Tacos and La Palapa fame) cordially attend to customers from this new location, which became their business as of January 2008. Mexican *antojitos* and seafood are the

THE *MICHELADA*

Mix Mexican beer, preferably Tecate, with a good amount of fresh-squeezed lime juice. Add optional flavorings, such as Worcestershire sauce, soy sauce, Tabasco, and black pepper. Serve the drink in a salt-rimmed glass, and you've got a Mexico original: the *michelada*, or, as we like to call it, a beer margarita.

main attractions; a book exchange and long-distance public phone draw information-starved travelers.

Victoria's Restaurant (tel. 200/124-9110, 6 A.M.–10 P.M. daily, US$5–15), at the Costa del Sol Hotel, features reasonably priced Mexican food, with fish and shrimp specialties, including *Pescado Encabronado* (Pissed-off Fish, as translated on the menu) and *Camarones a la Viagra* (Viagra Shrimp). Victoria bears more than a slight resemblance to salsa legend Celia Cruz.

Bahía de los Angeles now has a few legitimate grocery stores, too. The largest, **Super Xitlali,** on the south side of town at the turnoff to head out of town, is open 6 A.M.–11 P.M. daily and has just about anything one might find in similar stores in Guerrero Negro. Also well stocked are Casa Díaz and La Isla Market, among others.

INFORMATION AND SERVICES

There are now long-distance phones at many locations around town; Internet is also available through several of the hotels and camps, including Posada Cerrito Lindo and Villa Bahía, as well as at La Isla Market, which also has stamps and a mailbox. It seems inevitable that Wi-Fi will soon become available here, as it has in most other towns in Baja. A **TelNor** office on the main road offers long-distance phone service and Internet 9 A.M.–7 P.M. daily.

Credit cards are not widely accepted; bring cash. A Bahía de los Angeles resident maintains an informative website for visitors with up-to-date business listings at www.bahiadelosangeles.info.

GETTING THERE AND AROUND

The road from Highway 1 to Bahía de los Angeles was repaved in 2005 and was still in great shape at last check. Currently, the pavement extends north along the coast, as far as Los Vientos, and plans are to continue paving all the way to Punta la Gringa. Two new Pemex stations are now in business at the turnoff to Punta la Gringa. A mechanic located behind Casa Díaz can provide minor repair services and air for tires.

Unfortunately, public transportation is not an option for travel to Bahía de los Angeles; however, once there, you can reach just about everything on foot. Taxis offer service out to Punta la Gringa.

The 1,500-meter airstrip near Punta la Gringa was recently repaved. If you fly over the town once prior to landing, a taxi will meet you at the runway. Visit www.bajabushpilots.com for information.

South of Punta Prieta

SANTA ROSALILLITA

The kilometer-counter along Highway 1 begins anew as soon as you cross south of the Bahía de los Angeles junction. Between Km. 38 and 39 a paved road heads west 13 kilometers to the fish camp of Santa Rosalillita, one of the 28 nautical "steps" in the Mexican government's failed Sea of Cortez Project (Escalera Nautica). As part of this initiative, the port at Santa Rosalillita was expanded and the town received electricity in March 2008, and then all the activity came abruptly to a halt. Fonatur is looking to sell the marina. Antonio at **Tienda Comunitaria Diconsa** (tel. 615/161-1313, US$25) has four rooms with private baths for rent.

◖ SAN BORJA

Orchards planted by the Jesuits in the 18th century continue to support the family that oversees the Mission San Borja today. Located in the foothills of the Sierra San Borja, the village makes an interesting side trip for leisurely travelers who want to see some high-altitude scenery or follow the Jesuit mission trail and who are equipped for off-road driving.

There are two ways to reach San Borja, and each is about 35 kilometers long. The better of the two heads east from Rosarito on Highway 1. It should take less than an hour to reach the settlement via this route. The second, rougher option departs from the paved Bahía de los Angeles at Km. 44 and takes about 90 minutes.

Misión San Francisco Borja de Adác

In prehistoric times, the Cochimí established a settlement called Adác in the foothills of the Sierra San Borja, west of Bahía los Angeles, where two freshwater springs could support a small community. The Jesuits discovered the site in the 18th century and initially built a *visita*, or subordinate mission, to Misión Santa Gertrudis, which was located south of the present-day border between Baja California (Norte) and Baja California Sur. Jesuit Padre Wenceslaus Linck established Mission San Borja (1762–1818) in 1762, and the Franciscans took over five years later, in 1767, followed by the Dominicans in 1773. A stone church was completed in 1801, and in 1818, the mission was secularized. Some of the original church has been restored, and the local community uses it occasionally for services.

The mission is open 8 A.M.–6 P.M. daily. Caretaker José Angel Gerardo Monteón is a fourth-generation Cochimí, and his children offer walking tours to nearby hot springs. They can also guide you on a 1.5-hour driving tour

DESIERTO CENTRAL

to see some of the Sierra San Borja rock art sites. Fees are by donation. The family recently built five concrete-floor *palapas* for campers (US$5–10).

Rock Art

Historian Harry W. Crosby describes the rock art in this part of Baja as the "red-on-granite" school, for their use of a single color painted on the sides of large boulders, rather than on the walls and ceilings of caves. At least two major sites are accessible from San Borja: **Las Tinajitas** (more difficult to find) and **Montevideo.** Ask around in San Borja for a guide.

Surfing and Windsurfing

At the south end of Bahía Santa Rosalillita, off Punta Rosarito, is a surf break called **The Wall** that creates consistent, sizable, and well-formed waves in swells form any direction. When The Wall is too big, surfers in the know head 29 kilometers north to **Punta Santa Rosalillita,** where a long right point breaks during big west and northwest swells. Windsurfers also enjoy steady winds on the bay.

VILLA JESUS MARÍA

Thirty kilometers north of Guerrero Negro, this is a great place to stop for fuel for your car or yourself if you want to bypass Guerrero Negro or if you think you might run short

before you get there. Besides the Pemex, Jesus María boasts several eating establishments. All are good and specialize in slightly different Mexican foods, from fish and shrimp tacos at **Paulina's** to tasty *desebrada tortas* at **La Casita.** The classic tamales at **La Famosa Carmelita's** have a reputation for greatness among veteran Baja road-trippers. Each of these establishments is located along Mexico 1. All in all, the town makes a convenient and satisfying stop.

PARALELO 28

At Km. 128 and the 28th parallel, you can't miss the giant Mexican flag and 43-meter-high steel monument that mark the state line between Baja California (Norte) and Baja California Sur. You'll pass through a military checkpoint, where you may need to show your immigration papers. The time jumps ahead an hour here, as you change from the Pacific to Mountain time zone. Kilometer markers on Highway 1 reset at Km. 220 here and count down to Km. 0 at Santa Rosalía.

The town of Guerrero Negro lies seven kilometers south of this border, but before you get there, you'll need to stop at the immigration checkpoint and agricultural inspection station. In addition to checking immigration papers, officials may spray insecticide under your vehicle.

GUERRERO NEGRO TO BAHÍA CONCEPCIÓN

South of the border between Baja California (Norte) and Baja California Sur, a variety of Mexican and gringo communities invite exploration. This area begins with the saltworks town of Guerrero Negro, where travelers restock supplies, get on the Internet, and spend the night to wait for daylight driving hours. Nearby, the Laguna Ojo de Liebre draws a crowd for whale-watching tours. Beyond it, the protected Desierto de Vizcaíno forms a large peninsula that juts out into the Pacific Ocean.

Continuing south, the palm oasis of San Ignacio is home to an historic Spanish mission and colonial village, as well as a launching point for more whale-watching on the Laguna San Ignacio.

Back on the Gulf coast, the river town of Mulegé and white-sand beaches along Bahía Concepción have become seasonal homes for American and Canadian snowbirds. And deep in the interior of the Sierra de San Francisco and the Sierra de Guadalupe, more historic missions and mysterious rock art sites await.

PLANNING YOUR TIME

If you're in a hurry, you can make the 990 kilometers from Guerrero Negro to Cabo San Lucas in one long day of driving, with a stop for lunch in Loreto. But if your goal is to experience a little more of the outdoors (and to have a safer drive), you'll want to take more time.

The side trip out to the Vizcaíno Peninsula takes several hours, depending on road conditions. Once there, you might spend a couple of days, up to a week, exploring the coastal towns.

Allow 3–4 days for a whale-watching

HIGHLIGHTS

(Laguna Ojo de Liebre: Each winter, adult gray whales and their calves put on a spectacular show in this lagoon near Guerrero Negro (page 141).

(Reserva de la Biósfera Desierto de Vizcaíno: Mexico's largest natural reserve covers 2.5 million hectares of desert terrain and supports several hundred species of plants and mammals (page 148).

(Misión Nuestra Señor San Ignacio de Kadakaamán: This beautifully restored church on the plaza in a pretty oasis town played an important role in Jesuit mission history (page 155).

(Sierra de San Francisco Rock Art: This World Heritage site contains some of the best examples of Baja's prehistoric cave paintings (page 159).

(Laguna San Ignacio: Playful gray whales entertain groups of ecotourists with their spouting and spyhopping during the annual winter migration along the Pacific coast (page 160).

(Playa El Sombrerito: Watch the sun rise and listen to the birds calling from this beach at the mouth of the Mulegé River (page 170).

(Playa Santispac: This beautiful white-sand beach along Bahía Concepción has *palapa* shelters for picnics and overnight camping (page 177).

(La Purísima and Comondú: High in the Sierra de la Giganta range, these modern-day ranching communities trace their roots back to the Jesuit mission period (page 180).

LOOK FOR **(** TO FIND RECOMMENDED SIGHTS, ACTIVITIES, DINING, AND LODGING.

adventure in Laguna Ojo de Liebre of Laguna San Ignacio, since it can take several attempts to catch the right conditions and to see the whales up close. You can easily spend 2–3 days in and around San Ignacio; add at least two more for a trip into the sierra.

Mulegé and Bahía Concepción offer enough activities to occupy visitors for a couple of weeks—or an entire season—including hikes to nearby prehistoric cave paintings, snorkeling, scuba diving, fishing, clamming, birding, and kayaking.

Isla Cedros

Isla Natividad

To El Rosario

Santa Rosalillita

Bahía Santa Rosalillita

Rosarito

Isla Angel de la Guarda

Bahía de los Angeles

San Borja

MISIÓN SAN FRANCISCO BORJA DE ADDÁC

Central Desert of Baja California Nature Park

Bahía Sebastian Vizcaíno

Bahía de Tortugas

★ EAGLE MONUMENT

Guerrero Negro

Isla Salsipuedes

Isla Las Animas

Bahía San Rafael

Isla San Lorenzo

Parque Natural del Desierto Central

(**LAGUNA OJO DE LIEBRE**

Bahía de San Cristóbal

El Arco

BAJA CALIFORNIA
BAJA CALIFORNIA SUR

San Francisquito

MISIÓN SANTA GERTRUDIS

Cabo San Miguel

(**RESERVA DE LA BIÓSFERA DESIERTO DE VIZCAÍNO**

Vizcaíno Junction

Punta San Carlos

Bahía Asunción

Bahía La Asunción

Punta Priesta

Desierto de

(**SIERRA DE SAN FRANCISCO ROCK ART**

Sierra San Francisco

Punta Trinidad

Vizcaíno

S e a   o f   C o r t e z   (Gulf of California)

Bahía San Hipólito

(**MISIÓN NUESTRA SEÑOR SAN IGNACIO DE KADAKAAMÁN**

San Ignacio

Cabo Virgenes

(**LAGUNA SAN IGNACIO**

Punta Abreojos

Bahía Ballenas

Santa Rosalía

Isla Arena

Isla San Marcos

P A C I F I C

Punta Delgadito

Punta Chivato

(**PLAYA EL SOMBRERITO**

MISIÓN GUADALUPE

S i e r r a   d e   l a   G i g a n t e

Mulegé

Punta Concepcion

MISIÓN SANTA ROSALIA DE MULEGÉ

Bahía Coyote

C O A S T

Punta Santo Domingo

(**PLAYA SANTISPAC**

Bahía Concepcion

Punta Pequeña

Bahía San Juanico

(**LA PURÍSIMA**

San Isidro

Punta El Pulpito

GUERRERO NEGRO TO BAHÍA CONCEPCIÓN

Punta San Gregorio

LA PURÍSIMA CONCEPCIÓN DE CADEGOMÓ

MISIÓN COMONDÚ

(**COMONDÚ**

0   20 mi

0   20 km

(53)

(1)

To Loreto

© AVALON TRAVEL

Guerrero Negro and Vicinity

For most Baja road-trippers making their way down the peninsula, foggy Guerrero Negro (pop. 12,000) looms as a stopover town for refueling vehicles, loading up on supplies, and crashing for the night. Aside from marking the halfway point of a trip from Tijuana to Cabo San Lucas, the town is known for two things: gray whales and salt.

◖ LAGUNA OJO DE LIEBRE

Guerrero Negro is the Mexican translation for the name of a U.S. whaler, the *Black Warrior*,

which sank offshore in the 1850s. After depleting the population of gray whales by the late 19th century, the hunters moved on and remarkably, the whales were able to recover. Today whale hunting has been replaced by the sustainable activity of whale-watching. If you happen to visit in February or March, you'll catch the peak season for spotting—and maybe even petting—friendly gray whales. Head out to Scammon's Lagoon, known locally as Laguna Ojo de Liebre. In recent years, the whales have been arriving

© AVALON TRAVEL

THE GRAY WHALE TRAIL

Each year, the gray whale (*Eschrichtius robustus*) completes the longest known migration of any mammal in the world. It travels 16,000-19,000 kilometers round-trip from the shallow lagoons on the Pacific coast of the Baja Peninsula to the Bering Strait in the Arctic and back. The whales take about 2-3 months to complete the swim one-way. When migrating south, the gray whales cover about 161 kilometers a day, slightly less on the way north. Along the way, they stay within 3-5 kilometers of the shore.

ECOLOGY

Gray whales are the only kind of whales that feed on the ocean floor. They eat benthic (bottom-dwelling) amphipods — small shrimp-like crustaceans — by diving to the bottom, rolling on their sides, and gulping sand into their mouths. They use teeth-like baleen plates to filter water and sand out of their mouths, and then they swallow the trapped amphipods that are left behind. Adult whales eat about a ton of amphipods per day this way. They can stay underwater for 15 minutes at a time. Their natural predators are sharks and orcas.

Gray whales mate and feed primarily near the Bering Strait. Gestation takes 11-12 months, and females bear one calf every two years. They give birth in the shallow lagoons of the Southern Pacific — Laguna Ojo de Liebre, Laguna San Ignacio, and Bahía Magdalena. These lagoons provide safety from orcas as well as warmer water (important for babies that don't have much fat) and high salinity (which makes the newborns more buoyant).

Newborn whales weigh 500-680 kilograms and measure about 4.5 meters long, and they reach five or six meters in length within the first three months. Mature adults grow to about 16 meters and weigh 36 tons. The mothers nurse their young for 6-8 months, during which time the baby whales drink 190 liters of milk per day.

Grays live to ages of 30-50 years, some as long as 60 years. A recent sighting of a whale with harpoon scars suggests some may live to be more than 100 years old.

HISTORY AND CONSERVATION

The gray whale once inhabited the Atlantic Ocean, Baltic Sea, and North Sea as well as the Pacific Ocean. But Dutch, British, and American whalers hunted it to the point of extinction in the North Atlantic by the beginning of the 19th century. They almost wiped it out on the Pacific coast as well — reducing the population from 25,000 before the 1850s to just 250 by the 1930s. Charles Melville Scammon, a whaler from Boston, set the rapid slaughter in motion when he discovered the whales in Laguna Ojo de Liebre near Guerrero Negro in 1857, where he was able to trap and kill them using explosive harpoons. The introduction of floating whaling factories in the early 20th century pushed the species even closer to the brink of extinction.

Gray whales were given full international protection in 1947 by the International Whaling Commission, but many whalers didn't comply until the United States passed the Marine Mammal Protection Act of 1972.

The whale made a remarkable comeback at the end of the 20th century and now survives only in the Arctic-Pacific corridor with a population estimated at more than 26,000. It was removed from the endangered species list in 1994, but ocean pollution and fishing nets continue to pose a danger to these mammals.

In May 2010 a gray whale appeared in the Mediterranean Sea off the coast of Israel. The first sighting of a gray whale in the Atlantic in more than 300 years has scientists pondering whether a repopulation is possible. They surmise the whale must have found an ice-free route through the Northwest Passage; the only other means would be a swim through the Suez Canal or around Cape Horn at the tip of South America.

To learn more about the fascinating comeback of the gray whale, pick up a copy of *Saving the Gray Whale: People, Politics, and Conservation in Baja California,* by Serge Dedina or *Eye of the Whale: Epic Passage from Baja to Siberia,* by Dick Russel.

© NIKKI GOTH ITOI

watching for friendly whales

later than usual (late December) and leaving later so that the best months to watch them are now February and March; tours continue through the end of April. In February an official tally of whales in the lagoon resulted in more than 800 adults and more than 500 calves, significantly higher numbers than had been recorded in previous years.

There are two ways to see the whales: The first is to book a three-hour tour (US$50 pp) through an outfitter like **Malarrimo Eco-Tours** (Zapata, tel./fax 615/157-0100, www.malarrimo.com; reserve a day or more in advance), **Mario's Tours** (at Restaurant Mario's, Mexico 1, 615/157-1940, www.mariostours.com), near the Desert Inn, or **Laguna Tours** (tel. 615/157-0050) on Boulevard Zapata next to Motel San Ignacio. Of these options, Mario's created a strong impression on our last visit. This operation is fully certified and has been running tours since 1990. The staff is bilingual and includes whale and bird specialists. Mario's has expanded the restaurant to include a conference room for briefings before the tours.

The second way to see the whales is to drive to the lagoon and hire a *panguero* yourself. Take Highway 1 south of town nine kilometers and look on the right for a sign pointing toward the **Parque Natural de la Ballena Gris.** Follow this road six kilometers (with heavy washboard in places) to a gate that marks the beginning of the salt company property. After an attendant opens the gate, continue across the white salt flats to the lagoon (a total of 24 km). You may be asked to pay a small fee to park here for the day. Taxis are available at the bus depot in Guerrero Negro and will drive up to five passengers to the *panga* piers and back for about US$80. (They wait for you at the lagoon.)

You can often see the whales from the shoreline, but it's best to go out with a boat tour if you want the full experience.

Whale-watching is a morning activity because that's when conditions are calmest and visibility is best. Boats typically depart 9 A.M.–3 P.M. and stay out about 90 minutes. In January–March, there are usually several boats available at the park for hire (US$25 pp).

If you have your own boat, be aware that you won't be able to use it on Laguna Ojo de Liebre when the whales are in town. *Pangueros* must apply for permits to lead tours in the bay, and they know how to maneuver the boats without scaring mothers and their calves.

SALTWORKS

In order to export its seven million tons of salt per year, ExportadoraSal, S.A. (ESSA) employs around 1,000 people in Guerrero Negro—far more than all of the town's tourist businesses combined. Jointly owned by the Mexican government (51 percent) and Mitsubishi Corporation (49 percent), the company owns 182 square kilometers of salt flats surrounding the lagoon. The company gives tours of the plant and its vast network of concentration ponds. Of interest are the specially designed trucks and harvesting equipment used to transport the evaporated salt from the ponds to ships that take it to Isla Cedros and eventually overseas. Tours take about three hours; for information, inquire at **Hotel Malarrimo** (Zapata, tel./fax 615/157-0250, www.malarrimo.com).

DUNAS DE SOLEDAD

If the weather cooperates and you have time for a side trip, the Dunas de Soledad are worth a visit. Located north of town, four kilometers from the highway, the sand dunes reach heights of eight meters and they face **Playa Don Miguelito,** a pristine beach on the Pacific Ocean.

BIRD-WATCHING

North of the salt plant, near an old pier and lighthouse, is a bird sanctuary, a great place to catch beautiful views of the dunes at sunset. Baja California Sur Birds (www.bcsbirds.com) has thumbnail photos online. You can browse by image or by bird name.

SHOPPING

Inside Malarrimo Restaurant, **Casa El Viejo Cactus** (tel./fax 615/157-0250, casaelviejocactus.com) is a small gift shop with a nice selection of reasonably priced handicrafts, gray-

whale souvenirs, and a few English-language books. The line of Baja Desert soaps are locally made on the East Cape of the peninsula.

ACCOMMODATIONS

Guerrero Negro has a handful of modest hotels and motels, most of which are located along Boulevard Zapata.

Under US$50

Just off the main drag, the 14 rooms at **Motel Las Ballenas** (tel. 615/157-0116, US$25) are a pretty good deal, with TV and private bath, although the bed coverings are a little scary. Pets may be allowed in a couple of rooms, depending on who's at the desk. Las Ballenas has Wi-Fi, too. Near Malarrimo Restaurant, the **Motel San Ignacio** (tel. 615/157-0270, US$27) offers 24 basic rooms with a relatively late checkout time (1 P.M.).

Also in this category, the newly constructed **Baja Misión/Brisa Salina B&B, Hostel, and Camping** (Emiliano Zapato, tel. 615/157-0288) adds a fresh look to Guerrero Negro's somewhat outdated image with 14 rooms priced at US$30 per night (with breakfast for an additional US$3). This place also has reasonably priced camping spots and hostel-style accommodations for travelers on tighter budgets.

Adjoining Malarrimo Restaurant, **Hotel Malarrimo** (tel./fax 615/157-0250, www.malarrimo.com, US$45–50, no pets) rents standard rooms with a small TV, chair, and two beds that rest on hard wooden platforms. Sloped, beamed ceilings, yellow stucco walls, and a cactus decor add a cheerful touch. Bathrooms have old plumbing but plenty of hot water and good pressure. Threadbare towels, bare lightbulbs, and a few empty sockets remind you that this is Baja. The hotel offers free wireless Internet in its restaurant area.

Built in 2006, **◖ Hotel Los Caracoles** (Calz. de la República, tel. 615/157-1088, www.hotelloscaracoles.com.mx, US$45–65) has 13 rooms, with 5 more in the works. You can access the Internet from the lobby only; the first 20 minutes are free. This hotel is located north of Boulevard Zapata, along one of the first cross streets as you approach the town from Mexico 1. The owner is a retired manager from the saltworks.

More or less across from Los Caracoles and at approximately the same price point, **(Cowboy Hotel** (Zapata, tel. 615/157-2765, http://hotelcowboy.com/, US$45) opened in 2009 with 14 rooms and plans to expand. Showers are hot, parking is secure, Wi-Fi works, and pets are negotiable for an extra 100 pesos. The adjoining Asadero Cowboy restaurant draws a crowd for tasty tacos. Both businesses are cash only. There is an ATM in the Pemex next door. Rooms here get booked during the whale-watching season.

US$50-100
If you don't need to load up on supplies in town and don't mind paying a bit extra, the **Desert Inn** (formerly La Pinta, tel. 615/157-1304, toll-free U.S. tel. 800/800-9632, www.desertinns. com, US$85) has a hotel near the state border and Paralelo 28 monument, off Mexico 1.

Camping and RV Parks
The best spot for coastal camping near Guerrero Negro is inside the Parque Natural de la Ballena Gris, where you may be asked to pay US$5 per day to park. In town, **Malarrimo RV Park** (tel./fax 615/157-0100) has 40 sites with hookups and dump stations for US$18 up to 35 feet, US$20 over 35 feet, or US$14 for campers and vans. Tent sites cost US$12 per person. Rates include access to restrooms with hot showers.

The *ejido*-owned **Benito Juárez RV Park** (tel. 615/157-0025), just south of the state border, has 18 hookups (US$7–9) with restrooms and shower facilities but no shade. This place seems to be open sporadically, but probably can be counted on in the high season.

FOOD
Baja residents come from as far away as Bahía de los Angeles and San Francisquito to stock up on foods and supplies in Guerrero Negro. Most of its restaurants and supermarkets line the main avenue of Boulevard Zapata.

Few travelers make their way through Guerrero Negro without stopping at **(Malarrimo Restaurant** (Zapata, tel. 615/157-0100, 7 A.M.–10:30 P.M. daily, mains US$10–20) for fresh scallops, filet mignon, or gringo-style Mexican specialties. The adjoining gift shop has a great selection of souvenirs. Locals prefer **Don Gus** (tel. 615/157-1611) on Boulevard Zapata, past the Malarrimo and on the opposite side of the street.

Santo Remedio (Domingo Carballo Félix, tel. 615/157-2909, www.elsantoremedio.com. mx, 8 A.M.–10 P.M. daily) became the upscale dining venue of choice in Guerrero Negro when it opened in 2008. Since it's not on the main road through town, it can be difficult to find for travelers who arrive hungry after dark. Turn right at El Morro and before the Tiangis grocery store, and go two blocks to a sign. The restaurant will be on the left.

Closer to the highway, **Puerto Viejo** (no tel., 7 A.M.–11 P.M. daily, mains US$10–20) offers much of the same and free coffee with breakfast. Nearby, just inside the entrance to town, the clean **Las Cazuelas** (tel. 615/157-1303, 7 A.M.–11 P.M. daily, mains US$6–12) specializes in Spanish-style *mariscadas* (seafood stews); it also serves 12 types of meat dishes and a variety of seafood platters.

Tiangis (Zapata 5, tel. 615/157-0055) is the largest grocery store in town, with a variety of foods and housewares. It is located next to the Dunas Motel and before the water tower.

If you don't mind the limited selection, you can find discounted food items at the government-subsidized **Tienda ISSSTE** (no tel.) on Boulevard Zapata or **Tienda ESSA** (no tel.), across from the main entrance to the salt plant.

INFORMATION AND SERVICES
Tourist Assistance
Stop by the small tourist office (tel. 615/157-0100, 10 A.M.–2 P.M. and 4–7 P.M. daily) in front of Malarrimo Restaurant for local information. **Mario's Restaurant and Tours** (615/157-1940, www.mariostours.com), at the northern

GUERRERO NEGRO

entrance to town at the roundabout, is a reliable source of local information as well.

The Comisión Nacional de Areas Naturales Protegidas (CONANP) has an office in Guerrero Negro (Profesor Domingo Carballo Félix s/n, esquina Ruiz Cortinez, Col. Marcelo Rubio, www.conanp.gob.mx).

Money
The **Banamex** (8:30 A.M.–3 P.M. Mon.–Fri.) at the west end of Boulevard Zapata, has an ATM and currency-exchange service. The newer Pemex also has an ATM.

Telephone and Internet Access
Next to Motel Las Ballenas, **Café Internet Las Ballenas** (10 A.M.–1 P.M. and 4–9 P.M. Mon.–Sat.) offers high-speed Internet access for US$2 per hour. You can also use the public phone in front of Malarrimo Restaurant.

Laundry
You can wash your clothes across from Motel Las Ballenas on Calle Victoria at **Lavamática Express** (8 A.M.–9 P.M. daily).

GETTING THERE
By Air
Aereo Servicio Guerrero (tel. 615/157-0137, toll-free 800/823-3153, www.aereoserviciosguerrero.com.mx) operates flights to and from Isla Cedros four times a week (Mon., Wed., Thurs., Fri.). The flight time is about 30 minutes, and a one-way ticket runs US$65; the airline office, next to the police station on Boulevard Zapata, is open 9 A.M.–4 P.M. Monday–Saturday. The company also does charters upon request and flies to other destinations within Mexico such as Ensenada (US$137) and the Pacific coast of the mainland.

Guerrero Negro's airfield is located north of town, near the state line. Look for the turnoff between Km. 125 and 126.

By Bus
Guerrero Negro's bus station is located on Boulevard Zapata across from Malarrimo

Restaurant. **Aguila** (tel. 800/824-8452, www.autotransportesaguila.com) and **Autotransportes de Baja California** (ABC, tel. 800/025-0220, www.abc.com.mx) offer daily service north to Punta Prieta, El Rosario ($40) San Quintín, Ensenada, and Tijuana (US$80), and south to Vizcaíno (US$8), San Ignacio (US$17), Santa Rosalía (US$25), Mulegé (US$33), Loreto (US$49), Ciudad Constitución (US$67), and La Paz (US$90).

GETTING AROUND
The yellow **Infonavit-Centro** city buses (US$1) run along Boulevard Zapata and Calle Madero. You can usually find a few taxis at the bus station, and a ride within the town limits will cost about US$5. Taxis will drive up to five passengers to the *panga* piers at Laguna Ojo de Liebre and back for about US$80. (They wait for you at the lagoon.)

SAN FRANCISQUITO
If you have time for a day-long excursion (or more), the three- to four-hour drive east to the Sea of Cortez covers some beautiful mountain and desert scenery, ending at a seaside fishing camp on **Bahía Santa Teresa**. From Highway 1, watch for a turnoff to San Francisquito (signed for El Arco) about 30 kilometers south of Guerrero Negro. The road passes over a steep hill called Cuesta de la Ley (Slope of the Law), about 29 kilometers before San Francisquito. Some supplies are usually to be found in El Arco, 34 kilometers east of Mexico 1. A better stop is at **Rancho Piedras Blancas,** another 25 kilometers east of El Arco. Located in a spectacular setting among giant *cardóns*, cirios, and ocotillos inside the newly designated Valle de los Cirios national park, the ranch has been selected by the government as a site for the future development of ecologically sound cabins available for tourists.

An alternative route to San Francisquito comes from Bahía de los Angeles and takes about the same amount of time. The Baja 1000 road race uses this route, and some say this wrecks the road, while others claim it helps by creating good tracks that others can follow.

About 45–60 minutes into the drive from Bahía de los Angeles lies **Bahía San Rafael,** a beautiful bay with a population of one, an ex-shark fisherman from Guaymas named Pancho who has called San Rafael home for 20 years. He's on the eccentric side but is full of great stories and can sometimes provide meals and beer to travelers for a donation. He also has a rod for fishing from shore for halibut.

Each route generally has long stretches in good condition. Remember to fill your fuel tank wherever you begin and expect to find heavy washboard and incredible scenery along either route.

The two routes to San Francisquito meet near Rancho El Progresso, approximately 21 kilometers east of Bahía San Francisquito. The roads near the ranch are sometimes difficult to navigate: To stay on track toward the bay, choose the branch that heads due east from the ranch.

Accommodations

The former San Francisquito Resort is now closed, and the entire beach was sold in 2008 to a Mexican developer who plans to build a large luxury resort. In the meantime, you can still camp on the grounds of the resort or farther on along the bay for US$5.

Vizcaíno Peninsula

South and west of Guerrero Negro, the narrow Baja Peninsula widens to form the Vizcaíno Peninsula, a vast desert, mountain, and coastal region in which average annual rainfall amounts to a mere 70 millimeters and several years may pass without so much as a single rainstorm. And yet despite the harsh climate, the Desierto de Vizcaíno sustains one of the most fascinating ecosystems found anywhere in the world—so much so that the Mexican government decided to protect it in 1988, well ahead of current trends in green travel. At its northernmost point, the tip of the Vizcaíno Peninsula juts out into the Pacific Ocean, framing the southwest side of Bahía de Sebastián Vizcaíno, a large bay that encompasses the Laguna Ojo de Liebre whale sanctuary. Heading south from the tip, the coastline is shaped into a series of shallow bays with four fishing towns, where you'll find accommodations, food, and basic supplies. The southernmost bay, Bahía de las Ballenas, leads to Laguna San Ignacio, another breeding ground for gray whales and other endangered marine life.

In 1993 the United Nations Educational, Scientific, and Cultural Organization (UNESCO) designated the whale sanctuary of El Vizcaíno a World Heritage site, along with the rock paintings in the Sierra de San Francisco, an area that lies east of San Ignacio.

The majority of Baja road-trippers stop to refuel in Guerrero Negro and continue their journey south along Highway 1, skipping the Vizcaíno Peninsula altogether. But there are several good reasons to add a few days, or up to a week, to explore one of Baja's last remaining frontiers. You'll find beautiful sites for coastal camping, friendly local residents, and protected plant and animal life, supported almost entirely by a nearly constant layer of marine fog. Although the Vizcaíno Peninsula has changed considerably in recent years, it remains a wild and isolated place that gives travelers the sense of being at the very edge of civilization.

Anglers generally head to the coastal stretch between Bahía Asunción and Punta Abreojos to catch halibut, corvina, and croaker as well as sand, calico, and pinto bass.

VIZCAÍNO JUNCTION

Ejido Vizcaíno, along Highway 1, offers a number of services for motorists and truckers, but the larger town of Vizcaíno Junction (pop. 2,500) is located west of the highway.

Accommodations

A couple of hotels offer reliable accommodations here. **Hotel Olivia** (tel. 615/156-4524, US$30), across from the Pemex station at Km.

144, is a family-run establishment with 36 very clean rooms, each with two double beds, private hot-water bathrooms, seven channels of SKY TV, and 24-hour security.

The unique **Hotel Kadakaamán** (615/156-4112, kaadekaman@aol.com, US$40), on the west side of Highway 1 at Km. 143, was named after the former Jesuit mission site near San Ignacio, Misión San Ignacio Kadakaamán. It also offers air conditioning, hot-water bathrooms, 10 channels of SKY TV, and Wi-Fi in its 18 rooms. The artistic grounds feature a mural of the cave paintings found in the surrounding area.

Food
Highway 1 through Vizcaíno is dotted with many good, simple eating establishments, serving mainly homemade Mexican food, roasted chicken, and tacos. At Km. 140 on the east side of the highway, the very simple **Bar/ Restaurant Nancy's** (no tel., hours vary) features good homemade meals at reasonable prices, with main dishes ranging US$6–9. Similar food awaits at friendly **La Huerta** (no tel., 6 A.M.–11 P.M. daily, US$5–12), located by Hotel Olivia and attached to the bus depot.

Café Restaurant/Mezquite Grill Afrodita (daily, mains US$8–20) is the colorfully painted restaurant on the grounds of Hotel Kadakaamán. It specializes in varied cuts of steak. At Km. 142 on the west side of the highway is **Maximo's Pizza** (no tel., lunch and dinner daily, mains US$7–10), which operates a second location in Guerrero Negro.

Information and Services
Vizcaíno has a number of automotive stores (including Napa Autocar Center at Km. 141 on the west side) and *llanteras* (such as Llantera 2000 on the east side, 615/156-4582) as well as several long-distance phone and fax places. TelMex public phones are widely available.

Getting There and Around
An Aguila bus depot outside Hotel Olivia leads to all points on Highway 1 north and south. A van transports passengers to and from Bahía Tortugas on a daily basis for US$18 each way. Vans depart from the hotel at 10 A.M. each day and return at 3 A.M. The trip takes under two hours.

If you're driving, there are two ways to get to the Vizcaíno Peninsula's coastal attractions: You can turn off Highway 1 at Km. 144 and begin a 148-kilometer journey through the desert. As of early 2011 the road is now paved the entire way, and you can make it to Asunción Bay in about an hour.

Alternatively, if Punta Abreojos is your destination, you can turn off Highway 1 at Km. 98 and follow an 80-kilometer road to the coast.

If you want to make the trip into a loop, start by heading west to Bahía Tortugas or Bahía Asunción at Km. 144 on Highway 1, and then head south along the coast to Punta Abreojos, where you can turn back east and reconnect with Highway 1 at Km. 98.

RESERVA DE LA BIÓSFERA DESIERTO DE VIZCAÍNO
The desert that begins south of the 28th parallel is the largest such reserve in Mexico, covering some 2.5 million hectares. It holds 443 species of plants and 69 mammals, the most interesting of which is the rare *berrendo,* or desert pronghorn antelope, which gets its water only by eating succulents. An estimated 200 animals live in the reserve. Ford Motor Company has partnered with the Mexican government to sponsor a recuperation plan for the *berrendo.*

It is possible to view the *berrendos* in an area between Asunción and Abreojos, by turning off at a signed point on the road. Inquire at either town for specific instructions. Guided tours are also available. Chelo's in Abreojos and the SEMARNAT office in Asunción are good sources of information. There is also a CONANP office in Guerrero Negro where visitors can obtain current information.

BAHÍA ASUNCIÓN
Bahía Asunción (pop. 2,000) has undergone dramatic changes in recent years, from electricity and pavement to signed streets. It's a

THE ENDANGERED PENINSULAR PRONGHORN

The *berrendo* once roamed the Baja Peninsula from San Felipe to Bahía Magdalena, but now it survives only in the Vizcaíno Reserve of the Biosphere. Sometimes confused with an antelope, the animal stands about one meter high and weighs up to 50 kilograms. It "drinks" the dew that comes with coastal fog and feeds on plants with high moisture content. The *berrendo* can run up to 95 kilometers per hour. Only about 250 pronghorn live on the peninsula today. They are protected by the government, but poachers, cattle, and periods of drought continue to threaten its existence. The San Diego Zoo and Los Angeles Zoo both participate in conservation efforts.

town that appears to be prospering and receiving considerable attention both from foreign and national interests. For this reason, its days as a quaint and quiet destination may be numbered, especially now that the pavement is complete from the Vizcaíno road.

The town's main street is Benito Juárez, on which basically all services can be found, including a Pemex, SEMARNAT office (where you can get a permit for an island tour), airstrip, and two plants that process marine products, plus a clinic, library, post office/telegraph service, and a few eateries. Long-distance phones can be found at Farmacia Eduardo's, Farmacia Rosio, and Ultramarinos Asunción.

The waterfront in Bahía Asunción is not particularly attractive, but it does have a pier and a small beach located just north of town. The annual town festival, that of the Virgen de Asunción, is held in mid-August and includes a fishing tournament and surf competition.

Visit **Galería Bahía** (cell tel. 615/103-4432, www.galeriabahia.blogspot.com, hours vary,

daily Oct.–Apr.), where artist Nancy Pridham maintains a small art studio, with cards, paintings, and sculptures for sale. To find the gallery/home, follow the pavement through town and up the hill. Turn right at the stop sign at Atun street. Go two blocks and turn right to find the two-story mustard-yellow house.

Recreation

For most visitors, life at Bahía Asunción centers around sportfishing, socializing, and eating the daily catch. Throw a line into the surf for halibut and corvina, try spearfishing for grouper, or troll for yellowtail, dorado, wahoo and yellowfin tuna—all within a mile of shore. Otherwise, you can walk the beach and watch seawater spew out of the Bufadora. In June, you can snorkel at Isla Asunción, when thousands of baby sea lions are born. Surfers find numerous beach and reef breaks nearby. And you might be able to arrange a scuba diving trip through Mulegé-based Cortez Divers.

Juan Arce Murron is one of several local fishermen who offer guided trips. He and his wife, Canadian Shari Bondy, also offer guest accommodations and camping. Located across from the California Fishing Co-op near the point, **Kalicos Locos Sport Fishing and Excursions** (tel. 615/160-0241, cell tel. 615/107-3720, kalicosloco@yahoo.com) runs fishing tours as well as trips to Malarrimo Beach or to view the wild desert pronghorn. Camping and RV parking are free for clients.

Accommodations

The friendly **Hotel El Verduzco** (Juárez at Mantaraya, tel. 615/160-0004, US$$30) has clean, simple rooms with hot water and wireless Internet.

Fishing captain Juan Arce Murron built the **◖ Bufadora/Blowhole B&B** (tel. 615/160-0289, U.S. tel. 619/906-8438, US$60) one stone at a time, in between fishing trips. Perched on the side of a cliff, its two guestrooms are quiet and contemporary and overlook rocks and the blowhole below. From the patio, you'll enjoy views of Islas Asunción and San Roque just offshore. Amenities include

Wi-Fi, fridge, and microwave. Rates include full breakfast. The owners also have built several vacation rentals over the years, including a three-bedroom beach house (US$150/night for two people), rustic three-bedroom Casa Pargo (US$90/night for two people), and a one-bedroom bungalow (US$60 per night). You can also camp on their property for US$10 in a sheltered cove at the water's edge. One more option is the rustic fishing cabin at the abandoned San Roque fishing camp for US$40 per night. Camping is also possible here for US$10 per night.

Under the same ownership, centrally located **Campo Sirena** has tent camping and some hookups for RV travelers. It provides bathroom/shower facilities and a fee dumping station. Find the camp one block south of Benito Juárez near the entrance to town.

Kalicos Locos has both tent sites and ample space for large rigs. There are restrooms and showers and great views, and you'll be steps away from the *panga* boat launch in the morning. The camping is free if you book a chartered fishing trip with the owners.

Food

Restaurant Hotel El Verduzco (Juárez at Mantaraya, tel. 615/160-0004, 8 A.M.–10 P.M. daily, mains US$5–7) serves dependable Mexican staples. Next door to the hotel is the town's only Internet café, open to nonguests. At Campo Sirena, **Tide Pool Bistro** is open for breakfast, lunch, and dinner daily. The menu features fish tacos, abalone burgers, sushi/sashimi, and pizzas. You can bring your fresh catch or request box lunches for fishing or picnics.

Across from the fishing co-op at the three-way stop sign, **Lonchería Mari** (no tel., 8 A.M.–10:30 P.M. daily) is a relatively new establishment that offers seafood, burgers, tacos, and pizza and is open all day.

Plenty of taco and *antojito* stands line Benito Juárez, and the addition of new pavement along the beach heading out of town will probably lead to a revamping of some waterfront restaurants as well.

Getting There

There are two ways to reach Asunción from Tortugas: You can retrace your steps along the Vizcaino–Tortugas road to the fork and follow the southern branch (partially paved) southwest to the coast. Or you can take a more scenic and shorter route via San José del Castro.

PUNTA ABREOJOS

A longtime favorite of windsurfers and surfers alike, as well as a popular spot with the fishing crowd, Abreojos somehow remains a quiet, somewhat unchartered destination. In July 2007 the town's waterfront received a makeover with the installation of new pavement and streetlamps along its *malecón*.

The town has a Telecomm office for long-distance calls and a Western Union.

Accommodations and Food

Though most travelers who come to Abreojos choose to camp, the town does offer one good lodging, **Hotel Chelo's** (on town's main unnamed road, tel. 615/620-4515, US$35–40). Chelo's also has a bar/restaurant, open daily. Chelo herself is a good source of local information as well as a key player in a local movement to improve life in Abreojos in many ways. Her organization, MEAPA (Mujeres En Acción Punta Abreojos), is active on a variety of issues, from ecological conservation and beach cleanup to women's issues and townwide swim and surf camps. For travelers who want to donate their time or money to a good cause, Chelo is a great person to contact (tel. 615/104-2139).

Two other eateries are usually open: **Lonchería Las Palmas** (no tel., lunch daily, mains US$5), on the *malecón,* is open during the day only and serves tasty fish tacos and other basic Mexican staples. A couple of doors down, with Speedy Gonzalez painted on the front wall, is **Antojitos Juanita** (no tel., nightly, US$5), which opens for typical *antojitos* at night.

For groceries, bread, and other basic supplies, friendly **Super Zuniga** (on town's main road, no tel., 9 A.M.–6 P.M. daily) is well stocked.

VIZCAÍNO PENINSULA **151**

GUERRERO NEGRO

LA BOCANA

A fishing town between Bahía Asuncíon and Punta Abreojos, the settlement of La Bocana doesn't hold much to interest for travelers beside some reportedly good fishing, but it can make for a quiet rest between other destinations on the peninsula. It has one hotel, **Hotel Adriana** (on town's main road, no tel.) which is attached to the grocery store **Abarrotes Adriana** (no tel.). Rooms in this two-story building go for US$25, and a long-distance phone is also available. There are usually one or two eateries open for simple meals or *antojitos,* as well as gas from a barrel and a *llantera.* The road to Abreojos from here follows an unsigned mudflat; anyone in town can point you in the direction of it.

ESTERO DE COYOTE

In Bahía de las Ballenas, the next bay south of Bahía Asuncíon, anglers and bird-watchers will want to explore the Estero de Coyote, a lagoon and salt marsh area with a local *ejido.*

Campo Rene (tel. 615/103-0008 or 615/161-7360) has established itself on the estuary as a bar/restaurant/camping complex offering whale-watching, kayaking, surfing, and turtle observation. Campsites with a *palapa* and adjacent *asador* run US$15, while RV sites with power run US$10. Also available are 12 small wooden cabanas for US$20 and three trailers for US$15; all lodgings have use of shared hot-water bathroom facilities. Inquire about group and/or multiday discounts. An airstrip and *pangas* for rent (US$120 for a day's fishing trip with guide) as well as a full restaurant and bar (meals US$6–9) complete the experience. From the southern road into the peninsula, Estero de Coyote is only a 30-minute trip on a good paved road—it's well worth a visit.

BAHÍA TORTUGAS

The largest town on the Vizcaíno Peninsula (pop. 3,000) is Bahía Tortugas, a 160-kilometer journey from Highway 1. It seems to have declined somewhat in recent years, possibly since the closure of its cannery a decade ago. Residents remain optimistic, however, that by organizing their four fishing cooperatives, they'll be able to preserve the marine life that sustains their community.

Anglers here primarily catch lobster and two species of abalone. The cooperatives, both here and in Punta Eugenia, have night vigilance teams to prevent poaching, as well as abalone cultivating centers. Tourists usually arrive by boat to stock up on fuel and supplies or to take shelter.

The gray-sand beach closest to town was unfortunately covered with trash at last check. But near the airstrip, El Playón offers a suitable camping spot and is also a good place for a day at the beach. To find the beach, head to the airstrip following the road to Punta Eugenia and turn toward the ocean on any tracked road; they all funnel into a more established dirt road that leads to the beach. Once you arrive at the beach, rocky points to the left and right provide shelter from wind as well as decent breaks for surfing on occasion.

Bahía Tortugas fills during Carnaval celebrations every year (Feb.–Mar., dates vary) as well as during its new, annual Feria del Mar (Festival of the Sea; approx. mid-August), during which the town celebrates all facets of the sea through crafts made out of abalone and clam shells, seafood dishes, and a fishing tournament.

Accommodations and Food

Try **Motel Nancy** (tel. 615/158-0056, US$25) for basic rooms with private hot-water showers. The motel office is located inside Novedades Lupita, next door, where DVD rentals are also available. To find Nancy's, turn left as you are driving into the town and onto a downward-inclined dirt street just after a big minimarket and before the curve in the road at the TelCel office. On the southwest side of town, **Motel Rendón** (tel. 615/158-0232) has rooms inside a cinder-block building for US$25–35. Rendón's office is in El Moroco restaurant, next door.

There are a variety of taco stands and *antojito* spots in town. Down the street from Motel Nancy, toward the waterfront, is **Taquería Delia** (no tel., lunch and dinner daily, mains

US$5–8), which offers indoor seating for its tacos and *tortas*. Farther down the same road is the **Tortillería La Trinidad** (no tel., closed Sundays) for corn tortillas, with a taco and *birria* stand in front. **Alex's Pizza** (no tel., lunch and dinner daily, mains US$5–8), on the paved road through the center of town, is open for snacks and pizza in the afternoons and evenings daily. **Restaurant El Moroco** (no tel., 8 A.M.–10 P.M. daily, mains US$7–8), near Motel Rendón, serves a variety of fresh seafood dishes.

One of the best eateries in town is ◖ **La Palapa** (no tel., lunch and dinner daily, mains US$5–10), located right in the port. Carlos and Mercedes Jimenez started serving customers a decade ago as an extension of their family gatherings for the anglers who would come ashore looking for some food and company. This is a wonderful spot to spend an hour or two having a beer or some coffee with your home-cooked meal; Carlos, an ex-fisherman, is a fantastic source of local history and makes every visitor feel welcome in this sleepy town.

On the weekends, a disco on the hill above the Pemex is open for the younger crowd that fills the town when visiting family from school in Ensenada.

Information and Services

Services here include a Pemex station, several markets and cafés, a clinic, bakery, post office, and an out-of-use airfield. Western Union offers telegraph services, wires, and credit card advances.

Next door to the telegraph office is the town's only Internet place (no tel., 9 A.M.–1:30 P.M. and 4–9 P.M. Mon–Sat.).

There are many TelMex public phones spread throughout town for long-distance calls using public phone cards. **El Tortugo Tackle** (no tel.), right on the waterfront in the harbor, sells all manners of fishing supplies.

PUNTA EUGENIA

Follow the graded dirt road north from Tortugas for 26.5 kilometers to reach the small,

picturesque village of Punta Eugenia. This is the place to plan a boat trip to Islas Natividad, Cedros, and San Benito.

The scenic cliffs along Chest Camp are perfect for solitary camping. Enjoy great views of Islas Cedros and Natividad in the distance as well as Chester Rock, with the remains of a misguided shrimp boat. A local from Eugenia has constructed some palm-fringed shelters on one of the cliffs for a future tourist camp, and plans were to include a restaurant/café as well.

The drive out to Punta Eugenia and beyond is worth the extra time; the surroundings become increasingly more pristine as you get farther from Tortugas.

ISLA CEDROS

If you head northwest from Punta Eugenia by boat for 22 kilometers, you'll reach Isla Cedros (Island of Cedars). At 38 kilometers long, it's one of Mexico's largest islands, with a population of 1,350 as of 2005. Fishing and transporting salt from Guerrero Negro sustain the island's economy, but travelers also find the California juniper and Isla Cedros pine trees (mistaken long ago for cedars) of interest. The trees grow between the island's two 1,200-meter peaks. Aside from the unusual flora, there are a few beaches to explore, including **Punta Prieta,** at the southwest end of the island. Look for waves at Playa Elefante, also at this end of the island.

If you travel by air, you'll arrive at the saltworks town of Punta Morro Redondo at the southern tip of the island. The largest town on the island, **Puebla Cedros,** is located on the southeast side, facing the peninsula. Services include a port captain's office, CONASUPO, fish cannery, post office, church, bank, and a few eateries and guesthouses.

You can reach Isla Cedros by chartered boat from Punta Eugenia or Bahía Tortugas, or more easily by plane from Guerrero Negro via **Aereo Servicio Guerrero** (tel. 615/157-0137, toll-free 800/823-3153, www.aereoserviciosguerrero.com.mx). A one-way ticket for the 30-minute flight runs US$65, and planes

ISLA CEDROS

Punta Norte

Los Crestones
Punta Norte

PACIFIC

Arroyo El
Choyal

El Coloradito

OCEAN

Arroyo Vargas
Arroyo del
Gran Cañon

Cerro
Cedros

Cerro
▲ Redondo

Piedra
Colorada

LIGHTHOUSE
■ PIERS
Isla Cedros

Cabo San
Agustin
Bahía del Sur
Arroyo
Cedros

AIRSTRIP

LIGHTHOUSE Punta Morro
Redondo

0   5 mi

0   5 km
© AVALON TRAVEL

Package trips include ecotours to Isla Cedros and Islas San Benito (four days/three nights US$980) and sportfishing trips to Islas Cedros, San Benito, and Natividad (four days/three nights US$1,350). Prices include transportation from San Ysidro, California, as well as accommodations and meals.

ISLA NATIVIDAD

Between Isla Cedros and Punta Eugenia, tiny Isla Natividad (pop. 400) was a Cochimí settlement until a Jesuit missionary convinced the group to relocate to Misión San Ignacio. The island is better known today as a world-class surf destination, with the famous Open Doors break (south swell only). Open Doors breaks on the southeast side of the island, so the same westerly winds that blow the surf out along the mainland are barrel-grooming offshore waves all afternoon. Isla Natividad is known for advanced barreling waves and tough camping.

San Diego–based **Baja AirVentures** (toll-free U.S. tel. 800/221-9283, www.bajaair-ventures.com) runs all-inclusive, safari-style trips to Isla Natividad May–October, but only when a south swell is running. Trips are often planned on short notice, depending on the surf conditions. This is the way to get in and out for a surgical strike. A four-day trip costs US$1,495, and a six-day trip runs US$1,595. All trips depart from San Diego.

From Punta Eugenia, chartered boat service to Isla Natividad should cost about US$20 one-way, and the trip takes about 30 minutes. Planes also make the short trip to the island's dirt runway. Services are extremely limited here, but the island does have a clinic to handle small injuries.

ISLAS SAN BENITO

Divers who know this trio of tiny uninhabited islands say that its kelp beds are as rich with life as the Channel Islands were 75 years ago. Purple hydrocoral grow on underwater pinnacles, abalone and lobster hide in rocky crevices, and sightings of 9- to 18-kilogram yellowtail are common. Thriving populations

make the trip four times a week. Once you arrive, taxis are available for the short ride into town.

Note: Isla Cedros is part of the Ensenada municipality and lies above the 28th parallel, in the same time zone as Baja California (Norte). Set your watch back an hour if you arrive via Punta Eugenia or elsewhere in Baja California Sur.

Bilingual marine biologist Jose Sanchez-Pacheco offers a variety of guided trips through **Cedros Outdoor Adventures** (tel. 646/154-3085, cell tel. 646/193-2031, U.S. tel. 619/793-5419, www.cedrosoutdooradventures.com), which is based in San Ysidro, California.

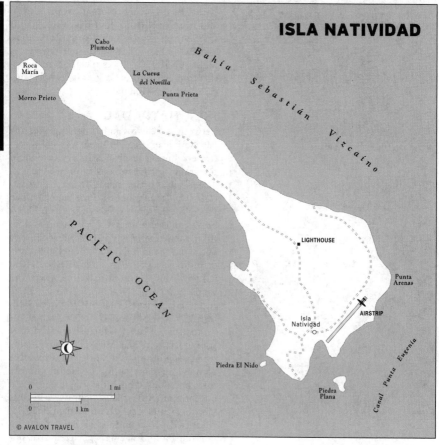

ISLA NATIVIDAD

Cabo
Plumeda

Roca
María

La Cueva
del Novilla

Morro Prieto

Punta Prieta

Bahía

Sebastián

Vizcaíno

PACIFIC OCEAN

LIGHTHOUSE

Punta
Arenas

AIRSTRIP

Isla
Natividad

Piedra El Nido

Piedra
Plana

Canal Punta Eugenia

0   1 mi

0   1 km

© AVALON TRAVEL

of California sea lions, giant elephant seals, and Guadalupe fur seals provide even more fun.

Islas Benito del Este, Centro, and Oeste are located about 80 kilometers west of Baja and about 450 kilometers south of San Diego—within reach of California-based liveaboard services. **Horizon Charters** (www.horizon-charters.com) occasionally runs an eight-day, seven-night dive trip to these islands. Boats depart from San Diego and stop at Isla San Martin on the way south.

Bilingual marine biologist Jose Sanchez-

Pacheco offers a variety of guided trips through **Cedros Outdoor Adventures** (tel. 646/154-3085, cell tel. 646/193-2031, U.S. tel. 619/793-5419, www.cedrosoutdooradventures.com), which is based in San Ysidro, California. Package trips include ecotours to Isla Cedros and the Islas San Benito (four days/three nights US$980) and sportfishing trips to Islas Cedros, San Benito, and Natividad (four days/three nights US$1,350). Prices include transportation from San Ysidro, California, as well as accommodations and meals.

San Ignacio and Vicinity

South of Vizcaíno Junction, Highway 1 begins to curve eastward on its way to meet the Sea of Cortez at Santa Rosalía. The drive presents views of the expansive Desierto de Vizcaíno to the west and the majestic Sierra de San Francisco to the east, with peaks up to 5,216 meters. In the middle of all this scenery is a spring-fed oasis surrounded by palms and the small colonial town of San Ignacio. Beyond the desert on the Pacific coast is the gray-whale sanctuary of Laguna San Ignacio.

SAN IGNACIO

Experienced Baja travelers often pass straight through Guerrero Negro and push on to San Ignacio (pop. 4,000) for an overnight stop on the way to points south. With its picture-perfect oasis, restored 18th-century Spanish mission, colonial buildings, and variety of places to stay and eat, the town offers an appealing combination of scenery, history, and visitor services.

Before the Jesuits arrived, the Cochimí knew San Ignacio as Kadakaamán (Creek of Reeds). Abundant freshwater made it a prime location for growing wheat and other crops during the mission period. Today the town consists of a small commercial and residential area surrounding the Misión San Ignacio Kadakaamán and plaza.

The weather here is moderate, compared to the surrounding Vizcaíno Desert. Nights can be chilly in the winter, and all the standing water makes for a healthy population of mosquitoes.

San Ignacio suffered severe flooding from Hurricane Jimena in 2009, and many businesses are still on the mend.

Sights
◖ MISIÓN NUESTRA SEÑOR SAN IGNACIO DE KADAKAAMÁN

If you visit only one mission along the entire Baja Peninsula, choose this one for the quality of its restoration, accessibility, and the important role it played in Jesuit history.

© NIKKI GOTH ITOI

bay scallop shell on the beach at Laguna San Ignacio

SAN IGNACIO

To Guerrero Negro
PEMEX/ GROCERIES
To Santa Rosalía
BUS DEPOT
NANG FONG HOTEL & CAFE
BAJA OASIS MOTEL
To Hotel Ricardo/ Rice and Beans
IGNACIO SPRINGS B&B
LOS PETATES
0   0.5 mi
0   0.5 km
DESERT INN/ LA PINTA HOTEL
EL PADRINO
BAJA EXPEDITIONS
POST OFFICE
CALLE MUJICA
INTERNET CAFE
MISIÓN NUESTRA SEÑOR SAN IGNACIO DE KADAKAAMÁN
CALLE MADERO
CASA LEREÉ
C. BENITO JUÁREZ
MUSEUM/INAH OFFICE
Plaza Ecotourismo
MERCADO LA HUERTA
HOTEL CABAÑAS
RESTAURANTE LA MISIÓN DE KADAKAAMÁN
RENE'S
CALLE HIDALGO
TORTILLERÍA LA MISIÓN
MOTEL LA POSADA
KUYIMÁ
© AVALON TRAVEL   To Laguna San Ignacio

The story of the Misión Nuestra Señor San Ignacio de Kadakaamán (1728–1840) begins with a visit to the arroyo in 1716 by Padre Francisco María Piccolo, who was stationed at the Misión Santa Rosalía de Mulegé. His soldiers built a hut of sticks and leaves to serve as a chapel, and he and Padre Sistiaga returned periodically to visit the indigenous people there over the next 12 years.

In 1728 Padre Juan Bautista de Luyando came to establish a mission. He funded the effort with his own money and lived in San Ignacio for seven years, during which the original chapel became a large adobe church. All that remains of the original structure is a line of foundation stones near the base of the mesa southwest of present-day San Ignacio.

Padre Sebastián de Sistiaga became head of the mission after Luyando and was joined by Padre Consag, who began construction of the stone building that is used today. The project was left incomplete upon his death in 1759, and Padre José Mariano Rotea became the new head of the mission until the Jesuits were expelled in 1768. With 2,000 baptisms recorded as of 1758, the Misión San Ignacio served as a base of Jesuit expansion into Central Baja.

In 1773 the mission passed from the Jesuits to the Franciscans and soon after to the Dominicans, and it was Dominican friar Juan Crisóstomo Gómez who completed the church in 1786, following the original plans of Padre Consag.

With walls more than a meter thick made of local volcanic stone, beams of lumber from the high sierra, and six-meter-high carved doors from mainland Mexico, the church is an impressive sight to see. Decorative stonework frames windows and doors. Inside is an altarpiece made of carved wood and covered with gold leaf. The church was restored beautifully in 1976, and the present-day community holds worship services inside.

MUSEO LOCAL DE SAN IGNACIO

Next to the church, the Instituto Nacional de Antropología e História (INAH) runs a museum (no tel., 8 a.m.–6 p.m. Mon.–Sat., free). Exhibits depict local history, including the rock art of the nearby Sierra de San Francisco. Although the exhibits have Spanish captions, a translated booklet is now available in English. The museum is open on Sundays during high season.

If you're planning a trip to the Sierra de San Francisco to view the cave paintings, stop by the **Unidad de Información y Manejo** (tel. 615/154-0222) next door to get the required permit.

Recreation
HIKING

For a good view of San Ignacio, you can hike a short way to the top of Mesa de la Cruz, which overlooks the town. If you have the time, descend down the other side to cool off in the Río San Ignacio springs. The trail begins behind Casa Lereé.

ORGANIZED TOURS
Servicios Ecoturísticos Kuyimá (Ecoturismo Kuyimá, tel. 615/154-0070, www.kuyima.com)

has an office and small gift shop facing the plaza in the old Bancomer building. Kuyimá specializes in whale-watching tours at nearby Laguna San Ignacio (US$115 pp per day or US$510 for four days/three nights) but can also arrange guided trips into the Sierra de San Francisco to view prehistoric rock art sites (day trips US$120). Kuyimá guides speak Spanish, English, and French.

Baja Expeditions (tel. 612/125-3828, U.S. tel. 800/843-6967, www.bajaex.com) also has an office on the plaza. With decades of experience running low-impact, environmentally focused trips, this outfitter recently merged with Antonio Ecotours to add a daily camping option to its weeklong chartered trips.

Events
The residents of San Ignacio celebrate their town fiesta on July 31 with the usual lineup of traditional Mexican music, food, and games.

Shopping
Casa Lereé (Madero s/n, near the plaza, tel. 615/154-0158) and **Ignacio Springs Bed & Breakfast** (tel. 615/154-0333, www.ignacio-springs.com) both carry a limited selection of English-language books about Baja. Casa Lereé also has arts and crafts made by local artisans. The shop is open 8 A.M. to 2 P.M. and 4–8 P.M. daily.

Accommodations
UNDER US$50
A kilometer south of San Ignacio on the west side of Mexico 1, the longstanding **Baja Oasis Motel** (tel. 615/154-0111, US$30) has 10 air-conditioned rooms. Some have king beds, others have queens or singles. All rooms include purified drinking water and hot showers. The quality of service seems to have slipped noticeably in recent years.

A better option at this price point is the new **Hotel Cabañas** (no tel.), just past the Mercado La Huerta, on the left side of the road as you head toward Laguna San Ignacio. (**Casa Lereé** (tel. 615/154-0158, www.casaleree.com) a single-story colonial near the town plaza, was constructed around 1885 as a family home and became the first guesthouse in San Ignacio

© NIKKI GOTH ITOI

Casa Lereé, just off the plaza in San Ignacio

around 1900. It has served many generations of travelers in the years since. Two small garden rooms (US$40) open onto a shady patio and share a full bath (each now has its own toilet in the room as well); a larger suite (US$75) in the main house has its own bath and anteroom. Gated parking is available. Owner Jane (Juanita) Bames has collected a number of historical sources, articles, and photos, and she offers guests and nonguests a free, self-guided tour through the house (guestrooms excepted). She also has created accurate town and hiking trail maps. Guests can use Wi-Fi inside the main house common area. Pets are okay. No TV or air-conditioning. Cash only. (Stop at an ATM before you get to town, as there are no ATMs in San Ignacio.)

Motel La Posada (tel. 615/154-0313), a few blocks from the central plaza, and **Motelito Fong** (tel. 615/161-8573), at the entrance of town, both offer simple rooms with private bathrooms and secure parking for US$25.

US$50-100

Next to the oasis as you drive toward the town center, Canadian expats Terry and Gary have rebuilt ◖ **Ignacio Springs Bed & Breakfast** (tel. 615/154-0333, www.ignaciosprings.com, US$65–125) little by little since Hurricane Jimena brought flash floods up to the ceiling of their property. Accommodations now include yurts in various sizes, some with private baths and others with shared facilities; one small *palapa casita* next to the river; and two block-style buildings with a shared shower facility. Each yurt is unique in style; for honeymooners, the China Wall yurt features Chinese tapestries, lamps, and silk robes along with a whirlpool bath—for sure the only suite of its kind in Baja. Prices include tax and a big, hearty home-cooked breakfast; credit cards are accepted. Kayaks and skiffs are available for guest use. Ignacio Springs has wireless Internet access for every yurt. Terry and her staff prepare home-cooked dinner for guests and nonguests (reservations required by 2 P.M. for dinner that evening). Her prix fixe menu changes according to what's fresh and in season, but she'll take

special dietary needs and allergies into consideration when planning the meal. The price of US$15–18 includes homemade pie or cake for dessert, and Terry usually has Starbucks coffee on hand to satisfy your espresso craving.

Ricardo's Rice and Beans (tel. 615/154-0283, http://ricardoriceandbeans.googlepages.com), the unofficial stopover for Baja 1000 motorheads, offers big rooms with air-conditioning and wireless Internet for US$50.

About 3.5 kilometers off Mexico 1 on the edge of town, the **Desert Inn** (tel./fax 615/154-0300, toll-free U.S. tel. 800/800-9632, www.desertinns.com, US$85) got a facelift in late 2006. Not much has changed since then. It offers 28 rooms with air-conditioning, plus a restaurant, pool, and billiards room. Rates are highest during the whale-watching season.

CAMPING AND RV PARKS

You can camp at several small campgrounds set in palm groves along the Río de San Ignacio (but beware the bugs). Almost opposite the Desert Inn, **El Padrino RV Park** (tel./fax 615/154-0089) has about 100 sites (20 with hookups). RV sites cost US$18 a night. Tent camping runs US$10 a night. Amenities include a dump station and bar/restaurant. The management arranges whale-watching and cave-painting tours for guests.

Camping Los Petates (no tel.) and **Camping Lakeside** (no tel.) are a step behind in terms of services, but they have the best location facing the river. Sites at Los Petates come with hot showers and electricity, and a small shop has camping supplies. Rates are US$12 for RVs and US$5 per person if you camp.

In addition to its hotel rooms, **Ricardo's Rice and Beans** (tel. 615/154-0283, http://ricardoriceandbeans.googlepages.com) has 20 RV spaces with full hookups and hot showers for US$25; tent sites are US$10.

Food

Palapa restaurant **Rene's** (cell tel. 615/103-0008, around 8 A.M.–9 or 10 P.M. Mon.–Sat., dinner only Sun., mains US$8–12), on the east side of the San Ignacio town plaza, prepares good-value seafood dishes and *antojitos*. If it's not too hot or buggy, you can sit outside under the brick arches for a pleasant outdoor dining experience.

Antojitos Mexicanos Fong (8 A.M.–11 P.M. daily), at the San Ignacio town entrance, has a simple menu featuring fresh ingredients. Nano Fong, who owns the restaurant and attached motel, is an ex-circus performer and marathon unicyclist (and Guinness-record holder); magic tricks and tales of his 50-hour unicycle marathons all over Mexico to raise money for various causes are free with your visit or meal. He is a living piece of Baja history.

Northwest of town, near the highway, **Ricardo's Rice and Beans** (tel. 615/154-0283, http://ricardoriceandbeans.googlepages.com, 7 A.M.–11 P.M. daily, dinner US$5–15, breakfast US$5–15) serves traditional Mexican and seafood dishes; to find it, make a U-turn at the Pemex station and follow the road parallel to the highway four blocks.

On Mexico 1, about three kilometers northwest of town, **Restaurant Quichule** (no tel., 8 A.M.–11 P.M. daily, mains US$5–10) is owned by Rancho El Carricito and uses homegrown meat, milk, and cheese in its dishes. The seafood cocktails and clam cakes are particularly good here.

San Ignacio has a new market in town, **Mercado La Huerta** (no tel.) which stocks a wide variety of supplies and produce. Look for the market on the road to the lagoon, just past the mission. You can find basic supplies at a few other *tiendas* and *miscelaneás* in town. Try **Mercados Mayoral López** (no tel.) or the **Diconsa** (no tel.) next to the Pemex on Mexico 1 for groceries, and **Tortillería La Misión** (near Rene's, just off the plaza, no tel.) for flour tortillas. You can also buy dates at various stands for about US$2 per kilogram.

Getting There

Aguila (tel. 800/824-8452, www.autotransportesaguila.com) and **Autotransportes de Baja California** (ABC, tel. 800/025-0220, www.abc.com.mx) buses stop at the bus terminal (7 A.M.–11 P.M. daily) a half kilometer north of town. There are six buses daily in both directions.

◖ SIERRA DE SAN FRANCISCO ROCK ART

The mountains northeast of San Ignacio hold some of the most spectacular prehistoric paintings found anywhere on the peninsula. It is for this reason that historian Harry W. Crosby described the Sierra de San Francisco as a "gallery of ancient art" and UNESCO designated the region a World Heritage site in 1993.

Getting there, however, takes some planning and a willingness to rough it in the backcountry for at least a couple of days. The Mexican government requires you to obtain a permit and hire a guide before visiting these sites, which you can do at the INAH offices in San Ignacio or La Paz. Then you'll need to make arrangements to travel by mule, bringing your own food and water.

First-time visitors to the Sierra de San Francisco typically head to the Arroyo de San Pablo, where a series of five rock art sites are relatively accessible: Cueva del Ratón, Cueva Pintada, Cueva de las Flechas, Cueva de la Música (Los Músicos), and Boca de San Julio. INAH categorizes all of these sites as Level 2, meaning they are open to any visitor with a permit and guide.

You need at least one night and two days to see Cueva de las Flechas and Cueva Pintada. Departing from San Francisco, on the first morning you'll ride down to the canyon floor, a 360-meter descent, and set up camp, and then visit the caves in the afternoon. On the second day, you'll climb out of the canyon and return to the village.

If you have more time, you can add up to three additional caves in the area to your itinerary: Cueva La Soledad, Cueva La Música, and Boca de San Julio.

San Francisco de la Sierra makes a good starting point for trips to rock art sites in other arroyos, including San Gregorio, El Batequí, and Santa Marta.

Cueva del Ratón

If the idea of camping overnight in the backcountry makes you uncomfortable, you might begin with Cueva del Ratón, a short hike (20 minutes) from the village of San Francisco de la Sierra. This is by far the most accessible rock art site in the Sierra de San Francisco. Measuring 12 meters long, the overhang is among the smaller canvases but nonetheless important for its relative completeness. Images include deer, desert bighorn sheep, rabbits, human figures, and a rare mountain lion. Park in the village near the set of stairs that ascends to the site, but remember to register with INAH and hire a guide in the village before setting out to view the rock art.

Cueva de las Flechas and Cueva Pintada

Two of the most striking cave paintings in all of Baja occupy opposing walls of a deep, palm-filled canyon in the Arroyo San Pablo. If you have just one night to spend in the Sierra de San Francisco, spend it on a trip to Cueva de las Flechas and Cueva Pintada. The setting alone makes it worth the ordeal of getting into the backcountry. And the art you'll see represents some of the most dramatic and best-preserved examples of Baja's prehistoric rock art.

The relatively small canvas of Cueva de las Flechas (Cave of the Arrows) features three large human figures notable for the many black arrows that appear to pierce their bodies. Historian Harry Crosby calls them three of the most elegant monos (human figures) found anywhere. You can see parts of Cueva Pintada (Painted Cave) from Flechas.

A 30-minute scramble over to the other side of the canyon reveals Cueva Pintada, the most well-known and most-visited rock art site in Baja. Discovered in 1962 by mystery writer Erle Stanley Gardner (and also known as Gardner's Cave), the cave features 150 meters of painted walls and ceilings with remarkably well-preserved figures. The back wall alone depicts more than 40 signature red and black images of humans, deer, and sheep.

"This grand cave is the most painted place in the most painted part of the entire range of the Great Murals. It may rightly be considered the focus of the phenomenon," wrote Harry Crosby in his beautiful photography book, *The*

Cave Paintings of Baja California: Discovering the Great Murals of an Unknown People. Other caves in the region are larger, but none rivals the quantity and quality of the art you'll see here.

Getting There

Look for a well-marked turnoff for San Francisco 36 kilometers northwest of San Ignacio. The rocky road climbs into the mountains and meanders along a mesa. Allow about two hours to reach the village at Km. 23.5.

VOLCÁN LAS TRES VIRGENES

Approximately 30 kilometers north of Santa Rosalía, the local *ejidatarios* have come together with the Mexican government (CONANP) as part of the Reserva de la Biósfera to construct bungalows (similar in style and concept to those of Valle de los Cirios) and a lodge, all with breathtaking views of this extinct volcano and surrounding area. Until recently, this part of the interior was inaccessible to most travelers except hunters who stalked the *borrego cimarrón* (desert bighorn sheep). Licensed guides now offer a variety of ecotours, including hikes to the top of the volcano (recommended mid-Oct.–mid-Apr.), tours to Laguna San Ignacio for whale-watching (Dec.–Mar.), hikes throughout the surrounding area to view the *borregos,* and tours to the cave paintings of the Sierra de San Francisco.

Simple cabanas provide visitors a chance to experience true desert tranquility. Interested visitors should contact Juan Villa Vicencio or Marcial Landeros Valdez (tel. 615/155-4241, desertsheep5@yahoo.com) ahead of time, or those with open travel plans should drive in and be prepared to stay or move on.

◖ LAGUNA SAN IGNACIO

If you've come to Baja in the winter to witness the gray-whale calving, the protected Laguna San Ignacio on the Pacific coast is a must-see destination. Discovered by whalers in 1860, Laguna San Ignacio is 58 kilometers from the town of San Ignacio and measures about 26

© NIIKKI GOTH ITOI

view of Volcán Las Tres Virgenes from the highway heading north

kilometers long and 8 kilometers wide. Along with the Vizcaíno Desert, it became part of the Reserva de la Biósfera in 1988. About 100 people live beside the bay and make their living from fishing and, increasingly, ecotourism. A major saltworks expansion effort was blocked recently by environmentalists.

Only two other bays, Laguna de Ojo Liebre to the north and Bahía de Magdalena to the south, offer comparable experiences for ecotourists. And for some reason, the whales here tend to come closer to boats and show off more for their audiences than at the other two sanctuaries (which is not to say that having an opportunity to touch one is a given).

To see the whales by boat, you need to hire a licensed *panguero*. There are two ways to do this: You can buy an all-inclusive package tour, which depart from San Ignacio or Loreto by ground transport or from as far away as San Diego via charter plane. Independent travelers may prefer to drive directly to the bay and purchase boat fare "à la carte" from one of several outfitters (US$40 pp, min. usually four people).

Boats typically depart at 9 A.M. and stay out for 3–4 hours. It's about a 60- to 90-minute drive from the town of San Ignacio to the camps (locals make it in 45 minutes), so day-trippers need to get an early start. Stop by the plaza in San Ignacio to arrange taxi service to the lagoon for around US$60 per person each way. (The larger the group, the lower the cost per person.)

At the south end of Laguna San Ignacio, a peninsula sticks out into the mouth of the bay close the main calving area. This can be a good vantage point from which to see the whales. With four-wheel drive, you can drive to the point; alternatively, a *panga* driver can also shuttle you there from one of the camps at the north end of the bay.

Two dirt roads connect Laguna San Ignacio to Bahía San Juanico: One leaves from the Kuyimá camp and traverses the Mesa Las Salinas, close to the coast, but may not be passable at high tide. The more reliable route is a continuation of the San Ignacio-Laguna San Ignacio road, and passes through several inland villages on the way to San Juanico.

GUERRERO NEGRO

© NIKKI GOTH ITOI

Several whale camps line the shores of Laguna San Ignacio.

Getting There

Laguna San Ignacio is 59 km from the plaza, and the whale camps are another 10–20 minutes past the point where the road meets the lagoon. The road to the lagoon is newly paved for the first 23 km, and this stretch is in better condition than the highway. After Km. 23, it becomes a graded dirt road the rest of the way. You may be able to make the trip in a standard sedan, but inquire about the conditions first. Loose rocks and sand drifts pose complications for low-clearance vehicles. Locals manage to complete the drive in about 45 minutes, but first-timers and more conservative motorists should count on one hour to 90 minutes. When you reach the lagoon, follow the road to the left, and note the sign for information if you need directions to a specific camp. Most of the camps have signs pointing the way, but it can be somewhat confusing the first time you venture out toward the point.

Whale-Watching Tours and Camping

A handful of outfitters offer whale-watching tours and trips January–April. Water and power are precious commodities at all the camps at

the lagoon, so it's important to reduce, reuse, and recycle at every opportunity.

With more than 35 years' experience running environmentally focused tours to Baja, **Baja Expeditions** (2625 Garnet Ave., San Diego, tel. 858/581-3311 or 800/843-6967, www.bajaex.com) offers a memorable catered-camping experience. Its camp has upgraded facilities following the merger with Antonio Ecotours. Guests on chartered trips stay in simple cabañas made of plywood and sleep on comfortable beds (full, queen, or two twins) with duvet covers, soft pillows, and cotton sheets. Each bungalow has a sink and tiled counter, and closet area, plus a small porch with two camp chairs. The bungalows are right on the beach, so you'll enjoy a front row seat for watching whales, birds, and other wildlife activity on the lagoon. When large groups or additional overnight visitors come to the camp, additional lodging is provided in safari-style tents equipped with cots, camp chairs, and lanterns. Every three tents share a toilet and hand-washing sink.

Family-style meals are a highlight of the experience here. Some of the standouts include a bay scallop ceviche called *aguachile*, fried flounder, tostadas with shredded beef *(machaca)*, and *chilaquiles.* Guests and staff dine together in a *palapa* lounge with two large tables, a comfortable sofa, fabulous library of books about Baja and gray whales, and computer for Internet access (no large file downloads due to limited bandwidth). Coffee, tea, soft drinks, beer, purified water, and baked treats are available anytime free of charge. When not on a boat looking for whales, visitors relax in the hammock, walk the beach, read in the library, play with the camp dogs, or sit by the fire and gaze at the stars. Guides are all trained in water safety/emergency rescue and knowledgeable about the local marine life.

Shared toilet facilities are outhouse style (and wheelchair accessible), so you need to rinse with a small bucket of water or scoop some sawdust each time you go. Solar showers are hot as long as the sun is shining. The entire camp is powered by sun, wind, and, when needed, diesel generator.

The overnight rate of US$210 per person per night, with a two-night minimum, includes two *panga* boat rides a day and all meals and drinks. Five-day packages cost US$2,395 per person based on double occupancy and include transportation from San Diego via chartered bus and a two-hour flight from Tijuana direct to the lagoon.

With an office in town and a camp close to the south end of the bay, **Ecoturismo Kuyimá** (Morelos 23, San Ignacio, tel. 615/154-0070, www.kuyima.com) is a full-service operation. Its campground has hot-water showers, composting outhouses, and a *palapa*-roofed dining area. Accommodations are either in one of 30 tent sites (US$12/night without the whale-watching package) or 10 cabins. If you don't have your own camping gear, you can rent a two-person tent, sleeping bags, and flashlights for US$40. Meals cost US$7–10. Best of all, you can often see the whale action from the shore.

For travelers who can get themselves to San Ignacio, Kuyimá's multiday packages are a good deal, especially when compared to the San Diego–based all-inclusive trips. For example, a four-day/three-night trip costs US$495 per person for cabin lodging, meals, and daily whale-watching excursions. Guests have use of bicycles, kayaks, a library, and video services. The packages include a trip to nearby salt fields and the expertise of the company's knowledgeable guides. Van transportation is available to or from San Ignacio for an additional US$120 for up to 10 people.

Near the mouth of the bay and even closer to the action, **Baja Discovery** (U.S. tel. 619/262-0700 or 800/829-2252, www.bajadiscovery.com) has run a safari-style camp for more than 25 years. Its strategic location on Rocky Point gives visitors front-row seats to the show—in season, whales will spout and spyhop right offshore. The downside for budget-conscious travelers is that to stay here, you must buy an all-inclusive package that starts and finishes in San Diego (US$2,395 pp for five days).

Santa Rosalía and Vicinity

Though it's not a top destination for most travelers, Santa Rosalía (pop. 9,700) leaves a lasting impression on those who do pass through. The reason is twofold: First, for drivers headed south on Highway 1, this former silver-mining hub is the first town you reach on the Sea of Cortez. After many hours of desert and mountain vistas, you'll likely never forget that first glimpse of ocean blue and the rapid descent to the water's edge.

Second, besides its proximity to the sea, the buildings in Santa Rosalía look very different from the rest of Baja. In contrast to the Spanish influence that dominates the peninsula, the colonial architecture here is distinctly French, thanks to the influence of a French mining company called El Boleo, which set up shop here in the 19th century and operated until 1954. Many of the original wood-frame houses are still intact. A famous French bakery and metal

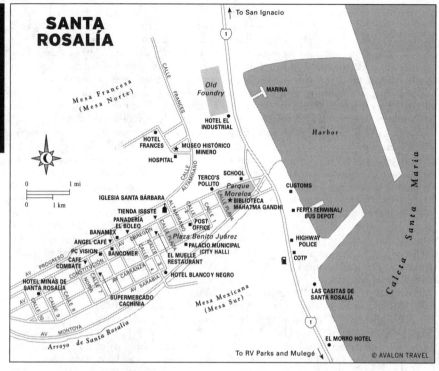

church, supposedly designed by none other than Gustave Eiffel, complete the effect.

Crowded into the mouth of a deep arroyo, the town's main commercial area runs perpendicular to the sea, with high mesa walls on either side. Old mining equipment and machinery still are visible in many places around town.

Today Santa Rosalía serves as a government and business hub for central Baja as well as a convenient place for travelers to stock up on supplies. A public library in Parque Morelos displays photos from the town's historic mining days.

If you visit June–October, be prepared for extremely hot temperatures. The town's waterfront promenade, or *malecón,* is a good place to catch an afternoon breeze.

HISTORY

Local ranchers first discovered copper deposits (called *boleos*) in the hills surrounding present-day Santa Rosalía in the late 1800s, and a French company bought rights to mine the area in 1884 and built the town that survives today. The infrastructure included 600 kilometers of tunnels, a large copper-smelting foundry, pier, and 30-kilometer mine railway.

By 1934 El Boleo had mined and smelted 14 million tons of copper ore. By the 1950s, the company's outdated process made the business unsustainable and El Boleo sold its facilities back to the Mexican government. A state-owned concern reopened the operation (without modernizing it) and ran it until the 1980s, when it was finally closed for good. But the story doesn't end there.

In 1992 the current management of Baja Mining Corp. briefly took control. After a decade of restructurings and changes of ownership, the mine returned to the same management team in 2001. Armed with more

© NIKKI GOTH ITOI

Santa Rosalía's harbor

advanced technology, deep pockets (US$962 million in funding to date), and agreements with the Mexican government and local *ejido,* Vancouver-based Baja Mining (www.bajamining.com) intends to extract value from the area's mineral deposits, including copper, cobalt, and zinc, once again.

The company has about 200 people on-site already, with a workers' camp, desalination plant, and cacti-relocation program in progress. Production—estimated at 56,000 tons of copper cathode, 1,500 tons of cobalt cathode, and 20,000 tons of zinc sulphate—is due to begin in 2010, with an expected life of 25 years.

SIGHTS
Iglesia Santa Bárbara de Santa Rosalía

Unlike the Spanish missions scattered across the peninsula, Santa Rosalía's church is a simple structure made almost entirely of metal. Long said to have been designed by French architect Gustave Eiffel for use in the country's African colonies, the origins of this unusual

church came into question in the 1990s and the true history remains a mystery. According to the Eiffel story, the church was exhibited at the 1889 Paris World Exposition, forgotten in a Brussels warehouse, and then rediscovered by an El Boleo manager, who had it shipped to Baja.

Today the local community uses the church for worship.

Mesa Francesa (Mesa Norte)

The mesa on the north side of town holds several well-preserved examples of French colonial architecture, including the **Hotel Frances** (Don Gaspar 210, tel./fax 615/152-2052) and, across from the hospital, the **Museo Histórico Minero de Santa Rosalía** (off Frances Altamirano, tel. 615/153-0471, 8 A.M.–2 P.M. and 5–7 P.M. Mon.–Sat., US$1.30), with exhibits that depict the town's mining past.

To get to the mesa from the town center, you can climb an old set of stairs from the Iglesia Santa Bárbara or follow Calle Altamirano.

FESTIVALS AND EVENTS

Santa Rosalía celebrates **Carnaval,** usually in mid-February, and the annual **Fiesta de Santa Rosalía,** is held around September 4 in honor of patron saint Santa Rosalía. A **founder's day celebration** also occurs in mid-October.

ACCOMMODATIONS
Under US$50

Housed in one of the town's mining-era wooden buildings, the **Hotel Blanco y Negro** (Sarabia at Calle 3, tel. 615/152-0080, US$18–30) has been a favorite among budget travelers for many years for basic, clean rooms with private baths. **Terco's Pollito** (Obregón at Calle Playa, opposite Parque Morelos, tel. 615/152-0075, US$35) has seven rooms, with air-conditioning and cable TV; its reception area is inside the adjoining restaurant (7 A.M.–7 P.M. daily). Two-hundred meters from the ferry terminal on Highway 1, **Hotel El Industrial** (tel. 615/152-1857, US$40) has safe parking, rooms with air-conditioning and cable TV, and 24-hour reception. **Hotel del Real** (Montoya 7, no tel.), is another good option for an overnight stop near the ferry terminal. New rooms on the back side of the building have air-conditioning and TV for US$35.

The business-oriented **⟨ El Morro Hotel** (tel./fax 615/152-0414, hotelmorro@aol.com, US$50) overlooks the Sea of Cortez about 1.5 kilometers south of town on Mexico 1 (btw Km. 194/195). Its 39 spacious rooms feature ocean views and remote-control air-conditioning, and there's secure parking, a restaurant/bar, and swimming pool. Wireless Internet, included in the price, is available in the lobby area. This place is pet friendly.

US$50-100

At the edge of a cliff that drops into the sea, **Las Casitas de Santa Rosalía** (tel. 615/152-3023, mariahsantarosalia@hotmail.com, US$60–70) has several modern cottages, plus a well-equipped gym, wireless Internet, and a terrace that overlooks the harbor.

In a French colonial building, the **Hotel Frances** (Don Gaspar 210, tel./fax 615/152-

2052, US$75) overlooks the old copper-smelting facility on Mesa Norte. Its 17 rooms have high ceilings, cable TV, wireless Internet, and air-conditioning. There is a small pool in the courtyard and the hotel restaurant is open daily for breakfast only. Coffee only on Sundays.

FOOD

Santa Rosalía has a handful of busy restaurants—several with outdoor seating—plus a number of tempting taco stands. Most of these establishments line Avenida Obregón. **Restaurant Terco's Pollito** (Obregón at Calle Playa, opposite Parque Morelos, tel. 615/152-0075, 8 A.M.–10 P.M. daily, mains US$5–7) does barbecued chicken right, and it's air-conditioned.

Several vendors sell tacos from carts around town. But at **Pavarotti's Tacos** (Obregén btw the church and the El Boleo bakery, no tel., lunch and dinner daily) there are stools from which one can enjoy the town's bustle for much the same price as other taco stands.

El Muelle Restaurant Bar (Calle 9 and the plaza, tel. 615/152-0931, 8 A.M.–11 P.M. daily) is a good spot for breakfast, seafood (US$9–14), or pizza ($9–12). Outdoor seating is a plus during cooler weather.

Angel Café (Calle 5, off Obregón, no tel.) prepares tasty *tortas,* plus burgers and breakfasts for US$3–5. **Café Combate** (Obregón btw Calles 5/6, no tel., 8 A.M.–1 P.M. and 3–6 P.M. Mon.–Fri., 8 A.M.–2 P.M. Sat.) has espresso drinks.

The government-subsidized **Super ISSSTE Tienda** (Obregón at Calle 3) is a dependable option for groceries and supplies.

A longtime favorite among locals and travelers alike, **Panadería El Boleo** (Obregón at Calle 4, tel. 615/152-0310, 8 A.M.–9 P.M. Mon.–Sat.) has been trumped by the newer Panadería Angel, on the mesa near the Hotel Frances and the museum.

For fresh flour tortillas, head to **Tortillería Santa Agueda** (Obregón near Calle 6, just west of the Bancomer, no tel.). **Tortillería Ranchería** (no tel.) near the west end of Obregón, makes corn tortillas.

At Constitución and Calle Noria is the well-stocked **Minisuper Delya** (no tel., 6 A.M.–9:30 P.M. Mon.–Sat., 7 A.M.–2:30 P.M. Sun.), whose vividly painted walls depict a bountiful harvest.

INFORMATION AND SERVICES

Bancomer and Banamex both have branches and ATMs on Obregón (8:30 A.M.–3 P.M. Mon.–Fri.).

Santa Rosalía's **post office** (no tel.) is located east of the plaza at Calle 2 and Avenida Constitución. You can use a public phone on the south side of the plaza for local and long-distance calls, and there are several TelMex Ladatel card phones along Obregón and elsewhere around town.

Head to **PC Vision** (corner of Obregón and Calle 6, tel. 615/152-2875, 10 A.M.–10 P.M. daily, US$2/hour) or air-conditioned **Dr PC** (Obregon and Calle Plaza, 10 A.M.–10 P.M. daily, US$1.50/hour) for Internet service.

For repairs and supplies, there is a hardware store (tel. 615/152-1234) on the east side of the plaza and a **Go4Value** (Calle 5 and Constitución, no tel.) discount store with food, cleaning supplies, and paper goods.

GETTING THERE

Domestic air service may be available from Palo Verde Airport (PVP) in San Bruno. At last check, Aéreo Servicio Guerrero (www.aereoserviciosguerrero.com.mx) was operating regular flights as well as an air taxi service between Baja and Hermosillo, Sonora, on the mainland. Daily flights are available from Guaymas and twice a week from Hermosillo, Sonora.

Santa Rosalía's **intercity bus depot** has moved to the ferry terminal. Several buses a day travel north to San Ignacio, Guerrero Negro, San Quintín, Ensenada, Mexicali, and Tijuana as well as south to Mulegé, Loreto, and La Paz.

A word of caution about filling up in Santa Rosalía: The Pemex station near the ferry terminal on Mexico 1 has long been known for scamming tourists. Watch the pump and count your change, or, better yet, fill up in San Ignacio or Mulegé instead.

Inside the harbor, **Marina Santa Rosalía** (tel./fax 615/152-0011) rents 20 moorings and sells fuel. Also here are the port captain, immigration, and customs offices.

SAN LUCAS COVE

The protected cove of San Lucas offers campers and travelers in small boats shelter from winter's northerly winds (small boats only, due to the shallow entrance).

Camping

This is the closest camping you can find to Santa Rosalía, 15 kilometers to the north, and it's a pleasant site. Access is via a sandy road that heads east from the highway.

San Lucas Cove RV Park (no tel.) and **Camacho RV Park** (no tel.) both offer campsites for US$7 per vehicle (no hookups). Facilities at the former include hot showers, a dump station, and a boat ramp.

SAN BRUNO

Thirty-two kilometers north of Loreto, Bahía San Bruno served as a launch pad for the first Spanish land expedition that sought to evaluate the Baja Peninsula for colonization. Padre Eusebio Francisco Kino and Admiral Isidro de Atondo y Antillón arrived in 1683 with a group of 50 soldiers and 100 loyal indigenous people from mainland Mexico and set up camp along this bay. Although they never established a permanent mission, they used the site as a base from which to explore the interior of the peninsula. And through these early efforts, they identified the future sites of the Comondú and La Purísima missions.

Modern-day San Bruno is a quaint fishing community with seemingly more *pangas* than residents. A new harbor and paved boat ramp were completed in 2006 with state government funding. This town also makes a good starting point for a trip to dive or fish around Isla San Marcos. Head to the harbor to charter a boat.

San Bruno celebrates its town festival in early October.

Services include gas from a drum, a bus stop, and a couple of *abarrotes* stores.

Accommodations
With prior experience at the Hotel Serenidad in Mulegé and Punta Chivato, Alberto Carrillo runs the first and only hotel in town. The new **Hotel Costa Serena** (tel. 615/153-9022, US$35) has a half dozen air-conditioned rooms in a single-story building facing the sandy beach. Each room is individually appointed with antique furnishings and named for one of Alberto's uncles. White bathrobes are a plus. Alberto has added a restaurant and spa, and his nephew offers *panga* tours to Isla San Marcos.

Getting There
To get to San Bruno, look for a turnoff on Highway 1 at Km. 173, north of the turnoff to San José de Magdalena.

ISLA SAN MARCOS
Directly offshore from San Bruno is a small island of San Marcos, known for abundant gypsum deposits and proximity to prime yellowtail fishing. Like Santa Rosalía, this is a company-built town. About 700 people live and work for the mining company, which has been in business since 1923 and for many years has been the top producer of gypsum in North America. The town's gypsum-block church was built in 1954.

There are no hotels and limited supplies on the island, available from one general store and a few *tiendas*. The island also has cell phone service and Internet.

Diving and Snorkeling
Head to Punta Piedra Blanca at the northwest end of the island for the best diving and snorkeling. On the east side, Punta Gorda and Punta La Chiva are also good sites to explore. Mulegé-based **Cortez Explorers** (www.cortez-explorers.com) runs boat trips to Isla San Marcos for US$110–135. Michael Hans Kanzler, a.k.a. **Isla San Marcos Mike** (cell tel. 415/244-8451, www.islasanmarcos.com) has run sportfishing charters on the island for

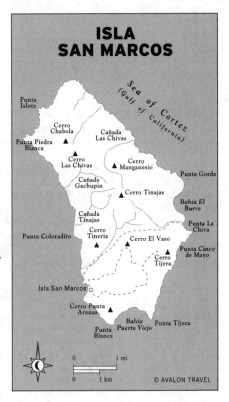

nearly 20 years. Rates are US$225 for trips around Isla San Marcos and US$275 for trips to nearby Isla Tortugas. Prices cover up to three people for a half day, starting at dawn and ending in the early afternoon. Rates are US$25 less for dive charters to the same destinations.

Getting There
The best way to get to Isla San Marcos is to hire a *panguero* at the harbor in San Bruno.

NORTHERN SIERRA DE GUADALUPE
South of San Ignacio and Santa Rosalía and west of Mulegé, the Sierra de Guadalupe rises to 1,200- to 1,500-meter peaks in a stretch of mountains that measures 128 kilometers long and 30–48 kilometers wide. The Jesuits

found the terrain suitable for mission life and the Misión Nuestra Señora de Guadalupe de Huasinapi operated from 1720 until 1795 as one of the most remote settlements on the peninsula. And in the early 20th century, mining company El Boleo bought and established numerous ranches throughout the northern part of the range to support its growing community of workers.

Two scenic roads leave the highway near San Bruno, heading into the mountains, but you'll need four-wheel drive to negotiate the twists and turns and rocks along the way. At Km. 188, south of the state prison, a 12-kilometer graded road heads west to **Santa Agueda.**

Local ranchers may be available to guide you to some of the closer cave painting sites, such as La Candelaria, San Antonio, or Los Gatos; however, you'll need to arrange for a permit in San Ignacio before you go.

The second access road leaves Mexico 1 at Km. 169, south of San Bruno, and leads to the remote farming community of **San José de Magdalena,** 14 kilometers west. After San José, the road continues another 48 kilometers to several ranchos and the mission ruins. There is little to see at the former mission site except parts of the foundation and adobe walls. This three-hour journey is best left to serious mission trail travelers.

Mulegé and Vicinity

Southbound travelers notice a distinct change in climate as they approach the mission town of Mulegé (pop. 3,300) on the Sea of Cortez. Temperatures and humidity climb to a tropical feel, and mosquitoes are ever present. Built alongside the mouth of the Río Santa Rosalía (also known as the Mulegé River), the town consists of a small network of narrow streets lined with colonial buildings. Agriculture, tourism, and fishing support the modern-day community. With its variety of restaurants, accommodations, and services, the town serves as a stopover for some and a destination in its own right for others.

In the last five years, Mulegé has experienced several devastating blows to its economy: two hurricanes (John in 2006 and Jimema in 2009) caused severe flash flooding that badly damaged many buildings around town. In between these events, drug wars at the border, the global slowdown in travel, and the swine flu epidemic all have conspired against this tropical outpost.

Although business have reopened, the recovery is slow-going and the town seemed almost deserted even in the peak winter season.

Though small in scale, Mulegé seems to have at least one of everything. There are laundry machines, auto mechanics and parts stores, grocery stores and minimarkets, restaurants, hotels, and campgrounds—and even a dive shop. And Mulegé offers enough water and land activities to keep you busy for a week or more.

SIGHTS
Misión Santa Rosalía de Mulegé
One of the earliest missions (1705–1828) established by the Jesuits in Baja California, the Misión Santa Rosalía de Mulegé was founded in 1705 by Padre Juan Manuel de Basaldúa. In 1770 a flood destroyed much of the original settlement on the Río Santa Rosalía, and the church was moved to a bluff overlooking the river. The mission continued to be active until 1828. The missions at San Ignacio and San Javier may be more elegant, but Mulegé's restored church offers great views of the town and river.

To find the church, follow Calle Zaragoza southwest under the highway bridge and then turn right to ascend the bluff by the church, about three kilometers from the bridge. It is usually locked, except when in use for services.

Museo Regional de Historia

The former town prison, on a hill that over-looks town, has been converted into a local museum (no tel., hours vary, by donation) with a small collection of historical artifacts, including a desk used by mystery writer Erle Stanley Gardner, who researched many of central Baja's rock art sites.

Playa El Sombrerito

The Mulegé River meets the Sea of Cortez at Playa El Sombrerito, forming a large estuary that supports a wide variety of marine birds. Sea views are especially dramatic at daybreak. There are a couple of restaurants and a few places to stay near the beach.

SPORTS AND RECREATION

Mulegé offers adventure travelers a full lineup of activities, both on land and in the sea.

Diving and Snorkeling

As the Sea of Cortez becomes more tropical, the underwater environment becomes more colorful and full of warm-water life. Green moray eels poke their heads out of rocky crevices; angelfish, damselfish, and parrot fish school along the reefs, while red, spiny Cortez, and slipper lobster hide in dark caves. Visibility and water temperatures are best June–November; it's not uncommon to see 30 meters at depth with temperatures of 30°C during these months. Bring or rent a full wetsuit for winter diving; in summer a Lycra dive skin is a good idea to protect against jellyfish.

The three rocky outcroppings known as **Islas Santa Inés** offer divers and snorkelers an opportunity to observe playful sea lions, schools of anchovies, and a variety of marine life along a shallow reef. Divers can explore the boulder fields below. Farther afield, **Bahía Concepción** has more diving and snorkeling sites, including **Pelican Reef, Isla Santispac, Isla Guapa, Isla Requesón,** and **Roca Frijole.**

Cortez Explorers (Moctezuma 75A, tel./fax 615/153-0500, www.cortez-explorers.com) has attained the highest level of PADI certification that a dive center can earn and offers a full-service operation. You can rent gear, fill tanks, take classes, and charter boats at the shop. A one-tank guided boat dive trip costs US$70, and a two-tank trip costs US$110. Guided shore dives cost less (US$50 and US$90, respectively). Snorkeling gear rents for US$21 per day. Credit cards are accepted. A two-tank dive to Isla San Marcos or Isla Santa Inés costs US$135. Stop in 10 A.M.–1 P.M. and 4–7 P.M. Monday–Saturday.

Kayaking
Paddlers can launch kayaks along the estuary for trips north to Bahía Santa Inés or south to Bahía Concepción; however, if Concepción is your target destination, there are better places to put in farther south. In a challenging five- to seven-day trip, you can paddle from Mulegé all the way to Loreto, 135 kilometers away. This trip is best attempted with an experienced guide or outfitter.

Fishing
Las Casitas (tel. 615/153-0019) and **Hotel Serenidad** (tel. 615/153-0530, www.hotelserenidad.com) can arrange sportfishing charters to Punta Chivato, Bahía Concepción, and nearby islands (US$180 per day in a *panga* for up to three people or US$200 per day for a five-person cruiser). For the best onshore fishing, head to the south side of the estuary, where you might catch yellowtail, roosterfish,

mackerel, or red snapper in winter; offshore catches in summer include dorado, yellowfin, and various billfish.

Organized Tours
Salvador Castro Drew (tel. 615/153-0232, cell tel. 615/103-5081, mulegetours@hotmail.com) offers guided cave-painting tours delivered in flawless English for US$40 per person, plus an additional fee charged by the rancho through which visitors must pass to get to the rock art site (US$7–10). Salvador can customize tours to include two of the following sites: Piedras Pintas, San Patricio, or La Trinidad; or he can cover all three in one day for a slightly higher fee. He also takes visitors to San Borjita, but this site requires a full day without time to see the other caves.

Salvador will pick you up in his air-conditioned van and share his knowledge of local natural and cultural history during the day. The standard tour includes stops at a local orchard, a rancho, and then the cave sites in La Trinidad. Participants need to bring photo ID to register at the INAH office and should also have good walking shoes, a hat, sunblock, camera, and water.

Salvador also leads walking tours through the towns of Mulegé (US$10), Santa Rosalía, and San Ignacio. And he can arrange bird-watching, clamming in Bahía Concepción, snorkeling, and sportfishing outings. Overnight trips include cave paintings in the Sierra Guadalupe and whale-watching at Laguna San Ignacio. Airport transportation is also available. If you don't reach Salvador by phone, inquire at **Hotel Las Casitas** (Madero 50, tel. 615/153-0019), on the town's main east-west street. As Mulegé's only guide certified to conduct all these tours, Salvador is highly respected around town.

ENTERTAINMENT
Hotel Las Casitas (Madero 50, on the town's main east–west street, tel. 615/153-0019) has invited *norteña* bands to play on Fridays and mariachis on Saturdays for many years. The small disco bar, **Danny Boy,** next to Tacos

Doney, on the Mexico 1 access road, opens 9 P.M.–3 A.M. on the weekends. Four kilometers east of town, off Mexico 1, the **Hotel Serenidad** (tel. 615/153-0530, www.hotelserenidad.com) hosts a pig roast with mariachis on Saturday nights.

SHOPPING

A general store in the truest sense, **La Tienda** (Martínez and Zaragoza, no tel., 9 A.M.–1 P.M. and 3–6 P.M. Mon.–Sat.) stocks fishing tackle and charts, books about Baja, gifts, swimsuits, wetsuits, and more. The Ladetel phone inside is a good place for a relatively quiet conversation. Credit cards are accepted as long as the power is on.

Adolfo's Tienda (Zaragoza across from Plaza Corona, no tel.) has a good selection of souvenirs, including hammocks and decorative crafts. **Curios Lupita's** (Martinez at Zaragoza, no tel.) specializes in crafts and wearable souvenirs such as sarongs and T-shirts. Several other curio shops remain open despite the drop in visitors to buy them.

ACCOMMODATIONS

Mulegé offers several choices in modest and budget hotels, plus a few bed-and-breakfasts and places to camp as well. Just about every hotel in town now offers free wireless Internet service to guests; however, some have Wi-Fi only in their reception areas.

Under US$50

Centrally located on Mulegé's main east–west street, the ever-popular **Hotel Las Casitas** (Madero 50, tel. 615/153-0019, fax 615/153-0190, US$35–55) once belonged to Mexican poet Vicente Gorosave. Its eight basic rooms have air-conditioning, and there is a pleasant patio restaurant on-site. No off-street parking.

Hotel Squid (tel. 615/153-0351, US$35–45) is located just around the corner from Minita's Internet. Its nine clean, modern rooms encircle a private parking area.

At the entrance to town, **Hotel Mulegé** (tel. 615/153-0090, US$44) offers clean rooms with air-conditioning, SKY TV, and parking.

On the south side of the river and about two kilometers east of town at Km. 132, the **Hotel Cuesta Real** (tel./fax 615/153-0321, US$39–59) has 12 air-conditioned rooms. An archway adorns the turnoff from the highway. Amenities include a small swimming pool, restaurant/bar, and laundry service. The hotel can make arrangements for fishing and cave-painting trips and tours. Credit cards are accepted.

US$50-100

Farther east along on the south side of the river, Mulegé's largest and best-known inn caters to fly-in guests. The **Hotel Serenidad** (tel. 615/153-0530, www.hotelserenidad.com, US$65–120) has 50 rooms, several two-bedroom cottages (with a/c and parking), and nicely laid-out grounds. Wi-Fi is available in the restaurant. Amenities include a pool and boat ramp. Its Saturday night all-you-can-eat pig roast with mariachis (US$14) is a famous Baja tradition.

Near the Oasis Rio RV Park on the south side of the river, ■ **Clementine's Inn** (www.clementinesbaja.com, US$50–65/night or US$205–355/week) has the most comfortable beds in Baja in this price range. Owners Cliff and Judith, who also run a top-rated bed-and-breakfast on the Oregon Coast, made a speedy recovery after both floods, with all-new beds, linens, appliances, and artwork for their guest accommodations. Four rooms and several *casitas* achieve a unique balance between upscale bed-and-breakfast (luxurious sheets, tiled baths, stylish light fixtures, extra towels, tea lights) and authentic Baja (wood-paneled ceilings, basic faucets, abalone shells for soap dishes). Rooms are decorated in warm colors and set around a large, well-equipped open-air kitchen, thoughtfully designed with the culinary enthusiast in mind. Appliances include a large refrigerator, double toaster, coffeemaker, and ice machine. A Weber gas grill, bottled water, and bug screens for covering prepared food are also provided. *Casitas* range in size from a studio to three bedrooms (US$90–160/night and US$450–800/week), and there is free wireless Internet. Prices vary by unit, and advance reservations are requested.

Closer to the sea, **Casa Granada** (Estero de Mulegé 1, tel. 615/153-0500, www.casagranada.net, US$75–85/night) has the most luxurious rooms in town. Its four rooms occupy a stone building with high ceilings, tiled baths, Talavera sinks, and remote-control air-conditioning. Guests enjoy sea views and a private setting along the estuary.

Vacation Rentals

Orchard Vacation Village (south side of Rio Mulegé, close to the highway, tel. 615/153-0516, www.bajalife.com/orchard, *casitas* $45–95) transformed itself after the 2006 floods. It now consists of a neighborhood of well-designed houses varying in size and amenities, sold individually and managed by the on-site office as rentals.

Camping and RV Parks

Shaded campsites for tents (US$7.50 pp) are a plus at **Villa María Isabel RV Park** (south of town, off Mexico 1, tel. 615/153-0246). It also has 30 RV campsites with full hookups for US$20. Rates include hot showers and the use of a swimming pool. The campground is located east of the highway and south of the river.

Across the river, near Playa El Sombrerito, **Huerta Don Chano's** (no tel.) offers RV and tent campsites at similar prices. **Hotel Serenidad** (tel. 615/153-0530, www.hotelserenidad.com) has 15 RV sites with hookups for US$12 for two people, US$2 per additional person.

The majority of campers spend part of a day exploring Mulegé and restocking supplies but set up camp farther south along Bahía Concepción, where the scenery is prettier and bugs are less of a nuisance.

FOOD
Restaurants

Mulegé's restaurants serve reasonably priced meals in an authentic setting. Don't be dissuaded by an empty dining room during off-peak months; the food is reliable anytime of year.

Second-story **Los Equipales** (Moctezuma, tel. 615/153-0330, 7:30 A.M.–10:30 P.M. daily,

mains US$10–23) overlooks a busy street and serves the best Mexican and seafood dishes around. The name refers to a type of leather-and-wood chairs that are part of the restaurant's decor.

On the south side of the river, past Clementine's Inn, **Jungle Jim** (no tel., lunch and dinner Mon.–Sat., mains US$6–12) feels a bit like an eating club, with regulars helping themselves to drinks at the bar. Decent burgers and seafood are the mainstays of a changing menu.

Popular among tourists, the restaurants at **Las Casitas** (tel. 615/153-0019, 6:30 A.M.–9:30 P.M. daily, breakfast mains US$4–6, dinner mains US$9–17) and **Hotel Serenidad** (tel. 615/153-0530, www.hotelserenidad.com, 6:30 A.M.–9:30 P.M. daily, mains US$5) offer moderately priced Mexican fare. The garden patio at Hotel Serenidad is a pleasant place to enjoy a signature daiquiri. Las Casitas also does a Friday night Mexican buffet with live music for US$10 during the high season.

Two places are worth a special trip to the beach to dine: On the beach where the road meets Playa El Sombrerito, the 21-year-old **El Patrón** (no tel., lunch and dinner daily, mains US$5–10) offers a complete menu of Mexican and seafood specialties. **Casa de Pancho Villa** (no tel., breakfast, lunch, and dinner daily, mains US$5–10), just a few steps away on the road to the beach, is newer and funkier. Both are reasonably priced and open daily and have spectacular views of the estuary and beach area.

Antojitos, Tacos, and Fast Food

Mulegé has several good taco stands. Try the *tacos de carne asada* or a quesadilla at **Asadero Dany's** (Romero Rubio, no tel., 8 A.M.–4 P.M. Thurs.–Tues). Better yet, **Tacos Doney Mely's** (no tel., 7:30 A.M.–10 P.M. Wed.–Mon., US$9–20), on Calle Moctezuma, across from the Hotel Mulegé, makes great tacos and even better *carnes* and seafood.

Taquitos Mulegé (Plaza Corona, no tel., 9 A.M.–1 P.M. daily) serves the best fish tacos in town. Right next door, **Mr. Pizza** (no tel.,

5–11 P.M. daily in summer, 3–11 P.M. daily in winter, 12" pizza US$10, 14" pizza US$15) offers pizza with additional toppings included in the price, as well as side portions of spaghetti and salad.

Eduardo's (Moctezuma, no tel., US$9–15) bakes pizza 6:30–11 P.M. Monday–Wednesday and Friday–Saturday but changes the menu on Sunday to prepare family-style Chinese food.

Several ice cream shops sell *nieve* (Mexican-style no-milk ice cream) and *paletas*.

Groceries

Among the town's *tiendas*, you'll find the widest selection of foods—both locally grown and some prepared—at **Casa Yee** (Madero 46, near Las Casitas, tel. 615/115-3018), **Abarrotes El Pingüino** (on the access road to/from the highway, near Hotel Mulegé), and **Mercado Alba** (on Plaza Corona, tel. 615/153-0030, 8 A.M.–9 P.M. daily). With advanced notice, **Saul's Tienda** (on Calle Madero where it becomes Calle Playa) can get just about any gringo-requested ingredients, including a Thanksgiving turkey.

The **Hielera Mulegé,** on "Ice House Road" (signed San Estanislao, no tel.), just north of town and west of Highway 1, has block ice and purified water. It's open 24 hours daily. Standard business hours for most *tiendas* is 9 A.M. to 6 P.M. daily.

INFORMATION AND SERVICES
Money

The Bancomer is located on Zaragoza, between Madero and Moctezuma. **El Pez de Oro** (Moctezuma 17, 9 A.M.–1 P.M. and 3–7 P.M. daily) is a money exchange that cashes travelers checks.

Communications

The post office (Martínez, tel. 615/153-0205, 8 A.M.–1 P.M. Mon.–Fri.) is just before the Pemex station on the right-hand side of the one-way street as you come into the town center. The Minisuper Padilla (corner of Zaragoza and Martínez, tel./fax 615/153-0190) has a long-distance telephone office.

Internet Minita (tel. 615/153-0212, 9 A.M.–9 P.M. Mon.–Sat.), at the end of Calle Madero, has eight desktop computers for rent for US$2 an hour. Baja Adventure Tours (Madero 3, tel. 615/153-0566) also has Internet service with printing and photocopying capabilities.

Next door to Cortez Explorers dive shop is a Western Union with telegraph service that is open 8 A.M.–noon Monday–Friday.

Laundry

Lavamática Claudia (Zaragoza and Moctezuma, tel. 615/153-0057, 8 A.M.–6 P.M. Mon.–Sat.) is the place to wash your clothes.

GETTING THERE AND AROUND

Loreto has the closest commercial airport. Mulegé does not have a bus depot or ticket office in town, so you have to buy your ticket on the bus (no reservations). Northbound and southbound **Autotransportes de Baja California** (ABC, tel. 800/025-0220, www.abc.com.mx) and **Aguila** (tel. 800/824-8452, www.autotransportesaguila.com) buses stop twice a day at the town entrance on Mexico 1. Check websites for schedules, but don't expect the arrival and departure times to be exact. Southbound buses arrive mid-morning and mid-afternoon; northbound buses arrive in the mid-afternoon and evening.

You can easily walk anywhere in town, even to or from the RV parks along the river. Mulegé's town center consists of narrow one-way streets—and not all of them are marked with arrows. Look before you turn.

There is a Pemex station in town, on Avenida Martínez, but a more convenient alternative is the modern Mulegé Pemex Centro on Mexico 1, located about 10 minutes south of town. You can pump your own gas here, and a café and minimarket with ice are on-site.

SOUTHERN SIERRA DE GUADALUPE

The largest concentration of rock art sites are located at the southern end of the Sierra de Guadalupe range, west of Mulegé. Hotels in town can arrange guided trips to the closest ones for US$35–45 per person.

La Trinidad

In a small canyon near Rancho La Trinidad, one wall remains of a cave that was once painted on all sides. The site is known for an image of a large deer painted in a striking orange-red color. The deer is filled with a checkerboard pattern, and beside it are two fawns. According to historian Harry Crosby, the deer represents a recurring theme in Baja rock art, and the one at La Trinidad is one of the best examples found anywhere on the peninsula.

To visit the site, you must secure a permit from **INAH** (San Ignacio, tel. 615/154-0222, La Paz, Calle Aquiles Serdán 1070, tel. 612/123-0399) and hire a licensed guide, either in Mulegé or at the ranch itself. The ranch is located 29 kilometers west of Mulegé. From there, a 6.5-kilometer hike, including several river crossings, leads to the site.

Plan to carry your own water and wear submersible footwear. It takes at least a half day to hike to the cave, and the canyon is scenic enough to consume an entire day. You can also make stops at several other ranchos along the way to watch leather tanning, cheesemaking, and other ranch activities.

There are two groups of murals at La Trinidad. To reach the first, you need only cross the river once. But the second site requires several more crossings. In years when the water level is high, one of these crossings may involve swimming 100 meters through a narrow stone gorge—a true backcountry thrill for the adventure-seeker.

Two experienced guides run half-day trips out of Mulegé: Salvador Castro Drew (tel. 615/153-0232, reserve tours by phone only) and Ciro A. Cuesta Romero (Rubio 27, tel./fax 615/153-0566, cirocuesta@hotmail.com) of **Baja Adventure Tours.** Trips cost about US$40 per person and can be arranged through any hotel in town.

If you decide to drive your own vehicle to the ranch, you'll need high clearance and sufficient spare parts. Guides at the ranch will be less expensive, but you'll have to navigate your way there along a network of unsigned roads. Hotels in town can provide specific directions to the ranch. The route begins on Ice House Road toward San Estanislao.

San Borjitas

The best-known cave painting in the Sierra de Guadalupe—and at one time in all of Baja—was discovered by virtue of its proximity to Mulegé, a town that has existed since mission times. The cave is located on the site of an abandoned ranch that belongs to the Gorosave family. To reach it, you need to drive 23 kilometers miles north of Mulegé to Km. 157 and then 30 kilometers (2 hrs.) west into the interior to Rancho Las Tinajas, where you must register with INAH. Mulegé-based guides can take you to San Borjitas in a long one-day trip, or you can drive yourself and hire a guide at the ranch.

Once signed in, you must drive several more miles through two locked gates (keys will be provided when you register) to Rancho Baltasar, where the hike (less than 1 km) to the cave begins.

The San Borjitas canvas measures 30 meters long by 24 meters deep with an average height of 3.5 meters. On it are some 50 human figures, painted in a uniquely Sierra de Guadalupe style. Colors are more varied than in other parts of the Great Mural region (red, black, ochre, gray, and white). Bodies are elongated with legs spread and arms stretched out to the sides, rather than overhead. And many of the figures are filled in with vertical lines. Another unusual characteristic of this site, according to historian Harry Crosby, is the appearance of adjacent and overlapping figures painted at right angles to each other.

BAHÍA SANTA INÉS AND PUNTA CHIVATO

North of Mulegé, near Km. 151, a sandy road departs Highway 1 heading east toward the wide and undeveloped bay of Santa Inés—a great place for a midday swim or beach stroll. There are multiple ways to reach the white-sand beach that lines the bay. Follow the network of sandy roads, choosing the most-traveled branches and taking care not to get stuck in patches of loose sand. Eventually you will end up at the low dunes that guard the beach. You can pitch a tent and spend the night here, although there are no facilities and you may be asked to pay a few dollars for overnight use of the site.

At the north end of Bahía Santa Inés (Km. 156), a 20-kilometer graded road leads to remote Punta Chivato, a popular sportfishing destination and a great spot to set up camp and snorkel the rocky point. A handful of *palapas* offer shade, and the beachfront camping area can accommodate RVs as well as tents.

Accommodations

The high-end **Posada de las Flores** (off the main, unnamed dirt road that leads to Punta Chivato, tel./fax 615/155-5600, U.S. tel. 619/378-0103, www.posadadelasflores. com, US$210–490/night) group took over the historic Hotel Punta Chivato, a onetime luxury fly-in resort that opened in 1966. Like its sister properties in Loreto and La Paz, the inn has large and stylish rooms with air-conditioning, private baths, fireplaces, and garden patios. Other amenities include a boat ramp, small desert golf course, pool, and sea kayaks. Rates include breakfast, snacks, and dinner, but don't include tax or a US$18-a-day service fee. There is a small *tienda* at the hotel.

You can also camp on the beach or contact **Costa Cardonal** (www.costacardonal. com) to inquire about vacation rentals that may be coming on the market as new homes are completed.

Bahía Concepción

South of Mulegé, stunning Bahía Concepción represents the best of all that Baja has to offer. Its string of a dozen protected white-sand beaches, small islands, and steady winds create a water-sports playground for snorkelers, divers, kayakers, and kiteboarders. The mouth of the bay faces north, and a long, narrow peninsula forms the eastern shore. As a national marine preserve, the bay supports a vibrant ecosystem of creatures big and small.

Mexico 1 hugs the coastline here, and every turn reveals a new and more breathtaking vista. Generally speaking, the beaches in the north are sandier and better protected than those at the south end of the bay. Most of the beaches belong to *ejidos,* which may collect camping fees of US$6–8.

In recent years, a number of American and Canadian expats set up semipermanent residences along several of the most protected coves. But in late 2006, local authorities asked them to remove all structures from the beach and leave the area, in preparation for sale of the property to a large Mexican real estate developer. A few years later, the campers were back, but to date, the makeshift structures have not been rebuilt. Development remains a future possibility. A small development of privately owned vacation homes called Posada Concepción crowds the shoreline at Km. 113. A small market here may have basic supplies for sale.

PUNTA ARENA

Windsurfers, kiteboarders, and summertime campers should head to windy Punta Arena, at the north end of the bay's western shore. Follow the signed, four-kilometer road and you'll find a group of *palapas* and *palapa* huts that rent for about US$8 a night. Look for the Punta Arena sign 13.2 kilometers from the Hotel Serenidad turnoff from the highway.

BAHÍA COYOTE

Near the opening of Bahía Concepción, Bahía Coyote encompasses several of the most popular beaches in the area (which doesn't necessarily mean they are the most crowded).

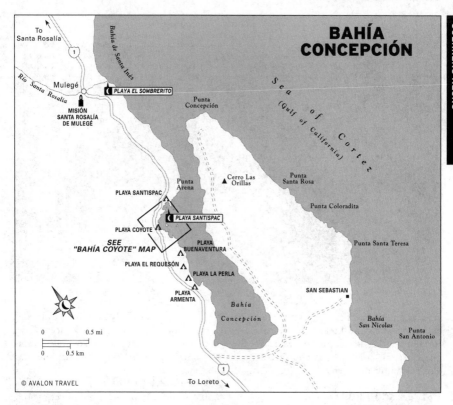

◖ Playa Santispac

Between Km. 114 and 115, Playa Santispac was once the most developed of the Bahía Concepción beaches; by 2008 all semipermanent structures had been removed, leaving many ruins of small gardens, tiled floor areas, and other boundary markers created by the snowbirds who formerly made Santispac their winter home. The beachfront area and its *palapa* shelters are now accessible to campers and travelers; those who were asked to leave the area have relocated mainly to Playa El Coyote and Posada Bahía Concepción. An entrance fee of US$7 per vehicle usually is collected here, whether or not you camp.

On the beach, **Ana's Restaurant Bar** (no tel., daily except Wed., 8 a.m.–10 p.m. winter, 2–10 p.m. summer, mains US$6–15)

is a full-service operation that specializes in fresh seafood and has a full bar known for its Bloody Mary cocktails. Ana's also prepares special dishes for its Saturday night music and dancing fiestas, and continues to have a faithful following among the ex-residents of the beach. Ana's has firewood, groceries, sundries, and propane as well as tools for repairing cars and boats. The owner, Russ, rents kayaks (US$25–35/day) and snorkeling gear (US$10/day). He can also arrange guided tours. Nonguests can use the showers for US$3.

B&B Casa de los Sueños (no tel., www.casadelossuenos.com), perched on the cliffs just north of Posada Concepción with its own clearly marked entrance, has a few rooms in its main house, as well as a separate *casita*. Prices

Playa El Burro

vary, and the owners prefer to send quotes via email. The bed-and-breakfast faces Isla San Ramón and has kayaks as well as a skiff for guest use; air-conditioning and Internet are also part of the deal here.

Playa Escondida

At Km. 111, an 800-meter road leads to several more beaches, ending at Playa Escondida. Larger RVs should avoid the narrow, bumpy track, which leads to a pretty, uncrowded place to lie in the sun, comb the beach, or set up camp (US$8/day).

Playa Los Cocos

Just north of Km. 111, Playa Los Cocos fronts a turquoise-colored cove whose beautiful color is a reflection of limestone in the cliffs above the beach. You can camp here under open *palapa* structures for US$6; the only other facilities are pit toilets. Between the beach and cliffs, a small lagoon is lined with mangroves.

Playa El Burro and Playa Coyote

Continuing south along the bay, the next beach is Playa El Burro with *palapas,* trash cans, and camping for US$8 per day. The adjacent Playa Coyote has a campground with pit toilets, *palapas,* showers, and drinking water (entrance fee US$8/vehicle).

Restaurant Bertha's (no tel., 8 A.M.–8:30 P.M. daily, US$5–11) serves very good, simple Mexican meals at Playa El Burro. It also has a well-stocked bar and friendly service. Across the highway is Abarrotes El Burro, a small supply store.

BEACHES TO THE SOUTH
Playa Buenaventura

Part coarse sand, part rock, this beach is occupied by the **Hotel San Buenaventura** (Km. 94.5, www.hotelsanbuenaventura.com, US$50–70), with clean rooms and campsites (US$10 to camp or US$3 for bathroom facilities with hot shower). Rooms are set around a small courtyard and have air-conditioning and ceiling fans.

George's Olé Sports Bar and Grill (no tel., 8 A.M.–10 P.M. daily, mains US$8–12) serves food and drinks; chessboards and a library of paperback books are available. The owners

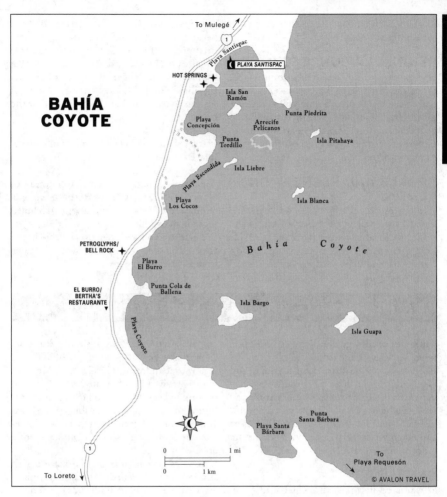

have a couple of *palapa* huts for rent (US$10) as well as a trailer and house. The restaurant has a pool table and kayaks for rent.

Playa El Requesón

A long sandbar running perpendicular to shore and connecting to a small island makes Playa El Requesón a whimsical place. Shallow coves border both sides of the sandbar. Drive your car out onto the hardened sand and the scene looks like something right out of an SUV commercial. You can camp in a tent or RV for US$6 per vehicle (pit toilets, *palapas,* no drinking water).

South of this point, the shoreline of Bahía Concepción becomes less appealing to beachgoers due to the presence of rocks and standing water. The southernmost beach on Bahía Concepción that you can reach by car is Playa Armenta, which faces northwest and has a few *palapas* and pit toilets for US$6. Look for the turnoff between Km. 90 and

91. The beach is about 800 meters down this road, after the ranchito.

PENÍNSULA CONCEPCIÓN

Few travelers venture out to the peninsula that forms the east side of Bahía Concepción because you have to drive a rough 60 kilometers to reach the point, and once there, you'll find no toilet facilities or water. If you really want to explore this part of the bay, a boat from Punta Arena is a better plan.

SPORTS AND RECREATION
Kayaking

With its protected white-sand beaches, tiny islands, and shallow reefs, Bahía Concepción makes an ideal kayaking destination. Aside from a couple of weeks a year of high winds, conditions tend to be warm and calm.

Playa Santispac is a good launch point because several islands are fairly accessible offshore, including **San Ramón, Liebre, Pitahaya (Luz),** and **Blanca. Arrecife Pelícanos,** or Pelican Reef, runs between the Liebre and Pitahaya islands. Thermal springs on the point at the south end of the beach are another popular destination for kayakers.

A few hundred meters east of Playa Coyote, **Isla Bargo** has a sandy beach that makes a pleasant campsite.

Around 2.4 nautical kilometers southeast of Playa Coyote, **Playa Santa Bárbara** can only be reached by boat. This is another secluded spot for an overnight stop.

There are no kayak rentals available in the area, so you should bring your own or rent one from a neighborhing town.

La Purísma, Comondú, and Vicinity

Southwest of Mulegé, the Sierra de la Gigante range separates three fertile valleys from the Gulf coast. San Isidro, La Purísima, and Comondú are worth a visit if you want to experience a slice of Jesuit mission history and see a couple of present-day ranch communities in action. For many travelers, the desert and mountain scenery alone justifies the extra miles of off-road driving.

SAN ISIDRO

Surrounded by orchards, San Isidro (pop. 1,000) has several *tienditas,* a post office, Western Union, and café/taco stand, which seems to be open at random hours. There is also a church, clinic, and barrel gas. Aside from these services, the town offers little to warrant a lengthy stay. Continue on to La Purísima for a larger town with a colorful mission history.

◖ LA PURÍSIMA

Abundant freshwater and surrounding volcanic cliffs made the settlement of Cadegomó suitable for mission life. Padre Nicolás

Tamaral established the Misión La Purísima Concepción de Cadegomó in 1720. The village was abandoned in 1822, and Mexican farmers revived it in the late 1800s. Many of the original date, citrus, and mango orchards survive today, along with the foundation ruins of the mission church (located a few kilometers north of town), which is now part of a private residence.

Services include Abarrotes Goruave as well as a minimarket, *llantera,* post office, pharmacy, and barrel gas at both ends of town.

A 48-kilometer graded road leads west and then north to Bahía San Juanico (Scorpion Bay), a popular surfing destination; from here, another graded dirt road connects to Laguna San Ignacio.

◖ COMONDÚ

Known collectively as Comondú, the twin towns of San José de Comondú and San Miguel de Comondú are beautiful rural communities with lively plazas and lots of architectural ruins from missionary times.

Travelers are not commonly seen here, but you'll be warmly welcomed if you visit. The towns lie about three kilometers apart from each other and about 20 kilometers south of La Purísima. Date palms are abundant here; farmers also grow figs, mangoes, bananas, citrus, corn, grapes, and sugarcane.

First identified by Padre Julián de Mayorga as one of the early Jesuit mission sites in 1709, Misión San José de Comondú had several false starts, with its location and status changing from *visita* to mission and back again. Most ruins, including a stone church built in the 1750s, have been incorporated into newer buildings. San José has a small plaza lined with a number of historic stone and adobe buildings.

San Miguel has barrel gas, a post office, medical center, and limited groceries. At **Restaurant Oasis** (no tel., 8 A.M.–8 P.M. daily year-round, mains US$5–10), located a few meters south of the main plaza, inside the owner's home, chef Martina serves regional dishes or whatever she happens to have on hand—which amounted to tortillas, avocados, beans, tomatoes, and cheese on a recent visit. She knows the area well and gives reliable directions.

GETTING THERE

The easiest route to La Purísima, San Isidro, and Comondú follows a paved road north from Ciudad Insurgentes and ends a few kilometers before La Purísima. From there, you can get to San Isidro, but the unpaved road to Comondú has been impassable since Hurricane John blew through in 2006. You need to return to the paved road and look for the Comondú turnoff in Ejido Francisco Villa. This is a beautiful 40-minute drive through deep canyons, palm groves, and traditional ranchos. The unpaved road surface is suitable for just about any type of vehicle.

A more scenic (and shorter but not faster) approach to La Purísima departs from Mexico 1 at a turnoff south of Bahía Concepción (Km. 60). The branch that forks to Comondú is not recommended.

If you want to turn this side trip into a loop, you can head southeast from San José to San Javier and then on to Loreto; however, the road was in pretty bad shape at last check. The first 32 kilometers can take more than 90 minutes due to rocks and holes, but the scenery is awesome. The last 20 kilometers improve considerably, for a total driving time of around two hours and 15 minutes.

Aguila (tel. 800/824-8452, www.autotransportesaguila.com) buses travel once a day between Ciudad Insurgentes and La Purísima.

BAHÍA SAN JUANICO (SCORPION BAY)

Frequented primarily by die-hard surfers, this off-the-grid bay on the Pacific coast provides access to a half dozen points that break in summer and winter swells. Novices and experienced surfers can often find suitable waves to ride, depending on the size of the swell and time of year.

Aside from a trickle of tourism revenue, fishing supports the local community. Electricity for the town comes from a combination of a diesel generator, solar power, and—in a 10-year pilot project—wind power. Services include gas, basic supplies, and an Internet café. A yoga studio called **The Jewel** holds classes twice a day for US$5 per class.

Accommodations and Food

About a 10-minute walk southwest of San Juanico, **Scorpion Bay Destination Surf Resort** (U.S. tel. 619/239-1335, www.scorpionbay.net) has a variety of accommodations. Camping is US$12.50 per person (free for children under age 7) and includes hot showers.

The resort has a restaurant called the Cantina that serves good and reasonably priced fish (US$11), burgers (US$4), and tacos (US$1.50), but it has been closed since Hurricane Jimena. The owners are working to reopen it soon. When open, hours are 7:30 A.M.–10 P.M. daily. You can use the Internet here for US$3 per half hour, but it costs half that if you go into town instead.

On the main road in town, **Pizzeria Don Alakran** (no tel., mains US$5–10) is open sporadically.

About a half dozen property owners have beachfront vacation rentals listed on VRBO's website (Vacation Rentals by Owner, www.vrbo.com). Prices range US$60–150 per night for two to four bedrooms.

Getting There

To get to San Juanico, follow a paved road out of Ciudad Insurgentes for 112 kilometers. The next 32 kilometers change to dirt and rocks, and the final 16 kilometers are paved again. You can also reach San Juanico from Laguna San Ignacio via a rough dirt road. This route takes about four hours.

LORETO AND BAHÍA MAGDALENA

Once considered just another sleepy coastal town along the Transpeninsular Highway, Loreto has become something of a destination in its own right. The combination of a dramatic setting at the base of the Sierra de la Giganta and a protected marine park directly offshore facilitates a wide range of outdoor activities, from snorkeling and scuba diving to kayaking and mountain biking. With deep roots in Baja California history, Loreto serves as a gateway to the Spanish mission trail and mysterious prehistoric rock art sites located high in the sierra.

Designated for development as a government-sponsored tourist corridor in the 1970s, Loreto remained primarily a sportfishing getaway until a few big-time real estate developers moved in with grand plans for large-scale vacation communities. But given the dismal economy and drop in tourism, progress has been slow, and compared to Los Cabos, Loreto remains relatively undiscovered.

Loreto has a one-terminal international airport, which was upgraded in 2009, plus a wide variety of accommodations and a handful of good restaurants. As such, it makes an easy weekend getaway for travelers coming from the West Coast of the United States.

© RICHARD JACKSON

LORETO

HIGHLIGHTS

◖ **Misión Nuestra Señora de Loreto Conchó:** Jesuit Padre Salvatierra founded the "mother of all California missions" in 1697, and visitors can tour the restored church on Loreto's town plaza (page 187).

◖ **Loreto *Malecón*:** Take a stroll along Loreto's waterfront promenade to see the sunrise, catch a breeze, or enjoy a seafood lunch with spectacular views (page 189).

◖ **Parque Marítimo Nacional Bahía de Loreto:** Mexico's largest marine preserve covers 2,000 square kilometers of the Sea of Cortez, including five major islands that are accessible from the town of Loreto (page 190).

◖ **San Javier:** One of the easiest side trips into Baja's mountainous interior is the winding road to San Javier, a former mission settlement with a beautifully restored church (page 203).

◖ **Whale-Watching in Bahía Magdalena:** Gray whales frequent Bahía Magdalena in winter when they come to bear their calves in the lagoon; whale-watching tours and a traditional Mexican fiesta accompany the annual migration (page 206).

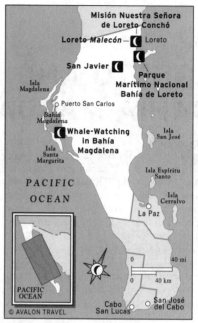

LOOK FOR ◖ TO FIND RECOMMENDED SIGHTS, ACTIVITIES, DINING, AND LODGING.

PLANNING YOUR TIME

In winter, whale-watching tours on the Pacific coast are popular excursions from Loreto-based resorts. Bahía Magdalena is one of only three places along the Pacific where you can watch gray whales up close as they migrate into the shallow lagoon to care for their calves.

For diving and fishing, summer is the best time to go. But temperatures are more moderate in March–May and November–December. January and February are the coldest months, when the north winds blow. The region is quietest during the rainy season in September.

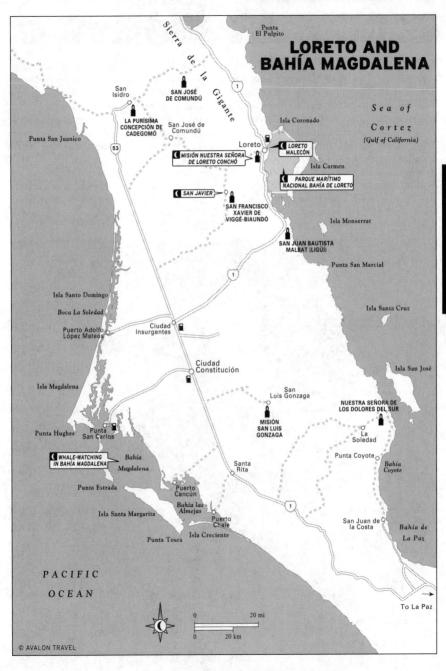

LORETO AND BAHÍA MAGDALENA

Punta El Pulpito

San Isidro

SAN JOSÉ DE COMUNDÚ

LA PURÍSIMA CONCEPCIÓN DE CADEGOMÓ

Punta San Juanico

San José de Comundú

Sierra de la Gigante

Isla Coronado

Sea of

Cortez

(Gulf of California)

Loreto

LORETO MALECÓN

MISIÓN NUESTRA SEÑORA DE LORETO CONCHÓ

Isla Carmen

PARQUE MARÍTIMO NACIONAL BAHÍA DE LORETO

SAN JAVIER

SAN FRANCISCO XAVIER DE VIGGÉ-BIAUNDÓ

Isla Monserrat

SAN JUAN BAUTISTA MALBAT (LIGÜÍ)

Punta San Marcial

Isla Santo Domingo

Boca La Soledad

Puerto Adolfo López Mateos

Ciudad Insurgentes

Isla Santa Cruz

Isla San José

Ciudad Constitución

San Luis Gonzaga

NUESTRA SEÑORA DE LOS DOLORES DEL SUR

Isla Magdalena

MISIÓN SAN LUIS GONZAGA

La Soledad

Punta Coyote

Bahía Coyote

Punta Hughes

Punta San Carlos

WHALE-WATCHING IN BAHÍA MAGDALENA

Bahía Magdalena

Santa Rita

Punta Estrada

Puerto Cancún

Bahía las Almejas

Isla Santa Margarita

Puerto Chale

San Juan de la Costa

Bahía de La Páz

Punta Tosca

Isla Creciente

PACIFIC

OCEAN

LORETO

0   20 mi

0   20 km

To La Paz

© AVALON TRAVEL

Loreto and Vicinity

For outdoor enthusiasts who would like to experience a little bit of history and culture, Loreto (pop. 17,000) makes an ideal home base. Fishing, kayaking, and diving here are all world-class; on land, town life centers around a historic plaza and mission church. With a newly restored lighthouse, Loreto's *malecón* is an attractive place to stroll. You won't have white-sand beaches, but with the largest National Marine Park in Mexico offshore and the Sierra de la Giganta in the background to the west, the scenery is plenty dramatic.

Once sleepy Loreto has experienced a roller-coaster ride of changes in recent years. A venture between Fonatur and the American- and Canadian-owned Loreto Bay Company went under, and a Mexican investor, Homex, took over in 2010. The resort's hotel is open once again after a prolonged closure during the financial crisis.

Although the real estate market has slowed to a crawl during the recession, locals are optimistic that the town can now better prepare itself for growth. Extensive road and sidewalk

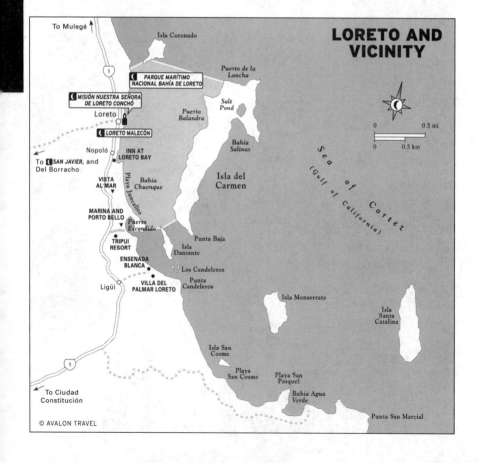

To Mulegé

Isla Coronado

LORETO AND VICINITY

PARQUE MARÍTIMO NACIONAL BAHÍA DE LORETO

Puerto de la Lancha

MISIÓN NUESTRA SEÑORA DE LORETO CONCHÓ

Salt Pond

Loreto

Puerto Balandra

LORETO MALECÓN

Nopoló

INN AT LORETO BAY

Bahía Salinas

To SAN JAVIER, and Del Borracho

VISTA AL MAR

Bahía Chuenque

Isla del Carmen

Playa Juncalito

MARINA AND PORTO BELLO

Puerto Escondido

TRIPUI RESORT

Punta Baja

Isla Danzante

ENSENADA BLANCA

Los Candeleros

Ligüi

VILLA DEL PALMAR LORETO

Punta Candeleros

Isla Monserrate

Isla Santa Catalina

0   0.5 mi

0   0.5 km

Sea of Cortez (Gulf of California)

Isla San Cosme

Playa San Cosme

Playa San Pasquel

To Ciudad Constitución

Bahía Agua Verde

Punta San Marcial

© AVALON TRAVEL

improvements have resulted in a pleasant historic district. With the opening of the new Villa del Palmar resort at Ensenada Blanca south of town, you'll likely encounter timeshare representatives at the airport, on the plaza, and elsewhere around town. Just say no thanks and continue with your trip, unless of course you'd like to go home the owner of one. The resort welcomed its first guests in early 2011 and is the first resort of its kind in the area.

The marina at Puerto Escondido, part of the failed Escalera Nautica project, remains in operation. Beyond these areas, more than 100 small ranching settlements and fishing communities remain much as they have always been.

HISTORY

Loreto holds a distinctive place in Baja California history as the site of the first permanent Jesuit mission and later as the first state capital. Its story begins with the arrival of an Italian Jesuit named Padre Juan María de Salvatierra on October 19, 1697. The Spanish had tried unsuccessfully for the preceding 167 years to establish a Baja California settlement. In a privately funded expedition conceived by Salvatierra and Padre Eusebio Kino, Salvatierra sailed from Sonora with a party of 10, landed at a place the indigenous people called Conchó, and renamed it Loreto in honor of his chosen patroness, Our Lady of Loreto. Ever the optimist, Salvatierra prevailed where others had failed because of his prior mission experience on the mainland, boundless energy, and deep commitment. He stayed in Loreto for 20 years, developing the mission into a base of expansion throughout the peninsula and the capital of Spanish California. When Spain expelled the Jesuits from the peninsula in 1767, the padres gathered in Loreto to await their fate. Franciscan Padre Junípero Serra, who would go on to establish the first Alta California mission, arrived in Loreto a few months later with 15 Franciscan padres.

Loreto served as the religious, civil, and military capital of both Alta and Baja California until 1776, when Monterey became the new capital. In 1829 an earthquake wiped out most of the town, prompting officials to move the regional government to La Paz. By the 1850s the mission era had come to a close and the town was left in ruins.

Loreto was forgotten until some Mexicans discovered its commercial fishing potential in the early 1900s. Soon after, adventurous fly-in anglers began to visit from the United States.

Present-day Loreto traces its roots to the completion of the Transpeninsular Highway in 1973. And about 20,000 tourists now visit Loreto each year. In 2011 Loreto voted in a new mayor (president) from the centrist former-ruling PRI party, Jorge Avilés Pérez. In keeping with local tradition, benches and lights along the *malecón* will likely be painted red, green, and white, the colors of the party.

SIGHTS
◖ Misión Nuestra Señora de Loreto Conchó

Several days after landing at Conchó, Padre Salvatierra and his team erected a tent next to a wooden cross on the mesa above the arroyo where they had landed and placed the Virgen de Loreto inside. This became the first place of worship for the expedition and its converts. The settlers began to build their first permanent church in 1699, outside the walls of the presidio compound, and completed it in 1704. The building was enlarged in the 1740s to accommodate a growing population. The church survived the 1829 hurricane as well as a devastating earthquake in 1877.

After several restorations and the addition of a bell tower in the 20th century, the church hosts regular worship services today. An inscription over the front doors to the church reads "The Head and Mother of the Missions of Baja and Alta California," with the mission founding date of October 25, 1697. The original Virgen de Loreto sits in a side room and is dressed in a new gown each year. The church also features a gilded altar restored from the mission era.

Next to the church, the **Museo de los Misiónes** (tel. 613/135-0441, 9 A.M.–1 P.M. and 1:45–6 P.M. Tues.–Sun., US$3) has a few

LORETO

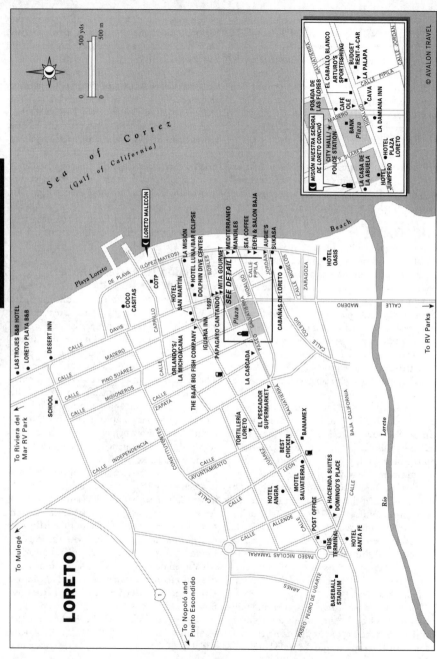

LORETO

To Mulegé

To Riviera del Mar RV Park

SCHOOL

CALLE

CALLE
CALLE

CALLE MADERO

CALLE PINO SUÁREZ

CALLE MISIONEROS

CALLE ZAPATA

CALLE INDEPENDENCIA

CALLE AYUNTAMIENTO

CALLE CONSTITUYENTES

CALLE

CALLE JUÁREZ

CALLE LEÓN

CALLE ALLENDE

CALLE

PASEO PEDRO DE UGARTE

PASEO NICOLÁS TAMARAL

ARNES

1

To Nopoló and
Puerto Escondido

BASEBALL
STADIUM

BUS
TERMINAL

HOTEL
SANTA FE

POST OFFICE

HOTEL
ANGRA

MOTEL
SALVATIERRA

DOMINGO'S PLACE

HACIENDA SUITES

BEST
CHICKEN

BANAMEX

EL PESCADOR
SUPERMARKET

TORTILLERÍA
LORETO

LA CASCADA

THE BAJA BIG FISH COMPANY

ORLANDO'S/
LA MICHOACANA

CALLE

CALLE DAVIS

DE PLAYA

CARRILLO

HOTEL
SAN MARTIN

COCO
CASITAS

DESERT INN

LASTROJES B&B HOTEL

LORETO PLAYA B&B

COTP

LA MISIÓN

HOTEL LUNA/BAR ECLIPSE

DOLPHIN DIVE CENTER

IGUANA INN

PAPAGAYO CANTANDO

MITA GOURMET

1697

ROBLES

(LÓPEZ MATEOS)

Playa Loreto

LORETO MALECÓN

Sea of Cortez
(Gulf of California)

SEE DETAIL

Plaza

SALVATIERRA

HIDALGO

CALLE PIPILA

JORDAN

MEDITERRANEO

MANDILES

SEA COFFEE

EDEN & SALON BAJA

AUGIE'S

SUKASA

Beach

CABAÑAS DE LORETO

CALLE MORELOS

ZARAGOZA

HOTEL
OASIS

PASEO

CALLE COLEGIO

CALLE MADERO

CALLE BAJA CALIFORNIA

CALLE SALVATIERRA

Río Loreto

To RV Parks

To Parks

N

500 yds
500 m

© AVALON TRAVEL

DETAIL INSET

MISIÓN NUESTRA SEÑORA
DE LORETO CONCHÓ

POSADA DE
LAS FLORES

EL CABALLO BLANCO

SALVATIERRA

CALLE JORDAN

BUDGET
RENT-A-CAR

ARTURO'S
SPORTFISHING

LA PALAPA

CAVA

CALLE PIPILA

CAFÉ
OLÉ

LA DAMIANA INN

CITY HALL/
POLICE STATION

BANK

MADERO

Plaza

HOTEL
PLAZA
LORETO

HIDALGO

P. SUÁREZ

LA CASA DE
LA ABUELA

HOTEL
JUNIPERO

© NIKKI GOTH ITOI

The historic Misión de Loreto dates to 1699.

interesting exhibits on life before and after the Spanish conquest. View historic maps, iron-forged scissors and other tools, and large copper kettles used for making pozole.

Paseo Salvatierra, Plaza Salvatierra, and *Palacio Municipal*

The cobblestone plaza that extends southwest of the church is named for Padre Salvatierra, and a bronze bust of him sits in the center of the plaza, facing the front doors of the church.

A shaded pedestrian walkway, Paseo Salvatierra, begins where Avenida Salvatierra meets Calle Independencia and connects to the small plaza in front of the church. It's lined with a few casual eateries and shops selling all sorts of souvenirs and handicrafts. The activity center here is run by the Villa Group and may include a timeshare pitch. Continue along Salvatierra past the church another two blocks, and you will reach the *palacio municipal,* or city hall, and a beautifully restored

plaza—dedicated in April 2010—where local kids like to take their new Rollerblades for a test ride. On the west side of this plaza, past the BBVA Bancomer bank and historic Posada Las Flores hotel, the walkway continues all the way to the sea. Several upscale restaurants have opened on the west side of the plaza, including 1697, Mita Gourmet, and El Papagayo.

◖ Loreto *Malecón*

Though not as busy or picturesque as its counterpart in La Paz, Loreto sports a pleasant, tree-lined waterfront promenade that runs the length of Boulevard López Mateos, connecting about 10 blocks between the marina and Hotel Oasis, with beaches to explore at either end. This is the place for a sunrise stroll or to catch a breeze on a hot and sticky afternoon. The west side of the street is lined with a handful of restaurants, inns, and private residences.

Nopoló and Puerto Escondido

Loreto counts itself among Cancún, Huatulco, Ixtapa, and Los Cabos as a coastal region designated by the Mexican government for development as a tourist corridor. To date, most of the development activity has focused on Nopoló, located eight kilometers south of Loreto, which has a hotel, tennis center, golf course, and residential area—all connected by a network of wide, palm-lined boulevards with curbs (an unusual sight in much of Baja).

Over the years, various commercial entities have partnered with Fonatur in attempting to profit from Loreto's real estate opportunity. The latest of these is Homex, based in Monterrey, Mexico, which came in when the previous investor, Loreto Bay Company, collapsed.

The same streetlamps and curbs that are found in Nopoló line the road to Puerto Escondido, where yachts can take shelter in a protected harbor. Here, as in La Paz, Fonatur has completed a three-story grayish-green building to house the marina operations. It has a classy restaurant on the second level, Porto Bello, which serves good lunch fare in a contemporary space if you happen to stop by when it's open. Wi-Fi is available here as well.

LORETO

LORETO

▣ Parque Marítimo Nacional Bahía de Loreto

More than 2,000 square kilometers of waters offshore from Loreto comprise Mexico's largest marine preserve, designated a UNESCO World Heritage site in 2005. Extending 60 kilometers from **Isla Coronado** in the north to **Isla Catalana** in the south, the Parque Marítimo Nacional Bahía de Loreto (Loreto Bay National Marine Park) is part of the federal Sistema Nacional de Areas Protegidas (SINAP), which prohibits trawling and commercial netting for 35–47 kilometers offshore along the length of the park. Five islands within the park are accessible by boat from Loreto: Coronado, Carmen, Danzante, Monserrate, and Santa Catalina. There is a park fee of about US$2 per day.

SPORTS AND RECREATION

Loreto offers outdoor enthusiasts a rare combination of desert, water, and mountain activities, all of which you can pursue independently or through an experienced outfitter.

Boating

Loreto offers easy access to a string of islands offshore, including Isla del Carmen (18 km from Loreto, 8 km from Puerto Escondido), with several pleasant beaches. Arrange for a *panga* through any hotel that offers fishing trips or at the harbor at the north end of the *malecón*. To launch your own small boat, head to the north end of the *malecón*, the Loreto Shores Villa and RV Park (www.loretoshoresvillasandrvpark.com), or Playa Juncalito or Puerto Escondido, south of Loreto. Larger boats should anchor at the deeper and protected marina at Puerto Escondido. Boat launch fees run US$3 for Loreto (through the port captain's office) and US$10 for Puerto Escondido.

The port captain's offices are located in Loreto (tel. 613/133-0656, fax 613/133-0465, VHF radio channel 16) and at Puerto Escondido.

Kayaking

From Loreto, you can easily paddle to Isla Coronado or the north end of Isla Carmen.

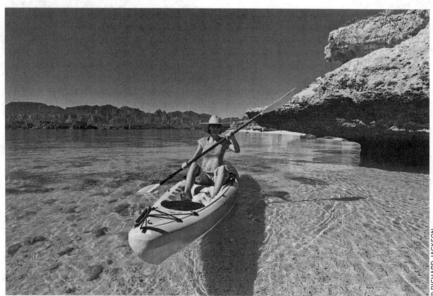

paddling the islands offshore of Loreto

© RICHARD JACKSON

Puerto Escondido is a better starting point for the trip to the southern or eastern shores of Isla Carmen, Isla Danzante, and Los Candeleros. Advanced kayakers might attempt to paddle all the way to Isla Monserrate or Isla Santa Catalina.

Loreto Kayak Tours (U.S. tel. 707/942-4550 or 800/398-6200, www.tourbaja.com), also called Paddling South, is a Loreto-based operation with variety of multiday trips. Cofounders Trudi Angell and Douglas Knapp have been leading trips since 1983. Trudi graduated from the National Outdoor Leadership School (NOLS) Baja course, while Doug has sailed the Sea of Cortez in a catamaran. They also organize mountain biking, horseback riding, and sailing trips.

Sea Kayak Baja Mexico (tel. 613/113-8262, www.seakayakbajamex.com) is another option for multiday guided paddles, training, and rentals.

As a safety measure, the Loreto port captain asks kayakers to file a float plan for any overnight paddling trip.

Kiteboarding and Windsurfing

Loreto is not a wind sports destination per se, but a few pioneers report that winds are strong enough in winter to launch a kite from the beach in front of the **Hotel Oasis** (at the south end of Calle de la Playa/Blvd. López Mateos). As of press time, **La Misión** (Rosendo Robles) was planning to offer rental equipment.

Sailing

You can set sail on the Sea of Cortez with **Loreto Sailing** (www.loretosailing.com.mx). Services include sailing instruction, daytrips, and overnight charters.

Diving

Divers visit Loreto to explore rock reefs, seamounts, underwater caves, and a few wrecks around five nearby islands (Carmen, Coronado, Danzante, Monserrate and Catalina). These waters support some 800 species, including dolphins, whales, sea lions, sea turtles, giant mantas, hammerheads, dorado, roosterfish,

yellowfin tuna, and even seasonal whale sharks. Water temperatures can exceed 27°C in summer and fall, dropping to 20–23°C in winter and spring. Visibility typically exceeds 15 meters and can reach 30 meters on the best of days.

Several shops lead guided dive trips and offer equipment rentals and instruction. Conveniently located a half block from the marina, **Dolphin Dive Center** (Juárez btw Davis/Mateos, tel. 613/135-1914, www.dolphindive-baja.com) is a PADI shop that leads dive tours and courses. Two-tank boat trips to Carmen, Coronado, or Danzante cost US$120. Rinse stations for gear and cameras and a secure room for overnight drying minimize the number of times you'll have to lug your gear across town. This outfitter also offers a special night dive to view the nearly two-meter-long Humboldt squid, which migrates through the area in summer and early fall. These unusual underwater adventures take place in a protective cage with surface-supplied air and cost US$200.

Arturo's Sportfishing (tel. 613/135-0766, www.arturosport.com) runs dive trips through 2M (Dos Mundos) Dive Center (tel. 613/135-0961, cell tel. 613/114-7128, www.bajadosmundos.com, 8 A.M.–1 P.M. and 4–7 P.M. Mon.–Sat.). Boats leave at 9 A.M. Dive-and-stay packages are available. Two-tank dives cost US$95–115, depending on the island you visit. Night dives are US$65 per person. A dive-gear rental package is US$20. Located in the Hotel Junipero, **Cormorant Dive Center** (Hidalgo at Misioneros, tel. 613/135-2140) runs dive trips to Coronado, Carmen, and Danzante islands (US$95–115) as well as SSI Discover Scuba classes and whale-watching tours.

Fishing

Anglers know Loreto first and foremost for its summer dorado catch. A number of other game fish (yellowtail, marlin, roosterfish, yellowfin tuna, cabrilla, grouper, and sailfish) are also abundant, though less so these days than in decades past. Loreto-based fishing charters visit the islands offshore for shelter from wind and to access a variety of fishing

LORETO

© RICHARD JACKSON

A fisherman lands a record-sized mahimahi.

environments. A day of fishing typically begins with a 6 A.M. departure from the marina, returning in the early afternoon.

Many hotels in town arrange fishing trips and offer activity packages that include accommodations. With more than 25 years of experience, **Arturo's Sport Fishing** (Hidalgo, tel. 613/135-0766, www.arturosport.com) has a staff of 20 and fleet of 17 boats. In 2008 it purchased new motors for its boats, upgraded its radio system, and added two new super-*pangas* to the lineup. Current price for a day of fishing in a super *panga* is US$285 for up to three anglers. Deluxe super-*pangas* run US$440 for four people, and cabin cruisers run US$550 for four people. Hotel Oasis also has its own fleet and serves an early breakfast at 5 A.M. Its prices (super-*panga* US$300/day, super-*panga* deluxe US$360/day) include fish filleting, vacuum packing, freezing, and taxes.

Record-setters bring their catch to **The Baja Big Fish Company** (Mateos, tel. 613/135-1603, www.bajabigfish.com), Loreto's official IGFA weighing station, on the Malecon, inside the Mediterraneo restaurant. Baja Big Fish leads conventional and fly-fishing trips in small groups. *Panga* fishing costs US$268 for up to two anglers, US$298–333 for up to three in a super- or deluxe super-*panga*. Half-day rates are US$150 for a standard *panga* and US$170 for a super-*panga*. Its Fly Shop is open 2–8 P.M. Monday–Saturday June–August. In the fall, you can stop in by appointment.

Based at the Tripui Trailer Park, **Jose Torres Fishing Charters** (tel. 613/104-4030, www.loreto.com/josetorres) is run by a local fisherman who takes anglers, divers, and snorkelers out on a fleet of three *pangas*.

Golf

After many years of neglect, the 18-hole **Campo de Golf Loreto** (Blvd. Misión San Ignacio, Nopoló, tel. 613/133-0788) is in good condition at last. Greens fees are US$65 for 9 holes, or US$40 for nine holes. An electric cart costs US$36, pull carts are US$15, and Calloway clubs rent for US$25. Villa del Palmar has a new designer course under development at Ensenada Blanca, south of Loreto.

Spas

Las Flores Spa & Boutique (tel. 613/135-1162, U.S./Canada tel. 877/245-2860, www.spalasflores.com) offers massage therapy, facials, and manicures/pedicures. Walk-ins are welcome.

La Misión also provides massage and body treatments at a poolside spa (US$50>–60 per hour). **Norma's Salon & Spa** (Hildalgo btw Madero/Missioneros, tel. 613/135-0455, normas_salon@msn.com) offers a 3.5-hour basic spa day package for about US$140.

Guided Tours

Most of the outfitters that specialize in one activity also dabble in the others, so if you like your boat crew, you can probably go with the same shop to see the cave paintings or the gray whales. Most trips require a minimum of two or three people.

In addition to overnight paddling expeditions, **Loreto Kayak Tours** (U.S. tel. 707/942-4550 or 800/398-6200, www.tourbaja.com) offers multiday horseback, mountain biking, and sailing trips as well as combination trips.

You can see San Javier by ATV tour through **Cormorant Dive Center/Loretours** (Hidalgo at Misoneros, tel. 613/135-2140, www.loretours.com, US$90). This outfitter also has Mongoose bikes for guided trips to San Javier (US$123) and Primer Agua (US$55).

Desert and Sea Expeditions (Hidalgo btw Colegio/Suarez, tel. 613/135-1979, www.desertandsea.com) leads trips to San Javier, local cave painting sites, Pacific and Gulf-side whale-watching, and Coronado Island.

In addition to these trips, several organizations are supporting conservation efforts in the area and offer ways for visitors to get involved: Licensed gray whale watching guide and Wilderness First Responder Pancho Mayoral (panchomay@yahoo.com) has been leading wilderness trips in the area since 1996. He is an outdoor educator for the National Outdoor

Leadership School (NOLS), and he recently began a sea turtle monitoring program.

SHOPPING

A handful of shops line the streets surrounding the plaza, with handicrafts, silver jewelry, home furnishings, and Mexican-style apparel for sale. In some of these stores, prices for crafts are about two or three times higher than for the same items elsewhere in Baja. In general, shop hours can vary by season and sometimes at the owner's whim.

In front of the mission, **La Casa de la Abuela** (no tel.) sells an assortment of handicrafts in a building as old as the mission itself (1744). **Artesanias Colibrí** (Salvatierra at Independencia, no tel.) carries a nice selection of ceramics, jewelry, maps, and handicrafts.

A retired schoolteacher from New Mexico, Jeannine Perez, opened **El Caballo Blanco** (Hidalgo 19 at Madero, no tel., jeannine1220@yahoo.com, 9 A.M.–7 P.M.

GUIDED TOUR COSTS AT A GLANCE

GUIDED DIVE AND SNORKEL TOURS

Snorkel trip	US$55
Two-tank dive to Coronado Island	US$80-95
Carmen Island	US$100
Danzante Island	US$120
Las Ánimas	US$200 (min. 5 divers)
Extra tank	US$45
Night dive	US$65
Discover scuba course	US$110-150
Open-water certification	US$400
Advanced certification	US$300
Scuba rental package	US$30

OTHER GUIDED TOURS

San Javier Mission	US$120
Cave paintings	US$115
Whale-watching	US$120

LORETO

Mon.–Sat.) in 2005 with thousands of used books, plus new Baja titles and art supplies, for sale. Jeannine has published a personal account of Loreto history, sights, and attractions, including her own sketches.

The **Baja Big Fish Company** (tel. 613/135-1603, www.bajabigfish.com, 9 A.M.–5 P.M. Mon.–Sat.) on Juárez, two blocks from the waterfront, carries a wide selection of flies, plus leaders and lines. Credit cards are accepted.

One block west of the mission, **El Alacrán** (Salvatierra at Misioneros, tel. 613/135-0029, 9 A.M.–7 P.M. Mon.–Sat.) is a fine-art gallery and upscale gift shop with unique ironworks, silver jewelry made in Taxco, and colorful scarves and wraps from Chiapas.

Next to Café Lolita, **La Biznaga** (Salvatierra 10, tel. 613/135-0961, Tues.–Sun.) has reasonably priced gifts and clothes as well as inexpensive bike rentals.

ENTERTAINMENT AND EVENTS
Bars

The majority of nightlife spots in Loreto are sports bars, where expats and Mexicans alike gather to watch American football and international soccer games. The second-story bar at La Misión is a new favorite for the Super Bowl and other big game nights. An open *palapa* bar on the second story of the Hotel Luna, **Bar Eclipse** (Vizcaíno btw Davis/Mateos, tel. 613/135-2288, www.hotellunaloreto.com, 7 P.M.–midnight Wed.–Sun., till 1 A.M. Fri.–Sat.) has a 42-inch plasma screen for viewing sports events. Enjoy cocktails and espresso drinks while taking in sea and mountain views. On the same block, next to the Dolphin Dive Center, **Giggling Dolphin** (Juárez btw Davis and the *malecón,* no tel.) has a bar made out of a converted boat.

Outside town, Tripui Resort has live music on Sunday afternoons 2:30–4:30 P.M.

Augie's Bar and Bait Shop (Blvd. López Mateos, tel. 613/135-1224, mains US$5–10), near the south end of the *malecón,* offers a menu of soup, salads, and burgers as well as fresh fish and seafood dishes. Air-conditioning

in the main room is a plus on hot summer days, and the second-story deck offers prime views of the bay. **Bar Coronado** (south end of Calle de la Playa/Blvd. López Mateos) at the Hotel Oasis features live music 10 P.M.–2 A.M. Wednesday–Saturday. The margaritas are strong, and the mojitos are top-notch if the bartender has mint on hand. Domingo's has a cozy bar and pours the best margaritas in town. Restaurant 1697 serves several locally made Baja Brewing Company draft beers. To dance the night away, head to **Salon Baja** on the *malecón* at the corner of Fernando Jordan. It's open 9 P.M.–4 A.M. Friday and Saturday nights.

Festivals and Events

The **Loreto Dorado International Fishing Tournament** takes place each June. Loreto celebrates the **Virgen de Loreto** with music, food, and dancing on the first weekend of September and the **founding of the city** in the last week of October.

Cruisers gather at Puerto Escondido in late April or early May for **Loreto Fest,** which is sponsored by the Puerto Escondido Hidden Port Yacht Club (www.hiddenportyachtclub.com). In its 15th year in 2011, the event features live music, food, and boating races. A portion of the proceeds is donated to the local community.

Bar Coronado (south end of Calle de la Playa/López Mateos) at the Hotel Oasis hosts a traditional clambake with live music every Friday evening starting at 7 P.M.

ACCOMMODATIONS

Most visitors choose downtown Loreto for their home base in this area for access to a wide variety of travel services; however, there are a few upscale options south of town if you'd like to get away from it all or don't mind the drive.

Loreto offers budget travelers several convenient options, and for those who seek a few more amenities, a number of moderately priced hotels and bed-and-breakfasts are scattered throughout the area. Some have sea views, others have equally pretty mountain views, and almost all are within walking distance of the marina, shops, and restaurants. Vacation rentals are another option as more homes come on the market.

Under US$50

Rooms are bare-bones at the **Hotel Posada San Martín** (Juárez 14 btw Madero/Davis, near the plaza, tel. 613/135-0442, US$35) but they do come with hot water, fans, private bathrooms, and purified drinking water in the courtyard. Bright yellow **Hotel Junípero** (Hidalgo, near the mission, tel. 613/135-0122, US$35–40) has expanded with additional rooms in a separate building across the street. Rooms that face the church on the backside of the original hotel building are quietest and have pleasant views of the plaza. Large rooms have air-conditioning, hot showers, cable TV, and double or king-size beds. Wi-Fi is available.

US$50-100

Next door to the Hotel San Martín, **Iguana Inn** (Juárez btw Madero/Davis, tel. 613/135-1627, www.iguanainn.com, US$45–55) has four bungalows, each with its own kitchenette, two queen beds, and a large tiled shower. Rates include tax.

Hotel Plaza Loreto (Hidalgo 2, tel. 613/135-0280, www.loreto.com/hotelplaza, US$62) occupies a two-story, neocolonial building one block from the mission church. Its 29 plain rooms have hot water, air-conditioning, Internet, and cable TV; a small restaurant/bar is on-site.

Popular **Hotel Luna** (Vizcaíno btw Davis/Mateos, tel. 613/135-2288, www.hotelluna-loreto.com, US$65, tax included) has three clean rooms with queen beds, cable TV, and Wi-Fi in a convenient location. Kayakers often stay a night or two at the start or end of their overnight paddles. Owners Alberto and Karla help their guests feel right at home.

Sukasa (corner of Paseo López Mateos and Jordán, tel. 613/135-0490, www.loreto.com/sukasa, US$55–85), on the *malecón,* has two bungalows in a brick duplex, a one-bedroom *casita,* and a yurt. Units are furnished with queen- or king-size beds, air-conditioning,

TV/VCR (Spanish channels only), Wi-Fi, and basic cooking equipment. No pool, satellite TV channels, or phones. Daily maid service is a plus.

A few blocks from the town center, American-owned ◖ **Coco Cabañas** (Davis 71, tel. 613/135-1729, www.cococabanasloreto.com, US$89) consists of a group of well-built cottages set around a pool. Thick walls and airtight windows block the sound of wind, dogs, and roosters in the residential surroundings. Cottages come with air-conditioning, hot water, a small TV, and the best kitchenettes we've seen anywhere in Baja; spotless appliances include a blender, and there's matching dishware and ice cubes already made from purified water. Bathrooms are tiny but clean and functional. Beds on metal frames are a little squishy. Hand-painted vines over doorways add a nice touch. Inside the gated compound are a small swimming pool and barbecue area. It's a five-minute walk to the waterfront. Rates include tax.

Adjacent to the cabanas, the owners recently opened **Coco Casitas de Loreto** (Davis 71, tel. 613/135-1729, www.cococasitasloreto.com) with five new units. One- and two-bedroom *casitas* are offered at an introductory rate of US$99/177, including tax. Amenities include comfortable furnishings, California King beds, large baths, and a small swimming pool. A single-story one-bedroom *casita* is wheelchair accessible.

At the beginning of the main drag through town, a bit far from the beach, **Hacienda Suites** (Salvatierra 152, tel. 800/224-3632, toll-free U.S. tel. 866/207-8732, fax 613/135-0202, www.haciendasuites.com, US$70) is a modern hotel with rooms set around a central courtyard and swimming pool. Amenities include air-conditioning, phones, TVs, minibars, and in-room safes. Parking is secure, and the hotel offers Wi-Fi. Rooms come with breakfast. The hotel's Rancho Viejo and Bar la Molienda are both pleasant spaces for a drink or full meal.

At ◖ **La Damiana Inn** (Madero btw Hidalgo/Fco. Jordan, www.ladamianainn.com, US$62–75), owners Debora and Gerardo

LORETO

maintain six guestrooms in a historic home, each with a large private shower. There is an outdoor kitchen and garden/patio area that dates back to the 1930s. Wi-Fi and secure parking are a plus; as with any hotels right near the plaza, the location can be noisy.

North along the waterfront, on Calle Davis, the **Desert Inn** (formerly La Pinta Hotel, tel. 613/135-0025 or 800/026-3605, toll-free U.S. tel. 800/800-9632, http://desertinns.com/Loreto/, US$89–110) offers large, air-conditioned rooms with terraces and views of the sea.

One row back from the waterfront at the southern edge of town, [**Las Cabañas de Loreto** (Morelos off the *malecón*, tel. 613/135-1105, U.S. tel. 707/933-0764, www.lascabanas-deloreto.com, US$95) has four modern studios set around a beautiful courtyard, a small pool with comfy chaise lounges and hammocks, and a fire pit. You can prepare simple meals in the private kitchenette in your unit or use the outdoor kitchen and barbecue to grill your fresh catch. The main house, also available for rent,

has an ocean view from the upstairs deck; studios have garden views. A new two-bedroom, one-bath casita was also available at last check for US$1,200 per week.

Studios have TV/VCR, air-conditioning, free Wi-Fi, and secure off-street parking, but no satellite or phones. The owners provide bikes, guest laundry, a video and book library, and beach equipment. They also arrange excursions to the islands as well as custom classes in Mexican cooking, Spanish language, and nature photography. This place fills up well in advance; check availability online and make reservations. There's a three-night minimum.

Six blocks north of Plaza Salvatierra and beyond the Desert Inn, **Las Trojes Bed & Breakfast Hotel** (Davis Norte, tel. 613/135-0277, www.loreto.com/costa2.htm, US$50 and up) offers guests a unique opportunity to sleep in converted Native American granaries that the owner originally found in the mountainous interior of the mainland state of Michoacán, transported to La Paz, and reassembled on the beach in Loreto. Amenities include air-

Guest studios surround a pleasant courtyard at Las Cabañas de Loreto.

COURTESY OF LAS CABAÑAS DE LORETO

conditioning, ceiling fans, and private showers as well as free bicycles and Internet access. You can stroll through the cactus garden to reach the beach bar and waterfront. Rates include continental breakfast.

Hotel Angra (Juárez btw Allende/Marquez de León, tel. 613/135-1172, www.hotelangra. com, US$55) has 12 basic guestrooms with air-conditioning, cable TV, private baths, Wi-Fi, and parking. Some rooms are pet friendly, and there is an attached café.

US$100-150

A perennial favorite within the sportfishing community, **Hotel Oasis** (south end of Calle de la Playa/Blvd. López Mateos, tel. 613/135-0211, toll-free U.S. tel. 800/497-3923, www. hoteloasis.com, US$120–130) is the only hotel in town that has its own beach. For anglers, the best part about a stay here is that breakfast service begins at 5 A.M. The 39 air-conditioned rooms are large and simply furnished and not well lighted. Bright orange cotton bedspreads cover sagging mattresses. Other properties in town offer more modern accommodations at a lower price, but the Oasis has history and charm, plus its own fishing fleet, a pool, tennis court, free Wi-Fi, and a swing set for kids.

At the north end of the *malecón,* **Loreto Playa Bed and Breakfast** (tel. 613/135-1129, www.loretoplaya.com, US$145–195) has two suites and a beach house for rent. Accommodations come with king-size beds, bubble bath, and robes; the use of mountain bikes and kayaks; and a full breakfast.

US$150-250

For charming accommodations in a historic setting, the **Hotel Posada de las Flores** (tel. 613/135-1162, toll-free U.S. tel. 877/245-2860, www.posadadelasflores.com, US$150–180) fits the bill; however, rooms were musty and the place was in need of some sprucing up at last check. Housed in a colonial building on Plaza Salvatierra, the inn has a small rooftop pool with a glass bottom through which sunlight shines into the lobby below. Its 15 rooms contain antique furnishings, pottery, tile, and

wrought iron from the mainland. Amenities include air-conditioning, satellite TV, wireless Internet, and a gift shop and spa on the ground floor (9 A.M.–5 P.M. Tues.–Sun.). Enjoy some of Loreto's best ocean and mountain views from the second-level terrace.

On the *malecón,* **La Misión** (Rosendo Robles, tel. 613/135-0524, toll-free U.S. tel. 877/887-2939, www.lamisionloreto.com, US$148–250) has been the talk of the town since it opened a few years back. It has 65 rooms and three two-bedroom suites in a newly constructed five-story building with a swimming pool, bar, and restaurant that specializes in thin-crust pizza. As the name implies, the ambience is colonial, with lots of dark wood furnishings and marble accents. Rooms have keyless locks, marble baths, and small flat-screen TVs. A few lower-priced mountain-view rooms on the third and fourth floors face the town and Sierra de la Giganta beyond it. More expensive oceanview rooms have shaded balconies that overlook the pool, *malecón,* and Sea of Cortez. This hotel has exceptionally comfortable beds and plenty of hot water at very high pressure; the acoustics, however, can be a problem. Rooms close to the bar (210, 320, 410) hear music until around midnight. When guests arrive, suitcases with wheels make a racket as they bump over grooves in the tiles along the breezeways. If the place is full, you'll likely hear neighbors above and next door. Doors are drafty (a problem only on the coldest of days in winter), bathrooms were missing some finishing touches, such as towel racks not securely attached to the wall, and the hotel seemed understaffed on a recent visit. Bottom line: This place is a step above most other Loreto accommodations, but the quality of accommodations and service may not live up to expectations based on the high price.

At the traffic circle that marks the entrance to town, **Hotel Santa Fe** (Salvatierra at Ebanista, tel. 613/134-0400, http://hotel-santafeloreto.com, US$80)is affiliated with the Villa Group, which runs the new Villa del Palmar resort at Ensenada Blanca and several

LORETO

resorts in Los Cabos. This five-story white building, newly constructed, has studio rooms, and one-, two-, or three-bedroom suites—each with its own well-equipped kitchenette. Keyless entry, touch-on lamps, and rain showers are a few of the contemporary touches. Exterior walls are airtight; however, the interior walls are thin, and the rooms could use some additional furniture or fabrics to absorb the sound of moving furniture and closing doors. A restaurant and convenience store are located on the ground level, and there is a small pool and whirlpool tub in the interior courtyard.

Vacation Rentals

As new homes are constructed, a few have come on the market as vacation rentals. For example, **Stay in Loreto** (tel. 613/135-0791, www.stayinloreto.com, US$800–900/wk.) manages a beachfront condo, house, and suite for weekly or monthly rentals. The newly constructed properties are located 30 meters from the water, with granite counters, seaview decks, satellite TV, and air-conditioning. **La Giganta Real Estate** (Madero 22-C, tel. 613/135-0802, www.lagiganta.com) manages a few vacation rentals in the area starting at US$150 per night.

Camping and RV Parks

Close to town and near the beach, **Rivera del Mar RV Park and Camping** (Madero Norte 100, tel. 613/135-0718, www.riveradelmar.com, US$16–19) has 25 spaces with full hookups and limited shade, plus showers, hot water, laundry, and grills. Tent camping costs US$7. This park allows pets as long as they are leashed. The atmosphere tends to be very noisy at night, especially on weekends.

South of town on the other side of the Río Loreto, **Loreto Shores Villas and RV Park** (Colonia Zaragoza, tel. 613/135-1513, www.loretoshoresvillasandrvpark.com, US$26) has 36 spaces with full hookups enclosed within a five-acre park that fronts the beach; tent camping costs US$7 per person and includes hot showers. Wi-Fi is available for US$2 per day. Every seventh day is free. Loreto Shores

has a pool, laundry service, boat launch, and *palapas* on the beach.

You can camp for free at Playa Juncalito, 22.5 kilometers south of Loreto, and the snorkeling is also good here. The simple 🄲 **Vista al Mar** (Km. 103, Mexico 1, mains US$5–15) restaurant is Baja dining at its best: fresh clams, shrimp, and fish of the day under a *palapa* roof by the seashore. Look for a sign on the highway.

Outside Loreto

For some longtime Loreto expats, poking fun at the real estate development underway in Nopoló is serious sport. Though they may have mixed feelings about the building of a 6,000-unit community, many would gladly trade beaches with the **Inn at Loreto Bay** (formerly the Camino Real, tel. 613/133-0010 or 800/507-6979, toll-free U.S. tel. 866/850-0333, www.innatloretobay.com, US$135–330). Here, guests can choose from 155 oceanfront and oceanview rooms, all with Wi-Fi, set around a lawn and pool. New curtains and modern bathrooms make for cheerful decor, but beds are sagging; this remains a 20-year-old hotel in need of a more complete makeover. You can book trips and rent gear for the water sport of your choice from the hotel. The **Loreto Bay Restaurant** serves breakfast 7–11 A.M., snacks, and dinner 7–10:30 P.M. Bordering the grounds are an 18-hole golf course and the Centro Tenístico de Loreto (tennis center), both free for guests.

There is more than meets the eye at **Tripui Resort** (Puerto Escondido, tel. 613/133-0818, U.S. tel. 512/749-6070, www.tripui.com, US$85–130), an understated resort that has several comfortable hotels rooms and an adjoining RV park, all set around a pleasant garden and large swimming pool. Rates include breakfast. Amenities include a boat launch, boat storage space, restaurant serving standard Mexican fare, laundry service, bar, Internet, and grocery store. The resort is not on the beach, but you can walk to the Puerto Escondido harbor and launch a kayak, or you can drive about 12 miles to town.

FOOD

Loreto's restaurants are mostly casual places that serve a variety of Mexican specialties. Seafood and steak find their way onto just about every menu. A number of local eateries have formed an association that maintains a useful website at www.loretorestaurants.com.

Mexican

Domingo's Place (Salvatierra 154 at Ebanista, tel. 613/104-4016, 1–10 P.M. daily) serves tasty grilled steaks as well as lobster, shrimp, and fish specialties. The back patio is a highlight of dining here, and the margaritas are among the best in town.

La Terraza (tel. 613/135-0496, 1–10 P.M. daily), above Café Olé, overlooks Plaza Salvatierra. Order the house special if you go: grilled steaks of fresh Sonoran beef (US$15).

Under the same ownership as Domingo's Place, casual **La Palapa** (Hidalgo btw López Mateos/Callejón Pipila, tel. 613/135-1101, 1–11 P.M. daily, mains US$7–15) has locals hooked on tasty seafood and great service. Try the whole red snapper *(huachinango)* or the chocolate clams *(almejas chocoladas)*, which are baked and topped with melted cheese.

Mediterraneo (López Mateos at Hidalgo, tel. 613/135-2577, www.mediterraneo-loreto. com, 12:30–4 P.M. and 6–10 P.M. Tues.–Sun., mains US$15–20) is a second-story restaurant on the *malecón,* just north of Avenida Salvatierra. It serves mainly Italian cuisine as well as steaks and paellas. Texas BBQ is a recent addition to the menu. Owners Carol and Lee Boyd have opened a second eatery on the plaza, next to Mita Gourmet: **Papagayo Cantando** (tel. 613/135-2216, 3 P.M. till close Fri.–Wed., mains US$10–20) serves a great tapas menu in an enchanting garden setting. Seafood paella, smoked salmon, and crab cakes are some of the small plates. Entrées include rib eye, baby back ribs, and fajitas.

La Cascada (Salvatierra, 8 A.M.–9:30 P.M. Thurs.–Tues., mains US$7–20) is a simple affair with bright blue tables and chairs arranged in an open-air dining room just a few steps from the mission. For breakfast, try a large glass of fresh-squeezed orange juice with eggs made to order. For dinner, try the shrimp or scallops in mango sauce and garnished with peanuts, or just a burger topped with tomato, lettuce, onion, bacon, and mozzarella cheese. **Los Mandiles de Santa Lucía,** on the south end of the *malecón,* is another good choice for traditional Mexican dishes.

North of town on the beach, **La Picazón** (tel. 613/109-5078, lapicazon@hotmail. com, noon–6 P.M. Mon.–Sat.) is a local find. Seafood wraps—a flour tortilla stuffed with fish or shellfish, lettuce, tomato, and melted mozzarella cheese—are a house specialty. The owners also stock a full bar.

International

On the plaza, Kieran and Norma Raftery prepare Mexican cuisine with an Italian twist at **1697** (Davis 13, tel. 613/135-2538, 12:30–2:30 P.M. and 6–10 P.M. Tues.–Sun., mains US$10–20). For example, the chile relleno comes wrapped in a puff pastry and garnished with a poblano cream sauce. Start with a nopal salad or *queso fundido* chorizo and order a Baja Blond from the tap, or choose from a good selection of wines by the glass. Friday night salsa classes are a popular event.

Mita Gourmet (Davis 13, tel. 613/135-2035, www.mitagourmet.com, mains US$7–15), across from the city hall building on the plaza, specializes in seafood dishes (fish with garlic is a favorite) and hosts live guitar music most nights. Fish tacos are fried and come with lettuce instead of the traditional cabbage.

Antojitos, Tacos, and Fast Food

When it comes to fish tacos, the efficient husband-and-wife team who run **El Rey del Taco** (no tel., mains US$3–7) have won the hearts of many a Loreto regular—some of whom place their orders before they fly into town, in case the place is closed when they arrive. Located on the south side of Juárez near the Pemex, El Rey gets high marks for *tacos de cabeza* as well as *pescado.* Those in the know say the fastest way to get your tacos is to sit down at a table, rather than waiting at the window.

LORETO

FISH TRANSLATOR

- albacore tuna – *albacora*
- barracuda – *picuda*
- black sea bass – *mero prieto*
- bluefin tuna – *atún de aleta azul*
- blue marlin – *marlín azul*
- dolphinfish (mahimahi) – dorado
- grouper (generic) – *garropa*
- halibut – *lenguado*
- hammerhead shark – *cornuda*
- jack crevalle – *toro*
- ladyfish – *sabalo*
- mackerel – sierra, *makerela*
- manta ray – *manta*
- marbled scorpionfish – *cabezón*
- octopus – *pulpo*
- Pacific amberjack – *pez fuerte*
- perch (generic) – *mojarra*
- pompano – *palometa*
- puffer (generic) – *bolete*
- red snapper – *pargo*

- roosterfish – *papagallo, pez gallo*
- sailfish – *pez vela*
- sea bass (cabrilla) – cabrilla
- shark (generic) – *tiburón*
- shark (small) – *cazón*
- snook – *robalo*
- squid – *calamar*
- stingray (generic) – *raya*
- striped marlin – *marlín rayado*
- swordfish – *pez espada*
- triggerfish – *cochi*
- tuna – *atún*
- wahoo – *sierra wahoo, peto*
- whale shark – *pez sapo*
- white sea bass – *corvina blanca*
- yellowfin tuna – *atún de aleta; amarilla*
- yellowtail – *jurel*

Pez is the generic word for fish. Once fish has been caught and is ready for cooking (or has been cooked), it's called *pescado*.

El Rey is open from 9 A.M. until whenever the food runs out, usually by 2 P.M.

Another longtime favorite for quick, inexpensive snacks, **McLulu's** (Salvatierra, west of Colegio, no tel., 10 A.M.–6 P.M. daily) prepares *tacos de carne asada, tacos de guisado,* homemade chorizo, and *picadillo* (spicy meat-and-chili salad). The once-legendary fish tacos were on the soggy side last time we tried them. Three tacos and a soda cost US$5.

Just off the plaza, **Orlando's** (Madero 25, tel. 613/135-0549) snack bar is open for breakfast and lunch, with favorites like pancakes,

hamburgers, and cupcakes, 7 A.M.–3 P.M. In the evening, the owners serve ice cream and *paletas* at the adjoining **La Michoacana** (Madero at Juárez, tel. 613/135-0549).

Best Chicken (Salvatierra, near the Pescador store, no tel., US$5) does one thing well: flame-broiled chicken. Follow the parade of locals to the register and order a *medio* half) or *entero* (whole) and say if it's *para aqui* (for here) or *para llevar* (to go). Choose fries or a salad on the side. Grab a cold drink from the fridge, and dig in.

Asadero el Super Burro (Fernandez at

Colocio, tel. 613/135-1243) does *antojitos* right, with a menu of papas *rellenas, molcajetes,* tacos, and the namesake burritos. Homemade flour tortillas are a plus.

Cafés

On the plaza, **Café Olé** (Madero 14, tel. 613/135-0495, 8 A.M.–10 P.M. Mon.–Sat., mains US$3–6) is a Loreto institution, where expats and visitors gather to dine on reasonably priced breakfast and lunch fare while watching the world go by. Seafood omelets and freshly squeezed orange juice highlight the morning menu; lunch fare includes tacos, burgers, ice cream, and the like. Check the community bulletin board for rentals, sales, and other local information.

A relatively new option for café culture is air-conditioned **Sea Coffee,** near Augie's on the *malecón* (tel. 613/135-2096, 7 A.M.–2 P.M. and 4–7 P.M. daily).

El Mejicano (on Misioneros, north of Juárez, no tel.) has the best cold treats in town, including *paletas, agua frescas,* and *nieve.*

Groceries

El Pescador (Salvatierra btw Independencia/ Ayuntamiento, www.elpescador.com.mx), is Loreto's largest grocery store. Locals prefer to shop at the smaller but less expensive and cleaner **Chuco's** (Madero, tel. 613/135-0065), which is across the street from the owner's husband's hardware store. A government-sub- sidized **Tienda ISSSTE** (no tel., 8 A.M.–8 P.M., Sun. 8 A.M.–2 P.M. Mon.–Sat.) is located on Madero, north of the plaza.

Stock up on fresh tortillas and Mexican pastries at **Tortillería Loreto** (Juárez btw Ayuntamiento/Independencia). On Sunday mornings, there is a farmers market on Zaragossa.

Outside Loreto

Del Borracho Saloon and Grill (Camino a San Javier, no tel., 8 A.M.–6 P.M. Wed.–Sun., closed June–Sept., mains US$7–15) is an or- der-at-the-counter kind of place. It's run by two hard-working Americans whose support

for the local community is widely known and respected. The restaurant is located about 800 meters from the highway on the road to San Javier. Eggs, pancakes, and waffles make up the breakfast menu; burgers, fries, and corn- dogs are for lunch.

At Playa Juncalito, stop at ◖ **Vista al Mar** (mains US$5–15) for Baja dining at its best: fresh clams, shrimp, and fish of the day, at a plastic table on the sand under a *palapa* roof by the seashore. This place also has a cute toy boat structure for kids. Look for a sign on the high- way. There are two dining options at Puerto Escondido: **Restaurante & Bar Tripui** (Lote 1, Manzana 1, Puerto Escondido, 8 A.M.– 9:30 P.M. daily) serves traditional Mexican food, including chicken mole, fish filets, and lobster in season. Contemporary **Porto Bello** (Lote 1, Manzana 15, San Carlos, Bahía de las Palmas, Puerto Escondido, tel. 613/133-0189) is located in a second-story space inside the ma- rina complex. (Porto Bello also has a second location inside the airport.)

In Nopoló, the **Loreto Bay Restaurant** (tel. 613/133-0010 or 800/507-6979, www.in- natloretobay.com) was going through a change in ownership at press time and may or may not be open.

INFORMATION AND SERVICES
Tourist Assistance

SEMARNAT, the government agency respon- sible for issuing permits to visit the protected islands near Loreto, has an office at the ma- rina (tel. 613/135-0477, www.semarnat.gob. mx, 8 A.M.–3 P.M. Mon.–Fri.).

Loreto's **tourist office** (Salvatierra at Madero, tel. 613/135-0411, 8 A.M.–8 P.M. Mon.–Fri.) occupies a street-level space in the Palacio de Gobierno on the plaza. There are a few brochures, but the staff has not been particularly helpful on recent visits. If you are in Nopoló and need information, stop by the **Fonatur office** (tel. 613/135-0650).

The Loreto Hotel Association maintains a marketing website at www.gotoloreto.com. A more informative site is the Loreto Adventure

Network (www.loretoadventurenetwork.com), representing several of the environmental organizations and local businesses that are leading conservation efforts.

Money

Loreto has several banks with ATMs that dispense pesos. One of the most convenient is the **Bancomer** (Mexico 1 at Paseo Ugarte) located at the highway, just north of the entrance to town. There is a **Banamex** on Avenida Salvatierra near the Pemex between the Hacienda Hotel and Pescador Market and another Bancomer on the plaza. The banks will not currently exchange U.S. dollars to pesos. They will exchange traveler's checks and Euros, Canadian dollars, and most other currencies for pesos. Some of the hotels may exchange currency but at a lower rate.

Post and Telephone

Loreto's post office (Allende btw Salvatierra and Juárez) is open 8 A.M.–4 P.M. Monday–Saturday. Public phones are widely available, and there are several Movistar and Telcel stores in town for mobile phone needs.

Internet Access

Most hotels now have wireless Internet for guests traveling with their own laptops and a desktop machine or two for those who are traveling sans electronics. Internet cafés/business centers are located on Calle Madero and Calle Vizcaíno near Independencia.

Emergencies

Loreto's new **Hospital de la Comunidad de Loreto** is on the highway at the south end of town. Call 066 for emergencies.

GETTING THERE AND AROUND
By Air

At press time, Alaska Airlines was the only major airline servicing Loreto's small international airport (LTO) with one small flight a day from Los Angeles; however, the Villa Group has been working hard to get one or two other airlines to reenter the market, as well as possibly a charter service or two. Delta, Aero California, and Continental had all initiated service and then pulled out due to the depressed economic climate. The newly constructed airport terminal has one shop and one restaurant (Porto Bello) inside. Even though the airport is a small operation, it's important to arrive early for your flight, because the same staff that handles ticketing and check-in will also do the boarding process once you are inside.

By Bus

Loreto's bus terminal is located at the intersection of Paseo Ugarte, Calle Juárez, and Calle Salvatierra. The schedule often changes, but you can usually count on about six ABC buses per day running in each direction. Fare to La Paz is approximately US$42 and about US$127 to Tijuana.

By Taxi

Head to the intersection of Calles Madero and Hidalgo to hail a cab or call 613/135-0047 for pickups. Taxi service from the airport to Loreto or Loreto to Nopoló costs about US$7 *colectivo* and US$23 private. Rides within town cost around US$5.

By Car

Loreto has several rental car agencies: **Budget/Fox** (tel. 613/135-1090, www.budgetbaja.com), on Hidalgo near the *malecón;* Alamo on Avenida Salvatierra (tel. 613/135-1773, www.alamoloreto.com) and **Europcar** (tel. 613/135-2260), at the intersection of Independencia and Salvatierra. In most cases, the desk at the airport and office in town are managed by the same manager; an exception is Hertz. If you book a reservation online, you'll get the Hertz at the airport. The location in town is under different management and looked closed at last check. These companies also have desks at the Loreto airport. Even with this many brands, the rental car companies frequently run out of cars on busy weekends, and they give cars to customers on a first-come, first-served basis, regardless of whether you have a reservation. Be flexible, as it's likely you may end up taking a cab to town and waiting a day or so until a vehicle becomes available. In the case of a problem with your rental, the agency should reimburse you for the cab fare at the end of your rental. Keep the receipt.

SAN JAVIER

If you make only one excursion into the mountains on a drive along the Transpeninsular Highway, let timeless San Javier in the rugged Sierra de la Giganta be the one. Located 36 kilometers southwest of Loreto at an elevation of 425 meters and along the deep Arroyo San Javier, this agricultural village of thatched-roof stone and adobe houses holds one of the best-preserved Spanish mission churches anywhere in Baja. Onions are San Javier's major crop, but local farmers also grow citrus, guavas, figs, papayas, grapes, corn, chilies, and dates. December 3 is San Javier's patron saint day, and the week before this date is an especially festive time to visit.

Misión San Francisco Xavier de Viggé-Biaundó

Italian Padre Francisco María Píccolo founded the Mission San Javier (1699–1817) along the Arroyo San Javier in 1699, just two years after Padre Salvatierra established Baja's first permanent mission in Loreto. Little remains of the structures that were built on the first San Javier site, which Píccolo abandoned a few years later due to a threatened revolt. But Padre Juan de Ugarte revived the mission in 1702, choosing a new location a few kilometers downstream. He planted seeds brought from the mainland to grow a variety of fruits and vegetables and also introduced cotton and sheep, from which the indigenous people learned to weave fabrics.

The church that survives today was constructed 1744–1758, under the guidance of Padre Miguel del Barco. It features detailed stonework around its doors and windows and a gilded altarpiece with a statue of San Javier. A glass cabinet in the sacristy displays precious vestments worn by the resident padres.

On Thursdays a priest from Loreto holds mass. Caretaker Francisca Arce de Bastida gives informal tours of the church (7 A.M.–6 P.M. daily, by donation).

Accommodations and Food

Most visitors spend only a day in San Javier, but if you want to stay overnight, there are a couple of options. The family that lives in the farmhouse behind the church rents a very rustic cabin for US$40. **Casa de Ana** (tel. 613/135-0112, fax 613/135-0795, US$35), at the east end of the cobblestone road that leads to the church entrance, rents several *palapa*-roofed cabanas with private baths. For more information, contact Ana Gloria at Hotel Oasis (tel. 613/135-0112, loretooasis@prodigy.net. mx) in Loreto.

La Palapa San Javier (no tel., 8 A.M.–8 P.M. daily, mains US$5) has a limited menu of Mexican staples and homegrown olives. A couple of small *tiendas* sell basic supplies.

Getting There

The road to San Javier begins at Km. 118 on the highway and follows part of the original Spanish *Camino Real*. It takes about an hour to traverse the narrow road from the highway to the village. The first few kilometers are now paved, and after that, the road is suitable for just about any vehicle in dry weather, as long as you don't mind the steep grades.

If you don't have your own car, you can either rent one in Loreto or join a guided tour.

Ensenada Blanca to Ciudad Constitución

South of Puerto Escondido, Mexico 1 hugs the Gulf Coast for about 20 kilometers more and then veers west across the peninsula toward Ciudad Insurgentes before turning south again to Ciudad Constitución.

ENSENADA BLANCA

About 40 kilometers south of Loreto, near the fishing village of Ligüí, Ensenada Blanca consists of a string of white-sand beaches, dunes, and estuaries that are now under development by the Villa Group. At press time, a crew of 400 builders were rushing to complete the first phase of construction so the **Villa del Palmar Loreto** (Km. 83, Carr. Transp., Ensenada Blanca, toll-free U.S. tel. 877/845-5247, www.villadelpalmarloreto.com) could open its doors in March 2011. Finished plans call for 2,200 rooms on its 728-hectare property. Part hotel, part timeshare, the resort was planning to open several restaurants, an activity center, kids' club, spa/gym, tennis courts, golf course, and swimming pool in the shape of a giant turtle. Studios have kitchenettes with stainless steel appliances; one-bedroom units have full kitchens. Every suite has a private balcony. Introductory rates start at US$150 per night, but prices are sure to climb as the resort operation gets into full swing.

AGUA VERDE

Between Km. 64 and 63, where the highway turns west toward Ciudad Constitución, a narrow and winding gravel road heads southeast for 41 kilometers to the fish camp of Agua Verde and a series of remote bays that make a good starting point for overnight kayak trips. The route traverses steep terrain with drop-offs of several hundred meters, frequent washouts, and no guardrails; as such, it is not suitable for trailers and RVs.

Along the way, **Rancho El Carricalito** (no tel.) offers basic accommodations and meals, and tortillas and goat cheese for sale. You can camp along the rocky shore here for about

US$5 or continue on to the end of the road at Puerto Agua Verde, where the local *ejido* charges a few dollars a day to camp. Some supplies may be available at the *tienda* in the village of Agua Verde.

CIUDAD INSURGENTES

This community of about 10,000 people has fuel, supplies, and food. Although it is not a destination itself, Ciudad Insurgentes is a point of departure for excursions to La Purísima (102 km), Comondú (101 km), and Puerto Lopez Mateos (17.7 km). Drivers should note that the kilometer markers finish their countdown from Santa Rosalía here and start over at Km. 236.

CIUDAD CONSTITUCIÓN

Ciudad Constitución, the next major town along Mexico 1, gets relatively little attention from travelers, given its size (pop. 37,000). But it has plenty of hotels and restaurants if daylight is waning and you need a place to crash. As the capital of Municipio de Comondú, Ciudad Constitución is an agricultural center for the central peninsula. There are several Pemex stations, banks with ATMs, auto repair places, grocery stores, and a hospital.

Accommodations
UNDER US$50

[Hotel Oasis** (Guerrero 284, btw Prieto/Farias, tel. 613/132-4458, www.hoteloasis.com, US$40), located three blocks off the main drag, is one of the best hotels in town. Modern, clean rooms come with air-conditioning, phones, and TVs, and there's parking, plus a pool and wireless Internet throughout.

Another good choice is the **Posada del Ryal Hotel** (Victoria btw Olochea/Lerdo de Tejada, tel. 613/132-4800 or -4690, US$40), where clean rooms have new bath fixtures. This hotel has secure parking, wireless Internet throughout the hotel, and a pleasant courtyard; there is a laundry next door.

Hotel El Tesoro (Olachea 239, at Independencia, tel. 613/132-8156, mmhoteleltesoro@hotmail.com, US$40) is conveniently located right on the main boulevard, on the south side of town. Its basic rooms come with cable TV and wireless Internet, and the hotel has 24-hour security/lobby hours, and parking and accepts Visa and MasterCard.

CAMPING AND RV PARKS

Misiones RV Trailer Park (Km. 213, Mexico 1-D, tel. 613/132-1103, http://misionesrvpark.com), on the east side of Boulevard Olachea at the north edge of town, has a large camping area with trees for shade. Rigs can pull through or back in. Amenities include a large swimming pool, Wi-Fi, and meals upon request. The owners are happy to arrange whale-watching tours for guests and offer tourist advice in general. The park has hookups that run US$14–18 a night (dry/full) and tent camping for $6 per person. There is also a swimming pool. If you aren't camping, you can rent a room for US$40.

Food

On Sunday afternoons, lines form at **Taquería Karen** (corner of Hidalgo/Olochea, no tel., mains US$5–7) for *cabeza, pescado,* and other tacos. **Tortas and Tacos Las Tortugas** (corner of Olochea/Bravo, no tel., mains US$5–7) makes *tortas, carne asada,* and Cuban sandwiches for US$2–3. At **Brismar** (Olochea at Zapata, tel. 613/137-0270, 8 A.M.–9 P.M. daily, till 8 P.M. Sun., mains US$6–10), a friendly staff serves *mariscos* and *carnes* in a pleasant, clean, and air-conditioned space.

For a taste of something different, **Baja Teriyaki** (Olachea at Bellsario Dominguez, tel. 613/132-7092 or tel. 613/132-8378 for delivery from another branch on Cervantes del Rio and Morelos, lunch and dinner daily, mains US$5–7) is a local chain that serves Mexican-style Japanese dishes accompanied by the usual Mexican salsas and pickled condiments. They have rice bowls, teriyaki of all varieties, and some sushi rolls and fried dishes.

One of the better *asaderos* in town is **Asadero Tribi** (Olachea and Suarez, tel.

LORETO

© NIKKI GOTH ITOI

typical *mariscos* restaurant by the sea

613/132-7353, 8 A.M.–midnight Tues.–Sun.) which does everything from hearty breakfasts for around US$5 to grilled meats, chicken, and seafood entrées in the US$8–12 range. Or you can order tacos with any grilled specialty for US$1.50 apiece. A clean restaurant and full bar round out the experience here.

The best options for groceries are **Super Ley** (Agustín Olachea Aviles btw Ignacio Ramírez/Pelayo, tel. 613/132-6873) and **La Americana** (Agustín Olachea Aviles s/n, no tel.), both on the main drag through town.

MISIÓN SAN LUIS GONZAGA CHIRIYAQUI

If you're following the Spanish mission trail, Ciudad Constitución is the departure point

for a trip to the short-lived San Luis Gonzaga mission (1737–1768). The site was a *visita* before it became a full-fledged mission in 1737 under the leadership of German Padre Lamberto Hostell. Made of sandstone, this simple but sturdy church lacks the ornate features of its counterparts located elsewhere on the peninsula. But it is well preserved, easily accessible, and a pleasant spot for bird-watching and camping. The church is used today by a local community of ranchers and farmers.

There are two turnoffs from Mexico 1 that lead to San Luis Gonzaga. The better option, signed La Presa Iguajil, begins at Km. 195. Follow this road 42 kilometers to reach the settlement.

Bahía Magdalena

At the western edge of the Magdalena plain on the Pacific coast, a long string of barrier islands protects a series of shallow bays that fill with gray whales during calving season, January–March. The surrounding estuaries and mangrove swamp supports a unique and vibrant marine ecosystem. Sheltered Canal Gaviota links the two largest bays in the system, Bahía Magdalena and Bahía Almejas, to create some of the best kayaking and windsurfing conditions anywhere on the peninsula. Visitors here enjoy paddling the bay, climbing 30-foot sand dunes, bird-watching, and gray-whale encounters.

In 2009 Hurricane Jimena, a Category 3 storm, made landfall at Magdalena Bay, leaving 35,000 people in Centra Baja without homes, food, power, and water. Airports, roads, bridges, power lines, and cell towers were destroyed by high winds, flash floods, and mudslides. The state of Baja California Sur was declared a natural disaster. The most severe damage occurred in the area around Isla Magdalena, Bahía Santa María, Puerto López Mateos, Puerto San Carlos, and Punta Abreojos. Given the unfortunate timing of the

disaster, in the midst of a global recession, the path to recovery has been extremely slow for these coastal communities.

Two environmental organizations play an active role in conservation efforts around the bay: Vigilantes de Bahía Magdalena, A.C. (www.propeninsula.org/window/1/8.html) and Guardianes del Agua, A.C. (La Paz Coastkeeper, www.guardianesdelagua.org). Both organizations are affiliated with the International Waterkeeper Alliance.

◖ WHALE-WATCHING

Just 45 minutes by car from Ciudad Constitución and about 2.5 hours from Loreto, Bahía Magdalena is the southernmost of the three gray-whale calving lagoons on the Pacific coast of the Baja Peninsula. (Laguna Ojo de Liebre near Guerrero Negro and Laguna San Ignacio are the other two.) Whale-watching tours that depart from Mulegé, Loreto, or La Paz generally head for this bay.

It is possible on some days to view the whale activity from a distance on shore near Puerto López Mateos, but this doesn't compare to the experience of getting up close on a boat. Look will be slim and the danger factor will be unnecessarily high.

Boat drivers must be licensed to drive in the lagoons during the whale- calving season. Ask at Hotel Brennan in San Carlos for a guide or head down to the embarcadero on the west side of town near the lighthouse to hire someone directly.

Viajes Mar y Arena (tel. 613/136-0076, fax 613/136-0232), **Brennan's y Asociados** (tel. 613/136-0288, fax 613/136-0019, turismo@balandra.uabcs.mx), and **Unión de Lancheros y Servicios Turísticos de Puerto San Carlos (ULYSTOURS)** (tel. 613/136-0253, Crispín Mendoza) are all licensed to run guided boat tours.

In Puerto López Mateos, several operators are authorized to take tourists on whale-watching tours. They include **Unión de Lancheros Touristicos** (tel. 613/131-5114), **Aquendi** (tel. 613/131-5164 or -5105 or -5306, US$80/hour, up to 6 people), and **Renta de Lanchas Juana Rosas III** (tel. 613/113-9195 or 613/131-5123) The offices for all these businesses are located at the port.

☾ Baja Expeditions (U.S. tel. 858/581-3311 or 800/843-6967, www.bajaex.com) offers highly recommended "catered camping" trips to Bahía Magdalena for US$240 per person per night (double occupancy). During the day, you'll go whale-watching, kayaking, or beach walking, and in the evening, you can hear guest speakers talk about local marine life.

Family-run **Mag Bay Tours** (U.S. tel. 215/667-8470, www.magbaytours.com) started out as a surf camp and then added whale-watching and sportfishing services; the company emphasizes a sustainable, low-impact approach to tourism. It has two semipermanent base camps: Its surf camp is located on the northern point of Bahía Santa María, and the whale-watching camp is inside Bahía Magdalena. Guests stay in dome-shaped tents that are big enough to stand up in. Each has a porch area that is protected from the wind. The camp provides sleeping bags, pillows, and cots with air mattresses. In winter you can book day trips from

for a viewing area with a parking lot north of the fish-processing plant.

A three- to four-hour *panga* tour costs about US$65 per person for up to four people, and prices are likely to fluctuate with fuel prices. It can be difficult—and dangerous—to cruise the lagoon when the winter winds kick up, so tour operators generally recommend that you allow an extra day or two on your visit in case the weather doesn't cooperate. In addition to the whales, you'll likely spot sea lions and a variety of marine birds. Beware of any *panguero* who offers to take you out in inclement weather; your chances of seeing the whales three to five hours in length or overnight packages that include all meals and transportation from San Carlos. A basic "eco-adventure" package (US$250 per person) includes two days and one night of accommodations with about seven hours of whale-watching over the two days. In summer eight-day surfing trips cost US$1,360.

Aside from watching for whales in winter and surfing in summer, clam-digging, campfires, bird-watching, and beachcombing are all part of the experience.

PUERTO SAN CARLOS

The largest town in the area is Puerto San Carlos (pop. 5,200), with the only other deepwater port on the Pacific coast of Baja besides Ensenada.

During the whale-watching season, Puerto San Carlos hosts the **Festival de Ballena Gris** (Gray Whale Festival), with music, food, and crafts festivities every weekend from the middle of February through the end of March.

Puerto San Carlos has a Pemex station,

several *tiendas,* a post office, and government offices for port captain, customs, and immigration. Public long-distance TelMex phones are scattered throughout the town.

PUERTO LÓPEZ MATEOS

North of Puerto San Carlos, tiny Puerto López Mateos offers a similar array of services but on a much smaller scale. It has a cannery, post office, and Pemex, plus several *tiendas,* hotels, and restaurants. TelMex public phones are scattered throughout town.

The town celebrated its 16th **Festival Internacional de la Ballena Gris** in February 2009. It also has a local fiesta on the last weekend in April or first weekend in May.

Several whale-watching tour operators have offices at the port, and booths of vendors sell all kinds of *artesania* in the high season.

PUERTO CANCÚN AND PUERTO CHALE

These two fishing camps are located in the shadow of Isla Santa Margarita. They have basic

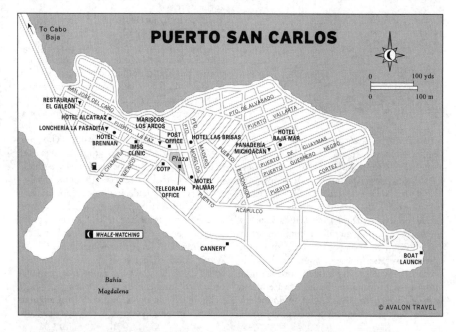

supplies, good camping, and an abundance of fresh clams, lobster, and other seafood.

SPORTS AND RECREATION
Fishing and Boating
Sportfishing remains a major attraction in the area, especially in the high season of July–November. Anglers catch halibut, yellowtail, red bass (mangrove snapper), corvina, and snook close to shore and big game fish farther out. For clams, you can simply walk along the shallows of either bay and dig.

San Carlos has a concrete boat ramp for launching small boats, as do Puerto López Mateos and Puerto Chale.

Kiteboarding and Windsurfing
Windsurfers and kiteboarders flock to Bahía Magdalena for the best wind conditions on the Pacific coast of the Baja Peninsula. Beginners take shelter in the relatively calm bay, while advanced boarders venture out to the *bocas* for stronger winds and bigger waves.

Surfing
South/southwest swells roll into Bahi Santa Maria beginning in May or June through November. Surfers enjoy three right point breaks here—Cuevas, Campsites, and Betadines—and the estuary mouth provides a fast beach break. Mag Bay Tours offers all-inclusive weeklong surf camps (Sun.–Sun.).

South of Bahía Magalena, committed surfers frequent remote Punta El Conejo, a point that juts far enough out into the open ocean to catch north and south swells. The left here holds the larger swells, while the right will close out. Beware the urchins on the rocks on the inside.

There are no facilities, but you can camp among the dunes here. Local lobster fishermen may come by in the evening to sell their sadly undersized catches. Normally, someone from the property will come and collect US$5 per car in exchange for collecting garbage and maintaining the primitive but sheltered bathrooms. This land and the access to it is private, but the owners don't mind leaving it open to visitors.

windsurfing on Bahía Magdalena

With a sturdy vehicle, you can follow the coastal road south another 17 kilometers to reach **Punta Márquez,** another surf spot. This same road continues all the way to Todos Santos (124 km from El Conejo), passing a number of remote beach breaks along the way.

ACCOMMODATIONS
Puerto San Carlos
The best place to stay in this town is **Hotel Brennan** (Puerto Acapulco, tel. 613/136-0288, www.hotelbrennan.com.mx, US$65), where the still-basic rooms have extra amenities such as ceiling fans, air-conditioning, kitchenettes, and satellite TV. The hotel has a restaurant and bar and can arrange guided outdoor activities for guests.

A popular place for tour groups, **Hotel Alcatraz** (Puerto La Paz, tel. 613/136-0017, www.hotelalcatraz.net, US$65–120), on the main road through town, has nicely tiled rooms set around a courtyard. In-room amenities include TVs, hot water, and minibars. Its restaurant-bar, El Patio, is open 6 A.M.–10 P.M. daily.

© RICHARD JACKSON

LORETO

There is laundry service, plus free Internet, boats and kayaks for rent and secure parking.

You can camp at the northwest and southeast ends of the peninsula for around US$5 per vehicle.

Puerto López Mateos

Hotel Posada Tornavuelta (Abelardo L. Rodríguez, tel. 613/131-5106, US$30) offers several clean rooms with private baths. Check in at the house next door. This hotel stays open year-round, and there is an adjacent restaurant in the works.

Cabañas Dunas, affiliated with the Aquendi complex, which includes a restaurant, bar, and tours (tel. 613/131-5293, cabanas_dunas@hotmail.com, US$40), is on the left as you head into the port. Its new, duplex-style cabanas each have private hot-water bathrooms and small patios. **El Camarón Feliz** (Abelardo L. Rodríguez, tel. 613/131-5032) also has five rooms for rent at US$30, each with its own bath.

FOOD
Puerto San Carlos

For fresh seafood, head to **Restaurant El Galeón** (no tel., lunch and dinner daily, mains US$10–15), close to Hotel Brennan. It serves beef and chicken dishes, as well as delicious shellfish and fish. **Mariscos Los Arcos** (Calle La Paz, no tel., 8 A.M.–10 P.M. daily, mains US$5–15, lobster around US$30) prepares seafood, *antojitos,* and Mexican breakfasts.

Another option for reasonably priced and delicious fresh food is **La Cocina de Tere** (no tel., mains US$5–10), just up from Hotel Alcatraz. The menu varies according to what's fresh, and your server will tell you what's available that day.

Puerto López Mateos

A few restaurants in town serve good seafood dishes, but they are usually open only January–April, when the whale-watchers are around. **El Camarón Feliz** (Abelardo L. Rodríguez, tel. 613/131-5032, mains US$5–10) is the place to stop for fish tacos. **Restaurant Ballena Gris** (no tel., mains US$10–15), on the right as you come into town, prepares fresh fish and shellfish.

GETTING THERE AND AROUND

You can drive the paved highway Mexico 22 from Ciudad Constitución to Puerto San Carlos (57 km west) in under an hour, or catch one of three buses a day that connect the two towns (US$5 pp). Bus fare from La Paz is US$34 one way.

To get to Puerto López Mateos, take the paved route west from Ciudad Insurgentes. And for Puerto Chale, turn off the highway at Km. 157.

The 1:250,000-scale INEGI La Paz map (G12-10-11) will help you find roads along the coast of Bahía Magdalena and Bahía Almejas.

LA PAZ AND VICINITY

If you've been making your way down the peninsula visiting small towns, fishing villages, and remote coastal stretches, the state capital of La Paz (pop. 226,000) and the largest city in Southern Baja may come as quite a shock. But once you've settled in and adjusted to the sight of more cars, shops, hotels, restaurants, and people, La Paz begins to show its true colors.

For many travelers, this city achieves the perfect balance: Nestled at the southern end of the largest and one of the most beautiful bays along the Gulf coast, it is tropical and picturesque, with a five-kilometer-long bayside promenade and plenty of opportunities for outdoor adventure. Protected islands offshore entertain paddlers, snorkelers, and scuba divers. Remote beaches, mountain scenery, and even

surf on the Pacific coast are all only a short drive away.

And yet La Paz conveys the feel of a real place with real people and its own distinct history and culture. The first Europeans to set foot on the peninsula arrived at La Paz in the 16th century, and the city was a pearling center long before it became a tourist destination. It is a hub for government, commerce, education, medical services, and environmental conservation. This is not a purpose-built resort town. La Paz is ideal for the traveler who wants more than a beach-and-booze vacation; here, you'll get some history, eco-adventure, and a taste of the real Mexico. The locals go about their business, and tourists can take it or leave it. And that's exactly why many visitors fall in love with the city.

HIGHLIGHTS

◖ *Malecón* Álvaro Obregón: You haven't experienced La Paz until you've strolled the waterfront promenade at sunset. Visitors and residents alike pause to watch the dramatic display of color. Take a break for a cocktail or an ice cream and enjoy the afternoon breeze (page 217).

◖ Museo Regional de Antropología e Historia: Think you know your Baja history?

Save time for a tour of the fossils, minerals, and maps of rock-painting sites in this well-run museum. Exhibits depict prehistoric and colonial life throughout Central and Southern Baja (page 219).

◖ Playa El Tecolote: A drive to the end of the road along Bahía de La Paz leads to this wide, sandy beach. Wade into clear, shallow waters and enjoy views of Isla Espíritu Santo across the channel. A steady breeze keeps the bugs away if you decide to spend the night (page 221).

◖ Isla Espíritu Santo: The best-known of the islands offshore from La Paz entertains paddlers, divers, and boaters with white-sand beaches and rock reefs. You can camp in several places on the island and enjoy endless opportunities for outdoor adventure (page 222).

◖ Carnaval: Like several other Mexican cities, La Paz celebrates Carnaval with great fanfare in mid-February. Time your visit with this annual event to experience the heart and soul of the city. The entertainment includes live music, colorful parades, and amusement rides, plus plenty of tequila and cerveza (page 235).

◖ Bahía de la Ventana: A short drive south of La Paz, this L-shaped bay offers ideal winds for kiteboarders and windsurfers, plus easy access to Isla Cerralvo for scuba diving adventures. Enjoy the remote feel while it lasts (page 252).

LOOK FOR ◖ TO FIND RECOMMENDED SIGHTS, ACTIVITIES, DINING, AND LODGING.

Marine biologists on sabbatical from universities in the United States, young professionals from mainland Mexico, vacationers cruising on their yachts, and baby boomers looking to live comfortably in their retirement are all making La Paz their home base. If you want to move to Southern Baja yet still have some of the conveniences of urban life, La Paz may well be your place.

Despite the feverish pace of real estate activity, the city that John Steinbeck described as *antigua* has protected its deep-rooted traditions, many of which came from the mainland along with the earliest immigrants. Then, as now, people who came over from Mexico City and other large cities were searching for a slower pace and a better quality of life.

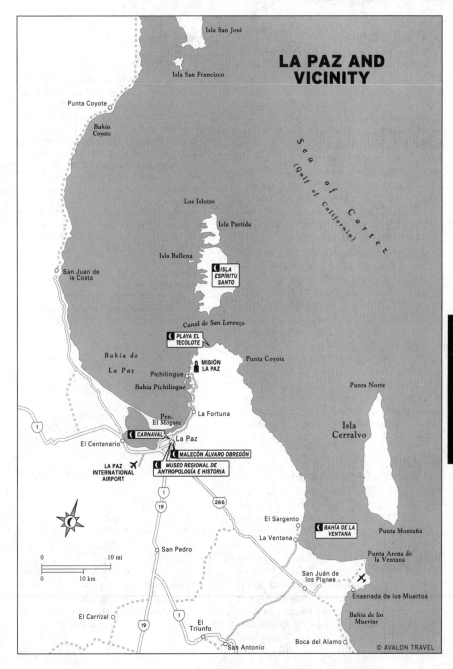

LA PAZ AND VICINITY

Isla San José

Isla San Francisco

LA PAZ AND VICINITY

Punta Coyote

Bahía Coyote

S e a   o f   C o r t e z
(Gulf of California)

Los Islotes

Isla Partida

Isla Ballena

San Juan de la Costa

ISLA ESPÍRITU SANTO

Canal de San Lorenzo

PLAYA EL TECOLOTE

Bahía de La Paz

Punta Coyote

MISIÓN LA PAZ

Pichilingue

Bahía Pichilingue

Punta Norte

La Fortuna

Pen. El Mogote

CARNAVAL

La Paz

Isla Cerralvo

El Centenario

MALECÓN ÁLVARO OBREGÓN

LA PAZ INTERNATIONAL AIRPORT

MUSEO REGIONAL DE ANTROPOLOGÍA E HISTORIA

266

19

El Sargento

La Ventana

BAHÍA DE LA VENTANA

Punta Montaña

Punta Arena de la Ventana

San Pedro

0   10 mi

0   10 km

San Juán de los Planes

Ensenada de los Muertos

El Carrizal

19

El Triunfo

Bahía de los Muertos

San Antonio

Boca del Alamo

© AVALON TRAVEL

HISTORY
Spanish Explorers

Two nomadic tribes, the Guaicura and Pericu, inhabited the area around present-day La Paz before the Spanish arrived in the 16th century. They knew the Bahía de La Paz as Airapí. In 1533 Hernán Cortés sent the *Concepcion* to sea to explore the Gulf of Mexico. After staging a mutiny and killing the ship's captain, the crew landed at La Paz in search of water, only to be attacked by the indigenous people. A few survivors were able to sail back to the mainland, and their tales of a beautiful bay filled with pearls lured Cortés himself back to Antigua California. He landed near Pichilingue in 1535 and stayed for two years, trying unsuccessfully to colonize the indigenous people.

Sebastián Vizcaíno landed next, in 1596, as part of a voyage around the entire Antigua California coast. He bestowed the name Bahía de La Paz (Bay of Peace) upon the area as a reflection of how well the indigenous people treated his crew.

Repeated attempts to establish a permanent settlement in the 17th century failed due to the scarcity of food and water and tension with the indigenous people. During this time, the bay became a hiding place for pirates seeking to attack the Manila Galleons. The Spanish needed a stronghold on the peninsula, but it would be 150 years before the first mission succeeded in Loreto in 1683.

Misión Nuestra Señora del Pilar de la Paz Airapí

Although La Paz hosted many of the first European explorers in the 16th century, it took nearly 200 years and several failed attempts for the Spanish to establish a permanent settlement. Jesuit padres Juan de Ugarte and Jaime Bravo eventually succeeded in 1720, but their mission was short-lived. The Pericú burned the city to the ground during the rebellion of 1734, and the mission never fully recovered. The Jesuits abandoned it in 1748. The precise location of the mission is lost to history but believed to be near the modern-day Plaza Constitución and the 1861 Catedral

de Nuestra Señora de La Paz. The twin towers of the church overlook the plaza. Inside, little evidence remains of the original mission.

The 19th Century

In the post-missionary period, a group of farmers and fishermen gave La Paz new life, and it ascended to a position of importance in 1829 when the municipal capital of Southern Baja was moved from Loreto to La Paz following a severe hurricane.

American forces occupied La Paz during the

THE PEARLS OF LA PAZ

When the Spanish began to explore the Sea of Cortez and the coastline near La Paz in the 16th century, they found abundant oyster beds near Isla Cerralvo. The pearls were well known to the indigenous people, who wore them as necklaces. Word of the treasure spread, and commercial expeditions began making the trip from the mainland to harvest saltwater pearls, which were sent back to Europe to adorn the Spanish clergy and royalty.

During the mission period of 1697-1768, the Jesuits limited pearl-diving activities, but the industry came back to life in the 19th century, when entrepreneurs contracted Yaqui divers from the mainland to dive the Gulf coast from La Paz to Mulegé.

Modern diving technology introduced in the 1870s allowed divers to reach deeper oyster beds and harvest mass quantities of the shelled mollusks. Only a small percentage of oysters harvested contained a natural pearl, and the oysters were all but depleted during this time. In the late 1930s, a disease – rumored but never confirmed to be introduced by the Japanese – attacked the few pearl oyster beds that remained, and by the time John Steinbeck arrived in La Paz, Southern Baja's world-famous pearling industry was a thing of the past.

Mexican-American War (1846–1848) until the Treaty of Hidalgo divided California into Alta and Baja territories.

In the years following the Mexican-American War, La Paz was known mainly for its pearl trade. Its economy diversified after World War II, when the government declared La Paz a duty-free port. People from mainland Mexico began traveling to La Paz to buy discounted imports, and some decided to make Baja California their home.

The 20th Century

People from the United States began arriving in the 1950s to fish the Sea of Cortez, and La Paz became known briefly as a celebrity resort town. The paving of the Transpeninsular Highway in 1973 heralded the next major change, transforming La Paz into a more accessible and popular travel destination. When Baja California Sur became a Mexican state in 1974, the government designated La Paz the state capital.

With modern transportation possible by air, land, and sea, La Paz expanded into a major center of commerce serving the greater Southern Baja region.

Tourism and Real Estate Development

Since the turn of the century, the Baja California Sur state government has invested heavily in infrastructure improvements and tourism-related services in the area around La Paz. Former BCS Governor Leonel Cota Montaño (1999–2005) cited the development of La Paz as his personal mission and did wonders for the city, including offering the governor's mansion as the city's new aquarium.

As the real estate market becomes saturated in Los Cabos, developers are looking northward. Three large-scale resort developments are under way. Like Cabo San Lucas, La Paz now has its own hilltop Pedregal (www.pedregal.com) gated community, at the northeastern edge of town on the way to Pichilingue. Cobblestone roads and utilities are the first step in the creation of a 52-hectare private, gated

© PAUL ITOI

on the sidewalks of downtown La Paz

community of 370 lots; a 200-room hotel; condos; and a shopping plaza. Nearby, a second beach development, the 500-acre CostaBaja Resort & Marina (www.costabajaresort.com) has an operational 280-slip marina and Fiesta Inn resort. The development also includes 50 villas, plus shops, restaurants, and a golf course. Real estate fever has spread to the south as well, with five hotels, a residential neighborhood, and airport planned for the Bay of Dreams development.

Another development is taking shape on the fragile Mogote Peninsula, a spit of land edged with mangroves that juts out in the bay. Linked to the *malecón* by water taxi, the Paraíso del Mar (www.paradiseofthesea.com, US$150–200) project consists of two golf courses, a 535-slip marina, 2,000 hotel rooms, and 2,000 private homes. At last check, the builders had completed one set of buildings and left the second set an empty concrete shell for now. Builders say they are taking environmental precautions—by planning to build two desalination plants, for example, and designing golf greens that use

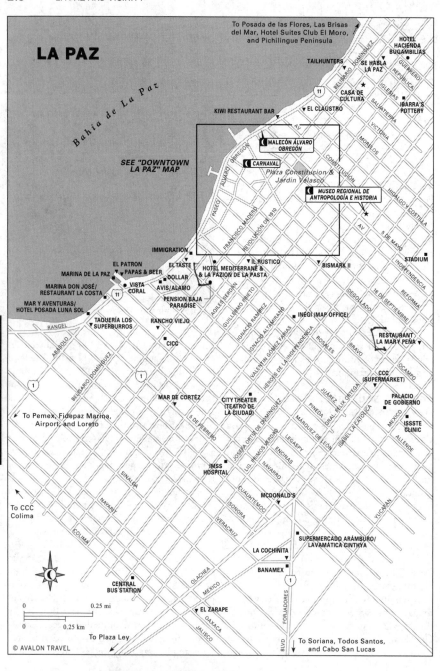

LA PAZ AND VICINITY

LA PAZ

To Posada de las Flores, Las Brisas del Mar, Hotel Suites Club El Moro, and Pichilingue Peninsula

Bahía de La Paz

SEE "DOWNTOWN LA PAZ" MAP

TAILHUNTERS

SE HABLA LA PAZ

CASA DE CULTURA

KIWI RESTAURANT BAR

EL CLAUSTRO

HOTEL HACIENDA BUGAMBILIAS

IBARRA'S POTTERY

MALECÓN ÁLVARO OBREGÓN

CARNAVAL

Plaza Constitución & Jardín Velasco

MUSEO REGIONAL DE ANTROPOLOGÍA E HISTORIA

IMMIGRATION

EL PATRON

PAPAS & BEER

MARINA DE LA PAZ

MARINA DON JOSÉ/ RESTAURANT LA COSTA

MAR Y AVENTURAS/ HOTEL POSADA LUNA SOL

VISTA CORAL

EL TASTE

DOLLAR

AVIS/ALAMO

PENSION BAJA PARADISE

IL RUSTICO

HOTEL MEDITERRANÉ & LA PAZION DE LA PASTA

BISMARK II

STADIUM

TAQUERÍA LOS SUPERBURROS

RANCHO VIEJO

CICC

INEGI (MAP OFFICE)

RESTAURANT LA MAR Y PEÑA

CCC (SUPERMARKET)

MAR DE CORTÉZ

CITY THEATER (TEATRO DE LA CIUDAD)

PALACIO DE GOBIERNO

ISSSTE CLINIC

To Pemex, Fidepaz Marina, Airport, and Loreto

IMSS HOSPITAL

McDONALD'S

To CCC Colima

SUPERMERCADO ARÁMBURO/ LAVAMÁTICA CINTHYA

LA COCHINITA

BANAMEX

CENTRAL BUS STATION

EL ZARAPE

To Plaza Ley

To Soriana, Todos Santos, and Cabo San Lucas

0   0.25 mi
0   0.25 km

© AVALON TRAVEL

Streets: BELISARIO DOMINGUEZ, DOMINGUEZ, REPUBLICA, GUERRERO, IGLESIAS, SALVATIERRA, VICTORIA, MORELOS, CONSTITUCION, HIDALGO Y COSTILLA, 5 DE MAYO, INDEPENDENCIA, REFORMA, 16 DE SEPTIEMBRE, DEGOLLADO, OCAMPO, BRAVO, MEXICO, ALLENDE, YUCATAN, FORJADORES, ÁLVARO OBREGÓN, PASEO, FRANCISCO MADERO, REVOLUCION DE 1910, AQUILES SERDAN, GUILLERMO PRIETO, IGNACIO RAMIREZ, IGNACIO ALTAMIRANO, VALENTIN GOMEZ FARIAS, HEROES DE LA INDEPENDENCIA, ROSALES, JUAREZ, GRAL. FELIX ORTEGA, ISABEL LA CATOLICA, PINEDA, MARQUEZ DE LEON, LEGASPY, ENCINAS, NAVARRO, LIC. PRIMO VERDAD, JOSEFA ORTIZ DE DOMINGUEZ, 5 DE FEBRERO, CUAUHTEMOC, SONORA, VERACRUZ, ISONORA, OLACHEA, MEXICO, OAXACA, JALISCO, RANGEL, ABASOLO, BELISARIO DOMINGUEZ, SINALOA, NAYARIT, EQUIMA native plants; however, conservationists continue to raise concerns that the development will permanently destroy hundreds of hectares of mangrove essential to the health of the local marine ecosystem. The impact remains to be seen, but, regardless, the development has permanently changed the skyline of La Paz.

PLANNING YOUR TIME

Allow several days to explore the city and surrounding beaches—a week or more if you plan to fish, snorkel, dive, or kayak around the islands just offshore. If you're coming to learn Spanish, local schools recommend a minimum stay of two weeks and up to a month if you can swing it. Travelers planning to take the ferry to Mazatlán should allow an extra day or two to arrange permits and reservations.

February is La Paz's busiest month for tourists. But even then, hotel rooms are usually easy to find. One exception is when the Baja 1000 off-road race comes to town in mid-November. With the race finish just outside the city limits, every room, condo, and vacation rental books up months in advance. If you roll into La Paz without reservations, you'll likely have to continue south to Los Barriles to find a place to crash for the night.

Sights

◖ MALECÓN ÁLVARO OBREGÓN

The most defining feature of downtown La Paz is the five-kilometer promenade that parallels Paseo Álvaro Obregón and hugs the shoreline from Calle 5 de Febrero at the southwest end and the Hotel El Moro at the northeast end. Along the way are a couple of marinas, numerous restaurants, shops, car rental agencies, hotels, a tourist pier, *panga*

© PAUL ITOI

holiday spirit on the *malecón*

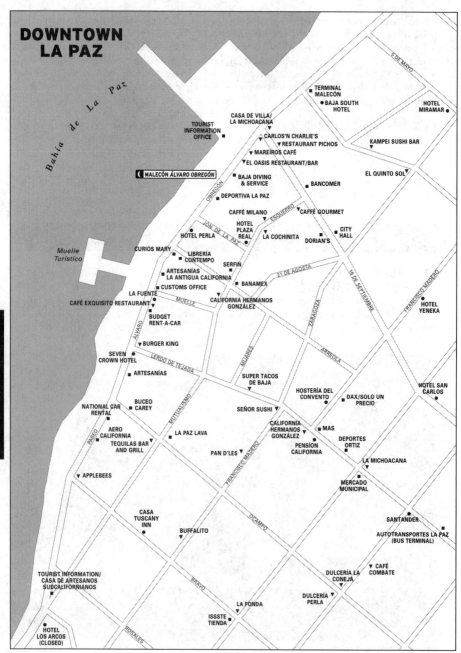

DOWNTOWN LA PAZ

Bahía de La Paz

Muelle Turístico

TERMINAL MALECÓN
BAJA SOUTH HOTEL
HOTEL MIRAMAR
CASA DE VILLA/ LA MICHOACANA
TOURIST INFORMATION OFFICE
KAMPEI SUSHI BAR
CARLOS'N CHARLIE'S
RESTAURANT PICHOS
MAREIROS CAFÉ
EL OASIS RESTAURANT/BAR
EL QUINTO SOL
MALECÓN ÁLVARO OBREGÓN
BAJA DIVING & SERVICE
BANCOMER
OBREGÓN
DEPORTIVA LA PAZ
CAFFÉ MILANO
ESQUERRO
CAFFÉ GOURMET
JON DE LA PAZ
HOTEL PLAZA REAL
LA COCHINITA
CITY HALL
HOTEL PERLA
DORIAN'S
CURIOS MARY
LIBRERÍA CONTEMPO
SERFIN
21 DE AGOSTA
16 DE SEPTIEMBRE
FRANCISCO MADERO
ARTESANÍAS LA ANTIGUA CALIFORNIA
BANAMEX
CUSTOMS OFFICE
HOTEL YENEKA
LA FUENTE
MUELLE
CALIFORNIA HERMANOS GONZÁLEZ
CAFÉ EXQUISITO RESTAURANT
ÁLVARO
BUDGET RENT-A-CAR
ZARAGOZA
BURGER KING
MILARES
ARREOLA
SEVEN CROWN HOTEL
LERDO DE TEJADA
ARTESANÍAS
SUPER TACOS DE BAJA
HOSTERÍA DEL CONVENTO
DAX/SOLO UN PRECIO
HOTEL SAN CARLOS
NATIONAL CAR RENTAL
BUCEO CAREY
MOTUALISMO
SEÑOR SUSHI
CALIFORNIA HERMANOS GONZÁLEZ
MAS
PASEO
AERO CALIFORNIA
LA PAZ LAVA
DEPORTES ORTIZ
TEQUILAS BAR AND GRILL
PAN D'LES
PENSIÓN CALIFORNIA
LA MICHOACANA
FRANCISCO MADERO
APPLEBEES
MERCADO MUNICIPAL
CASA TUSCANY INN
BUFFALITO
SANTANDER
OCAMPO
AUTOTRANSPORTES LA PAZ (BUS TERMINAL)
TOURIST INFORMATION/ CASA DE ARTESANOS SUDCALIFORNIANOS
DULCERÍA LA CONEJA
CAFÉ COMBATE
BRAVO
DULCERÍA PERLA
HOTEL LOS ARCOS (CLOSED)
LA FONDA
ISSSTE TIENDA
ROSALES

boats, and a small beach area. A fixture since the early days of the city, the *malecón* is looking better than ever these days. Decorative paving, recently painted crosswalks, and white wrought-iron benches invite visitors and residents to take a sunset stroll along the Bahía de la Paz, just as the afternoon breeze kicks up. Water quality has improved, too, making it possible to swim once again (though most people continue northeast to the beaches along the Pichilingue Peninsula).

◖ MUSEO REGIONAL DE ANTROPOLOGÍA E HISTORIA

As Southern Baja's cultural center, La Paz has a wonderful anthropology and history museum, the Museo Regional de Antropología e Historia (5 de Mayo and Altamirano, tel. 612/122-0162, 9 A.M.–6 P.M. daily, US$2–3, free Sun. and holidays). Its three floors contain exhibits that begin with a depiction of life in Baja California before the Europeans arrived—including photos and depictions of prehistoric cave paintings—and progress all the way up through the Mexican-American War of the 19th century. Fossils and minerals tell the story of the geologic past of the peninsula. The knowledgeable and enthusiastic staff speaks limited English, and exhibit signs for the permanent exhibits are only in Spanish. The on-site gift shop has replicas of Amerindian pottery and other souvenirs for sale as well as books, music, and guides focused on the history, geology, and anthropology of Mexico.

PLAZA CONSTITUCIÓN AND JARDÍN VELASCO

La Paz's central plaza and garden take up a full block between Avenida Independencia and Calle 5 de Mayo and between Calles Revolución de 1910 and Madero. With its gazebo and wrought-iron benches, this is a good place to get your bearings and begin a walking tour. Note the fountain with a representation of the Mushroom Rock that stands just offshore in Balandra Bay. In the evening you might catch a live performance or a game of Mexican bingo.

On the southwest side of the plaza (Revolución de 1910 btw 5 de Mayo/ Independencia) stands the 1871 Catedral de Nuestra Señora de La Paz, built by the Dominicans as a replacement for the original Jesuit mission church.

LA UNIDAD CULTURAL PROFESOR JESÚS CASTRO AGÚNDEZ

This cultural center (Navarro btw Altamirano/ Independencia, tel. 612/125-0207, 8 A.M.–3 P.M. Mon.–Fri.) has art exhibits, classes, and the 1,500-seat city theater, which stages dance performances, concerts, and plays year-round. In the complex, **Galería de Arte Carlos Olochea** (tel. 612/122-9196) hosts temporary and permanent exhibitions by renowned national artists. The city's central library and historical archives are also located here.

ACUARIO DE LAS CALIFORNIAS

A welcome addition to the La Paz waterfront is the long-anticipated aquarium, housed in the historic governor's mansion, three miles northeast of downtown. This is a good place to get acquainted with the local marine life by viewing exhibits of red snappers, sea turtles, lobster, and more than 300 other species. Built with state and federal funds as an engine for environmental education and conservation, the aquarium is open 9 A.M.–2 P.M. Monday–Saturday and located on Playa El Caimancito, near the La Concha Beach Resort on the road to Pichilingue.

Beaches

BAHÍA DE LA PAZ

A series of public beaches line the Bahía de La Paz, from the city center all the way to the tip of the Pichilingue Peninsula. As a general rule, the beaches become prettier as you get farther away from the city. To find them, follow the La Paz-Pichilingue Road (Paseo Obregón becomes this road at the northeast end of the *malecón*), which is paved all the way to El Tecolote at the northern tip of the peninsula.

Palmira, El Coromuel, and El Caimancito

At Playa Palmira, closest to downtown La Paz (Km. 2.5), resort development has encroached on the sand—so it's best to continue another kilometer to Playa El Coromuel (Km. 4.3), a small beach with a restaurant, bar, *palapa* structures for shade, and restrooms. Playa El Caimancito, at the La Concha Beach Resort (Km. 6), has a rock reef close to shore suitable for snorkeling and an aquarium called the Acuario de las Californias.

Playa El Tesoro and Punta Colorada

Playa El Tesoro (Km. 13) has *palapas* and a hit-or-miss restaurant. The dirt road that heads southwest from the beach goes to Playa Punta Colorada, a secluded swimming cove.

Playa Pichilingue

The next beach east of the ferry terminal (Km. 17–18) has restrooms open 24/7 for visitors who want to camp. Its simple *palapa* restaurant (tel. 612/122-4565, 11 A.M.–9 P.M. daily, mains US$5–15) serves a variety of Mexican fare, but the real reason to go is the shellfish: clams, lobster, mussels, and crab. A taxi from the *malecón* to the ferry terminal will run about US$20.

Playa Balandra

The best beach for snorkeling along this stretch is Playa Balandra, which came under protection by the La Paz City Council in 2008—a victory for local environmental organizations. Known for Mushroom Rock, which balances offshore, this sometimes-crowded beach is protected from the wind (good for calm water and chilly days, but not so good for bugs when camping). Swim out to the coral reef at the south end of the beach for the best underwater scenery. To get the best views, you'll have to scale the rock cliffs behind the beach. Look for an access road about five kilometers past the ferry terminal.

◖ Playa El Tecolote

Continue another three kilometers beyond the road to Playa Balandra and you'll reach Playa El Tecolote, an exposed beach that faces the Canal de San Lorenzo and Isla Espíritu Santo to the north. A handful of *pangas* are moored here, and you can swim in a roped-off area, or anywhere along the beach. The slope is gentle leading into the water and the bottom is sandy, so you can wade quite far from shore before having to swim. Campers often come here to escape the bugs. Two beachfront restaurants, **El Tecolote** (tel. 612/127-9494, mains US$8–15) and **Palapa Azul** (tel. 612/122-1801, mains US$8–15), offer food and drinks as well as rental gear (chairs, umbrellas, fishing equipment) and boat tours (US$$40–50). There are pay showers and public *palapas* for shade.

Though you are well away from the city, don't leave valuables unattended. Theft is rare, but readers have reported that it happens.

Playa El Coyote

After El Tecolote, a dirt road continues around to the east side of the Pichilingue Peninsula to Punta Coyote. Coves along this stretch are rocky and sand is gray or brown instead of white. The road effectively ends here, although the most adventurous off-roaders might attempt to find their way through a maze of sand roads to Puerto Mejia and Las Cruces.

Las Cruces

When Hernan Cortés sailed from the mainland to Antigua California in 1535, he supposedly landed at Las Cruces, about 50 kilometers southeast of La Paz on the Canal de

Cerralvo. Today three stone crosses perched on a bluff mark the historic place. The port here became a key part of the pearl trade but was abandoned by the 1930s when the oyster supply had been depleted.

Believing he had found a diamond in the rough, Abelardo L. Rodríguez Montijo, grandson of Mexico's interim president (1932–1934), decided to invest. In 1949 he built a luxury fly-in resort on 8,000 hectares, designed to attract wealthy Hollywood celebrities—and went on to found the original Palmilla hotel in Los Cabos in 1957.

Though still a private organization, Rancho Las Cruces has opened its guestrooms to the public again (www.rancholascruces.com).

PENÍNSULA EL MOGOTE

The closest land you see when standing on the *malecón* is the thumb-shaped Mogote Peninsula. Extending 11 kilometers in an east–west direction, it joins the main Baja Peninsula via a narrow sand spit on the north side of the Ensenada de La Paz. Mangroves grow along the Mogote's southern shore, which faces the city; the opposite shore features a long, sandy beach.

Once the domain of kayakers and other adventure-seekers, the area is now under development as the US$240 million Paraíso del Mar (tel. 612/125-5199, toll-free U.S. tel. 888/207-2825, www.parasiseofthesea.com, stay-and-play packages starting at US$129 and up) real estate project takes shape. Plans call for two golf courses, a clubhouse, hundreds of homes, a shopping mall, church, hotels, marina, and park. Necessary infrastructure will include desalination plants, water and sewage treatment plants, and a ferry terminal. (Although there is a dirt road leading out to the peninsula from El Comitá, north of La Paz, primary access for visitors will be by water taxi, since the distance is only 800 meters from the *malecón*.)

The project has encountered criticism from environmentalists, including Greenpeace, for endangering hundreds of acres of mangroves, which provide a habitat and nutrients for thousands of marine species in the Sea of Cortez. But the developers are taking steps to protect the fragile ecosystem by landscaping the golf courses with native plants, for example.

Accommodations today consist of a few newly finished condos and rental houses. The resort has an office on the *malecón* in the Vista Coral Plaza near Papas and Beer, where guests check in and catch the water taxi to the peninsula. Activities so far are mainly centered around golf tournaments, but you can also walk the beach, borrow a kayak, and play volleyball, tennis, horseshoes, or boccie. Transportation within the resort is via golf cart (US$20 per day). A free shuttle is also provided. The golf course (tel. 612/165-1818) is open 7 A.M.–7 P.M. Tuesday–Sunday. A restaurant on the course is open the same hours. La Tiendita, a small convenience store, is open 11 A.M.–7 P.M. daily.

Islands

You haven't fully experienced La Paz until you've explored the group of undeveloped barrier islands that guards the entrance to the bay. Along the shores of Isla Espíritu Santo and Isla Partida, protected coves in shallow bays provide a safe environment for swimming, rock and coral reefs attract abundant marine life, and steep cliffs lead to stunning bay views.

◀ ISLA ESPÍRITU SANTO

Closest to the Pichilingue Peninsula, Isla Espíritu Santo is 22.5 kilometers long. Its southwest side is scalloped with a series of narrow bays, each with one or more fingers reaching deep into the interior of the island. The shoreline on the northeast side is smoother, with fewer protected places to land small boats and snorkel or swim.

Formerly owned by a local *ejido,* this island was "sold" to the Mexican government in 2003 through the cooperative efforts of several nonprofits, which raised US$3.3 million to compensate *ejido* members for the land. For the traveler in search of outdoor adventure, this means the island has a good

ISLA ESPÍRITU SANTO, ISLA PARTIDA, AND LOS ISLOTES

Los Islotes

Isla Partida

El Embudo

Arroyos

Punta Tintorera

Ensenada Grande

Punta Tijeretas

Las Cuevitas

El Cardonal

FRESHWATER WELL

Sand Spit

El Cardonalcito

Caleta Partida

El Cardonalcito

Bahía El Mesteño

Arroyo

Isla Espíritu Santo

S e a   o f   C o r t e z

(Gulf of California)

FRESHWATER WELL

Arroyos

Caleta El Candelero

Bahía La Salinita

Punta Lobos

Isla Ballena

Playa Ballena

ISLA ESPÍRITU SANTO

Arroyos

HOT SPRINGS

Isla Gallo

Playa Gallina

Isla Gallina

LIGHTHOUSE

Punta Bonanza

Puerto Ballena

Arroyo

Arroyo

Bahía Bonanza

Playa Coralito

Bahía de La Paz

Punta Morito

Punta Prieta

Bahía San Gabriel

Punta Lupona

Punta Colorada

Playa Dispensa

Punta Dispensa

0   1 mi

0   1 km

To La Paz

LEAVE NO TRACE

Visitors intent on setting foot on the delicate islands of the Sea of Cortez should heed the recommendations proffered by Conservation International as follows:

• Check your equipment and provisions thoroughly before landing to avoid the introduction of rats, mice, insects, or seeds from other islands or from the mainland. Check your shoes and cuffs.

• Don't bring cats, dogs, or any other animals to the islands.

• Don't take plants, flowers, shells, rocks, or animals from the islands.

• The animals and plants that live on the islands are not used to human presence. Keep this in mind during your visit.

• Keep a minimum distance of 45 meters from all seabird and sea lion colonies, and keep at least 300 meters away from pelicans during their nesting period (Apr.-May).

• Don't cut cacti or shrubs. Don't gather wood; plants take a long time to grow on these arid islands. Dry trunks are the home of many small animals. If you need to cook, take your own stove and avoid making fires.

• Don't make new walking paths. Don't remove stones or dig holes; you will cause erosion.

• Don't camp on the islands unless you are familiar with low-impact techniques. Conservation International Mexico can provide you with that information.

• Help keep the islands clean. Don't throw or leave garbage on the islands or in the sea. Help even more by bringing back any garbage you find.

• To camp or even land for any activity on the islands of the Sea of Cortez you need a permit from the Secretaría de Medio Ambiente y Recursos Naturales (SEMARNAT). To obtain a permit, contact Instituto Nacional de Ecología, Dirección de Aprovechamiento Ecológico, Periferico 5000, Col. Insurgentes Cuicuilco, C.P. 04530, Delegación Coyoacán México D.F. 01049, México, www.ine.gob.mx.

For more information, contact Conservation International, Calle Banamichi Lote 18 Manzana 1, Lomas de Cortés, Guaymas, Son. 85450, México, tel./fax 622/221-1594 or 622/221-2030, m.carvajal@conservation.org, www.conservacion.org.mx, or its main U.S. office at 1919 M St., NW Suite 600, Washington, DC 20036, tel. 202/912-1000 or 800/406-2306, www.conservation.org.

chance of remaining undeveloped, even as large real estate projects take shape on the peninsula.

Due to the presence of numerous reefs and underwater rock formations, this island is a popular stop for snorkeling and scuba diving tours. **Bahía San Gabriel** near the southwest tip of the island features ruins from a former pearl-fishing operation.

For a good hike, begin at the beach at Caleta el Candelero on the northwest side of the island. Find the arroyo and follow it inland, where a deep canyon is carved into the volcanic bluffs. Along the way are wild fig and plum trees; keep your eyes peeled for the rare black jackrabbit.

ISLA PARTIDA

The next major island heading north from Pichilingue is the much smaller Isla Partida, which has more beaches, dive sites, and opportunities for hiking and views. Fish camps at either end of the island sometimes have freshwater, but it isn't guaranteed. Plan to bring your own drinking water. If you are navigating your own boat, beware the sandbar that almost connects Isla Partida with Isla Espíritu Santo. The channel is extremely narrow.

LOS ISLOTES

Hundreds of playful sea lions live on and around this group of small jagged rock islands north of Isla Partida. Roughly a one-hour boat ride from Pichilingue, they are a popular destination for snorkeling, scuba diving, kayaking, and sportfishing.

CAMPING

Because the islands near La Paz are protected by the Mexican government, a permit (US$4/day) is required to camp on them. Visit the local **SEMARNAT office** (2nd floor, Ocampo 1045 btw Rubio/Verdad, tel. 612/128-4171, www.semarnat.gob.mx, 8 A.M.–3 P.M. Mon.–Fri.) before you head out to sea. Pets are prohibited, as is harvesting wood for campfires. The availability of freshwater limits camping options on the larger islands, and camping is not allowed on Ensenada Grande or Playa Ballena.

Two of the bays, Caleta El Candelero on Isla Espíritu Santo and El Cardonalcito on Isla Partida, have freshwater wells where you can bathe. You'll need a bucket and five meters of rope to reach the water level. Purify the water if you must use it for drinking. (Plan to bring your own purified water and only use the well water in an emergency.) It's also a good idea to bring multi-fuel stoves for camping to increase your chances of finding the canisters you need while in Baja.

GETTING TO THE ISLANDS

There are several ways to reach the islands. Most visitors book a daylong kayak, snorkeling, or scuba diving tour. You can also join a guided multiday kayak/camping trip, or arrive by private yacht. Experienced paddlers can rent a kayak in La Paz and paddle the 6.5 kilometers across the channel from Pichilingue (Playa El Tecolote is the closest launch point) to the islands. Wind, current, and tides make this a challenging trip, even though the distance is relatively short. At Playa El Tecolote, you can also hire a *panga* for an excursion to the island. Rates are around US$150 per boat, including lunch. A one-way shuttle out to the island costs about US$75.

Sports and Recreation

FISHING

The best fishing near La Paz takes place May–November, and the typical catch includes wahoo, dorado, and tuna as well as sailfish and blue, black, and striped marlin. The El Bajo seamount is exposed to the wind but has developed a legendary reputation for some of the biggest marlin, tuna, and dorado.

The waters around the far side of the Pichilingue Peninsula near Isla Cerralvo, Punta Arena de la Ventana, and Bahía de los Muertos have more consistent fishing than the bay and islands closer to La Paz. For this reason, many fishermen choose the relative ease of a one-hour van ride and launch at Punta Arena de la Ventana over the *panga*-pounding journey by sea to the same fishing grounds.

If the wind is blowing too hard to get to the pelagics offshore, you can try for inshore species such as barred *pargo,* snapper, mackerel, sea bass, and grouper. Ceviche made from fresh mackerel is a fine consolation prize for getting blown off the big water. The norm for inshore fishing is live sardines with a few thrown in around your bait as chum.

Roosterfish *(pez gallo)* are available in the Punta de la Ventana area and can reach world-record size. The all-tackle world record, weighing 51.7 kilograms, was landed off La Paz in 1960. In 2007 an angler caught an estimated 54-kilogram roosterfish, but it was never weighed. Whether you are fishing or not, there is nothing more exciting than the moment when the spiked comb of the *pez gallo* breaks the surface of the turquoise waters and tears across a shallow bay on Isla Espíritu Santo. Your first instinct might be to run.

SHARK NORMA OFICIAL MEXICANA 029: A COMMERCIAL LONG-LINE FISHING LEGISLATION

Official Mexican Norma 029, commonly seen on bumper stickers and banners throughout Southern Baja as NOM-029, is a highly controversial legislation regulating commercial long-line fishing in the Sea of Cortez and along the Pacific coast of Mexico.

After years of opposition to the *norma* (regulation) by ex-president Vicente Fox, the legislation went into effect only five months after Felipe Calderón took office, in mid-May 2007.

Proponents hail the bill as promoting responsible fishing of sharks and rays; among other things, it restricts new shark fishing permits for the area, prohibits shark finning, and increases protected areas for sharks, sea turtles, and sea lions.

However, opponents claim that problems overlooked by the bill will actually contribute to a decline in the general health of the marine environment, especially in the Sea of Cortez. The problem is that the law legalizes the retention of incidental "by-catch" – around 80 percent of which is usually marlin, sailfish, and other fish until now officially designated to sportfishing purposes only and previously subject to much tighter bag limits. Even though more areas have been designated protected areas for marine life, the bill opens up a greater zone with closer coastal access limits than before; many activists claim that, with surveillance and enforcement being a point of weakness in Mexico, the entire sportfishing industry will soon be wiped out by the encroaching presence of long-liners in areas once restricted for tourism.

A heated debate continues over the purpose and efficiency of achieving the stated purpose of NOM-029. Many NGOs, such as Greenpeace Mexico, International Fund for Animal Welfare (IFAW), and Conservation of Marine Mammals of Mexico (COMARINO), support the bill. They claim that its attempts at regulating the commercial fishing industry are better than nothing (though not enough), and that recognizing and protecting several species of shark – as well as prohibiting their finning, among other positive features of the bill – is a step in the right direction.

Opponents are numerous and vocal, consisting of other prominent marine ecology organizations, such as SeaWatch and Oceana, as well as local unions of sportfishing operators and hotel and restaurant unions of Los Cabos.

IGFA representative and union head Minerva Smith, who owns Minerva's Baja Tackle Shop in Cabo San Lucas, has been recognized for her conservation efforts over the years and is one of the most articulate opponents of the Shark Norma.

Both sides agree that endangered sharks and rays need government protection. Unfortunately, the argument will only be settled through a trial-and-error approach. It's quite possible that allowing commercial long-lines and gillnets so close to the coast will end the sportfishing industry as we know it.

Charters

The fishing charter business in La Paz is well developed, with many professional operations, experienced captains, and well-appointed boats. Here are a few of the most popular choices: Owned by Southern California native Jonathan Roldan, **Tailhunter International** (Obregón 755 btw Salvatierra/Torre Iglesias, cell tel. 612/125-3311, U.S. tel. 626/638-3383, toll-free U.S. tel. 877/825-8802, www. tailhunter-international.com) often guides fly-fishing clients who want to catch roosterfish and dorado. It has two fleets: The La Paz boats head to Espíritu Santo and El Bajo; a separate Punta Arena fleet fishes the waters around Isla Cerralvo, Banco 88, and Bahía de los Muertos.

Jay Murakoshi's **C&J Fishing Adventures** (Flies Unlimited, U.S. tel. 559/449-0679, www. fliesunlimited.com) specializes in saltwater fly-fishing in tropical destinations around the world and leads charter trips to Bahía de la Ventana. Jay also sells his own saltwater and surf-zone flies.

Baja Pirates (toll-free U.S. tel. 866/454-5386, www.bajapiratesoflapaz.com) has a fleet of eight boats, from a standard 22-foot *panga* up to cruisers and a 26-foot Bay Liner. Boats are equipped with life jackets, marine heads (on 210 or larger), tackle, gear, and ice chests (with ice), along with breakfast and lunch. This company has package deals that include airfare out of LAX.

Other charter services include **Fishermen's Fleet** (tel. 612/122-1313, U.S. tel. 408/884-3932, www.fishermensfleet.com), specializing in complete *panga* packages. Fishing destinations include El Bajo, Isla Cerralvo, and Las Arenas. Owner David Jones has lived in La Paz with his family since the 1990s. His 38-foot Hatteras cruiser is a good option for large groups and multiday fishing trips.

The experts say if you bring your own gear, a seven-foot rod with something like Penn 500 loaded with 30-pound test will work for most situations. You can pick up fishing tackle and related supplies at **Deportiva La Paz** (Mutualismo, tel. 612/122-7333), one block in from the Applebee's on the *malecón*.

DIVING AND SNORKELING

La Paz has one of the largest scuba diving communities anywhere in Mexico. The islands offshore from La Paz present divers of all skill levels with some of the most interesting underwater topography in the Sea of Cortez as well as opportunities to spot some of the largest pelagics in the sea. Sea lions frolic at Los Islotes, while hammerhead sharks school around the El Bajo seamount and giant mantas cruise against the current. From the surface, you may see flying mantas, schools of dolphins, and giant bait balls.

Unlike the reef and wall diving in Cabo Pulmo and Cabo San Lucas, where dive sites are a 5- to 15-minute boat ride from shore, long, choppy boat rides (45–60 minutes) are the norm here—hence the higher rates. Remember to take your seasickness medicine the night before. (Many divers swear by Bonine, found over the counter in the United States and Mexico.)

A day of diving typically begins around 7–8 A.M. and finishes in the late afternoon. Lunch is usually included at no extra cost.

Most operators require a minimum of at least two divers to send a boat out to the islands. Some require four divers to visit the more remote sites.

Dive Sites

Most boats frequent about a dozen different sites around the islands offshore from La Paz. A sea lion colony at Los Islotes (7–15 meters) provides loads of underwater entertainment. Also suitable for beginners, the *Salvatierra* wreck (18 meters) presents an opportunity to explore the remains of a cargo ferry that sank in 1976. If conditions permit, advanced divers might request a trip to the El Bajo seamount (18–30 meters) in hopes of encountering a school of hammerhead sharks as well as giant mantas, whale sharks, and towers of schooling amberjacks and tuna.

Day Trips

In business since 1992, **Buceo Carey** (Legaspy and Topete, tel. 612/128-4048, toll-free U.S. tel. 877/239-4057, www.buceocarey.com) is one of the more respected dive centers in town. A staff of local captains and international dive guides leads one-day and multiday dive trips to Espíritu Santo sites for US$85 a day, and to El Bajo and Isla Cerralvo for US$95. The cost includes lunch, transportation, guide, unlimited sodas and beer, weight belt, and two tanks. Rental equipment includes regulators, BCDs, wetsuits, masks, snorkels, fins, tanks, weight belts, booties, and portable air compressors. The company has a second office at Marina de La Paz. Inquire about accommodations packages.

The largest dive operation in La Paz is Fernando Águilar's **Baja Diving and Service** (BCS. 11/Carr. a Pichilingue, past the ferry terminal, tel. 612/122-7010, www.clubcantamar. com). Based at the Club Cantamar Resort and

DIVING AND SNORKELING COSTS

GUIDED DIVE/SNORKEL TOURS

Discounts apply for multiday dives (overnight in La Paz hotel, typically the Los Arcos). Hotel/dive packages are available.

Snorkel tour (equipment included)	US$50-65
Two- or three-tank boat dive	US$85-150
Night dive	US$60-70
Package of two days/three nights, with accommodations and meals	US$300-400
Package of six days/seven nights, with accommodations and meals	US$700-800
Nondiver passenger	US$10-15

LIVEABOARD DIVE TRIPS

Types of liveaboard trips: Socorro Island, Whale Shark Expedition, Island Tour

Six days/seven nights	US$1,900
Eight days/nine nights	US$1,500-3,000
Night dive on liveaboard trip	US$30

DIVE INSTRUCTION

Open-water certification (classroom and dives)	US$450-500
Discover Scuba/resort course (introduction to scuba)	US$125
Advanced certification	US$350-400
Nitrox certification	US$250

GUIDED KAYAK TOURS

Day trips	US$50-100
Two-day trip	US$250-300
Four-day trip	US$400-500
Six-day trip	US$1,100
10-day trip	US$2,000

DIVE AND KAYAK EQUIPMENT RENTAL

Snorkel gear (usually included with tour)	US$6-15
Scuba package with dives (discounts for multiday dives)	US$20-30/day
Rebreather	US$65
Airfills	US$5
Nitrox refills	US$8-12
Panga shuttle to Espíritu Santo (round-trip from Playa Tecolote)	US$200-400
Double kayak	US$60/day
Single kayak	US$40/day
Truck shuttle to Playa Tecolote	US$25
Island camping fee	US$4

Sports Centre on the Pichilingue Peninsula, the company operates a fleet of eight vessels, including some of the largest dive boats on the Sea of Cortez, holding more than 20 divers. Its custom-built 53-foot *Liberación* features air-conditioning and hot water, two heads, and a pleasant sundeck for warming up after each dive. The boat accommodates 30 divers for day trips and 10 divers as a liveaboard. They also run *pangas* for divers who consider the larger boats to be too much like cattle cars. Besides the sheer scale of the operation, shorter boat rides are a significant advantage of diving with the Cantamar staff. Boats typically depart at 8:30 A.M. and return by 5 P.M. For divers who aren't staying at the resort, a shuttle service is provided at no additional cost.

Dive rates are US$119 per person per day for two or three tanks, depending on conditions. Day trips include transportation, boat ride, lunch, and drinks. The resort has an ultralight plane used for spotting whale sharks (extra charge of US$20 pp). Shorter boat rides also make the more distant dive sites like Las Animas and the San Diegito Reef more accessible for day-trippers (extra charge of US$25 per diver for trips to these sites).

Dive packages for 3–14 nights, lunch and breakfast included on dive days, cost US$400–1,705; Nitrox and rebreather dive packages are also available at additional cost. Round-trip airport transfers are also included.

Rental gear is available (snorkel set US$7/day, dive gear US$23/day). Certified divers can also get nitrox refills for US$8–12 and rent rebreathers for US$65. New divers can get certified in the resort's own pool (US$420, includes two days of open-water dives) or try an introductory Discover Scuba course (US$157). Advanced certification costs US$370. Nitrox certification is US$220. In case of a dive emergency, the Cantamar has the only recompression chamber in La Paz. For more information or to make a reservation, drop in at the Cantamar's downtown sales office (Paseo Obregón 1665-2, Plaza Cerralvo, near the Hotel Perla, tel. 612/122-1826, 9 A.M.–8 P.M. daily).

Another multiboat operation is based at the La Concha Beach Resort. **The Cortez Club Dive Center** (Km. 5, Carr. a Pichilingue, tel. 612/121-6120, www.cortezclub.com) has 12 dive boats, its own classroom for dive instruction, and a private jetty and ramp. Rates are a little higher than other shops.

Day excursions aboard Baja Expeditions' 45-foot *Don Cano* or 48-foot *Pez Sapo* cost US$125 per day (Mar.–Dec.), which covers three dives, breakfast, lunch, snacks, and happy hour (tel. 612/125-3828, toll-free U.S. tel. 800/843-6967, www.bajaex.com).

Liveaboard Trips

If viewing underwater marine life is the focus of your trip to La Paz, consider a multiday trip aboard one of these custom-designed dive boats. Packages typically include the first and last nights in a La Paz hotel. Rates shown here are for double occupancy. An additional fee often applies for single occupancy.

Baja Diving and Service (tel. 612/122-7010, www.clubcantamar.com) runs several liveaboard trips through the summer and fall months on the Sea Escape. An eight-day/seven-night trip to Socorro Island (with eight days of diving) costs US$2,850. A seven-day/six-night trip to Cabo Pulmo is US$1,900. **Buceo Carey** (Legaspy and Topete, tel. 612/128-4048, toll-free U.S. tel. 877/239-4057, www.buceocarey.com) runs multiday trips on two boats: *Marco Polo* holds 6–8 divers and offers six days/five nights for US$1,399. **Baja Expeditions** (tel. 612/125-3828, toll-free U.S. tel. 800/843-6967, www.bajaex.com) offers liveaboard trips on the air-conditioned, 80-foot *Don José*. Trips are booked out of the U.S. office, but you can sometimes sign up in La Paz if the boat isn't full. An eight-day trip aboard the *Don José* (offered June–Nov.) starts at US$1,625 per person. Three eight-day whale shark–viewing trips take place in May and June (from US$1,795 per person). The boat holds 16 divers. The *Don José* has a loyal following, since the staff allows divers to go on their own schedule by running constant shuttles to many different sites.

Deportiva La Paz (Mutualisimo, tel./fax

612/122-7333) sells scuba diving equipment and fills air tanks but does not run dive trips.

Snorkel Tours

Most dive and kayak outfitters also run snorkel tours. Less-expensive trips visit the beaches along the Pichilingue Peninsula; the more expensive ones go to the islands for the day. For example, **Buceo Carey** (Legaspy and Topete, tel. 612/128-4048, toll-free U.S. tel. 877/239-4057, www.buceocarey.com) offers snorkeling trips for US$65 to Playa Encantada and the sea lion colony. **Baja Diving and Service** (tel. 612/122-7010, www.clubcantamar.com) at the Cantamar does local snorkel trips for US$65. One of the best values among organized trips is the snorkeling trip to Espíritu Santo run by **Azul Tours** (Paseo Obregón 774, tel. 612/125-2596, www.azultourslapaz.com, azultours@gmail.com). The staff is knowledgeable, well equipped, and safety-conscious. The adventure takes the better part of a day and includes a delicious lunch, prepared by its sister restaurant, Palapa Azul, for US$65 per person.

El Tecolote Restaurant/Bar/Playa (tel. 612/127-9494) transports snorkelers to Espíritu Santo in *pangas* for US$40 per person. The price includes gear and lunch. Boats depart between 10 and 11 A.M. for a four-hour tour. Stop by the booking office, just off the plaza next to the Hotel Miramar, for more information. El Tecolote also offers WaveRunners, kayaks, banana boats, and waterskiing.

Marlin Adventures (Obregón 460, at Ocampo, tel. 612/125-7842, cell tel. 612/137-4495, www.marlin-adventures.com, 8 A.M.–7 P.M. daily) offers snorkeling tours as well as diving, instructor certification, whale-shark tours, fishing, and kayak rentals at Playa Tecolote (US$60 for a four-hour tour, including lunch and gear). It has three 28-foot *pangas,* which are fully insured and have oxygen and first aid on board.

WHALE-WATCHING

There are several ways to observe gray and blue whales near La Paz, and several dive and kayak outfitters offer special whale-watching tours.

Some tours go to the Sea of Cortez, while others go to Laguna San Ignacio or Magdalena Bay on the Pacific side of the Baja Peninsula. Some trips involve snorkeling and paddling; others are just boat cruises. You can go for one day or eight, depending on your budget and how much time you want to spend with the mammals.

Baja Outdoor Activities (tel. 612/125-5636, toll-free U.S. tel. 888/217-6659, www.kayakinbaja.com) offers a package with two three-hour boat trips plus an overnight stay and all meals for US$250 per person.

Johnny Friday and Maldo Ficher lead ecotours in the area through **Baja Adventure Company** (tel. 612/125-9081, toll-free U.S. tel. 877/506-0557, www.bajaecotours.com), a division of Mar de Cortez sports. Its marine biologists, zoologists, and other professionally trained guides lead whale-watching trips.

A pioneer in environmental education and sustainable tourism, **Baja Expeditions** (tel. 612/125-3828, toll-free U.S. tel. 800/843-6967, www.bajaex.com) offers multiday whale-watching trips to Magdalena Bay and Laguna San Ignacio and in the Sea of Cortez.

KAYAKING

The islands near La Paz are some of the best places in the world to kayak, and several companies provide highly recommended tours. Day trips are possible, but given the amount of gear and transportation logistics involved, many day-trippers end up feeling rushed and wish they had chosen a multiday tour instead. Most trips fall into one of two categories: a four-day paddle along the west side of Isla Espíritu Santo (usually north to south) and a seven-day (or more) paddle all the way around Isla Espíritu Santo and Isla Partida (56 km).

Overnight package trips usually include the first and last nights in hotel accommodations, with camping on the nights in between. Meals, transportation to the islands, and airport transfers are also typically covered by the price. Some trips return to a base camp every night, while others move to a new place each day. Some have motorized support boats to move camping gear from place to place and shuttle paddlers to the best snorkeling sites for the particular conditions each day. Some outfitters supply camping gear; others ask that you bring your own.

Many companies book kayak tours, but often they are brokers for the actual outfitter. In general, it's better to book directly so you can get complete information about the itinerary and equipment before you sign up for a trip. Two of the most popular operators are Mar y Aventuras and Baja Outdoor Adventure.

Owned by a La Paz native, **Mar y Aventuras** (Topete 564, btw 5 de Febrero/Navarro, tel. 612/123-0559, toll-free U.S. tel. 800/355-7140, www.kayakbaja.com), near La Marina Don José and Marina de La Paz, leads one-day and multiday trips and rents kayaks and gear to experienced paddlers (reserve well in advance if you want to rent). Its boats are a mix of doubles and singles made of fiberglass and some plastic. All have rudders. A half-day coastal trip costs US$45. Full-day trips range US$75–100 per person, depending on the destination and size of the group. Multiday tours start at US$590.

If you want to explore El Mogote or the islands on your own, you'll have to convince the staff that you know what you're doing. For safety reasons, they are reluctant to rent to novice and intermediate paddlers. Single sea kayaks rent for US$45 a day, with a PFD (personal flotation device), paddle, bilge pump, and spray deck. Double kayaks cost US$65 a day. You can also rent snorkeling gear and camping equipment. Boat shuttles out to Isla Espíritu Santo cost US$200–400 round-trip for one or two people; a truck shuttle to Playa El Tecolote for launching from the beach to Espíritu Santo costs US$25 one-way for one or two people. You can pay the US$4-per-day camping fee at the Mar y Aventuras office.

Baja Outdoor Activities (BOA) (tel. 612/125-5636, www.kayakinbaja.com) offers two different styles of kayak trips: "Cooperatively catered" trip participants carry their own gear each day and help guides prepare meals, making for a more self-sufficient

experience but with heavier boats to paddle. Others prefer a fully catered trip, in which guides prepare all meals and camping supplies are transported by motorboat. Four-day island tours start at US$590. Daily dolphin sightings are common on the 10-day Loreto to La Paz trip (US$1,280). Participants should expect to paddle about four hours per day on this trip.

The half-day tour for US$45 is a nice way for beginners to get a feel for the sport without committing to a full-day adventure. BOA also offers a one-day tour of Balandra Bay for US$75. BOA rents sit-on-top kayaks and sea kayaks by the day or week (US$35–60/day and US$110–220/week).

Baja Expeditions (tel. 612/125-3828, toll-free U.S. tel. 800/843-6967, www.bajaex.com) has been running seven-day trips to Espíritu Santo (US$1,125) since 1985. Other destinations include Loreto to the La Paz coast (10 days) and Magdalena Bay (eight days). An aggressive 10-day, open-water kayak trip hops among the islands of Espíritu Santo, Los Islotes, San José, Santa Cruz, and Santa Catalina (Oct.–Apr. only).

BOATING

With the largest bay along the Gulf Coast, La Paz is far and away the frontrunner in all of Baja when it comes to boating services and supplies. Even Cabo San Lucas pales in comparison. There are numerous public and private marinas, boatyards, and marine supply stores, with new businesses opening and old ones upgrading all the time.

Marinas

At the west end of the *malecón,* the **Marina de La Paz** (Topete 3040 at Legaspy, tel. 612/122-1646, www.marinadelapaz.com) has completed numerous upgrades in the last decade: New docks and a new layout came in 2004, followed by a fixed breakwater system in 2005, and an additional 37 meters of fixed breakwater plus a new 50-meter dock for accommodating large vessels in 2006. Facilities at this floating marina now include a launch ramp, diesel fuel dock, grocery store with marine supplies,

LA PAZ AND VICINITY

Marina de La Paz

The Dock Café (tel. 612/125-6626, 8 A.M.–10 P.M. daily), water and electricity outlets, cable TV, laundry, showers, restrooms, wireless Internet, a chandlery, and boat and vehicle maintenance and storage. Local nonprofit **Club Cruceros de La Paz** (no tel., www.clubcruceros.org, 9 A.M.–6 P.M. Mon.–Sat.) has a clubhouse at the marina with a book exchange. It also provides incoming mail service.

Rates for one of the marina's 150 slips range from US$22 per day for a 30-foot craft to US$103 per day for a 90-foot craft. Discounts also apply for stays of 4–21 days, if paid in advance. Showers cost US$1.50. Parking for slip clients is US$1 daily or US$25 per month. Prices include tax.

Well known on the yachting circuit, the marina typically fills up in the high season, November–May; check for vacancies before sailing in. A US$200 deposit will hold your space on the waiting list. Reserve online or by mailing a personal check.

Northeast of town, at Km. 2.5, the **Marina Palmira** (tel. 612/123-7000 or 877/217-1513, www.marinapalmira.com) offers 186 full-service slips suitable for yachts up to 130 feet long and 12 feet deep. The marina recently reinforced its breakwater and launching ramp. There is free wireless Internet, and a free shuttle to downtown is available at various times each day. Guests can use dry-storage facilities, laundry, water, showers, bathrooms, a pool, hot tub, and tennis court. There are also a market, two restaurants, a bar, 24-hour security, parking for one car per registered guest, a public phone, marine supplies, a fuel dock with diesel and gas, and boat launch. You can charter boats here, with or without a crew. Monthly slip rates are US$13–28 per foot per month; electrical service costs extra. You can rent condos and hotel rooms at several resorts nearby by the day, week, or month.

Based at the Club Cantamar Resort and Sports Centre, **Marina Pichilingue** (tel. 612/122-7010, www.clubcantamar.com) has 35 slips for boats up to 75 feet long. Water, electricity, and dry storage are available.

Farther out on the Pichilingue Peninsula,

Marina CostaE tel. 612/121-6225, www.
costabajaresort.com, rooms US$140–330)
can accommodate mega-yachts up to 220 feet
in 250 slips. Liveaboards require special permission from the marina. Amenities include
Internet, TV, and phone, and at-slip pump-
out service, dry storage, restrooms and showers, parking, pool, and shuttle to La Paz. Some
travelers who have used this marina report
problems with black soot from the nearby oil
refinery damaging canvas on their boats. A reservation form is available online.

Near the airport, **Singlar Fidepaz Marina**
(Mexico 1/Constituyentes, tel. 612/124-2206),
part of the Mexican government's failed
Escalera Nautica Sea of Cortez Project, was up
for sale at last check.

If you're hauling your own boat, you can use
ramps at Marina de La Paz, Marina Palmira,
and Pichilingue. Smaller boats and kayaks can
launch from any of the public beaches.

Parts and Repairs
Marina de La Paz is the one-stop shop in town
for boating questions, services, and supplies;
Ferretería Marina SeaMar (SeaMar Marine
Chandlery, Topete and Legaspy, tel. 612/122-
9696, 8:30 A.M.–1:30 P.M. and 3–6 P.M. Mon.–
Fri., 8:30 A.M.–1:30 P.M. Sat.), across from
the marina entrance, carries basic supplies.
López Marine Supply (Vista Coral Plaza, tel.
612/125-4160, 8 A.M.–5 P.M. Mon.–Sat.) accepts credit cards. Club Cruceros keeps a list
of local marine service providers at www.club-
cruceros.org/services.html.

Boat Charters
If you like the idea of cruising but don't
have your own boat or any experience on the
water, you might book a trip with **Baja Coast
SeaFaris** (Dock B, Marina de La Paz, tel.
612/111-7335, www.bajaseafaris.com). This
company offers full-service charters with a bilingual crew aboard *Tesoro del Mar,* a Beneteau
50 that has space for six adults. Privacy is the
distinguishing factor with this outfitter. All
trips are private, whether for a party of two or
six; pricing varies with the size of the group.

Multiday trips (3–5 days or longer) include
stops at Espíritu Santo, Isla Partida, and Los
Islotes for swimming with sea lions, scuba
diving, kayaking, tubing (for kids), sailing,
beachcombing, whale-watching, bird-watching, snorkeling, or fishing. Rates are US$795
per night for two persons and US$165 addi-
tional per night for additional adults, US$115
additional per child. The price covers all meals,
snacks, and cocktails while on board the yacht;
a night of lodging on the final evening; and
round-trip airport transfers. The boats are fully
equipped with kayaks and other gear. Scuba
diving and rental gear are also arranged upon
request. Book well ahead (several months) for
peak travel times. Miscellaneous taxes, permits, and island and port fees will add about
15 percent to the total trip cost.

Inquire about a 10 percent discount for families and special occasions like honeymoons
and anniversaries. "Learn to sail" trips are another option. Deposits must be paid by personal check, money orders, or bank wire.

The owner of Baja Coast SeaFaris has compiled a thorough list of FAQs for novice and
experienced sailors that covers topics related
to cruising in Baja at www.bajaseafaris.com/
cruise.html.

Baja Expeditions (tel. 612/125-3828, toll-
free U.S. tel. 800/843-6967, www.bajaex.com)
offers custom-designed sailing charters aboard
El Mechudo, a catamaran with four en suite
cabins, which can accommodate up to eight
adults for US$2,250 per day.

MOUNTAIN BIKING
Co-located in the Baja Outdoor Activities
(BOA) office next to the El Moro hotel,
Mexican-owned **Katún** (tel. 612/348-7758,
www.katuntours.com) runs guided tours of the
Sierra de La Laguna or combo kayak/bike trips
for US$1,190 for seven days. And the weeklong
Jesuits trail tour traces historic routes through
the Sierra la Giganta, from the Sea of Cortez
to the Pacific (US$1,199). Day trips of 10 to 30
miles lead riders along nearby desert roads and
coastal trails or around the abandoned silver
mines at El Triunfo (US$50–70).

Katún also rents 2006 Giant Yukon bikes with front suspension for US$10 an hour, US$15 for four hours, or US$20 per day.

Baja Challenge (Obregón 460-1, btw Ocampo/Degollado, tel. 612/128-6089, www.bajachallengetours.com, 9 A.M.–11 P.M. daily; US$2–4 per hour) rents mountain bikes, cruisers, tandems, and Rollerblades and operates a five-kilometer mountain biking course across from the Hotel Marina.

HIKING AND HORSEBACK RIDING

Antonio Moller (tel. 612/123-1370) leads one-day and overnight trips into the Sierra de la Laguna from La Paz. Day trips (US$45–65 pp, min. 3 people) include transportation from La Paz to the biosphere, lunch at a local ranch, and a one-hour horseback ride. Student discounts available. **Eduardo's Tours** (tel. 612/166-1657 or 612/152-1213, www.eduardostours.com, US$85 pp) is another option for a day of horseback riding in the desert. The price includes transportation, a bilingual guide, food, drinks, and about two-and-a-half hours of riding time.

SPA SERVICES

Several La Paz hotels, including the Costa Baja and Grand Baja resorts, offer spa services to guests as well as those who wish to visit just for the day. At La Concha Beach Resort, Nautilus Spa (tel. 612/121-6161, ext. 1452, cell tel. 612/127-1190) offers a full menu of massage services and body treatments as well as manicures and pedicures. Nautilus Spa has additional locations at the Hotel Marina (tel. 612/121-6323) and Seven Crown Hotel.

ORGANIZED TOURS

Travel companies and outfitters offer a variety of guided tours and organized activities, from island kayak trips and whale-watching to language immersion and cooking classes. A number of the newer ones are committed to promoting environmentally aware tours and trips. Since each outfitter may partner with others to offer unique trips, it's difficult to keep up with all the options.

Aside from the activity-specific outfitters mentioned earlier in this chapter, **Espíritu & Baja Tours** (Obregón #774-A, btw Allende/Juárez, tel. 612/122-4427, www.espiritubaja.com) runs professional and reasonably priced trips, such as snorkeling at Espíritu Santo (US$65 pp), whale-watching trips to Bahía Magdalena (US$120 pp), sportfishing (US$240 per boat), kayaking along the Pichilingue Peninsula (US$70 pp), and airport transfer services (airport to hotel US$15, hotel to airport US$7).

Readers have reported pleasant outings with **Eduardo's Tours** (tel. 612/166-1657 or 612/152-1213, www.eduardostours.com). Eduardo Gomez provides ground transportation and leads guided trips to Los Cabos (US$110 pp), Todos Santos (US$80 pp), and El Triunfo (US$80 pp). A La Paz city tour costs US$32 per person, and a tour of several beaches along the Pichilingue Peninsula is US$32. Whale-watching tours (US$120 pp, includes two hours of whale-watching but is a full-day trip with a long drive to Bahía Magdalena and back) and snorkeling (US$80 pp, US$95 pp with kayaks) are also possible. Travelers with more time can arrange multiday trips to the missions in Loreto and Mulegé or to see nearby cave paintings in the mountains.

In addition to hiking and horseback riding tours, **Antonio Moller** (tel. 612/123-1370) offers guided trips to El Triunfo and the nearby cactus sanctuary. Tours cost US$40 per person, with a minimum of three people, and last approximately six hours (8 A.M.–3 P.M.).

Besides catering to divers and kayakers, **Baja Expeditions** (tel. 612/125-3828, toll-free U.S. tel. 800/843-6967, www.bajaex.com) offers wildlife cruises, open-water swim clinics, and a wide variety of custom-designed group trips that usually blend an element of adventure with a conservation-minded approach.

ATV Tours

ATV tours have become a popular way to explore the Baja Peninsula, and La Paz has joined the crowd. **Espíritu & Baja Tours** (Obregón #774-A, btw Allende/Juárez, tel. 612/122-4427, www.espiritubaja.com) offers a two-hour tour at Playa Tecolote for US$85 per person.

Entertainment and Events

NIGHTLIFE

La Paz nightlife is more diverse and vibrant than that of San José del Cabo, but not as crazy and tourist-oriented as what you'll find in Cabo San Lucas. Many Baja expats who live in surrounding towns come to La Paz for live concerts and other performances. A former journalist and Canadian expat maintains an up-to-date website (www.rozinlapaz.com) that describes all the venues and lists most of the goings on around town. Most venues are open nightly until at least midnight or later on weekends.

One of the oldest watering holes in town is **Tequilas Bar and Grill** (Ocampo 310 E. at Mutualisimo, tel. 612/121-5217) with simple decor, pool tables, and a cigar bar. It has a full kitchen and will happily cook your fresh catch for you. **Bar Salsipuedes** (Obregón 2130, btw Allende/Juárez, tel. 612/128-5594) seems to attract a concentration of the city's marine biologists. Besides serving drinks, it shows films, arts exhibits, and sports events.

Carlos'n Charlie's, on Paseo Obregón, has an attached dance club called **La Paz Lapa** (Obregón and 16 de Septiembre, tel. 612/122-9290). Above Pizza Fabula **Casa de Villa** (Obregón and 16 de Septiembre, tel. 612/122-5799) is a rooftop bar and nightclub that's popular with locals.

The Hotel Perla's **Nightclub La Cabaña** (Obregón 1570, tel. 612/122-0777, 9 P.M.–3 A.M. daily) hosts *norteña* bands, usually on Thursdays and Sundays.

On the *malecón,* sportfishing outfitter Jonathan Roldan has opened the **Tailhunter Bar & FUBAR Cantina** (Obregón 755 btw Salvatierra/Torre Iglesias, cell tel. 612/125-3311, U.S. tel. 626/638-3383, toll-free U.S. tel. 877/825-8802, www.tailhunter-international.com, mains US$6–14) with nine flat-screen TVs showing all the major sporting events. Enjoy a margarita or cold beer on tap while you work out the details of your fishing trip. The kitchen will prepare and serve your fresh catch or vacuum-seal it to go. You can also order from a menu of traditional Mexican dishes with a Hawaiian flair. For example, the Hawaiian burger comes with teriyaki sauce, cheese, pineapple, mushrooms, lettuce, and tomato.

With locations in Rosarito, Ensenada, and now La Paz, **Papas and Beer** (Vista Coral Plaza, Márquez de León at Topete, tel. 612/128-5145, www.papasandbeer.com) prides itself on providing a wild spring-break experience for the college crowd. It seems a bit out of place in La Paz, although unlike the Baja California (Norte) establishments, this one attracts more of a local crowd. Its beach club serves a menu of seafood and Mexican dishes.

CINEMA

The only cinema in town is the 15-screen **Cine Gemelos** in the Soriana shopping complex on Boulevard Forjadores at the corner of Avenida Luis Donaldo Colosio.

FESTIVALS AND EVENTS
🅲 Carnaval

La Paz is known throughout Mexico for its all-out celebration of Carnaval, a six-day festival held throughout the world in mid-February or early March on the days leading up to Ash Wednesday. Like Mardi Gras in New Orleans, Oktoberfest in Munich, or Burning Man in the Nevada desert, this is a destination event—something every traveler should consider experiencing at least once. There are daily parades along the *malecón,* brightly colored costumes, the crowning of a queen, amusement rides, fireworks, music, and food stands—with tequila and cerveza flowing freely all the while.

The Carnaval tradition came to Mexico from Spain and is believed to have evolved as the last chance for Christians to party before the fasting time of Lent. Some interpret the name Carnaval as deriving from the Latin *carne vale,* which means "farewell to meat."

Fiesta de La Paz

The Fiesta de La Paz (officially known as Fiesta de la Fundación de la Ciudad de La Paz) takes place on May 3, the anniversary of the city's founding. Contact the state tourism office (tel. 612/124-0100, turismo@correro.gbcs.gob.mx), between Km. 5 and 6 on Mexico 1 (Avenida Abasolo), for festival venues and events.

Baja 1000

The Baja 1000 off-road race comes to town in mid-November. Produced by SCORE International (U.S. tel. 818/225-8402, www.score-international.com), the event is the sixth and last in a series of desert races that take place in the southwestern United States and Mexico each year. The Baja 1000 attracts more than 400 pro contestants who drive trucks, motorcycles, ATVs, and every imaginable variation of off-road vehicle. They start in Ensenada and cruise at breakneck speeds through the desert to the outskirts of La Paz. Only about half of the race entrants complete the challenging 1,000-mile course.

In its 43rd year in 2010, the race draws thousands of support crew and spectators to the most remote parts of the peninsula. The course opens for pre-running approximately three weeks before the race start. Travelers on Mexico 1 during this time will often see vehicles kicking up a cloud of dust in the distance, moving at speeds faster than highway drivers go. This is one of the only times a year you may encounter traffic on the more remote stretches of Mexico 1. Watch the 2005 documentary *Dust to Glory* for a fascinating inside look at the sport.

Shopping

La Paz serves as a vital commerce center for all of Southern Baja. Its many shops and department stores cater not only to local residents but also to those of towns as far away as Todos Santos and the East Cape. The result is a greater variety of items at competitive prices. Two large shopping centers were in the works at press time, which promise to bring high-end department stores and boutiques similar to the Puerto Paraíso Mall in Cabo San Lucas.

DEPARTMENT STORES

The two **Sears** (16 de Septiembre at Esquerro, tel. 612/125-9373, Forjadores, tel. 612/121-3843) used to be home to Dorian's, La Paz's largest department store. The original **La Perla de La Paz,** a good bet for housewares and the like, never reopened after a fire in 2006, but it does have an annex that is open for business across the street (Arrival at Mutualismo, no tel.).

For clothing at discounted prices, try **MAS** (Madero at Degollado, 9 A.M.–9 P.M. daily). Next door, **DAX** (Arreola at Zaragoza, tel. 612/125-2480, 8 A.M.–9 P.M. Mon.–Thurs., 8 A.M.–10 P.M. Fri.–Sat.) has a pharmacy, cosmetics, and toiletries. And next to DAX, **Solo Un Precio** ("Only One Price," Madero btw Tejada/Arreola, 8 A.M.–9 P.M. daily) is the Mexican equivalent of the dollar store. Everything in the store is 10 pesos.

For everyday needs, La Paz now has a Walmart and Home Depot.

HOME FURNISHINGS

One of 28 **Segusino** (Álvaro Obregón 2140, Loc.1, tel. 612/125-1703, www.segusino.com) furniture stores has opened in La Paz, selling beautiful contemporary and rustic Mexican furniture. With headquarters in Puebla on the mainland, the company advocates a fair trade approach in choosing its materials.

ART GALLERIES

La Paz has about 20 up-and-coming fine-art galleries, representing mostly contemporary Mexican artists working in a variety of media and styles. Housed in a restored colonial building, **Galería Galería** (Revolución 590, at Juárez, tel. 612/125-6973, 9 A.M.–4 P.M. Mon.–Sat.)

© PAUL ITOI

shops in downtown La Paz

is both a working studio for local artists and an interior design store. Attend a workshop or simply browse the shelves for the perfect something to accent your home. Next door is a new **children's library.** Both are reportedly funded by Christy Walton of Walmart.

Near the post office, **Galería de Arte Tonantzin** (Constitución 320 btw Serdán/Revolución, 10 A.M.–2 P.M. and 5–8:30 P.M. Mon.–Sat., cell tel. 612/154-8136) has contemporary works from Latin American artists. Call or stop by for a schedule of music concerts.

ARTESANÍA

Several tourist-oriented shops line the *malecón* between the bus terminal and the Applebee's. They sell handicrafts, T-shirts, jewelry, and postcards. **La Antigua California** (Obregón 220, tel. 612/125-5230) has a good selection of arts and crafts made primarily in mainland Mexico. **México Lindo** (Álvaro Obregón at 16 de Septiembre), next to Carlos'n Charlie's, is another option.

The government-run **Casa de Artesanos Sudcalifornianos** (Paseo Obregón at Bravo, tel. 612/128-8707), next to the Tourist Information/Tourist Police office and skate park, stocks *artesanías* from all over Southern Baja.

You can watch artists at work when you visit **Ibarra's Pottery** (Prieto 625 btw Iglesias/República, tel. 612/122-0404, 9 A.M.–3 P.M. Mon.–Fri., 9 A.M.–2 P.M. Sat.) The outdoor store contains several aisles of plates, mugs, pitchers, vases, pots, and the like—mostly in bold patterns and colorful designs. **Artesanía Cuauhtémoc** (Abasolo btw Jalisco/Nayarit, no tel.), in a white building near the CCC (Centro Comercial California), has Oaxacan-style textiles, including rugs, blankets, and table linens.

Artesanías Colibri (Paseo Obregón btw Muelle/Arreola, tel. 612/128-5833, 10 A.M.–1 P.M. and 3–8:30 P.M. Mon.–Sat.) carries a good selection of *artesanías,* rustic furniture, and decorating accessories, plus cute clothes for babies and kids.

Bargain-hunters in search of clothing, housewares, or leather goods might check out the **Mercado Municipal Francisco E. Madero**

(Revolución de 1910 at Degollado). **Santander** (Serdán and Degollado, tel. 612/125-5962) has saddles, guitars, and huaraches.

Next to Allende Books, **Las Manitas ARTesanias** (Independencia at Prieto, 10 A.M.–4 P.M. daily and by appointment) serves as the gift shop for guests at El Angel Azul. It carries clothing, sculptures, jewelry, and a variety of handicrafts.

SPORTING GOODS

Deportes Ortiz (Degollado 260, almost opposite Pensión California, tel. 612/122-1209) carries basic camping, diving, and other sports gear, plus some athletic apparel.

BOOKSTORES

La Paz has a wonderful English-language bookstore, **Allende Books of La Paz** (Independencia 518, btw Serdan and Prieto, tel. 612/125-9114, www.allendebooks.com, 10 A.M.–6 P.M. Mon.–Sat.). Open since 2007, it's located in the same historic building as El Angel Azul B&B and carries maps, dictionaries, cookbooks, history books, and contemporary fiction. The store also holds occasional events such as book signings, children's story time, and book club meetings.

Librería Contempo (Arriola at Paseo Obregón) carries Mexican newspapers as well as a few American magazines.

Accommodations

In general, rooms in La Paz are more affordable than their counterparts in Los Cabos, but they aren't the same bargains you might have found a decade ago. There are hotels in all budget categories, many with kitchenettes, plus bed-and-breakfasts, condo complexes, and private vacation rental homes. Rates do not include tax or service fees, but many places offer discounts for stays of a week or longer.

Despite the planned construction of several large luxury hotels, most rooms in La Paz still fall in the US$50–125 range. Some of the older establishments could use a makeover, but the time warp is also part of their charm. You'll pay a bit more to stay right on the water rather than along the *malecón*. And none of the bay-front hotels are within easy walking distance of the *malecón* or downtown La Paz, although taxis are always available.

Most times of year, you can wing it and find a room when you arrive. But if you plan to visit during mid-November, check the Baja 1000 event schedule and make reservations well in advance.

UNDER US$50

Budget accommodations tend to be centrally located but noisy and typically do not have air-conditioning, which can be problematic for travel during the hot-weather months of July–October.

Run by two Japanese women and popular with divers, **Ⓒ Pensión Baja Paradise** (Madero 2166, tel. 612/128-6097, www.baja-paradiselapaz.com, US$25–45) offers basic but immaculate accommodations in a multilevel building. Rooms have private baths, air-conditioning, refrigerators, Wi-Fi, and TV—amenities not often found at this price point. Guests share an outdoor kitchen and courtyard.

A mainstay on the budget travel circuit, bohemian **Pensión California** (Degollado 209, btw Revolución de 1910 and Madero, tel. 612/123-3508, fax 612/122-2896, misioner@bcs1.telmex.net.mx, US$25) occupies a former 18th-century convent. Its basic rooms have lots of beds, a relatively fresh coat of paint, and ceiling fans, which may or may not work. Rooms around the courtyard have TV and cost a few dollars more per night. Showers can be hot, as long as you turn on the water heater well beforehand. Most guests opt to use the cold water only. The open-air common space has a fridge, stove, sink, and chairs, but it's not equipped well enough to prepare more than the simplest of meals. There is a computer with Internet access at the front desk (30-min. limit), and free Wi-Fi in the common areas, but it doesn't quite reach to all the rooms. Guests here tend to be young and social. Pets are allowed. This is not the best place to choose for a quiet night's sleep.

Around the corner, **Hostería del Convento** (Madero 85, tel. 612/122-3508, fax 612/123-3525, misioner@bcs1.telmex.net.mx, US$20) is owned by the same family and has similar rooms, but the scene is a bit older and quieter.

The **Hotel San Carlos** (16 de Septiembre btw Serdán/Revolución de 1910, tel. 612/122-0444, fax 612/122-3991, US$25, US$30 with a/c) has 30 basic rooms.

Posada Hotel Yeneka (Madero 1520, btw 16 de Septiembre/Av. Independencia, tel./fax 612/125-4688, ynkmacias@prodigy.net.mx, US$25) has made a name for itself among global backpackers. A courtyard filled with greenery, a rusting Model T, and collection of junk give the place a flea-market feel. Its dark rooms have little in the way of amenities, but the location is convenient and there is a laundry facility on-site.

If you're just passing through and want to bypass downtown La Paz, **Hotel Calafía** (Km. 4, tel. 612/122-5811, hotelcalafia@gmail.com, US$40) is a good option for affordable rooms with secure parking and a pool. Rates include tax.

US$50-100

The 56-room **Hacienda Bugambilias** (formerly Las Gardenias, Serdán Norte 520, tel. 612/122-3088, www.hotelgardenias.com.mx, US$62) has a residential location (three blocks from the waterfront and six blocks north of the plaza), which makes for a much quieter night's sleep than you'll get at other downtown hotels. Rooms come with tiled floors, rustic furnishings, air-conditioning, phone, and TV. The hotel restaurant serves breakfast and lunch fare. This is a popular place for Mexican visitors. Enter on Guerrero between Serdán and Guillermo Prieto.

A block up from the *malecón,* **Hotel Miramar** (5 de Mayo at Domínguez, tel. 612/122-8885, fax 612/122-0672, www.hotelmiramarlapaz.com, US$60) sometimes has rooms available when other properties at this price level are booked. Amenities include air-conditioning (noisy units), small TVs, and secure parking. Rooms get very little daylight, especially on the lower of its three floors. Beds rest on concrete platforms and slope a bit. Some rooms have balconies and bay views.

Above the Mar y Aventuras offices, **Hotel Posada Luna Sol** (Topete 564, btw 5 de Febrero/Navarro, tel. 612/123-0559 or 612/122-7039, www.posadalunasol.com, US$65–75) offers 14 clean rooms, all with local TV, air-conditioning, private baths, and hot water; some also have bay views. Enjoy a sunset cocktail under the rooftop *palapa.* In recent years, the property has added a new top-floor suite and a room with a small kitchen. Rates include tax.

The historic **Hotel Perla** (Paseo Obregón 1570, tel. 612/122-0777, toll-free Mex. tel. 800/716-8799, toll-free U.S. tel. 888/242-3757, www.hotelperlabaja.com, US$75–100) has been hosting foreign and domestic visitors since 1940. The building and 110 guestrooms (28 with bay views) have been well cared for over the years, but the overall impression is more business hotel than vacation destination. And rates seem to be climbing without substantial renovations in recent years. Rooms are small but very clean; decor is minimal, which means noise carries in hallways. High ceilings at least create the illusion of more space. Amenities include air-conditioning, TVs, and phones. There is Wi-Fi in the lobby only. A small pool on the mezzanine level may not be heated in winter months; the rooftop playground entertains young kids.

You can't beat the Perla's location right in the middle of the action on the *malecón.* In fact, the hotel's La Terraza restaurant is a great place to grab breakfast or lunch and watch the city life stream by. Bottom line: Stay here if a central, waterfront location and secure indoor parking are important and the price is acceptable.

Under Swiss ownership, the charming ◀ **Hotel Mediterrané** (Allende 36, tel./fax

612/125-1195, www.hotelmed.com, US$65–95) has nine immaculate rooms in a blue and white stucco building just steps from the *malecón*. In keeping with the Mediterranean theme, its large and pleasant guestrooms are named for the various Greek islands. They come with air-conditioning, refrigerators, and TVs; some have bay views, but these are also the closest to the street and pick up a little more noise than those at the back of the hotel. A rooftop sundeck with lounge chairs invites visitors to catch a breeze and enjoy the bay views. The owners have loaner kayaks, canoes, and bikes available. **Restaurant La Pazion** (4–11 P.M. Wed.–Mon., mains US$10–20) and the **Hotel Mediterrané Café** are downstairs; the café opens at 7 A.M. daily and has wireless Internet.

At the northeast end of the *malecón*, on the way to Pichilingue, the **Club El Moro** (Km. 2, Carr. a Pichilingue, tel./fax 612/122-4084, www.clubelmoro.com, US$80–122) is a popular choice for families and travelers planning to take the ferry across to Mázatlan. A Moorish design and nicely landscaped pool and bar area are highlights of the property. Both rooms and suites come with air-conditioning, satellite TV with HBO, reliable wireless Internet, and a private terrace. Standard rooms are a little small for the price, but at US$112, the large junior suites are a great value. There is off-street and gated parking. The adjoining **Café Gourmet** serves great espresso as well as breakfast and lunch every day. Hotel guests receive free coffee and a coupon for US$2.50 per day. Friendly staff and an attractive frequent-guest program bring repeat visitors back year after year. You can easily catch a city bus during daylight hours to cover the two kilometers to the downtown area. In the evening, you'll have to walk or take a cab.

Next to the Baja Ferries terminal in Bahía Pichilingue, **Club Cantamar Resort and Sports Centre** (BCS. 11/Carr. a Pichilingue, tel. 612/122-7010, www.clubcantamar.com, US$78–220) caters to serious scuba divers and other water enthusiasts. This family business has grown steadily since it opened in 1994 with one 22-foot *panga* and an old 40-horsepower outboard engine. A boat ramp and tank-filling station paved the way to a full-scale resort.

Today guests sleep in a four-story lodge with 45 standard rooms, eight double condos, and two junior suites; a separate building contains four apartments, each with two bedrooms, two bathrooms, kitchenette, dining room, living room, and private balcony. Rooms are decorated in desert colors, with stucco walls and rustic furnishings. Air-conditioning and satellite TV are included, and most rooms have phones, too. Other resort amenities include a 35-slip marina, swimming pool overlooking the ocean (deep enough for scuba training), bar, dockside restaurant, and swim-up bar. Other adventure-oriented amenities include a boat ramp, kayaks for rent, private beach, fishing fleet, dive shop, and recompression chamber. Proximity to the industrial ferry terminal, with semitrucks coming and going, is one disadvantage of the location. Night owls will find the Cantamar much too remote, but for those who want to maximize their time on the water, this resort is a fine home base. Rates include breakfast and taxes.

Behind the bus terminal, the four-story **Baja South Hotel** (Independencia 907, at Callejón 18 de Marzo, tel. 612/129-4231, baja_south@hotmail.com, US$50–75) has 10 rooms with air-conditioning, Wi-Fi, and views of the *malecón* from the upper floors.

Ten large-sized rooms at **La Casa Jalisco** (Jalisco 480, tel. 612/128-4311, US$55–75) have air-conditioning, balconies, Wi-Fi, and satellite TV. The location in a residential neighborhood of the Pueblo Nuevo district is outside the tourist area, 10 blocks away from the beach, and 15 blocks from the *malecón*.

On the west side of the La Paz–Pichilingue Road, the **Araiza Palmira** (Km. 2.5, Carr. a Pichilingue, Alberto Alvarado, Fracc. Lomas de Palmira, tel. 612/121-6200, toll-free Mex. tel. 800/026-5444, toll-free U.S. tel. 877/727-2492, www.araizahoteles.com, US$60–95) is primarily a business hotel, with conference rooms, ballrooms, and guestrooms that look out on a lush garden. Amenities include a swimming pool, tennis court, and restaurant/bar. This hotel is one of many that have dropped their prices dramatically during the recession years.

US$100-150

On the *malecón,* the **Seven Crown Hotel** (corner of Paseo Obregón and Lerdo de Tejada, tel. 612/128-7788, toll-free U.S. tel. 800/276-9673, www.sevencrownhotels.com, US$95–130) is a modern 50-room property that has all the basics but lacks the character and history of La Perla. Amenities include a gym, parking, and wireless Internet. Suites (US$130) have ocean views and kitchenettes. There is a rooftop restaurant (El Aura), bar, and whirlpool tub.

La Concha Beach Resort and Condos (Km 5., Carr. a Pichilingue, tel. 612/121-6161, toll-free Mex. tel. 800/716-8603, toll-free U.S. tel. 800/999-2252, www.laconcha.com, US$115) has the closest beachfront location to town, but the beach itself is much less attractive than those found farther out along the Pichilingue Peninsula and the accommodations are in need of some serious attention. There are hotel rooms as well as condos with lovely bay views, and there have been some improvements such as new air-conditioners in some units; however, for the most part, the property is run-down.

Across from the Araiza Palmira and next to the Club de Yates Palmira, the **Hotel Marina** (Km. 2.5, Carr. a Pichilingue, tel. 612/121-6254, fax 612/121-6177, toll-free U.S. tel. 800/826-1138, www.hotelmarina.com.mx, US$93–180) has 150 suites and master suites with somewhat saggy beds and older furnishings. The resort has tennis courts, a large swimming pool, and an outdoor bar.

Part of the new 500-acre CostaBaja Resort & Marina (www.costabajaresort.com), the **Fiesta Inn La Paz** (Km. 7.5, Carr. a Pichilingue, tel. 612/123-6000, www.fiestainn.com, US$85–133) is popular with families as well as boaters, who can anchor at the on-site marina. The resort has 120 guestrooms, including some that

are wheelchair accessible; amenities include wireless Internet and a separate lap-swimming lane in addition to the main pool. The location far from town and near an oil refinery may disappoint some travelers. To find the hotel, look for a signed entrance on a rise on the seaside of the road to Pichilingue.

US$150-250

Some of the classiest accommodations in town are found at the **❰ Posada de las Flores** (Paseo Obregón 440 btw Militar/Guerrero, tel. 612/125-5871, fax 612/122-8748, www.posadadelasflores.com, US$150–290). With its signature coral-colored building and beautiful landscaping, this property looks out on the bay from the west side of the *malecón.* Rooms are designed in a rustic Mexican style, with tile floors and marble baths. Amenities include air-conditioning, wireless Internet, cable TV, and small refrigerators. Guests can also rent a larger *casa* next door. Bikes and kayaks are complimentary, and rates include breakfast. Posada de las Flores also has sister properties in Loreto and Punta Chivato.

Southwest of town, at Km. 5.5 on northbound Mexico 1 (it turns north eventually), the three-story **Grand Plaza Resort** (Lte. A, Marina Fidepaz, tel. 612/124-0830, www.grandplazalapaz.com, US$100–160) is a typical airport business hotel with 50 bayside suites. Rooms are on the dark side and beds sag a bit, but the pool is large and bay views are a plus (no swimming). Notable amenities include free wireless Internet in the lobby and restaurant area, plus a sauna, pool tables, gym, hot tub, tennis court, massage room, and restaurant/bar. Rooms come with air-conditioning and refrigerators. The hotel stands opposite the state tourism office and next to the Singlar Fidepaz Marina.

BED-AND-BREAKFASTS

If you like cozier accommodations and the opportunity to socialize with your host, bed-and-breakfast-style accommodations can be a wonderful way to meet Mexican and expat-families during your stay in La Paz.

A branch of the same family that runs the popular Club El Moro hotel runs **Baja Bed and Breakfast** (Madero 354, tel. 612/123-1370, www.bajabedandbreakfast.com, US$55–90) in a centrally located home just off the plaza. Two street-level rooms share a bath and a patio with a small swimming pool and barbecue. Above, a spacious first-floor apartment for rent by the night or week has a kitchen, separate bedroom, and living room. The owners completed a renovation in 2007. Next door, the owners have added four rooms with private baths. Rates include tax and wireless Internet.

Owner Cecilia Moller serves a multicourse breakfast each morning on the third-floor terrace that's attached to her own kitchen. You'll start your day with fresh breads, fruit, juice, coffee or tea, and eggs, quesadillas, *chilaquiles,* or other Mexican specialties. Cecilia is the life of the party here, so be sure to time your visit for a time when she's in the house. Some of La Paz's hottest new restaurants are less than a block away, and the *malecón* is a two-block walk.

Near the governor's palace, Italian-run **Gemma Inn B&B** (Durango 2090, at Allende, tel. 612/123-5508, www.gemmagroup.it, US$90) has four rooms and one suite surrounding a small swimming pool.

◖ **Casa Tuscany Bed and Breakfast** (Bravo 110A, tel. 612/128-8103, www.tuscanybaja.com, US$95–140, tax included) has a new proprietor, Carol Dyer. Four colorful guestrooms overlook a garden courtyard behind the main house. Each room has a comfortable queen bed, private bath, ceiling fan, and remote-control air-conditioning. Prices include tax and full hot breakfast that varies each day. The new owner has remodeled one room, the Firenze Suite. Two dedicated parking spots in front of the inn are not enclosed.

In ◖ **El Ángel Azul** (Independencia 518, tel./fax 612/125-5130, www.elangelazul.com, US$100–165), Switzerland native Esther Ammann has converted an abandoned 19th-century courthouse into a modern-day bed-and-breakfast, with guidance from the

Rooms face a pleasant courtyard at the Casa Tuscany Bed and Breakfast.

© PAUL ITOI

National Institute of Anthropology and History (INAH). The result is a living piece of La Paz history with a contemporary flair. Nine rooms and one suite are arranged around a beautiful courtyard garden designed and maintained by the owner. Brightly colored rooms have queen or twin beds, bath with shower, air-conditioning, and a radio. Locally created artwork adds to the ambience, and there is secure off-street parking for guests.

CAMPING AND RV PARKS

You can camp on the beach for free north of the ferry terminal at Playas Pichilingue, Balandra, El Tecolote, and El Coyote. Among these options, only El Tecolote has freshwater; plan to bring all your supplies from La Paz. Two restaurants at El Tecolote sell food and drinks. Though not common, theft unfortunately does occur at these beaches. Keep valuables out of sight if at all possible.

Only a couple of RV campgrounds remain as real estate development continues in the greater La Paz area. **Oasis RV Park** (Km. 15, El Centenario, tel. 612/124-6090 or 612/125-6202, open year-round, US$14) is one of the survivors. It has a good location on the Ensenada de La Paz; however, its 25 sites are best reserved for self-contained rigs, as services have been limited in recent years. Tents are welcome, too.

Much closer to town and with much better facilities, popular **Casa Blanca RV Park** (Km. 4.5 at Pez Vela, Fracc. Fidepaz, tel. 612/124-1746, rv.casablanca@gmail.com, Nov.–May) has more than 40 full-hookup sites for US$20 per night or US$400 per month. The property is surrounded by a high white concrete wall and the park provides 24/7 security. Inside, facilities include hot showers, flush toilets, laundry, and a small convenience store—but there is no dump station. Guests may use the swimming pool, tennis court, and spa. The park does not have Internet, but there is an Internet café open to the public just a short walk away.

You can also camp on the Isla Espíritu Santo, which is protected by the Mexican government. Permits cost US$4/day. Visit the local **SEMARNAT office** (2nd floor, Ocampo 1045, btw Rubio/Verdad, tel. 612/128-4171, www.semarnat.gob.mx, 8 A.M.–3 P.M. Mon.–Fri.) before you head out to sea. Pets are prohibited, as is harvesting wood for campfires. The availability of freshwater limits camping options on the larger islands, and camping is not allowed on Ensenada Grande or Playa Ballena.

Two of the bays, Caleta El Candelero on Isla Espíritu Santo and El Cardonalcito on Isla Partida, have freshwater wells where you can bathe. You'll need a bucket and five meters of rope to reach the water level. Purify the water if you must use it for drinking. (Plan to bring your own purified water and only use the well water in an emergency.) It's also a good idea to bring multi-fuel stoves for camping to increase your chances of finding the canisters you need while in Baja.

Food

La Paz has become a culinary destination of sorts, with outstanding meals to be found in every price category, from street-side tacos to fresh seafood and gourmet cuisine.

MEXICAN

A new generation of chefs up and down the peninsula is working hard to define a distinct identity for Baja regional cuisine, which centers around fresh seafood prepared with a Mediterranean influence. La Paz enjoyed its first such restaurant debut with the opening of **Las Tres Virgenes** (Madero btw Constitución/Hidalgo, tel. 612/165-6265, 1–11:30 P.M. Tues.–Sun., mains US$10–30) in 2006. Its name refers to three mountains, one of which is a dormant volcano, visible in the distance on the drive from San Ignacio to Santa Rosalía. Think tuna *tataki,* rose-petal quesadillas, venison tostadas, and damiana crème brûlée, and you'll have a good idea of

what culinary delights the menu holds in store. Wines are reasonably priced. In 2010 the chef/owner began serving a lunch menu from 1 to 4:45 P.M.

Carlos'n Charlie's (Paseo Obregón at 16 de Septiembre, tel. 612/122-9290, www.carlosandcharlies.com, noon–1 A.M. daily, mains US$6–17) is part of the same chain as El Squid Roe and Señor Frog's in Cabo San Lucas, but the atmosphere is less touristy and zany, so it attracts some local and visiting Mexicans as well as foreigners. The menu features traditional Mexican dishes, plus some local specialties, such as a *ceviche paceño.* There is outdoor seating on a terrace facing the *malecón,* where you can often catch the afternoon breeze.

Off the beaten track, **El Zarape** (Av. México 3450, btw Oaxaca/Nayarit, tel. 612/122-2520, www.elzarapelapaz.com, 8 A.M.–10:30 P.M. daily, mains US$10–15) does traditional Mexican dishes right: On Saturday evenings, the kitchen prepares a buffet of *cazuelas* (large, open clay pans) filled with moles and other dishes from central and southern Mexico. Sunday buffet is served 1–6 P.M. (US$10). The daily breakfast buffet is also a good bet for traditional foods (8 A.M.–noon, US$10).

Corazón Café (formerly El Aljibe, Revolución 385 at Constitución, tel. 612/128-8985, 8 A.M.–11 P.M. Mon.–Sat., mains US$15) specializes in *Comida Mexicana,* or traditional fare. The play chalkboard and kitchen in one corner of the restaurant provide entertainment for little ones. Sit indoors under open-sky seating or out in the courtyard. Walmart's Christy Walton, who lives in town, has provided funding for the business as well as the restoration of the small park across the street.

SEAFOOD

Ultra-fresh fish is the theme at **Restaurant La Costa** (Navarro and Topete, no tel., 10 A.M.–11 P.M. daily, mains US$10–15), a waterfront *palapa* restaurant near the Marina de la Paz. From *ceviche de pescado* to *huachinango* and *albondigas de camerones*, air-conditioned **Restaurant La Mar y Peña** (16 de Septiembre btw Isabel la Católica/Albañez, tel. 612/122-9949, noon–10 P.M. daily, mains US$10) serves one of the widest ranges of fish and shellfish entrées anywhere in Baja. In fact, it is the wholesale supplier to most of the other restaurants in town. The decor is casual, the margaritas are fresh, and credit cards are accepted.

Long ago a well-kept secret, **Bismark II** (Degollado at Altamirano, tel. 612/122-4854, 8 A.M.–10 P.M. daily, mains US$10–20) has become a mainstay within the local expat crowd. Lobster, abalone, and carne asada are its hallmark dishes, but the ceviche is also worth a try. On the *malecón,* **Bismarkcito** (Paseo Obregón, near Constitución, tel. 612/128-9900, lunch and dinner daily, mains US$10–15) is a waterfront offshoot of its parent restaurant and appeals more to visitors. The menu includes all manner of seafood cocktails, and fish and shellfish entrées; Peñafiel brand Mexican sodas are a treat.

The popular **Mariscos Moyeyo's** (corner of Paseo Obregón and Héroes del 47, no tel.,

lunch and dinner daily, mains US$5–15), just past El Moro hotel, packs a crowd on weekend afternoons, when locals stop in for towering seafood cocktails. The floor is sand and the tables and chairs are plastic. It takes a dozen servers to keep the fresh catch flowing. The restaurant has occasional live music.

Near the Posada las Flores on Obregón, **Las Brisas del Mar** (Paseo Obregón at Militar, tel. 612/123-5055, lasbrisasdelmbcs@hotmail.com, dinner daily, mains US$13–27) serves seafood cocktails, fish *a la parilla, empanizado,* shrimp, lobster, and red meat from Sonora.

The owners of Rancho Viejo have expanded with **Mariscos La Palapa** (Pineda at Obregón, tel. 612/126-1886, 7 A.M.–midnight daily, lunch/dinner mains US$8–20), a two-story restaurant that overlooks Marina de La Paz. Order ceviche or a seafood cocktail to start, followed by a plate of *arranchera* tacos. Enjoy patio seating in the second-level bar, where a pitcher of margarita costs US$35.

The secret to the tacos at **Taco Fish La Paz** is a tempura batter (Márquez de León at Héroes de Independencia, 8:30 A.M.–4 P.M. Tues.–Sun.). See if you can tell the difference.

In an open-air restaurant across from Las Varitas nightclub, **Kampei Sushi Bar** (Independencia btw Dominguez/15 de Marzo, tel. 612/128-8757, caballero_sk8@hotmail.com, 1–11 P.M. daily) makes *nigiri* sushi (US$2–3 per order), *maki* rolls (US$4–8 per roll), and sashimi (US$7–10) at reasonable prices. The bar is filled with locals in the evening.

ITALIAN

Owned and run by an Italian-Chinese husband-and-wife team, **Caffé Milano** (Esquerro 15, btw Callejón de la Paz/16 de Septiembre, tel. 612/125-9981, www.caffemilano.com.mx, 1–11 P.M. Mon.–Sat., mains US$6–18) prepares traditional Italian fare that wows discerning diners from around the globe. Start with an order of fried oysters with caviar and move on to a homemade pasta or a hearty main dish like *frutti di mare.* Homemade *limoncello* is a fitting way to end the meal. Look for the tall, light blue wooden doors.

Decorated in pastel colors and original artwork, **La Pazion de la Pazta** (Allende, adjacent to Hotel Mediterrané, tel. 612/125-1195, 7 A.M.–11 P.M. Wed.–Mon., 7 A.M.–3 P.M. Tues., mains US$10–15) prepares a mix of Italian and Swiss dishes, including pastas, pizzas, and fondues. Choose from an impressive list of wines from Italy, the United States, Chile, and Baja.

The former Toscana Pizza Gourmet has changed hands to become **Alforno Pizza** (Dominguez and Constitución, tel. 612/122-1444, 5–11 P.M. Mon.–Sat., mains US$10–30). The menu includes some pasta dishes as well as a handful of gourmet pizzas and several wines by the glass to complete the meal. Dine at six pine picnic tables outside or at window counter seating inside.

Two blocks from the *malecón,* **Il Rustico** (Revolución de 1910 btw Rosales/Bravo, tel. 612/157-7073, 2–11 P.M. Wed.–Sat. and Mon., 2–11 P.M. Sun.) serves tasty thin-crust pizzas with creative toppings.

ECLECTIC

On the east side of the *malecón,* **Kiwi Restaurant Bar** (Paseo Obregón btw 5 de Mayo/Constitución, tel. 612/123-3282, 8 A.M.–midnight Sun.–Thurs., until 2 A.M. Fri. and Sat., mains US$6–15) has good views and a menu of passable seafood, Mexican, and international dishes. The people-watching is better than the food, but this is not a bad choice for lobster.

At the Hotel Perla, open-air **La Terraza** (Paseo Obregón 1570, tel. 612/122-0777, breakfast, lunch, and dinner daily, mains US$10–20) serves everything from seafood and Mexican fare to steak and Italian dishes. The crowd is a mix of visitors and locals and the prices are reasonable.

AMERICAN

Near the plaza and across from Baja Bed and Breakfast, **Buffalo BAR-B-Q** (Madero 1420, tel. 612/128-8755, 6 P.M.–midnight Mon.–Fri., 2–10 P.M. Sat.–Sun., mains US$10–20) continues to earn praise from locals and visitors for its steaks and burgers, made of Angus and Sonora beef. Owner Carlos Valdez is passionate about wine, and the restaurant's wine list shows it. But by the end of his first year in business, Carlos's little brother had proved with 🄲 **Buffalito Grill** (Madero btw Ocampo/Nicholas Bravo, tel. 612/140-1142, buffalitogrill@gmail.com, 2–11 P.M. Tues.–Sun., 6–11 P.M. Mon.) that he has the chops to live up to his older brother's establishment. Locals now rave about the little brother's fries, juicy burgers, and casual ambience.

An upscale option on the waterfront near the Marina de La Paz, **El Patrón Bar & Grill** (Plaza Vista Coral, tel. 612/125-9977, www.el-patronbarandgrill.com, 1–11 P.M. Sun.–Wed., 1 P.M.–midnight Thurs.–Sat., mains US$15–40) serves lamb, Sonora beef, grilled fish, tequila shrimp, and Cornish game hens in a casual indoor/outdoor setting. Prices reflect the waterfront location.

The yachting crowd frequents **The Dock Café** (Topete/Legaspy, tel. 612/125-6626, 8 A.M.–10 P.M. daily, mains US$10–15) inside the Marina de La Paz. This casual diner prepares a long list of American standbys, including fried chicken, burgers, fish-and-chips, bagels, salads, and steaks—and even homemade apple pie.

Restaurant Grill Campestre (Km. 5.5, Mexico 1, tel. 612/124-0454, lunch and dinner daily, mains US$10–15), opposite the Fidepaz building, is popular with gringos and Mexicans alike for barbecued ribs, Cobb salad, and other American specialties.

CHINESE

A number of decent Chinese restaurants have opened around town, serving unique Mexican-Chinese fare at inexpensive prices. For example, **Jeon-San** (Revolución 1440, btw Reforma/Independencia, tel. 612/122-0606, noon–8 P.M. daily, myli.wv@gmail.com, mains US$7) offers à la carte plates and combinations, all in large portions and delivered with friendly service. These days, local foodies prefer the simple **Lonchería Nuevo Oriental** (Marcelo

Rubio btw 16 de Septiembre/Reforma, no tel., 1–6 P.M. Tues.–Sun., mains US$5–10).

ANTOJITOS AND FAST FOOD

It's easy to find **◖ Rancho Viejo** (Legaspy, a half block from the Marina de La Paz, tel. 612/128-4647, 24 hrs. daily, dinner mains US$12–17) from the smell of the grill wafting up the street. Sit at a picnic table on the sidewalk or in either of two dining rooms inside to get away from the smoke. *Tacos de arranchera,* carne asada, or *pastor* arrive with the usual tray of fresh condiments. You can also order by the kilo. Service is prompt and friendly, and you can't beat the prices. Rancho Viejo has expanded to include a new space next door and has also opened a satellite location on the *malecón,* near Carlos'n Charlie's and the Thrifty Ice Cream shop. Instead of staying open 'round the clock, this one closes at 3–4 A.M.

A half block from the *malecón* on 16 de Septiembre, **Restaurant Pichos** (no tel., 8 A.M.–11 P.M. Tues.–Sun., mains US$3–6) serves delicious *tortas, licuados,* tacos, burgers, and *chilaquiles.* The *Hamburguesa Mexicana* comes with carne asada instead of ground beef, bacon bits, cheese, sliced avocado, tomato, and shredded lettuce, all on a lightly toasted bun. Two people can easily have lunch here for less than US$10, including sodas.

Street vendors open in the afternoons around the plaza and along Calle 16 de Septiembre. They typically sell hot dogs, tacos, stuffed baked potatoes *(papas rellenas),* burgers, and seafood cocktails. One of the best for fish and shellfish tacos as well as *aguas frescas* is **Super Tacos de Baja California Hermanos González** on Calle Esquerro (no tel.). There is a second location on Degollado at Madero, next to Pensión California, and a larger restaurant location on Degollado at Mijares. **Taquería Los Superburros** (Abasolo btw 5 de Febrero/Navarro, no tel.) is another popular choice for cheap eats.

Loncherías in the **Mercado Municipal Francisco E. Madero** (Revolución de 1910 and Degollado, no tel.) serve a good mix of *antojitos* and *comidas corridas.*

La Cochinita (Forjadores and Veracruz, tel. 612/122-1600, 10 A.M.–10 P.M. daily, mains US$5–10) is an only-in-Mexico option for Japanese fast food. A second branch is located on Calle Mutualismo, next to Bar El Misión.

CAFÉS

The espresso business is booming in La Paz. Several chains now have multiple locations, and new ones seem to open every month. Starbucks look-alike **5th Avenida Coffee** has wireless Internet in various locations, including 5 de Mayo on the plaza and Avenida Abasolo near the Marina de La Paz. **Café Exquisito** has a *malecón* location with sidewalk tables (Paseo Obregón, south of La Fuente, 6 A.M.–10:30 P.M. Mon.–Sat., 8 A.M.–10:30 P.M. Sun., drinks US$1–3), plus two drive-through espresso stands north and south of town on Mexico 1 and one more at the airport. **Café Combate** has at least two locations in town: Serdán between Calles Ocampo and Degollado, and on Calle Bravo at the southeast entrance to Mercado Bravo.

Aside from these chains, air-conditioned **Caffé Gourmet** (Esquerro and 16 de Septiembre, tel. 612/122-6037, 8 A.M.–10 P.M. Mon.–Sat.) has a counter full of sweets to go with your coffee, plus a selection of smoothies, Italian sodas, cigars, and liquors. Breakfast is served until 3 P.M. There is a nonsmoking section in the back and a newer second location on the *malecón.*

Also air-conditioned, **Mareiros Café** (Paseo Obregón, no tel., 8 A.M.–11 P.M. Mon.–Sat., 9 A.M.–5 P.M. Sun.) has sandwiches and salads to go with its full menu of hot drinks. There is outdoor seating and Internet access. **Hotel Mediterrané Café** (tel. 612/125-1195) opens at 7 A.M. daily. It serves excellent espresso drinks made from imported Italian Illy brand coffee, as well as cocktails, beer, and wine. There is air-conditioning, wireless Internet is free, and a desktop computer is available.

Café Gourmet (Km. 2, Carr. a Pichilingue, tel./fax 612/122-4084, www.clubelmoro.com, 7 A.M.–4 P.M. daily, mains US$5–15), attached to the El Moro hotel, is a good place to stop for breakfast on the way to Pichilingue.

El Quinto Sol (Domínguez and Independencia, tel./fax 612/122-1692) prepares vegetarian *tortas, comida corrida,* pastries, salads, granola, fruit and vegetable juices, and yogurt. You can also stock up on healthy foods in the attached store.

GROCERIES

Vendors in the **Mercado Municipal Francisco E. Madero** (Revolución de 1910 at Degollado) sell fresh fish, meats, fruit, vegetables, and baked goods, and there is a *tortillería* at the corner of Revolución de 1910 and Bravo.

The government-subsidized **ISSSTE Tienda** (Revolución de 1910 at Bravo) has the lowest prices but limited inventory.

La Paz has two large **Chedraui** (formerly Centro Comercial California/CCC) stores (Abasolo at Colima s/n, tel. 612/146-2263, Isabel La Católica 1915 at Bravo, tel. 612/129-3810). They stock U.S. and Mexican brands, but prices are relatively high. **Supermercado Arámburo** also has three branches in town: 16 de Septiembre at Altamirano, Madero at Hidalgo y Costilla (tel. 612/122-1599), and Durango 130 Sur (btw Ocampo/Degollado), plus another on Boulevard Forjadores at Cuauhtémoc (tel. 612/123-9210).

For big-box stores with groceries and more, head to **Plaza Ley** on the eastern edge of town (Las Garzas at Teotihuacán), **Walmart** (Lázaro Cárdenas 2200, tel. 686/568-0579), or **Soriana** (Forjadores de Sudcalifornia at Luis Donaldo Colosio s/n, tel. 612/121-4771) and **City Club** (Forjadores de Sudcalifornia at Luis Donaldo Colosio s/n, tel. 612/165-4990), which are in a shopping plaza on Boulevard Forjadores at the corner of Luis Donaldo Colosio. The Mega chain was building a new store at press time.

Sabores de México (Madero btw Constitución/5 de Mayo, no tel., www.saboresdemexico.mx) specializes in organic foods made only in Mexico, such as pure vanilla extract, sea salt, olive oil, and the like.

On Tuesdays and Saturdays a recently established **farmers market** takes place 9:30 A.M.–noon in the small park at the corner of Constitución and Revolución, across from the post office and Corazón Café. Enjoy fresh produce and organic foods at the twice-weekly local food fest. In addition to seasonal fruits and veggies, you can find fresh mozzarella, eggs, young chickens, jams, and flavored sea salts (without the added fluoride and iodine).

BREADS AND SWEETS

A day in La Paz isn't complete without an icy treat, and the downtown area has lots of options for *nieves* (Mexican-style ice cream), *paletas* (popsicles), and the like. **La Michoacana** (no tel.) is a chain with branches on Paseo Obregón and Calle Madero. But the most popular stand in town by far is ◖ **La Fuente** (Paseo Obregón btw Degollado/Muelle, no tel.), known for its long list of flavors, some of which are quite unusual. Look for a polka-dot tree in front of the entrance.

A couple of *dulcerías* (sweet shops) are located at the intersection of Calles Ocampo and Serdán. **Dulcería Perla** (no tel.) sells traditional and modern Mexican candies, while **Dulcería La Coneja** (no tel.) on the opposite corner makes piñatas.

Run by an accomplished pastry chef from California known in La Paz as "the bread guy," **Pan D'Les Bakery** (Madero btw Ocampo/Degollado, tel. 612/119-8392, loaves US$3 and other treats US$1–2 each) combines domestically sourced flours, yeast, salt from the Sea of Cortez and local water to make handcrafted artisan breads that reflect the colonization period in Mexico's history. Each day of the week brings a different special loaf (US$3 each)—rustica and ciabatta on Monday, multigrain and sourdough on Tuesday, and so on. For a sugar fix, order muffins, cookies, scones, cinnamon buns, and other irresistible treats. Chef/owner Les Carmona also writes an informative blog, Eating through La Paz (http://eatingthroughlapaz.blogspot.com).

Information and Services

TOURIST ASSISTANCE

Baja California Sur's state tourism office, **Fideicomiso de Turismo Estatal de BCS** (Km. 5.5, Mexico 1, tel. 612/124-0100, www. explorebajasur.com, 8 A.M.–8 P.M. Mon.–Fri.) is a few kilometers north of downtown on Mexico 1 (Abasolo), opposite the Grand Plaza Resort. Also here is the Attorney for the Protection of Tourists. More convenient is the information booth on the *malecón,* near the Applebee's, which has maps and brochures (Paseo Obregón at Allende, 8 A.M.–8 P.M. Mon.–Fri.).

The La Paz Hotel Association, **La Paz Emprhotur** (16 de Septiembre at Domínguez, tel. 612/125-6844, www.visitlapaz.org) maintains an advertiser-driven site, not to be confused with the tourist office site.

MONEY

Unlike in the Los Cabos area, you will need pesos for making cash purchases at many businesses in La Paz. Three banks with ATMs are clustered near the intersection of Calle 16 de Septiembre and the *malecón.* They provide currency-exchange service 9 A.M.–noon Monday–Friday. If you need to exchange money in the afternoon or on a Saturday and you can't use an ATM, **Tony Money Exchange** (Mutualismo, near La Perla, and nearby on 16 de Septiembre near the *malecón,* 9 A.M.–9 P.M. Mon.–Sat.) usually has acceptable rates. On Sundays the larger hotels are the only option.

POST AND TELEPHONE

The main La Paz post office is at the intersection of Revolución de 1910 and Constitución, one block northeast of the cathedral. It's open 8 A.M.–3 P.M. Monday–Friday, 9 A.M.–1 P.M. Saturday.

DHL (Abasolo at Nayarit, tel. 612/122-8282) offers domestic and international shipping.

INTERNET ACCESS

Most hotels and cafés now offer high-speed wireless Internet access for free. The 5th Avenida and Café Exquisito chains offer wireless access, as do most of the marinas. Hotels with wireless connections include the Mediterrané, Fiesta Inn, Seven Crown, El Moro, and Posada de las Flores. Air-conditioned **Hotel Mediterrané Café** (Allende 36, tel. 612/125-1195, 7 A.M.–11 P.M. daily) has a desktop computer set up for customer use; wireless access is free if you bring your own computer.

In addition, a number of Internet cafés are still in business along the *malecón.* **Omni Services** (Paseo Obregón 460-C, tel. 612/123-4888, toll-free Mex. tel. 877/805-7372) has Internet, PCs, and copy and fax services. Rates in La Paz are generally a reasonable US$2 per hour.

GAS

The most central Pemex to downtown is located on 5 de Mayo between Serdán and Prieto. A second is 10 blocks away at the intersection of Isabel la Católica, and a third is on Avenida Abasolo as you leave La Paz headed toward the airport.

LAUNDRY

Close to the *malecón,* **La Paz Lava** (Ocampo at Mutualismo, tel. 612/122-3112, 8 A.M.–9:30 P.M. daily) is a self-service or full-service facility that also can deliver your clothes to your hotel. The marinas in town have their own laundry services as well.

LANGUAGE COURSES

Swiss-run **Centro de Idiomas, Cultura y Comunicación (CICC)** (Madero 2460 at Legaspy tel. 612/125-7554, www.cicclapaz.com, 8:30 A.M.–1 P.M. Mon.–Fri., 9:30 A.M.–1 P.M. Sat.) teaches Spanish-language students of any level. Its standard program (US$780) includes four weeks of intensive study (22 hrs. per week); a homestay with a Mexican family costs extra. A one-week travel Spanish course costs US$99. The school also offers business-Spanish and medical-Spanish programs.

LA PAZ PHONE NUMBERS

- La Paz Area Code: 612

- Baja Ferries Office (Pichilingue): 123-0208

- COTP (Captain of the Port): 122-0243 or 122-4364

- Green Angels: 124-0100 or 124-0199

- Highway Patrol/Federal Police: 122-0369

- Immigration: 125-3493 or 124-6349

- IMSS Hospital: 122-7377

- Police, Fire Department, Red Cross (Emergency): 066

- SEMATUR Ferry Office (Pichilingue): 122-5005

- State Tourism Department: 124-0100 or 122-0199

Se Habla La Paz (Madero 540, tel./fax 612/122-7763, www.sehablalapaz.com) also offers more expensive classes and homestays for travelers and medical or legal professionals. Costs include a US$75 registration fee that covers student/family matching for homestays and airport pickup. Lessons run US$25 per hour for a private session and US$12.50 for group lessons. A one-week course is US$250 (20 hrs.) and a four-week program costs US$850 (80 hrs.). Payment is accepted via PayPal.

NEWSPAPERS AND MAGAZINES

La Paz has two Spanish-language dailies: *Diario Peninsular* and *El Sudcaliforniano* (www.elsudcaliforniano.com.mx). **Librería Contempo** (Arriola at Paseo Obregón) carries mostly Mexican newspapers as well as a few American periodicals.

The Baja Citizen (www.bajacitizen.com) is a free biweekly newspaper published by Gari-Ellen Donohoe for the gringo community.

IMMIGRATION

La Paz has an immigration office on Paseo Obregón between Allende and Juárez (tel. 612/125-3493, 8 A.M.–8:30 P.M. daily). Another immigration office at the airport also is open daily, and a third office, at the Pichilingue ferry terminal, opens about an hour before each ferry departure.

EMERGENCIES

La Paz has two hospitals: Hospital Fidepaz (Km. 5.5, Mexico 1, tel. 612/124-0400), on the Transpeninsular Highway near the tourist office, and Hospital Juan María de Salvatierra (tel. 612/175-0503), off Boulevard Forjedores. Dial 066 for emergencies and tel. 612/122-5939 for information and the tourist police.

LA PAZ AND VICINITY

Getting There and Around

GETTING THERE
By Air

Márquez de León International Airport (LAP) (tel. 612/124-6307) is located 12 kilometers south of La Paz; look for the access road at Km. 9. Services include fast food (Burger King, Chili's), a duty-free shop, at least eight major car rental companies, Ladatel public phones, and a Scotiabank ATM.

Direct service from the United States has been on-again, off-again as the economy rises and falls. At last check, Alaska Airlines was the only airline making the trip; Delta had put its service on hold indefinitely. All other carriers required a connection in mainland Mexico, which adds significant cost and time to the trip.

Transporte Terrestre (tel. 612/125-3274) runs a shuttle service between downtown and the airport in yellow and white vans; prices are about US$12 pp for *colectivo* (shared ride), US$25 for private service *(especial)*, and US$50 for a larger van. A regular taxi to the airport should cost around US$25. Some hotels offer airport shuttles for US$5–10 per person. **Espíritu & Baja Tours** (Obregón #774-A, btw Allende/Juárez, tel. 612/122-4427, www.espiritubaja.com) offers airport transfer services in addition to its other tours (airport to hotel US$15 pp, hotel to airport US$10 pp).

By Bus

La Paz has two bus terminals. The main one is on Calle Jalisco at Avenida Independencia, about 10 blocks inland from Avenida Abasolo. The second one, called the *terminal turistica,* is on the *malecón*. **Aguila** (tel. 612/122-3063 or 612/122-4270, www.autotransportesaguila.com) has daily northbound service from the main terminal with stops at the tourist terminal to Ciudad Constitución, Puerto San Carlos, Puerto López Mateos, Loreto (US$40, twice daily), Mulegé, Santa Rosalía, San Ignacio, Vizcaíno Junction, Guerrero Negro (US$90, several times daily), San Quintín, Ensenada (US$120, four times daily), Tijuana (US$130, four times daily), Tecate, and Mexicali. You can now check schedules and prices online.

Southbound buses all depart from the **Terminal Turistica** (tel. 612/122-7898). Only one bus (5 P.M.) runs through the towns of El Triunfo, San Antonio, San Bartolo, Los Barriles (US$9), Santiago, and Miraflores, terminating in La Ribera/Las Cuevas. Most run via Mexico 19 through Todos Santos (nine buses per day, beginning at 7 A.M., US$7), continuing to Cabo San Lucas (US$17) and San José del Cabo (US$19); the 3 P.M. bus continues all the way to La Ribera.

Southbound travelers have another option: **Autotransportes La Paz** (tel. 612/122-2157) has a more central terminal on Calle Degollado at Guillermo Prieto, which has several departures a day to Los Cabos via Todos Santos. Fares are competitive with the Aguila fares.

By Boat

The busy ferry port at Pichilingue lies 16 kilometers northeast of downtown La Paz via Mexico 1, also known as the Carreterra a Pichilingue. It offers passenger and vehicle service to Mazatlán and Topolobampo on the mainland through **Baja Ferries** (Pichilinque Terminal, tel. 612/123-0208, downtown office: Allende 1025 at Rubio, tel. 612/123-6600 or 800/122-1414, www.bajaferries.com, 8 A.M.–5 P.M. daily). You can book tickets in advance online, in downtown La Paz, or at the ferry terminal.

You must obtain a **temporary vehicle import permit** (Expedición de Permisos de Importación Temporal de Vehículos, IITV, approx. US$30 payable at a Banjercito bank) in order to drive your vehicle in mainland Mexico. The purpose of this document is to make sure that you take the vehicle with you when you leave, instead of selling it illegally and avoiding the import tax. There are several ways to take care of this paperwork:

- Visit a Mexican consulate in the United States (Albuquerque, Chicago, Dallas, Houston, Los Angeles, Sacramento, San Bernardino, San Francisco, or Phoenix).
- Apply on the Banjercito website (www.banjercito.com, pages and forms are available in English), and then complete the process in person at a Banjercito branch in Mexico.
- Go to customs *(aduana)* in Tijuana, Tecate, or Mexicali when you enter Baja.
- Go to customs at the ferry terminal in La Paz.

To get the permit in La Paz, go to the customs *(Aduana Maritima)* office (9 A.M.–1 P.M. and 5–7 P.M. Mon.–Sat.) at the ferry terminal. It's a slow and sometimes frustrating experience, and it's best to allow an extra day or two to be sure all the paperwork gets done in time for your departure.

Wherever you apply, you will need the following documentation in order to get the permit:

- Vehicle title or registration, to prove you own the vehicle: original plus three copies.
- Certificate of canceled import permit for any prior temporary import permits.

- A letter from the owner authorizing you to take the vehicle into Mexico (if you have leased, rented, or borrowed the vehicle)
- Major credit card (in the vehicle owner's name), for securing the temporary import deposit, which guarantees that you'll bring the vehicle out of Mexico when you leave. If you don't bring a credit card, you'll need to leave US$200–400 in cash, depending on the age and value of the vehicle; the deposit is refunded when you cancel the permit at the end of your trip.
- Valid driver's license
- Passport with valid Mexican visa
- Proof of Mexican auto insurance policy

If you arrive with all the requisite paperwork, the permit can usually be issued on the spot, after long waits in several lines. Once issued, the permit is valid for six months.

For travelers arriving and departing by private boat, La Paz is an official port of entry into Mexico, and foreign vessels must follow the appropriate procedures for checking in and out of the country. The port captain's office is located near the Marina Palmira. The staff at any of the major marinas in town can process paperwork required for clearing the port. The Marina de La Paz has published a detailed FAQ with information about the official entry and exit requirements at www.marinadelapaz.com.

GETTING AROUND

Except on the hottest of days, downtown La Paz is best explored on foot. Narrow one-way streets filled with people and vehicles can be intimidating to navigate for the first-time visitor, but if you stick to the perimeter streets—Avenida Abasolo, Paseo Obregón, Boulevard Forjadores, etc.—it's fairly easy to get around by car as well. City buses and taxis are readily available, too.

If you are driving into La Paz from the south and want to head directly to the Pichilingue Peninsula and the ferry terminal, you can take a shortcut just after the university on Boulevard Forjadores. Look for a sign for Libramiento Norte heading off to the right. If you get to Soriana and Office Depot, you've missed the turn and it's best to continue on into the city and make your way to the waterfront.

By Bus

Municipal buses and *colectivo* shuttles congregate around the Mercado Municipal on Calle Degollado and head out in all directions from there. Routes may be indicated by the name of the street the bus will follow (e.g., G. Prieto) or the district to which it is heading (e.g., El Centro). To get to the Soriana mall on Boulevard Forjadores, look for buses labeled Soriana.

Frequent Aguila buses connect the downtown area to the Pichilingue Peninsula. Catch them at the Terminal Malecón (Paseo Obregón 125, tel. 612/122-7898). Buses to Playa Balandra and Playa El Tecolote depart at noon and 2 P.M. on weekends only.

By Taxi

Taxis are easily found along the west end of Calle 16 de Septiembre and in front of the La Perla hotel. Fare for rides within the downtown area should be under US$5, about US$5 to Soriana, US$15 to the airport, and US$20 to the ferry terminal. There are no meters, so be sure to agree on a price before you hop in.

By Car

A handful of international car rental agencies have airport and downtown locations in La Paz. Rates start around US$25 per day for unlimited miles, not including tax and insurance.

La Paz has numerous Pemex stations, all selling *magna sin* (unleaded), premium, and diesel.

Construction is under way to widen Mexico 19 to a four-lane highway connecting La Paz and Cabo San Lucas. So far, the entire stretch between La Paz and Todos Santos is complete. On the other side of the city, the government is working on another stretch of highway, to create a four-lane bypass around La Paz, from El Centenario to Mexico 1 south and on to Mexico 19.

Southeast of La Paz

Two scenic bays southeast of La Paz—Bahía de la Ventana and Bahía de los Muertos—are joined to the city via paved BCS 286, which departs Mexico 1 at Km. 211 and extends 43 kilometers to the farming town of San Juan de los Planes. In between, the peaks of the Sierra de la Laguna range rise to more than 1,200 meters. (The mountains here are also called the Sierra de las Cruces on the north side of the highway and the Sierra el Novillo and Sierra la Trinchera on the south side.) The descent affords stunning views of the sea and Isla Cerralvo just 16 kilometers (10 miles) offshore.

Combine the culture and history of La Paz with a more rustic outdoor experience along one of these bays and you have a near-perfect Baja itinerary.

Information and Services

La Paz has the closest hospital and other emergency services, but there is a **BlueMedicalNet** clinic (tel. 624.104-3911, 24/7 daily) at Km. 55, on the road from La Paz to Los Planes.

You can get gas and supplies in Los Planes; there are also a few convenience stores in El Sargento.

Getting There

Most people reach La Ventana and Los Muertos by car from La Paz. It takes about 35 minutes to get to La Ventana from downtown La Paz and about 45 minutes from the airport. Once on BCS 286, look for the La Ventana turn-off at Km. 38—it's a paved road that branches northeast. Follow this road along the edge of the bay about eight kilometers to La Ventana and 11 kilometers to El Sargento.

Shuttles from La Paz to La Ventana cost around US$120 (US$350 from Los Cabos). Pubic transportation is an option, albeit a complicated one. It's about a US$15 taxi from the airport to the La Ventana bus stop. From there, a bus leaves daily at 2 P.M. for US$5.

If you are on the East Cape heading to Bahía de los Muertos, you have two options: Follow the 47-kilometer dirt road between Los Barriles and Los Planes, or follow the Transpeninsular Highway north and use the now-paved connector between Mexico 1 and BCS 286. The dirt road begins with a relatively smooth ride, but after El Cardonal (13 km. into the drive), the road narrows and ascends into the sierra, where the going gets pretty rough. You don't need four-wheel drive, but this is not a drive for those prone to vertigo or anyone in a hurry. Many of the curves have steep drop-offs, and you'll have to take it slow.

If you are coming from the south on Mexico 1, a paved route connects BCS 286 and Los Planes to the town of San Antonio. This road is straight and flat, and its east end begins on BCS 286 about 3.5 kilometers south of the turnoff for La Ventana and El Sargento. The road is not marked when approaching the turn-off from northbound Mexico 1. Look for a few handmade signs pointing the way to kiteboarding schools.

The private **Aeromar las Arenas** airfield offers tie-down service and 24-hour security for guests of the Bay of Dreams resort. Currently 1,500 meters long, the strip will be expanded to nearly 2,000 meters in the future. Current flights must clear customs and immigration in La Paz, Loreto, or Los Cabos; however, the resort is working to get on-site customs and immigration, which would allow direct service from the United States.

◖ BAHÍA DE LA VENTANA

Once a pair of quiet fishing villages, Bahía de la Ventana and neighboring **El Sargento** were discovered by windsurfers in the 1990s and kiteboarders soon after. In winter months when the powerful *El Norte* winds blow through the narrow Canal de Cerralvo, sailboards fill the bay—as well as the campgrounds that surround it.

Other times of year, the towns attract scuba divers/free divers, beachgoers, and sportfishing enthusiasts.

LA VENTANA AND
EL SARGENTO

VENTANA BAY RESORT

EL CHAPITO
MINIMARKET

BAHÍA DE LA
VENTANA

EL SARGENTO

TORTAS Y
HAMBURGUESAS
ANDREA
TOLON FISHMARKET

LUPITA
MINIMARKET

TACOS
"LA TORRE"

TACOS LEON

TORTILLERÍA LAS BRISAS

TAQUERÍA EL SARGENTO

POLICE

LAS PALMAS

EL AMIGO PANCHO
MINISUPER BELLE

PIZZA VELA

CTRA. A EL SARGENTO

LA VENTANA

CAPTAIN KIRK'S

PALAPAS VENTANA

RAFA'S

LA VENTANA
CAMPGROUND

PABLO'S
MINIMARKET

KIJOTE COFFEESHOP

LA VENTANA FISHMARKET

DON RUBEN MINIMARKET

EL RINCÓN DE LA BAHÍA

PLAYA CENTRAL

CASA VERDE

0   0.25 mi

0   0.25 km

EL NORTE

BAJA JOE

© AVALON TRAVEL

Though it's still relatively undeveloped compared to nearby La Paz or the Los Cabos corridor, the word is out on La Ventana; the area has been experiencing a real estate boom for the last few years, with dozens of properties for sale and many new buildings taking shape each year.

Expats here support the local community through annual fundraising contests, English language instruction, and other events. The result is an integrated community that gives a warm welcome to its visitors.

Sports and Recreation

Though the area is best known for wind sports, there is an activity for just about every weather condition: Calm seas mean short boat rides and good visibility for snorkeling or diving; windy days are good for sails—or a hike. Big swells are an excuse to head to the Pacific side to catch some waves.

WINDSURFING AND KITEBOARDING

Windsurfers discovered the ideal conditions at La Ventana in the 1990s, but in recent years, the rising popularity of kiteboarding has brought many more adventure-seeking travelers to the area. Kiteboarders say La Ventana is one of the best places in the world to learn the sport, because the shoreline of the bay curves around to catch those who drift downwind on white-sand beaches. Experienced windsurfers say the wind at La Ventana isn't as strong as at Los Barriles but it tends to be more consistent. The wind typically picks up around 11 A.M. and holds steady until just before sunset.

Several schools certified by the **International Kiteboarding Organization (IKO)** rent gear and offer lessons for windsurfing and kiteboarding. (They'll also come get you if you have trouble staying upwind.) Radio-assisted lessons are a great way to get minute-by-minute coaching. The student wears a waterproof helmet system, and the instructor gives directions from the shore. Watercraft-assisted lessons are another option for beginners. "Downwinders," offered by many of the schools, eliminate the need to worry about staying upwind. Take a

LA PAZ AND VICINITY

BAHÍA DE LA VENTANA

LIGHTHOUSE

El Sargento

BAHÍA DE LA VENTANA

La Ventana

SEE "LA VENTANA AND EL SARGENTO" MAP

Punta Arena de la Ventana

LIGHTHOUSE

266

San Juán de los Planes

Bahía de los Muertos

0   2 mi

0   2 km

To El Triunfo

© AVALON TRAVEL

shuttle ride to the north end of the bay and enjoy a two-hour sail back to camp.

One of the first to set up shop in the early 1990s was **Captain Kirk's Windsurfing** (U.S. tel. 310/833-3397, www.captainkirks.com), with headquarters in San Pedro, California. The shop also rents several vacation homes, ranging from US$60–300 per night. For example, there is a two-bedroom home with kitchen (US$275/night) and a *casita* with two double beds and bath (US$160/night). Rentals come with free use of mountain bikes, sea kayaks, and snorkeling equipment. Breakfast is included. A windsurfing or kiteboarding gear package is US$65 per person per day. Other activities include stand-up paddling and yoga.

With headquarters in Hood River, Oregon, the **New Wind Kite School** (U.S. tel. 541/387-2440, www.newwindkiteboarding.com, Nov. 15–Mar. 15) offers lessons for new and experienced kiteboarders (US$216–280/day, depending on the number of students; US$85 for a 1.5-hr session). Custom instruction runs US$89 per hour for one person, with a two-hour minimum. Board rentals cost US$39 per day, kite-only rentals are US$70 per day, kite and bar rentals are US$89 per day, and a full

setup goes for US$119 per day. This school also has a beach house next door, Casa del Sol (beachfront suite US$150/night, courtyard room US$105/night, rates include tax). Store your gear and use the air compressor to inflate your kite for free.

British Columbia–based **Elevation Kiteboarding School** (Canada tel. 604/848-5197, www.elevationkiteboarding.com) offers private lessons for CDN$115 per hour (two-hour minimum), a full day (about four hours) for CDN$325 per person, and multiday kiteboarding camp packages. The school is located at Baja Joe's Resort. **Sheldon Kiteboarding** (U.S. tel. 707/374-3053, www.sheldonkiteboarding.com) maintains summer headquarters in Rio Vista, California, and winter headquarters at La Ventana. Owner Bruce provides beds and mattresses for camping, plus a shared kitchen, and bath with a hot-water shower. Bring your own sleeping bag. Bruce offers lessons, equipment, and repairs.

Baja Adventures at **Ventana Bay Resort** (tel. 612/128-4333, www.ventanabaykiteboarding.com) is a full-service operation that provides equipment rentals and lessons. It replaces its rental gear each season, selling the previous year's equipment at reduced prices. Kiteboarding equipment is the latest lines from North Kites. You can also rent K2 full-suspension mountain bikes from the shop.

South of the campground, **Kitemasters** (www.kitemasters.com) offers six hours of lessons for US$600 or US$85/hour. Student use radio helmets and NAISH gear.

SNORKELING, SCUBA DIVING, AND SPEARFISHING

Palapas Ventana (tel. 612/114-0198, www.palapasventana.com) has a certified PADI dive shop on-site that leads guided trips to Isla Cerralvo year-round. The 26-foot super-*panga* has a four-stroke engine and takes up to six divers per trip. Trips cost US$125 for a two-tank dive, including all gear and lunch. Snorkelers pay US$50, including all gear and lunch. Boats depart at 7:45 A.M. and return at 3 P.M. Scuba certification packages are

© NIKKI GOTH ITOI

Divers meet at Palapas Ventana before heading out to explore Isla Cerralvo.

available (six days/five nights for US$679 pp, min. three people). Captain Tavo is a shark fisherman and dive instructor. Several of the windsurfing and kiteboarding resorts dabble in scuba trips as well.

The small reef in La Ventana Bay provides a good introduction to the underwater life in the area. Watch for urchins during entry/exit and keep an eye out for the local frogfish on the reef. The best snorkeling from shore is at Las Arenas reef, a 20-minute drive. Follow BCS 286 east through Los Planes and turn left at the airstrip, before you reach Bahía de los Muertos. Follow this road about a mile, past several guard stations, until you reach an abandoned hotel at the coast.

For a more adventurous day of snorkeling, accompany researchers on a day of whale-shark observation in La Paz Bay (US$75 pp). Boats depart from the Costa Baja Marina near Pichilingue, north of La Paz. The drive along BCS 286 and the bypass around La Paz takes about 45 minutes from La Ventana. Palapas Ventana can arrange your trip.

For those who want to catch their dinner, Palapas Ventana offers spearfishing instruction and guided trips. Students learn to identify edible fish and test their aim on an underwater target (US$50 pp from shore, US$85 pp by *panga*).

STAND-UP PADDLING

Stand-up paddling has come to La Ventana, and you can rent or borrow gear at several shops along the bay, including Captain Kirk's, Casa Verde, and Palapas Ventana, where rentals cost US$10 per hour or US$30 all day. Guided tours cost US$40 for three hours.

FISHING

The waters surrounding Isla Cerralvo, Bahía La Ventana, Punta Arena de la Ventana, and Bahía de los Muertos offer more consistent fishing than Bahía de La Paz and the islands near the city. Many charters will drive BCS 286 from La Paz and launch at Punta Arena or Los Muertos, rather than traveling by boat across the choppy water. The Canal de Cerralvo is known for roosterfish and *pargo colorado* January–July and for marlin and dorado in the summer months. It is also a world-class spearfishing destination. The 88 bank area off Cerralvo is known for marlin, dorado, and yellowfin tuna.

Sportfishing with Lalo (tel. 612/114-0335, cell tel. 612/151-9921, www.fishlalo.com) offers fly-fishing, live bait, and trolling services. Run by Captain Nono, **HOOKUP** offers trips aboard a 23-foot (US$200) or 26-foot *panga* (US$250). Boats depart at 6:30 A.M. and return at 3 P.M., or earlier upon request. Contact Palapas Ventana (tel. 612/114-0198, www.palapasventana.com) for reservations.

You can launch small boats easily from the beaches at Bahía de la Ventana, Punta Arena, and Bahía de los Muertos. Fishing licenses cost US$15 per day.

SEA TURTLES

In winter green sea turtles nest along the bay, and lucky visitors might catch the hatch on a full moon. Leatherback turtles nest later in the spring. Nesting areas are marked with hand-painted signs that give a zone number and read *Cuida Los Nidos* (Protect the nests). Nests are marked with tape. Needless to say, do not disturb them.

HIKING

Inquire at Palapas Ventana about a six-mile loop trail to see a 1,500-year-old **cave painting** of a yellowfin tuna and wahoo. Your guide will point out palms, birds, and native plants along the way, and you'll learn about the mining history of El Sargento. The trip takes about 4.5 hours and costs US$45 with a two-person minimum.

A shorter hike begins in a canyon just west of El Sargento, called Las Canoas Arroyo. Vegetation includes wildflowers and cacti. You might also spot gray foxes, iguanas, and many types of birds. Inquire at Palapas Ventana for directions and/or a guide (US$25 pp, two-person minimum).

SPAS

Get a relaxing Swedish massage from Teresa or Marcela at Palapas Ventana (US$45 for one

hour, reservation required), or book a massage, body wrap or mani/pedi at the new **Spa Verde** (tel. 612/114-0214, www.laventanaspa.com), located at Casa Verde. A 30-minute massage is US$25.

OTHER ACTIVITIES

Several businesses in town arrange Spanish classes, cooking classes, and other group activities. Stop by the offices at Casa Verde, Palapas Ventana, Captain Kirk's, or any of the kiteboarding schools to find out what's going on during your stay.

Festivals and Events

The **La Ventana Classic** is a fundraising kiteboarding race held in January every year. Participants start at Isla Cerralvo and finish on the shore of Bahía de la Ventana. Proceeds are donated to the town for schools and other community needs. Contact **Palapas Ventana** (tel. 612/114-0198, www.palapasventana.com) for information.

La Ventana and El Sargento celebrate their **annual town festival** in late October with three days of live music, carnival rides, and street food.

Accommodations and Camping

Located about 800 meters past El Sargento, the **Ventana Bay Resort** (tel. 612/128-4333, www.ventanabay.com, US$110–140) has clubhouse rooms on the beach or private bungalows set back from the beach. Amenities include tiled floors and showers, rustic wooden furniture, ceiling fans, private patios, and hammocks strung between palms on the beach. The resort offers a variety of packages that combine accommodations, meals, and windsurfing/kiteboarding or other activities. For example, a seven-day kiteboarding package includes accommodations, two meals per day, and unlimited use of kiteboarding gear for US$875–1,050. A "sports" package for US$595–695 includes unlimited use of mountain bikes, sea kayaks, snorkeling gear, and Hobie Cats. Wireless Internet is available at additional cost. The resort also manages a

© NIKKI GOTH ITOI

RVs set up for the season on Bahía de la Ventana.

few private homes as vacation rentals. Its **Cisco Restaurant** serves breakfast, lunch, and dinner. Fresh fruit margaritas are a popular way to pass the afternoon.

Between La Ventana and El Sargento, ◖ **Palapas Ventana** (tel. 612/114-0198, www.palapasventana.com) has two types of newly constructed *palapa*-roof *casitas*. Regular ones sleep two in a king or in two twin beds with shared shower and bath and air-conditioning (US$60 pp double occupancy). Specialty *casitas* sleep four (in one room) with private tiled bath and air-conditioning (US$77.50 pp double occupancy). Extra touches include high ceilings (with fans), Mission-style furnishings, hammocks, purified water dispensers, and rain showers. Also on-site are a dive shop, gated parking area, Internet café, and restaurant. The resort offers kiteboarding lessons, stand-up paddle surfing lessons and rentals, kayaks, fishing/spearfishing, whale-shark research trips, and surf trips to the West Cape as well as guided hikes to local cave paintings. Stay-and-dive packages include five days/four nights of accommodations; three days

of diving (two tanks per day); breakfast every day and lunch on dive days; and free use of kayaks, snorkeling gear, and sailboats (US$655 pp, min. three people).

Mokie's (tel. 612/114-0201, U.S. tel. 541/478-2199, www.mokies.com, US$550/wk. or US$1,500/mo., payment via PayPal) rents studio and one-bedroom *casitas* on 1.4 fenced hectares fronting the beach. Both *casitas* come with full-size bed, kitchen (including margarita glasses), two full-size futons, bath with large shower, mountain and sea views, and an outdoor terrace. Guests store their gear in a beachfront loft just 10 meters from the water's edge, or walk to shops that rent gear and offer lessons. When not on the water, you can enjoy a partially shaded beachfront terrace that has a glass wall for shelter from the wind.

Kurt-n-Marina (tel. 612/114-0010, U.S. tel. 509/590-1409, www.ventanakiteboarding.com) offers several *casitas* with *palapa* roofs and tiled baths (US$55) as well as camping (RV spaces US$12, tent camping US$8) and a spacious outdoor kitchen area for guests to share.

Lush gardens, comfortable beds, and seven stylish rooms (called *casitas*) are a plus in relatively new ◖ Casa Verde (tel. 612/114-0214, U.S. tel. 509/228-8628, www.bajmahal.com, US$110, tax included). Enjoy natural light, private baths, small refrigerators, and sea views in each one. Two stand-alone houses on the property rent for US$150 per night. Three Native American lodges are set up for camping (US$30/40 s/d); guests may use a main kitchen or garden kitchen and shared bath with hot showers. Bikes, kayaks, stand-up paddle boards, and wireless Internet are included as well. The resort has teamed up with Kitemasters to offer seven-night, all-inclusive packages that cover accommodations, all meals, and eight hours of lessons for two people, plus the use of kayaks and mountain bikes (US$1,800, including tax). Tee Pee Camping (US$55) in one of the resort's three Native American lodges is a unique option for budget travelers. These are simply furnished with beds, and guests use shared bath and kitchen facilities. The on-site espresso stand is a plus while you're waiting for the wind to pick up. RV camping and a new spa are great additions to the guest experience at this property.

Steps from the sea, **Baja Joe's** (tel. 612/114-0001, www.bajajoe.com) has several *palapa*-roof cabins for rent (US$50–110). Some share a bath; others have their own. All have air-conditioning and a small refrigerator. RV cabanas have private kitchens, while economical bunkhouse rooms (US$40/50 s/d) have use of a shared outdoor kitchen and one of six baths on the property. Rates include use of mountain bikes, sea kayaks, snorkel equipment, and a storage area for gear. No children under age four. Discounts for long-term stays. Baja Joe's rents windsurfing and kiteboarding equipment, or you can stop by its store to buy new or consigned gear. Its instructors use WaveRunners and helmet radios to facilitate faster learning.

The main camping area is called **La Ventana Campground,** located along the beach just north of the village of La Ventana, and it packs in the sailboarders during the windy season. This barebones campground has around 50 simple tent sites (US$7–8/night) close to the water—and the road. There are toilets and cold showers. RVs are welcome, but there are no hookups for utilities. **Yoyo's Campground** at the entrance to La Ventana, is similar, with hot showers (tel. 612/114-0015, cell tel. 612/348-0004, US$8/day up to two people, US$8/day each additional person).

Between La Ventana and El Tecolote on a remote stretch of beach accessible by private aircraft, **Rancho Las Cruces** (tel. 612/125-5639, U.S. tel. 858/764-4122, www.rancholascruces.com), has poolside rooms (US$185–275 pp) and cabanas (US$290 pp) that are open to nonmembers. Rates include all meals, and children ages 5–12 are 20 percent off when they stay in the same room as their parents. (No charge for ages four and under.) Guests enjoy hikes on trails through the expansive property, a private golf driving range, tennis courts, and croquet courts, plus sunbathing and sportfishing. The resort is closed mid-July–mid-October.

Food

Each winter season brings a new wave of eateries to these sleepy bayside towns. Expect to find several small minisupers (no supermarkets), a few traditional Mexican restaurants, several newer gringo establishments, a number of taquerias, and a *tortillería* (on the paved part of the road in El Sargento). Prices are generally low, and the atmosphere is casual. If you plan to cook most of your own meals, stock up on supplies in La Paz.

New in winter 2010, **Playa Central** (www.laventanakiteboarding.net) aims to create a much-needed gathering place for the kiteboarding community. Run by the twentysomething children of a Mexican family from Cozumel, the business occupies a former shrimp factory near the arroyo in La Ventana. A small patch of grass in front of the yellow building makes it easier to pump up and wrap kites. In its first season, Playa Central opened a bakery and pizzeria. Accommodations consist of a writers' bunk with four beds, hostel style, for US$14 a night, and two basic apartments, each with a king-size bed and loft area, for US$65 a night. The not-yet-renovated interior of the warehouse is large enough to host music events during the high season.

On the way to El Sargento, before the pavement ends, **El Amigo Pancho** (no tel., 8 A.M.–10 P.M. daily, breakfast mains US$2–5, dinner mains US$4–7) is one of the few eateries that stays open late. Follow the smell of meat sizzling on the grill to a simple *palapa* structure next to Minisuper Belle, where you can order Mexican specialties, including chicken mole, burgers, enchiladas, and fish prepared various ways such as *al mojo de ajo, a la veracruzana,* or *al diablo.* During breakfast hours, the restaurant offers *licuados, chilaquiles,* and various egg dishes.

About 200 meters south of the pubic campground, **Rincón del Bahía** (no tel., hours vary, mains US$7–13) serves tasty seafood and Mexican fare on the beach. Owner Joaquin will serenade you while you dine. The stuffed fish with shrimp has been popular since the restaurant opened in the 1990s. Just south of Palapas Ventana, **Tacos Rafa** (no tel., hours vary) grills fish tacos for US$6–13. The restaurant at **Palapas Ventana** (tel. 612/114-0198, www.palapasventana.com, breakfast and lunch daily, plus dinner Fri.–Sat. and live music in winter, mains US$8–13) prepares lasagna, steaks, BBQ ribs, fresh grilled fish (all of it caught by the staff themselves). Try the coconut wahoo. Enjoy local wines, an icy margarita, or a Negra Modelo on tap (the only draught beer available in La Ventana) with your meal. Reservations are recommended.

Look for **Tacos en la Torre** "Tower Tacos" (no tel., hours vary, mains US$4–7) at the base of the radio tower in El Sargento, with a menu of *chilaquiles, tortas cubanas,* and *flautas.* On the west side of the road in El Sargento, behind Mini Super Corona, **Tacos Leon** (no tel., hours vary) has hot dogs, *papas rellenas,* and enchiladas for US$4–10. Long a favorite among campers, **Viento del Norte** (mains US$4–9) serves hearty breakfasts, enchiladas, and jumbo margaritas.

In a yellow two-story building on the beach, **Las Palmas** (no tel., 8 A.M.–10 P.M. daily; dinner mains US$5–8) prepares omelets, *flautas, machaca,* and espresso drinks for breakfast and a menu of enchiladas, tacos, *mariscos,* and pastas for lunch and dinner. The fish tacos, made of fresh-caught cabrilla, come with an exceptionally fresh medley of avocado, lettuce, cucumber and tomato. There are tables on both levels. Head upstairs for the bar and the best views. The restaurant is located at the end of the pavement, about a mile past La Ventana and across from the police station. **Pizza Vela** (500 meters north of Palapas Ventana on the beach side of the road, no tel., hours vary, mains US$5–15), offers an alternative to Mexican fare; you can order a fresh salad and a glass of wine to go with your pie. Wine bottles are stored in a wine refrigerator, ensuring the right temperature on the hottest of days. At **Mariscos El Cone** (beach side of the road in El Sargento, diagonally across from MiniSuper Los Delfines, no tel., breakfast, lunch, and dinner), start with the raw scallop or shrimp *aguachile* plate, and then move on to the *pescado al mojo de ajo.*

Information and Services

Many local resorts and campgrounds now have wireless Internet; most offer it for free. Across from the main beachfront campground, **El Norte Restaurant** has satellite Internet for US$3 for 30 minutes. You can use the restaurant's computers or bring your own. Mobile phones work here but get spotty signals. There are public pay phones as well; pick up a Ladatel card at one of the mini-supers. Palapas Ventana has long-distance service.

Near the end of the pavement in El Sargento are a hardware store, mechanic, pharmacy, and Internet café as well as **Miscellania Lupita.** A couple of launderettes offer drop-off or self-service. El Sargento also has a Centro de Salud (Public Health Clinic) and a place where you can buy barrel gas.

ISLA CERRALVO

Less than 16 kilometers offshore from Bahía de la Ventana is Isla Cerralvo, one of the largest islands in the gulf and once a key destination in the historic pearl-oyster trade. Few travelers make their way out to this island because it is a long boat ride from the charters in La Paz, but it has several good dive and sportfishing sites around its shores. Scuba divers can explore rock reefs, coves, and wrecks. Presently, Palapas Ventana (www.palapasventana.com) is the only PADI-certified dive operation in La Ventana.

SAN JUÁN DE LOS PLANES

Los Planes, as this agricultural town is usually called, has several markets, a café, *dulcería, tortillería,* taxi stand, and around 1,500 inhabitants who make a living growing cotton, tomatoes, beans, and corn, or by fishing the nearby bays. There is a Pemex station where the road from San Antonio joins BCS 286. During the windy season, dust blowing from cultivated fields on either side of the highway can cause a complete whiteout. Once you leave the main drag in Los Planes, there is little in the way of commercial businesses until you reach Restaurant 1535 on Bahía de los Muertos.

BAHÍA DE LOS MUERTOS

BCS 286 ends at Los Planes, but if you follow the graded road that continues east, you'll end up at the Bay of the Dead. The dark name of this pretty bay dates back to the 18th century, but its exact origins are unknown. At least two later incidents in history validated the name: In 1885 a Chinese ship landed and lost a crew of 18 to yellow fever after port authorities in La Paz refused to admit the ship. And in the early 1900s, when a group of farmers from the United States attempted to cultivate the land around the bay, the effort for some ended in starvation. Another possible explanation is that an El Triunfo Mining company named the bay after burying train axles underwater to provide moorings for its barges.

Long-abandoned **Ensenada de los Muertos** dates back to the 1920s, when it was used for transporting ore from mines in the Sierra de la Laguna.

Panga boats still line the shore, but the bay is changing little by little each year as a massive luxury real estate development takes shape to the south.

Bahía de los Sueños

When complete, the Bahía de los Sueños (Bay of Dreams, toll-free U.S. tel. 866/202-0789, www.bahiasuenos.com) project will encompass 1,700 hectares with an 18-hole golf course designed by Tom Doak, 432 homes, and 192 villas and condos. Inside the Bay of Dreams development, **Gran Sueños** sits on 25 landscaped acres with tennis courts, a nine-hole golf course, multiple swimming pools, a fitness facility, and a long list of luxury amenities—including an on-site chef service and concierge. Its seven villas have king-size beds, rain showers, Viking barbecues, satellite TV, wireless Internet, private or shared pool and spa, and complimentary Internet calling to the United States. One-bedroom villas range US$350–750 per night; two-bedrooms are US$650–1,050 per night.

Food

The former Giggling Marlin restaurant on Bahía de los Muertos has changed hands several times in recent years. At the moment, it is called **Restaurant 1535,** in reference to the year that Hernán Cortés landed in the bay. Casual fare is overpriced, but it's the only option in the area and the setting is ideal for at least a *limonada* or cold beer after a morning snorkel. Live blues, jazz, and reggae music play on Thursday evenings 6:30–9:30 P.M.

PUNTA ARENAS DE LA VENTANA

About four kilometers before you reach Los Muertos, a smaller dirt road heads northeast to Punta Arenas de la Ventana (8 km), the site of an abandoned hotel and a good spot for snorkeling and fishing. Roosterfish are said to be unusually large here. You might be able to hire a *panguero* from the beach next to the former Las Arenas Resort for US$60–85 per day. Just south of the resort, snorkelers can explore the reef off **Punta Perico** (Parakeet Point).

THE EAST CAPE AND THE SIERRA DE LA LAGUNA

The promise of calm seas, steady winds, and abundant game fish lures many adventure-seekers away from the resorts of Los Cabos to the remote beaches and rocky points of the East Cape—and increasingly also to the traditional ranchos and freshwater springs hidden deep in the mountainous interior.

Some of Baja's prettiest and most secluded beaches line the Gulf coast between Bahía de las Palmas and San José del Cabo, at the southern tip of the peninsula. And along this stretch, the opportunities for deep-sea fishing, windsurfing, kiteboarding, kayaking, and scuba diving are among the best in the world. The region contains a few larger towns, such as Los Barriles, Santiago, and La Ribera, but for the most part, civilization consists of tiny fishing villages alternating with newer gringo enclaves. The vibe is low-key and in many places, the lifestyle is still off the grid, with dirt roads, *palapa*-roof bungalows, solar power, and satellite-only Internet and phone service.

Coastal development began to accelerate rapidly around the year 2000 and continues along the entire coastline, although the global recession has slowed or stalled most of the larger-scale development efforts. *Propriedad Privada* signs line both sides of the coastal road, but many of the spec homes sit empty and prices for lots have dropped substantially. Once you find access to the sea, the beach still feels pretty secluded.

In September 2006 Hurricane John made

HIGHLIGHTS

Isla Espíritu Santo

La Paz

Isla Cerralvo

La Ventana

San Pedro

Bahía de los Muertos

El Triunfo

Arroyo San Bartolo

Picacho de la Laguna

Los Barriles

Todos Santos

Cañon de la Zorra

Santiago Town Plaza

Santiago

Miraflores

Cabo Pulmo

Playa Migriño

La Fortuna

San José del Cabo

Banco Gorda

Cabo Falso

Cabo San Lucas

PACIFIC OCEAN

0   10 mi

0   10 km

© AVALON TRAVEL

❰ Los Barriles: Anglers, kiteboarders, and divers all find paradise in the Sea of Cortez near Los Barriles, the most developed town for visitors between La Paz and San José del Cabo (page 266).

❰ Cabo Pulmo: Reef-building corals, crystal waters, and white-sand beaches attract divers, snorkelers, and kayakers to Bahía Pulmo and Playa La Sirenita (page 281).

❰ Banco Gorda: Six miles from shore, this pair of seamounts offers unrivaled marlin and wahoo fishing as well as a chance for scuba divers to see hammerheads and whale sharks (page 289).

❰ El Triunfo: This ghost town in the mountains along Mexico 1 was once a silver-mining boomtown and the largest community in Southern Baja (page 291).

❰ Arroyo San Bartolo: A freshwater spring in the sierra keeps this palm-filled riverbed lush and green (page 293).

❰ Santiago Town Plaza: Shaded by mature trees and lined with a row of colonial buildings, this plaza is a perfect place to relax after a trip to the nearby hot springs or waterfall (page 295).

❰ Cañon de la Zorra: At the edge of the Sierra de la Laguna, near Santiago, a 10-meter waterfall plunges over smooth granite rock into a swimmable lagoon (page 296).

LOOK FOR ❰ TO FIND RECOMMENDED SIGHTS, ACTIVITIES, DINING, AND LODGING.

landfall at Bahía de los Frailes, causing severe wind and flood damage. Although roofs and roads took a beating, the towns in its path had mostly recovered by year-end.

The East Cape, particularly along the *Camino Costero Rural*, became the center of several large land disputes during the spring and summer of 2007, though by now many have been either resolved or forgotten, remnants of the uproar dot the landscape. Heavy

barbed-wire fences, aggressive signage, and abandoned (and some still occupied) guards' camps abound, lending a somewhat hostile look and feel to the area; the reality, though, has not changed, and visitors can still feel the same pervading sense of tranquility and isolation as has always been the area's hallmark.

When you've had your fill of white-sand beaches and salty air, the Sierra de la Laguna

THE EAST CAPE
AND
THE SIERRA DE
LA LAGUNA

beckons, with 2,100-meter peaks and cascading waterfalls. No longer the sole domain of experienced backpackers, parts of the range are doable in a half-day excursion, with or without a guide, depending on your comfort level with navigating networks of dirt roads and missing a turn here or there. The reward is a rugged part of Baja that few travelers even know exists.

PLANNING YOUR TIME

Towns along the East Cape are small and don't take much time to explore; you could easily take in a little of each in a four- to five-day trip. However, if you've come to the East Cape for a specific activity, such as fishing, diving, or windsurfing, you'll likely want to stay in one place for a while. If fishing is your top priority, then it makes sense to stay in Los Barriles or Buena Vista and add a day of diving. But if diving is the draw, it's best to head north or south to be closer to the dive sites. And if you plan to drive along the Coastal Road, as opposed to Highway 1, note that the unpaved 77-kilometer stretch between El Rincón and San José del Cabo can take up to four hours, depending on your vehicle and its ability to handle washboard roads.

Santiago, at the foothills of the Sierra de la Laguna, is an easy day trip from San José del Cabo or a good place to stretch your legs during the drive between San José and La Paz. Allow 3–5 nights if you want to explore the backcountry of the Sierra de la Laguna.

THE EAST CAPE

Bahía de las Palmas

After winding its way over the Sierra de la Laguna heading southeast from La Paz, Mexico 1 reaches the Gulf coast once again at Los Barriles, more or less in the middle of the wide and exposed Bahía de las Palmas. The bay is roughly 32 kilometers long, extending from Punta Pescadero in the north to Punta Arena at its southern end. The area experienced its first heyday in the 1960s as a fly-in resort for anglers. Fishing is still a draw in summer; however, a new pair of sports have taken center stage in the winter months: Strong winds blowing out of the north combined with thermals generated by the inland peaks create ideal conditions for kiteboarding and windsurfing.

As with the rest of the Southern Baja coastline, land development is fast changing the profile of communities beside the bay. Second homes owned by retirees from the United States rim the shore, with a few resorts mixed in. In general, the bay gets less developed the farther north you go, but even the famed Hotel Punta Pescadero has expanded to become a full-service luxury resort.

PUNTA PESCADERO

There are now two ways to reach the northern end of Bahía de las Palmas and the southern end of Bahía de los Muertos: A sandy, washboard road, narrow in parts, heads north from Los Barriles right along the water—the turnoff from Mexico 1 is signed Punta Pescadero. The road traverses two wide arroyos that could be flooded in heavy rains. Alternatively, a paved road built in 2005 continues along a scenic inland route from Los Barriles directly to El Cardonal. Watch for potholes and broken sections along this otherwise good road.

At the far north end of Bahía de las Palmas (13.6 km. north of Los Barriles), the historic **Hotel Punta Pescadero Paradise** (tel. 612/141-0101, toll-free U.S. tel. 800/332-4442, www.puntapescaderoparadise.com, US$95–150; pets of any sort strictly prohibited) is transforming from a low-key sportfishing establishment to an exclusive luxury property, complete with timeshares, gourmet food, and guided tours. A development master plan shows planned growth well beyond what is now in operation, with villas, beach clubs, "villages," spas, and a pier all included in the design. The resort has long been popular with private pilots, since it has a paved landing strip (1,065 m, Unicom 122.8, US$25 landing fee), and you'll likely hear regular fly-in guests trading stories at the bar. (As at other Baja airfields, plane theft is a very real concern here; throttle locks and prop chains are essential. Contact Baja Bush Pilots, www.bajabushpilots.com, for more information. Baja Bush Pilot and AAA discounts available.) A row of houses lines the airfield facing the sea.

Each of the 24 spacious rooms comes with a view of the bay, private terrace, air-conditioning, satellite TV, and refrigerator; some have cathedral ceilings and fireplaces for keeping warm on chilly winter nights. All rooms were renovated in 2005. King-size beds are made in crisp white linens with fluffy pillows and down comforters. During the windy season, ask for a room that faces southwest for a terrace that's sheltered from the El Norte gusts. A gracious staff speaks excellent English, and public areas include a restaurant with large picture windows, outdoor patio dining, small pool, lighted tennis court, and rental equipment for free diving (US$14/day), kayaking (US$10/hr), boating (US$15/hr), fishing (30-foot cruiser US$510/day, 28-foot cruiser US$400/day, super-*panga* US$300/day, *panga* US$250/day), and ATVs (US$20/hr).

The resort restaurant is open to the public with theme-night menus, such as a traditional suckling pig roast on Saturdays and romantic Italian nights beachside on Fridays—and Sunday brunch. Guided trips include city tours of La Paz, a visit to the closely guarded local petroglyphs, and tours to the sites of former Spanish missions. Tour prices range US$50–460 and range 2–8 hours in length.

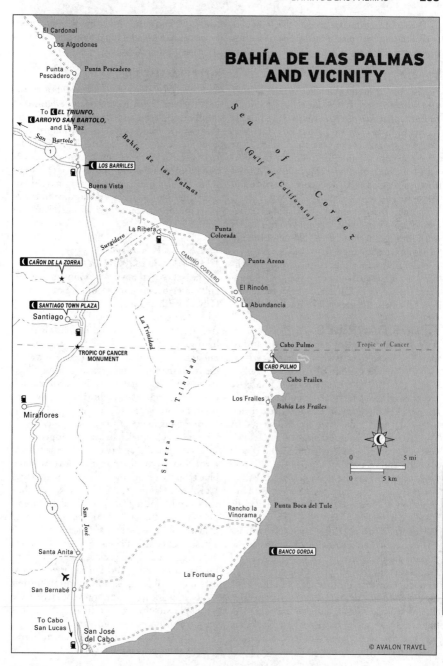

BAHÍA DE LAS PALMAS AND VICINITY

El Cardonal
Los Algodones
Punta Pescadero
Punta Pescadero

To ◖EL TRIUNFO,
◖ARROYO SAN BARTOLO,
and La Paz
San Bartolo
1

Sea of Cortez
(Gulf of California)

Bahía de las Palmas

◖LOS BARRILES
Buena Vista

La Ribera
Punta Colorada

Surgidero
Punta Arena

CAMINO COSTERO

◖CAÑON DE LA ZORRA
★

◖SANTIAGO TOWN PLAZA
Santiago

La Trinidad

El Rincón
La Abundancia

Cabo Pulmo
TROPIC OF CANCER MONUMENT
★
Tropic of Cancer

◖CABO PULMO
Cabo Frailes

Miraflores

Sierra la Trinidad

Los Frailes
Bahía Los Frailes

0   5 mi
0   5 km

1

San José

Rancho la Vinorama
Punta Boca del Tule

Santa Anita
✈
San Bernabé

◖BANCO GORDA

La Fortuna

To Cabo San Lucas
San José del Cabo

© AVALON TRAVEL

THE EAST CAPE

The reef that extends out from the point here is among the best places in the Sea of Cortez for snorkeling.

EL CARDONAL

A new, paved highway makes it much easier and faster to reach El Cardonal, located north of Punta Pescadero, at the south end of Bahía de los Muertos (23 km. from Los Barriles). You can snorkel among the coral heads close to shore, hire a guide for a look at the local cave paintings, or simply enjoy the views from the beach. Canadian-owned **El Cardonal's Hide-A-Way** (tel. 612/348-9793, www.elcardonal.net) offers lodging, meals, and activities. The owner, Eddy, can put you in contact with local guides for a two-kilometer hike to nearby cave paintings.

After El Cardonal, the road continues northward along the coast and then veers west to traverse the Sierra El Carrizalito before reaching San Juan de los Planes southeast of La Paz.

◀ LOS BARRILES

The defining image of day-to-day life in Los Barriles these days is that of early retirees happily speeding along dirt roads on ATVs, which they ride to the supermarket, hardware store, beach, and everywhere in between. No longer the sole domain of sports fishermen and windsurfers, the town has broadened its appeal with more guest accommodations, restaurants, and services—and a vibe that is friendly and relaxed.

A strip mall on the main access road from Mexico 1 is the de facto town center, with another row of commercial businesses along Calle 20 de Noviembre, heading north to Punta Pescadero. A row of gringo McMansions front the beach behind a stone retaining wall, and several developments are in varying stages of completion in the hills above and to the north of town. However, those in search of the "real" Baja should not despair; Los Barriles retains an authentic *tortillería,* plus roosters that roam the streets, a cement factory where blocks are still made by hand, numerous taco stands, and countless other family-owned businesses. Local

Mexicans know each other by their *sobrenombres* (nicknames), and the untamed backcountry is just minutes away.

BUENA VISTA

Smaller and quieter than its neighbor to the north, Buena Vista attracts a similar crowd of families, anglers, and retirees—many of them former law enforcement professionals from Southern California. It won't be long before the two towns are connected by the homes and businesses that are spreading out between them. Southbound travelers may have difficulty finding the unsigned entrance to town: Look for the turn on a curve between Km. 104 and 105.

LA RIBERA AND PUNTA COLORADA

As the last coastal town with municipal power and water heading south until San José del Cabo, La Ribera (pop. 2,000) has evolved into a busy commercial center. The town has its first ATM, two Pemex stations, a few small hardware and grocery stores, and several restaurants. One of two large real estate developments in the works has broken ground: Cabo Riviera (Calle Santa Maria de La Ribera, tel. 624/105-1005, www.caboriviera.com.mx) will have multiple golf courses, a 285-slip marina, plus the requisite condos and hotels. The main channel has been dredged, two breakwaters built, and two man-made islands formed inside the harbor. You can't miss the blue flags that mark the office on the way into La Ribera. Nearby, Cabo Cortés (www.cabocortes.com), located at Bahía El Rincon, has plans to build out to 30,000 beds, three golf courses, and a marina for 400 boats on 10,000 acres of coastal land, but SEMARNAT recently suspended the project due to environmental concerns. Cabo Pulmo Vivo (www.cabopulmovivo.org) is an organization that has been working hard to prevent large-scale developments that will drain already limited resources from moving forward.

Punta Colorada lies to the south, marking the southern end of Bahía de las Palmas.

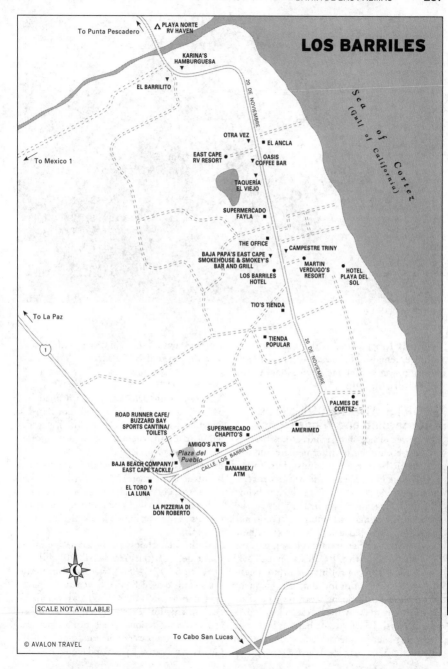

LOS BARRILES

To Punta Pescadero

∧ PLAYA NORTE RV HAVEN

KARINA'S HAMBURGUESA

EL BARRILITO

20 DE NOVIEMBRE

To Mexico 1

OTRA VEZ

EL ANCLA

EAST CAPE RV RESORT

OASIS COFFEE BAR

TAQUERÍA EL VIEJO

SUPERMERCADO FAYLA

THE OFFICE

CAMPESTRE TRINY

BAJA PAPA'S EAST CAPE SMOKEHOUSE & SMOKEY'S BAR AND GRILL

MARTIN VERDUGO'S RESORT

HOTEL PLAYA DEL SOL

LOS BARRILES HOTEL

To La Paz

TIO'S TIENDA

1

TIENDA POPULAR

20 DE NOVIEMBRE

PALMES DE CORTEZ

ROAD RUNNER CAFE/ BUZZARD BAY SPORTS CANTINA/ TOILETS

SUPERMERCADO CHAPITO'S

AMERIMED

AMIGO'S ATVS

Plaza del Pueblo

CALLE LOS BARRILES

BAJA BEACH COMPANY/ EAST CAPE TACKLE/

BANAMEX/ ATM

EL TORO Y LA LUNA

LA PIZZERIA DI DON ROBERTO

Sea of Cortez (Gulf of California)

SCALE NOT AVAILABLE

To Cabo San Lucas

© AVALON TRAVEL

THE EAST CAPE

church in La Ribera

Below La Ribera, several tiny seaside communities remain off the grid—though mainstream power and phone service loom in the not-too-distant future.

SPORTS AND RECREATION
Kiteboarding and Windsurfing

The powerful side shore winds at Los Barriles are best attempted by intermediate and advanced kiteboarders and windsurfers. In the peak season, November–April, wind speeds frequently exceed 20 knots and rarely drop below 18 knots. Beginners can usually get in the water during calmer early morning conditions. Instructors say windsurfers should know how to water-start or plan to take a lesson to learn how when they arrive. By 11 A.M. most days, the winds kick up a rolling swell (no breaking waves) that is fun for jumping. Frequent "downwinders" to Buena Vista are a particularly fun way to enjoy the breeze. The trip begins at North Beach in Los Barriles and ends two hours later in Buena Vista, with a shuttle ride back to Los Barriles. Water temperatures

average about 22–24°C in winter, with air temperatures around 26–27°C.

INSTRUCTION

The **Vela Windsurf Resort** (U.S./Canada tel. 541/387-0431 or 800/223-5443, Los Barriles, www.velawindsurf.com, Nov.–Mar.) provides windsurfing instruction, rental gear, and accommodations packages. At last check, it had more than 80 Starboard- and JP Australia-brand boards and more than 100 Neil Pryde sails—the largest stock of equipment anywhere in Baja.

Vela also has a kiteboarding program through a partnership with ExotiKite (US$75 per hour).

Both Vela schools are based at the Hotel Playa del Sol (tel. 624/141-0050, toll-free U.S. tel. 877/777-8862, www.vanwormerresorts.com, closed Sept.). Seven-night packages start at US$1,000–1,300 and include all gear, instruction (except for novice windsurfers), accommodations, meals, tax, and service. No-meal options were a new addition in 2010. Guests may borrow kayaks and mountain bikes

SURFING THE EAST CAPE

The lower East Cape gets decent waves in summer and early fall (May–Oct.), when *chubascos* off the mainland to the south send large swells to the region. If there is any south swell in the water, you will get waves at the lower breaks. On large south or southeast swells, you can surf as far north as Punta Colorado, but don't plan your trip around spots that far north. If it's flat, drive down to the Los Cabos Corridor or hop across to the Pacific and surf near Todos Santos. If you are day-tripping from Los Cabos for a day of surfing, make sure you stock up the night before on water and then more water, and bring your own shade, sunscreen, and food.

The closest break to San José (15 km north along the Coastal Road), called Shipwreck, is also the most consistent spot on the East Cape with the steepest waves. The point typically breaks in sections, so the crowds spread out a bit. If you like lefts, look for a small reef in the middle of the bay that breaks on the larger swells. The sandy beach out front is a good spot for spectators and post-surf picnics. Don't bother scanning the bottom for the shipwreck; it was washed away by a hurricane years ago.

Heading north, the next reliable break is Nine Palms. The palms have grown in numbers, so don't bother counting them. This is a good longboarding wave but can get steeper as it goes overhead. About 800 meters north of the Crossroads Country Club at Boca de la Vinorama, Punta Perfecta is a right reef break that can produce decent barrels on larger swells.

anytime during their stay for no charge. Other activities free of charge include snorkeling, tennis, and volleyball. Scuba diving, kiteboarding lessons, and horseback riding cost extra.

Fishing

Bahía de las Palmas is an exciting place to fish because the sea floor drops to great depths not far from the shoreline. The reef extending out from Punta Pescadero is great for triggerfish, barred pargo, and cabrilla. Less than a mile from land, you can find depths that exceed 100 fathoms. The popular **Tuna Canyon**, 6.5 kilometers south of Punta Pescadero, is the place to catch yellowfin tuna. Several charter services based along the bay offer trips on *pangas* (US$200–260/day) and cruisers (US$200–325/day). Bait costs around US$20–25 per day. A popular day trip when the conditions aren't too windy is to travel north by boat to Bahía de los Muertos, fish on the way, and stop for lunch at **Restaurant 1535.**

In Los Barriles, Martin Verdugo's Beach Resort (tel. 624/141-0054, www.verdugos-beachresort.com) and the Hotel Palmas de Cortez (tel. 624/141-0050, toll-free U.S. tel.

877/777-8862, www.vanwormerresorts.com) offer fishing packages; the concierge at the Hotel Palmas de Cortez (tel. 624/141-0050, toll-free U.S. tel. 877/777-8862, www.vanwormerresorts.com) can arrange fishing trips for guests and nonguests. In addition, **Baja's Awesome Sportfishing** (tel. 624/141-0231, U.S. tel. 208/726-1955, www.eastcaperv.com/awesome_sportfishing.html), headquartered at the East Cape RV Resort, operates two cruisers, a 30-foot island hopper, and a 32-foot Blackfin sportfisher. The most popular captains in Los Barriles and Buena Vista, including Julio Cota and Chuy Cota, book a year in advance for weekend visits, so plan your trip early.

Juan Carlos of **La Capilla Sportfishing and Eco Tours** (tel. 624/141-0611) runs charters on a diesel-powered *panga*.

Fish with Me (toll-free U.S. tel. 800/347-4963, www.fishwithme.com) owner Jerry Hall has been fishing the East Cape since 1973 and organizes group trips several times a year.

SHORE FISHING
Since the sea floor plunges to great depths so close to shore, it's possible to catch unusually

THE EAST CAPE

large fish simply by casting into the surf from the shoreline. Punta Pescadero, Punta Colorada, and Punta Arenas are three of the best places to try; roosterfish and jack crevalle are common catches.

KAYAK FISHING

East Cape Kayak Fishing (U.S. tel. 619/461-7172, www.eastcapekayakfishing.com) offers several guided trips a year out of the Hotel Punta Colorada and Rancho Leonero, with an emphasis on paddling and angling instruction. Owner Jim Sammons is famous for having landed a marlin from a kayak, the only person to date to have done so. An all-inclusive package that includes five nights and four days of fishing starts at US$1,032 per person, all-inclusive (double occupancy). In addition to scheduled small-group trips, the staff offers private trips.

FISHING GEAR AND SERVICES

East Cape Tackle (Plaza del Pueblo, Los Barriles, no tel., eastcapetackle@gmail.com, 9 A.M.–5 P.M. Mon.–Fri., 9 A.M.–2 P.M. Sat.) sells bait and tackle and also rents surf rods, pole spears, and snorkeling gear; plus, you can pay with plastic. **Todo de Pesca** (20 de Noviembre, Los Barriles, tel. 624/124-8061, 9 A.M.–2 P.M. and 4–6 P.M. Mon.–Sat.), run by Ricardo Reyes, is a new fishing store well stocked with all the basics, plus some spearfishing gear.

Baja Papa's East Cape Smokehouse (20 de Noviembre at Calle Don Pepe, tel. 624/141-0294, www.bajapapas.com, 9 A.M.–6 P.M. daily) offers processing services for your catch. Allow 48 hours turnaround time to have them smoke (US$3.50 per pound of fillet) or freeze (US$1.25 per pound to flash freeze fillets) and package it for your trip home. The smoking process uses natural smoke from imported sugar maple and hickory woods, local fresh fish, sea salt, brown sugar, and organic honey. The store has started a travel club that extends discounts on auto insurance and other services to its members.

Scuba Diving

Buena Vista has a reputable dive center located on the beach, next to the Vista del Mar trailer park. **Vista Sea Sport** (tel. 624/141-0031, Buena Vista, www.vistaseasport.com) is run by two PADI-certified dive instructors from Southern California who own three super-*pangas* and one cruiser. However, boat rides to the major sites—Cabo Pulmo, Los Frailes, Punta Pescadero, and Isla Cerralvo—are long and rates are higher (US$125–140 for a two-tank dive) than at shops based in La Paz or Cabo Pulmo. Scuba gear rental is US$30 with a tour. Airfills cost US$10; snorkeling gear US$10. Look for a giant earthmover that serves as the boat launch. To find the shop from Mexico 1, take the turn across from the Calafia Hotel and then turn left at the T in the dirt road and follow the signs.

ATV Tours

ATVs are a popular mode of transportation in Los Barriles. Inquire about rentals and tours at **Amigos ATV Tours** (Calle Los Barriles near Plaza del Pueblo, Los Barriles, tel. 624/141-0430, www.amigosactivities.com) on the main access road. Tours cost US$60–70 for a single rider and US$75–90 for a double. Rental rates are US$20 per hour or $100 per day. Amigos also rents WaveRunners and leads horseback rides and snorkeling tours. Other possibilities include hikes, bird-watching, mountain biking, and snorkeling. You can book any of these activities through the concierge at the Hotel Palmas de Cortez, whether or not you are staying at the resort.

Quadman (tel. 624/168-6087, cell tel. 624/168-6087, www.quadman.net), across from the Amerimed clinic on the north side of Calle Los Barriles near the T intersection at 20 de Noviembre, also rents ATVs (US$85/day) and Rhinos (US$135/day). Rhinos seat four people, and you must be 35 or older to drive. ATVs have racks for fishing poles, though riders must stay at least 20 meters from the high-tide line to protect turtle nests.

Mountain Biking

Vela Windsurf Resort (Los Barriles, U.S./Canada tel. 541/387-0431 or 800/223-5443, www.velawindsurf.com) at the Hotel Playa del

Sol rents Specialized mountain bikes for coastal and desert rides. Clip-less pedals are an option, so bring your shoes. They also have children's bikes, a trail-a-bike, and a kid's trailer.

Spa Services

Above the gym in the Hotel Palmas de Cortez, at the end of Calle Los Barriles, **Spa de Cortez** (tel. 624/141-0050, ext. 616, spadecortez@ yahoo.com) offers Swedish, therapeutic, and sports massage, plus aromatherapy, body scrubs, facials, and waxing services. A one-hour massage is US$80 and a 90-minute treatment is US$115.

SHOPPING

Los Barriles has the only real shopping in this part of Baja: **Tío's Tienda** (20 de Noviembre at Los Barriles, Los Barriles, tel. 624/141-0330, 7:30 A.M.–10 P.M. daily), next door to Tío Pablo's, carries everything from fishing tackle and souvenirs to apparel, gift wrap, and office supplies. It also stocks one of the most impressive collections of books about Baja California found on either side of the border. Many of the titles are self-published memoirs written by gringo transplants; others are field guides, travel books, and novels that take place in Mexico. **Baja Beach Company** (Plaza del Pueblo 8, Los Barriles, no tel., 9 A.M.–5 P.M. Mon.–Fri., till 2 P.M. Sat.), in the strip mall near Buzzard Bay, has ceramics, textiles, gifts, and a few books and maps. In the same plaza, **La Casa** (Plaza del Pueblo 10, Los Barriles, tel. 624/124-8057) sells kitchenware and other goods for the home. **Big Tony** (Plaza Libertad, Los Barriles, no tel., 9 A.M.–7 P.M. Mon.–Sat.) has good-quality beach clothing, shorts, bikinis, and accessories. Back on the highway, across from the main entrance to town, **El Toro y La Luna** (Mexico 1, Entrada a Los Barriles, Los Barriles, tel. 624/141-0696, www.eltoroylaluna.net, 8 A.M.–5 P.M. daily) carries ceramic sinks, tiles, and other home furnishings. The store has a second branch in La Ribera (Av. Santa Maria, La Ribera, tel. 624/141-0698, www.eltoroylaluna.net, 8 A.M.–5 P.M. daily), at the turn for the road to Cabo Pulmo.

DESERT SOAPS

Browse the boutique shops in Los Cabos and La Paz and you may come across this line of organic soaps and lotions, all handmade from material such as torote bark, aloe vera, and dried *palo de arco* flowers extracted from the surrounding desert. The business is the brainchild of an expatriate couple that has restored a historic ranch in the hills of the East Cape and trained local workers in the lost art of soap-making. Natural ingredients, solar energy, minimal packaging, employment for rural women – you can purchase these gift items knowing this is about as sustainable as it gets.

Desert Soaps (www.desertsoaps.com) are currently available in these stores and hotels:

- El Cactus Viejo, inside the Malarrimo Hotel in Guerrero Negro

- La Tienda in Mulegé

- Manos Mexicanos, Hotel California, La Esquina, in Todos Santos; Rancho Pescadero, in El Pescadero

- Dos Lunas, Chile y Anis, The Bungalows, Esperanza Resort & Spa, Capella Pedregal, in Cabo San Lucas

- Indigenous, Mexicanisimo, Antigua Los Cabos, Playa Azul, El Armario, Curious Carmela, Cabo Surf Hotel and Spa, Los Cabos Airport Terminals, in San José del Cabo

- Villa del Faro, on the East Cape

ACCOMMODATIONS

Accommodations along Bahía de las Palmas range from all-inclusive hotels to modest hotels and RV parks to private vacation homes available for rent either by the owner or through a property manager. Los Barriles has the greatest concentration of options, but Punta Pescadero, Buena Vista, and La Ribera all have at least a couple of options.

THE EAST CAPE

Punta Pescadero

At the far north end of Bahía de las Palmas (13.6 km north of Los Barriles), the historic **Hotel Punta Pescadero Paradise** (tel. 612/141-0101, toll-free U.S. tel. 800/332-4442, www.puntapescaderoparadise.com, US$174–199; pets of any sort strictly prohibited) has 24 spacious rooms, each with a view of the bay, private terrace, air-conditioning, satellite TV, and refrigerator; some have cathedral ceilings and fireplaces for keeping warm on chilly winter nights. All rooms were renovated in 2005. King-size beds are made in crisp white linens with fluffy pillows and down comforters. During the windy season, ask for a room that faces southwest for a terrace that's sheltered from the El Norte gusts. A gracious staff speaks excellent English, and public areas include a restaurant with large picture windows, outdoor patio dining, small pool, lighted tennis court, and rental equipment for free diving (US$14/day), kayaking (US$10/hr), boating (US$15/hr), fishing (30-foot cruiser US$510/day, 28-foot cruiser US$400/day, super-*panga* US$300/day, *panga* US$250/day), and ATVs (US$20/hr).

The resort restaurant is open to the public with theme night menus—such as a traditional suckling pig roast on Saturdays and romantic Italian nights beachside on Fridays—and Sunday brunch. Guided trips include city tours of La Paz, a visit to the closely guarded local petroglyphs, and tours to the sites of former Spanish missions. Tour prices range from US$50–460, and range 2–8 hours in length.

El Cardonal

El Cardonal's Hide-A-Way (tel. 612/348-9793, www.elcardonal.net, US$69) offers six sparsely furnished suites. There are also spaces for RV (US$13/day for full hookups) and tent (US$10–12/day) camping. Each of its large beachfront studios comes with two full-size beds, a sofa, kitchen, and ceiling fan. Amenities and services include a dump station, fishing boats, hot showers, 24-hour restaurant, laundry facilities, public telephone, horseshoe pit, volleyball net, picnic tables, ice, and rental shop with equipment for fishing, windsurfing, diving, kayaking (free with stay), and snorkeling. You can pick up the Wi-Fi signal from the restaurant/patio area. An all-inclusive fishing packages run US$599 for four days/three nights/two days of fishing and all meals.

Los Barriles

US$50-100

Martin Verdugo's Beach Resort (20 de Noviembre, approximately two blocks north of Calle Los Barriles, Los Barriles, tel. 624/141-0054, www.verdugosbeachresort.com, US$65–75) has updated air-conditioning units in each of its 29 rooms, located in a two-story hotel next to the beach. Facilities include a small pool, boat launch, and restaurant. Kitchenettes are a plus here (though not in every room). When the wind is blowing hard, the pool at the Los Barriles Hotel offers more shelter. Service was a bit gruff on a recent visit.

Off the beach but within walking distance to restaurants and shops, the exceptionally clean **C Los Barriles Hotel** (20 de Noviembre, approximately one block north of Calle Los Barriles, Los Barriles, tel. 624/141-0024, www. losbarrileshotel.com, US$73) looks unremarkable from the outside but feels something like a well-kept Swiss chalet inside. It has 20 spacious rooms set around a swimming pool with hot tub, each with high ceilings, two firm but comfortable queen-size beds, large tiled showers, and remote-controlled air-conditioning. Minimal but quality furnishings include rustic wooden dressers, tables, and headboards. Popular with families, this hotel is a great value for the price.

US$100-150

The Van Wormer family runs two all-inclusive resorts in Los Barriles, including **Hotel Playa del Sol** (tel. 624/141-0050, toll-free U.S. tel. 877/777-8862, www.vanwormerresorts.com, US$120–130, closed Sept.), on the beach off 20 de Noviembre north of Calle Los Barriles. This property has 26 air-conditioned rooms, a pool that overlooks the beach, tennis and volleyball courts, a restaurant with outdoor seating, and bar with satellite TV. The resort rents windsurfing, kayaking, and fishing gear as well as mountain bikes. You can charter boats for a day of sportfishing (US$250–385 per day, not including fishing permits) or sign up for windsurfing lessons.

The second Van Wormer resort in Los Barriles is located on the beach at the end of Calle Los Barriles, a little south of Hotel Playa del Sol; the **Hotel Palmas de Cortez** (Los Barriles, tel. 624/141-0050, toll-free U.S. tel. 877/777-8862, www.vanwormer-resorts.com, US$130–160) offers 50 poolside, oceanfront, and garden-view rooms, plus several cabanas and condos that sleep up to six guests. Rates include three meals a day. Amenities include a driving range, infinity pool, and tennis and racquetball courts. You can rent windsurfing gear and fishing equipment and charter a fishing boat (US$275–500, not including fishing permits) through the resort. The Van Wormer family also runs the Hotel Punta Colorada farther south along the East Cape.

Run by the owner/driver of a California-based motorsports team, the **Agave Hotel & Cantina** (Km. 108, Mexico 1, U.S. tel. 760/275-0339, www.agavehotelandcantina.com, US$85–250, tax included) is a renovation of the former Casa Miramar Hotel. Its nine rooms enjoy a hillside location overlooking the beach, just off Mexico 1, across from the Pemex station. The property consists of a two-bedroom house and separate beachfront *casita*. It can accommodate up to 25 people. Owner Rick Johnson and Team Agave compete in the Baja 1000 each year. Although not on the premises, they can share a wealth of information about Baja via email or phone. They can also arrange cooking classes, massages, transportation, and other services for guests. This hotel operates somewhat like a vacation rental in the sense that the property managers do not stay on-site. They live nearby and stop in daily to attend to guests' needs. Additional highlights include a swimming pool, ocean views, and convenient beach access. The town center of Los Barriles is a short walk away.

OVER US$250

Among the newest accommodations in town are the suites at the **Villas de Cortez** (Los Barriles, tel. 624/141-0050, toll-free U.S. tel. 877/777-8862, www.vanwormerresorts.com, US$280–380), next door to the Hotel Palmas de Cortez, which is under the same ownership. Meal packages are available through the sister resort, or you can enjoy outstanding gourmet fare in the villas' new restaurant, **La Taberna di Don Roberto,** which impressed local foodies from the get-go with its authentic Italian cuisine (tel. 624/141-0050, 5–10 P.M. Tues.–Sun.).

CAMPING AND RV PARKS

A trendsetter among parks in Mexico, the **East Cape RV Resort** (20 de Noviembre at Ocean, Los Barriles, tel. 624/141-0231, U.S. tel. 208/726-1955, www.eastcaperv.com) designed its property with big rigs in mind. Located a short walk from the beach, the resort has 51 spaces with full hookups (US$25/150/525 per night/week/month). Another dozen spaces with limited hookups are located in an adjacent palm garden that sometimes floods during the rainy season (US$18/105 per night/week). Bathrooms are modern and clean, and there's a pool as well as a hot tub. High-speed wireless Internet costs US$4/15/40 per day/week/month. Washing machines and dryers require U.S. quarters. Owner Theresa Comber is the closest thing Los Barriles has to a chamber of commerce. Ask her for advice on day trips and activities in the area.

North of Hotel Playa del Sol, **Martin Verdugo's Beach Resort** (20 de Noviembre, approximately one block north of Calle Los Barriles, Los Barriles, tel. 612/141-0054, www.verdugosbeachresort.com) caters to families and retirees with lower rates and a beachfront location. It has dump stations, flush toilets, showers, boat ramps, laundry facilities, and full hookups for US$15 for two people, plus US$3.50 for each additional person. Weekly and monthly rates are US$100 and US$260, respectively (credit cards are accepted). Tent sites cost US$12 per night. Kids play Marco

Polo in the beachfront swimming pool, and locals gather for breakfast in the third-story restaurant. Fishing rates are US$390 for a 28-foot cruiser and US$240 for a 23-foot super-*panga*. Inquire about fishing packages that include accommodations and meals, and be sure to make reservations well in advance during the peak windsurfing season (Jan.–Mar.).

About five minutes' drive north of town, another big-rig- and caravan-friendly park has one of precious few remaining waterfront locations in Southern Baja: **◖ Playa Norte RV Haven** (20 de Noviembre, Los Barriles, U.S. tel. 425/252-5952, www.playanortervpark.com, US$22–33 per day) is situated in Bahía de las Palmas between two wide arroyos, San Bartolo to the north and Buenos Aires to the south.

The park encompasses 10 hectares of landscaped property, divided into 85 sites with separate areas for tent camping, caravans (45 sites), permanent RV sites, and seasonal RV sites. A number of the sites are pull-through style for larger rigs, and many also have individual septic and power. The sites are divided into three rows that parallel the beach. The first row (24 sites) costs a few dollars more per day than the second and third rows. The owners have completed a number of improvements in recent years, including new laundry facilities, more restrooms and showers, and wireless Internet.

Power and electricity cost extra (US$3 for 15–30 amp, US$5 for 50 amp). Book early if you want a site with these conveniences. There is a US$5 fee for use of the dump station (caravans and guests of longer than one week excepted). Tent sites have free access to drinking water, hot showers, parking, and Internet.

This park is a good choice for travelers with pets because they can run on the beach or in the arroyo outside the park—and there is even an on-site veterinary clinic; however, management requires pets to stay at their own site while inside the park, and it goes without saying that you should clean up after your dog.

Free primitive camping is available in the area north of these parks, usually referred to by gringos as Playa Norte.

Buena Vista

UNDER US$50

Hotel Restaurante-Bar Calafia (Km. 107, Mexico 1, tel. 624/141-0028, US$45) has nine basic but new and clean rooms with air-conditioning above a simple Mexican restaurant.

At **Ramada Baja** (Km. 105, Mexico 1, tel. 624/141-0038, www.bajaramada.com, US$37/$200 per night/week, tax included) guests sleep in one of four yurts, one of which is two stories tall. Each has a private bath.

US$100-150

In business since 1952, **Rancho Buena Vista** (Km. 106, Mexico 1, U.S. tel. 805/928-1719 or 800/258-8200, www.ranchobuenavista.com, US$105 pp) opened to host Hollywood celebrities for fly-in sportfishing vacations. Today the scene is much less glitzy—downright worn down in many ways—but the fishing tradition continues and longtime guests appreciate the simplicity of the accommodations and the quality of the food. The resort has more than 50 cottage-style rooms, all with air-conditioning, ceiling fan, and tiled floor and shower. All meals are served in one restaurant; breakfast is made to order, lunch and dinner are fixed menus that rotate throughout the week. Boxed lunch is available for days on the water. The grounds include a swimming pool, whirlpool tub, and tennis and volleyball courts. The resort has fishing tackle, including fly-fishing gear, as well as its own cruisers, a boat ramp, and boat storage.

It can be difficult to find the turnoff to Rancho Buena Vista if you're heading south on Mexico 1. Watch for the entrance on the left just after a small mountain pass and a blue hotel sign on the right.

US$150-250

Popular with families and retirees, the **Hotel Buena Vista Beach Resort** (Km. 105, Mexico 1, tel. 624/141-0033, U.S. tel. 619/429-8079 or 800/752-3555, www.hotelbuenavista.com, US$185–215 all-inclusive) has 60 Mediterranean-style bungalows with air-conditioning, private baths, and private terraces. Buildings are arranged close together against a hillside, and the resort feels somewhat dated, but the location just across from the beach is ideal. A lush tropical garden surrounds the resort's two pools, one of which has a swim-up bar. If you're not fishing, activity choices include spa treatments, kayaking, horseback riding, and snorkeling. The resort organizes trips to nearby cave paintings and waterfalls as well as bird-watching, hiking, and snorkeling tours. Most guests choose the American plan, which includes three meals a day, but European plans (meals à la carte) are available as well if you want more flexibility in where you dine. Inquire about fishing and diving packages. The fleet of boats at this hotel includes a 23-foot *panga* (US$270), 28-foot cruiser (US$415), luxury 29-foot twin-engine cruiser (US$485), and 31-foot twin-engine cruiser (US$630). (Tax, tips, tackle, bait, and fishing licenses cost extra.) The resort's U.S. reservations office can arrange round-trip or one-way transportation from the airport.

Near the southern end of Bahía de las Palmas, the secluded **Rancho Leonero Resort** (tel./fax 612/141-0216, U.S. tel. 760/438-2905 or 800/646-2252, www.rancholeonero.com, US$150–250) sits on a mesa overlooking the bay. This resort was founded in the 1960s as one of the original fly-in fishing destinations in Baja, and a sense of history oozes out of the rustic *palapa*-roofed bungalows on the property. All guestrooms have sea views, but there are no in-room TVs or phones. The grounds are well cared for, and the overall effect is something like family camp meets hunting lodge. As at Punta Pescadero, a small development now adjoins the resort, with new homes built on land sold by the owner of Rancho Leonero.

Amenities include a restaurant and bar, swimming pool with hot tub, dive center, sportfishing fleet, and a network of hiking trails. You can snorkel the rock reef in front of the hotel. Three meals a day are included in the room price. Fishing charters start at US$275 for a super-*panga*, US$425 and up for cruisers.

Snorkeling equipment costs US$10 per day. The resort also arranges horseback riding, kayaking, scuba diving, and hiking trips.

La Ribera

At the south end of town, near the beach, **RV Park La Trinidad** (Esq. 16 de Septiembre, La Ribera, tel. 624/158-9837, http://latrinidadrvranch.com, US$25/150/500 per day/week/month) has more than 20 full hookups, a swimming pool, and an incredible ratio of bathrooms and showers per site (there are eight of each). There are a few tent camping sites and a restaurant/bar that serves a Mexican/seafood buffet for US$16–18. To find the park from the highway, follow the exit at Las Cuevas east to La Ribera and drive straight through town until you reach the beach road (Calle Hacienda Eureka). Turn right (south) and go about 800 meters to a Pemex station; then turn left (east) and look for the entrance on your left.

Punta Colorada

The southernmost of the original Baja fishing resorts was established in 1966 and overlooks Punta Colorada at the south end of Bahía de las Palmas. Friendly and unassuming to this day, the **(Hotel Punta Colorada** (tel. 612/121-0044, U.S. tel. 818/222-5066 or 800/368-4334, www.vanwormerresorts.com, US$130–180) has reputation throughout the sportfishing community as *the* place for catching roosterfish, described by veteran anglers as reel-melting fighters that will keep you coming back for more. The conditions off Punta Arena, the next point south from the hotel, are as good as it gets in Baja, as evidenced by the photo of a record-setting 42-kilogram catch on the wall in the bar. Guided fishing trips start at US$245 a day for a super-*panga* and US$330–385 for cruisers; half-day trips cost 70 percent of the full-day price. The hotel teams up with partners to offer kayak fishing and fly-fishing tours.

The hotel has 39 large rooms, all but eight of which have ocean views. Free wireless Internet is available in the lobby/courtyard area.

TO BUY OR NOT TO BUY: TIPS FOR PURCHASING REAL ESTATE IN BAJA

The real estate frenzy in Baja California began as a trickle at the start of the 21st century, progressed into a full-scale land rush by about 2003, and then died about as suddenly as it began when the global recession hit. As Mexican law and real estate services have made it easier for foreigners to own property, many Baja-bound Americans and Canadians continue to answer the call.

1. THE TERMS

Foreigners can only purchase coastal property (within 50 km of the coast) in Mexico through a limited real estate trust *(fideicomisos)*. Trusts are renewable every 50 years, with no limit on the number of renewals. In most cases, you will need a Mexican real estate attorney to complete a transaction.

2. FINANCING

You can finance the purchase through several lenders: Mortgages are now available for financing up to 70 percent of appraised property values with terms of 15-20 years. Lending rates run around 3 percent higher than in the United States, and closing costs for a mortgage deal are high.

Some sellers ask that the full purchase price be paid up front. Because a large number of gringos buy land in Mexico with cash, some Mexicans assume this is customary for all Americans and Canadians. Paying up-front is not the typical procedure for Mexicans them-

selves, who usually make down payments and send in monthly time payments; mortgage terms similar to those found in Canada and the United States are available in Mexico, though they are difficult for nonresidents to obtain. Even if you have the cash, don't hand over more than half the full amount until you have the *fideicomiso* papers in hand.

3. TITLE INSURANCE

You can purchase title insurance, previously unavailable, from several providers.

4. PRICES

Prospective buyers can find small plots in subdivisions near the beach from US$20,000. Completed small vacation homes range US$200,000-500,000, and full-scale mansions are in the millions. These days, there are deals to be found, as many sellers and developers have fallen on hard times with the drop in tourism.

5. REAL ESTATE AGENTS

Choose a reputable agent and check his or her references thoroughly. The larger tourism offices are a good place to find listings of available properties. Local residents can usually advise on the better agents to work with. Brokers do not have to get a license to operate in Mexico, so it pays to do your homework up front before committing to real estate deals of any sort.

Three meals daily are included in the price, and the locally renowned restaurant serves a Mexican buffet dinner open to the public on Wednesdays and Saturdays as well as a seafood buffet on Sundays. Call by noon for reservations. The hotel also has an indoor/outdoor bar and its own airstrip (1,000 m, Unicom 122.8). Tap water at the resort comes from a mountain well, so you can drink it. The hotel is closed in January, February, and September through the first week of October.

Vacation Rentals

Many owners rent their Baja vacation homes by the night, week, or month. **East Cape Property Management and Vacation Rentals** (Plaza del Pueblo, tel./fax 612/141-0381, www.abajavacation.com, 10 A.M.–2 P.M. Mon.–Sat.) handles rental properties in Los Barriles, Buena Vista, Punta Pescadero, Rancho Leonero, and Los Frailes. **Sunset Rentals** (20 de Noviembre, just past the Hotel Los Barriles, tel. 624/141-0416) offers short- and long-term rentals in studios as well as one- and two-bedroom condos. All have kitchens, garages, balconies, wireless Internet, and air-conditioning. **Vacation Rentals by Owner** (www.vrbo.com) also has a few dozen East Cape listings. Rates range US$75–195 a night for one-bedroom homes.

FOOD
There are a number of casual eateries along the shores of Bahíia de las Palmas, with the greatest variety in Los Barriles. Seafood takes center stage on most menus. Los Barriles also has the only large-size grocery store in the area, **Supermercado Chapito's** (7:30 A.M.– 10 P.M. daily).

Punta Pescadero
The restaurant at **Hotel Punta Pescadero Paradise** (tel. 612/141-0101, toll-free U.S. tel. 800/332-4442, www.puntapescaderoparadise. com) is open to the public with theme dinners on different nights of the week. Turn off Mexico 1 in Los Barriles and follow a dirt road nine miles north until you reach the resort.

El Cardonal
El Cardonal's Hide-A-Way offers meals to guests and other visitors at **Restaurante Acuario** (no tel., hours vary) and serves whatever is fresh—lobster, shrimp, and fish as well as local eggs and produce—with homemade tortillas and salsas. This is an out-of-the-way place, on a dirt road along the coast, and hours vary according to demand. Reservations are recommended. Expect to wait 35–45 minutes if you arrive unannounced.

Los Barriles
The number and variety of restaurants in Los Barriles is multiplying every season. Today's menus feature grilled fish and meats, traditional Mexican *platos,* pasta, sushi, pizza, sandwiches, soups, espresso, and, of course, mouthwatering tacos.

SEAFOOD
Another favorite among locals for dinner, **◖ El Barrilito** (20 de Noviembre, tel. 624/121-

5856, elbarrilito@hotmail.com, lunch and dinner daily, mains US$6–15) serves large portions of fresh seafood under a large *palapa* at the bend in the road heading out toward Pescadero. Ceviche is a standout. In a smaller *palapa* next door, the same owners have opened **Kenichi Sushi & Bar** (no tel., lunch and dinner daily) with à la carte dishes and all-you-can-eat specials for US$20. More sushi can be found at **Yako's Sushi-Bar** (tel. 624/141-0050, noon–7 P.M. daily, mains US$10–20) in the Hotel Palmas de Cortez, on the beach at the end of Calle Los Barriles.

If you don't have your own fish to smoke, stop by **Smokey's Bar and Grill** (20 de Noviembre at Calle Don Pepe, tel. 624/141-0294, www.bajapapas.com, 9 A.M.–6 P.M. daily) to enjoy someone else's fresh catch. The bar has four flat-screen TVs and serves beer, sandwiches and, of course, smoked fish.

MEXICAN
Run by the same owners as the once-famous Restaurant Balandra in Cabo San Lucas, which closed more than 30 years ago, **◖ Campestre Triny** (20 de Noviembre at La Laguna, across from the East Cape Smokehouse, tel. 624/124-8067, campestre_triny@hotmail.com, noon–10 P.M. daily, mains US$9–20) offers freshly prepared traditional Mexican fare, including specialties of *huachinango frito* (whole fried red snapper), paella, and imperial shrimp. High-quality ingredients and a somewhat upscale presentation are reflected in menu prices. This is also one of the few places in town that serves Negro Modelo beer. You can dine family style under a canopy of trees behind the main house or at your own table on the porch. Check out the collection of arrowheads hanging on the wall while you're there.

ITALIAN
Tío Pablo's (20 de Noviembre, Los Barriles, tel. 612/142-1214, 11 A.M.–10 P.M. daily, mains US$7–20) is popular among gringos for pizzas and does orders to go. Look for the restaurant on the west side of the main north–south street through town.

278 THE EAST CAPE AND THE SIERRA DE LA LAGUNA

An Italian chef bakes pizzas in a wood-heated oven at (**La Pizzeria di Don Roberto** (at the south-end entrance to town on Highway 1, tel. 624/141-0303, noon–9 P.M. Tues.–Sun.), open since early 2008. Variations include the simple Margarita (US$10) and a Calzone Classico (US$17). Foodies rave about the quality of the food and level of service here. It's an unusual find in this part of the peninsula.

The **Bay View Bar & Grill** (tel. 624/141-0050, toll-free U.S. tel. 877/777-8862, www.vanwormerresorts.com, 11 A.M.–10 P.M. daily) is open to the public for dinner. It offers a menu of pasta, fish, and seafood dishes prepared in an Italian style.

AMERICAN
In a strip mall just off Mexico 1 on the access road to Los Barriles, **Buzzard Bay Sports Cantina** (Plaza del Pueblo 21, Calle Los Barriles, Los Barriles, no tel., lunch and dinner daily, mains US$7–15) makes burgers, sandwiches, and pub fare, with tables inside and on a small sidewalk patio that adjoins the parking lot.

Martin Verdugo's Restaurant (20 de Noviembre, approximately one block north of Calle Los Barriles, tel. 612/141-0054, 6 A.M.–noon daily, mains US$4–7) is a third-story restaurant that serves Americanized breakfast fare. *Chilaquiles* arrive smothered in melted cheese but without the signature *queso fresco* on top. Omelets come with seasoned hash browns and a choice of toast or tortillas. Sea views and air-conditioning are the main draw. Service is friendly, though slow even by Mexican standards.

Also on 20 de Noviembre, **Otra Vez** (tel. 612/141-0249, 5–10 P.M. Mon.–Sat., mains US$8–20) is popular with local gringos, and the menu includes freshly prepared parrot fish, burgers, steaks, fresh salads, and pasta dishes.

ANTOJITOS AND FAST FOOD
During American football season, you're likely to find a number of tourists watching the game at (**Taquería El Viejo** (20 de Noviembre, near El Oasis Coffee and Baja Land Deals, tel. 624/141-0826, breakfast and lunch daily). The

restaurant has about a dozen shaded outdoor tables where you can enjoy a breakfast of eggs, omelets, or *chilaquiles* for US$5–6, tacos for US$1–2, and burgers for US$5. Lunch specials vary daily (US$7–8).

Taquería Los Barriles (no tel., breakfast, lunch, and dinner daily), at the junction with the beach road, is packed all afternoon and evening for the great seafood and carne asada tacos; the breakfasts are cheap. The enormous super burros at **La Palma Taquería** (no tel., dinner daily) are a great value, too. Look for the sign on a surfboard just off 20 de Noviembre near Tío Pablo's.

Across the street from El Barrilito, on the inside of the bend that turns to Pescadero, **Karina's Hamburguesas** (no tel., dinner daily) serves carne asada (US$4), *papas rellenas* (US$5), and other quick meals from a restaurant cart.

Back on Mexico 1, heading toward La Paz, **Baja Cactus** (north of the Pemex, no tel.) serves good Mexican food at reasonable prices.

CAFÉS
Oasis Coffee Bar (20 de Noviembre, past The Office, tel. 624/141-0711, daily) serves coffee for US$2 as well as hot and cold espresso drinks and smoothies for US$2–4. It shares the space with Baja Land Deals, so you can browse pictures of real estate for sale while you wait for your drink. High-speed wireless Internet service is free, and there are a few shaded tables outside.

Roadrunner Café (Plaza del Pueblo 5, no tel., 7 A.M.–4:30 P.M. Mon.–Fri., 7 A.M.–2 P.M. Sat.–Sun.) has very good coffee and espresso (US$2) and eggs any style (US$3.50–6) served at tables inside or on the patio. Free wireless Internet is a plus. **Caffe Paradise** (20 de Noviembre, across the street from Campestre Triny, no tel., 7:30 A.M.–3:30 P.M. Wed.–Mon.) has the best smoothies (US$3–5) in town, as well as coffee, espresso, sandwiches, burgers, and eggs.

GROCERIES
On Calle Los Barriles, the main access road from Mexico 1, between Plaza del Pueblo and

20 de Noviembre, **Supermercado Chapito's** (7:30 A.M.–10 P.M. daily) is the largest grocery store in town (or anywhere on the bay, for that matter), and it has a separate pharmacy inside. Newer **Tienda Popular** (7 A.M.–10 P.M. daily), west of 20 de Noviembre, about one block north of the intersection with Calle Los Barriles, has opened just up the hill from Tío Pablo's. **Supermercado Fayla** (8 A.M.–6 P.M. Mon.–Sat.), on 20 de Noviembre just past the Hotel Los Barriles, has basic food supplies as well as souvenirs, videos, and U.S. newspapers on Fridays. During the peak winter season, a bakery truck from La Paz visits town on Fridays and a fresh produce vendor comes on Saturday mornings.

Buy frozen or smoked fish or have yours prepared and vacuum-packed at the **Baja Papa's East Cape Smokehouse** (20 de Noviembre at Calle Don Pepe, tel. 624/141-0294, www.bajapapas.com, 9 A.M.–6 P.M. daily). Allow 48 hours turnaround time.

For a sugar fix, head to **Charlie's Chocolates** (Calle Los Barriles, across from AmeriMed, no tel.) for a box of strawberries dipped in chocolate and topped with nuts.

Buena Vista

Hotel Restaurante-Bar Calafia (Mexico 1, Km. 107, tel. 624/141-0028, 7:30 A.M.–8:30 P.M. daily, mains US$10–20), on the west side of the highway near the local police station, makes tasty shrimp tacos and chiles rellenos, and its outdoor tables have nice views of the bay. **La Concha** (no tel., hours vary, mains US$5), at the north end of town, serves up a delicious ceviche in a taco-stand environment. A **Tienda Popular minimarket** (no tel.) is located on the east side of the highway, north of the main entrance to town.

La Ribera

Close to the beach and a few blocks from the Trinidad RV Park, **La Costa** (no tel., 11 A.M.–6 P.M. Tues.–Sun, main US$5–10) does a good shrimp ceviche as well as large-sized fish and scallop tacos.

Mercado Rey (7 A.M.–10 P.M. daily), on El Camino Rural Costero, just past the Y and across from the Pemex, carries tools, propane tank parts, chains, and beer, plus basic groceries and a good selection of American liquors.

At the entrance to La Ribera, **Vianey's Restaurant** (La Ribera, cell tel. 624/158-0938, vianeyslaribera@hotmail.com, 8:30 A.M.–10 P.M. Thurs.–Tues.) does egg dishes for breakfast; tacos, meat, and fish dishes for lunch; and more elaborate meat and fish dinners. Thursday is a special pork rib and chile rellenos combo. Lunches range US$5–7, dinners US$10–15. The restaurant makes its own bread to serve with dinner entrées.

INFORMATION AND SERVICES

Most travel-related services for towns along Bahía de las Palmas are located in Los Barriles. East Cape RV Resort owner Theresa Comber in Los Barriles is the closest thing the area has to a chamber of commerce. Stop by to ask for advice on restaurants, day trips, and activities in the area. The larger resorts are also a good source of visitor information.

La Plaza del Pueblo shopping center in Los Barriles, near the highway on the main access road, has clean public restrooms and public telephones. The post office in Los Barriles closed a few years ago. Near the end of the main access road to Los Barriles, an **Amerimed Clinic** is open 8 A.M.–2 P.M. and 4–6 P.M. Monday–Saturday for medical needs. Call 624/141-0797 for emergencies.

If you don't already have a car, **National Car Rental** (20 de Noviembre s/n, tel. 624/142-2424, 8 A.M.–4 P.M. daily) maintains an outpost at the Hotel Palmas de Cortez in Los Barriles, but in most cases an ATV would be a better vehicle for getting around town. The closest Pemex is just south of Los Barriles on Mexico 1.

For airport transportation, contact TurisPancho (tel. 624/127-3122, www.turispancho.com). **El Lavadero/The Washroom** (20 de Noviembre, no tel., hours vary Mon.–Sat.), near the Los Barriles Hotel, and the new **Lavamatica** (Plaza Libertad, no tel., 10 A.M.–6 P.M. Mon.–Sat.) are the only places

THE EAST CAPE

to have your clothes washed, unless you're staying at one of the full-service RV parks.

East Cape RV Park, Sunset Rentals, and many cafés and private home-owners have wireless Internet. And some keep a computer set up for guest use.

A number of businesses in these towns accept credit cards, but you'll still need cash (dollars or pesos) for tacos and the like. There is a Banamex (no tel., 9 A.M.–4 P.M. Mon.–Sat.) in Los Barriles at Plaza Libertad, which can exchange dollars to pesos and has the only ATM in the area.

La Ribera has a new health center as of 2010, thanks in part to funding from local developers. Find the **Centro de Salud La Ribera** (tel. 624/130-0067, 24 hours daily) next to the athletic fields on the way into town, on the south side of Avenida Santa María, past the turnoff to Cabo Pulmo.

El Camino Rural Costero

The historic El Camino Rural Costero (Rural Coastal Road) begins south of La Ribera and follows the Gulf coast south to Pueblo La Playa, outside San José del Cabo. The road is graded but not paved beyond the first few miles south of La Ribera. Most standard rental vehicles—and even small RVs—can negotiate the washboard and patches of soft sand, but the going will be slow, especially as you get farther south, where the road tends to be in pretty bad shape. High clearance is always helpful. During the rainy season, the road may be washed out in parts. Ask for updates before you plan your drive.

The government has had plans to pave the entire Coastal Road from La Ribera to San José del Cabo for at least a decade. So far it hasn't come to pass. In early 2006 local government officials staged a press event to commemorate the beginning of work on a eight-kilometer-long paved road to Los Frailes; however, the earthmover that was to be the star of the show reportedly got a flat tire and the event was canceled. The machine stayed by the side of the road for weeks after, but no dirt was ever moved. Plans to pave the road have been repeatedly delayed in recent years, to the relief of local residents, who fear the arrival of mainstream power and phone service will change their towns forever.

In spite of the difficult access (or perhaps because of it), a few enclaves along the way are growing into full-scale developments. You can

following the Camino Costero to Cabo Pulmo

still camp for free on the beach in places, but as is the case all along the coast, access is becoming increasingly limited as new developments lay cinder blocks and finish their first few homes.

In the midst of all the change, a few traditional ranchos continue to raise livestock—typically without fencing to keep the animals off the road.

THE EAST CAPE

© PAUL ITOI

EL CAMINO RURAL COSTERO

Laguna Salina

La Ribera

Sea of Cortez
(Gulf of California)

La Trinidad

Salinas Punta Colorada

Matanza

Punta Colorada
Punta Colorada

Punta Arena

Tropic of Cancer   Miramar

Los Mangles

Parque Marina Nacional Cabo Pulmo

Cabo Pulmo

CABO PULMO

La Boquita

San Miguel

BANCO GORDA

Los Frailes

Cabo Frailes

0   2 mi
0   2 km

© AVALON TRAVEL

To reach the Coastal Road from the north, take the paved road signed La Ribera east at Km. 93 off Mexico 1 (at Las Cuevas) and go 20 kilometers to a Y intersection near the Lighthouse restaurant and town athletic fields. Bear right here, and you're on the beginning of the Coastal Road. It is paved for the first few miles and then becomes dirt the rest of the way south.

PLAYA EL RINCÓN

At the point where the pavement ends on the Coastal Road is a wide, sandy beach that still feels somewhat deserted even though it's right in the middle of a major real estate project. The developers have put in an access road next to the airstrip.

◖ CABO PULMO

About 10 kilometers from where the pavement ends, the Coastal Road climbs over a rise and presents a panoramic view of Bahía Pulmo—a shallow bay rimmed with a mix of coarse white sand and cobblestones—and the eight fingers of coral reef that are its main attraction. The road descends to parallel the beach along the bay and then passes through the center of a tiny fishing village-turned-vacation-and-retirement-community.

Modern-day Cabo Pulmo is a close-knit community made up mostly of older expats and several branches of a local Mexican family that has fished the area for generations. The oldest vacation homes were built right on the beach, but in recent years, construction has expanded west across the road and into the hills.

Most visitors these days come to explore the reef, from above and below, and to relax on the white-sand beaches that line the bay. The surface of the beach varies with the seasons: in winter, there are usually more stones and pebbles, particularly at the north end of the bay; in summer, the sand comes back and the rocks roll back into the sea.

The government has stepped up its conservation efforts in recent years, posting large signs, patrolling the park by boat, and collecting a US$4 park use fee from those who snorkel or dive in the bay. At last check, beachgoers did not have to pay the fee—only those who go into the water to view the coral.

There are several scuba diving operations in town, *panga* fishing charters, kayak rentals, and a long list of excursions up and down the coast and into the desert.

Given its small size, proximity to the beach, and comfortable accommodations, Cabo Pulmo is an excellent place for families with young kids (though the nearest medical clinic is in La Ribera, a 15-minute drive, and the closest hospital is in San José del Cabo).

THE EAST CAPE

ENDANGERED SEA

In 2005 the United Nations Educational, Scientific and Cultural Organization (UNESCO) added the Gulf of California (referred to in this book as the Sea of Cortez) to its World Heritage List of outstanding natural and cultural value around the globe. Citing its striking beauty and critical role as a natural laboratory for the study of thousands of marine species, UNESCO identified a site of 244 islands, islets, and coastal areas within the Gulf of California. Also important was the fact that all major oceanographic processes occurring in the planet's oceans take place in this body of water.

Environmental conservation groups heralded the designation as a critical step forward in curbing severe damage wrought by commercial fishing and bottom trawling, which destroy eelgrass beds and shellfish that sustain many other species in the sea. But World Heritage status is only the beginning of a long and costly battle. Several international organizations, including Conservation International (www.conservation. org), the Environmental Defense Fund, and the World Wildlife Fund (www.worldwildlife. org) are funding projects in the area in an effort to protect the fragile ecosystem for generations to come. Meanwhile, the Mexican government is stepping up its commitment to fund marine parks and conservation activities throughout the region.

© PABLO NOBILI

baby turtles headed to the sea

Playa Los Arbolitos

A large new marine park sign marks the way to this white-sand beach at the south end of Bahía Pulmo. Follow the Coastal Road south about five kilometers from the village of Cabo Pulmo and look for the only dirt road on the left without a fence or gate. The turn is the last road you can take before passing Los Frailes Mountain. Rent snorkeling gear and/or kayaks in Cabo Pulmo before you go.

Playa La Sirenita

The most attractive beach on Bahía Pulmo goes by many names: La Sirenita (The Mermaid) seems to be the most common one, but it is also known as Los Chopitos (The Squids) and Dinosaur Egg Beach. All the more enchanting for its difficult access, the beach is hidden at the base of a cliff that frames the southern end of the bay. You can only reach it by small boat or kayak or by walking along a path from Playa Los Arbolitos to the north, which has a small parking lot. The beach is narrow but covered in white sand and dotted with rocks. The cove and beach are protected from winds coming out of the south, and you can snorkel around the rocks just offshore. A towering boulder pile marks the divider between Bahía Pulmo and Bahía de los Frailes; on its south-facing side lives a colony of sea lions.

Pulmo Reef System

The fragile hard-coral reef in Bahía Pulmo is one of only three coastal reefs in North America and the only living one in the Sea of Cortez. It plays a vital role in the health of the Sea of Cortez ecosystem and for this reason was designated a national marine park in 1995. Commercial fishing and sportfishing are banned within the park (this means no shore fishing, either), as is anchoring on the reef or anywhere in the bay. Both foreign and Mexican residents are committed to protecting the water and land from pollution, but they worry that runoff from developments on land—especially from the mega-resorts that are just breaking ground—poses a serious threat to the reef.

The reef is made up of eight separate fingers, four of them close to shore and the other four farther out in the bay. Depths range 4.5–10.5 meters close to shore and as deep as 33 meters in the outer bay.

The abundance and variety of marine life here rivals anything you'll find in the Caribbean. The fact that the reef begins within a few meters from the shore makes it even more appealing. For divers, boat rides are a quick five-minute jaunt out into the bay; snorkelers can skip the boat ride altogether and hop right in from shore. You can find a wide variety of tropical fish, eels, and rays—as well as the occasional nurse shark—in waist-deep water.

Sports and Recreation
DIVING AND SNORKELING

You can dive at Pulmo year-round, but the best conditions are in summer and early fall, when water temperatures exceed 26°C and visibility exceeds 30 meters. Guided drift diving is the norm here. Divers board a *panga*

boat at the beach, zip over to the morning's dive site, and roll backward into the water to begin the dive. While divers drift with the current along the reef below, the boat captain follows the bubbles on the surface. The sides of the reef are jam-packed with colorful marine life. Green moray eels poke their heads out of rocky crevices, schools of tropical fish dart here and there, and the occasional sea turtle cruises by. It only takes a few dives to begin to recognize the telltale pile of shells in front of an octopus's den or the antennae of a spiny lobster hiding in a cave.

Besides the natural reefs, the wreck of a tuna boat called *El Vencedor* has evolved into an artificial reef. Dive boats also take groups to El Islote, a lone rock on the southern side of the bay, and to a sea lion colony near Bahía de los Frailes.

Three dive centers, located within 100 meters of each other, run guided tours from Cabo Pulmo. In the village center, the **Cabo Pulmo Beach Resort** (El Camino Rural Costero, tel. 612/141-0884 or -0885, U.S. tel./fax 562/366-0398, www.cabopulmo.com) operates a PADI-certified dive center with two boats, well-maintained gear, and experienced, professional dive guides. A two-tank boat dive costs US$75 and an equipment rental package is US$20 with a boat dive. You do not need to be a guest of the resort to snorkel or dive with the shop. The dive center often hosts groups of day-trippers from resorts in the Cabo San Lucas area. These dives tend to be more crowded with novice divers. Call ahead to check the schedule if you want to do more advanced dives. Snorkeling tours are US$40 with gear, and single kayaks rent for US$35 a day.

Cabo Pulmo Divers (tel. 624/130-0235, cell tel. 612/157-3381, www.cabopulmodivers.com) is another option, located in the Castro family complex, next to the Miscellanea Market. Rates at both are comparable to those at the Cabo Pulmo Beach Resort.

Next to La Palapa restaurant, in a blue building with a marine-life mural painted on its side, is **Cabo Pulmo Eco Adventures** (no tel.). Owner Juanito offers snorkel trips for US$35 and kayak rentals by the hour or day, and can arrange taxi service to La Sirenita beach. Juanito is very knowledgeable, bilingual, and the only person in town who can arrange trips to the nearby waterfall and hot springs.

The dive operators are also happy to arrange boat trips for non-divers interested in touring the bay, Playa La Sirenita, and the sea lion colony.

Newcomer **Cabo Pulmo Water Sports** (tel. 624/130-0367 www.cabopulmowatersports. com) offers dive trips and gear rental at competitive rates. It can also arrange fishing trips with local fishermen.

FISHING

Commercial fishing and sportfishing are no longer permitted anywhere in Bahía Pulmo. *Panga* boats that launch from Pulmo have to go beyond the national marine park limit (8 km from shore) before putting in lines. On land, you have to travel about eight kilometers north or south of Pulmo proper to fish from shore. Kiki and Paco Castro offer half-day (US$180) and full-day (US$260) tours in their super-*pangas,* including gear and bait. Tuna and dorado are common offshore catches. Inquire at Cabo Pulmo Divers (www.cabopulmodivers.com) behind the La Palapa beachfront restaurant.

Accommodations

As new owners build and acquire properties in Cabo Pulmo, the number of rental options has increased—although the location remains off the grid, so don't expect air-conditioning, TV, Internet, and the works in the places you find here. Most high-season rates climb even higher during the peak season around Christmas and New Year.

For many years, **Cabo Pulmo Beach Resort** (El Camino Rural Costero, tel./fax 612/141-0244, -0884, or -0885, U.S. tel. 562/366-0398, U.S. tel./fax 208/726-1306, toll-free U.S. tel. 888/997-8566, www.cabopulmo. com, US$70–200) was the only option for short-term visitor accommodations in the area. The village has grown, bringing more properties and management services onto the market,

but this beach resort is still a good option for beachside bungalows within steps of the water. All of its *palapa*-roofed units feature kitchenettes or full kitchens, and some have barbeque grills. Many have second-story roof decks for catching a breeze in the afternoon or watching activity on the bay. Sheets and towels are provided. Like all accommodations in the village, power here is solar, with generators for backup only.

Marly Rickers also manages a handful of rentals in the same group of *casitas* for US$75–150 per night. Contact **Cabo Pulmo Casas** (tel. 877/754-5251, www.cabopulmocasas.com).

Across the dirt road from the Cabo Pulmo Beach Resort, Kent Ryan rents **Baja Bungalows** (www.bajabungalows.com, US$75–85), with a main house that has spectacular views from the upstairs master suite, plus a two-bedroom unit on the lower level and an additional bungalow and *palapa* suite with shared bath and full outdoor kitchen. Kent recently added another house to his list of rental properties: Located on an adjacent lot, the house features two separate units (upstairs and down) and has spectacular sea and mountain views from the upstairs unit. The house once belonged to musician (and former local character) Jimmy Ibbotsen of the Nitty Gritty Dirt Band. The house has been adapted to rental standards but holds many a good story from the musician's stay in Pulmo. The beach is a three-minute walk away.

For upscale accommodations, check out **Villa and Casa del Mar** (U.S. tel. 208/726-4455 or 888/225-2786, www.bajaparadise. com, US$210–450). This property includes a main house (US$450 per night for two guests) and attached studio (US$210 per night). Air-conditioning is available, although as with any Cabo Pulmo rental, it can only be used as long as there is enough power to run it. A few steps farther from the beach and centrally located in the village, the **El Nido** cottage (US$255 per night) has a full kitchen.

El Encanto de Cabo Pulmo (U.S. tel. 619/618-1248, www.encantopulmo.com, US$90–170) brings a new standard of luxury to Cabo Pulmo. Think air-conditioning (extra cost), an espresso machine, and surround-sound entertainment with satellite TV. Designed by an artist and her husband, the home is indeed beautiful; the only caveat is that in Pulmo, there's always a chance that the power-intensive amenities won't be working when you visit. This town is an off-the-grid location that runs on solar and generator power, and when those sources of electricity run out, the air-conditioning unfortunately turns off. (Most guests find the ceiling fans adequate for cooling the home on all but the hottest of nights.) The house has three suites—two in a two-story main house and a third in a separate *casita*. Its garden setting is lovely (though not really private if both suites and the main house are in use). This property would work best for a group of six or more that rents out the whole property together. Wireless Internet is included. Individual suites rent for US$90–170 per night, and the whole house rents for US$325 per night.

Another vacation rental, **The Jewel of Cabo Pulmo** (Cabo Pulmo village, U.S. tel. 831/440-8811), has a master bedroom in the main house and a separate garden *casita* (US$160 for the for the house alone, and US$250 for both house and *casita*). This property is pet friendly. No smoking.

Reinhard's Rentals (www.reinhardsrentals.com), across the street from Baja Bungalows at the metal palm-and-dolphin sculpted gate, offers two houses each for US$80 a night and an additional house, called Paradise with an Ocean View, for US$90 a night. These rentals are popular with the fishing crowd and owned and operated by one of the town's true characters, Reinhard and his dog, Max. Another plus for pet owners: These rentals are dog friendly.

At the other extreme, you can **camp for free** on the beach at the south end of Bahía Pulmo or for US$5 per night at the north end.

Food

Cabo Pulmo's restaurants are notoriously understaffed, even during peak season. It can take up to 45 minutes or longer to be served, even at lunch. As with the other businesses in Cabo Pulmo, restaurants are clustered together along the coastal road, so the best thing to do is find a point of reference, like the Cabo Pulmo Beach Resort, then ask around if you have questions about where a specific place is.

Adjacent to the Cabo Pulmo Beach Resort, **Nancy's Restaurant and Bar** (no tel., hours vary Thurs.–Tues., mains US$16–20) began as a trailer and two tables and has evolved into a full-scale restaurant with a rustic collection of tables beneath a *palapa* shelter. Fresh guacamole with homemade chips is a delightful way to begin the meal. Lobster enchiladas, crab cakes, and fresh catch (yours or Nancy's) are accompanied by crisp side salads.

The **Coral Reef Bar and Grill** (no tel., hours vary Wed.–Mon., mains US$10–20) is a cozy restaurant with a TV and bar located above the blue building that serves as the Cabo Pulmo Resort dive center. Miguel Angel, a professional chef who came from San José del Cabo, serves up tasty seafood specialties.

Restaurant El Caballero (no tel., 7 A.M.–10 P.M. Fri.–Wed., mains US$6–14), on the opposite side of the road near Nancy's, has a varied menu of Mexican fare. It also has a bar and small assortment of groceries, drinks, and snacks for sale.

La Palapa (lunch and dinner Mon.–Sat., lunch plates US$4–10, dinner mains US$8–18), on the beach in front of the Cabo Pulmo Beach Resort, offers casual beachfront dining from a menu of fish tacos, carne asada, and other traditional fare. The great family-style, traditional Mexican seafood, always fresh and simple, is served by smiling Angeles—the sister of Juanito at Cabo Pulmo Eco Adventures.

In the Castro family complex, near Cabo Pulmo Water Sports, **Alicia's Restaurant** (mains US$4–7) is a great new option for simple Mexican dishes served outside under a *palapa* roof. The chiles rellenos are a top pick here. Hours vary day to day and there is no phone, so it's best to stop by on your way to or from the beach.

On the main road near Nancy's, **Tito's** (no tel., days and hours of operation vary) offers a popular Saturday buffet for dinner during the high season and a standard menu of Mexican dishes and beer on other days.

For groceries, several vendors make the rounds through town during the week. A bakery truck comes from La Paz on Wednesdays; Ysidro delivers fish, scallops, and shrimp on Tuesdays and brings similar seafood selections on Saturday mornings. The **Miscellanea Market** (9 A.M.–7 P.M. daily, limited summer hours), with colorful snails painted on the side of the building, is located next to Cabo Pulmo Divers and stocks basic supplies, including dairy, juice, produce, bread, toiletries, candy, and canned goods. For a long stay, it's best to load up on groceries at Soriana or one of the other supermarkets in San José del Cabo or at Supermercado Chapitos in Los Barriles. Mexican food brands generally cost less than their U.S. counterparts. It's a good idea to buy ice, as the propane refrigerators in most Cabo Pulmo rentals cool very slowly, and a car full of groceries will take a long time to chill.

Information and Services

Internet access via satellite is possible in Cabo Pulmo, but service is by no means reliable, and you cannot download large files, due to bandwidth restrictions from the service providers. A few private places throughout the village have Wi-Fi set up and you may be able to get permission to use one of those networks. In an emergency, the owners of the different rentals can usually get a message out. For casual correspondence, plan to connect in San José or Los Barriles.

There are no banks or ATMs in Cabo Pulmo or Los Frailes, and few places except the largest resorts accept credit cards. U.S. or Mexican currency is accepted, and you can load up on cash at an ATM machine in San José, Los Barriles, or La Ribera. Be sure to get plenty of small bills, as many businesses cannot change larger bills. Some places accept traveler's checks, but it would be best not to count on it.

Basic medical services are available in La Ribera and Los Barriles, and the closest hospital is in San José.

Getting There

Most visitors fly to Los Cabos, rent a car, and drive to Cabo Pulmo via El Camino Rural Costero. From San José del Cabo, follow Highway 1 north 50.6 kilometers to an overpass at Las Cuevas and bear right (east) onto the single-lane road to La Ribera. From La Paz, pass Buena Vista heading south and take the exit for La Ribera. As you approach La Ribera (9.6 km), turn right before the soccer field. Follow the Coastal Road 26 kilometers south to Cabo Pulmo. The drive should take about 40 minutes from the time you leave Highway 1.

If you are flying into San José and plan to drive the same day to Cabo Pulmo, aim to arrive no later than noon. By the time you get through passport control, retrieve your luggage, rent a car, and buy your groceries, several hours will have passed, and it is not advisable to drive the highway or Coastal Road after dark. If you arrive in the afternoon, consider staying overnight in San José before departing for Cabo Pulmo the next day.

The closest gas to Cabo Pulmo is at La Ribera to the north. Be sure to fill up before heading south along the Coastal Road.

Aguila bus service from San José will get you as far as Las Cuevas for about US$5 one-way, but from there you'll have to hitch a ride or arrange in advance for someone to pick you up. Another option for traveling sans auto is to contact one of the companies that transport divers from the Los Cabos area to Cabo Pulmo for the day. For example, **Impala Transportation** (tel. 624/141-0726 or cell tel. 624/173-1476) has a van that holds 14 passengers. With notice, Cabo Pulmo Resort can arrange round-trip transportation from Los Cabos airport for a fee; a stop at a grocery store near the airport on the way up can be included.

BAHÍA DE LOS FRAILES

When winds out of the north whip Bahía Pulmo into a frothy mess, the next bay south, Bahía de los Frailes, is usually calm enough for snorkeling, diving, and fishing. The bay plunges to depths of 210 meters, which makes for slightly colder water temperatures than in Bahía Pulmo.

Following the Coastal Road, it's about eight kilometers to the turnoff for this white-sand beach. Since Los Frailes lies just outside the national marine park, the fishing onshore and inshore tends to be especially good here. Anglers often catch roosterfish by casting into the surf; charters catch yellowfin tuna, grouper, dorado, and marlin within a couple miles of the shoreline.

Accommodations and Camping

Villa Los Frailes (El Camino Rural Costero, U.S. tel. 206/390-1700, www.bajavilla.com, US$600 per night) is an oceanfront home that sleeps 10 people in four bedrooms and five baths, plus a hot tub and pool deck. Cabo Villa Rentals manages a few vacation properties along the East Cape, including **Casita Luna Azul** at Estancia (U.S. tel. 310/943-7614, toll-free U.S. tel. 877/473-1946, www.cabo-villarentals.com). This one-bedroom *casita* is set on a point overlooking the sea and costs US$225 per night.

You can camp on the beach along the north end of the bay—a fee of US$2–3 per site may be charged.

SOUTH TO SAN JOSÉ DEL CABO

Below Los Frailes, the road continues to hug the coast, climbing over hills and swerving inland here and there. The scenery alternates between traditional ranchos and new gringo developments, with beautiful desert flora in between. These days, the road is in pretty good shape between Los Frailes and Boca de la Vinorama and even on to Punta Gorda, but the last few miles before La Playita will test the sturdiness of the vehicle as well as the patience of the driver.

From Los Frailes to La Vinorama, a number of small real estate developments are popping up on the east side of the road: Boca del Salado has El Salado, with a small group of homes up on a bluff overlooking the sea. Rancho del Sol has another 34 home sites in the vicinity.

Between Los Frailes and Vinorama, a trio of Mexican, U.S., and Canadian flags marks the entry to the **Castillo de Arena** community, where a few vacation rentals are available to short-term visitors. Check Vacation Rental by Owner (www.vrbo.com) for listings. Beach access is via the arroyo to the south, a 15-minute walk or short drive.

Boca de la Vinorama

About 18 kilometers below Los Frailes and 34 kilometers up the Coastal Road from La Playita, Boca de la Vinorama refers to a river mouth, a rancho, and a growing expat community, all located just north of the Palo Escopeta turnoff, which heads west toward Mexico 1 and the Los Cabos airport. The development consists of 140 lots and at least one gated community. The only business here is the **Crossroads Country Club** (Camino Costero Rural, no tel., 7 A.M.–9 P.M. daily, breakfast mains US$5–7, dinner mains US$8–16, cash only), which had moved from a *palapa* into the owner's main house at last check. Crossroads has a bar and restaurant with Internet service, public phone, and book exchange. There are also a few grocery items (but not ice), postcards, and T-shirts designed by a local artist for sale. The Desert Soaps on display are made from plants and extracts found in the surrounding desert. For breakfast, choose eggs any style for US$4. For lunch or dinner, there are fish tacos (US$6), quesadillas, sandwiches, and pasta with or without seafood (US$8–14). On Saturday nights open-mic sessions draw a crowd. Internet costs one peso (about 8 cents) per minute.

Swimming pools are a rare find in this off-the-grid location, but **Villa del Faro** (Camino Costero Rural, no tel., www.villadelfaro.net, US$140–425) has one that measures 60 feet. Once a private home for a large family, the property consists of four well-appointed *casitas* and a primitive stone cottage on the beach. Rates are higher than some of the options to the north, but true solitude is hard to come by,

THE EAST CAPE

even in these remote parts, and the visit does include breakfast each day.

Palo Escopeta

Just south of the Crossroads Country Club, a graded dirt road in good shape heads west over the lower Sierra la Trinidad hills, past a series of ranchos, to the 100-person pueblo of Palo Escopeta. From there, the road continues southwest to Santa Catarina, where it joins Mexico 1, just north of San José Viejo. The total distance from the Coastal Road to Mexico 1 is 34 kilometers, about the same distance you'd travel from La Vinorama to San José del Cabo on the Costal Road. The difference is a much smoother and faster ride, plus a change of scenery from coastal desert to ranchos and sierra foothills.

The route to the East Cape via Palo Escopeta is relatively easy to find and drive, but for first-time travelers, the turns may not be as obvious as the locals would have you believe. Here is the best set of directions we've found, courtesy of Villa del Faro:

From the Los Cabos airport, head south (right) toward San José del Cabo for three kilometers and watch for the Palo Escopeta road on the left after the sign for Veterinaria Chiapa. Signs on both sides of the road here say *No Tire Basura*. Under each one, another small sign says Palo Escopeta. A set of *topes* (speed bumps) are another indication that the turn is imminent. Approaching from San José, turn right at the *No Tire Basura* signs. If you pass a Pemex and Veterinaria Chiapa, turn around. You have gone too far. Once you are off the highway, follow the paved road downhill at first, about 1.5 kilometers, until it ends, just past a now-closed bar called Catarina Beach. The road turns to dirt and crosses an arroyo; then it becomes paved again through the town of Santa Catarina. At the town monument, the road turns left; keep going along this road until it becomes a dirt road again. From here, the road will wind back and forth. Ignore any lesser-traveled branches and stay on the main route. Approximately 8.4 kilometers after leaving Mexico 1, the road will

fork. Bear left toward Palo Escopeta. If you go straight, you'll find yourself at the town dump. Continue 9.3 kilometers, staying on the road most traveled, into the village of Palo Escopeta. Veer left toward the ball court, which marks the halfway point of the route, and continue winding down the hills through the ranchos. Watch for cows in the road from here to the coast. Keep going straight for another 14.3 kilometers until you reach the Sea of Cortez at a T intersection. This is El Camino Costero Rural (Coastal Road), and you've reached Boca de la Vinorama. Turn left (north) to reach Bahía de los Frailes and Cabo Pulmo, or right (south) to Punta Gorda and Los Zacatitos.

This route is equally straightforward coming from east to west. The turns through Palo Escopeta are easy to spot; when you get close to Santa Catarina, the turns might be a bit less obvious, but you can see the highway across the arroyo and there aren't all that many options to throw you off course. When in doubt, stop and ask, *"Donde está la carretera?"* The answer will likely be *"Todo derecho."* (Straight ahead.)

If you opt to stay on the Coastal Road south of the Palo Escopeta turnoff, you'll pass two more ranchos and a small dairy farm called La Fortuna. Nearby (21 kilometers north of Buzzard's Bar and Grill in La Playita), Oregonians Lloyd and Marti Miesen host a one-unit bed-and-breakfast, **Boca de Las Palmas** (U.S. tel. 503/922-0465 or 866/781-8159, www.martimiesen.com, US$275). Accommodations are in a one-bedroom guesthouse with a king-size bed, private bath, and luxury linens; an additional guestroom is available in their home on the same property for an additional US$75 (only with rental of the guesthouse). For surfers, this B&B is conveniently located between the Shipwrecks and Nine Palms breaks. Amenities include satellite Internet, washer/dryer, filtered water (no bottles needed), and use of kayaks, boogie boards, and surfboards. Horseback riding is also available to guests and the public.

Punta Gorda

About 10.3 kilometers north of Pueblo La Playa, Punta Gorda is a reliable spot for onshore/inshore fishing, as well as surfing during the south swells of late summer and fall.

A number of new real estate projects are taking shape here. The farthest along of these is Los Zacatitos, which has a few artist residents. The development's first restaurant opened in late 2008. Run by Paul and Angel Rini, **Zac's Bar and Grill Restaurant** (tel. 624/168-4696, www.zacsbar.com, 1–8 P.M. daily, mains US$5–15) occupies a second-story, open-air space. The menu is a mix of Mexican, Italian, and American staples, including pizza for Monday night NFL. A new addition is locally brewed Baja Blond beer on tap. Check the Zacatitos homeowners association website, www.loszacatitos.net, for community news.

The Mexican resort developer Mayan Group and Pueblo Bonito each own large properties in the area.

South of Punta Gorda, the Navarro Group owns a large chunk of coastal land, and there has been talk about the potential of another marina. On the outskirts of San José, the Laguna Hills development has views of the Estero San José and Punta Palmilla in the distance. Close to Buzzard's Bar and Grill and about three miles from La Playita, El Encanto is another group of waterfront homes and luxury condos.

Banco Gorda

About 10 kilometers offshore from Punta Gorda, two seamounts known officially as

---

GORDO OR GORDA BANKS?

The name of this prime diving and sport-fishing destination in the southern part of the Sea of Cortez has been the source of much confusion, so we attempted to get to the bottom of the issue. The word *gordo/gorda* is an adjective that means "fat" in Spanish. When used to modify feminine objects, it takes an "a," as in Punta Gorda. When used to modify a masculine object, it should take an "o," as in Banco Gordo. Not so, according to the Secretaria de Pesca (fishing secretary) of the Mexican government, whose national sportfishing map uses the name Banco Gorda. To add to the confusion, many gringos have adopted the name Gordo Banks, as in Gordo Banks Pangas. It seems in this case, either name will get you to the right place.

Banco Gorda, but more commonly called Gordo Banks, are of interest to serious sport-fishing enthusiasts and advanced scuba divers. Fishing boats head out this way in search of marlin and wahoo, while scuba divers come for a chance to see schools of hammerheads and the occasional whale shark.

If you want to fish the banks, it's best to hire a *panga* at La Playita, or book a charter out of Cabo San Lucas. For dive trips, try **Eagle Divers** (tel. 624/125-0008, www.eaglediver. com) in Cabo San Lucas.

THE EAST CAPE

Sierra de la Laguna and Vicinity

Most travelers who drive Mexico 1 from La Paz to San José via Los Barriles and the East Cape blaze right by the historic mountain towns along the way. But a quick visit to any of these communities gives you a sense of what Baja California was like during the 19th-century silver-mining boom as well as a snapshot of present-day Mexican life in the peninsula's interior.

In the 19th century, two neighboring settlements in the Sierra de la Laguna formed the epicenter of Baja California's gold- and silver-mining boom; today El Triunfo and San Antonio are smaller, quieter communities sustained by agriculture and basket weaving, although there is talk and much controversy over proposed plans to begin mining operations again.

SIERRA DE LA LAGUNA AND VICINITY

To La Paz

San Pedro

Bahía de los Muertos

Boca del Alamo

El Cardonal

Los Algodones

Punta Pescadero

SIERRA

☾ EL TRIUNFO

San Antonio

☾ ARROYO SAN BARTOLO

El Carrizal

San Bartolo

San Bartolo

▲ Picacho de la Laguna

DE

Los Barriles

Santo Domingo

☾ LOS BARRILES

Buena Vista

LA

El Tarayse

San Dionisio

Salsial

LAGUNA

MISIÓN TODOS SANTOS

☾ CAÑON DE LA ZORRA

Santiago

Tropic of Cancer

★ ☾ SANTIAGO TOWN PLAZA ★

Todos Santos

TROPIC OF CANCER MONUMENT

San Bernado

PACIFIC

El Pescadero

Miraflores

MISIÓN SANTIAGO

El Sesteadero

Portezuelo

OCEAN

19

El Aguaje

To Cabo San Lucas

La Matanza

San José

To Cabo San Lucas

To Cabo San Lucas

Santa Anita

0   5 mi

0   5 km

San Bernabé

© AVALON TRAVEL

Miners first discovered silver in the area in the mid-18th century, near present-day San Antonio (then called Real de Minas de Santa Ana). The town became the first Baja municipality founded without a mission. In 1862 better mineral deposits were discovered near El Triunfo, and the Progreso Mining Company arrived in 1878, bringing with it thousands of workers from Europe and China. A thriving company town emerged with a population around 10,000 that was in many ways similar to the mining town that grew at the same time around Santa Rosalía, on the Gulf coast to the north. The miners built towering smokestacks, the largest of which, La Ramona, stands ten stories high. Historic photos of El Triunfo's mining towers are on display at the Centro Cultural in Todos Santos.

The two towns prospered until a hurricane flooded the mines in 1918. By 1926 the mines had closed and the towns were almost abandoned.

◖ EL TRIUNFO

A short distance from the intersection of Mexico 19 and Mexico 1, modern-day El Triunfo (pop. 350) makes an intriguing stop on the drive from Los Barriles to La Paz or Todos Santos. You'll know you've arrived at this ghost town when you reach the only bend in the road lined with aging brick structures and a few small businesses hoping to catch travelers passing through.

Begin with a walk around the mining ruins on the southwest side of the highway. These and a few restored colonial homes are the only signs of the town's glorious past. Browse the handicrafts, including handwoven baskets at **El Mirador Artesanias** (no tel.), which is two blocks west of the highway, at the south end of town. Then stop in for a bite to eat at ◖ **Café El Triunfo** (one block west of the main road, tel. 612/157-1625, 8 A.M.–6 P.M. daily)—an unexpected find serving pizza, coffee drinks, and a tempting assortment of fresh breads.

Before you leave, visit the famed **Piano Museum** (Mexico 1, no tel., 9 A.M.–6 P.M. Mon.–Sat., US$2) to reflect on the town's

IS WATER WORTH MORE THAN GOLD?

Los Cabos-area residents have defeated, for the moment, a potentially disastrous international gold-mining venture at Picacho Blanco in the Sierra de la Laguna near El Triunfo. Two Canadian companies are in discussions with the Mexican government to excavate a 163-square-mile site using cyanide and arsenic in an open-pit mining operation. Environmentalist have raised concerns that the mine could poison the water supply of Los Cabos, further harm the health of local fisheries, and deepen unemployment in the region. The area surrounding the mine is a buffer zone of the UNESCO-designated Sierra de la Laguna Biological Reserve and is the sole source of drinking water for Los Cabos and Baja California's East Cape.

BajaSurViva (www.bajavivaur.com) and Human SOS are among the environmental groups fighting the mine. Residents from Cabo San Lucas to Todos Santos to La Paz have organized to vocally oppose the mine, and in January 2011 they made some progress when Mexico's two main environmental agencies, SEMARNAT and CONANP, denied the companies the required federal land-use permit.

glorious past. During its most prosperous years, classical music came into vogue, and pianos were shipped from Europe. Pianist Francisca Mendoza entertained the well-to-do with weekend concerts, and many of the instruments are on display inside the museum with bilingual signs. If you're lucky, the curator, known among gringos as the Liberace of Baja, might play for you. Look for an orange and white brick building on the east side of the highway. A small blue *Museo* sign points the way, but it's easy to miss.

Save time to explore the **Santuario de Cactus** (Cactus Sanctuary, Ejido El Rosario, Km. 167, Mexico 1, no tel., dawn till dusk daily, US$4) just outside town. This is the place remains of silver mining operations in El Triunfo

to get acquainted with the flora of the desert. Bring along a copy of the *Baja California Plant Field Guide,* by Norman C. Roberts, for your stroll. About two hectares in size, the park has a short interpretive path with signs to identify the different species. If your Spanish is up to it, the enthusiastic caretaker likes to chat. The turnoff is on the west side of Mexico 1 between Km. 167 and 168. Follow the dirt road about 10 minutes to the park entrance.

A few of the tour operators based in La Paz and Todos Santos lead guided trips here. Contact Todos Santos Eco Adventures (Cerro La Poza, Calle Guaycura, tel. 612/145-0780, www.tosea.net) or **Eduardo's Tours** in La Paz (tel. 612/166-1657 or 612/152-1213, www.eduardostours.com).

San Antonio

At the junction of the paved road to Los Planes, a part-cobblestone, part-dirt road leads south into San Antonio, now a center of commerce for local ranchers with a few minisupers. Drive about a half mile and turn left at the T, and you will see an attractive town plaza on the left, followed by a large church. Tall palms and cobblestone streets border the plaza. Buy a cold drink at **La Realeña** (no tel.), a mini-market on the east side. There are public restrooms next to the school—oddly, three toilets in one open room. (Bring your own paper and hand sanitizer.)

San Antonio's town festival, the feast of St. Anthony, takes place on June 13, and residents from both towns show up for the celebration.

Information and Services

San Antonio (pop. 800) has a Pemex, post office, and several markets. And there are two options for basic groceries in El Triunfo: **Abarrotes La Escondida** (on Mexico 1, no tel.) and the **Tienda Comunitaria** (off Mexico 1 in the center of town, no tel.).

Getting There

If you're driving south from La Paz, you'll encounter El Triunfo (pop. 300) first, at Km. 163, 48 kilometers south of La Paz, and San Antonio seven kilometers farther south.

If you're driving north along Mexico 1 from Los Barriles and want to head over to the coast at Bahía de la Ventana or Bahía de los Muertos, you can take a recently paved shortcut from San Antonio (btw Km. 158 and 159). The road is 22 kilometers long and meets state highway BCS 286 in San Juan de los Planes. The unsigned road is easy to miss. (Look for an intersection near the school zone.) Once you reach BCS 286, turn left (north) for La Paz and La Ventana, or right (south) for Los Planes, Los Muertos, and the Sea of Cortez coast. There is a Pemex station at this intersection as well.

SAN BARTOLO

As Mexico 1 emerges from the sierra and prepares to descend to the coast once again, it passes through the farm settlement of San Bartolo (pop. 550) at Km. 128. An attractive row of markets and eateries line both sides of the highway. You can buy mangoes, avocados, and other locally grown produce from markets along the road—or pick out a bag of homemade candies. Then grab a seat on a wrought-iron bench and enjoy the vista looking down on the palm-filled arroyo. **Restaurant El Paso** (no tel., hours vary, mains US$4–8) and **Dulcería Daniela's** (no tel., hours vary, mains US$4–8), on the east side of the highway, serve simple Mexican dishes as well as sweets. **El Oasis** (no tel., hours vary, mains US$4–8) sells fruit-filled *dulces* and snacks and prepares simple meals. It's also a popular stop for guided tours from Los Cabos.

San Bartolo celebrates its patron saint day on June 19, just a week after San Antonio's town festival.

◖ Arroyo San Bartolo

San Bartolo has one of the best water supplies anywhere in Southern Baja, and waterfalls along its arroyo are a popular way to cool off on balmy days. Organized tours from Los Barriles often travel here via ATV. But if you want to drive yourself to the falls, head to the village of San Bartolo and inquire at Rancho Verde for directions.

Recreation

Rancho La Venta (Km. 144.5, Mexico 1, tel. 612/156-8947, www.rancholaventa.com) offers guided horseback rides (US$50 for up to 2 hrs., US$70 for up to 3 hrs., US$550 for overnight ride with meals and drinks) and trails for hiking and bird-watching.

Accommodations

Rancho Verde (Km. 143/142, Mexico 1, tel. 612/126-9103, U.S. tel. toll-free 888/516-9462, www.rancho-verde.com) advertises itself as a private RV community with lots for sale, but it does rent sites by the night as well (RVs US$12/day, US$72/week; tents US$8/day). Set on more than 1,200 hectares of sierra wilderness, this park offers a refreshing contrast to the increasing crowds and real estate development that are overtaking much of the Baja coast. Amenities include water, sewer, hot showers, and free Wi-Fi.

Just up the road, in a historic location on the mission trail, **Rancho La Venta** (www.rancholaventa.com, US$75) offers a few *casitas* for rent, meals included. Owners Bob and Liz Pudwell ran a popular fish taco restaurant in Alaska before moving permanently to Baja. Now they grow organic vegetables on their ranch.

SANTIAGO AND VICINITY

The largest town along this stretch of Mexico 1, Santiago, was founded as a mission settlement and has evolved into a modern-day agricultural commerce center with a population of around 2,000. Located two kilometers west of Mexico 1, the town is overlooked by most Baja visitors, which allows it to retain an authentic Mexican feel despite its proximity to the Los Cabos tourist corridor.

The Arroyo de Santiago divides the town into two halves, Loma Norte and Loma Sur (North Hill and South Hill). All around the slopes are mango, avocado, and palm orchards. Local farmers now grow much of the organic produce that appears on many Los Cabos menus, and the town's palm orchards supply the palms used to make the ubiquitous *palapa* roofs used up and down the peninsula.

SANTIAGO TO MIRAFLORES

To Cañon San Dionisio and La Laguna

To ☾ EL TRIUNFO and La Paz

☾ CAÑON DE LA ZORRA ★

▲ Cerro el Tepetate

Palo Verde

Santiago

San Jorge

☾ SANTIAGO TOWN PLAZA

GRADED ROAD

SANTA RITA (HOT SPRINGS)

El Encinal

San Jorge

Mesa Cerralvo

1

Agua Caliente

Las Cabras

Tropic of Cancer

EL CHORRO (HOT SPRINGS)

Agua Caliente

★ TROPIC OF CANCER MONUMENT

Las Escobas

Las Vinoramas

Mesa Las Vinoramas

▲ Cerro La Ventanita

To Cañon San Bernardo

Boca de la Sierra

GRADED ROAD

▲ MISIÓN DE SANTIAGO EL APÓSTOL AIÑINÍ

Miraflores

El Ranchito

0   2 mi

0   2 km

San Martín

Mesa El Capulín

La Tinaja

Mesa Los Difuntos

Boca de la Sierra

1

GRADED ROAD

Caduaño

To Cañon San Pablo

To San José del Cabo

© AVALON TRAVEL

Set at the base of the sierra foothills, Santiago is also an access point for backpacking trips into the Sierra de la Laguna.

The town has one well-known restaurant and hotel, plus a few *tiendas* and produce markets.

Santiago is the last town you'll see on Mexico 1 southbound before crossing the Tropic of Cancer (latitude 23.5°N). Although the climate has likely felt tropical since Mulegé, this crossing makes it official.

Misión de Santiago El Apóstol Aiñiní

Italian Padre Ignacio María Nápoli founded the mission (1724–1795) at Santiago after attempting to build settlements on Bahía de las Palmas on the East Cape and at Santa Ana in the Sierra de la Laguna. As was the case at the other Southern Baja missions, the Pericú resisted the Catholic way of life. Santiago was the first mission attacked in the massive Pericú rebellion of 1734. Missionary buildings and possessions were burnt to the ground and the padre in residence was murdered.

Survivors began to rebuild the settlement in 1736, but uprisings and epidemics continued, and the Dominicans abandoned the site in 1795, moving the last remaining indigenous people to San José. A modern church (1958) on Santiago's Loma Sur (South Hill) is believed to have been built on the ruins of the original mission.

◖ Santiago Town Plaza

On the north side of Santiago is the ever-charming town plaza, with tall trees for shade and a handful of colonial buildings around its perimeter. The plaza makes a relaxing stop for a stroll or a place to enjoy a picnic lunch after a trip to the hot springs or waterfall nearby. Santiago hosts its town festival on July 25, the feast day of St. James. Services on the plaza include a post office, gas station, minimarket, produce market, and a few stores.

Accommodations and Food

Decorated with local fossils, the highly regarded ◖ **Palomar Restaurant-Bar** (tel. 624/130-2019, 10:30 A.M.–7 P.M. Mon.–Sat., mains US$11–15), south of the plaza on the

© PAUL ITOI

the town plaza in Santiago

THE EAST CAPE

east side of Calzada Misioneros, serves seafood, enchiladas, steak, and burgers. Fresh guacamole is made from avocados grown in the courtyard. Homemade soups and *pescado al mojo de ajo* (fish cooked in garlic butter) are house specialties. It also offers six plain but clean rooms with air-conditioning around a shady courtyard for US$45.

Past the Hotel Palomar on the north side of town, a road heads northwest to Rancho San Dionísio (23.5 km) and the Cañon San Dionísio approach into the Sierra de la Laguna. Owner Sergio Gomez (tel. 624/130-2019) can also contact guides from Rancho San Dionísio for hikers.

Tacos La Cascada (no tel., dinner daily), 200 meters from the plaza on the way to the waterfall, offers excellent carne asada, *mixto* (*carne* and cheese), and fish tacos for US$1.50 each.

Getting There

To get to Santiago, turn west off Mexico 1 at the Pemex station at Km. 84–85 and follow this road for two kilometers to a boulevard that eventually meets the plaza.

Eight kilometers northeast of Santiago on Mexico 1 (around Km. 93), Las Cuevas marks the exit ramp for La Ribera and El Camino Costero Rural. Services include a mini-super and bus stop.

Buses stop at Santiago, for access to the Sierra de la Laguna, and at La Ribera/Las Cuevas, Km. 93, for access to Cabo Pulmo (no connecting service).

Hot Springs

Several waterfalls and hot springs are a short drive into the sierra from Santiago. Finding them involves navigating a series of turns along mostly unsigned dirt roads, although the state is beginning to make the area more visitor friendly with more pavement and signs at each of the ranchos to indicate what they grow or produce—and what they may have for sale.

The main hot springs are called Agua Caliente, El Chorro, and Santa Rita—and all three are just a few kilometers from town.

DRIVING WASHBOARD ROADS

Whether you rent a car or drive your own, exploring Baja's back roads takes a toll on vehicle and driver alike. Follow these tips to enjoy a safe and smooth ride:

- **Less is more:** Lower the air pressure in your tires for driving on softer sand.

- **Stay to the side:** You can often find a smoother track on the far left or right side of the road.

- **Pick up the pace:** Faster speeds often smooth out the bumps, but be sure to slow down when approaching turns to avoid skids and unexpected obstacles.

- **Know your clearance:** Watch for large rocks and deep potholes that can wreak havoc on low-hanging oil pans.

- **Travel with tools:** At a minimum, a spare tire and jack are essential. Old carpet remnants work well for getting traction on soft sand.

- **Ask around:** For less-traveled routes, inquire when the road was last graded and what kind of vehicle you need to pass through safely.

Many residents and hotel managers along the East Cape can provide accurate turn-by-turn directions to these sites. The Hotel Palomar (tel. 624/130-2019) is a good place for information. A nominal admission fee (around US$3–5) may be required to enter the sites.

Cañon de la Zorra

Freshwater is a sight to behold in the Baja desert landscape. For those travelers who would like to venture into the sierra but do not have time for a multiday hike, there is a 10-meter waterfall just 9.6 kilometers beyond Santiago that has a swimmable lagoon and is reachable by foot. At the far end of the divided avenue that leads into Santiago (as you approach the plaza), turn right and set your trip odometer to zero. At 0.48 kilometer, go straight through the dirt road intersection and head up the hill, past a sign for San Dionísio. At 1.29 kilometers and the crest of the hill, turn left. At 1.77 kilometers, turn right across a small arroyo and follow this road to 4.02 kilometers, where the road forks and there is a sign pointing to the right fork marked Cañon de la Zorra. Follow this fork to the end of the road at 9.66 kilometers and park at the trailhead. Small wooden outhouses are popping up in remote areas of the cape, and you'll find one of them here. Go through the gate and follow the trail for 10 minutes down to the river bottom and the falls. The state has installed concrete steps to get to the waterfall now, instead of the rope, which used to scare off some potential visitors. And there is an entrance fee now of US$5. Note: As part of the Sierra de la Laguna Biosphere Reserve, this is a protected area, and pets are not allowed inside the park. The use of sunscreen is also prohibited if you are going to swim.

Rancho Ecológico Sol de Mayo (Calle Guadalupe Victoria 40-B, tel. 624/130-2055, www.ranchoecologicosoldemayo.com) offers rental cabanas and guided trips into the mountains. Stop by the office in town to make arrangements.

MIRAFLORES

Continuing south along Mexico 1 from Santiago, the next town off the west side of the highway is Miraflores (pop. 3,000), a center for agriculture, leatherwork, and handmade furniture. Follow the paved access road from the Pemex at Km. 71 about 2.5 kilometers to the town center. You'll pass a few *carnicerias*—where the town population seems to congregate on Sunday afternoons—a Tienda Popular minimarket, and several other businesses. Turn left at the T to find the small plaza, town church, and a couple of eateries. There's not much for visitors to see here, but **Curtiduría Miraflores** (Miraflores Tannery, tel. 624/355-0254, 7 A.M.–7 P.M. daily), on the way into town (left side of the road),

makes leather saddles and other ranching gear as well as a limited assortment of hats, belts, and purses.

Two annual events in Miraflores would make for an especially festive visit: Fiesta Guadalupana on December 12 and the Miraflores town fiesta on July 20.

A dirt road leaves Miraflores heading northwest to the village of Boca de la Sierra (Mouth of the Sierra), which is located at the entrance to Cañon San Bernardo, an access point for hikes into the sierra. Another dirt road southwest of town goes to Cañon San Pablo, another trail into the mountains. The leather shop is a good place to inquire about hiring a guide for a hike.

SIERRA DE LA LAGUNA

In between the tranquil Sea of Cortez and the powerful Pacific Ocean, a range of 1,500–2,100-meter granite peaks runs north to south, from the plains south of La Paz to the edge of San José, dividing the East Cape and West Cape regions of the Baja Peninsula. Its freshwater springs, unique flora and fauna, and dramatic weather patterns contrast radically with the desert-tropical environment along the coast. And yet the access points for the Sierra de la Laguna are only minutes away from the Transpeninsular Highway and Mexico 19. There are good reasons why *Backpacker* magazine calls this area the best midwinter trail hiking on the Baja Peninsula.

There is some dispute about the highest peak in the range, but **Picacho de la Laguna** (elev. 2,161 m) is most often cited as the tallest. The meadow that stretches the 6.4 kilometers between Picacho de la Laguna and Cerro las Casitas is called La Laguna, since it used to be a lake until around 1870. (The lake was drained to support agriculture and mining operations in the late 1800s.)

The peaks are a genuine cloud forest in the late summer months and can receive more than 100 centimeters of rain a year.

The range's unique position between the desert to the north and the water on the other three sides creates a rare ecosystem of lush

THE EAST CAPE

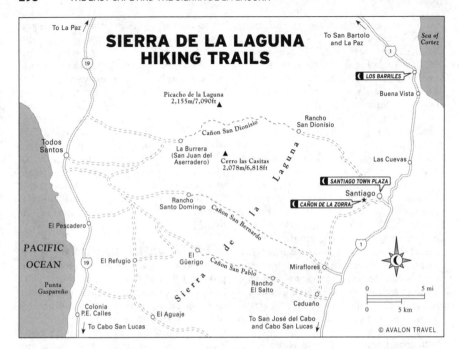

subtropical, alpine, and desert vegetation. The waterfalls that run until late spring add to the stunning scenery.

The peak hiking season here is late October through early spring, after the summer storms have subsided and the waterfalls are running. Temperatures at La Laguna can drop below freezing during the winter months, when the daytime highs range 10–20°C. In spring, daytime temperatures climb to around 25°C.

Sierra de la Laguna Biosphere Reserve

Drenched with far more annual precipitation than any other part of the peninsula, La Laguna has become an isolated microclimate that sustains plants and animals long gone from the desert plains below. There are more than 900 plant species growing in the range, 70 of them indigenous. More striking than the number of species is the unusual combination of plants typically associated with opposite climates.

This is a place where moss grows next to cacti and palms thrive beside willows. Naturally, the area is popular with avid bird-watchers.

In 1994 the Mexican government designated the Sierra de la Laguna a "biosphere reserve," a designation long sought by local environmentalists. The reserve encompasses 11,300 hectares, divided into a core zone, in which development is prohibited, and a buffer zone, where ranchers may graze livestock.

Hiking

Hikes in these mountains typically follow canyons, trails, or cow tracks—or a combination of the three. There are three main routes into the sierra from the east side of the range: Cañon San Dionísio, with access from Santiago; Cañon San Bernardo, with access from Miraflores; and Cañon San Pablo, with access from Caduaño (4 km south of Miraflores). The main access point from the west side is at La Burrera, between Pescadero

CARMEL TSABAR

view on a hike through the Sierra de
la Laguna

and Todos Santos. A couple of representative hikes are described here; local guides can make additional recommendations based on current conditions and client preferences.

LA LAGUNA AND PICACHO DE LA LAGUNA SUMMIT

The most popular hike in the area is a round-trip summit of the highest peak in the range via Cañon San Dionísio, with an overnight stop to camp in the oak meadow at La Laguna. The summit is best attempted from west to east because the terrain in this direction is more direct and easier to navigate. You do not need a guide to do this hike; however, SEMARNAT, the government agency that manages the biosphere reserve, asks hikers to obtain a permit from its office in La Paz (Ocampo 1045, second floor, tel. 612/123-9313, US$1 pp).

The total distance for the hike is 24 kilometers, with 1,800 meters of elevation gain. Many people leave before sunrise under a full moon to get off the exposed face before the sun hits the west slope. There are a few forest ranger and military buildings in the meadow.

Access to this hike begins at the village of La Burrera, near Todos Santos. Look for a dirt turnoff from Mexico 19, about 100 meters south of the road to Punta Lobos. After the old water tower, take the first left and continue straight through several intersections until the road ends

at a gate and parking area. From the gate, follow the dirt road all the way to La Burrera, about 25 minutes more. Continue on the same road for 20 minutes more until you reach a clearing on the right that has been used for camping; a sign here reads *No Tire Basura* (Don't Throw Trash). Just past the sign, the road climbs a small rise, and the trail begins from here.

Enjoy the first few steps of flat terrain because the trail gets fairly steep in a hurry. The trail to La Laguna is 11 kilometers, which takes 5–8 hours, depending on your pace. As you approach the meadow, the dense vegetation gives way to panoramic views of the mountains and ocean below. In the southeast corner of the meadow is a waterfall and swimming pool. Pack enough drinking water to get you to La Laguna, as there is no permanent source of water along the trail.

If you need transportation to the trailhead, stop by the Siempre Vive grocery store (Juárez at Márquez de León, Todos Santos) in the late morning, or check with Todos Santos Eco Adventures (www.tosea.net) for organized trips. Taxis waiting at the taxi stand by the town park will also drive you there.

Guides are strongly recommended to do this trip from the eastern approach, due to the complex network of cow tracks. (Ask in Santiago.) Most hikers allow 3–4 days to cover the 12.8 kilometers to La Laguna. Make sure to bring enough water for the whole journey.

TRANS-SIERRA HIKE

Cañon San Bernardo presents the easiest route for crossing the range from east to west. From the village of Boca de la Sierra, you climb to an elevation of 1,000 meters over the course of about 16 kilometers and then descend to Santo Domingo on the west side. There is drinking water in year-round pools along the way. Allow 4–5 days to complete the 22.5-kilometer hike.

Information and Services
SUPPLIES

At a minimum, you need a reliable compass and topographic map for any of these hikes.

THE EAST CAPE

© PABLO NOBILI

a caballero ready to guide hikers through the Sierra de la Laguna

Relevant topo maps include El Rosario F12B23, Las Cuevas F12B24, Todos Santos F12B33, and Santiago F12B34. Pack warm layers and sleeping bags for the higher elevations, even in the spring. Long pants and sturdy footwear can protect bare skin from the getting jabbed by cactus needles.

Although some routes have water along the way, it's best to bring your own and use what's there as backup. Remember to purify any water you collect from mountain pools.

GUIDES

For hikes from the east side of the sierra, guides are recommended and readily available Santiago and Miraflores. Rates are about US$30–35 per day per person, plus an extra US$15 per day per pack animal. Rancho San Dionísio charges US$30 for a guide without mules, no matter how many people are hiking.

A guide is not essential to hike from the west side, although it helps to have someone show you to the trailhead. In Todos Santos, **Fernando Arteche** (sierradelalaguna@hotmail.com) has been leading trips for many years. He speaks excellent English and knows a lot about the Sierra de la Laguna. Trips are on mule or by foot. **Juan Sebastián López** (onejohnone@hotmail.com) runs three-day trips

on horseback, with packhorses to carry your gear. At **Rancho Pilar** (Km. 73, Mexico 19, ranchopilar@hotmail.com), artisan and amateur naturalist Cuco Moyron can arrange mule trips into the Sierra de la Laguna and is a good source of information about sierra flora. He'll need about a week to make the arrangements.

Todos Santos Eco Adventures (www.tosea.net) leads organized group trips into the sierra.

Getting There and Around

With high clearance and a sense of adventure, you can drive across the mountains from Mexico 1 north of San José del Cabo to Mexico 19 on the Pacific side via an ungraded road called Los Naranjos. The road is 42 kilometers long and ends at the village of El Aguaje, near El Pescadero.

From the Los Cabos airport, head north until you pass Santa Anita and go about eight kilometers more. Turn left onto Los Naranjos road, which ascends from the flats up into the sierra.

Bring along a copy of the *Baja California Plant and Field Guide,* by Norman C. Roberts.

Follow the switchbacks to a plateau and then continue west until you glimpse the Pacific Ocean in the distance. At this point, the road frequently washes out and may not be passable. If it's clear, you can continue on to El Pescadero.

LOS CABOS

Something magical happens at the point where the cool green Pacific Ocean crashes into the blue sapphire Sea of Cortez at Land's End. The fish that inhabit these waters drew the original visitors 30 years ago—wealthy Hollywood types who arrived by yacht or private plane to fish the Marlin Alley. Then the anglers began to bring their golf clubs, dive gear, and college-age kids. Today stunning geography, perfect weather, endless opportunities for outdoor recreation, and federal funding from the Mexican government have transformed the area from a cluster of fishing villages into a full-scale tourist corridor.

From Cabo San Lucas to San José del Cabo and everywhere in between, landscaped highway exit ramps are replacing dirt-road turnoffs, new resorts and condo buildings are under construction, seaside golf courses are opening, and restaurant menu prices are reaching for the stars. Some say Los Cabos is well on its way (if not already there) to becoming Mexico's most expensive destination.

Adventure travelers, fear not: Los Cabos offers much more than nine-bedroom villas and 100-foot yachts. Beneath the upscale veneer, quaint bed-and-breakfasts, modest hotels, free snorkeling beaches, authentic taquerías, and affordable *panga* boat tours invite exploration.

The tip of the Baja Peninsula consists of two large towns connected by a 29-kilometer-long stretch of white-sand beaches, exclusive golf courses, and luxury resorts—known as the Corridor—which the government has divided

HIGHLIGHTS

◖ **Plaza Teniente José Antonio Mijares:** San José del Cabo town life centers around this cobblestone plaza in front of an elegant 1940 church built on the site of the original Jesuit mission (page 309).

◖ **Historic Art District:** Historic adobe buildings in the San José Art District house a number of contemporary art galleries. More than a dozen galleries participate in Thursday evening Art Walks, which draw visitors and locals alike (page 312).

◖ **Estero San José:** Spanish colonists were originally drawn to the tip of the Baja Peninsula by the promise of fresh water. Here, a large estuary, home to hundreds of species of birds, connects the Pacific Ocean to an underground river that flows out of the sierra (page 312).

◖ **Bahías Chileno and Santa María:** Two of the Corridor's most popular and accessible beaches offer safe swimming and good snorkeling (page 333).

◖ **Finisterra (Land's End):** Every tour boat in Cabo visits Finisterra and its 62-meter-high arch. This granite rock formation marks the end of the Baja Peninsula and the point where the Sea of Cortez merges with the Pacific Ocean (page 344).

◖ **Playa del Amor:** This two-sided beach just outside the Cabo San Lucas harbor faces calm waters on its eastern Bahía San Lucas side and pounding surf on the western Pacific side (page 345).

LOOK FOR ◖ TO FIND RECOMMENDED SIGHTS, ACTIVITIES, DINING, AND LODGING.

into several development zones or *fraccionamientos.* These towns and zones make up the Los Cabos *municipio* (county).

With its signature rock arch and large, protected harbor, Cabo San Lucas is situated on the west side of the peninsula, at the place where the Sea of Cortez and Pacific Ocean meet. Cabo San Lucas is busier, noisier, more Americanized, and more touristy than unassuming San José del Cabo. On any given day, multiple cruise ships may deliver thousands of day-trippers into the Cabo San Lucas marina.

They mingle with expats, snowbirds, and the adventure-seekers who come to fish, dive, cruise, and party.

On the east side of the peninsula, San José del Cabo is quieter and prettier, with a historic plaza and numerous restored colonial-era buildings. Its growing art district holds a handful of well-respected galleries, representing artists from all over Mexico as well as some from the United States.

That said, San José is experiencing some growth pains of its own. Its new Puerto Los

a cave near Finisterra (Land's End)

© NIKKI GOTH-ITOI

extended from Cabo San Lucas to San José and up to Cabo Pulmo on the East Cape. Early Spanish explorers took interest in the vicinity of San José del Cabo when they discovered freshwater in the Río San José. While the Spanish set up camp near San José, favoring its protected estuary and abundant freshwater, English pirates, including Francis Drake and Thomas Cavendish, dominated the cape and bay at San Lucas. In a major blow to the Spanish, Cavendish captured, looted, and sank the 600-ton Manila galleon *Santa Ana* in 1578, in the same waters where modern cruisers troll for game fish.

The Pericú proved to be less tolerant of the Spanish than neighboring tribes to the north had been. Following a series of uprisings in the 1720s, Jesuit Padre Nicolas Tamarál came from La Purísima in 1930 to establish a permanent mission and military outpost that would guard the estuary from further attacks by pirates and indigenous people. He planted orchards and moved the mission site around a few times before settling on the current town center, which afforded views of the harbor without all the bugs.

Padre Tamarál baptized more than 1,000 Pericú in the first year of the mission, but peace lasted only until 1734, when the Pericú rebelled once again, this time to protest a Spanish decree against polygamy. They burned four missions in Southern Baja and killed Tamarál in the battle.

Few of the Pericú remained by 1767, when the Jesuits were expelled from Baja California. But the mission persevered under the Dominicans. In the following decades, the Spanish built a garrison at San José, turning the mission into a military outpost that resupplied the Manila galleons on their way to and from the Philippines. To learn more about the earliest settlers of the area, visit the Museum of Natural History in Cabo San Lucas.

In a rarely documented chapter of the Mexican-American War (1846–1848), a group of 20 U.S. marines from the sloop *Portsmouth* briefly occupied the city of San José from barracks in a former mission building, which

Cabos Marina has brought power, Internet, and a modern sewage system to the village at La Playita. But with these amenities come the owners of US$80 million yachts, the noise and mess of constant construction, threats to coastal wildlife, higher prices, and increasing traffic congestion. In many ways, San José is becoming unaffordable for the local residents whose families have lived here for generations.

The global economic recession continues to take a toll on Baja-based businesses. Construction on just about all major developments came to a halt, at least temporarily, and most of the workers' camps were empty. Overall, business is down an estimated 30–50 percent, depending on whom you ask. In this climate, many businesses have had to close. The good news for visitors is that there are plenty of great deals to be found, even at peak travel times.

HISTORY

The Pericú first inhabited the Los Cabos area. They were a nomadic people whose territory

To Todos Santos and La Paz
19
Hong Kong
El Manglito
LOS CABOS
SORIANA
CCC SUPERMARKET
HOME DEPOT/ COSTCO
CABO SAN LUCAS
SANLUQUEÑA BULLRING
CABO SAN LUCAS COUNTRY CLUB
VAGABUNDOS RV PARK
CLUB CABO MOTEL/ CAMPGROUND
LA EUROPEA
CABO DEL SOL (DESERT COURSE)
Playa El Médano
Bahía San Lucas
MISIONES DEL CABO
Playa Cementerio
FIESTA AMERICANA
CABO DEL SOL (OCEAN COURSE)
Bahía Chileno
PLAYA DEL AMOR
Cabo El Arco
FINISTERRA (LAND'S END)
Isla Cerro La Bufadora
Isla Cerro Blanco
ESPERANZA RESORT
SHERATON HACIENDA DEL MAR
Punta Cabeza de Ballena
Playa Barco Varado
BAHÍA SANTA MARÍA
© AVALON TRAVEL

is now preserved as the town's Casa de la Cultura. The U.S. forces were given a nine-pounder carronade (a type of cannon) and 75 carbines to hold the town against about 150 Mexican insurgents. When Mexican lieutenant José Antonio Mijares attempted to invade the barracks and capture the cannon in 1847, he failed and was shot by the marines, but the heroic effort earned him a place in local history. Boulevard Mijares and Plaza Mijares are both named in his honor.

A 21-day siege of the U.S. force's barracks in San José took place in early 1848, even as U.S. President James K. Polk was claiming victory in the Californias. The Americans were eventually rescued by a party of 102 men from the sloop *Cyane*. In the end, the Treaty of Guadalupe Hidalgo, signed on February 2, 1848, did not give the United States possession of Baja California. The U.S. forces that had held the garrison withdrew 18 months after the conflict had begun. Many expressed disappointment in the outcome, believing that the United States had abandoned its promise

to take lower California under its wing and left its supporters at the mercy of their own government.

After the Mexican-American War and a short-lived mining era, San José experienced a period of agriculture in the 1930s. The mission church was rebuilt in 1940, and San José began to attract its first sportfishing tourists in the 1960s.

Cabo San Lucas first became a port town near the end of the 19th century, when it began to export the bark of the *palo blanco* tree, which was used as an agent for tanning leather. The Faro Viejo (Km. 2, Mexico 19) lighthouse was built at Cabo Falso in 1890.

Next came the era of tuna canning and the opening of the Compania de Productos Marinos, S.A. de C.V. in 1927, which spurred growth and development in the area for a couple of decades. (The pioneering company moved to Puerto San Carlos in the 1980s.) A road was constructed to join San José to San Lucas. Today it's known as the Camino Viejo a San José (the old road to San José). The

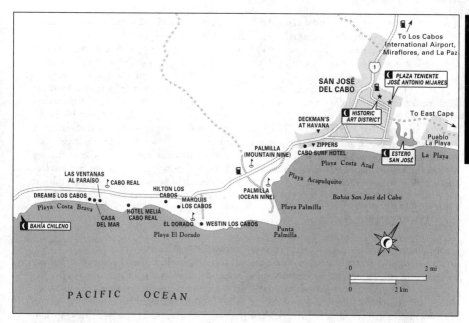

canning business declined rapidly after a severe hurricane damaged the equipment in 1941.

With an infrastructure in place, visitors began to arrive at the port after World War II, and a small tourism business evolved around sportfishing. In the 1960s the original road was replaced by a paved highway that became part of the Transpeninsular Highway, which was completed in 1973. By this time, the population of Cabo San Lucas had grown to about 1,500.

The new highway ushered in a new phase of road travel, bringing a steady stream of visitors to the tip of the peninsula. Mainland Mexican residents began moving to Los Cabos in the mid-1970s, when ferry service commenced between Puerto Vallarta and La Paz. Around this time, the Mexican government designated the Los Cabos corridor for tourism investment and development, and the opening of the Los Cabos International Airport in the 1980s began to bring mainstream travelers en masse.

Today tourism and related construction are the engines of growth for the Los Cabos economy; however, the development comes at the expense of limited natural resources. Already in short supply, freshwater remains a serious concern, as does the protection of endangered sea turtles, whose habitat continues to erode. As the ocean becomes increasingly polluted and overfished, the very ecosystem that has captured the imagination of so many visitors may disappear for good. For environmentally aware travelers, there are many opportunities to engage in sustainable tourism and participate in local conversation efforts. Take the time to seek them out and support their efforts, and you'll leave knowing you've made a real difference in protecting the future of the destination.

PLANNING YOUR TIME

In a couple of days, you can easily explore the main sections of downtown San José and sample a few restaurants, plus have time for the beach. Add extra days for any special activities, such as scuba diving, fishing, or mountain biking. The drive from San José del Cabo to

Cabo San Lucas along the Corridor takes about 30–45 minutes. Surfers and beachcombers can happily spend a full week at a resort along the Corridor. But aside from the beaches (which are spectacular) and associated activities, there is little else to see—meaning, you don't need a lot of time to cover the area if you're just passing through.

For some travelers, a half day in Cabo San Lucas will be more than enough time; others will be content to spend a week. It all depends on whether you prefer nightlife or a more remote setting for your vacation.

CHOOSING AN ACCOMMODATION

Whether you are a first-time or veteran Los Cabos visitor, finding a place to stay involves an overwhelming variety of choices. There are all-inclusive resorts, boutique hotels, basic motels, bed-and-breakfasts, condominiums, timeshares, and villas of all sizes. (And some resorts mix and match, to give even more choice.) You can be at the beach, on a golf course, or in town. You can book directly with a resort or private owner or use a booking service or property management company. And you can spend US$50–950 a night, depending on your budget and the level of comfort you seek.

If you'd like a quieter location where you can look at the beach but swim in a pool, the Corridor or hotel zone of San José would be a good choice. If you want to surf, consider Playa Costa Azul, just outside San José. For swimming and nightlife within walking distance of your hotel, head to Cabo San Lucas.

High-end resorts feature a full list of amenities, usually including air-conditioning, direct-dial phones, satellite TV, multiple swimming pools, swim-up bars, tennis courts, hot tubs, fitness centers, kids' club, and beach *palapas,* plus on-site restaurants and bars. Some resorts also have their own dive centers, spa services, horseback riding, and ATV rental services. High-speed wireless Internet, VoIP phones (free long distance), and flat-screen TVs are some of the newest amenities that hotels and condo owners are adding to differentiate themselves.

Vacation rental condos or villas, or condo-style hotels, afford the most flexibility, as you can cook some of your own meals and venture out for others. Many of the newest condo complexes are concentrated near Playa Costa Azul, between San José and the Corridor. Most are on or near the beach, and many have tennis courts, swimming pools, and laundry facilities; however, the persistent sound of traffic on Mexico 1 is a drawback to this location. You can rent units directly from private owners by searching for listings online (on www.craigslist.com and www.vrbo.com, for example) or by contacting a property management service. (Many of these services also advertise on the private-owner sites.)

Planning Ahead

If you are thinking about a year-end holiday vacation, book as far in advance as possible. Repeat visitors reserve many of the most popular rooms and rentals as much as a year in advance for the weeks around Christmas and New Year's Day. February and March are popular, too, and despite the number of choices for accommodations, there are a handful of resorts—including the One&Only Palmilla, Dreams, and Riu Palace—that seem to be full almost all the time. Flexible travelers need not plan so far ahead, and they are often rewarded with better deals.

Booking Services and Property Management Companies

If you haven't yet decided on a specific location within Los Cabos, or you have a very specific set of criteria for choosing a place to stay, contact a booking service agent, who can give you an overview of several different properties that meet your criteria and your budget. The following companies specialize in Los Cabos-area bookings: **Delfin Hotels & Resorts,** also called **Cabo Hotels** (toll-free U.S. tel. 800/524-5104), lists a wide variety of villas, condos (Terrasol, Las Mañanitas, Mira Vista, Mykonos) all-inclusive resorts, and bed-and-breakfasts. It also publishes several Cabo accommodations websites, including www.

cabohotels.com, www.cabocondos.com, and www.allinclusivescabo.com. **Baja Properties** (Doblado and Morelos, San José tel. 624/142-0988, Cabo San Lucas tel. 624/143-2560, toll-free U.S. tel. 877/464-2252, www.bajaproperties.com) has 20 years of experience in Los Cabos real estate marketing, eight office locations, and a team of 25 agents.

Watsonville, California–based **Earth, Sea & Sky Vacations** (ESSV, toll-free U.S. tel. 800/745-2226, www.cabovillas.com) specializes in luxury vacation packages to the Los Cabos area. It represents 90 villa rentals, ranging from two- to nine-bedroom units, starting at US$1,500 per night, as well as 30 resorts. For an extra fee, ESSV staff will stock your villa prior to your arrival with the foods and supplies you request. Guests can also opt for in-villa services, such as Pilates or yoga classes, spa treatments, and chef services (for one special meal or three meals daily). Since ESSV also handles activity bookings for whale-watching, fishing, and snorkeling, many travelers work with the company to coordinate group trips, such as large family vacations or small weddings.

Companies that focus exclusively on Cabo San Lucas or San José del Cabo (as opposed to the entire region) are listed in the *Accommodations* sections for those towns.

GETTING THERE

The majority of Los Cabos visitors arrive by air, but you'll meet many who have traveled by car, boat, or bicycle or even on foot. Public transportation by bus is also a possibility. Once you've arrived, you can do without a car if you plan to stay at an all-inclusive resort or at a hotel in town. Rent a car if you want to take a day trip to the East Cape or Todos Santos.

By Air

Los Cabos International Airport (SJD, Km. 44, Mexico 1, tel. 624/142-5111, http://aeropuertosgap.com.mx/english/airports/loscabos-airport) serves San José del Cabo and Cabo San Lucas. The airport does not have Jetways, so have your shades at the ready as you exit the plane and climb down the stairs to the tarmac. Additional airport information is available at www.sjdloscabosairport.com, but this is not the official airport website.

The process of going through passport control and customs can take as little as 15 minutes or more than an hour, depending on how many people are working and if other flights have arrived at the same time. After you go through passport control, you'll proceed to the baggage claim area. Claim your bags and have your paperwork ready to show the customs official. You'll be asked to run your bags through a scanner and to press a button that determines whether your bags will be randomly searched. Sometimes, you'll cruise through immigration only to find yourself in a much longer customs line with one x-ray machine scanning luggage from multiple flights. Relax and enjoy the people-watching. The wait is all part of the experience.

The airport has two terminals served by several major airlines (as well as a cargo-only terminal), including:

• Terminal 1: Domestic flights on AeroCalifornia, Aeromexico, Mexicana, and Volaris
• Terminal 2: International flights on American, AmericaWest, Continental, United Airlines
• Terminal 3: Domestic and International flights on Aeroliteral/Mexicana, Alaska, Frontier, and Virgin America

Each terminal has a few fast-food options and souvenir shops, but seating is limited in the waiting areas for arriving flights.

Several international rental car agencies have desks in the terminals. For most brands, you'll need to ride a shuttle to off-airport pickup locations, all of which are very close to the terminal. These days, you'll almost always get a better deal if you reserve ahead of time. During busy holiday periods, most agencies will sell out of cars entirely. They tend to give cars on a first-come, first-served basis, regardless of whether you have a reservation or not.

A shuttle (*colectivo*) into the San José area

runs US$13 per person, US$15 per person to the Cabo San Lucas area. A private taxi from the airport to San José del Cabo costs US$50 for up to four passengers or US$75 to Cabo San Lucas.

BY PRIVATE AIRCRAFT

Private pilots will find a 1,550-meter paved airstrip just north of Cabo San Lucas. Contact **Baja Bush Pilots** (www.bajabushpilots.com) for up-to-date information about making the trip to Los Cabos.

By Car

Most of the big auto rental agencies have desks at Los Cabos International Airport as well as offices in or near San José and San Lucas. Rates are similar across most companies, and since car rentals don't require a deposit up front, it doesn't hurt to make a reservation in advance. You can always cancel if you change your mind. When you reserve or prepay for a car online, the price typically will not include Mexican liability insurance. Be sure to factor this cost (around US$25 per day for the minimum required coverage of US$50,000) into your travel planning. Vehicles range from standard transmission subcompact sedans to SUVs, wagons, Jeeps, pickup trucks, and vans. Independent agencies sometimes include insurance in the rates.

If you're driving yourself, there are two ways to reach the towns along the Los Cabos Corridor from the airport: Follow signs for Mexico 1 south through town, passing through several stoplights before you reach the town of San José. Continue on Mexico 1 another 10–20 minutes for destinations along the Corridor or about 30 minutes to Cabo San Lucas. Alternatively, if you don't mind paying a toll of about US$2.25 (MEX$28), you can exit the airport onto the *quota,* a fast four-lane road with no exits until you enter San José at the junction of Paseo Los Cabos and the Mega grocery store plaza. If you pick up a rental car off-site, you'll have to return to the terminal to get to the toll road. The roundabout at the intersection with Highway 1 can

be an intimidating entry into town, especially if you are trying to go left into downtown San José. Wait for a break in the traffic or turn right and go about one mile to the *Retorno* sign. Exit right and then turn left under the highway and left again to reenter the highway heading back toward San José.

By Bus

A steady stream of **Aguila** (tel. 624/143-5020, www.autotransportesaguila.com) buses provide transportation between Los Cabos and La Paz and on to other points north. Schedules and fares are posted online, and you can purchase tickets in advance online. Current fares are about US$15 from Cabo San Lucas to La Paz and US$20 from San José to La Paz. Note: La Paz via Todos Santos is the shorter and less mountainous route (3.5 hours from Cabo San Lucas); the route to La Paz via the East Cape takes about an hour longer due to the terrain and number of stops. The Cabo San Lucas bus terminal is on Mexico 19, north of the Mexico 1 junction and across from the Pemex station. San Jose's main bus terminal is on Calle Gonzales near Mexico 1.

If you're headed all the way to Tijuana (a 27-hour trip that costs US$150), you'll need to catch the 9 A.M. or 4 P.M. departure, which will stop in Ciudad Constitución, Loreto, Mulegé, Guerrero Negro, and Ensenada.

By Sea

The nearest ferry service to the mainland operates between La Paz and Mazatlán. You can book tickets in La Paz or online through **Baja Ferries** (tel. 612/123-0208, 612/123-6600, or 800/122-1414, www.bajaferries.com).

There are now two full-service marinas in the Los Cabos area. **Marina Cabo San Lucas** (Lote A-18 De la Dársena, tel.624/173-9140, www.igy-cabosanlucas.com) is still the main docking facility for those arriving by sea. But the new **Marina at Puerto Los Cabos** (Paseo de los Pescadores, Col. La Playa, tel. 624/105-6028, www.marinapuertoloscabos.com) is open and designed to hold up to 500 boats, including the largest luxury yachts.

San José del Cabo

An elevated plain above a narrow estuary at the mouth of the Río San José gave early Spanish settlers protection from pirate raids and up-risings by indigenous peoples. The first Jesuit missionaries arrived in 1730 from settlements to the north and tried several sites before choosing the current town center as the permanent location for a mission.

Surrounded by *huertas,* modern-day San José consists of a historic downtown with an attractive plaza and church as well as many restored colonial buildings. The newer part of town includes a nine-hole golf course and beachfront hotel zone. There is also a busy commercial area along Mexico 1. The town is the municipal seat for Los Cabos. Many expats, especially artists, have taken up residence in San José in recent years, but for the most part they seem committed to restoring and preserving their adopted community of Josefinos, and so far the town retains an authentic Mexican feel.

SIGHTS
◖ Plaza Teniente José Antonio Mijares

The center of all the action in San José is a wide brick plaza with a white gazebo-like structure in the middle. On the west side of the plaza, where the original mission once stood, is the 1940 Iglesia San José. Opposite the church, a relatively new fountain has a continuous light show at night. And behind it a row of statues pays tribute to important leaders in Mexican history. Mature trees provide ample shade, while street performers entertain adults and children alike. Restaurants and shops line the plaza on Calles Zaragoza, Hidalgo, and Obregón and Boulevard Mijares. At sundown a handful of food carts open for business. A nice alternative to a formal sit-down meal is to sample a taste of each: tamales, empanadas, *paletas,* and more. A variety of town festivals take place here, including events every Sunday evening during the Christmas season.

THE BIG DIG

San José del Cabo's new Puerto Los Cabos marina has set some records in terms of its size and scale. Its 430 slips can accommodate yachts up to 180 feet long. When complete, the facility will be the largest marina in all of Mexico, with more than 21,000 linear feet of dock space at a price tag of US$50 million.

To form the protected harbor, construction crews shuttled 400,000 tons of granite blasted from a local quarry, with individual capstones weighing 60 tons apiece. They also removed some 650,000 cubic meters of earth from the site. Dump trucks were on the move six days a week for eight months straight to get the job done.

The new marina puts yachts and sportfishing boats one hour closer to Banco Gorda than the Cabo San Lucas marina, with a supposedly easier approach to navigate.

Misión San José del Cabo Añuiti

The Jesuit mission (1730–1840) at San José was founded in 1730 when Father Nicolas Tamarál traveled south from La Purísima and baptized more than 1,000 indigenous people in the first year.

The current church, painted a creamy yellow color, was built in 1940 with two symmetrical towers and a mosaic over the main entrance, which depicts the murder of Father Tamarál by the Pericú who rose up against him. The church holds regular worship services for the people of San José.

Palacio Municipal (City Hall)

This striking 1831 building on Boulevard Mijares just off the plaza has a neoclassical facade and a tower with a wrought-iron balcony and large clock. In the 19th century the

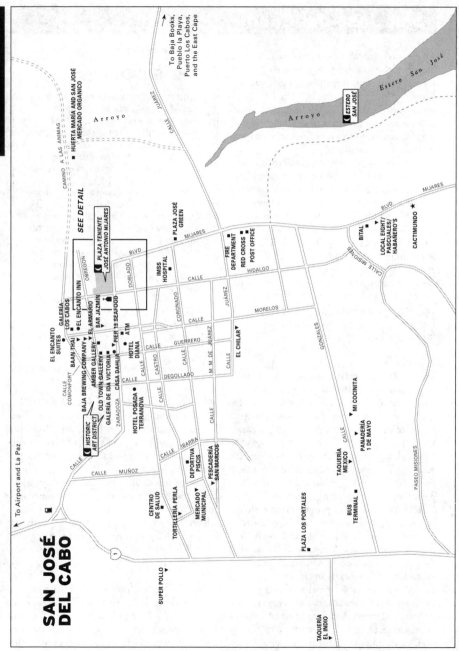

SAN JOSÉ DEL CABO

To Airport and La Paz

To Baja Books, Pueblo la Playa, Puerto Los Cabos, and the East Cape

Arroyo

Estero San José

Arroyo

ESTERO SAN JOSÉ

HISTORIC ART DISTRICT

SEE DETAIL

CAMINO A LAS ÁNIMAS

HUERTA MARIA AND SAN JOSÉ
MERCADO ORGÁNICO

PLAZA TENIENTE JOSÉ ANTONIO MIJARES

PLAZA JOSÉ GREEN

EL ENCANTO INN
EL ARMARIO
BAR JAZMIN
PIER 19 SEAFOOD
ATM

EL ENCANTO SUITES
GALERIA LOS CABOS
BAAN THAI
AMBER GALLERY
OLD TOWN GALLERY
GALERÍA DE IDA VICTORIA
CASA DAHLIA
HOTEL DIANA
BAJA BREWING COMPANY

HOTEL POSADA TERRANOVA

DEPORTIVA PISCIS
PESCADERIA SAN MARCOS

TORTILLERÍA PERLA
MERCADO MUNICIPAL
CENTRO DE SALUD

SUPER POLLO

TAQUERÍA EL INDIO

PLAZA LOS PORTALES

BUS TERMINAL

TAQUERÍA MEXICO

PANADERÍA 1 DE MAYO

MI COCINITA

IMSS HOSPITAL

FIRE DEPARTMENT
RED CROSS
POST OFFICE

BITAL

LOCAL EIGHT/ PASCUALES/ HABAÑERO'S

CACTIMUNDO

CALLE OBREGÓN
CALLE MIJARES
BLVD MIJARES
BLVD
CALLE DOBLADO
CALLE HIDALGO
CALLE MORELOS
CALLE JUAREZ
CALLE CORONADO
CALLE GUERRERO
CALLE M. M. DE JUAREZ
CALLE CASTRO
CALLE DEGOLLADO
CALLE ZARAGOZA
CALLE COMONFORT
CALLE IBARRA
CALLE MUÑOZ
CALLE GONZALES
CALLE MISIONES
PASEO MISIONES
EL CHILAR

© AVALON TRAVEL

© NIKKI GOTH ITOI

Easy-to-find signs mark the Historic Art District in San José del Cabo.

building housed the municipal council for San José. Today it contains a number of local government offices.

Historic Art District

About a dozen of the historic adobe buildings in downtown San José have been converted into fine-art studios and galleries representing artists from all over Mexico and Central and South America as well as the United States. Most of the galleries are concentrated in the blocks between Calles Guerrero and Hidalgo and Calles Zaragoza and Comonfort. On display are stone sculptures, paintings, photography, pottery, and jewelry. On Thursday evenings, the galleries stay open late for the weekly Art Walk (5–9 P.M. Nov.–June). This is an unguided opportunity to visit the galleries at your own pace. Some serve refreshments, and some allow you to watch the artists at work in their studios.

Casa de la Cultura

U.S. marines stayed in this mission-era building just off the plaza in 1847–1848, during the Mexican-American War. Today the blue and green building hosts art exhibits as well as music, dance, and theater performances. The cultural center is located on Calle Obregón at the end of Boulevard Mijares, on the north side of the plaza. The building is open to the public 9 A.M.–8 P.M. Monday–Saturday. Call tel. 624/142-2960 for a schedule of events.

Estero San José

The Río San José, the largest source of freshwater in Southern Baja, originates in the Sierra de la Laguna, travels about 48 kilometers (much of it underground), and empties into a long, narrow estuary that measures 50 hectares. Sebastián Vizcaíno called the estuary Bahía San Bernabé. At the mouth of the river, a sandbar encloses a lagoon ringed by towering Tlaco palms and marsh grasses, which form a sanctuary for more than 200 species of birds.

Unfortunately, this fragile ecosystem is shrinking in size and biodiversity as the town of San José grows, the water table lowers, and the Puerto Los Cabos marina and development encroaches on the preserve.

To reach the estuary, walk or drive to the northeast end of the *zona hotelera* and park outside the Presidente InterContinental. Walk toward the beach and you'll see the estuary on the left. The area was flooded during our last visit, and it wasn't clear if and when the trail would reopen.

Zona Hotelera

San José's government-designated hotel zone encompasses more than 1,600 hectares that parallel the coastline from the Estero San José to Playa Costa Azul. To date, about a dozen large resorts and several condo complexes are complete. Some of the newcomers include the Royal Solaris, The Grand Mayan, and Cabo Azul resorts. As more properties have opened for business, Paseo de San José has become a busy thoroughfare, with several car rental offices and a few new shops and restaurants. Condos and vacation homes surround a nine-hole golf course, now owned by The Grand Mayan. You can walk the beach all the way from the estuary to the surf break known as

Zippers at Playa Costa Azul, but swimming is generally not a good idea, as the undertow is strong most of the year.

Cactimundo Botanical Gardens

The brainchild of two cacti collectors, Cactimundo (Mijares, btw downtown/ *zona hotelera,* tel. 624/146-9191, www.cactimundo.com, 8 A.M.–6 P.M. daily, US$3) has committed itself to the promotion, conservation, and reproduction of rare desert plants. It has 850 succulent species and more than 5,000 plants on display in a small public garden and nursery, some of which are visible from the street. Call or check the website for free gardening classes. Guided tours are available by appointment. The entrance is on Boulevard Mijares, about 0.25 mile before the traffic circle at Paseo San José. Park on the street. There is a small gift shop inside the gardens with T-shirts, books, and other desert flora souvenirs.

Pueblo La Playa

Once an isolated fishing village frequented only by *panga* fishermen and adventurous travelers, Pueblo La Playa and its sandy beach, **La Playita,** are now linked to San José del Cabo via a paved road and bridge across the wide arroyo that separates the two.

The 800-hectare **Puerto Los Cabos** project includes a US$50 million marina designed to accommodate luxury mega-yachts, as well as a couple of designer golf courses, five-star accommodations, and beachfront lots that are selling for US$6–8 million.

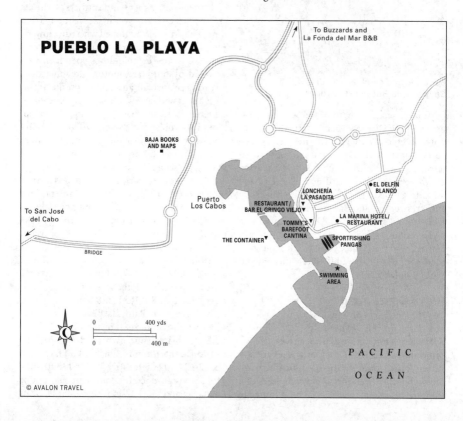

PUEBLO LA PLAYA

To Buzzards and
La Fonda del Mar B&B

BAJA BOOKS
AND MAPS

Puerto
Los Cabos

• EL DELFÍN
BLANCO

LONCHERÍA
LA PASADITA

RESTAURANT/
BAR EL GRINGO VIEJO

LA MARINA HOTEL/
RESTAURANT

To San José
del Cabo

TOMMY'S
BAREFOOT
CANTINA

THE CONTAINER

SPORTFISHING
PANGAS

BRIDGE

SWIMMING
AREA

0   400 yds
0   400 m

PACIFIC

OCEAN

© AVALON TRAVEL

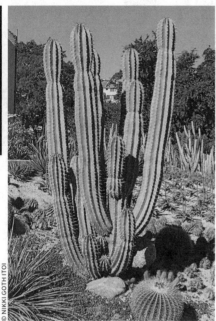

Cacti big and small are on display at Cactimundo Botanical Gardens.

At last check, the harbor was open for business and the first few yachts were sailing into port. Pueblo La Playa had Internet access, paved streets with curbs, and a new, modern sewage system in the works. A *panga* marina and beachfront park features a play structure for kids; a roped-off, protected swimming area; clean restrooms; and the fanciest fish-cleaning tables found anywhere in Baja.

To reach La Playita, turn east off Boulevard Mijares onto Calle Juárez. Follow this four-lane road over the bridge and watch the signs at each roundabout.

Playa Costa Azul

On the outskirts of San José, under a lookout point on the Transpeninsular Highway (Carretera Transpeninsular) near Km. 28–29, somewhat protected Plaza Costa Azul attracts surfers, beachcombers, and occasionally swimmers who walk from the condo complexes that front the beach. For travelers coming from San José, there is a new and unmarked exit ramp just after the Deckman's at Havana restaurant and before the wide arroyo. Turn left off the ramp and park in the sandy lot that divides Mira Vista condos and Zippers Restaurant.

SPORTS AND RECREATION
Fishing

Whether you're a seasoned veteran or you've never fished a day in your life, there are plenty of options near San José. For newbies, your captain and crew will find the right spot for the day, rig up the bait, and handle boating the fish. All you have to do is reel and smile for the picture. Later, top off the day by taking your fresh catch to a local restaurant to have it prepared to your liking.

Fishing boats for hire fall under two general categories: *pangas* and cruisers. Cruisers are the larger boats you'll see in the marina slips. They're often equipped with tuna towers, enclosed cabins, a bathroom, and other amenities. *Pangas* are the ubiquitous open launches, powered by outboard motor and sometimes featuring a sunshade and center console. If you see a *panga* with a newer four-stroke outboard, center console, sunshade, and mounted radio, jump in—you've got a winner. The fish don't care what kind of boat you're in, but the cruisers can handle the larger game fish and a nonfishing passenger in comfort.

Don't forget to pack a hat, sunglasses, sunscreen, water, food, waterproof camera, sandals, and a windbreaker. Take motion sickness medicine the night before and morning of the trip if you are prone to seasickness (or if you aren't sure).

All hotels in the *zona hotelera* can arrange guided fishing trips. Well-known **Francisco's Fleet** (formerly Victor's Sportfishing, toll-free U.S. tel. 800/521-2281, www.jigstop.com) is based at Palmilla Beach. A six-hour super-*panga* trip for two or three people costs US$195; bring your own food and drinks. **Gordo Banks Pangas** (Pueblo La Play, tel./fax 624/142-1147, toll-free U.S. tel. 800/408-1199, www.gordobanks.com) launches out of La Playita and rents 22-foot *pangas* for US$210 (six hours, 1–3 anglers) or 23-foot super-*pangas* for US$250 (six hours, 1–3 anglers) and cruisers for US$380–470. **Jaime Castro** (Pueblo La Playa, cell tel. 624/154-9110, U.S. tel. 858/922-3355, US$200–280 per boat) runs *panga* fishing charters by day and manages the kitchen at Buzzard's by night. Boats depart at 6 A.M. daily from B dock at the La Playita marina and return at noon. Bait, lunch, drinks, and fishing license cost extra. Reserve online.

There are a few extra costs to factor into the planning: Tips for the captain and fish-cleaning crew are the norm. Live bait is often not included in the cost of the *panga*, so expect to pay US$20 per boat. Fishing licenses cost US$8 a day or US$20 a week. You do not need a fishing license to fish from the shore. Licenses can be purchased online through the state tourism office at www2.ebajacalifornia. gob.mx/Pesca.

For tackle, bait, and fishing books, head to **Deportiva Piscis** (Castro and Green, San José del Cabo, 1 block south of the Mercado Municipal, tel. 624/142-0332, 8 A.M.–7 P.M. daily).

Snorkeling and Diving

San José visitors must head to the East Cape, the Corridor, or Cabo San Lucas for suitable snorkeling and diving sites. Expert divers who are comfortable in strong currents and choppy seas and interested in exploring the offshore Gordo Banks seamounts may be able to hire a *panga* from La Playita; however, be aware that even groups of experienced dive instructors have run into complications when attempting to turn an angler into a dive-boat captain for the day. The safer approach is to book a trip through one of the PADI-certified dive shops in Cabo San Lucas.

Surfing

Summer is the peak season for catching waves in Los Cabos, but good-sized swells occasionally roll through as late as mid-November. Playa Costa Azul has three of the best-known breaks anywhere in Southern Baja. Enter from a sandy beach but beware the rocks at low

tide. You can scope out the scene from a lookout on Mexico 1 before taking the plunge. Longboarders and beginner surfers favor the Playa Acapulquito (Old Man's) reef break, in front of the Cabo Surf Hotel. Directly below the lookout, The Rock is another right. Localism is alive and well at Zippers, but only when the waves are pounding. The rest of the time you can easily paddle out to enjoy this short and fast break. Just flash a smile and be prepared to wait your turn.

There are many lesser-known breaks along the Corridor that break on different sized swells, plus a handful of breaks on the East Cape.

EQUIPMENT

Several shops near San José rent boards and other equipment. The **Cabo Surf Shop** (Km. 28, Carr. Transp., San José del Cabo, tel. 624/172-6188, U.S. tel. 858/964-5117, www. cabosurfshop.com), located at the Cabo Surf Hotel, offers private or group instruction on Playa Acapulquito through the Mike Doyle Surf School (8 A.M.–6 P.M. daily, until 7 P.M. in summer, group rate US$70 pp for two hrs., private lessons US$95/hr.) as well as board rentals. Drop-ins are welcome. The **Costa Azul Surf Shop** (Km. 28, Carr. Transp., Plaza Costa Azul, San José del Cabo, tel. 624/142-2771, 8 A.M.–7 P.M. Mon.–Sat., 9 A.M.–5 P.M. Sun.) rents short boards, hybrids, and longboards to experienced surfers, as well as beginner boards with rubber fins, and offers lessons. Stop in for beach umbrellas, beach chairs, and snorkeling gear, too. You can also rent boards right on the beach, next to Zippers Restaurant.

Golf

Most of the now world-famous golf courses are located in the Corridor between San José and Cabo San Lucas; however San José proper has a few courses of its own. Centrally located in the hotel zone, the **Mayan Resorts Golf Course** (tel. 624/142-0905, US$130/18 holes) is a convenient and affordable option for beginners and intermediate players. Rates are considerably lower for resort guests (US$90).

Discounted twilight rates (US$70) begin at 2 P.M. The clubhouse is located on the south side of Mexico 1, between Paseo de los Cabos and Paseo Finisterra.

At Km. 119, **Club Campestre San Jose Golf** (tel. 624/173-9400) is an 18-hole, par-71 course designed by Jack Nicklaus. Nicklaus is also the mastermind behind the **Puerto Los Cabos Golf Club** (Paseo de los Pescadores, Pueblo La Playa, tel. 624/144-1200), an 18-hole, par-72 course.

Yoga

San José now has about a half dozen yoga studios, but some instructors seem to come and go each season. Caryl Leffel (tel. 624/137-3278, www.kaleidoscopeyoga.com, US$10–25 per class) teaches yoga classes in two locations: Cabo Danza (Plaza Tamarindo on Calle Gonzales, 7:45 A.M. and 6:20 P.M. Mon., Wed., Fri.), a private dance studio, and Laguna Hills (9 A.M. Tues. and Thurs.), on a beachfront terrace along the East Cape.

Spa Services

Ixchel Salon & Spa (Morelos 133, San José del Cabo, tel. 624/142-2330, www.elencantoinn.com/Spa/Archivos/Spa.html, 9 A.M.–8 P.M. Mon.–Sat., 10 A.M.–6 P.M. Sun.), inside the El Encanto Inn, offers a full menu of treatments, including massages (50 min. for US$70), facials (50 min. for US$80), manicures, and pedicures. In addition, the Hola Grand Faro, Grand Mayan, and other resorts have on-site spas that are open to the public.

Organized Tours

Most Los Cabos hotels have an activity desk with a binder full of brochures advertising guided tours, excursions, and recreational activities. You can choose from whale-watching cruises, snorkeling tours, ATV tours, horseback rides, sunset cruises, and more. Hotels generally do not charge an additional fee when they book these activities for their guests. A note for the environmentally aware: Ecotours have overtaken spas as the latest marketing tool for companies looking to earn a share of your tourist dollars. This means just about every operator will tell you they offer eco-something. This does not necessarily mean that every hotel and outfitter in business follows a safe and low-impact approach with their trips and has experienced guides who really understand the fragile Baja ecosystem. Do some homework before you book: Understand where the business buys its supplies, how it supports the local community, what materials it reuses and recycles, and what kind of training it requires of its guides. Emergency training and environmental education should be top considerations.

Here are a few of the larger and better-known outfitters:

Baja's Activities (Paseo del Malecón, San José del Cabo, tel. 624/142-2922, www.bajas-activities.com, 9 A.M.–6 P.M. daily) organizes horseback rides along the estuary and beach (US$35/hr., US$55/2 hrs.), snorkeling tours to Santa María Bay (US$35 pp), and ATV tours of the East Cape (US$65/single, US$85/double). **Rancho Tours** (tel. 624/143-5464, www.ranchotours.com) leads walking tours of La Paz and Todo Santos for US$65 per person, as well as glass-bottom boat tours and ATV rides near Cabo San Lucas.

Baja Wild Outfitters (tel. 624/172-6300, www.bajawild.com) leads a variety of adventure trips, including kayaking, snorkeling, surfing, hiking, ATV, Jeep safaris, whale-watching, and turtle-release programs. Half-day trips range US$70–85, and all-day trips are US$110–650, depending on the activity. Group and multi-sport packages are available.

Desertica (Km. 61.8, Carr. Transp., tel. 624/146-9601, www.desertica.com.mx, US$35) has brought its amusement-park style of outdoor entertainment to Baja, with canopy tours on eight different zip lines, plus trails for ATVs, buggies, and horses. Four-hour tours begin at 9 A.M., noon, and 3 P.M. daily (minimum age seven and maximum weight 250 pounds).

You can also tour the back roads of Baja in a fleet of Hummers with **Baja Outback** (tel. 624/142-9200, www.bajaoutback.com, US$135–183 pp). Single- and multiday tours go to Todos Santos, Santiago, Rancho La Verdad, and Rancho Antares (btw Cabo Pulmo and Los Frailes).

ENTERTAINMENT AND EVENTS
Bars and Nightclubs

San José nightlife is low-key compared to the famous clubs in Cabo San Lucas, where you can dance the night away, but there are a handful of places where you can enjoy a few drinks and listen to live music.

Enjoy a glass of wine and tapas on a second-story balcony overlooking the plaza at **La Internacional** (Plaza Mijares, near the fountain, noon–midnight Tues.–Sun.).

Baja Brewing Company (Morelos 1227, btw Comonfort/Obregón, San José del Cabo, tel. 624/146-9995, www.bajabrewingcompany.com, noon–2 A.M. daily, mains US$10–15) quickly became a popular watering hole when it opened next to Baan Thai in December 2007. As the only brewery in Baja California Sur, it crafts eight different artisanal beers, including a Baja Blonde and Cactus Wheat brew, and you'll find them on menus as far north as Loreto. Order a brew-tender and get five pints for the price of four, conveniently served from a mini-tap at your table. The brewery uses its barley, yeast, and beer to make a delicious pizza dough. Spicy chicken wings are another crowd pleaser.

Tropicana Bar and Grill (Mijares 30, San José del Cabo, tel. 624/142-1580, 8 A.M.–midnight Sun.–Thurs., till 2 A.M. Fri.–Sat.) has been a mainstay among gringos for many years. It plays regional Mexican music from 6:30 P.M. to 8:30 P.M. Wednesday–Monday.

Morgan's Restaurant and Cellar (Hidalgo and Doblado, San José del Cabo, tel. 624/142-3825, morgans@prodigy.net.mx, 6–11 P.M. daily) frequently has live jazz. Canadian-owned **Shooters Bar & Grill** (Doblado and Mijares, San José del Cabo, tel. 624/142-9900, lunch and dinner daily, bar open until 11 P.M. nightly, later on weekends), above Tulipán Restaurant,

is an open-air rooftop bar with seating in plastic chairs and usually jazz music.

The nautical theme is a bit cheesy and tunes are country oldies, but otherwise the **Cielito Lindo Sky Bar** (Paseo del Malecón, San José del Cabo, tel. 624/142-9292, 5–11 P.M. Tues.–Sun.), in the lighthouse tower of the Hola Grand Faro resort, is a great place to catch the sunset.

Behind the Mega shopping center, the **Baja Blue Bar and Grille** (formerly the Rusty Putter, Paseo del Malecón, San José del Cabo, tel. 624/142-4546, lunch and dinner daily, bar open until 11 P.M. nightly, later on weekends) is a large sports bar and restaurant with live music on weekends, plus satellite TV and an 18-hole miniature golf course.

Expats who live near Playa Costa Azul convene at **Deckman's at Havana** (Km. 29, Carr. Transp., tel. 624/142-2603, www.deckmans.com, breakfast–late night daily), on the north side of the highway, for nightly live jazz. Across the street and a little farther west, **Zippers** (Km. 28.5, Carr. Transp., tel. 624/172-6162, 11 A.M.–10 P.M. daily) plays oldies for the baby-boomer crowd on Friday and Saturday nights.

Festivals and Events

On weekend evenings during the high season, you can almost always find a fiesta in progress at Plaza Mijares, complete with music, dancing, cotton candy, mimes, and piñatas.

The weekly **Art Walk** on Thursday evenings (5–9 P.M.) has become a town-wide celebration during the high season, with wine and food served at many of the galleries. The streets close to traffic and Cuban dancers perform in front of the Centro Cultural. When the galleries close, the party moves to the Baja Brewing Company, which stays open late.

San José celebrates the **feast day of its patron saint** on March 19, a day of more music, dancing, food, games, and a parade.

On June 1, San José celebrates the annual **Día de la Marina,** a national day of honor for the Mexican navy, with great fanfare, including a fishing tournament, carnival, music, and even a greased pig.

SHOPPING

From souvenirs to collectible furnishings, you can find a little of everything along the streets of San José. And unlike in Cabo San Lucas, here you can browse at a leisurely pace without worrying about aggressive shop owners encouraging you to make a purchase.

Arts, Crafts, and Souvenirs

A handicraft market has opened on Boulevard Mijares near Plaza La Misión. About a dozen vendors sell reasonably priced arts and crafts, including hammocks, handmade toys for children, T-shirts, ceramics, sombreros, and more. Another handful of vendors sell inexpensive arts and crafts along the north side of Boulevard Mijares, between Calles Coronado and Juárez. These stands are open 11 A.M.–9 P.M. daily. For better selection and quality, at higher prices, check out the shops that are closer to Plaza Mijares and the art district.

Antigua Los Cabos (Mijares 5, San José del Cabo, tel. 624/146-9933, antiguabcs@yahoo.com) has some antiques as well as handmade rugs, folk art, ceramics, and tequilas. **Sol Dorado** (Mijares 33, across from the Tropicana, San José del Cabo, tel. 624/142-1950) is a multilevel store filled with ceramics, glassware, ironworks, mirrors, and furnishings. For large or fragile items, the store ships via DHL (fully insured). It will also deliver purchases to your hotel for US$10–85, depending on the location. The smaller **Mejicanisimo** (Zaragoza 8, San José del Cabo, tel. 624/142-3090, 9 A.M.–10 P.M. daily), next to the plaza, has much of the same.

Cinthya Castro stocks **El Armario** (corner of Morelos and Obregón, San José del Cabo, tel. 624/105-2989, elarmario@gmail.com, 10 A.M.–8 P.M. Mon.–Sat.) with an artistic mix of ceramics, paintings, locally made Baja Desert soaps, and other crafts made in Mexico.

Shop 12 Leather Factory (corner of Mijares and Coronado, no tel., 9 A.M.–8 P.M. daily) has been in business since 1927 with a large selection of leather goods, including purses, shoes, belts, and even shotgun cases.

Jewelry

Several stores sell high-quality Mexican fire opals and other gemstones. Ask to see the opals in natural light—the more "fire," the higher the price. If you don't see what you want, ask to see individual stones. Most stores offer 24-hour turnaround for custom settings, but don't plan your pickup time to the minute or you may be late to catch your flight home.

Martha Rodriguez at **El Rincón del Ópalo** jewelry factory (Mijares 6, San José del Cabo, tel. 624/142-2566, beltran_018@hotmail.com, 9 A.M.–9 P.M. Mon.–Sat., till 2 P.M. Sun.) can help you choose a stone and setting in a pleasant gallery off the main plaza. **Jewelry Factory** (Mijares 5, San José del Cabo, tel. 624/142-6394, 9 A.M.–8 P.M. daily), on the plaza next to Antigua Los Cabos, has some of the highest-quality jewels in town, and service to match. **La Mina** (Mijares 33, San José del Cabo, tel. 624/143-3747, lamina788@hotmail.com, 9 A.M.–8 P.M. daily) displays costume jewelry on the porous walls of a small cave and has a second location in Cabo San Lucas.

Fine Art

San José has a thriving art district that is home to about 20 galleries, many of them first-rate. Galleries tend to be run by expats, but the artists are a fairly even mix of Mexicans and foreigners. Run by a graduate of the Parsons School of Design in New York City and a full-time Los Cabos resident, the three-story **Galería de Ida Victoria** (Guerrero 1128, San José del Cabo, tel. 624/142-5772, www.idavictoriaarts.com, 10 A.M.–7 P.M. Mon.–Fri.) has been recognized as one of the finest art galleries south of Los Angeles. State-of-the-art lighting and hanging systems were custom designed to showcase paintings, photography, sculpture, and other works of art.

The **Old Town Gallery** (Obregón 20, San José del Cabo, tel. 624/142-3662, www.oldtowngallery.net, 10:30 A.M.–7:30 P.M. Mon.–Sat., till 9 P.M. Thurs.) displays works by contemporary Mexican, American, and Canadian artists. **Galería Arenas** (Obregón

© NIKKI GOTH ITOI

Vendors hope to catch the eye of the passersby.

10, San José del Cabo, vicjorge71@hotmail. com, 10 A.M.–2 P.M. and 4–8 P.M. Mon.–Sat.) has original Mexican pottery.

Amber Gallery (Obregón 18, San José del Cabo, tel. 624/105-2332, www.amberart.net, 10 A.M.–6 P.M. daily) features the work of artist Ronsai, who travels to Chiapas, where the gem is mined by hand, to select raw stones to make jewelry, sculptures, and perfume bottles. The most unusual part of his collection features perfectly preserved fossils of various flowers and insects such as cockroaches, crickets, spiders, and termites.

Home Decor

Second-home owners looking to furnish their new condos and villas with authentic Mexican design elements will find just about everything they need in San José. For a rustic look, head to **Galería Los Cabos** (Hidalgo north of Obregón, San José del Cabo, tel. 624/142-0044, 9 A.M.–8 P.M. Mon.–Fri.), which has some antiques as well as rattan pieces, and barrel-back chairs made by local craftsmen. **Casa Paulina**

(Morelos at the corner of Comonfort, San José del Cabo, tel. 624/142-5555), across from El Encanto Suites, is a beautiful store to browse, even if you aren't in the market to buy. It has wood and upholstered pieces as well as ceramics and other decorative items displayed on two levels. **Adobe Design** (Plaza San José, Km. 32, Carr. Transp., San José del Cabo, tel. 624/142-4281) carries furniture and interior design materials for both antique and modern home styles.

Sporting Goods

On the north side of Mexico 1 in a small shopping plaza, the **Costa Azul Surf Shop** (Km. 28, Carr. Transp., San José del Cabo, tel. 624/142-2771, www.costa-azul.com.mx, 8 A.M.–7 P.M. Mon.–Sat., 9 A.M.–5 P.M. Sun.) has board rentals and surf and snorkel maps. You can also have your board repaired after a rough day in the water.

The **Cabo Surf Shop** (Km. 28, Carr. Transp., San José del Cabo, tel. 624/178-6188, www.cabosurfshop.com, 8 A.M.–8 P.M. daily), located at the Cabo Surf Hotel, offers board rentals.

Deportiva Piscis (Castro, San José del Cabo, tel. 624/142-0332, 8 A.M.–7 P.M. daily), on the south side of Calle Castro near the Mercado Municipal, has fishing tackle, bait, and fishing-related books and gear.

Bookstores

The most comprehensive selection of English-language titles related to Baja California anywhere on the peninsula is to be found at **Baja Books and Maps** (Camino a La Playa, La Choya, tel. 624/165-5596, U.S. fax 415/962-0588, 9:30 A.M.–6 P.M. Mon.–Sat.) in the pueblo of La Choya on the way to La Playita. Owner Jim Tolbert is a distributor of English-language books to shops throughout the central and southern peninsula. He also sells inventory online at www.bajabooksandmaps.com. A true bibliophile, Jim is a wealth of information on all things Baja.

At the conveniently located **Spider Web** (tel. 624/105-2048, bajabookcenter@yahoo.com.mx, 9 A.M.–6 P.M. Mon.–Sat.), you can trade used paperback books and browse a limited selection of new titles. Used pocket fiction books cost US$3. There are a few PCs available for Internet access (US$4/hr.). The store is located on an alley just west of the Mega shopping plaza.

Deportiva Pisces (Castro, San José del Cabo, tel. 624/142-0332, 8 A.M.–7 P.M. daily) stocks a few books related to sportfishing, **El Armario** (corner of Morelos and Obregón, San José del Cabo, tel. 624/105-2989, elarmario@gmail.com, 10 A.M.–8 P.M. Mon.–Sat.) has a small selection of design books, and the gift shop at **Buzzard's** (Laguna Hills, U.S. tel. 951/302-1735, www.buzzardsbar.com) has a few books for sale as well.

ACCOMMODATIONS

Besides the major hotels and "condotels" in the *zona hotelera* along the beach, San José offers some smaller, reasonably priced inns in the town itself. A downtown location puts you close to shops and restaurants, with a short drive or long walk to the beach. Condos and hotels along Playa Azul are about a 5- to 10-minute drive from town, depending on traffic. Rates are given for double occupancy in the high season (holiday rates may be higher) and do not include 12 percent tax and 10 percent service charge, unless otherwise noted. Discounts may be available for stays of a week or longer.

Hotels in Town
UNDER US$50

Two budget hotels are located on Calle Zaragoza opposite the church. The accommodations are minimal and you'll hear noise from the street below, but the prices are about the lowest you'll find anywhere in town. Manager Señor Félix provides clean, if basic, accommodations at **Hotel Ceci** (Zaragoza 22, opposite the church, tel. 624/142-0051, US$35). It has 14 rooms with ceiling fans, air-conditioning, TV, and hot water. The rooms at **Hotel Diana** (Zaragoza 30, tel. 624/142-0490, US$30) also have air-conditioning, TV, and hot water.

Steps from Plaza Mijares, on the same block as the Casa de la Cultura, the charming **[Posada Yuca Inn** (Obregón 1A, tel. 624/142-0462, www.yucainn.com.mx, US$40–50) is something of a mix of a hostel, bed-and-breakfast, and motel. It has three simple hotel-style rooms, each with its own refrigerator, remote-control air-conditioning, and private bath. Additional bunk rooms offer even less-expensive hostel-style accommodations for US$16 per person and US$25 for two. The inn has its own water purification system, so you don't need to buy drinking water. Walk to the Organic Market on Saturday mornings and return to the inn to prepare your meal in the shared *cocina*. The owner, Rogelio Lopez, whose nickname is Yuca, grows Mexican oregano, epazote (used in enchilada sauce), and other herbs, as well as vegetables, in several raised beds in the courtyard of the inn; plus there are numerous fruit trees on the property—grapefruit, oranges, *guanabano,* and lemons. Guests are welcome to pick whatever is ripe. Amenities include a swimming pool, Wi-Fi, and parking at the backside of the building. The inn does not typically offer daily maid service but will change your towels as needed.

Next door, **Hotel Posada Señor Mañana**

(Obregón 1B, tel./fax 624/142-1372, US$40–70) has several rooms connected by a labyrinth of ramps and ladders. Each room has a ceiling fan and private bath with hot water.

US$50-100

One of the oldest hotels in town, **Hotel Colli** (Hidalgo btw Zaragoza/Doblado, tel. 624/142-0725, US$50) has a dozen small and clean rooms with simple furnishings, newly tiled baths, and hot water in a building just off the plaza. Its rooms come with ceiling fans, air-conditioning, and private baths. Bottled water is a plus, and the friendly service makes for a comfortable stay. As with any of the downtown hotels, noise is likely to be a minor nuisance at night, but all is usually quiet by about 11 P.M. There is secure parking under the hotel.

Many travelers enjoy the authentic Mexican surroundings and hospitality at **Hotel Posada Terranova** (on Degollado, just south of Zaragoza, tel. 624/142-0534, www.hterranova.com.mx, US$60), located between Plaza Mijares and the Mercado Municipal. Over the years this large residential property has been renovated to hold 29 guestrooms, each with two beds, air-conditioning, phone, and satellite TV. This hotel has a pleasant terrace and a dependable Mexican restaurant (7 A.M.–10 P.M. daily, mains US$10–15).

The **Best Western Hotel & Suites Las Palmas** (Km. 31, Carr. Transp., tel. 624/142-2131, www.suiteslaspalmas.com, US$85) makes a satisfactory stop for a night on your way in or out of the area. The pros: a friendly staff, reasonable rates, and the possibility of substantial discounts during peak travel times. Easy access to the more local eateries is another plus, and small kitchenettes mean you can stock up on groceries at the Mega the night before a drive to the East Cape. The cons: a front-row seat next to Highway 1 means the sound of traffic will lull you to sleep. Decor is about as basic as it gets. On a recent visit, the room and bath were clean enough, but they didn't exactly sparkle. Dishes in the cabinet were sticky, and the dish sponge had been recycled.

US$100-150

In the heart of San Jose's growing art district, **El Encanto Inn** (Morelos 133, tel. 624/142-0388, U.S. tel. 512/465-9751, www.elencantosuites.com, US$100–160) encompasses two buildings on Calle Morelos. Fluffy towels, king-size beds, and remote-control air-conditioning are a few of the special touches at the newer property, El Encanto Suites. The two-story hacienda surrounds a small swimming pool and courtyard. More economical standard and garden suites are in the original inn. Rooms here are popular with travelers who plan a one-night stopover before heading to or from the East Cape, but recent guests have complained about duplicate charges and other complications with advance reservation payments. A café near the pool serves breakfast and drinks, and you can park for free in a gated, but not guarded, lot across the street. The on-site Ixchel Salon & Spa offers manicures, pedicures, and massage treatments.

Behind the Tropicana Bar and Grill and set back from busy Boulevard Mijares, the **Tropicana Inn** (Mijares 30, tel. 624/142-1580, www.hoteltropicana.com, US$130–180) has 37 rooms and several suites set around a pleasant courtyard, with a fountain, heated swimming pool (a nice feature for winter stays), and several cages of tropical birds to greet you each day. Rooms and baths are on the small side and should be up for renovation soon, but all the standard amenities are there: phones, air-conditioning, Wi-Fi, small fridge, coffeemaker, and satellite TV. Rooms on the ground level tend to be noisy as other guests pass by or linger by the pool. Inquire whether the multi-course continental breakfast is included with your rate—it's a pretty good deal. The inn has a spa with a full menu of treatments.

OVER US$250

Internationally acclaimed **C Casa Natalia** (Mijares 4, tel. 624/142-5100 or 888/277-3814, www.casanatalia.com, US$150–335) sets the standard for luxury boutique hotel accommodations in Los Cabos. It has become a favorite venue for small weddings and the honeymoon suite at the Tropicana Inn

other formal celebrations. Its 14 rooms and two suites are designed with a contemporary, European flair, including original artwork. Private (though extremely small) terraces with hammocks face a heated swimming pool. And the attached Mi Cocina restaurant (6:30–10 P.M. daily, mains US$18–32), run by owner Natalie Tenoux's husband, Loïc Tenoux, is just steps away. This is not the place for children under the age of 13.

Beach Hotels

Occupancy rates for the hotels along Playa Hotelera have been climbing in recent years to match those of their busier Cabo San Lucas peers, though you may still be able to negotiate a deal during off-peak seasons. Whether you choose a hotel or condo, beware that demolitions, renovations, and new construction are in progress all over this area, even during the peak travel season. There's a good chance you'll end up next to, above, or below a noisy construction zone. The hammering, sawing, and drilling typically begins at 8:30 A.M. and lasts till 5:30 P.M. Do your homework before you book.

OVER US$250

Situated between the Desire and Posada Real resorts along the Zona Hotelera, **Barceló Los Cabos** (formerly The Grand Baja, Paseo del Malecón 5D, tel. 624/146-7500, toll-free U.S. tel. 800/227-2356, www.barcelo.com, US$250 and up) has one-, two-, and three-bedroom suites and was under renovation by a new owner, Spain-based Barceló, in 2009.

At the far northeastern end of the *zona hotelera,* next to the Estero San José, the 400-room **Presidente InterContinental Los Cabos Resort** (Paseo del Malecón, tel. 624/142-0211, toll-free U.S. tel. 888/567-8725, www.ichotelsgroup.com, US$290–425) serves some of the best meals around for all-inclusive package guests.

ALL-INCLUSIVE RESORTS

Rooms at the Best Western **Hotel Posada Real Los Cabos** (Paseo del Malecón, tel.

624/142-0155, toll-free U.S. tel. 800/528-1234, www.posadareal.com.mx, US$120–210 pp) are among the better-value all-inclusive options. They come with air-conditioning, phone, and satellite TV. The property has a pool with two hot tubs and swim-up bar, plus its own restaurant. Most rooms have views of the ocean, too. Rates cover meals, drinks, tips, and tax.

Next door, the **Hola Grand Faro Los Cabos** (formerly Crowne Plaza Los Cabos, Paseo del Malecón, tel. 624/142-9292, toll-free U.S. tel. 866/365-6932, www.cploscabos.com, US$220 pp and up) is one of few resorts in Los Cabos where you can enjoy a stay free of condo sales pitches, as the property does not have timeshares on-site. Large guestroom terraces and a saltwater infinity pool are two more distinguishing features. Children aged four and up can play in the kids' club while adults relax by the pool. Meals are standard resort buffets, served in several on-site restaurants. High-speed Internet access costs US$15 per day. The on-site Natura Room offers a full menu of massage, body, and facial treatments (US$90–110 for 50 minutes). The resort offers free and secure parking underground.

On the northeast side of the Crowne Plaza, the **Royal Solaris Los Cabos Hotel** (Paseo del Malecón Lte. 10, Zona Hotelera, tel. 624/145-6800, toll-free U.S. tel. 866/289-8466, www.clubsolaris.com, US$145–175 pp) has a water park for kids and serves a breakfast that's popular among resort-goers. Most of its 389 rooms have ocean views. Entertainment options include a Tehuacan dinner theater show. A free snorkeling tour comes with a stay of six nights or more.

Clothing is optional at **Desire Resort & Spa Los Cabos** (formerly the Fiesta Inn, Paseo del Malecón, tel. 624/142-9300, toll-free U.S. tel. 888/201-7551, toll-free Can. tel. 800/655-9311, www.desireresorts.com, US$170 pp and up). Reactions ranged from shock to awe when this couples-only establishment opened in 2006, catering to upscale, "liberated" adults. A red and dark brown

ALL-INCLUSIVE RESORTS

If making decisions about food adds stress to your vacation experience, look for a rate plan that includes meals, activities, and entertainment. The following resorts offer all-inclusive packages:

SAN JOSÉ DEL CABO

- Hola Grand Faro Los Cabos – Business conventions
- Presidente InterContinental Los Cabos Resort – Good variety and quality of food
- Hotel Posada Real Los Cabos – Good deal for the money
- Royal Solaris Los Cabos Hotel – Families with young kids
- Desire Resort & Spa Los Cabos – Clothing optional

THE CORRIDOR

- Dreams Los Cabos Suites Golf Resort & Spa – Weddings, honeymoons, anniversaries
- Meliá Cabo Real – Safe swimming beach

CABO SAN LUCAS

- Riu Palace Cabo San Lucas – Largest of the all-inclusive set, with 642 guest rooms
- Wyndham Cabo San Lucas Resort – College students on spring break

Delfin Hotels & Resorts maintains a current list of all-inclusive resorts in the Los Cabos area at www.allinclusivescabo.com.

color scheme with hand-painted murals of scenes from the *Book of Kama Sutra* set the mood. A clothing-optional pool and whirlpool tub, L'Alternative Disco, and Sensuous Playroom take it over the top. The resort's 150 rooms and suites have king-size beds and flatscreen TVs, among a complete list of standard amenities. From the beach, curious onlookers can recognize the resort by shoulder-height bamboo screens on the terraces that allow for private sunbathing.

The **Grand Mayan Los Cabos** (Paseo del Malecón, toll-free U.S. tel. 866/802-0674, www.mexicomayanresorts.com/thegrandmayan/los-cabos/index.php, US$155 and up), which opened in 2007, has a stunning reception area and offers a Wednesday-evening Mayan dinner theater performance.

Pueblo La Playa and La Playita
US$50-100

At **El Delfín Blanco** (Delfínes, Pueblo La Playa, tel. 624/142-1212, tel./fax 624/142-1199, www.eldelfinblanco.net, US$50–80), Osa Franzen maintains several clean cabanas that are situated about 300 meters from the beach with views of the water. The place attracts independent travelers who seek an authentic Mexican experience as well as a good value in accommodations. You may hear the wind rustling through palm-thatched roofs and dogs barking at night, but you'll also be steps away from the new marina and park at La Playita. Walk to several restaurants or shop in town and cook your own meals in the shared outdoor kitchen.

About 6.5 kilometers past La Playita and Puerto Los Cabos, on the coastal road that hugs the East Cape, 【 **La Fonda del Mar Bed and Breakfast** (Laguna Hills, U.S. tel. 951/302-1735, www.buzzardsbar.com, US$75–95) has three rooms with *palapa* roofs, American-style beds, and tile floors. Each has its own half bath but shares a shower. For families, there is a larger suite with a pullout couch and private bath. Guests may order anything off the Buzzard's menu for breakfast, including the famed eggs Benedict on Sundays. The inn is situated almost on the beach, and it's a very short walk along an arroyo to the water's edge. To find La Fonda del Mar, follow the road to La Playita, turn left at the first traffic circle, and go about 6.5 kilometers, following signs for Laguna Hills and El Encanto. The inn changed hands in 2010 and is now under Canadian ownership.

Just steps from the new *panga* marina, **La Marina Inn** (formerly La Playita Inn, Pueblo La Playa, tel./fax 624/142-4166, US$60–100) has managed to stay its course through all the development and change around it. This three-story Mexican-style inn is a good choice if you are planning to fish or simply want to stay away from the hustle and bustle of downtown San José. Its air-conditioned rooms each have large showers and two queen beds. There is a small pool and an authentic Mexican seafood restaurant, La Marina.

Condominiums and Condo Hotels

Condominium complexes are sprouting up on the outskirts of San José as fast as all-inclusive resorts. Las Olas (closest to the lookout point at Zippers surf break), El Zalate (next to the Coral Baja timeshare resort), and Sampiguita (closer to the hotel zone) are just a few of the more recent properties to open. Owners rent vacant units to visitors for anywhere from US$120 a night for a studio or one-bedroom to around US$450 or more for a deluxe two- or three-bedroom unit. Rates can vary quite a bit even within the same complex, depending on location and views and how the unit is furnished. Be sure to inquire how close the unit is to the highway and whether there is construction underway inside the building. At Mykonos and other complexes nearby, the persistent sound of heavy traffic on Mexico 1 can drown out the sound of waves crashing onto the beach. Discounted weekly and monthly rates are sometimes available.

The payment process for a condo is different from reserving a hotel room: Property managers typically require a deposit of 50 percent of the rental fee by check or direct deposit to a U.S. bank account and the remaining amount by cash upon arrival. Cleaning fees are often added to the rental fee. Sometimes full payment is required before arrival—all the more reason to get the information you need before committing to a particular unit.

Mediterranean-inspired **Mykonos Bay Resort** (Km. 29, tel. 624/142-3789, one-bedroom US$130–290) rents one- and two-bedroom condos in three buildings, each with air-conditioning, satellite TV, kitchen, and washer/dryer. Amenities include a basic gym and lighted tennis court. Buildings B and C have larger units and are closest to the beach and quieter than Building A, which has smaller units and picks up more noise from the highway.

Within walking distance of the Mega shopping plaza as well as the beach, the sprawling **C Las Mañanitas** complex has some of the nicest condos around for US$225–475 per night. Next door, **Sampaguita Luxury Townhouse/Condominiums** is newer and smaller, with only 14 units in a quiet, gated complex that has a pool, hot tub, and tennis court. Two-bedroom units run about US$200–300 per night. To inquire about these properties you need to contact the individual owners through www.vrbo.com, www.craigslist.org, a booking service, or property management company.

Booking Services and Property Management Companies

Baja Properties (Doblado and Morelos, tel. 624/142-0988, toll-free U.S. tel. 877/462-2226, www.bajaproperties.com) manages one-, two-, and three-bedroom rentals in Las Mañanitas for US$250–525 per night as well as a few less expensive locations. **Nash Group Properties** (Paseo Finisterra #107, www.baja-holidays.com), run by the owners of the Casa del Jardín B&B, manages several rental properties in Mykonos, Las Olas, and a few other complexes. **SeaSide Vacations** (tel. 624/142-3789, Canada tel. 604/484-8488, www.sea-side.com) has a variety of units in several buildings in the area.

FOOD

For many travelers, San José del Cabo has become a culinary destination. Renowned chefs from Baja, mainland Mexico, and the United States are using local foods and, in many cases, organic ingredients to prepare creative interpretations of traditional Mexican cuisine. From the organic farmers market to fresh tortillas

and carnitas by the kilo, you can find it all in and around the streets of San José.

Traditional and Contemporary Mexican

San José del Cabo is the epicenter of a culinary trend in Baja called *alta cocina mexicana,* or gourmet interpretations of traditional Mexican dishes. One of the trailblazers in this category was **Tequila Restaurant** (Doblado 1011, west of Mijares, tel. 624/142-1155, www.tequilares-taurant.com, dinner daily, mains US$20 and up). The setting is cozy, and the menu suggests Asian, Mexican, and Mediterranean influences. The restaurant cooks with organic produce, and the tequila menu is, of course, top-notch.

A member of the Slow Food movement emphasizing locally grown and prepared foods, **C Don Emiliano** (Mijares 27, tel. 624/142-0266, 6–11 p.m. daily, mains US$20–36) is run by a well-known chef from Mexico City, Margarita C. de Salinas. Try the six-course tasting menu paired with Mexican wines or order à la carte. European-inspired **Mi Cocina** (Mijares 4, tel. 624/146-7100, 6–11 p.m. daily, mains US$20–30), inside Casa Natalia, serves creative fare at high prices in an intimate and contemporary garden setting.

Next to the plaza, **La Panga Antigua** (Zaragoza 20, tel. 624/142-4041, www.lapanga.com, lunch and dinner daily, mains US$20) offers colonial ambience, with a courtyard, lounge bar, and wine cellar. A menu of contemporary Mexican cuisine with a focus on seafood is prepared by a chef who is a graduate of the Culinary Institute of America.

Chilies in all their forms take center stage at **El Chilar** (Juárez 1497 at Morelos, tel. 624/142-2544, 3–10 p.m. Mon.–Sat., mains US$10–30). An Oaxacan chef prepares an ever-changing menu of Mexican specialties at this small restaurant located near the Telmex tower. Cash only.

In the art district, **Restaurant Bar Jazmín** (Zaragoza and Obregón, tel. 624/142-1760, 7 a.m.–10 p.m. daily, mains US$13–40) serves *huachinango* (whole red snapper) and *carne* *asada a la tampiqueña* on sizzling hot platters. The atmosphere is casual, and the menu includes *licuado* and *chilaquiles* for breakfast and *tortas,* tacos, and fajitas for lunch and dinner. Credit cards, including American Express, are accepted.

If you don't mind the strip-mall setting, **Habañeros Gastro Grill and Tequila Bar** (Mijares in Plaza La Misión, tel. 624/142-2626, www.habanerosgastrogrill.com, 11 A.M.–10 P.M. Mon.–Sat., lunch mains US$7–15, dinner mains US$10–30) has some creative Mexican fusion dishes in store. Try the chipotle tequila BBQ baby back ribs or Cajun filet mignon with grilled prickly pear ratatouille. The Shrimp Extravaganza consists of seven different preparations, including coconut, Parmesan, gingered tequila tamarind, and "frazzled." The Sushizza blends the flavors of sushi rice, cream cheese, and tamarind. Choose from 100 different kinds of tequila to go with your meal.

Another art district option for straightforward Mexican is **Salsita Cocina y Cantina** (Obregón 1732, tel. 624/142-6787, www.salsitascocinaycantina.com, 7:30 A.M.–11 P.M. daily, mains US$10–20), in a pretty aqua and white building just behind the plaza and a block from the Cultural Center. Order shrimp tacos, tamales, enchiladas, *carne en su jugo* (beef slow-cooked in its juice), *clamatos,* and chiles rellenos. In the same vicinity, a long-popular Cabo San Lucas restaurant, **Mi Casa** (Obregón 19, tel. 624/146-9263, www.micasarestaurant.com, mains US$20) has expanded with a second location in San José. Start with stuffed clams or the traditional tortilla soup and then move on to *cochinita pibil* or the signature El Mole Poblano.

First-time visitors to San José del Cabo often grab a sidewalk table at the **Tropicana Bar and Grill** (Mijares 30, tel. 624/142-1580, 8 A.M.–10:30 P.M. daily, mains US$10–23) for their first meal. They can take in the scene on Boulevard Mijares as they down their first *limonada,* cerveza, or margarita. Inside and in the garden dining area behind the building, a regular clientele visits the restaurant for American-style fare and nightly live music

and dancing. The menu is vast; the prices are for tourists.

Breakfast is a good value at the understated **Posada Terranova** (Degollado, south of Zaragoza, tel. 624/142-0534, 7 A.M.–10 P.M. daily, mains US$5–18), a family-run restaurant inside the hotel of the same name. It has indoor and outdoor tables, and the menu covers all the basics of Mexican food.

◖ Mariscos Mazatlán II (Km. 35, Mexico 1, tel. 624/143-8565, lunch and dinner daily, mains US$10–14), near Soriana on the way to the airport, is a favorite among expats for fresh fish at reasonable prices in a non-touristy atmosphere. Look for an orange and blue *palapa*-roof building with outdoor seating on the west side of Mexico 1. There is also a sister location in Cabo San Lucas.

American and International

El Tulipán (The Tulip Tree, Doblado at Mijares, tel. 624/146-9900, lunch and dinner daily, mains US$10–20), below Shooter's Bar, serves casual fare such as burgers, steaks, salads, and pasta dishes. Booth seating and the varied menu make it a good place for young kids.

Regulars praise the lamb dishes at **Baan Thai** (Morelos and Comonfort, tel. 624/142-3344, noon–10:30 P.M. daily, mains US$10–25). You can also order pad thai, wok-tossed salmon, and an assortment of curries. In business for many years, this restaurant draws patrons from the East Cape and beyond for a refreshing change from everyday Mexican cooking.

Dinner at **Morgan's Restaurant and Cellar** (Hidalgo and Doblado, tel. 624/143-3825, morgans@prodigy.net.mx, 6 P.M.–midnight daily, dinner till 10 P.M. only, closed Sept., mains US$20 and up) begins with a basket of homemade bread. A variety of wines from around the world complement the menu of Mediterranean entrées. **Morgan's Encore** (Morelos and Obregón, tel. 624/142-4727, 6 P.M.–midnight daily, dinner till 10 P.M. only, closed Sept., mains US$20–40), near the El Encanto Inn, can accommodate large groups in its main open-air dining area. The menu includes seared scallops, grilled fish, shrimp fettuccine, and spaghetti and meatballs. This is also the kind of place where you might happily order a couple of the creative starters for your main meal.

In a relatively new plaza behind the Casa Paulina interior design store, **Voila! Bistro** (Plaza Paulina on Morelos and Comonfort, tel. 624/130-7569, www.voila-events.com, lunch and dinner daily, mains US$10–30) serves a few wines by the glass as well as soup, salads, and entrées like rib-eye steak.

You can watch the staff make your personal, thin-crust pizza from a patio table at **La Dolce Ristorante Italiano & Pizzeria** (Plaza Mijares, Hidalgo and Zaragoza, tel. 624/142-6621, 2–11 P.M. daily, mains US$10–20). The menu includes bruschetta to start and tiramisu to finish.

Every table seems to have its own private corner at elegant **Local Eight** (Plaza la Misión, Mijares, tel. 624/142-6655, www.localeight.com, dinner daily, mains US$15–25), where you dine in a second-story garden terrace located about midway between downtown and the hotel zone. Mediterranean loosely defines the cuisine, but flavors come from all over the world, with entrées ranging from Arabian snapper to gazpacho to pork tenderloin served with a tamarind sauce and fried plantains. An extensive wine list features bottles from Mexico, Chile, California, France, and Germany. Sink into the comfortable cushions, admire the unusual colored lights, and enjoy the relaxed ambience for the evening.

In Plaza La Misión, chef/owner Pasquale Matero and his wife, Alicia, serve thin-crust pizza, osso buco, and other Italian delights at **Pasquales Pizzeria and Ristorante** (Plaza La Misión, Loc. 6, tel. 624/142-0496, www.pasqualescabo.com, noon–11 P.M. Mon.–Fri., 2–11 P.M. Sat.–Sun., mains US$9–18).

Many restaurants in San José serve excellent seafood. **Pier 19 Seafood & Bar** (Zaragoza s/n btw Morelos/Guerrero, tel. 624/130-7453, 11 A.M.–5 P.M. lunch, 6–11 P.M. dinner) is one of only a few that stakes its reputation on it. The owners were brave enough to open during the depths of the global recession. The raw

oyster bar is reason enough to give it a try. Live music plays on Wednesday nights.

New American and contemporary Mexican themes shape the menu at **H Restaurant** (Obregón 1505, tel. 624/105-2974, www.hrestaurant.com.mx), located in a two-story colonial in the Historic Art District. That translates into starters such as tortilla chowder *gratinada* and entrées such as seafood cannelloni and flounder encrusted in sunflower seeds. Chef Luis Herrera Thatcher is originally from Mexico City, trained at the prestigious Culinary Institute of America in Hyde Park, New York, and has recent experience as executive chef at Club Golf de Querencia and the Club Ninety Six beach club.

Taquerias and Street Food

Cheap eats are clustered around the Mercado Municipal and close to the highway, near Calle Doblado. Try any of the *loncherías* near the market (6 A.M.–6 P.M. Mon.–Sat., 6 A.M.–4 P.M. Sun.). Or order *tortas* and *comida corrida* at **Mi Cocinita** (Gonzales, south of the 1 de Mayo bakery, tel. 624/142-6660, 8 A.M.–5 P.M. Mon.–Sat., mains US$5), a cute place with plastic tables and floral tablecloths. The staff here speaks English. At **Taquería Erika** (Doblado at Mexico 1, no tel., lunch and dinner daily), where two *tacos al pastor* cost about US$2.50. Longtime favorite **Taquería Rossy** (tel. 624/145-6755, tacos US$1) is on the other side of Mexico 1, near the light for Calle Pescador.

Adventurous eaters should head to **Taquería El Ahorcado** (Pescadores and Marinos, tel. 624/172-2093, 6 P.M.–midnight Tues.–Sun., mains US$5–10), in the Chamizal neighborhood across Mexico 1, for beef-tongue tacos and a full menu of creative quesadillas. It's known among gringos as The Hangman and is famous for its eclectic decor. Bring your own beer and enjoy live music while you dine.

In the same neighborhood, **Guacamaya** (no tel., dinner daily, mains US$8–12), off Calle Doblado, on the north side of Mexico 1, is under new ownership. Hopefully, its mouthwatering *tacos al pastor,* carved from a rotisserie spit and served with the signature toss of a pineapple slice, will stay just the same. Huge stone bowls filled with flank steak and avocado were a super deal for about US$7.

Near the bus terminal, **Taquería México** (González s/n at Profesores, Col. 1 de Mayo, tel. 624/128-8953, 1 P.M.–close Mon.–Fri., 4 P.M.–close Sat.–Sun., mains US$4–12) draws a crowd of local gringos for lunch under a large *palapa* roof with at least a dozen ceiling fans that keep the air moving on warm days. Sit at plastic tables and chairs beside a busy street and order a plate of tacos or a super burrito, Mexican-style hamburger, *papas rellenas,* or an entire *huachinango* (red snapper). This restaurant has a few large round tables that work well for a large group.

When the sun goes down, a handful of street carts roll onto Plaza Mijares. The longest line tends to form at ◖ **Tamales Doña Nina.** Order them *de pollo* with *salsa verde* or *de rajas* (chile) with cheese. Don't miss the sweet rice for dessert. Empanadas, tacos, and cups of *elote* (corn kernels) dusted with chili powder and a squeeze of lime are also popular evening fare.

Breakfast and Cafés

It's hard to resist the strong coffee and sweet pastries once you've discovered the **French Riviera** (corner of Hidalgo and Doblado, tel. 624/142-3350, www.frenchrivieraloscabos. com, 8 A.M.–11 P.M. daily, breakfast mains US$5–10, lunch mains US$10–15). Order to go from the counter or grab a table for a full breakfast. Early risers note: Though the posted hours say the place opens at 7:30 A.M. and the staff will let you wander in and take a seat, you likely won't get served even a cup of coffee until they are fully ready, closer to 8 A.M.

In the art district, **Casa Dahlia Gallery** (Morelos btw Obregón/Zaragoza, tel. 624/142-2129, www.casadahlia.com, 10 A.M.–3 P.M. and 6–9 P.M. Mon.–Fri., 10 A.M.–3 P.M. Sat.) serves coffee and tea in a pleasant garden behind a 100-year-old adobe building and has wireless Internet.

Next to the store of the same name, **El Armario Café** (corner of Morelos and Obregón, San José del Cabo, tel. 624/105-2989, elarmario@gmail.com, 10 A.M.–8 P.M. Mon.–Sat.) offers reasonably priced light fare such as yogurt with fresh fruit and granola for US$2 and a baguette sandwich with chips and *limonada* for US$5.

Mi Ensalada is a corner café at the end of Plaza La Misión on Boulevard Mijares. Sit inside or out on the shaded patio while you enjoy a latte and update your Facebook wall.

La Michoacana, on Zaragoza opposite the church, is the place to go for *paletas* and other frozen treats. There is another location on Doblado at the intersection with the highway.

Groceries

These days, the best place to stock up on food and other supplies is the **Mega** supermarket (tel. 624/142-4524), at the intersection of Paseo Los Cabos and Mexico 1. Choose from a full array of Mexican and American brands, decent produce, and a wide selection of cheeses and meats. There is a well-stocked pharmacy, and those traveling with youngsters will find all manner of supplies, from pacifiers to bouncy seats. In the adjoining plaza are a Telcel store, surf shop, public restrooms, and numerous fast-food options. Beware the timeshare reps who pose as grocery store clerks and offer to help you find your way around the store.

For a more authentic shopping experience, the small **Mercado Municipal** (no tel., dawn to dusk daily) between Calles Castro and Coronado in the west part of town, has separate stands for meat, fish, produce, and crafts. There is a *tortillería* that makes corn tortillas next door on Calle Castro (no tel., opens daily at 5 A.M.) and another that makes flour tortillas across the street.

A half kilometer north of town on the east side of Mexico 1, **Soriana** (tel. 624/142-6132) is a Walmart-style store with everything from beach towels to deli meats. If you are heading directly to the East Cape, this is a good place to stock up on supplies for the week.

On Calle Gonzalez, near the Corona supermarket and down the street from the bus terminal, **Panadería 1 de Mayo** (no tel.) has freshly baked breads and pastries with the usual tray-and-tong service.

If you're in town on a Saturday, head to the **Organic Market** (Huerta Maria, Camino a las Animas, 9 A.M.–3 P.M. Sat.), which draws some 50 vendors, many from as far away as La Paz and Todos Santos. They gather at a site located off the road to La Playita. In addition to fresh produce, you can buy cheese, ice cream, bread, books, and leather goods. There is usually music and rotating themes such as alternative medicine and ecofriendly living. Look for a sign and dirt trail on Avenida Centenario, behind the Yuca Inn. It's about a five-minute walk from the plaza.

Pueblo La Playa and La Playita

On the road to La Playita, near the sportfishing *panga* area, **Tommy's Barefoot Cantina** (tel. 624/142-3774, www.tommysbarefootcantina.com, noon–10 P.M. Thurs.–Tues., mains US$7–30) is owned by the gregarious TJ, originally from the San Francisco Bay Area; he entertains a well-heeled clientele with a slice of the old Baja. The menu consists of fresh seafood, American-style beef, and a variety of Mexican staples. This is a good place to go in the afternoon, when the fishing boats return with their catch. There is also live music and dancing on the weekends during the high season.

The friendly husband-and-wife team that previously ran Mariscos El Puerto has moved a few doors closer to the beach to open **La Marina Restaurant** (hotel tel. 624/142-4166, 9 A.M.–5 P.M. Tues.–Sun., mains US$5–10). The same colorful checked tablecloths are now clustered on a shaded patio next to the La Marina Inn lobby. Ceiling fans keep the air moving on hot afternoons. On a recent visit, the wahoo filet was extremely overcooked, but the *arranchera* tacos, served with the same signature tray of fresh condiments, were fantastic. The restaurant and hotel are located across from the *panga* marina, next to Tommy's.

For a quick bite to eat in La Playita, order a *torta* or some tacos at **La Pasadita** (no tel., mains US$3–5), next to Lilly's salon on the way to the beach. The decor is barebones—a *palapa* roof with a dirt floor and live chickens running about—but the food is tasty and cheap. La Pasadita is open for dinner only, and days vary; if you see the sand in front of the restaurant hosed down, that's a likely sign it will be open for business that evening.

At the main Puerto Los Cabos Marina (not to be confused with the *panga* fishing area at La Playita) **The Container Bar-Restaurant** (tel. 624/105-6211, 8 A.M.–9 P.M. Tues.–Sun., mains US$3–7) is a refurbished shipping container with a wooden deck that is perched on a hillside with nice views of the marina below. It has a full bar, and margaritas cost US$8. Prices are in U.S. dollars. Follow Boulevard Juárez over the bridge and take the first right turn into the marina and stay on this dirt road up and over the hill until you see the marina and restaurant on your left.

Beyond Puerto Los Cabos on the lower part of the East Cape, **Buzzard's Bar and Grill** (Laguna Hills, U.S. tel. 951/302-1735, www.buzzardsbar.com, 8 A.M.–8:30 P.M. Mon.–Sat., 9 A.M.–2:30 P.M. Sun., mains US$10–20) makes a tasty platter of coconut shrimp as well as a popular eggs Benedict for Sunday brunch. Dinner entrées are served all day, but the side dishes may not be ready until 5:30 P.M. To find Buzzard's from downtown San José del Cabo, follow the road to La Playita and turn left at the first traffic circle, following the coastal road (it reaches the coast at Buzzard's) and signs for Laguna Hills.

Playa Costa Azul

For casual, beachfront dining, head to **Zippers** (Km. 28.5, tel. 624/172-6162, 11 A.M.–10 P.M. daily, mains US$10–20), where you can watch surfers try to catch the waves out front while you dine under the shade of a *palapa* roof. The menu is a mix of Mexican and pub fare. Cash only.

Mama Mia, at the Worldmark Coral Baja resort (Km. 29.4, tel. 624/142-3939, lunch and dinner daily, mains US$7–14) offers casual beachfront dining with friendly and attentive service. Juicy burgers come with grilled onions and lots of pickles. Chicken fajitas are accompanied by the requisite basket of warm tortillas and a healthy serving of guacamole. The menu features many organic ingredients.

INFORMATION AND SERVICES
Tourist Assistance
The Baja Sur **state tourism office** (tel. 624/146-9628, www.loscabos.gob.mx) is located in Plaza San José (Loc. 3&4) on Mexico 1, near the intersection of Calle Valerio González Canseco.

Money
There are now ATMs aplenty in San José, with numerous options downtown, behind the Mega, and in several plazas in between. Several scams have been reported recently at ATMs in the supermarkets and other non-bank locations. It's safer to withdraw your pesos at an official branch location.

Post and Telephone
The *correos* (post office, 8 A.M.–5 P.M. Mon.–Fri.) has moved to the new Plaza Cabo Ley (Paseo de los Misiones) on the west side of Mexico 1. **Mail Boxes Etc.** has a local branch in Plaza Las Palmas on Mexico 1 (Km. 31, tel. 624/142-4355, fax 624/142-4360).

You can place long-distance phone calls from the **public telephone office** on Calle Doblado, across from the hospital, but there are also numerous Ladatel booths downtown. The pharmacy counter of the Mega supermarket sells Ladatel phone cards, as does Deckman's, at Havana near Plaza Costa Azul. You can use a Skype account from most of the Internet cafés around town; some also allow you to plug in your own computer and VoIP headset. There is a Telcel shop in the Mega grocery store plaza and another on Zaragoza, across from the plaza.

Internet Access
Next to the Mega shopping center, on an alley just off Mexico 1, **Spider Web** (tel. 624/105-2048) has a few computers connected to the Internet. Rates are US$1 for 15 minutes, or

---

SAN JOSÉ DEL CABO PHONE NUMBERS

- San José del Cabo Area Code: 624
- Police (emergency): 060
- Red Cross: 065 or 624/142-0316
- AmeriMed: 105-8550
- Fire Department: 142-2466
- General Hospital: 142-0180 or 142-1681
- Tourism Office: 142-3310, turismolosca-bos@gmail.com

US$4 per hour. Most people use Wi-Fi at their hotel or a nearby café.

Medical Services
For emergencies, dial 066. The main *centro de salud* (hospital, tel. 624/142-2770) is located on Calle Doblado between Colegio Militar and Márquez de Leon.

An AmeriMed hospital has opened in Plaza Cabo Ley (Paseo de los Misiones s/n, tel. 624/105-8550, 24 hrs.). For medical assistance, visit the **Walk-in MediClinic** (Km. 28, tel. 624/130-7011) in the El Zalate Plaza on Mexico 1. The facility has an emergency room, lab, pharmacy, and ambulance. Two other options are **BlueMedicalNet** (tel. 624/104-3911), which operates a clinic in the Plaza Misión, next to HSBC Bank, and **Médica Los Cabos** (Zaragoza 128, tel. 624/142-2770), near the Pemex station. All will respond to emergencies 24/7.

Laundry
Blue Lavandería, on Calle Obregón, near Morgan's Encore, is a full-service laundry open 8 A.M.–9 P.M. Monday–Saturday and 8 A.M.–3 P.M. Sunday. A small load costs about US$5. Other laundry options are located near the Mercado Municipal

(tel. 624/130-7979, 8:30 A.M.–12:30 P.M. and 2:30–7 P.M. daily, US$5 wash and dry) and on Calle Green, near the art district (8 A.M.–8 P.M. daily, US$2 per load).

RV Service and Supplies

Those who drive their own home on wheels depend on **Wahoo RV Center** (Calle Misión de Mulegé, tel./fax 624/142-3792, www.wahoorv.com, 8 A.M.–1 P.M. and 2:30–6 P.M. Mon.–Fri., 8 A.M.–1 P.M. Sat.), near the CFE electric utility office in Colonia Chula Vista, off Mexico 1 (turn west btw the Super Pollo and the turnoff for the Pemex station), for RV parts and accessories as well as maintenance and repair services. It has Direct TV satellite dishes and a dump station.

Canadian Consulate

The office of the Canadian consulate is on the second floor of Plaza José Green (Mijares near Juárez, tel. 624/142-4333, www.loscabos@canada.org.mx, 9 A.M.–1 P.M. Mon.–Fri.).

Veterinarians

San José has a number of respected veterinarians, should your pet need attention during your travels. One is usually available at the **Chiapas feed store** (Prolongacion Ave. Providencia, tel. 624/142-1095). **Veterinaria las Palmas Felipe Martinez** (Km. 32.5, Mexico 1, tel. 624/142-2928) comes highly recommended. If you fall in love with one of Baja's stray animals, it may be possible to bring it home, as long as it is in good health and you can show proof of a rabies vaccinations at least 30 days prior to entry into the United States. Talk to a local vet and then contact your airline for more information.

Language Courses

With an office in the Mega shopping plaza, **Interlingua** (tel. 624/142-0070, www.interlingua.com.mx) offers monthly Spanish courses for small groups of students at four different levels.

GETTING AROUND

Detailed information on how to get to Los Cabos is given at the beginning of this chapter.

Once you've arrived, you can get around by foot, bike, bus, rental car, taxi, or shuttle.

By Bus

The main bus station is located on Calle González (tel. 624/142-1100), near Mexico 1. **Aguila** (www.autotransportesaguila.com) and **Autotransportes de Baja California** (ABC, www.abc.com.mx) offer frequent service to La Paz via Todos Santos (shorter distance/fewer stops, US$20) and Los Barriles (longer distance/more stops, US$15). A few buses a day from La Paz continue on to the ferry terminal on the Pichilingue Peninsula. About six buses a day go to Cabo San Lucas (US$2–3). The Flecha Verde and Estrella de Oro bus lines run hourly connections to Cabo San Lucas. Another option is the municipal Subur Cabo buses that connect San José and San Lucas. These buses stop at many places along Mexico 1, including near the Worldmark Coral Baja Resort at Playa Costa Azul, and the fare is only a few pesos (less then US$2). Buses run until 10 P.M. most nights.

By Car

You can do without a car if you plan to stay at an all-inclusive resort or a downtown hotel. Rent a car if you want the convenience of being able to drive yourself into town from a more remote location or if you plan to take a day trip to the East Cape or Todos Santos. Most of the big auto rental agencies have desks at Los Cabos International Airport as well as offices in or near town (many have opened locations along the hotel zone). Note: When renting in Mexico, you must buy Mexican liability insurance (typically about US$25/day). On business days, expect heavy traffic getting into San José in the morning from points north and out of town in the evening.

By Taxi and Shuttle

Except during the hottest months, San José is pleasant to explore on foot. As congestion increases around the plaza, it is a convenience to leave the car behind. Cabs are available on Boulevard Mijares near the plaza, at the bus station, and along the Paseo del Malecón in the *zona hotelera* (US$4–6 from the *zona hotelera* to the plaza downtown or from downtown to Pueblo La Playa, about US$40–50 from town to Los Cabos airport or to Cabo San Lucas). Call 624/142-0401 or 624/142-0105 for pickups.

The Corridor

In between San José del Cabo and Cabo San Lucas, a 29-kilometer stretch of beautiful coastline has evolved from a no-man's land into a luxury resort corridor. In front of and in between the resort properties are a number of sandy beaches, hidden coves, and exposed rocky points. Unfortunately for independent travelers, access to many of these prime coastal areas becomes more difficult by the month as new hotels go up; however, though builders may discourage the public from attempting to visit the beach by installing gates and security guards, they cannot legally prohibit access entirely. You may have to ask permission to pass or park at the highway and walk, but you should be able to get to the beach, one way or another.

There aren't really separate towns along the Corridor; instead, the area is divided into several *fraccionamientos,* or districts for development, each containing several resorts, golf courses, spas, and the like. At Km. 19.5, the Cabo Real development presides over scenic Bahía El Bledito and comprises the Marquis Los Cabos, Meliá Cabo Real Convention Center Beach and Golf Resort, Hotel Casa del Mar, and Casa del Mar Condos as well as the renowned Cabo Real Golf Course and the Jack Nicklaus–designed El Dorado Golf Course. Stretching between Km. 10 and Km. 20, Cabo del Sol consists of the Sheraton and Fiesta America resorts and the Cabo del Sol golf course.

© NIKKI GOTH ITOI

Escape the heat of the sun under a palm-thatched *palapa*.

Driving along the Corridor is easy compared to driving around the rest of Baja. Mexico 1 is a four-lane highway between San José and San Lucas, with a mix of paved and dirt roads running perpendicular into the resorts and developments. Off-ramps are still the exception rather than the rule, so in some cases, you may have to pass your destination and make a U-turn to get to the other side of the road.

BEACHES

Pristine sunbathing beaches are the primary reason why so many high-end resorts have decided to build along the Corridor. To find the most easily accessible beaches, look for blue and white signs that say *Acceso a Playa* with an image of a snorkel and mask or a swimmer. (Some signs have just the picture and not the words.) Ocean swimmers should be aware that strong undertows and rocks make many of these beaches unsafe for wading and bodysurfing. Playas Chileno and Santa María are two exceptions. You may also be able to get in at Playa Palmilla.

Playa Palmilla

The beautifully landscaped access road may trick you into thinking that Playa Palmilla (Km. 26) is private. At the moment, it's not. It does serve as the main beach for several upscale resorts, but there is a good-sized public parking lot, several *palapas* for shade, and plenty of sand to go around. The beach is pleasant for swimming or snorkeling. Palmilla is also the only place along the Corridor where you can watch the fishing *pangas* launch the old-fashioned way—without a paved boat launch or dock.

Playa El Bledito (Tequila Cove)

In front of the Hilton and Meliá resorts in Cabo Real, a breakwater protects swimmers from the pounding surf. You can rent personal watercraft on the beach, and the Hilton offers day passes for use of its pool and facilities. Look for an access road at Km. 19.5 or enter through either of the resorts.

◖ Bahías Chileno and Santa María

If you want to swim and snorkel during your stay in Los Cabos, chances are someone will direct you to one of these two accessible beaches on the Corridor. Construction is in progress around both of these bays, so access may change as yet more golf courses and resorts go up. Many land and sea tours bring groups of tourists to these bays because they are protected from the surf and have rocky points that attract a variety of marine life. Both have ample parking in dirt lots, though you may have to pay a few dollars to the security guard monitoring the lot. Shade and commercial services are lacking at both locations, though vendors seem to come and go each season. There are public restrooms at Chileno (Km. 14) and snorkeling rentals at Santa María (Km. 12). Both these beaches can get crowded with shoulder-to-shoulder snorkelers when the tour boats come in mid-morning to mid-afternoon. It's best to get an early start if you'd like to have the bay to yourself. Playa Chileno has an exit ramp from a new stretch of the highway, which has moved inland to give way to a new development.

Playa Las Viudas (Widows Beach)

At Km. 12.5, between the now-demolished Twin Dolphin and up-and-running Fiesta Americana resorts, a shallow bay with rocky points offers good snorkeling and swimming, when conditions are calm. The sand can get deep, but most vehicles seem able to traverse the access road intact.

SPORTS AND RECREATION
Surfing

Late summer storms bring a strong south swell to the Los Cabos coast, and several breaks offer fairly consistent rides. Close to Cabo San Lucas, Monuments breaks left over a rock reef located below the Misiones del Cabo condo complex at the west end of Playa Cabo Bello. Expect a crowd on good days, and beware the rocks and urchins.

El Tule is a dependable right at Km. 16, and the right point break at Punta Palmilla (Km. 27) may be worth the long paddle on a super big day.

Diving

Bahías Santa María (5–18 m) and Chileno (9–21 m) both have rocky reefs for underwater exploration. Due to the crowds, sea life near the shore is limited compared to what you'll see in protected marine parks elsewhere on the peninsula. These two bays are best suited for snorkeling or shallow beginner dives. Offshore from Bahía Santa María, a site called the Blowhole (12–30 m) features a wall dive where divers often see giant mantas, sea turtles, and schooling jacks and grouper.

Punta Palmilla (Km. 27) is another good spot to put on your mask and fins. A zebra eel slithered about in broad daylight during a recent snorkel here.

Golf

Designer golf courses have popped up all over Southern Baja, luring players away from the competition in Arizona and California. Jack Nicklaus, Robert Trent Jones II, Tom Fazio, Tom Weiskopf, and Roy Dye all have had a hand in shaping the Los Cabos golf experience.

Gray water irrigates most of these courses, but even so, keeping all those fairways groomed and green in a desert environment doesn't come cheap: Greens fees average US$250 for 18 holes. Discounted twilight rates begin at 2 P.M., earlier in summer. Rates typically include tax, use of a golf cart and driving range, bottled water, and club service, and prices may vary according to the travel season and day of the week.

PALMILLA

Jack Nicklaus was the mastermind behind the arroyo, mountain, and ocean courses at the **One&Only Palmilla** (Km. 26, Carr. Transp., Palmilla, tel. 624/144-5250, US$200 for 18 holes), which form the center of a 384-hectare resort community. Most of its 27 holes have

views of the ocean. Palmilla is known for a 440-yard, par-4 Mountain Five hole, which challenges the golfer to a long drive across two desert arroyos. Callaway rental clubs cost US$55.

CABO REAL

Open since 1989, the 18-hole, par-72 **Cabo Real Golf Course** (Km. 19.5, Carr. Transp., Cabo Real, tel. 624/144-0040, toll-free U.S. tel. 877/795-8727, www.caboreal.com, US$180–280 for 18 holes) covers 6,400 meters with three oceanfront holes. Guests of the Westin Los Cabos, Meliá Cabo Real, and Casa del Mar resorts get 10 percent off the greens fees. King Cobra–brand golf club rentals are US$50.

Jack Nicklaus designed the world-renowned 18-hole, par-72 **El Dorado Golf Club** (Km. 19.5, Carr. Transp., Cabo Real, tel. 624/144-5450, US$280 for 18 holes) with an oceanfront driving range and clubhouse. Although it was initially designed as a public course, the El Dorado has now gone private, and four of the nine original oceanfront holes have been converted into home sites.

CABO DEL SOL

The golf community at Cabo del Sol (Km. 10.5, Carr. Transp., Cabo del Sol, tel. 624/145-8200, toll-free U.S. tel. 877/703-4394) includes two separate courses, with more in the plans. The ocean course (US$265–350) was designed by Jack Nicklaus and opened in 1994. Built to preserve a natural look and feel, the course extends from a kilometer and a half of oceanfront property, with 7 of the 18 holes on the water. This is the only course in Mexico named to the 2007 *Golf Magazine* Top 100 Courses in the World list (#88) and one of only two courses in Mexico on the *Golf Digest* list of 100 course outside the United States (#28). The adjacent desert course (US$165–220) was designed by Tom Weiskopf, his first anywhere in Mexico. TaylorMade clubs at either course rent for US$65. Guests of the Fiesta Americana and Sheraton resorts in Cabo del Sol receive a 10 percent discount.

CABO SAN LUCAS COUNTRY CLUB

Palo Blanco trees, *cardón* cacti, and other desert flora form the backdrop for a challenging 18-hole course designed by Roy Dye (Palo Blanco 501, tel. 624/143-4653 or -4654, toll-free U.S. tel. 888/298-1132, www.golfincabo.com). Enjoy stunning views of Bahía Cabo San Lucas, including the rock formations at Land's End. Winter greens fees are US$105–204; summer rates are lower. The adjacent **Los Cabos Golf Resort** (tel. 624/145-7100 or 877/496-1367) has rooms with kitchenettes starting at US$235. The largest units have three bedrooms and full kitchens.

Spa Services

Most of the resorts listed in this chapter have their own spa facilities, with treatments from body wraps and massages to facials and pedicures. Services are typically offered inside or under a tent on the beach. Standouts include heavenly body wraps at **The Spa at the Westin Los Cabos** (Km. 22.5, Carr. Transp., tel. 624/142-9000, toll-free U.S. tel. 800/598-1864, www.westinloscabos.com), and the indoor steam caves and waterfalls, plus holistic treatments using local fruits and vegetation, at **Esperanza Resort** (Km. 7, Carr. Transp., Punta Ballena, tel. 624/145-6400, toll-free U.S. tel. 866/311-2226, www.esperanzaresort.com), where 90-minute treatments cost US$235–250. The **Marquis Los Cabos** (Km. 21.5, Carr. Transp., tel. 624/144-2000, toll-free U.S. tel. 877/238-9399, www.marquisloscabos.com) also boasts a gorgeous 929–square meter spa with six additional massage tents on the beach. A 50-minute facial runs US$100–115; deep-tissue, Shiatsu, Thai, or sports massage services are US$115–125 for 50 minutes; mud therapy treatments are US$115 for 50 minutes; and body scrubs are US$79 for 25 minutes. Nonguests can use the spa facilities (steam room, whirlpool tubs, and spa swimming pool) without reserving a treatment for US$25.

SHOPPING

For jewelry, clothing, antiques, and home furnishings, head to the upscale **Shoppes at Palmilla** (Km. 27.5, Carr. Transp., Palmilla, tel. 624/144-6999, www.lastiendasdepalmilla.com), on the north side of Mexico 1 at the Palmilla Resort exit. Among other boutiques, the eclectic **Galería Pez Gordo** (tel. 624/144-5292, www.pezgordogallery.com, 10 A.M.–8 P.M. Mon.–Sat.) represents more than 40 contemporary artists based in Baja and throughout Mexico. Works range from oil and acrylic to wax, collage, and photography.

At Km. 16, across from the Marbella Suites Hotel, the **Regional Center of Popular Arts and Crafts** (9 A.M.–5 P.M. Mon.–Sat.) has a small glassblowing factory and several artisan workshops. Prices here are lower that what you'll find in San José or San Lucas.

ENTERTAINMENT

Most of the hotels along the Corridor have nightly music of some kind—though some of it can be pretty cheesy. Behind the Costco just outside of Cabo San Lucas, **Latitude 22 Roadhouse Inn** (Km. 4.5, tel. 624/143-1516, www.lat22nobaddays.com, 8 A.M.–11 P.M. Wed.–Mon.) hosts live music 7–10 P.M. Thursday–Saturday. It attracts Corridor residents and Baja old-timers with ocean views, reasonably priced cocktails, and giant flat-screen TVs, and offers a Croatian-influenced menu.

The Marquis, Westin, and Esperanza resorts also host musicians and vocalists from time to time. The **French Riviera Restaurant & Beach Club** at Club Ninety Six (tel. 624/144-6013) in the Villas del Mar at Punta Palmilla also has live music nightly.

ACCOMMODATIONS

Travelers with deep pockets head to the Corridor's posh resorts to see and be seen. Prices for these resorts begin around US$300–400 for the Sheraton and Hilton, climb to US$500 for the Westin and Marquis, and top out at US$700–1,000 per night or more for the Palmilla, Esperanza, and Las Ventanas. The lowest rates at each resort typically require full payment at the time of booking, and cancellation fees apply. Travel club memberships such as AAA can yield a discount of US$100 or more per night. The standard rates do not include 12 percent tax and 15 percent service, unless otherwise noted.

Cabo Surf Hotel

When the waves are rolling in at Playa Acapulquito, surfers and surfing spectators fill the 22 rooms, suites, and villas of the Cabo Surf Hotel (Km. 28, Carr. Transp., tel. 624/142-2676, U.S. tel. 858/964-5117, www.cabosurfhotel.com, US$265–625). The hotel is part of a Mexican-owned hotel company. Highlights here include marble floors, satellite TV, and in-room Wi-Fi. The largest villas accommodate up to eight guests. You can book a lesson through the Mike Doyle surf school, and when you've had enough of the action in the water, retreat to the on-site spa to recuperate. Then you can dine under an open-air *palapa* at the **7 Seas,** where choices include blue crab tostadas, fresh Baja clams au gratin, and a sea bass and spinach–stuffed chile pepper.

Sheraton Hacienda del Mar

You won't have to get up at the crack of dawn to reserve a chaise lounge at the Sheraton (Km. 10.5, Carr. Transp., Cabo del Sol, tel. 624/145-8000, toll-free Mex. tel. 800/903-2500, toll-free U.S. tel. 888/625-5144, www.sheratonhaciendadelmar.com, from US$400); an abundance of patio furniture was part of the resort design. Even better, a poolside concierge helps guests plan the day's activities without having to leave the pool.

Mediterranean defines the look and feel of this sprawling resort, which has 270 rooms and 31 suites; the latter were renovated in late 2006. The hotel has several options for dining and entertainment. Best known among these is **Pitahayas** (tel. 624/145-8010, breakfast, lunch, and dinner daily, mains US$15–40), which prepares variations on a Pacific Rim theme. You can also dine inside or out at the more casual **Tomates** (tel. 624/145-8000, breakfast, lunch, and dinner daily, mains US$10–15), serving a fusion of Mexican and international dishes.

Look for the beautifully landscaped Cabo del Sol exit ramp near Km. 10.

Dreams Los Cabos Suites Golf Resort & Spa

A favorite among wedding parties, honeymooners, and anniversary celebrants, Dreams Los Cabos (Km. 18.5, Carr. Transp., Cabo Real, tel. 624/145-7600, toll-free U.S. tel. 866/237-3267, www.dreamsresorts.com, from US$600) has 308 large and private luxury suites and all the amenities of a full-service resort. Its honeymoon packages include a champagne breakfast in bed. Book ahead if you have your heart set on a stay at Dreams; this popular resort has one of the highest occupancy rates in Los Cabos.

Hilton Los Cabos Beach & Golf Resort

Next door, the Hilton (Km. 19.5, Carr. Transp., Cabo Real, tel. 624/145-6500, wwww.hiltonloscabos.com, from US$400) features Mediterranean architecture, a beautiful infinity pool, and a complete list of luxury-style amenities, plus a favorable location near Playa Bledito. Rooms were recently renovated by designer Paul Duesing and have large baths with soaking tubs, separate showers, and L'Occitane products.

Meliá Cabo Real

The Meliá Cabo Real (Km. 19.5, Carr. Transp., Cabo Real, tel. 624/142-2222, toll-free U.S. tel. 888/956-3542, www.solmelia.com, from US$245) is an all-inclusive resort with more than 300 rooms situated near the Cabo Real Golf Course. Most have marble baths, balconies, and ocean views. This is one of few resorts along the Corridor that's located on a swimmable beach, thanks to a man-made jetty.

Zoëtry Casa del Mar Los Cabos

On a smaller scale, the 32 suites at the hacienda-style Casa del Mar (Km. 19.5, Carr. Transp., tel. 624/145-7700, toll-free U.S. tel. 800/227-9621, www.zoetryresorts.com/casadelmar, US$500 and up), now run by Zoëtry Resorts, come with ocean views, luxury bed

TYING THE KNOT

Destination weddings are big business in Los Cabos. Inviting your friends and family to a seaside marriage ceremony and wedding reception will create memories to last a lifetime. But the choices can be overwhelming, and there seems to be no upper limit on what you can spend. Consider these tips before you start planning the big day:

HIRE A WEDDING COORDINATOR

Different legal system, languages, and business norms can make for a difficult planning process. Do yourself a favor and get help early. Dozens of wedding specialists operate from the area and can advise on reception sites, flowers, music, and food. Booking service **Earth, Sea & Sky Vacations** (www.cabovillas.com/weddings.asp) works with a professional coordinator to plan weddings in the area. **Baja Weddings** (www.bajawedding.com) is another reputable service.

CHOOSE YOUR PRIORITIES

When planning from afar, you won't be able to oversee every last detail of the event in person. Decide in advance what matters most and focus your attention there. Leave the other details in the hands of the wedding coordinator.

FIND THE RIGHT SETTING FOR YOU AND YOUR GUESTS

An all-inclusive resort may simplify the logistics for some couples; others will prefer to select food, music, cake, photography, and flowers à la carte.

SET A BUDGET AND STICK TO IT

You may fall in love with the gourmet lunch at the One&Only Palmilla, but it may not be the place to host your 100-person event.

READ THE FINE PRINT BEFORE YOU BOOK

Are you committing to rent all the rooms in the inn? Make sure you know the terms of the deal before you pay a deposit.

DIG FOR DEALS

Join an online forum, such as **CaboWeddings** on Yahoo! Groups (http://groups.yahoo.com/group/CaboWeddings), to learn from the experience of others. Brides report finding bands and vendors for as low as half the cost of vendors their coordinator recommended. The **Los Cabos Guide** keeps an online list of local wedding service providers (www.loscabosguide.com/services/weddings.htm).

---

linens, teak furniture, marble baths, and Mexican artwork. This is a boutique property with six swimming pools, four lighted tennis courts, and a European-style spa.

Fiesta Americana Grand Los Cabos

Adjacent to the Cabo del Sol golf course is the family-oriented Fiesta Americana Grand Los Cabos (Km. 10.3, Carr. Transp., Cabo del Sol, tel. 624/145-6200, toll-free U.S. tel. 800/343-7821, www.fiestaamericana.com, US$450–600), with 250 oceanview guestrooms and suites and a secluded beach. Rooms are spread across six floors and feature private balconies. The resort's restaurant, **Rosato** (tel. 624/145-6200, dinner daily, mains US$15–20), serves northern Italian cuisine.

Westin Resort & Spa Los Cabos

A dramatic architectural interpretation of the arch at Land's End stands at the center of the Westin Los Cabos (Km. 22.5, Carr. Transp., tel. 624/142-9000, toll-free U.S. tel. 800/598-1864, www.westinloscabos.com, US$350–700). Mexican architect Javier Sordo Magdaleno designed the hillside resort with bright colors and views from every vantage point.

The chain's signature Heavenly Beds are reason enough to stay here. Separate tubs and showers in large marble bathrooms add even more of a distinctive touch.

Several restaurants on-site provide a variety of dining experiences; they include eclectic **Arrecifes** and **La Cascada,** which serves tapas from around the world.

A European-style spa offers body wraps, mud baths, and massage treatments inside or on the beach. Guests have golf privileges at the Cabo Real Golf Course, about 2.5 kilometers southwest.

Marquis Los Cabos

From the inlaid turquoise stones that accent resort corridors to perfectly filtered light in the spa rooms, meticulous attention to detail and contemporary Mexican decor set the tone for a stay at the Marquis Los Cabos (Km. 21.5, Carr. Transp., tel. 624/144-2000, toll-free U.S. tel. 877/238-9399, www.marquisloscabos.com, US$450–700). Opened in 2003, the Mexican-owned resort was designed to reveal ocean views from every angle. Guests can move from their room to a restaurant, the spa, or the gym without losing sight of the sea. The Marquis' 237 rooms have soaking tubs and showers, Bulgary bath fixtures, mahogany woodwork, flat-screen TVs, and exquisite linens. Each morning, hotel staff delivers breakfast to guests through a private pass-through alcove. In addition, rooms and common areas showcase contemporary Mexican paintings and sculpture. And if you fall in love with the eclectic furnishings, as many guests apparently have, you can buy your own from a furniture store on the premises. Twenty-eight *casitas* have their own swimming pools. A 929–square meter spa and an award-winning 21-seat French restaurant, **Canto del Mar,** sets the hotel apart. Close proximity to the highway and small balconies are the only obvious disadvantages at this resort. A service charge of US$35 per day is added to the daily room rate.

Las Ventanas al Paraíso

Romance defines the experience at Las Ventanas (Km. 20, Carr. Transp., tel. 624/144-0300, toll-free U.S. tel. 888/767-3966, www.lasventanas.com, junior suites US$600 and up), which celebrated its 10th anniversary in 2007. Accordingly, one of your first choices upon arrival here will be selecting bed linens from the sheet menu. Known for its underground service tunnels, designed to hide some of the infrastructure and busy staff that keeps the place running, the property is run by Rosewood Hotels and Resorts. Colors are earthy and warm for an intimate ambience.

Large guest suites feature inlaid stone-and-tile floors and adobe fireplaces. Computerized telescopes help guests find whales offshore. Three spa suites have space for in-room treatments, as well as rooftop terraces with outdoor hot tubs. Everyone else can book treatments at the on-site spa. A large infinity pool has "high-tech" pebbles that change color according to the color of the sky and sea.

A tequila- and ceviche-tasting bar hosts Friday evening Tequila Nights, open to guests and nonguests. Private movie nights on the beach, complete with wine and gourmet Mexican *botanas,* are another signature Las Ventanas diversion. Multiday spa and meal packages are available. For guests who want to venture away from the resort, Mini Cooper S convertibles, BMW motorcycles, and off-road Hummers are available for rent.

Esperanza Resort

By many accounts, Esperanza (Km. 7, Carr. Transp., Punta Ballena, tel. 624/145-6400, toll-free U.S. tel. 866/311-2226, www.esperanzaresort.com, US$600–850) leads the pack for outstanding guest service. Located close to Cabo San Lucas, its 50 *casitas* and six suites feature original Mexican artwork and handcrafted furnishings. A signature spa has indoor steam caves and waterfalls, with treatments that incorporate local fruits and vegetation. The oceanfront Mediterranean restaurant, the **Signature Restaurant at Esperanza,** open for breakfast, lunch, and dinner, completes the picture. Esperanza also has its own art gallery with works by contemporary Mexican painters and sculptors for sale. A four-night minimum stay is required for all weekend bookings January–April except February and March, when a seven-night stay is required.

One&Only Palmilla

The oldest resort in Los Cabos is also one of the destination's most expensive—and most popular—places to stay. Originally built in 1956 by "Rod" Rodríguez, son of former Mexican president Abelardo Luis Rodríguez, the One&Only Palmilla (Km. 27, Carr. Transp., tel. 624/146-7000, toll-free U.S. tel. 866/829-2977, www.oneandonlyresorts.com, US$600 and up) has a prime location against a cliff on Punta Palmilla near San José. Over the years, it has grown from one hotel to encompass an entire resort community. Like Esperanza, this is a place for travelers who want to be pampered and are willing to pay for the personal service—which includes everything from loaner iPods and sunglasses cleaning at the pool to golf cart shuttles to get you to and from your room. The result is a private and relaxing five-star vacation. Activities include yoga, spa treatments, and golf. You can dine at Charlie Trotter's **Restaurant C** or the Mediterranean **Agua Restaurant.**

FOOD

Most restaurants along the Corridor are tucked inside full-service resorts. Expect to pay at least US$100 for two (without drinks) at most of the restaurants in this section. Here are a few stand-alone eateries and some of the resort standouts.

Seafood and International

Pecan-encrusted sea bass, mesquite-grilled prawns, and live lobster anchor the menu at **Pitahayas** (Km. 10, Carr. Transp., Cabo del Sol, tel. 624/145-8010, 5:30–10:30 P.M. daily, mains US$15–40), at the Sheraton Hacienda del Mar. An underground wine cellar complements the menu of fresh seafood and mesquite-grilled entrées. You'll need to wear formal resort attire if you plan to dine here.

At the Cabo Surf Hotel, **7 Seas** (Km. 28, Carr. Transp., tel. 624/142-2676, www.7seasrestaurant.com, 7 A.M.–10 P.M. daily, lunch mains US$7–13, dinner mains US$15–30) serves breakfast, lunch, and dinner under an open-air *palapa*. The dinner menu features Mexican, Mediterranean,

and seafood entrées with a decent wine list. Seafood-stuffed poblano peppers is one of the more unusual dishes.

At the Westin Los Cabos, **Arrecifes** (Km. 22.5, Carr. Transp., tel. 624/142-9000, dinner daily, mains US$15–25) is the more formal of the two main restaurants; jazz music plays over the sound of waves crashing on the beach below, and the menu emphasizes seafood dishes with an international twist. The other restaurant, **La Cascada** (Km. 22.5, Carr. Transp., tel. 624/142-9000, breakfast and dinner daily, mains US$15 and up), underwent a US$900,000 renovation in 2006. It features illuminated onyx cube tables, a fire-pit lounge, and a menu of creative *tapas del mundo,* or small plates from around the world paired with wines that match the flavors of the food.

And at the One&Only Palmilla, diners can choose between the *palapa*-style **Agua Restaurant** (Km. 7.5, Carr. Transp., Palmilla, tel. 624/146-7000), featuring Mediterranean cuisine and a view of the sea, and Charlie Trotter's first overseas restaurant, called **Restaurant C** (Km. 7.5, Carr. Transp., Palmilla, tel. 624/146-7000, www.charlietrotters.com, mains US$20 and up). Entrées at C include rockfish with ratatouille, quinoa, and a black olive–caper vinaigrette, and steamed and spit-roasted duck with spiced carrots, parsnips, and a tangerine-merlot reduction. Both restaurants are open for breakfast, lunch, and dinner.

The Mediterranean-inspired **French Riviera** in San José has a new branch in the exclusive Club Ninety Six beach club at Punta Palmilla (Km. 27.5, Carr. Transp., Palmilla, tel. 624/144-6013, www.frenchrivieraloscabos.com, noon–11 P.M. daily, mains US$30).

Italian and Continental

In the Misiones del Cabo complex, **Sunset da Mona Lisa** (formerly Da Giorgio, Km. 5.5, Carr. Transp., tel. 624/145-8160, www.sunsetmonalisa.com, 8:30 A.M.–11 P.M. daily, mains US$15–35) draws a crowd for sunset views and Italian fare. A multilevel patio overlooks the bay and Cabo San Lucas.

Dinner at the award-winning French restaurant **Canto del Mar** (Km. 21.5, Carr. Transp., tel. 624/144-2000, dinner only, prix fixe US$60 pp), inside the Marquis Los Cabos resort, is an Old World affair, complete with acoustic guitar music and a collection of masks from Florence on the walls. There are just 21 seats in the house for the nightly six-course tasting menu. An adjoining cigar room has a hardwood floor and ornate upholstered armchairs.

Mexican

Close to Cabo San Lucas, ◖ **Puerta Vieja** (Km. 6.3, Carr. Transp., tel. 624/104-3252, www.puertavieja.com, mains US$10–25) offers a fantastic view and hearty fare like Sonora beef and fresh shellfish, prepared with Asian accents and offered at incredibly reasonable prices—a rare find along the Corridor. One more kilometer east, the same owners run the popular **Villa Serena Restaurant** (Km. 7.5, Carr. Transp., tel. 624/145-8244, 7 A.M.–10 P.M. daily, mains US$12–25), next to the Villa Serena RV Park. Tasty seafood platters or beef and chicken dishes are a great deal.

Groceries and Supplies

If you want to stock up on fine wines, spirits, and gourmet foods, **La Europea** (Km. 6.7, Carr. Transp., tel. 624/145-8755, 9 A.M.–8 P.M. Mon.–Fri., 9 A.M.–9 P.M. Sat.) is the place to shop. Look for the main store at the first stoplight as you enter Cabo San Lucas from the east. Credit cards are accepted. Near Costco, **Vinoteca** (Camino del Cerro 225 Int. Local 2, Colonia Pedregal, Cabo San Lucas, tel. 624/143-7795, www.vinoteca.com) is a Mexican-owned chain selling wine from around the world and liquor, including tequila.

Costco (Km. 4.5, Carr. Transp., tel. 624/146-7180, 9 A.M.–9 P.M. daily) and **Home Depot** (Km. 6.5, Carr. Transp., tel. 624/105-8600) have also opened stores close to Cabo San Lucas. Other big-box stores in the vicinity include Office Max, Office Depot, Walmart, and Sam's Club.

INFORMATION AND SERVICES

Pemex stations are located at Km. 5, just outside Cabo San Lucas, and near the Westin, between Km. 24 and Km. 25. Most of the resorts offer Internet access and phone services for guests.

For medical needs, see *Information and Services* in the *San José del Cabo* and *Cabo San Lucas* sections.

GETTING AROUND

Resorts along the Corridor are a 30- to 60-minute drive from the airport. Many, including the Westin, offer shuttles to San José del Cabo and Cabo San Lucas for guests who want to see a little more than their hotel grounds. Car rental agencies have offices at many of the larger resorts.

Cabo San Lucas

Baja travelers tend to love or hate Cabo San Lucas (pop. 56,800) with great passion. Some relish the crowded beach clubs, two-for-one happy hours, all-you-can-drink sunset cruises, and late-night dance clubs. The scene is anything but Mexican, but the energy and pure silliness are infectious, and with all this partying going on, it would seem impossible not to have a good time.

For other travelers, the intensity is too much, the timeshare sale pitches too aggressive, and the overall experience far too Americanized to be enjoyable.

Whether you love it or hate it, there's no denying that Cabo San Lucas is one of a kind. Its natural beauty is hard to beat: The dramatic arch stands at Land's End; Playa del Amor connects the Pacific Ocean to the Sea of Cortez; and the peaks of the Sierra de la Laguna rise in the distance.

The town attracts a surprising variety of visitors, from partying singles to thirty-somethings with kids, and from cruise-ship passengers to scuba divers and sportfishing enthusiasts. Food and accommodations are correspondingly diverse. Cabo has luxury resorts and vacation rental villas as well as modest condos, budget motels, and trailer parks. You can eat world-class sushi, shrimp by the kilo, or simple Mexican *antojitos*. The downtown shopping plazas sell everything from Sergio Bustamante sculptures to hand-embroidered dresses. Venture away from the immediate tourist area and you'll find a grid of dirt roads lined with ordinary Mexican homes and small businesses.

As the second-largest municipality in Baja California Sur after La Paz, Cabo San Lucas has struggled to cope with fast-paced growth over the past two decades. Most of the development has centered around the hillside Pedregal neighborhood, along Playa El Médano, and most recently on the Pacific coast north of Playa Solmar.

In 2010 the town completed a series of infrastructure improvements that resulted in new road surfaces, sidewalks, traffic lights with pedestrian signals, and spiffy new signage. Services related to tourism and the construction business drive the local economy today.

CABO SAN LUCAS MARINA

Much of the Los Cabos tourist activity takes place at or near the Cabo San Lucas Marina and along a wide boulevard that wraps around the harbor. A number of the most popular bars and restaurants are clustered here along the waterfront. You can hire water taxis and book all kinds of recreational tours from the many vendors who compete aggressively for your business. Many snorkeling tours and sunset cruises depart from the main dock, located on the southwest side of the marina, near the mouth of the inner harbor.

Several plazas along the marina contain a variety of cafés, shops, and service businesses.

At the north end of the harbor, the **Puerto Paraíso Mall** is a three-level shopping center with a cinema, bowling alley, art galleries, boutiques, and American food chains such as Häagen-Dazs and Johnny Rockets. Plaza Bonita has an outdoor coffee stand and Internet café.

The Wyndham Cabo San Lucas Resort, with its labyrinth of hallways and passages, occupies a long stretch of the marina on the southwest side of harbor.

A gray five-story cinderblock building remains an unfortunate eyesore on Boulevard Marina. It was abandoned in the late 1980s and has been in an ownership dispute ever since.

On busy days, multiple cruise ships shuttle thousands of passengers into this downtown area. They wander the streets looking for souvenirs and familiar shops like Diamonds International. But at day's end, they return to their cabins, leaving the nightlife to those who've arrived by air and car.

PLAZA AMELIA WILKES

Set back a few blocks from the tourist corridor, the original town plaza (btw Hidalgo/Av. Cabo San Lucas, cross streets Madero and Lázaro Cárdenas) has a pretty gazebo and several benches where you can enjoy a break from the frenzy at the marina. The plaza hosts various festivals, often with live music and dancing.

It is also home to a small natural history museum, **Museo de Historia Natural Cabo San Lucas** (tel. 624/105-0661, mcsl@loscabos.gob.mx, 10 A.M.–2 P.M. Mon., 10 A.M.–7 P.M. Tues.–Fri., 10 A.M.–2 P.M. and 4–8 P.M. Sat., 10 A.M.–8 P.M. Sun.), that has been open since 2006. Exhibits in seven different rooms cover the astronomy, geology, paleontology, archeology, biodiversity, and history of the region. In one quick visit, you'll learn about plate tectonics, the Pericú, the Jesuit missions, and the flood of 1939. Admission is by donation.

Across from the plaza on Avenida Cabo San Lucas is the unassuming Iglesia de San Lucas, which dates back to the 18th century and holds regular worship services today.

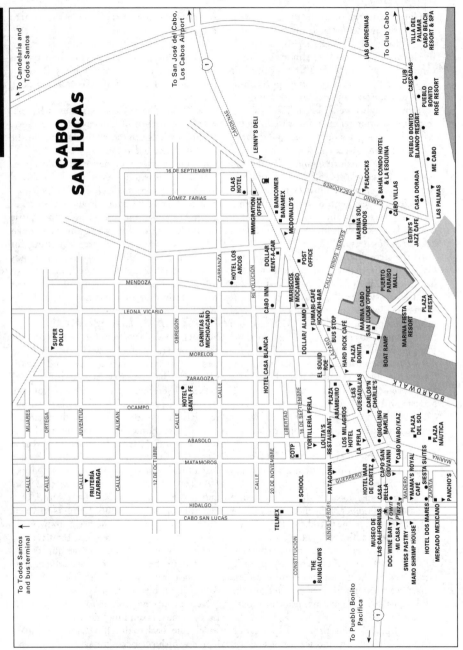

CABO SAN LUCAS

To Candelaria and Todos Santos

To San José del Cabo, Los Cabos Airport

To Club Cabo

LAS GARDENIAS

VILLA DEL PALMAR
CABO BEACH RESORT & SPA

CLUB CASCADAS

PUEBLO BONITO BLANCO RESORT

PUEBLO BONITO ROSÉ RESORT

ME CABO

CASA DORADA

LAS PALMAS

CABO VILLAS

EDITH'S

JAZZ CAFÉ

PEACOCKS

BAHIA CONDO HOTEL & LA ESQUINA

16 DE SEPTIEMBRE

GÓMEZ FARIAS

OLAS HOTEL

IMMIGRATION OFFICE

BANCOMER
BANAMEX

McDONALD'S

LENNY'S DELI

CARDENAS

PESCADORES

CAMINO

MARINA SOL CONDOS

MENDOZA

LEONA VICARIO

SUPER POLLO

CARNITAS EL MICHOACANO

OBREGON

MORELOS

ZARAGOZA

HOTEL CASA BLANCA

CARBANZA

REVOLUCIÓN

HOTEL LOS ARCOS

CABO INN

DOLLAR RENT-A-CAR

POST OFFICE

MARISCOS MOCAMBO

FUMABI CAFÉ HOOKAH-BAR

CALLE NIÑOS HEROES

PUERTO PARAÍSO MALL

MARINA CABO SAN LUCAS OFFICE

PLAZA FIESTA

MARINA FIESTA RESORT

DOLLAR/ ALAMO

EL SQUID ROE

HARD ROCK CAFÉ

BUS STOP

PLAZA BONITA

BOAT RAMP

EL LAZO

BOARDWALK

HOTEL SANTA FE

MIJARES

ORTEGA

JUVENTUD

AUKAN

OCAMPO

ABASOLO

MATAMOROS

HIDALGO

CABO SAN LUCAS

12 DE OCTUBRE

16 DE SEPTIEMBRE

LIBERTAD

TORTILLERIA PERLA

LOLITA'S RESTAURANT

PLAZA ARAMBURO

LOS MILAGROS HOTEL

LA PERLA

LAS QUESADILLAS

CARLOS'N CHARLIE'S

GIGGLING MARLIN

CABO WABO/KAZ

PLAZA DEL SOL

PLAZA NÁUTICA

MARINA

FRUTERIA LIZARRAGA

CALLE

CALLE

CALLE

CALLE

CALLE

CALLE

CALLE

CALLE

20 DE NOVIEMBRE

COTP

SCHOOL

PATAGONIA

GUERRERO

HOTEL MAR DE CORTEZ

CASA BELLA

CAPO SAN GIOVANNI

MAMA'S ROYAL CAFÉ

SIESTA SUITES

MADERO

ZAPATA

PANCHO'S

MUSEO DE LAS CALIFORNIAS

DOC WINE BAR

MI CASA

SWISS PASTRY

MARO SHRIMP HOUSE

HOTEL DOS MARES

MERCADO MEXICANO

Town Plaza

CONSTITUCION

NIÑOS HEROES

TELMEX

THE BUNGALOWS

To Todos Santos and bus terminal

To Pueblo Bonito Pacifica

FINISTERRA (LAND'S END)

PLAYA DEL AMOR

Los Frailes

Bahía San Lucas

Playa El Médano

HACIENDA

Playa Escondida

OLD CANNERY PIER

Playa Balconcito

OLD CANNERY

HOTEL SOLMAR SUITES

US CONSULATE

Cabo San Lucas Marina

SPORTFISHING

Playa Solmar

MARINA

SIGHTSEEING BOATS

Tianguis Marina

Plaza Gali

TERRASOL CONDOMINIUMS

WYNDHAM CABO SAN LUCAS RESORT

BLVD

P

P

TUTTO BENE!

ROMEO & JULIETA

ENTRANCE TO PEDREGAL

HOTEL FINISTERRA

200 yds

200 m

0

0

© AVALON TRAVEL

One boutique hotel, Casa Bella, and several trendy restaurants line the streets surrounding the plaza.

PLAYA EL MÉDANO

Cabo San Lucas offers the rare combination of a large tourist destination with a well-developed beach area within walking distance of the town, plus several pristine beaches just minutes away by boat. And when you've exhausted all these possibilities, the beaches along the Corridor and closer to San José are only a short drive away.

The partying crowd congregates at beach clubs along Playa El Médano (Dune Beach) beginning in the late morning. This long, sandy beach starts at the entrance to the inner harbor and parallels the old road to San José (Camino Viejo a San José) for several kilometers heading northeast. A wide range of travelers crosses paths on this beach each day: Families mingle with college kids who swim with their bottles of beer; fortysomethings stroll by in string bikinis, dogs chase Frisbees in the surf, and

a constant parade of vendors sells silver and beaded jewelry, sombreros, embroidered bracelets, ceramics, beach wraps, hammocks, and, best of all, fresh fruit. You can swim here any time of year, though the water is warmest July–October. On busy days, keep an eye out for boats landing on the beach. Inexperienced Jet Ski drivers routinely cruise into the roped-off swimming areas. You can book just about any water activity from the beach, including rental of personal watercraft, kayaks, stand-up paddle boards, boogie boards, catamarans, and snorkeling gear. Options for food and facilities at the beach include *palapa* bars, beach clubs, and resort restaurants.

◖ FINISTERRA (LAND'S END)

You know you've reached the end of the road in Baja when the towering granite rock formations and signature arch at Finisterra, or Land's End, come into view. Just about every tour boat that departs the Cabo San Lucas Marina heads to the 62-meter El Arco to stage a postcard-perfect photo op. In most conditions, the boat

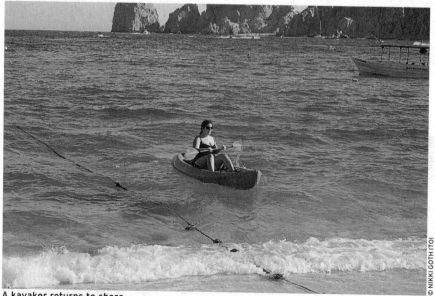

A kayaker returns to shore.

© NIKKI GOTH ITOI

captain can pull right up to the arch. On rare, exceptionally low tides, sand appears under the arch and you can walk through the passage. Nearby rocks host a colony of sea lions, while pelicans congregate at the Roca Pelicano, a popular snorkeling and scuba diving site.

If you're the sort of traveler who avoids the well-beaten tourist path, consider making an exception for this sight. It's generally not as crowded as you might expect, and the dramatic effect of sunlight dancing on the cliffs and wildlife playing in the sea spray is truly spectacular.

◖ PLAYA DEL AMOR

At the southernmost tip of the cape, Playa del Amor (Love Beach), also known as Playa del Amante (Lover's Beach), offers a rare opportunity to dip a toe in two different bodies of water from the same beach. This two-sided beach touches both the Sea of Cortez in the Bay of San Lucas and the Pacific Ocean (where the beach is called Playa Divorceado). The beach is narrow on the bay side and opens into a wide, sandy expanse on the ocean side. You can swim and snorkel on the bay side, but heavy surf pounds the exposed western shoreline, creating a dangerous undertow.

Water taxis and glass-bottom boats from the Cabo San Lucas marina shuttle passengers to and from the beach for US$8–12 round-trip. (Ask to see the boat before you pay, as some are in much better shape than others. Should the engine fail and cut your trip short, the person you paid will likely be nowhere in sight.)

There are no docking facilities at the drop-off point, which is on the narrow bay side of the beach. *Panga* drivers drift as close as possible to shore, but passengers inevitably get wet on the way in and out. Wear water shoes and protect any electronic gear. Shade is limited to a few rocky overhangs (get there early to claim a spot or bring your own umbrella), and there are no commercial services at the beach, except for an occasional vendor selling cold drinks. Bring a cooler and pack your own lunch.

Another option for getting to Playa del Amor is to rent a kayak (US$10 pp/hr.) on Playa El

© NIKKI GOTH ITOI

Playa del Amor goes by many names.

Médano and paddle across the bay. It's best to go in the morning, when the water is calm; the paddle takes about 40 minutes one-way.

PLAYA SOLMAR

To escape the crowds or cool off in an ocean breeze, head to Playa Solmar on the Pacific Coast. This exposed beach has a steep slope and strong undertow, making it unsafe for swimming. But for sunbathing and whale-watching, it's a find. Follow Boulevard Marina to the sign for the Hotel Solmar on the right, and park at the resort.

SPORTS AND RECREATION
Fishing

Fish counts may not what they used to be a few decades ago, but recreational fishing remains a popular activity throughout the Los Cabos area, and Cabo San Lucas has the widest variety of charters and related services. The legendary Bisbee Tournament takes place each October, with thousands of boats on the bay. In the peak season, hundreds of boats depart the Cabo San Lucas marina each morning in search of prized billfish (blue, black, and striped marlin and sailfish), plus tuna, wahoo, and dorado. It's not uncommon for boats to hook 1,000-pound marlin and multiple billfish in one outing. Depending on the season, you might also catch red snapper, yellowtail, sierra, jack crevalle, roosterfish, and grouper.

Cabo San Lucas boats report an average of almost one billfish per departure, and multiple catches are not unusual. Fortunately, the boats also report a high release rate (95 percent or better), meaning they return the fish to the water to fight another day. A universal system of flags reveals the action that took place on any given boat that day: A red flag with a T means the boat caught and released a billfish, while a blue triangular flag means the crew caught and killed a billfish. Boats may legally keep one billfish per boat, but most charter operations strongly discourage the practice.

For marlin fishing, captains generally head to San Jaime Banks, 29 kilometers southwest of Cabo Falso, or Golden Gate Banks,

31 kilometers west of Cabo Falso. Anglers frequently catch dorado and wahoo as well in these areas.

There are three ways to fish the waters near Cabo San Lucas: by cruiser (motorboat equipped with fish-finders, tackle, captain's chairs, and wells for live bait), in a *panga* (simple aluminum skiff), or from shore (surf casting).

SPORTFISHING CRUISERS

Numerous outfitters arrange sportfishing trips aboard cruisers (US$350/day on a 28-foot boat with up to four anglers; US$550/day on a 36-foot boat with up to six anglers). A few outfits charge extra for the license, gear, tax, and ice, but most include these items in the daily fee. Bait, however, always costs extra. **Pisces Fleet** (Blvd. Marina at Madero, tel. 624/143-1288, U.S. tel. 619/819-7983, www.piscessportfishing.com) is one of the oldest and most conservation-minded fishing operations in Cabo. It offers two different rates: Bareboat prices, in which customers bring their own lunch and handle their own catch when they return, are US$445 for a 28-foot cruiser for up to four people, US$580 for a 31-foot Bertram for up to six people, and US$900 for a 31-foot Cabo Express (up to six people). The bareboat rate includes crew, ice, tackle, coffee, and sweet rolls before departure. All-inclusive packages add drinks, box lunches, fishing licenses, and live bait, plus filleting and freezing services for your catch. The fleet includes yachts of every size, all the way up to the 111-foot *Crystal* (US$9,500 for up to 12 anglers). Half-day rates are available for many boats.

After many years of fishing the Baja Peninsula from a home base in the United States, "Renegade" Mike moved to Cabo San Lucas, bought a 31-foot Bertram, and set it up the way he wanted to fish. He has earned a reputation for top-notch service and high-quality gear, including two-speed reels and bamboo gaffs, which he makes himself. Within his first few months of operation, Mike had completed several days of two-digit marlin releases. Contact him at **Renegademike Sportfishing**

Charters (tel. 624/129-9581, U.S. tel. 619/591-8969, www.renegademikesportfishing.com, US$550/day).

Dream Maker Sportfishing (Locale 20, Wyndham Cabo San Lucas Resort, tel. 624/143-7266, www.dreammakercharter.com) leads five-hour and eight-hour trips with a fleet of nine boats that includes everything from a 22-foot *panga* (US$175/5 hrs.) to a 42-foot sportfisher (US$1,250 all-inclusive or US$1,050 boat only).

Located at the Bahía Hotel, **Gaviota Sportfishing** (toll-free U.S. tel. 800/932-5599, www.gaviotasportfishing.com) has experienced captains and 11 boats ranging from 26- to 36-foot cruisers. All-inclusive packages for four (US$755, including tax, or US$595 boat charter only) come with tackle, bait, lunch, and a case of beer, soda, or bottled water. The same package for two aboard a 26-foot cruiser is US$440 (US$360 boat charter only). Boats leave at 7 A.M. and return at 3 P.M.

If you don't want to contact an outfitter directly, you can arrange guided fishing trips through any major hotel. A few, including the Solmar and Finisterra, run their own fleets.

First-timers are sometimes surprised and frustrated by the amount of time it takes before they actually have lines in the water. Getting bait, cruising out to the banks, and returning to the harbor are all part of the time that will be spent on a day of fishing. You can save time by buying bait in advance and requesting to fish destinations closer to shore.

PANGA FISHING

The most economical—and exhilarating—way to plan a Baja fishing adventure is to hire a local *panguero* for a few hours; however, options for these simple skiffs are limited in Cabo San Lucas, where most visitors prefer the luxury cruiser experience. The best bet is to head to La Playita near San José del Cabo. If you can find one, a day of *panga* fishing will cost around US$175 for five hours in a three-person, 22-foot boat. **Dream Maker Sportfishing** (Locale 20, Wyndham Cabo San Lucas Resort, tel. 624/143-7266, www.dreammakercharter.

com) is one of the few outfitters that has a *panga* in its fleet. Typical catches include cabrilla, grouper, and sierra, but even marlin are possible with the right captain in the right place at the right time. Prices won't include rental gear or fishing licenses. Some will fillet the fish you catch for no additional cost. Be forewarned, if you happen to go out on a *panga* when the fish are on, you may well tire of the action long before your captain is ready to return to shore. As one *panguero* told us in the midst of a prolonged fishing frenzy, "When the fish are here, you fish!"

SURF CASTING

If you want to fish without parting with the cash for a full day aboard a cruiser, you might try casting into the surf from shore. You don't need a license, and your catch might include sea bass, sierra, and red snapper. Playa Solmar offers the best conditions, but it is a dangerous location because of the strong undertow. Sleeper waves often strike here, catching even the most experienced anglers off guard. A safer place to try is the old pier at the entrance to the harbor. Fishing is permitted at the northeast end of Playa El Médano.

BAIT, TACKLE, AND FISH PROCESSING

Minerva's Baja Tackle (Blvd. Marina at Madero, tel. 624/143-1282, 9 A.M.–7 P.M. Mon.–Sat.), next door to Pisces Fleet, carries a wide selection of gear and tackle for your fishing adventure. It is also the designated Los Cabos representative to the International Game Fish Association (IGFA).

You can buy fresh bait at the docks along the marina for a few dollars and hire local pros to clean and fillet your catch. Another option for cleaning, processing, vacuum-packing, and freezing is **Gricelda's Smokehouse** (Loc. 19 and 20 in the Tesoro Hotel complex, tel. 624/143-7266, www.dreammakercharter.com) on the marina.

Diving and Snorkeling

Cabo San Lucas offers a variety of unique opportunities for underwater exploration. A

SAND FALLS

Many scuba divers come to Cabo San Lucas hoping to see the unusual sand falls – rivers of sand flowing between rocks and over the edge of a canyon wall beginning 30 meters below the surface. The sand falls lie within the national marine preserve, close to Playa del Amor.

The Scripps Institute of Oceanography first discovered the phenomenon in 1960, and Jacques Cousteau later made the sand falls famous in his television series.

Divers should note that the sand rivers typically run in stormy weather; during extended periods of calm seas, when diving conditions are otherwise best, you may not be able to see the falls in action. But there is plenty to see at the site, whether or not the sand is flowing. The canyon walls support marine life big and small. Graceful eagle rays, good-sized grouper, and tiny zebra eels are just a few of the sightings divers may experience on these dives.

strategic location between tropical and temperate zones and the presence of a vast submarine canyon bring large pelagics such as giant mantas, hammerhead sharks, and amberjacks very close to shore, along with a colorful mix of tropical species. Boat rides are relatively short (as little as five minutes to the closest sites), and the terrain is dramatic. There are wall dives, submerged boulder fields, drift dives, and a one-of-a-kind dive that begins in the Sea of Cortez, rounds the point at Land's End, and ends in the Pacific Ocean.

Playa del Amor is a great place to snorkel on your own or with a guide. Just offshore from this beach, **Pelican Rock** is another good snorkeling site, though given its proximity to the harbor, it can get crowded during the high season. Boats out of San Lucas make the trip to Bahías Chileno and Santa María on the Corridor for snorkeling and shallow diving, but you can also reach these sites yourself by car.

Guided scuba dives tour many of the same sites as snorkelers, making it convenient to accommodate mixed groups (but also making it more crowded, both above and below the surface). Also, given the proximity of these dive sites to the harbor, the loud and constant rumble of boat traffic overhead makes for an annoying distraction.

The most popular dive sites in the Cabo Marine Preserve include Pelican Rock, Neptune's Finger, and the point at Land's End. Pelican Rock and Neptune's Finger begin at shallow depth (6–8 m) and then descend over boulders or along a wall into a vast submarine canyon, as diver skill, air consumption, and visibility allow. All these dives take place in a protected marine preserve, an unusual feature to have so close to a town the size of Cabo San Lucas.

The Land's End dive begins in the surge under a sea lion colony on the bay side of the point and ends with an underwater swim around to the Pacific side, covering varied underwater topography along the way. Guitarfish, schooling amberjack, green sea turtles, and countless other species are likely to make an appearance on this dive.

Cabo San Lucas dive shops can also arrange trips to Cabo Pulmo on the East Cape for reef dives in a protected marine park and the Gordo Banks, where advanced divers with experience in deep dives and strong currents have the opportunity to view hammerheads, whale sharks, and giant mantas, among other pelagics. The dive usually circumnavigates the top of a seamount at a depth of about 41 meters.

DIVE GUIDES AND OUTFITTERS

Just about any local resort or hotel can arrange guided dive trips and equipment rentals for their guests. Some have their own shops on-site, while others book through one of the many independent shops in town. Dive operators typically organize two outings per day, weather permitting. Morning boats leave the harbor around 9 A.M., and the afternoon shift departs around 1 P.M. Mornings tend to be less crowded above and below the surface. In the afternoon, the wind kicks up and boat traffic increases, making water entries and exits a little trickier.

DIVING AND SNORKELING COSTS

GUIDED DIVE AND SNORKEL TOURS
Discounts apply for multiday dives.

Snorkel tour (equipment included)	US$25-45
One-tank boat dive	US$50-75
Two-tank boat dive	US$85-100
Night dive	US$65-70
Cabo Pulmo day trip	US$120-175
Gorda Banks day trip	US$120-185
Nondiver passenger	US$15-25

SCUBA INSTRUCTION

Open-water referral (four dives, for students who have completed classroom and pool work prior to arrival)	US$210-250
Open-water certification (classroom and dives)	US$400-500
Discover Scuba/resort course (introduction to scuba)	US$100-130
Refresher dive	US$120
Advanced certification	US$280-330
Rescue diver course	US$350

EQUIPMENT RENTAL

Snorkel gear	US$5-15 (usually included with tour)
Scuba package with dives	US$25-35/day (discounts for multiday dives)
Weight belt and weights	US$8
Regulator	US$12
Tanks	US$12
BCD	US$12
Wet suit	US$8
Airfills	US$4-5

Manta (Blvd. Marina #7D Local 37 Int. Plaza Gali, tel. 624/144-3871, www.caboscuba.com) is a professionally run PADI shop conveniently located at Playa El Médano. Its custom-designed 35-foot boat holds 15 divers comfortably; additional 28-foot and 26-foot boats accommodate up to 10 divers each. All three boats are equipped with radios, first-aid kits, and oxygen. For local dives in the Cabo Marine Preserve, advanced and novice divers often share the same boat but have separate dive guides, since easy and advanced dives start at the same points. (Experienced divers go deeper and stay under longer than beginner groups.) Knowledgeable boat captains and a friendly international guide staff make for a safe and enjoyable dive experience. An earlier morning start at 8:30 A.M. helps avoid the crowds. Rental gear is in good shape, with Sherwood regulators; Aqualung and Genesis BCDs; and Akona, Body Glove, and Scuba Pro wetsuits. In addition to standard 80-cft tanks, smaller (63 cft) and larger (100 cft) sizes are available. A two-tank dive costs US$85. The office has moved from Camino de los Pescadores to Boulevard Marina.

Underwater Diversions (tel. 624/143-4004, U.S. tel. 949/226-8987, www.divecabo.com) is another reputable shop in the Plaza Marina.

Local dive instructors prefer PADI-certified **Eagle Divers** (Plaza Embarcadero Local 3, tel.

© NIKKI GOTH ITOI

divers near Pelican Rock in Bahía San Lucas

624/125-0008, www.eaglediver.com) for advanced diving. A trip to Gordo Banks runs US$165. This shop also offers scuba courses for kids aged eight and older.

LIVEABOARDS
Amigos del Mar (tel. 624/143-0505, fax 624/143-0887, toll-free U.S. tel. 800/344-3349), next to Solmar Fleet on the west side of the harbor, arranges luxury liveaboard dive trips to the Socorro Islands, Guadalupe Island, Gordo Banks, Los Frailes, El Bajo, Cabo Pulmo, and other more remote sites aboard the 112-foot *Solmar V* (www.solmarv.com, US$1,795/eight days). The boat holds a maximum of 22 divers and 10 staff members.

SNORKEL TOURS
Pez Gato (Camino del Cerro 215, El Pedregal, tel. 624/143-3797, www.pezgatocabo.com, tours 10 A.M.–2 P.M. daily, US$45) organizes four-hour sail and snorkeling tours to Bahía Santa María, along the Corridor, aboard one of three catamarans. The tour includes two hours of water exploration at Santa María, plus lunch and cold drinks. Kids under 12 are free.

SunRider Adventure (tel. 624/143-2252, U.S. tel. 619/240-8669, www.sunridertours. com; US$55, kids under 10 free) has three boats and prepares Mexican buffet meals onboard. A snorkeling lunch tour to Playa Santa María for US$55 per person includes the buffet and an open bar. Cash only.

EQUIPMENT
Most dive shops rent snorkel and dive equipment in packages or à la carte, so if you forget your fins or your mask strap breaks, you'll be able to borrow a replacement for the day. Repairs are a different story, however. If you're bringing your own gear, have it serviced before you leave home; check your computer batteries and bring spare parts. Despite the number of dive shops, replacement parts are difficult, if not impossible, to come by in Baja.

RECOMPRESSION
Clínica de Especialidades (Lopez Mateos btw Morelos/Vicario, tel. 624/143-3914 or -2919) has a hyperbaric recompression chamber that is available to recreational divers for emergencies.

Surfing

Cabo San Lucas proper is not a surf destination, though the action isn't far away by car. In summer there is surf along the Corridor, and in winter the closest waves are north along the Pacific near Todos Santos.

Kayaking

Playa El Médano is calm enough most of the time for launching kayaks easily, and you can rent from a number of vendors along the beach for US$10 per person per hour or US$50 for a half day.

The water is calmest in the morning, and it takes about 40 minutes to get to Playa del Amor, so it's best to get an early start. Beware of larger watercraft on the bay, and if you are a beginning paddler, stick close to the beach, regardless of the conditions.

Boating

The **Cabo San Lucas Marina** (Lote A-18 de la Dársena, tel. 624/173-9140, www.igy-cabosanlucas.com) is now owned by Island Global Yachting, a company that develops and manages luxury marinas around the world. Its 380 slips line the inner harbor and can accommodate yachts up to 200 feet in length. Services include 24-hour security, wireless Internet, and a desalination plant for water. There is a swimming pool, laundry facilities, hot showers, storage, a two-lane boat ramp, and a state-of-the-art fuel dock with both diesel and gasoline. The on-site boatyard and 75-ton lift can handle just about any standard repair. Rates are US$340 per week or US$1,250 per month for a 20-foot boat, and up to US$2,814 per week or US$10,325 per month for a 79-foot boat. Reservations are accepted online. Office hours are 9 A.M.–5 P.M. Monday–Saturday, 10 A.M.–3 P.M. Sunday.

Cabo San Lucas offers a greater variety of shops, restaurants, and services within walking distance of the marina than the new Puerto Los Cabos marina at La Playita near San José. As an official port of entry into Mexico, Cabo San Lucas has a **port captain's office** (Calle Matamoros at 16 de Septiembre).

Cape Marine (Plaza Marina, Local J2-3, tel. 624/143-4970, 8 A.M.–6 P.M. Mon.–Sat.) carries hardware, apparel, yachting supplies and tools, and fishing equipment. Credit cards are accepted.

Cruises

An abundance of glass-bottomed tour boats depart frequently from the marina and from Playa El Médano 9 A.M.–4 P.M. each day. The standard 45-minute tour costs US$8–12 per person and covers Pelican Rock, the famous Land's End arch, and the sea lion colony. For no extra charge, the crew will let passengers off at Playa del Amor near the arch; you can flag down any passing boat from the same fleet and catch a ride back to the marina later in the day. Be sure to see the boat you will board before you pay, as engines can be old and unreliable, and you may not get your money back if the trip is aborted due to engine failure. **Dos Mares** (tel. 624/143-4339) is one of the oldest fleet operators; **Esperanza's Fleet** (tel. 624/144-4666, US$12 or US$22 with snorkeling gear rental) is another option, with four large glass-bottomed *panga* boats.

A handful of larger boats head out of the harbor in the late afternoon to catch the sunset over the Pacific Ocean. The usual route is to head out to the arch and around the point, up as far as the Hotel Solmar and Pueblo Bonito hotels. These sunset cruises usually include all the beer and margaritas you can drink, which can make for an entertaining boat ride. You can make reservations directly through the cruise companies or at any hotel in town (for no extra charge).

The all-the-margaritas-you-can-drink sunset cruise aboard one of the **Pez Gato** (Camino Del Cerro 215, El Pedregal, tel. 624/143-3797, www.pezgatocabo.com, Mon.–Sat.) catamarans is a memorable experience. The tunes are all from the 1980s—from Toto and Abba to Bon Jovi—and the crowd is a mix of older couples and families. A hardworking staff from the mainland sees that drinks are replenished and no one falls overboard. **Jungle Cruise Tours** (tel. 624/143-7530, www.cabobooze-cruise.com,

US$35 pp) does a similar cruise, except it's adults-only. Boats leave from the marina at 6 P.M. in spring and summer and 5 P.M. in fall and winter.

A larger cruise ship, **Caborey** (Blvd. Marina, inside the Wyndham Cabo San Lucas Resort, tel. 624/143-8269, toll-free U.S. and Canada tel. 866/460-4105, www.caborey.com) runs a dinner cruise for US$89 per person and a margarita cruise with appetizers for US$45. Kids under 10 are half price.

Two modern-day pirate ships take passengers back to the days when the English stalked the Spanish Manila galleons from hiding spots behind the rocks at Land's End. The 29-meter **Buccaneer Queen** (Dock 1, Cabo San Lucas Marina, near the Hacienda Resort, tel. 624/144-4218, www.buccaneerloscabos.com, US$45–69 pp) races around the bay and heels like it's racing in the America's Cup (passengers must wear life preservers). Choose among the whale-watching, snorkeling, or sunset tours. The **Sunderland** (tel. 624/143-2714, www.pirateshipcabo.com.mx) is a historic tall ship built in 1885. Tours are family friendly, except for the loud noise from the cannon.

Whale-Watching

During the winter months, adult and juvenile gray whales entertain resort-goers all along the Los Cabos coast with their spouting and breaching. Many of the glass-bottom boat operators also offer whale-watching cruises to get you a little closer to the action; however, note that these are not the close encounters that you can have in the breeding grounds farther north. If you are determined to touch a whale, you'll need to head to Bahía Magdalena, Laguna San Ignacio, or Laguna Ojo de Liebre near Guerrero Negro.

In business for more than a decade, **Cabo Expeditions** (Blvd. Marina, Wyndham Cabo San Lucas Resort, tel. 624/143-2700, www.caboexpeditions.com.mx, US$85 pp) does a better job than most at training its staff in safety procedures and knowledge of marine life. Guides must be PADI-certified rescue divers with emergency response training. The

organization is active in whale rescue, beach cleanup, and other local conservation programs. Tours on inflatable Zodiac boats depart at 8 A.M., 10:30 A.M., 1 P.M., and 3:30 P.M. mid-December–mid-April. In addition to whale-watching, Cabo Expeditions offers snorkeling, parasailing, and some underwater experiences for noncertified divers: "snuba" (underwater helmet diving) and rides aboard a semisubmersible vessel, Cabo Submarine (painted bright yellow, of course). Look for the Cabo Expeditions office inside the Wyndham Cabo San Lucas Resort on the marina.

ATVs and Personal Watercraft

When you've had enough of the water, you might begin to explore the area's kilometers of open beaches and inland attractions via ATV (not permitted near swimming or turtle-nesting areas). A number of outfitters offer these tours, and any hotel or activity stand along the marina can make a reservation. Current prices are around US$60 per person single/US$80 double. **Baja's Activities** (tel. 624/143-2050, www.bajasactivities.com) has locations at the Hilton, Tesoro, and Villas de Palmar hotels, plus an outpost on Highway 19 on the way to Playa Migriño. It allows two riders per ATV at a discounted rate. **Amigos Moto Rental** (tel. 624/144-4161) rents ATVs for US$25 per hour or US$120 per day. Guided tours of Migriño Beach and/or Candelaria cost US$70–90 for a single rider.

On a calm day, a WaveRunner or Jet Ski can be a fast and fun way to explore the bay and Playa del Amor, and you don't have to be a speed demon to enjoy the ride. A number of vendors along Playa El Médano offer rentals for around US$40 per half hour.

Horseback Riding

Several stables offer horseback tours along Playa El Médano and into the mountains nearby. The going rate is about US$30 per hour. **Red Rose (La Rosa) Riding Stables** (Km. 4, across from Cabo San Lucas Country Club, tel. 624/143-4826) offers custom trips and lessons. **Rancho Collins** (Camino Viejo a

San José, tel. 624/143-3652, 8 A.M.–noon and 2–6 P.M. daily), across from Club Cascadas, has 45 horses that are healthy and in good shape. Look for a pretty palomino near the road or book through your hotel.

Skydiving and Parasailing

Look for **Skydive El Sol** (tel. 624/129-7173, www.skydiveelsol.com, daily year-round), a relative newcomer to Cabo San Lucas, near Club Cascadas on Playa El Médano. The going rate is US$250 for a tandem jump that includes one minute of free-fall time. Plan on a two-hour outing from start to finish. For an additional US$130, you can return home with a video and photographs of the entire experience. Skydive El Sol needs at least two jumpers to book a trip.

The *Caborey* luxury cruise ship (tel. 624/143-8260, www.caborey.com) offers parasailing trips at a rate of US$35 for an 8- to 10-minute ride.

Golf

Just beyond the Cabo San Lucas city limits, the 300-hectare **Cabo San Lucas Country Club** (Km. 3.7, Carr. Transp., tel. 624/143-4653 or -4654, toll-free U.S. tel. 888/298-1132, www.golfincabo.com, US$79–200) is one of the more reasonably priced courses in Los Cabos. There are many other more exclusive and more expensive options along the Corridor.

Yoga

Cabo Mind Body Fitness offers Pilates and Bikram yoga sessions in the privacy of your own villa, but prices are correspondingly steep: Pilates sessions run US$125–225 per person per hour (or US$45 pp per hr. for groups of seven or more). Yoga classes cost US$110–160 per person per hour (or US$30 pp for groups of 10 or more). Discounts apply for pairs and triples, too, so it pays to buddy up. Visit www.cabovillas.com for details.

Spa Services

Most of the larger Cabo resorts have their own spas on site. One of the nicest is the **Armonia**

Spa (Playa El Médano s/n, tel. 624/142-9696, www.pueblobonito.com) at the Pueblo Bonito Pacifica resort, which offers 50-minute massage treatments for US$110. Choices include hot stone, Shiatsu, four-hands, deep-tissue, Swedish, and pregnancy massage. Located in the basement of the hotel, the spa setting is a bit cave-like but quiet and peaceful, with a friendly and professional staff. To find the resort and spa, follow the main street through Cabo San Lucas (Lázaro Cárdenas), past the plaza and up the hill. The road will curve to the right and back to the left, and the name will change to Boulevard Herrera. Keep going up the hill about a kilometer and a half until you reach a stop sign with the Pueblo Bonito entrance and sign on the left. Currently, the sign says Pueblo Bonito Sunset Beach, but this is also the entrance for the Pueblo Bonito Pacifica.

ENTERTAINMENT AND EVENTS

With an emphasis on booze and music, Cabo nightlife begins early and ends late. On any given night, there are dozens of options for entertainment. The drinking begins at the bars along the marina and moves to the dance clubs around midnight. The clubs stay open until 3 or 4 A.M., at which point the party moves to any hotel that will tolerate the noise.

Bars

You won't have any trouble finding a watering hole in Cabo—there are far too many for a comprehensive list here. One of the most famous is the **Giggling Marlin** (Matamoros at Blvd. Marina, tel. 624/100-6956, www.gigglingmarlin.com) with a nightly dance show and signature block-and-tackle hoist from which well-imbibed patrons hang upside down like hooked marlins. **Carlos'n Charlie's** (Blvd. Marina, tel. 624/143-1280, 11 A.M.–midnight daily, mains US$10–20) is a tourist-oriented chain with a popular bar and decent Mexican food.

Among the row of bars and restaurants along the marina in Plaza Bonita, **The Nowhere**

Bar (tel. 624/143-4493, www.nowherebar. com, 11 A.M.–1 A.M. daily, margaritas US$5) is a popular stop, especially during March Madness NCAA basketball championships. At happy hour (5–9 P.M.), you'll get two drinks (served in glasses, not plastic) for the price of one, whether you need them or not.

For sunset views, head to the newest outpost of the **Baja Brewing Company** (tel. 624/143-9199, noon–11 P.M. daily), atop the Cabo Villas resort, on Camino de los Pescadores, a short walk up from Playa El Médano. Artisanal beers on tap are made of water, barley, yeast, and hops—about as simple as it gets, and a most unusual find in Southern Baja. There is live music on Monday, Thursday, and Saturday. Order from a menu of pub fare. The hamburger buns are made fresh daily on-site.

At **Hemingway's** (Guerrero btw Cárdenas/ Madero, tel. 624/143-9845, www.jnjhabanos. com), you can order a sip of tequila for US$150 (the bottle costs more than US$1,000). Or the knowledgeable bartenders can help you taste a variety of high-end tequilas in the range of US$7–10 per taste. There are more than 345 tequilas from which to choose. The immense walk-in humidor has a full selection of Cuban cigars from Cohiba, Montecristo, and Partagas. A cigar roller, or *torcedor*, rolls well-made cigars for US$11–15.

Fumari Café Hookah Bar (Lázaro Cardénas, across from the Paraíso mall, 4–11 P.M. Mon.– Thurs., 4 P.M.–2 A.M. Fri.–Sat., drinks US$2–4) is a cozy second-story café with several tables inside and a large roof deck outside. Curl up on a sofa and play a game of chess while you smoke a flavored hookah (US$13) or sip a chai tea.

Friday is tango night at super-chic **Barometro** (tel. 624/143-1466, 10 P.M.–2 A.M. daily) on the Plaza Marina.

For nightly jazz music, try **Edith's** (tel. 624/143-0801, www.edithscabo.com, 6 P.M.–1 A.M. daily), a block from Playa El Médano, on the west side of Camino de los Pescadores.

Two-story **Desperados Restaurant and Cantina** (Morelos at Niños Heroes, tel. 624/143-4331, 1 P.M.–midnight Mon.– Thurs., 1 P.M.–3 A.M. Fri., 1 P.M.–4 A.M. Sat.,

1 P.M.–11 P.M. Sun., mains US$10–30) serves hearty fare with a Mexican/Tex-Mex theme— think seafood kabobs and baby back ribs. Free Wi-Fi makes this a good place to stop in for just a drink and some Ultimate Nachos. You can also watch whatever sports event happens to draw the biggest crowd that day. On Saturday nights a Latin rock band called La Flaca plays 10:30 P.M.–2:30 A.M. Pay a US$12 cover and your cervezas cost just 1 peso each the rest of the night.

Dance Clubs

Cabo's discos are empty before 11 P.M. and packed from midnight on. Among them all, none embodies the party-till-you-drop Cabo spirit better than **El Squid Roe** (Lázaro Cárdenas at Zaragoza, tel. 624/143-0655, noon–3 A.M. daily). Giant margaritas and piña coladas appear two at a time to set the mood. Balloons and confetti fall from the sky, while staff and patrons climb on tables, form 50-person centipedes, and whoop it up on the dance floor.

Rock-and-roll music artist Sammy Hagar often celebrates his birthday by performing at the club he owns, **Cabo Wabo** (Guerrero btw Madero/Lázaro Cárdenas, tel. 624/143-1188, www.cabowabo.com, 7 P.M.–2 A.M. daily). Open since 1992, the club plays recorded and live music. Hagar often makes a New Year's Eve appearance as well.

Zoo Bar & Dance (Blvd. Marina across from Plaza Bonita, tel. 624/143-5500, 9 P.M.–4 A.M. daily) targets the younger crowd.

Cinema

On the second floor of the Puerto Paraíso mall, **Cinema Paraíso** (Cabo Bello at Gómez Farais, tel. 624/143-1515), with 10 theaters, shows a mix of blockbusters and independent films from Mexico, the United States, and elsewhere around the world. The VIP area has comfortable reclining leather seats.

Festivals and Events

Bike races, fishing tournaments, golf tournaments, music festivals, and national holidays are just a few of the gatherings that take place in Cabo San Lucas each year. The Los Cabos Guide (www.loscabosguide.com) has the most up-to-date listing of events online.

The annual **Stars and Stripes Fishing & Golf Tournament** (www.starsandstripestournament.com) takes place in June and raises money for children in Mexico and the United States. This is a family-friendly event, and the fun continues well into the night. Performers such as Super Diamond provide the Friday night entertainment. The largest of the fishing tournaments is **Bisbee's Black and Blue Marlin Jackpot Tournament** (tel. 624/143-1622, www.bisbees.com), held for three days each October.

The **San Lucas Fiesta** takes place on October 18 and includes a traditional mix of music, dancing, crafts, and foods.

SHOPPING

The streets of Cabo are chockablock with places to buy souvenirs, apparel, fine art, tequila, cigars, and more. A number of upscale shops line the Plaza Fiesta, near the Marina Fiesta hotel, and most of the luxury stores inside the Puerto Paraíso mall are open for business.

Arts, Crafts, and Souvenirs

Across from the main dock, the **Marina Mercado** (Cabo San Lucas Marina, Lot 4, 9 A.M.–5 P.M. daily) is an arts and crafts market with dozens of vendors selling embroidered dresses, carved ironwood figures, ceramics, and jewelry. Sellers expect to bargain. Inquire about prices at several places before you decide to buy.

Taxco (Guerrero and Blvd. Marina, tel. 624/143-0551, 9 A.M.–6 P.M. daily) has a good selection of silver jewelry. **Joyería Alberto** (Matamoros btw Niños Héroes/Lázaro Cárdenas, no tel., 9 A.M.–6 P.M. daily) is a satellite of a well-regarded Puerto Vallarta jeweler.

Dos Lunas (Plaza Bonita and Puerto Paraíso locations, tel. 624/143-1969, 9 A.M.–6 P.M. daily) has pretty sundresses, handbags, and the like, and **Cartes** (Plaza Bonita, tel. 624/143-1770, 9 A.M.–9 P.M. Mon.–Sat., 9 A.M.–4 P.M.

© NIKKI GOTH ITOI

Embroidered name bracelets, like the kind this artisan carries, are a fun souvenir for kids.

Sun.) carries rustic furniture, Talavera pottery, and classy accents for the home.

Across from Mi Mariscos restaurant at the corner of Paseo a la Marina and Camino Viejo a San José, **Chile & Anis** (tel. 624/143-7454, 9 A.M.–8 P.M. Mon.–Sat.) is a Baja arts and crafts store with silver jewelry, wood crafts, mirrors, and ceramics for sale. Upscale crafts line the shelves of **Mi Mexico Magico** (Loc. 52, tel. 624/143-5153, 8 A.M.–9 P.M. daily) in the Marina Fiesta plaza.

Fine-Art Galleries

In the lobby of the Wyndham Cabo San Lucas Resort, a **photography gallery** (U.S. tel. 831/480-4411) displays prints by Tomas Spangler (www.fotomas.com), whose work depicts images and scenes unique to the Baja Peninsula. A representative is available 10 A.M.–2 P.M. Monday–Saturday.

Golden Cactus Gallery (Guerrero and Madero, tel. 604/628-2233 or 624/143-6399, www.goldencactusgallery.com) features the works of artist Chris MacClure in a second-story studio. MacClure's work captures local Baja imagery, and he has created commissioned paintings of yachts, airplanes, and the like for celebrity clients, including John Travolta.

Cigars

Many stores sell Cuban cigars in Los Cabos, but fakes are rampant. Buy from a reputable merchant if you want the real thing. And remember, Cubans never go on sale. **La Casa del Habano** (formerly J&J Habanos, Blvd. Marina near Madero, tel. 624/143-6160 or 877/305-6242, www.jnjhabanos.com) has a walk-in humidor and a few tables inside. Prices are steep, but you can be confident that you're getting what you pay for. The owners also run a cigar bar called **Hemingway's** (Guerrero btw Cárdenas/Madero, tel. 624/143-9845, www.jnjhabanos.com) across from the entrance to Cabo Wabo.

Wine and Liquor

La Europea (tel. 624/145-8755, 9 A.M.–8 P.M. Mon.–Fri., 9 A.M.–9 P.M. Sat.) has opened a small street-level store in the Puerto Paraíso complex. This satellite of the larger main store on the Corridor has the best selection and most competitive prices on wines from around the world, plus a fairly complete list of liquors and gourmet foods.

Sporting Goods

Head to **Cabo Sports Center** (Plaza Náutica, tel. 624/143-4272, 9 A.M.–7 P.M. daily) for beach gear, water shoes, and basic supplies for golf, swimming, surfing, snorkeling, boogie-boarding, and mountain biking. **Minerva's Baja Tackle** (Blvd. Marina at Madero, tel. 624/143-1282, 9 A.M.–7 P.M. Mon.–Sat.), next door to Pisces Fleet, is the one-stop shop for lures and tackle.

Books and Magazines

Cabo San Lucas does not have a dedicated English-language bookstore; however, several shops in town stock a few titles. They include **Minerva's Baja Tackle** (Blvd. Marina at Madero, tel. 624/143-1282, www.minervas.com) for fishing books and **Bahías Jiromar** (Puerto Paraíso Local #284, tel. 624/144-3250) for newspapers, magazines, and some books. In addition, most of the larger resorts carry at least a few pocket fiction titles.

Puerto Paraíso

Upscale Puerto Paraíso (tel. 624/144-3000, www.puertoparaiso.com, 9 A.M.–10 P.M.), a shopping mall on the east side of the marina, is the first of its kind in Southern Baja. Most stores are now open, and the mall contains a mix of luxury boutiques, international chains, and entertainment venues. You'll find everything from Sergio Bustamante artwork to Diamonds International and many familiar brands such as Tumi, Kenneth Cole, and Nautica. There is even a Curves exercise center. Food options include Ruth's Chris Steak House, Häagen-Dazs, Houlihan's, and Johnny Rockets. There is also a bowling alley on the third level. Clean public restrooms and underground parking are added conveniences.

ACCOMMODATIONS AND CAMPING

You can find just about any type of accommodations in Cabo San Lucas, from simple and reasonably priced motels to boutique inns and luxury resorts. There are condos and villas for rent as well. The one exception is camping, for which there are relatively limited options. Most visitors prefer to stay at the beach, but the better values are downtown or on the outskirts of town, away from the water.

Downtown and Marina
UNDER US$50

Near the bus terminal, **Hotel Casa Blanca** (Revolución at Morelos, tel. 624/143-5360, US$40) has 20 adequate rooms with king-size beds and air-conditioning. In the same vicinity, **Olas Hotel** (Revolución at Gómez Farías, tel. 624/143-1780, fax 624/143-1380, US$50) feels more like a hostel, with 35 rooms (some with one king-size bed, others with two single beds). Amenities include cable TV, fan, fridge, microwave, and patio. Budget travelers might also check out relative newcomer **Hotel Oasis** (US$35–45), across from the CCC (Centro Comercial California), on the west side of Mexico 19 just north of the junction with Mexico 1.

US$50-100

You can easily walk to the marina and the Puerto Paraíso mall from the two-story **Cabo Inn Hotel** (20 de Noviembre btw Vicario/Mendoza, tel. 624/143-0819, U.S. tel. 619/819-2727, www.caboinnhotel.com, US$50–70), but with the central location comes a whole lot of noise, and readers have shared disappointing experiences in staying here. Here are some factors to consider before you book: Its 22 rooms are mostly small and dark, especially the ones without windows. Beds have foam mattresses and baths have curtains instead of doors. Air-conditioners are old and often loud. Some rooms have refrigerators. Two rooftop *palapa* rooms give travelers a sense of the real Baja; one has its own whirlpool tub and both come with bug nets over the beds. There is a full kitchen and shared TV in the common area, as well as a very tiny "social" pool. The managers do ask guests to adhere to a number of house rules, which are reasonable, but the tone in which they are presented may not sit well with some travelers. The owner has installed wireless Internet throughout the property. Credit cards are accepted for advanced reservations only; you'll need cash if you show up unannounced.

◖ Siesta Suites Hotel (Zapata btw Guerrero/Hidalgo, tel. 624/143-2773, toll-free U.S. tel. 866/271-0952, www.cabosiestasuites.com, US$60–75) completed a top-to-bottom remodel in 2007. Highlights include granite counters, new bath fixtures, and new queen beds. In business since 1992, it is owned by a couple originally from Southern California who converted an old apartment building into the hotel. Several of Cabo's best restaurants are steps away. The hotel has 15 suites with kitchenettes (including microwaves and toaster ovens) and separate bedrooms and five hotel-style rooms. All are air-conditioned and come with satellite TV. Repeat guests enjoy the sundeck, BBQ, and "social" pool; secured parking is another plus. Wi-Fi for guests costs a onetime US$5 fee but does not reach to all the rooms, and several PCs in the lobby are available to guests and the public for US$3 an hour.

The **Hotel Los Arcos** (Vicario and Revolución, tel. 624/143-0702, hotelplazalosarcos@hotmail.com, US$55) opened in December 2005 with 32 clean rooms in a two-story building with cable TV, air-conditioning, and wireless Internet.

The centrally located and well-worn **Hotel Mar de Cortez** (Blvd. Lázaro Cárdenas at Guerrero, tel. 624/143-0032, toll-free U.S. tel. 800/347-8821, www.mardecortez.com, US$50–67) has seen better days, but it is much loved by its loyal patrons, many of whom return for the same week year after year, and still manages to stay full in the high season. The prices haven't gone up in the last five years. Its *muy tranquilo* setting provides a welcome respite from the noisy, crowded streets of downtown Cabo San Lucas—yet puts guests

LOS CABOS TIMESHARES

Few visitors board their flight to Los Cabos intending to buy a timeshare. Yet the timeshare market is booming as the destination evolves. Timeshares now command higher prices and higher occupancy rates than hotels. Nearly six million people now participate in fractional ownership vacation models (also called vacation clubs), and they spend US$1 billion a year on their condos and villas. How do so many travelers come to change their minds between arrival and departure?

LOS CABOS IS A BEAUTIFUL PLACE
It's a lot easier to pack up and head home when you know you can return again and again.

THE PITCH IS ALL AROUND
Timeshare salespeople disguise themselves as activities coordinators, concierges, restaurant hosts, rental car agency staff, and even grocery store clerks. Their goal is to draw unsuspecting visitors into a friendly conversation – *Is this your first time in Los Cabos? Where are you staying? Would you like to go whale-watching today? Can I help you find the sugar?* – and then invite them to

a 90-minute presentation over breakfast in exchange for any number of giveaways. With prices ranging US$15,000-25,000, "owning" a timeshare in a world-class destination can be an attractive proposition. Why not hear what they have to say?

THE FREEBIES ARE ENTICING
Salespeople may offer US$200 in cash, free whale-watching or snorkeling tours, sunset horseback rides, restaurant coupons, and more. The deal gets better the longer you resist. Not a bad way to finance part of your trip if you don't mind giving up part of a day.

Everyone thinks they can work the system, and many who participate in a presentation do resist the temptation to buy. Some even sign up for a second pitch on their next visit. But here's the catch:

TIMESHARES ARE NOT REAL ESTATE
They are vacations. When you buy a timeshare, you prepay for vacations at a discounted rate. If you like the idea of returning to a familiar place in Los Cabos for one or two weeks each year, this model can make a lot of sense.

conveniently close to all the action (except the beach, which is a 20-minute walk). Clean, air-conditioned rooms each have one queen and one twin bed, some with a bit of a slope, and dimly lit baths. There are no TVs and no phones, but there is free Wi-Fi. Guests can rent a small refrigerator for US$10 per day. Enjoy the small pool and patio area, which are shaded by date palms, or dine in the on-site restaurant and outdoor bar.

Friendly and attentive service makes for a memorable stay at █ **Los Milagros Hotel** (Matamoros 116, tel. 624/143-4566, U.S. tel. 718/928-6647, www.losmilagros.com.mx, US$85), which has a dozen large rooms with air-conditioning and private baths; a few rooms include kitchenettes as well. There is a cactus garden on the roof, a tiny pool in the courtyard, and free Wi-Fi.

Now owned by The Villa Group (www.villagroupresorts.com), **Hotel Santa Fe** (southwest corner of Zaragoza and Obregón, tel. 624/143-4401, toll-free U.S. tel. 877/845-5247, gerenciasantafe@prodigy.net.mx, US$40-80) is a well-maintained property with 46 studios surrounding a pool. Each studio has a sliding glass door, tile floor, renovated bath, kitchenette, and relatively new furnishings as well as air-conditioning, satellite TV, and phone. Amenities include wireless Internet, off-street parking, 24-hour security, a small counter restaurant with outdoor seating (7 A.M.–7 P.M. daily), laundry, and a mini-super (7 A.M.–7 P.M. daily). A free beach shuttle service is provided.

One block off the marina, on the second floor of Plaza de la Danza, **Viva Cabo Hotel** (Blvd. Marina, Plaza La Danza, tel./fax 624/143-5810, US$90–100) has eight studios,

IT'S HARD TO SAY NO

Sales reps choreograph every aspect of the pitch, from the upbeat music to the champagne and cheers of congratulations echoing around the room. They face intense pressure to sell, so if the first approach doesn't win you over, there will be one or two more pitches as you attempt to leave the room. (Biannual weeks? Off-season weeks? Trial membership? Free Jet Ski tour? Take our survey before you go?) As prices come down, the deal gets sweeter, and suddenly you either begin to feel guilty for accepting all the freebies or you think you're crazy for not taking advantage now that you've negotiated the terms so low. Bottom line: That 90-minute breakfast presentation could result in a US$10,000 charge on your credit card.

YOU MAY NOT GET WHAT YOU PAID FOR

Timeshare developments typically begin selling when construction has just begun – sometimes they don't get finished, or when they do, they don't always shape up as promised. Stories abound of frustrated timeshare purchasers who don't get the weeks they originally bought or whose reservations seem to get lost every time they book. Services may not be available as promised, and the quality of the accommodations may change as the years go by.

Also, because timeshare owners aren't year-round residents, they usually lack both a sense of community and a sense of responsibility toward the local environment. For the developer, timeshares mean huge profits, as the same space is sold repeatedly in one-week segments. Because land in Baja is relatively inexpensive, considering the charming scenery and climate, it seems to attract get-rich-quick developers who show a decided lack of respect for the fragile Baja environment.

PROCEED WITH CAUTION

Timeshares are not all bad, and attending a presentation may be a worthwhile experience for a variety of reasons. Just be sure you know what's coming before you give away any of your precious vacation time. And don't buy without considering all the options.

each with two double beds or one king, kitchenette, air-conditioning, and satellite TV. Guests have access to a pool and fitness center next door.

US$100-150

Close to downtown but also within easy walking distance of Playa El Médano, **Marina Sol Condominiums** (tel. 624/143-3231, toll-free U.S. tel. 877/255-1721, www.marinasolresort.com, US$110–140) has basic one- and two-bedroom condos arranged around a pretty courtyard and swimming pool. A wheelchair-accessible room is available. The lobby has several independently operated businesses, including a convenience store, day spa, and laundry service.

On the east side of the marina, next to the Marina Fiesta Hotel, between downtown and the beach, the **Marina Cabo Plaza** condominium hotel (Blvd. Marina 39, tel. 624/143-1833, www.marinacaboplaza.com, US$100/day or US$700/week) has 63 rooms with tiled floors and balconies with impressive views of the marina below. Guests share a swimming pool.

US$150-250

Elegant **⟨ Casa Bella** (Hidalgo 10, tel. 624/143-6400, U.S. tel. 626/209-0215, www.casabellahotel.com, Oct. 1–July 31, US$160–190) brings a San José del Cabo feel to downtown Cabo San Lucas. Its 11 rooms are set in a restored colonial-style home across from the town square and Mi Casa restaurant. Rooms have ornate wooden doors, antique-style furnishings, oversized tiled showers, and remote-control air-conditioning. An enclosed patio has a small pool with several chaise lounges. You will be hard-pressed to find this kind of intimacy and elegance so close to the marina and nightlife anywhere else in town.

It's impossible to miss the sprawling **Wyndham Cabo San Lucas Resort** (formerly Tesoro Los Cabos Hotel) (tel. 624/173-9300 or 800/716-8770, toll-free U.S. tel. 800/543-7556, www.wyndham.com, US$65–130 European plan or US$183–194 American plan) on the west side of the marina. It is the most basic all-inclusive resort you'll find in Los Cabos, but new management as of January 2011 may be planning to change that. As of this writing, all 286 rooms have air-conditioning, phone, and refrigerator, and the hotel has a beach club on Playa El Medano. Hard beds, low water pressure, and inattentive service rank among the top complaints.

Not quite as large as the Wyndham, but still an imposing presence on the marina, is the **Marina Fiesta Resort & Hotel** (tel. 624/145-6020, toll-free U.S. tel. 866/998-3767, www.marinafiestaresort.com, US$240–380). This property gets high marks for a central location, but the noise coming from nearby bars and round-the-clock construction has bothered many recent guests. Amenities include a swimming pool and views of the marina, but guestrooms could use a cosmetic overhaul. The timeshare pitch comes on strong from the moment you walk in the door. The resort seems overpriced at its current rates.

Playa El Médano
US$50-100
East along Playa El Médano, and set back a ways from the beach, clean and cozy **Club Cabo Hotel and Campground Resort** (tel./fax 624/143-3348, www.clubcaboinn.com, US$55–85) is also dog friendly. It has a handful of suites and bungalows, some with *palapa* roofs, all with air-conditioning and king-size beds. Owners Irene and Martin Rozendaal, a Mexican and Dutch husband-and-wife team, have been in business since 1992. Their property borders the only remaining expanse of mesquite forest in the area, which is also a bird sanctuary. On the grounds are laundry

machines, a large fridge for storing freshly caught fish, and a swimming pool with an attached whirlpool tub. The hotel provides wireless Internet and a shuttle to town (a 15–20 minute walk).

US$100-150
Bahía Hotel (Pescador s/n, tel. 624/143-1889, U.S. tel. 914/432-3307, www.bahiacabo.com, US$130–180), just off Camino de los Pescadores above Playa El Médano, has lost most of its ocean views due to construction of the Casa Dorada complex right in front. Its studios have minimally equipped kitchenettes, air-conditioning, satellite TV, and direct-dial phones. Giant sculpted concrete shells frame the beds as headboards, and bamboo doors enclose the bathroom and closet. Faucets and tiling have aged a bit. The property includes laundry facilities, a decent restaurant, pool with hot tub and swim-up *palapa* bar, and free parking in a gated lot. Rates here include tax. Like most affordable Cabo San Lucas locations, the place is overrun with college students on spring break during the month of March. The outdoor **Bar Esquina** (lunch mains US$6–12, dinner mains US$15–25) is a nice addition to the casual dining options in the neighborhood.

US$150-250
Families particularly like **Villa del Palmar Cabo Beach Resort & Spa** (Km. 0.5, tel. 624/145-7000, toll-free U.S. tel. 877/845-5247, www.villadelpalmarloscabos.com, junior suites US$200–400, including tax, three-night minimum), with 458 junior suites and one- to three-bedroom oceanview deluxe suites. Each unit has a kitchenette, marble bath, and balcony. There are two pools (one with a bar), two lighted tennis courts, a fitness center, and restaurants. Some units are available only by the week. The on-site Spa at Villa del Palmar offers individual and package treatments in a European-style spa.

Part of the Trading Places International network of timeshares, **Club Cascadas de Baja** (Camino Viejo a San José, tel. 624/143-1882, toll-free U.S. tel. 800/365-9190, ext. 400, www.clubcascadasdebaja.com, one-bedroom US$200), at the east end of El Médano, has 110 thatched-roof villas, plus two swimming pools and tennis courts. You can make reservations online.

Near Edith's on Camino de los Pescadores and a short walk up from Playa El Médano, **Cabo Villas** (tel. 624/143-9166, fax 624/143-2558, cabovillasresort@prodigy.net.mx, US$180–500) has one-bedroom, one-bath units and two-bedroom, two-bath units in two white towers.

OVER US$250

Next door to the Villa del Palmar, **Villa La Estancia** (Km. 0.5, Camino Viejo a San José, tel. 624/143-8121, U.S. tel. 619/683-7883, www.villalaestancia.com, US$215–300) has 156 units ranging in size from one bedroom to three bedrooms as well as standard guestrooms and junior suites. Brand-new **Villa del Arco** (tel. 624/145-7000, toll-free U.S. tel. 888/880-8512, www.villadelarcocabo.com, US$285–340) has three buildings with junior

suites as well as one- and two-bedroom units. Prices at both of these resorts include tax, and there is a three-night minimum.

The **ME Cabo** (Playa El Médano, tel. 624/145-7800, toll-free U.S. tel. 800/336-3542, www.solmelia.com, US$220 and up) is a Spanish-owned Sol Meliá property with 88 remodeled rooms and suites built in a horseshoe shape around a large pool and patio area. Reasonable prices, a convenient location, trendy beach club, and inviting spa make this a popular spot for younger travelers, many of them European. On the plus side, most rooms have ocean views, towels are large and fluffy, baths feature Aveda products, and hotel service is prompt. As for the minuses, rooms on the fifth floor, three levels above the club (and presumably other floors as well), echo sound from the lobby and disco/bar below. As with most places this close to the El Medano beach scene, the resort attracts a fun-loving crowd that's here to party hard.

The Pueblo Bonito chain has four properties in Cabo San Lucas. The original **Pueblo**

© NIKKI GOTH ITOI

Guestrooms have balconies at ME Cabo.

Bonito Los Cabos (Playa El Médano s/n, tel. 624/142-9797, toll-free U.S. tel. 800/990-8250, www.pueblobonito-loscabos.com, US$400 and up) is a white adobe five-story building designed in a Mediterranean theme. From the tiles on the roof to the chaise lounges, blue and white form the dominant color scheme. Its 148 junior and luxury suites surround an attractive free-form swimming pool. Room features include kitchenettes and views of the bay.

Farther away from downtown along the beach, the **Pueblo Bonito Rosé** (tel. 624/142-9898, toll-free U.S. tel. 800/990-8250, www.pueblobonito-rose.com, US$400 and up) has a striking Baroque-themed lobby, but its 260 suites leave less of a dramatic impression. Not-especially-new rooms have decent beds, private balconies, and hand-painted terra-cotta floors.

About five kilometers east of Cabo San Lucas, beachfront **Hotel Riu Palace Cabo San Lucas** (Km. 5.5, Camino Viejo a San José, tel. 624/146-7160, toll-free U.S. tel. 888/666-8816, www.riu.com, US$300–450) comprises a town unto itself, with 642 guestrooms—booked almost all the time, according to travel agents—and all-inclusive (only) meal plans. Part of a large international hotel chain, the lively Riu has so many dining and entertainment options that most guests never leave the resort during their visit. Rates include taxes.

One of the newest luxury properties to open along Playa El Médano is **Casa Dorada** (Pescador s/n, tel. 624/163-5757, toll-free U.S. tel. 866/448-0151, US$200 and up), where guests enjoy mango margaritas upon arrival. Modern kitchens, large baths, contemporary design, and a stellar location are some of the pros. Suites range in size from studio to two-bedroom. There have been some maintenance issues, and rooms above the Mango Deck are reportedly noisy. Its Saltwater Spa offers a full menu of massage and body treatments with products from Pevonia Botanica.

After several years of demolition and construction, the new **Hacienda Beach Club and Residences** (tel. 866/300-0084, www.haciendacabosanlucas.com) has opened on 22 acres in a prime location on Playa El Médano yet also close to downtown and the marina. Luxury vacation rentals range from one to four bedrooms in size. Prices start at US$695 per night.

Pacific Beach
US$150-250

One of the oldest hotels in Cabo, the **Hotel Finisterra** (tel. 624/143-3333, toll-free U.S. tel. 800/347-2252, www.finisterra.com, US$115–180) stands on a ridge overlooking the Pacific Ocean. There are two parts to this resort: an original building built into the hillside but set back from the beach, and two newer towers collectively called the Palapa Beach Club, which are on the beach and overlook the pool. A well-equipped business center makes for a comfortable office away from home. It has leather chairs, five flat-screen TVs, and several Dell computer stations. Wireless Internet costs US$10 a day. A 1,040–square meter swimming pool with whirlpools and a swim-up bar sits on the beach at the foot of the Palapa Beach Club. Beds are on the firm side, and there are a variety of views on the older Finisterra side of the resort. Be sure to request city, marina, garden, or ocean views when you book. Guests can use lighted tennis courts, a sauna, and swimming pool. There is a spa and wedding chapel on-site.

Another historic property close to Land's End is the **Hotel Solmar Suites** (tel. 624/143-3535, U.S. tel. 310/459-9861 or 800/344-3349, www.solmar.com, US$140–280), which features 180 rooms and suites on the beach with separate timeshare/condo units overlooking the beach. An older section of units directly on the beach has lower ceilings and less natural light; newer units are set back from the sand but have high ceilings, better lighting, and newer furnishings. Amenities include tennis courts, an aquatic center, and two heated pools with swim-up bars and hot tubs. The hotel's La Roca restaurant (6 A.M.–10 P.M. daily, mains US$6–15) cooks your fish any way you like it. The Solmar is well known among anglers for its fishing fleet and among divers for its luxury liveaboard boat, the *Solmar V* (www.solmarv.com).

Next door to the Hotel Solmar and walking distance to the beach, **Terrasol Condominiums** (tel. 624/143-1803, toll-free U.S. tel. 800/524-5104, www.terrasolcabo.com, one-bedroom US$130–250) has studio, one-bedroom, and two-bedroom units. Each has a full kitchen, ocean view, and wireless Internet access. Amenities include two pools, a tennis court, swim-up bar, and snack bar.

OVER US$250

The sparkling new **Capella Pedregal** (Camino del Mar 1, tel. 624/163-4350, www.capellahotels.com/cabosanlucas, US$575) has 66 ocean-view rooms in a five-story building, plus villas and *casitas* for rent. Beds are king-size, and rooms come with a long list of luxury amenities, including a spa, private plunge pool, and twice-a-day maid service so your sheets are turned down before you retire. Pets are even allowed. There are three restaurants on-site: Don Manuel serves traditional Mexican dishes in an elegant setting. El Farallon is modeled after a seafood market. And the Beach Club serves more casual fare. Learn to make ceviche, tamales, or salsa and moles in one of the resort's one-day cooking classes (US$70 pp). To find the hotel, turn right off Marina Boulevard onto Camino del Mar; then take the immediate left turn into Capella Pedregal.

Open since 2002, the **Pueblo Bonito at Sunset Beach** (Cabo Pacifica, tel. 624/142-9999, toll-free U.S. tel. 800/990-8250, www.pueblobonitosunsetbeach.com, US$190–330) has 327 suites on a 20-hectare hillside overlooking the Pacific, behind the Pedregal development. Amenities include a hilltop "sky pool," a main pool that overlooks the beach, tennis courts, and a free shuttle into town (drop-off at the Pueblo Bonito Blanco on Playa Medano). Fitness facilities cost extra (US$15/day), and massages run a steep US$130 at the Spa at Sunset Beach (8 A.M.–7 P.M. daily). Two-for-one happy hour lasts exactly one hour, so it's best to load up on beverages during that time. Eat tacos and chicken sandwiches and the like poolside, or enjoy sushi in the bistro.

In the vicinity, the newest Pueblo Bonito property, **Pueblo Bonito Pacifica** (Cabo Pacifica, tel. 624/142-9696, toll-free U.S. tel. 800/990-8250, www.pueblobonitopacifica.com, US$400–500), opened in 2005. Couples in search of a romantic getaway like the no-kids factor at this boutique-style resort. Its 154 rooms, including 14 suites, are appointed in minimalist fashion, with a sand and ivory color scheme. Those who want a little more nightlife find the location a bit too remote. Strolling along the beach is discouraged due to heavy surf; you can, however, rent a bed on the beach for US$20 an hour. There is a free shuttle to town or cabs for US$10 one-way. Meals at **Siempre,** the resort's main restaurant, are pricey, and food quality gets mixed reviews. The on-site **Armonia Spa** offers a variety of massage treatments, including hot stone, Shiatsu, four hands, deep-tissue, Swedish, and pregnancy massage (US$100 for 50 minutes).

To get to any of the Cabo Pacifica resorts, follow Lázaro Cárdenas, the main boulevard through town, west past Plaza Amelia Wilkes, until it curves to the right and becomes Herrera. Go through a traffic circle and continue following this street around a few S-turns and up the hill toward the Pacific Ocean. Along the way, two blue and white signs indicate the way to Cabo Pacifica. At the stop sign, turn left into the driveway that says Pueblo Bonito Sunset Beach. This is the entrance for all the Cabo Pacifica resorts at press time. Tell the attendant at the gate which resort you want to visit, and then proceed along a long landscaped boulevard that descends down the ridge to the resorts and beach below.

Bed-and-Breakfasts
US$50-100

A few blocks from the town center, **Casa Pablito Bed and Breakfast Hotel** (Hidalgo and Ortega, tel. 624/143-1971, toll-free U.S. tel. 866/444-1139, www.casapablitoloscabos.com, US$90) was originally built to house employees of the Club Cascadas resort. A few years back, the building was converted into a traditional Mexican hacienda-style inn with 14 suites set around a pool and *palapa*-shaded breakfast area. Rooms have either one queen or two twin beds, plus kitchenettes, air-conditioning, and cable TV. This location will work for you if you don't mind a fairly long walk to most of the shops and restaurants downtown.

US$100-150

Another place that's removed from most of the action downtown is **The Bungalows Breakfast Inn** (Dorado and Lienzo Charro, tel. 624/143-5035, toll-free U.S. tel. 888/424-2226, www.cabobungalows.com, US$95–175), a good option for small groups or any travelers who like to stay off the beaten path. Its eight newly painted suites have separate sleeping areas, air-conditioning, kitchenettes, and TVs. A honeymoon suite has its own terrace with city views. Six two-bedroom bungalows can accommodate 4–6 guests each. There's no smoking, inside or out. The small but nicely designed grounds hold a swimming pool, hot tub, and BBQ. Full breakfast is a treat to start the day. Guests here unanimously praise owner Eric for his personal service and attention to detail.

US$150-250

About one and a half kilometers east of Cabo San Lucas and 800 meters above Mexico 1, **Casa Contenta** (tel. 624/143-6038, www.cabocasacontenta.com, US$160–195/day or US$1,050–1,300/week) has five air-conditioned rooms with private baths in a three-story home with a swimming pool and wireless Internet throughout. Take a yoga class, book a spa treatment, or simply enjoy the view of Land's End on the rooftop terrace. There's a three-night minimum.

Booking Services and Property Management Companies

Delfin Hotels & Resorts (toll-free U.S. tel. 800/524-5104) has condos in the Terrasol complex. It also books for Casa Contenta B&B and most of the all-inclusive resorts. **Cabo Villa Rentals** (toll-free U.S. tel. 877/473-1946, www.cabovillarentals.com, 8:30 A.M.–5 P.M. daily) manages condos in the Terrasol and

Villa La Estancia complexes and three- to five-bedroom villas in the Pedregal development. **Earth, Sea & Sky Vacations** (toll-free U.S. tel. 800/745-2226, www.cabovillas.com) represents 90 luxury villa rentals, ranging from two- to nine-bedroom units, with a starting price of US$1,500 per night, as well as 30 resorts. **Pedregal Escapes** (Camino de La Plaza 145, Fraccionamiento Pedregal, tel. 624/144-3222, www.pedregalescapes.com) is the vacation rental division of the company that developed the Pedregal gated community on the west side of Cabo San Lucas. It manages two- to five-bedroom villas, plus even a few larger homes. Prices start at about US$450 per night, and some properties require a security deposit.

Camping and RV Parks

Three kilometers northeast of Cabo San Lucas off Mexico 1, the Mexican-owned **Vagabundos del Mar RV Park** (Km. 3, tel. 624/143-0290, www.vagabundosrv.com) has 52 slots with full hookups but no dump station. Rates are US$24 per day or US$140 per week, with a 10 percent discount for members of the Vagabundos del Mar travel club. The park is not on the beach; however, campers return year after year to enjoy the peaceful surroundings, comfortably away from the frenzy of activity in downtown Cabo San Lucas. There are four double-size pull-through spaces, and more than half of the spaces are designated annual rentals with *palapas*. Book early if you want to get a spot at this popular park. No caravans. Facilities include a restaurant, bar, flush toilets, *palapas,* showers, a pool, and new laundry machines.

In the same vicinity, the campground part of **Club Cabo Hotel and Campground Resort** (tel. 624/143-3348, www.clubcaboinn.com, US$16–19) has 10 sites for tent camping and another 10 for small RVs. Guests may use clean restrooms, hot showers, and a hot tub. There is a lounge area with hammocks, table tennis, a swimming pool, wireless Internet, and secure parking.

Villa Serena RV Park (Km. 7.5, toll-free U.S. tel. 888/522-2442, US$21/day, US$112/week, US$391/month) has 54 spaces with full

CABO SAN LUCAS **365**

LOS CABOS

hookups but no shade, as well as laundry, restrooms, and hot showers. In the adjacent *palapa* restaurant, a La Paz native serves delicious food (coconut shrimp, whole *huachinango*/red snapper) at reasonable prices (tel. 624/145-8244, 7 A.M.–10 P.M. daily, mains US$12–25). Visit www.gaviotasportfishing to make a reservation online.

For primitive camping on the beach, you need to head out of town to the Pacific beaches along Mexico 19 or the Gulf coast along the East Cape.

FOOD

Cabo San Lucas offers a wide range of culinary delights, including some world-class dining; however, many of its restaurants are expensive tourist-oriented establishments, rather than authentic local eateries. You'll have to venture away from the marina district to find enjoy real Mexican food at uninflated prices.

Mexican

Located in one of the oldest adobe buildings in town, **Mi Casa** (Av. Cabo San Lucas, opposite the plaza, tel. 624/143-1933, www.micasarestaurant.com, dinner 5:30–10:30 P.M. daily, lunch noon–3 P.M. Mon.–Sat., mains US$15–30) prepares authentic Mexican specialties, including *chile en nogada* (a traditional Independence Day dish) and *cochinita pibil* from the Yucatán.

The restaurant has its own tortilla station and makes its own *mole poblano* from scratch, and it takes a staff of 15 cooks to keep up with the demand. The ambience is festive, with hand-painted murals on the walls of an indoor/outdoor dining area, primary colors for chairs and tables, and mariachi groups passing through all evening long. In recent years, though, many readers have reported underwhelming and inconsistent dining experiences here.

The more contemporary **O Mole Mío** (Plaza del Sol, Blvd. Marina, tel. 624/143-7577, 11:30 A.M.–11:30 P.M. daily, mains US$10–20) specializes in various kinds of chicken mole. An artist from Guadalajara designed

WABORITA, THE SIGNATURE CABO WABO DRINK

The signature Cabo Wabo drink looks like a tropical fish – blue on the bottom and green on top. Here's how to make one when you get home:

- 1 oz. tequila
- ½ oz. Damiana liqueur
- ½ oz. orange liqueur
- ½ oz. lime juice

Shake and serve straight up with a dash of blue curaçao.

the unique interior of the restaurant with glass and metal accents.

At **Edith's** (tel. 624/143-0801, www.edithscabo.com, 6 P.M.–1 A.M. daily, mains US$20–30), near Playa El Médano on the west side of the Camino de los Pescadores, you can enjoy views of Bahía Cabo San Lucas and Land's End as long as the sun's up and a hearty dinner of prime rib, rack of lamb, or any number of regional specialties through the evening hours.

Join the locals at **La Perla** (Lázaro Cárdenas at Guerrero, no tel., 9 A.M.–4:30 P.M. Mon.–Sat., mains US$4–5) for inexpensive and tasty burritos, enchiladas, *chilaquiles,* tacos, *licuados,* and *comida corrida* (1–4 P.M., US$5). Another option for real Mexican food is **Lonchería Lolita's** (Niños Héroes at Matamoros, tel. 624/143-6586, 7 A.M.–7:30 P.M. Mon.–Sat., mains US$7–13), where you can order *huachinango* and *champurrado* (hot chocolate made with cornstarch).

Family-run █ **Las Gardenias** (Camino al Hacienda at Niños Heroes, no tel., 8 A.M.–5 P.M. Tues.–Sun., tacos US$2, mains US$10–25) is a mainstay that attracts a loyal following of visitors and locals. Plastic tables and chairs and minimal decor put the emphasis on the food: tacos of nearly every kind, including *barbacoa* (lamb), *nopales,* and *cochinita pibil,* and the house specialty, shrimp *molcajetes* served in a mortar.

Portions are large at **Pancho's Restaurant and Tequila Bar** (Hidalgo, off Blvd. Marina, tel. 624/143-0973, 7 A.M.–11 P.M. daily, dinner mains US$18–40) but prices still seem high. Breakfast is a slightly better deal, and the bar pours hundreds of different kinds of tequila. English is spoken.

Amber glassware and a free pomegranate tequila aperitif are nice touches at **Los Garcia** (tel. 624/143-4601, mains US$8–15), one of the newer restaurants located at the street level of the Puerto Paraíso mall, serving upscale tacos, barbecued ribs, lobster salad, and other Mexican fare.

Tequila shrimp, made with the restaurant's own label, and lobster burritos are standout entrées at Sammy Hagar's **Cabo Wabo Restaurant** (Guerrero btw. Madero/Lázaro Cárdenas, tel. 624/143-1188, www.cabowabo.com, 11 A.M.–11 P.M. daily, mains US$17–28). Try the Waborita cocktail to start the meal off right. Downstairs, the Cabo Wabo Cantina serves a more casual menu.

Known for its signature salsa bar, which has some 20 different variations on the theme, **Felix** (Zapata and Hidalgo, tel. 624/143-4290, 4–10 P.M., mains US$15–20) began serving tacos and has expanded to a full menu of shrimp and traditional Mexican dishes such as posole over the years. The restaurant shares its indoor and outdoor space with Mama's Royal Café during the day.

Desperados Restaurant and Cantina (Morelos at Niños Heroes, tel. 624/143-4331, 1 P.M.–midnight Mon.–Thurs., 1 P.M.–3 A.M. Fri., 1 P.M.–4 A.M. Sat., 1–11 P.M. Sun., mains US$10–30) serves hearty fare with a Mexican/Tex-Mex theme. Free Wi-Fi makes this a good place to stop in for just a drink and some *botanas.* You can also watch whatever sports event happens to draw the biggest crowds that day. On Saturday nights, a Latin rock band called La Flaca plays 10:30 P.M.–2:30 A.M. Pay US$12 cover and your cervezas cost just 1 peso each the rest of the night.

Happily removed from the bustle of downtown, **La Fonda** (Hidalgo btw Obregón/12 de Octubre, tel. 624/143-6926, 1–10 P.M. daily, mains US$10–30) serves some of the best traditional Mexican dishes in town. The menu features empanadas, *sopes,* ceviche, chicken mole, *cochinita pibil,* and, for adventurous eaters, some more exotic delights.

Seafood

Just about every Cabo San Lucas restaurant offers seafood on the menu. A few are willing to hang their hats on it: Casual **Mocambo de Los Cabos** (Vicario and 20 de Noviembre, tel. 624/143-6070, noon–10 P.M. daily, mains US$10–20) has an extensive menu of seafood cocktails, plus fish and shellfish entrées like a fish fillet gratin and a grilled *pargo* (red snapper) fillet.

Try the *pescado zarandeado* (red snapper served whole in a tomato-based broth) or grilled fish *meniore* style (in a sauce of garlic, butter, white wine, and capers) at **Mariscos Mazatlán** (Mendoza and 16 de Septiembre, tel. 624/143-8565, lunch and dinner daily, mains US$10–15). The menu also includes 12 different preparations of shrimp. This restaurant has a second, less touristy location in San José del Cabo, on the west side of Mexico 1 on the way to the airport. Near the Ace Hardware store at the corner of Camino Real and Paseo de la Marina, **Mi Casa de Mariscos** (tel. 624/143-1858, salesmicasa@gmail.com, 1–10:30 P.M. daily, mains US$13–29) has a raw bar with shrimp, scallops, and oysters; "barely touched" dishes like ceviche and seared fresh catch; and fully cooked entrées like *huachinango frito a la talla* (fried whole red snapper). The restaurant is located in a striking hacienda-style building, and it's owned by the same folks who operate Mi Casa and Peacock's.

Japanese and Mexican flavors meet at **Nick-San Restaurant** (Lte. 10, Blvd. Marina, tel. 624/143-4484, www.nicksan.com, 11:30 A.M.–10:30 P.M. Tues.–Sun., mains US$20 and up), and sushi connoisseurs cannot rave enough about the results: tuna tostada, *pulpo* carpaccio, cabrilla *misoyaki, hamachi* curry, and sashimi *serranito* are just a few examples. The restaurant ranks among the world's best in its class. Plan to spend about US$50–100 per person.

On the marina near the Marina Fiesta hotel, **Baja Lobster Co. Seafood Grill** (formerly El Shrimp Bucket, Blvd. Marina Locals 37–38, tel. 624/145-6011, 6 A.M.–11 P.M. daily, mains US$10–20 and up) specializes in all things lobster: tacos, curry, pasta, salad, bisque, and more. At **The Shrimp Factory** (Blvd. Marina at Guerrero, tel. 624/143-5066, noon–11 P.M. daily, mains US$10–20), you can order shrimp or lobster by the kilo (US$20–30 per half kilo)—served with bread, salad, and crackers—and go to town.

For upscale dining on the beach, you can't beat **Las Palmas** (Playa el Médano, a few buildings northeast of Camino de los Pescadores, tel. 624/143-0447, laspalmascabo@hotmail.com, 10 A.M.–11 P.M. daily, mains US$10–15). Choose a table on the raised patio or on the sand below, order the signature shrimp carousel dish, and enjoy the views.

On the marina, family-oriented **Solomon's Landing** (tel. 624/143-3050, 7 A.M.–11 P.M. daily, mains US$10–30), behind the Tesoro Hotel, prepares a variety of tasty shellfish entrées.

The shrimp and lobster combo (US$17) is the way to go at **◖ Maro's Shrimp House** (Hidalgo btw Madero/Zapata, tel. 624/355-8060, mains US$14–20), where owner Maro and his high-energy staff greet a loyal clientele by name. Start with a bowl of tortilla soup; then order the fresh shellfish by the kilo and the house-special Bulldog, if you dare. The best dish for landlubbers is the sizzling *molcajete* (stone bowl) with slices of skirt steak or chicken. For dessert, Maro's wife makes homemade coconut and chocolate ice cream as well as chocolate cake. This small open-air restaurant is easy to find across the street from La Dolce and Mama's Royal Café. A half kilo of medium-size shrimp costs US$14, and a half kilo of lobster is US$20.

On the marina next to Pisces Fleet and near the Tesoro Resort, **Captain Tony's** (tel.

© NIKKI GOTH ITOI

Maro's Shrimp House is a popular eatery.

624/143-6797, 6 A.M.–9:30 P.M. daily, mains US$11–30) will cook your fresh catch. A bucket of five beers goes for US$10.

Italian and Continental

On Plaza Amelia Wilkes, next to Mi Casa, newcomer **DOC Wine Bar** (Av. Cabo San Lucas btw Lázaro Cárdenas/Madero, tel. 624/143-8500, www.docwinebarcabo.com, 1–11 P.M. Mon.–Sat.; mains US$8–15) draws a crowd for wines by the glass and Italian fare.

Southern Italian defines the hearty cuisine at **Capo San Giovanni** (Guerrero at Madero, tel. 624/143-0593, 5–11 P.M. Tues.–Sun., mains US$13–32). The restaurant is located roughly across from Cabo Wabo.

Near the Solmar and Finisterra hotels, **Romeo & Julieta** (Camino al Pedregal, tel. 624/143-0225, 4–11 P.M. daily, mains US$10–20) aims to create a Spanish/Mediterranean feel with a menu of mesquite wood–fired pizza and homemade pasta dishes. In the plaza below the Puerto Paraíso mall, **Amarone** (Store #107, tel. 624/105-1035, lunch and dinner daily) prepares starters like antipasti or prosciutto and melon for US$12 and lobster or veal filet for US$38. Also downtown, **La Dolce Italian Restaurant & Pizzeria** (Hidalgo and Zapata, tel. 624/143-4122, 6–11 P.M. daily, mains US$10–20) serves a full menu of pastas and pizzas, plus Italian starters and desserts.

The appetizer list at **Peacocks Restaurant and Bar** (Camino de los Pescadores at Vicario, tel. 624/143-1858, 6–10 P.M. daily, mains US$20–30) demonstrates the creative powers of its chef: salmon tartar tower, calamari fusilli in a cilantro pesto, and sautéed lobster dumplings. Combined with the lovely garden setting, the menu makes for an enchanting evening.

Olé Olé (Plaza Bonita Loc. 3A, tel. 624/143-0633, 7 A.M.–11 P.M. daily, mains US$15–40) faces the marina at Plaza Bonita. The large outdoor tapas bar features Spanish cuisine and dinner combos. Paella (US$22) is served from 1 P.M. on Sunday (and sometimes on Friday).

Salvatore's Italian Restaurant (Zapata btw Guerrero/Hidalgo, tel. 624/105-1044) serves up hearty lasagna, chicken parm, and osso buco in a courtyard setting. The large portions of American-style lasagna, reasonably priced, are a hit.

American and Eclectic

Popular with Corridor residents and Baja old-timers, **Latitude 22 Roadhouse** (Km. 4.5, tel. 624/143-1516, www.lat22nobaddays.com, 8 A.M.–11 P.M. Wed.–Mon., mains US$10–20) prepares a Croatian-influenced menu of slow-roasted prime rib, steak, burgers, ribs, shrimp, fish, chicken fried steak, and pastas. Ocean views, reasonably priced cocktails, and giant flat-screen TVs add to the dining experience. Formerly a downtown hangout, "Lat 22" is now located next Costco and behind the power plant.

Serious carnivores have some choices: **Brasil Steakhouse** (Zapata at Hidalgo, tel. 624/143-8343, 5–11 P.M. daily, US$25 pp) serves an all-you-can-eat feast of top sirloin, New York strip, *arranchera,* sausage, ribs, and more. The chef slices meats from a serving skewer at the table while the waitstaff delivers fresh salads and vegetables. The chicken wings that come as an appetizer rival the best you can find in the United States. Try the *caipirinha* cocktail to start—essentially a mojito without the mint.

These days, the best steaks in town are grilled to order at the understated ◖ **Patagonia** (Niños Heroes near Matamoros, tel. 624/143-3874, www.patagonia.freevar.com, Mon.–Sat., mains US$15–30), an Argentinian steakhouse located just a few blocks away from the main restaurant zone. The setting is no frills, and the food is top-notch—as in grass-fed beef and sweetbreads that rank among the best anywhere. Order a bottle of red wine or an ice-cold beer to wash it down.

The English-speaking staff at the **Stop Light Bar and Grill** (Lázaro Cárdenas and Morelos, tel. 624/143-4740, breakfast, lunch, and dinner daily, mains US$6–19) serves a decent breakfast of eggs, pancakes, and *chilaquiles.* Portions are large, and cocktails are served in glasses, not plastic. Dinner fare includes ceviche, snails, sandwiches, salads, and enchiladas as well as lobster, steak, and pasta.

Taquerias and Quick Bites

To find the local fast-food options, you need to venture away from the marina. Calles Morelos and Ocampo are good bets for tacos, *tortas,* seafood cocktails, and the like. The **Carnitas Los Michoacanos** chain has two locations in town (Vicario btw Carranza/Obregón, tel. 624/105-0713, and on Mexico 19 across from Soriana, tel. 624/146-3565). For tacos *al pastor* (shepherd's style, served from a rotisserie grill), try **El Palacio del Taco** (16 de Septiembre btw Morelos/Vicario, cell tel. 624/147-6894, 8:30 a.m.–3 a.m. daily).

Las Quesadillas (Blvd. Marina at Lázaro Cárdenas, tel. 624/143-1373, 7 a.m.–2 a.m. daily, mains US$6–13), opposite Arámburo Plaza, is a good bet for late-night dining.

In the plaza below Cabo Wabo, **Taco Loco** (Guerrero btw. Madero/Lázaro Cárdenas, no tel.) serves bean, chicken, pork, and shrimp tacos for US$1 each. **La Luna** (Camino Real, tel. 624/105-0132, noon–10 p.m. Tues.–Sat., noon–6 p.m. Sun.), behind the Pueblo Bonito Rosé resort, serves wraps, burgers, and tacos.

Gordo Lele's (tel. 624/109-1778), on Calle Matamoros, does tacos with a twist: carne asada with tomatoes and corn mixed in, and a Beatles performance while you dine. Authentic it is not, but for most travelers, a meal here turns into a memorable experience.

Delicatessens

Across from the City Club on Paseo del Pescador, **Lenny's Deli** (tel. 624/143-8380, 7 a.m.–4 p.m. daily) bakes fresh bagels, sourdough, and rye breads daily and prepares authentic New York and Philly-style subs. Its box lunches are good sustenance for a day of fishing. You can also order sandwiches at **La Europea** (no tel., 9 a.m.–8 p.m. daily, mains US$5–12), just outside the Puerto Paraíso mall. There are a few tables out front, overlooking the marina. Air-conditioned booths are a comfortable place to grab a sandwich (and check your email with free Wi-Fi) at **Señor Greenberg's Mexicatessen** (tel. 624/143-5630, 24 hours daily, mains US$5–12), which has several locations, including a

new deli next to Johnny Rockets in the Puerto Paraíso mall.

Breakfast and Cafés

One of the best places to get breakfast in Cabo San Lucas these days is 🄲 **Mama's Royal Café** (Hidalgo btw Zapata/Madero, tel. 624/143-4290, 7:30 a.m.–2 p.m. daily, mains US$7–15). Brightly colored woven linens serve as tablecloths in this small indoor/outdoor café. Start with the signature mango mimosa, served in a giant sundae glass. Then move on to the traditional breakfast burrito or the chef's creative interpretation of *chilaquiles,* in which the tortillas are cut in strips instead of wedges and served with a medley of seasoned vegetables (avocado, mushrooms, spinach, and tomato) instead of smothered in sauce. The menu features exceptionally fresh ingredients. The only downside: no espresso drinks.

Starbucks has finally made an appearance in Cabo (Plaza Bonita), but so far, the cafés are holding their own. **Theory Café** (tel. 624/143-5518, from 10 a.m. daily, mains US$8–12), in the center of Plaza Bonita, serves lattes, mochas, and frappes, and plays music like the Red Hot Chili Peppers. Use your laptop or theirs for wireless Internet. **Cabo Coffee Company** (Hidalgo and Madero, tel. 624/105-1130) has expanded to a new Internet café with high-speed wireless connections, across from its original roasting facility. This is your stop for 100 percent organic brews. A satellite location is also available outside the Giggling Marlin (Matamoros at Blvd. Marina).

Among the many dockside restaurants by the marina, **Baja Cantina** (Dock L–M, tel. 624/143-1591, mains US$7–15) serves tasty jalapeño poppers, artichoke and spinach dip, and other starters for US$5–8, as well as fish, burgers, and Mexican plates for dinner. Wireless Internet is a plus. Look for a second location at Playa El Médano near where Camino Pescadores ends at the beach (tel. 624/143-9773).

Beach Club Bar/Restaurants

A string of dance club bar/restaurants lines the beach at Playa El Médano in front of Casa

Dorada: One of the best known among these is **The Office** (Playa El Médano at Camino Pescadores, tel. 624/143-3464, lunch and dinner daily), but travelers often cite inflated prices here.

A better option these days is **Nikki Beach,** the trendy beach club of the ME Cabo resort. A lounge music beat keeps people moving all day long and well into the night. Nonguests pay a day-use fee for access to the pool, towels, and lounge beds. Sunbathers eat from a menu of pricey sushi rolls (US$10–15), Kobe beef sliders (US$20), and fish tacos (US$15). Choose a shaded table on the deck, enjoy full sun at a table on the sand, or retreat to the poolside terrace restaurant. Drinks tend to be watered down, but the service is prompt and friendly.

Las Palmas (tel. 624/143-0447, lunch and dinner daily) offers a somewhat classier dining experience and a menu of burgers, seafood, and Mexican plates (lunch mains US$8–15; dinner menus are more expensive).

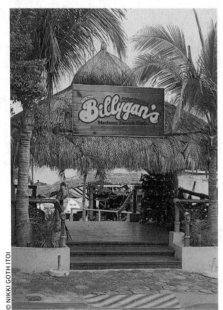
© NIKKI GOTH ITOI
the famous Billygan's Island beach club

In the same vicinity, **Billygan's Island** (tel. 624/143-0402, lunch and dinner daily) and the Mango Deck are similar.

Groceries

Most visitors buy supplies for their Cabo San Lucas stay at **Soriana** (Mex. 19/Carr. Todos Santos and Calle Guajitos, tel. 624/105-1290, www.soriana.com), a Walmart-esque superstore, or at Costco on the Corridor. But there are some smaller options right in town that carry brands from Mexico and the United States. They include **Almacenes Grupo Castro** (southwest corner of Morelos and Revolución, tel. 624/143-0566), **Supermercado Sánliz** (three locations: Blvd. Marina at Madero, Ocampo at Matamoros, and Vicario at López Mateos), and **Supermercado Arámburo** (Arámburo Plaza, Lázaro Cárdenas at Zaragoza, tel. 624/143-1450). There is also a **CCC** (Centro Comercial California, tel. 624/146-7200) on the east side of Mexico 19, just north of the junction with Mexico 1 and before the Soriana. On the east side of town, warehouse-style **City Club** (Blvd. Lázaro Cárdenas at Paseo del Pescador, tel. 624/143-9492, www.soriana.com) has groceries, produce, and baked goods.

Pescadería El Dorado (5 de Febrero btw Abasolo/Ocampo, tel. 624/143-2820) is a good bet for fresh fish and shellfish. You can buy fresh tortillas at **Tortillería Perla** (Morelos btw Hidalgo/Matamoros, tel. 624/143-1381).

Next to the entrance to the Pedregal community, **La Baguette** (Blvd. Lázaro Cárdenas, tel. 624/142-1125, 8:30 A.M.–7:30 P.M. Mon.–Sat.) specializes in pastries, bagels, and breads from Europe and the United States. For a sweet tooth, the **Swiss Pastry** (Hidalgo at Lázaro Cárdenas, across from the plaza, tel. 624/143-3494, 7 A.M.–4 P.M. Mon.–Sat.) has homemade chocolates and candies as well as a variety of pastries.

For fresh fruits and vegetables, head over to **Frutería Lizarraga** (Matamoros at Av. de la Juventud, tel. 624/143-1215). And for organic produce and imported wines, try **Tutto Bene!** (Blvd. Marina, opposite the Wyndham Cabo San Lucas Resort, tel. 624/144-3300, 9:30 A.M.–9 P.M. daily).

INFORMATION AND SERVICES
Tourist Assistance
The **Los Cabos Tourism Trust** (Fideicomiso de Turismo de Los Cabos) has an office on Lázaro Cárdenas Edificio Posada (tel. 624/143-4777, toll-free U.S. tel. 866/567-2226).

Money
There is no shortage of ATMs in Cabo San Lucas, and U.S. currency is accepted just about anywhere; however, in most cases, you'll get a better deal if you pay in pesos. You can exchange money 8:30 A.M.–noon Monday–Saturday at **Bancomer** (Lázaro Cárdenas btw Hidalgo/Guerrero, tel. 624/143-2992), **Banamex** (Hidalgo at Lázaro Cárdenas, tel. 624/143-0767), and **Santander Serfín** (in Arámburo Plaza, tel. 624/144-4730). Avoid exchanging money at the airport or other money-change stands in town, as they will always charge you more.

Post and Telephone
The local **post office** (Lázaro Cárdenas at 16 de Septiembre) is open 8 A.M.–4:30 P.M. Monday–Friday and 9 A.M.–1 P.M. Saturday. It's next to McDonald's and across from the Mini Market, in a yellow building with a clock on top. **Public telephone booths** are scattered around town, and long-distance services are often found inside Internet cafés.

Mail Boxes Etc. (Blvd. Marina 39-F, Plaza Fiesta, tel. 624/143-3033, fax 624/143-3031) carries mailing supplies, postage stamps, and magazines.

Internet Access
Cabo San Lucas has experienced a proliferation of Internet cafés, although they seem to come, change hands, and go faster than the taco stands. Coffee shops and real estate offices are good places to check. Prices have come down quite a bit in recent years, settling at about US$2–6 per hour. If you travel with your own computer, wireless Internet access is also widely available in Los Cabos hotels and

---

CABO SAN LUCAS PHONE NUMBERS

- Cabo San Lucas Area Code: 624
- Police (emergency): 060
- Police (non-emergency): 143-3977 or 143-5123
- Red Cross (emergency): 065
- Red Cross (non-emergency): 143-3300
- AmeriMed: 624/105-8500
- Fire Department: 142-3577
- Hyperbaric Chamber: 143-3666
- Immigration: 143-0135
- U.S. Consulate: 143-3566

---

campgrounds—and many also have public computers available for guest use.

The lobby of the **Siesta Suites Hotel** (Zapata btw. Guerrero/Hidalgo, tel. 624/143-2773) has three fast PCs (with USB ports) for US$3 per hour.

There are several places in town where you can enjoy a latte or cappuccino while you check your email: **Theory Café** (tel. 624/143-5518), in the center of Plaza Bonita, opens at 10 A.M. daily. **Cabo Coffee Company** (Hidalgo and Madero, tel. 624/105-1130, U.S. tel. 619/819-7953, www.cabocoffee.com) has expanded to an Internet café with high-speed wireless connections. A satellite location is also available outside the Giggling Marlin.

Laundry
Cabo has a number of self-serve and full-service laundry facilities scattered about town. One of the most reputable is **Lavandería Evelyn** (Matamoros and Mijares, tel. 624/143-0920, 7 A.M.–7 P.M. daily), which has a self-service option. **Marina Sol Condominiums** (Aquario btw Paseo del Pescador/Paseo de la Marina, tel. 624/143-5430) has an on-site laundry and

dry cleaning service with quick turnaround times: same day for laundry and next day for dry cleaning.

Magazines and Newspapers

The online **Los Cabos Guide** (www.loscabosguide.com) contains overviews of many Los Cabos businesses, including hotels, restaurants, and outfitters; much of its content is promotional in nature and some of the information is several years out of date, but the listings are fairly thorough. Another handy resource is the **Los Cabos Gringo Pages** (tel. 624/104-3887, www.thegringopages.com), an annual yellow pages listing covering the entire Los Cabos region, with some listings for Todos Santos and the East Cape as well.

The local Spanish-language newspaper is **El Heraldo de los Cabos.** The **Gringo Gazette** aims to get the inside scoop on all things Baja for an audience of expats and frequent visitors. **Destino** is another promotional paper that is available or free. The bilingual **Los Cabos News** reports on happenings from Cabo San Lucas to San José.

Bahía Jiromar also carries some English-language periodicals (Puerto Paraíso Local #284, tel. 624/144-3250).

Language Courses

California Conexion (locations vary, tel. 624/108-2095, thecaliforniaconexion@hotmail.com) holds Spanish classes for beginners and intermediate students.

Medical Services

Dial 066 for emergency situations. Check the *Los Cabos Gringo Pages,* available in many hotels, for English-speaking doctors and clinics. **AmeriMed** (Pioneros Building Loc. 1, Blvd. Lázaro Cárdenas, tel. 624/143-9670) has a bilingual staff trained to handle emergencies, along with OB/GYN care and a family practice. The clinic is open 24/7 and accepts most insurance policies. **BlueMedicalNet** (tel.

624/104-3911, 24/7 daily) operates a clinic in the Plaza del Rey, across from Home Depot.

Immigration

Cabo's *migración* office is on the north side of Boulevard Lázaro Cárdenas between Gómez Farías and 16 de Septiembre, across from the Banamex.

U.S. Consulate

The U.S. consular agency in Cabo San Lucas is at Plaza Naútica (C-4, Blvd. Marina, tel. 624/143-3566, usconsulcabo@hotmail.com, 10 A.M.–1 P.M. Mon.–Fri.). This is the place to go if you lose your passport or for other emergencies.

GETTING AROUND

The majority of Cabo San Lucas visitors get around by foot and by cab. A taxi ride around town should cost around US$6, but it's always a good idea to ask for a quote before you hop in.

You can hire water taxis from the marina in front of the Tesoro Hotel to Playa El Médano (US$3) and Playa del Amor (US$8–12, round-trip only).

For trips to the Corridor and beyond, a rental car comes in handy. Rates are lower from the airport, but if you only want the car for a day or two of a longer trip, then renting in town makes sense. Options include Budget/Fox (Wyndham Cabo San Lucas Resort, Lázaro Cárdenas, www.budgetbaja.com), Dollar (Lázaro Cárdenas s/n btw Vicario/Mendoza, tel. 800/801-0365, U.S. tel. 800/002-8343, www.dollarloscabos.com, 7 A.M.–8 P.M. daily), Avis (Hotel Pueblo Bonito Rosé, Playa El Médano, tel. 624/143-2422, ext. 2847, and Pueblo Bonito Sunset Beach, Predio Paraíso Escondido s/n, tel. 624/143-4607, 8 A.M.–10 P.M. daily, both locations), and Thrifty (ME Cabo, Playa El Médano s/n, tel. 624/144-0406).

Other ways to get around include mopeds and ATVs. Look for vendors advertising these services along Boulevard Marina.

THE WEST CAPE AND TODOS SANTOS

A few hundred meters past the modern Soriana shopping complex in Cabo San Lucas, the urban sprawl abruptly ends, cows reclaim the road, and the Pacific Ocean eventually pops into view. A lone trailer or two has set up camp along the shore, but you can't quite tell which dirt road they drove to get there. If it's late fall or early winter, wildflowers may still dot the landscape with a splash of color.

Don't get too lost in the scenery, however, or the Aguila bus driver tailgating you might very well decide to pass on a blind turn just as an 18-wheeler approaches from the opposite direction. Welcome to the West Cape, the least developed stretch of coastline on the lower part of the Baja Peninsula. Although paved, two-lane Mexico 19 (soon to be four lanes from start to finish) connects Cabo San Lucas to

Todos Santos and meets Mexico 1 just south of La Paz. Housing developments are still few and far between. Several large real estate projects are in the early stages near the farming community of El Pescadero and close to Cabo San Lucas, leaving the middle stretch to the pelicans, rancheros, fishermen, and the occasional ATV tour.

Once considered a stopover on the drive from La Paz to Cabo San Lucas, bohemian Todos Santos has become a destination in its own right. Surfers, artists, retirees, exotic bird rescuers, and yoga students all cross paths here, and at least several hundred of them are permanent expat residents. Over the last few years, Todos Santos has basked in the attention of its designation as a Pueblo Mágico—one of only 23 small towns in Mexico given government

HIGHLIGHTS

◖ La Candelaria: Experience the rancho way of life in this rural village set in the foothills of the lower Sierra de la Laguna. Book a trip with Todos Santos Eco Adventures or plan your own excursion (page 377).

◖ Playa Los Cerritos: Popular with novice surfers, swimmers, and sunbathers, this gently sloped beach lies comfortably protected from winter's northwest swell. Eagle rays, puffer fish, and other marine life await discovery (page 378).

◖ Playa San Pedrito (Playa Las Palmas): Rock cliffs at either end of the beach frame your view of the Pacific at this beach near Todos Santos. Bring a picnic and enjoy the secluded setting (page 380).

◖ Todos Santos Historic District: Explore narrow streets with rows of colorful, century-old facades and the signature large windows and doors of the Andalusian architecture style. Browse the galleries and then rest at an outdoor café (page 387).

◖ La Poza: A small freshwater lagoon within walking distance of Todos Santos is a paradise for bird watchers (page 389).

LOOK FOR ◖ TO FIND RECOMMENDED SIGHTS, ACTIVITIES, DINING, AND LODGING.

funding to make their culture and history more accessible to tourists and travelers. Foreign and Mexican locals alike remain optimistic that the town will be able to preserve its artsy character even as the number of visitors increases.

The busloads of visitors no longer come from Los Cabos, but a few development efforts have persevered through the global economic recession, notably at Playa Los Cerritos, in El Pescadero, and along the beaches north of Todos Santos. Longtime residents lament the addition of new hotels and homes, while business owners welcome potential new customers.

PLANNING YOUR TIME

The drive from Cabo San Lucas to Todos Santos via Mexico 19 and the West Cape takes approximately one hour—making it an easy day trip for visitors who are staying in the Los Cabos area—or a slightly longer drive (90 minutes) directly from the airport.

You can take in most of what Todos Santos has to offer in a full day of sightseeing, covering the historic buildings and galleries in town and a beach or two along the coast. But as with most other towns in Baja, you'll enjoy the West Cape infinitely more if you stay long enough to wander kilometers of virgin, as-yet-undeveloped beaches stretching north and south from Todos Santos along the Pacific, explore the steep western escarpment of the Sierra de la Laguna, or simply hang out and soak up the small-town ambience.

Backpackers often plan multiday trips into

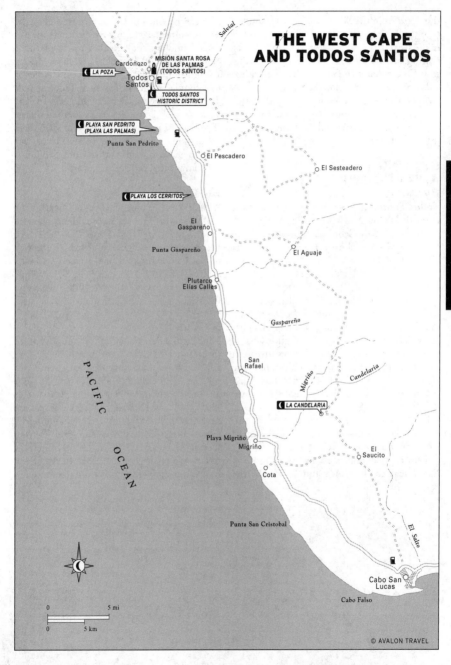

THE WEST CAPE
AND TODOS SANTOS

THE WEST CAPE

Salsial

Cardonozo
LA POZA
MISIÓN SANTA ROSA
DE LAS PALMAS
(TODOS SANTOS)
Todos
Santos
TODOS SANTOS
HISTORIC DISTRICT

PLAYA SAN PEDRITO
(PLAYA LAS PALMAS)
Punta San Pedrito

El Pescadero
El Sesteadero

PLAYA LOS CERRITOS

El
Gaspareño
El Aguaje
Punta Gaspareño

Plutarco
Elías Calles

Gaspareño

San
Rafael
Migriño
Candelaria
LA CANDELARIA

PACIFIC
Playa Migriño
Migriño
El
Saucito
Cota
OCEAN

Punta San Cristobal
El Salto

Cabo San
Lucas
Cabo Falso

0   5 mi
0   5 km

© AVALON TRAVEL

the sierra from the West Cape. If that sounds too challenging, guides also run half-day hikes as well as trail rides on ATVs. A day of fishing or surfing could also lengthen your stay. Of course, if you're into these activities, a day probably isn't enough. Surfers can easily spend a week or a month trying to master the winter breaks here. And the fishing—whether by boat, surf rod, or hand line—is just as addictive.

GETTING THERE AND AROUND
By Air
Todos Santos is more or less equidistant from the Los Cabos and La Paz airports. A shuttle from Los Cabos costs approximately US$150, while a shuttle from La Paz runs US$200–300.

By Car
Though not essential, most travelers will want to have a car while staying in the West Cape and Todos Santos, as the beaches and sights are spread out from the two small towns. If you don't rent a car at the airport or drive your own from the United States, you can rent one in Todos Santos. Mexican-owned **Fox Rent a Car** (formerly a Budget affiliate, Márquez de León 4, tel. 612/145-0615, toll-free U.S. tel. 866/496-2880, www.foxrentacar.com, 8 A.M.–6 P.M. Mon.–Sat.) offers a small fleet of cars from economy to SUV.

Mexico 19 connects Todos Santos to Cabo San Lucas to the south and La Paz to the north. From the Los Cabos airport, follow the Transpeninsular Highway (Mexico 1) toward Cabo San Lucas and take the turnoff for Todos Santos/Mexico 19. From La Paz, follow Mexico 1 south to the turnoff for Mexico 19, which is now four lanes the entire way to Todos Santos. There are numerous Pemex stations in La Paz, Todos Santos, Pescadero, and Cabo San Lucas. If you need a mechanic during your visit, there are a couple of options in Todos Santos, but you may have to head south to Cabo San Lucas for complicated transmission work.

By Taxi
A small fleet of blue vans parked next to the park in Todos Santos can provide taxi service around town for US$5 a trip. Taxi service to Pescadero is about US$20. A van all the way to Los Cabos International Airport will cost around US$200; vans can hold 8–15 people with luggage. Call 612/145-0063 for more information.

By Bus
Nine Aguila buses a day connect Todos Santos to La Paz and Cabo San Lucas. The La Paz and Cabo San Lucas bus trips take about two hours and cost about US$8 per person; a bus all the way around to San José del Cabo costs US$12 and to Tijuana, US$130. Tickets are sold on the buses, which arrive at and depart from Colegio Militar and Zaragoza (for San José del Cabo and Cabo San Lucas) or in front of Karla's Lonchería (for La Paz). In Pescadero, buses stop across the street from the Pemex.

The West Cape

A handful of beach communities fronting the Pacific Ocean compose the sparsely populated West Cape. In the shadow of the more established Todos Santos, El Pescadero is emerging as a small center for commerce and tourism.

CABO FALSO TO PLAYA MIGRIÑO

Early explorers once believed that a cape three kilometers west of Cabo San Lucas marked the southern tip of the peninsula. Later cartographers discovered the mistake and named the cape Cabo Falso. Today the wide, sandy beach is protected so that sea turtles can lay their eggs undisturbed; once a popular destination for ATV tours from Cabo San Lucas, the dunes are now off limits as well, due to pending development. An abandoned lighthouse, **El Faro Viejo,** was in operation from 1895 to 1961; some years back, the original lens was moved to a modern lighthouse located higher on the beach.

Inland from Cabo Falso, Mexico 19 enters the foothills of the Sierra de la Laguna and reaches the village of Migriño. The coast here consists of a long, sandy beach dotted with rocks and a small estuary at the mouth of Río Candelaria.

In winter surfers can find a right point break at the north end of the beach, but the camping is no more. Rancho Migriño has moved in, with new home sites for sale.

Playa Migriño is easily accessible from Cabo San Lucas (about 15 minutes by car), with access roads at Km. 94 and Km. 97. The beach is about 2.5 kilometers west of the highway on either road.

☾ LA CANDELARIA

A small ranching settlement in the sierra foothills, La Candelaria is worth a side trip if you want to get away from the crowded beaches and have an off-road adventure. Known for its pottery and *curanderos* (healers who specialize in herbal treatments), the

CABO FALSO TO PLAYA MIGRIÑO

town is most often visited by guided ATV tours, which stop to buy the inexpensive ceramics and swim in the palm oasis. Fewer than 100 people live here year-round, raising livestock and tending to crops of citrus, avocado, and mango. The village itself consists of simple homes with *palapa* roofs, a church, and a school.

THE WEST CAPE

Getting There

There are two ways to reach La Candelaria if you want to drive yourself. The most direct, via Migriño, requires four-wheel drive. The longer route has more turns and forks, but you can make it in most regular vehicles.

FROM PLAYA MIGRIÑO

The route follows the Río Candelaria 9.1 kilometers southwest from Mexico 19 near Playa Migriño. The turnoff is not signed. Look for a dirt road three kilometers south of Km. 94, or about a half kilometer north of the main Playa Migriño turnoff (Km. 97). The road is sandy and narrow in places. Do not attempt the drive in the rainy season.

FROM CABO SAN LUCAS

From downtown Cabo San Lucas, drive along Boulevard Lázaro Cárdenas east toward San José and turn left at Boulevard Constituyentes (also labeled Av. Reforma on some maps) and the sign for La Paz Via Corta. Follow this street northwest toward Todos Santos and La Paz, past a soccer field on the left. At the power plant on the right side, turn onto a wide dirt road (1.7 km from the intersection of Blvds. Lázaro Cárdenas and Constituyentes).

From here, La Candelaria is 22 kilometers away, assuming you manage to find all the correct turns on the first try. Turn right 4.3 kilometers from the highway at the sign for La Candelaria and Los Pozos. Pass through the fence and cattle guard—an attendant may be on guard to prevent livestock theft. Watch for cattle in the road from here on.

Twelve kilometers from the highway, the road forks. Stay left, ignoring the right branch, which goes to San Felipe and El Sauzal. Next come the ranches and adobe ruins of Los Pozos. There is a small chapel 14 kilometers into the drive (measuring from the highway). Keep following signs for La Candelaria and La Trinidad, ignoring any smaller branches off the main road.

Soon the Pacific Ocean comes into view. About 21 kilometers from the highway is a turnoff for Rancho San Ramón, after which

is another fork. Both branches will get you to La Candelaria, but the right fork is quicker. It crosses an arroyo, passes a turn to La Trinidad, and then arrives in La Candelaria.

ATV TOURS

An easy way to visit La Candelaria is by guided ATV tour. Several companies have rental stands along Mexico 19, near Playa Migriño. Contact **Baja's Activities** (Km. 104–105, tel. 624/143-2050, www.bajasactivities.com), **Motosol** (Km. 99.5, Mex. 19, Migriño, tel. 624/143-9393, www.atvsmotosol.com; 8 A.M.–7 P.M. daily; US$70–95), or Amigos (tel. 624/144-4161, www.amigosactivities.com) to make a reservation. Tours run US$65–90 for single riders, US$85–120 for doubles, and usually include helmets, goggles, bandanas, training, bottled water, and a bilingual guide.

EL PESCADERO AND VICINITY

In recent years, the area around El Pescadero has seen the rise of many new homes and businesses, most notably the stunning **Rancho Pescadero** resort. Happily, you can still get lost in the maze of unmarked dirt roads that lead from the highway to the beach.

Rancho Pilar

Originally from La Paz, Cuco Moyron (Km. 73, Mexico 19, ranchopilar@hotmail.com) is an artist, craftsman, and naturalist who uses recycled tire-rubber soles to make custom-fit sandals (US$35 a pair). He and his wife, Pilar, also make pottery, jewelry, and hats of woven grass. They have campsites available on their property. Cuco leads informative trips through the Sierra de la Laguna. Allow a week to make arrangements. At Km. 73, take the dirt road toward the beach until you see the Rancho Pilar sign on the left.

◖ Playa Los Cerritos

The West Cape's most popular beach awaits at Km. 64 (12.8 km south of Todos Santos). A handful of new businesses now provide food and accommodations, and some camping options are once again available.

EL PESCADERO AND VICINITY

To San Pedro and La Paz

To La Pastora, El Carrizal, and Las Playitas

Playa la Cachora

San Ignacio

MISIÓN SANTA ROSA DE LAS PALMAS (TODOS SANTOS)

La Poza

Todos Santos

Cerro La Calera

Cerro La Poza

Cerro Salado

LIGHTHOUSE

GRADED ROAD

Punta Lobos

Puerto Campechana

Puerto Algodones

PLAYA SAN PEDRITO (PLAYA LAS PALMAS)

Cerro San Pedro

CAMPO EXPERIMENTAL

Punta San Pedro

Cerro Los Viejos

Agua

Grande

Playa San Pedro

San Juan

RANCHO PESCADERO

El Pescadero

GRADED ROAD

GRADED ROAD

0   1 mi

0   1 km

Cerro Tecolote

Cerro El Gavilan

GRADED ROAD

Cuatro Vientos

Punta Pescadero

PLAYA LOS CERRITOS

To Cabo San Lucas

© AVALON TRAVEL

Road construction obscured the sign to Playa Los Cerritos at last check, but the dirt road to the beach is well traveled, and signs to Hacienda Cerritos point the way. From the turn, drive 2.7 kilometers southwest until you reach the sandy parking area. Sheltered by Punta Pescadero at its north end, the beach is usually safe for swimming, though you should ask at the surf shops about currents and riptides before getting in the water. Also keep a lookout for flying surfboards on busy days. Throw on a pair of goggles and you may even catch a glimpse of a spotted eagle ray gliding by just offshore. Boogie boarding is another popular activity.

This is generally a good beginner surf spot, but it can get big in the right conditions. Several surf shops rent boards and offer lessons.

The only food right on the beach comes from **Los Cerritos Beach Club** (tel. 624/143-4850, cell tel. 624/129-6315, www.cerritos-bcs.com, breakfast, lunch, and dinner daily, mains US$7–20), which offers a menu of ceviche, pasta, sandwiches, and the like. It has a full bar as well as restrooms for paying customers. A short walk uphill from the beach, toward the highway, **Miguel's** (10 A.M.–8 P.M. Thurs.–Tues., mains US$5–15), a well-known Todos Santos eatery, has opened a satellite location for tasty Mexican fare.

About five kilometers south, near Km. 75, a new real estate development, **Tortuga del Sol** (www.tortugadelsol.net) is taking shape with 123 home sites.

El Pescadero

As you approach El Pescadero from the south (Km. 62), hilly terrain gives way on the west side of Mexico 19 to a series of flat, cultivated fields fed by underground springs, most of which are bordered by a single row of tall corn stalks to break the wind. Between fields of cherry tomatoes and basil, a number of palm-lined dirt roads meander to the water's edge. Though still much smaller and more spread out than its neighbor to the north, El Pescadero has evolved in recent years from a cluster of simple *tiendas* and *loncherías* into a more developed business center with its own Pemex and Oxxo convenience store. The first major real estate development underway in the area is the 20-hectare gated community of **Playa Agave Azul.** More development is under way at nearby Playa Los Cerritos.

Local expat residents here are involved with turtle conservation efforts, through egg collection and baby turtle release programs as well as the building of an educational amphitheater, designed in the shape of a turtle, to promote ecological awareness. Visit www.bajaturtle.com for more information.

Dirt roads heading to the beach can be a bit tricky to navigate. There are few street names or signs, and many roads dead-end at someone's driveway. The easiest way to find most of Pescadero's waterfront attractions is to follow a wide dirt road with a row of palms in the median that meets Mexico 19 just across from the Sandbar restaurant. If you've rented a place along this stretch of coast, be sure to get specific directions to find it.

a taco stand in El Pescadero

Playa San Pedro

Playa San Pedro extends north from El Pescadero to Punta San Pedro. It is filled with cobblestones near the point but sandy the rest of the way south. Surfable waves break along the north end of the beach. The access road may be difficult to find at Km. 59 due to road construction. Once off the pavement, follow the dirt road 3.1 kilometers west to the beach.

Playa San Pedrito (Playa Las Palmas)

Harder to find, Little San Pedro Beach (Km. 56–57) also goes by the name of Palm Beach. With its fan palms and salt marsh, you might forget you're in the desert here. Enclosed by rocky points at either end, the beach can offer good swimming, shore fishing, and surfing, depending on the swell. Watch for riptides near the points. Beach camping is permitted on the sand. The access road to San Pedrito is across from the Campo Experimental buildings on Mexico 19. Stay left when you reach the ruined mansion and you'll arrive at the south end of the palm orchard. From here, it's a short walk to the water's edge.

Sierra de la Laguna

East of El Pescadero, you can navigate a network of dirt roads up into the foothills to palm-filled arroyos, remote ranches, and stands of *cardón* cacti. A high-clearance vehicle is a necessity; better yet, park in the foothills and hike in. It's easy to become lost here, so consider hiring a guide in El Pescadero or Todos Santos. At **Rancho Pilar** (Km. 73, Mexico 19, ranchopilar@hotmail.com), artisan and amateur naturalist Cuco Moyron can arrange mule trips into the sierra and provides interesting information about the local plants and animals. He'll need about a week to make the arrangements for your trip. In Todos Santos, **Todos Santos Eco Adventures** (Cerro La Poza, Calle Guaycura, tel. 612/145-0780, www.tosea.net) arranges one-day and multiday hikes, including a trip to visit a celebrated local mountain potter named Doña Ramona, who welcomes guests to experience her family's working ranch for a day. A variation of this day trip involves a back-roads jaunt over to La Candelaria to meet yet more potters.

The rugged, and often impassable, Naranjos road heads southeast from a point near Playa Los Cerritos and crosses the Sierra de la Laguna to join Mexico 1 between Santa Anita and Caduaño.

SPORTS AND RECREATION
Surfing
Surfable waves pound the West Cape in winter, from Playa Migriño all the way to Punta Márquez, north of Todos Santos. Beginning in the south, Migriño has an exposed right point and hollow beach break. Punta Gaspareño, a rock-bottomed right point break at Km. 73, breaks best in large west or northwest swells. Playa San Pedro (Km. 59, site of the former San Pedrito RV park) offers fairly consistent right reef and beach breaks; paddle out from the beach to avoid urchins on the reef. A little farther north, Playa San Pedrito has another beach break, best enjoyed during a west or north swell.

Popular with novice surfers, Playa Los Cerritos has several left and right beach breaks. Ask the local shops about currents and riptides before you hop in for the first time. Experienced surfers will enjoy the right break off the point on larger northwest and south swells. Vacation rentals in the Pescadero area are popular with some surfers, while others prefer to camp north of Todos Santos.

The **Pescadero Surf Camp** (Km. 64, www.pescaderosurf.com) offers cabanas, campsites, board rentals, and instruction. The Costa Azul Surf Shop and El Diablo Blanco rent boards at Los Cerritos from dawn till dusk. **Mario Surf School** (Cerritos Beach, tel. 612/142-6156, www.mariosurfschool.com) also rents boards (US$20/day) and offers lessons (US$60/hour), ding repair, and accessories you may have forgotten at home. Two blue beach umbrellas near the lifeguard tower serve as Mario's office, or look him up through Todos Santos Eco Adventures (www.tosea.net).

Skating
Also at Km. 64, the **Baja Life Camp** (Barrio Las Palmitas, tel. 612/141-9440, camping US$10) has a skate park (1–6 P.M. Tues.–Fri., 11 A.M.–6 P.M. Sat.–Sun., US$2).

Swimming
Most of the beaches along the West Cape are exposed to heavy surf; however, on calm days Playa Los Cerritos and Playa Las Palmas offer sheltered conditions for an ocean swim. At Las Palmas, the middle section of the cove is usually the safest. Toward the north and south ends, the water looks shallow and inviting, but riptides pose a danger.

Yoga and Spa Services
Yandara Yoga Institute (Km. 73, Mexico 19, www.yandara.com) offers yoga instructor courses several times a year. Students prepare most of their meals from the house *huerta*. At Km. 73, take the dirt road toward the beach until it ends and then turn left. Another studio at the Mini Super Los Arcos, across from the Pemex, offers **Hatha yoga** classes taught in Spanish (tel. 612/130-3006, 9 A.M.–10:30 A.M. Mon., Wed., Fri., US$5/class). **Rancho Pescadero** (www.ranchopescadero.com) offers morning yoga classes beginning at 9 A.M. daily, plus advanced classes at 4 P.M. on Sunday, Tuesday, and Friday (US$4 per class). Several massage therapists have set up tables on the beach at Playa Los Cerritos. Call Minerva at tel. 624/164-6766 to inquire or book on the spot (US$20 for 30 minutes or US$35 for a full hour).

In a brick building three rows in from the beach, **Los Bules Day Spa** (Playa Congrejos, El Pescadero, tel. 612/118-1062, www.pescadise.com) offers deep-tissue, hot-stone, or Swedish massage (US$50), body wraps (US$45), and facials (US$40–70)—plus a Native American *temazcal*, or sweat lodge (US$20). The proprietor, Maria, is also a gourd artist. Her gallery on the property contains pitchers, bowls, animals, candles, and teacups—all crafted from hard-shelled bottle gourds.

ENTERTAINMENT
When Todos Santos residents want to go out for a night on the town, they head to El Pescadero.

Todos Santos may have more shops and restaurants, but El Pescadero has the **Sandbar** (Km. 63, tel. 612/130-3209, 3 P.M. till late Wed.–Sat. and Mon., 9 A.M.–10 P.M. Sun.), with a pool table, live music, and daily happy-hour specials as well as occasional cook-your-own kebab dinners. Wednesday is all-you-can-eat pizza, and on Sundays, the restaurant shows NFL games all day and serves breakfast, lunch, and dinner.

SHOPPING

A string of *artesanías* selling colorful Mexican blankets, hammocks, and pottery lines the highway south of El Pescadero.

A handful of Candelaria artisans make pottery, baskets, and *palo escopeta*-style chairs. At Km. 69, **The Blanket Factory** (no tel.) is a popular stop for organized tours. Shop here for handmade rugs, blankets, clothing, and hammocks (US$60–80) or request a custom design.

ACCOMMODATIONS

Several longtime El Pescadero inns change hands each year, and new places are opening each season. The most celebrated opening of late is the high-end Rancho Pescadero. A number of private homes have opened up as vacation rental properties.

US$50-100

On the beach in Pescadero, 3.5 kilometers from the wide dirt road that leaves Mexico 19 across from the Sandbar, the **San Pedrito Surf Hotel** (www.sanpedritosurf.com, US$70–105) is a remodel of the former Casa Cyrene. Now owned by two families from Hawaii, the property has five *casitas*. The surf bunkhouse has been converted into a two-bedroom family *casita*. All have full kitchens and king-size beds. Other amenities include bottled water, basic cooking utensils and spices, and linens. There is a washer/dryer on the property.

Also in a beachfront location and a little south of the San Pedrito Surf Hotel, **Casa Simpatica** (http://todossantos.cc/casasimpatica.html, US$65, three-night minimum) features four clean, open air *casitas,* each with a queen-size bed and private bath; guests share an outdoor kitchen. Owner Gary Faulk provides Internet access.

At the San Pedrito surf break, **Las Palmas Tropicales** (www.tropicalcasitas.com, US$75–140) has five *palapa*-roof *casitas* (four with kitchens) with tiled baths and wireless Internet. Also close to the San Pedrito surf break, friendly Rob and Lorinda Costa from Santa Cruz, California, own **Sierra de la Costa** (www.sierradelacosta.com, US$75, three-night minimum), super-clean beach bungalow rentals with queen-size beds, tiled baths, private patios, and gas barbecues.

Set back from the water's edge at Playa Los Cerritos, behind Miguel's restaurant, **Hotelito Los Cardones** (Playa Los Cerritos, www.loscardonesbaja.com) has one ocean-view suite (US$50) and a camping *palapa* area (US$8). Still farther from the beach but with ocean views, Wi-Fi, and a small swimming pool, **Villas de Cerritos** (Playa Los Cerritos, tel. 612/151-3728, www.villasdecerritosbeach.com, US$60) has six two-bedroom villa rentals (US$120–160) and several studio bungalows for US$60 per night.

US$100-150

Near the San Pedro Surf Hotel, **El Pozo Hondo** (pozohondobcs@yahoo.com, US$100–110) is a bed-and-breakfast with two *palapa*-roof bungalows surrounded by mango, avocado, and citrus trees. Guellermo prepares excellent coffee for guests every morning.

Under the same ownership as the Hacienda Cerritos, the **Cerritos Surf Colony** (cell tel. 612/107-9935, U.S. tel. 503/926-8131, www.cerritossurfcolony.com; US$95–125) rents a few small bungalows steps from the surf. Introductory prices were set at US$95 for a studio, US$125 for a one-bedroom, and US$295 for a two-bedroom.

US$150-250

Marble floors, robes, Egyptian cotton sheets, and fluffy towels are just a few of the luxury amenities at **La Alianza** (tel. 612/118-3423, www.bajaturtle.com, US$110–195), a five-room property located between Cerritos and San Pedrito point. Guests share a third-floor *palapa*-roof deck and common kitchen. A separate two-bedroom *casita* has one bath and a kitchen for US$150. Commissioned works from local artisan Cuco Moyron add an authentic Baja twist to the grounds and home. This is the place to stay if you want privacy and that extra-special touch. Owner Debora McIntire is involved with local sea turtle conservation activities to protect the leatherbacks and olive ridleys that nest on the beach in Pescadero. Inquire about participating in a baby turtle release August–December.

Sunflowers bordering an organic vegetable garden lean in the breeze along the driveway that leads to **Rancho Pescadero** (tel. 612/135-5849, www.ranchopescadero.com, US$185–425). Its 26 guestrooms include continental breakfast delivered to your door, daily yoga classes, and the use of two swimming pools, fishing poles, and surfboards. Lounge in daybeds on the beach or book an oceanside massage. A beer lounge on the terrace and lower-level restaurant are open

to the public (7 A.M.–9 P.M. daily). No pets or kids under 12. Rancho Pescadero does not have a street address. To find the hotel, turn west on the first main dirt road south of the Pescadero Pemex. Follow this road for a mile toward the ocean and turn right at the T, and signs will point the way from there.

Over US$250

Perched atop Punta Pescadero, the imposing **Hacienda Cerritos** (Playa Los Cerritos, Km. 65, Mexico 19, cell tel. 612/107-9935, U.S. tel. 503/926-8131, www.haciendacerritos.com, US$295–495) overlooks the beach. This boutique hotel opened in 2010 with four pools, five spas, and 12 suites and bungalows.

Vacation Rentals

Several Todos Santos community websites list vacation rentals in the area. They include www.baja.com, www.bajawesternonion.com, www.todossantos.cc, and www.todosantosguide.com. Vacation Rental by Owner (www.vrbo.com) also has a few West Cape listings. Here are a few of the most popular homes:

© NIKKI GOTH ITOI
the ocean view at Rancho Pescadero

Osprey San Pedrito (Playa San Pedrito, www.bajaosprey.com, US$140–160) is a home divided into three suites, each with its own bedroom, bath, and kitchen. One of the suites on the main level has two bedrooms. The units may be rented separately or together. Cook your own meals in the fully equipped kitchen or walk along the beach to the bar/restaurant at Rancho Pescadero.

Featuring new construction and a location right on the beach, **Dr. Roberts Oceanfront Oasis** (no tel., www.bajaroberts.com, US$60–120) has a main house that sleeps seven and rents for US$350/night, plus a smaller apartment, surf room, and bungalows for smaller groups. Visit the website to make reservations.

For kids (and the young at heart), the highlight of a stay at **Villa del Faro** (U.S. tel. 707/468-0876, www.todosantosguide.com/villadelfaro, US$4,000/week) is the curved waterslide that deposits swimmers into a 12-meter saltwater pool rimmed with fiber-optic lights that glow after dark. Located at the south end of Pescadero Beach, the villa was built to handle a crowd, with three kitchens, five bedrooms, and a hot tub, plus massage and maid services and catering available by request. For more entertainment, there is a Ping-Pong table, volleyball court, and 52-inch television.

Between the Los Cerritos and San Pedrito surf breaks, **Alhaja de Baja** (no tel., www.alhajadebaja.com, US$990/week) is a recently remodeled two-bedroom house with king-size beds.

Camping and RV Parks

RV Park Baja Serena (tel. 612/130-3006, US$12) in El Pescadero offers eight spaces with water and sewer hookups (no electricity) that can be rented by the day, week, or month. The entrance is on Mexico 19, just south of Mini Super Los Arcos, and guests check in at the Los Arcos. **Rancho Pilar** (Km. 73, no tel., rates vary) has several campsites on the property.

At the moment, camping at Playa Los Cerritos is limited to a site here or there mixed in among the new businesses.

Free beach campsites along Mexico 19 await at the ends of several dirt roads that leave Mexico 19 between Km. 89 and 70—though these are quickly disappearing as developers move in.

Surf Camp

On the east side of the highway at Km. 64, **Pescadero Surf Camp** (tel. 612/134-0480, www.pescaderosurf.com, US$30–60) is a good place for die-hard surfers to meet kindred spirits. Options for lodging include a cabana for six with its own kitchen and bath or camping under a *palapa* (US$10 pp/night). Guests may use the swimming pool, hot showers, and shared outdoor kitchen.

FOOD

Restaurant Migriño (Km. 102, Mexico 19, no tel., hours vary, mains U$5), on the west side of the highway, serves basic *antojitos* and refreshingly cold beer. Another road stop is the dirt-floored **Los Idolos de Mexico** (Km. 79, Mexico 19, no tel., hours vary, mains US$5). They keep it simple but tasty with carnitas and tacos *de pescado* and *de camarón*.

Lonchería Rosita (tel. 612/130-3094, 8 A.M.–8 P.M. daily, mains US$5), on the east side of Mexico 19, near the Pemex, is small with a *palapa* roof. Try its pork tamales or *machaca* burritos.

The friendly **Marina's** (Km. 62, no tel., mains US$3–7) offers a nice variety of fish and shrimp tacos, plus quesadillas, a soup of the day, and the huge cheese/carne asada *mixto* (US$3).

Popular with locals and expats alike for its casual fare, **Ⓒ Felipe's Restaurant** (Km. 61, Mexico 19, no tel., hours vary Wed.–Mon., mains around US$8) makes delicious Mexican and seafood dishes at nongringo prices for breakfast, lunch, and dinner. This place serves an excellent shrimp chile relleno and even better *arrachera*.

Grill your own kebabs at the **Sandbar** (Km. 63, Mexico 19, tel. 612/130-3209, 3 P.M. till late Wed.–Sat. and Mon., 9 A.M.–10 P.M. Sun.) or just pop in for daily happy-hour specials as well as weekly all-you-can-eat pizza. Show up for all-you-can-eat spaghetti on Thursdays, reggae night with live music on Fridays (for which there is a US$2–3 cover charge), and disco nights on Saturdays.

The **Los Cerritos Club** (Km. 66.5, Mexico 19, Playa Los Cerritos, tel. 624/143-4850, cell tel. 624/129-6315, 7 A.M.–8 P.M. daily, mains US$5–20) is the perfect place for a beer and a burger after a good surfing session and to enjoy the sunset. Live music plays Friday and Saturday nights.

Regulars praise **Art & Beer** (Km. 69, Mexico 19, no tel., hours vary) for large signature cocktails—creative variations on the Bloody Mary—which comes generously garnished with all manner of shellfish. You must agree to buy a drink or a meal in order to view the art on display. When it's time to go, your eccentric hosts, Alfredo and Lourdes, may offer up a beer for the road. Fish dishes cost US$20. **Rancho Pescadero** (tel. 612/135-5849, www.ranchopescadero.com, 7 A.M.–9 P.M. daily) serves breakfast, lunch, and dinner during the high season, November–May. Dinner mains

such as posole verde, fish/pasta of the day, and grilled rib eye range US$20–30.

Mini Super Los Arcos (no tel.) on Mexico 19 stocks basic groceries, and the owners welcome special orders. **Mini Super Los Cerritos** (Km. 63, Mexico 19, no tel.) sells cold beer and ice as well as some arts and crafts. At Km. 61 you can buy strawberries direct from the farmers at US$1–2 per basket.

INFORMATION AND SERVICES

El Pescadero has the only Pemex between Cabo San Lucas and Todos Santos as well as an Oxxo convenience store. For emergencies, call tel. 612/145-0445 or head to Todos Santos or the Los Cabos area for medical services. Buses en route to La Paz and Cabo San Lucas stop across from the Pemex. Many places in the Pescadero area now have wireless Internet; otherwise, **Gonver's Coffee Shop** (located exactly across from the Pemex, no tel.) charges US$2 per hour for the use of one its computers, and the service is free if you buy a coffee or a muffin. This place makes great smoothies.

Todos Santos

About halfway from La Paz to Cabo San Lucas, at a kink in the highway, Mexico 1 passes through the 18th-century mission town of Todos Santos (pop. 5,000–7,000, depending on the season). When they discovered freshwater in an underground spring here at the base of the Sierra de la Laguna, the Jesuits developed this arroyo settlement, about two kilometers inland from the coast, as a farming supply station. When the silver mines were active on the east side of the sierra, wealthy families from El Triunfo began making Todos Santos their weekend getaway town.

After a period of booming sugar production in the early 20th century, the town became once again an agricultural center, supplying restaurants in Los Cabos and markets as far away as the United States with organic fruits and

vegetables year-round. The spring keeps Todos Santos lush and green, especially around the *huerta* (orchard) on the north side of town.

In recent decades, Todos Santos has become a haven for artists, retirees, snowbirds, and yogis who either live here permanently or return year after year to soak up the sun and the bohemian vibe. It is also a popular weekend place for La Paz residents looking to escape the summer heat.

The downtown area consists of a grid of mostly paved though dusty streets, many lined with 100-year-old brick buildings. There is a town plaza with a historic church, but it doesn't feel like the center of the action in modern-day Todos Santos. Most visitors congregate along the central blocks between Avenida Juárez and Calles Centenario, Obregón, and Márquez de León.

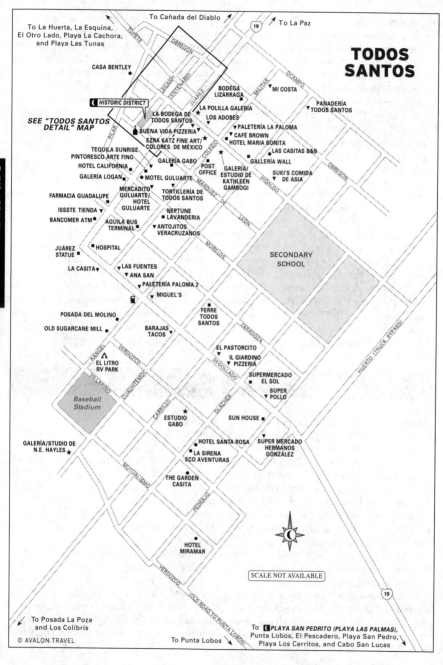

To Cañada del Diablo

19 To La Paz

To La Huerta, La Esquina,
El Otro Lado, Playa La Cachora,
and Playa Las Tunas

TODOS SANTOS

CASA BENTLEY

BODEGA
LIZARRAGA

MI COSTA

PANADERÍA
TODOS SANTOS

◀ HISTORIC DISTRICT

LA POLILLA GALERÍA

LOS ADOBES

*SEE "TODOS SANTOS
DETAIL" MAP*

LA BODEGA DE
TODOS SANTOS

BUENA VIDA PIZZERIA

PALETERÍA LA PALOMA

CAFÉ BROWN

HOTEL MARIA BONITA

TEQUILA SUNRISE
PINTORESCO ARTE FINO

EZRA KATZ FINE ART/
COLORES DE MÉXICO

LAS CASITAS B&B

GALERÍA WALL

HOTEL CALIFORNIA

GALERÍA GABO

SUKI'S COMIDA
DE ASIA

GALERÍA LOGAN

POST
OFFICE

GALERÍA/
ESTUDIO DE
KATHLEEN
GAMBOGI

MOTEL GULUARTE

MERCADITO
GULUARTE/
HOTEL
GULUARTE

FARMACIA GUADALUPE

TORTILLERÍA DE
TODOS SANTOS

ISSSTE TIENDA

NEPTUNE
LAVANDERIA

BANCOMER ATM

AGUILA BUS
TERMINAL

ANTOJITOS
VERACRUZANOS

JUÁREZ
STATUE

HOSPITAL

SECONDARY
SCHOOL

LA CASITA

LAS FUENTES

ANA SAN

PALETERÍA PALOMA 2

MIGUEL'S

FERRE
TODOS
SANTOS

POSADA DEL MOLINO

OLD SUGARCANE MILL

BARAJAS
TACOS

EL PASTORCITO

IL GIARDINO
PIZZERIA

EL LITRO
RV PARK

SUPERMERCADO
EL SOL

SUPER
POLLO

*Baseball
Stadium*

ESTUDIO
GABO

SUN HOUSE

GALERÍA/STUDIO DE
N.E. HAYLES

HOTEL SANTA ROSA

SUPER MERCADO
HERMANOS
GONZÁLEZ

LA SIRENA
ECO AVENTURAS

THE GARDEN
CASITA

HOTEL
MIRAMAR

SCALE NOT AVAILABLE

19

To Posada La Poza
and Los Colibrís

© AVALON TRAVEL

To Punta Lobos

To ◀PLAYA SAN PEDRITO (PLAYA LAS PALMAS),
Punta Lobos, El Pescadero, Playa San Pedro,
Playa Los Cerritos, and Cabo San Lucas

Beyond the immediate downtown area are sandy beaches with surf breaks and a freshwater lagoon called La Poza that supports a healthy population of birds.

As a newly designated Pueblo Mágico, Todos Santos has received access to government funding for improving infrastructure and developing cultural tourism. To date, the money has been used to remodel the park and repair the auditorium. Next on the project list: burying wires and cables in the town center, repairing the theater, and protecting the oasis and lagoon.

The feverish pace of real estate development stalled due to the dismal economy, but new homes have popped up at the other end of town, along Playa Las Tunas, as power and water infrastructure creep northward. Locals remain optimistic that Todos Santos will retain its small-town feel, even in the wake of increased development—with Carmel and Santa Fe as models, rather than Los Cabos or Cancún.

HISTORY

Spanish Jesuit Padre Jaime Bravo arrived in the Todos Santos area in the early 18th century to find the nomadic Guaicura tribe living off abundant freshwater and shellfish in a coastal oasis environment. He promptly set up a *misión de visita* (visiting mission) in 1724 as a support station for the struggling settlement at La Paz. Within a few years, Todos Santos was sending 200 burro-loads of *panocha* (raw brown sugar) a year, along with figs, pomegranates, citrus fruits, and grapes, to La Paz.

Misión Santa Rosa de las Palmas

Todos Santos' mission history begins with the founding of a *visita* by Jesuit Padre Jaime Bravo in 1724. The visiting station became a full-fledged mission called Misión Santa Rosa de las Palmas in 1733, with Padre Sigismundo Taraval in charge. A year later, the Pericú rebelled, destroying four Southern Baja missions, including Todos Santos. Taraval, however, escaped to Isla Espíritu Santo. Missionary activities resumed a year later, but the Pericú continued to resist conversion, and a number

of epidemics began to wipe out the population. When the mission in La Paz closed in 1748, Todos Santos was renamed Nuestra Señora del Pilar de Todos Santos. In 1768 the Franciscans moved several hundred Guaycura to Todos Santos from other missions in the central peninsula. The population continued to drop until the mission was secularized in 1840.

The earliest mission buildings were located about a kilometer and a half north of the current town center. A modern church and private residence are located on top of the ruins. The Iglesia Nuestra Señora del Pilar stands on the southwest side of the Todos Santos town plaza. Originally built by the Dominicans in the mid-19th century, the building was expanded in 1967. It contains a statue of the Virgin of Pilar, whom the town honors with a festival each year in October.

Sugar Mills

Following the mission period, Todos Santos built an economy based on sugarcane production. By the late 1800s there were eight sugar mills in the area, and the town grew rapidly. The sugar market crashed after World War II in the face of lower prices and lack of fresh water, and by 1965 all the mills closed. Todos Santos was virtually abandoned until the end of the century.

Around 1981 the spring filled once again with freshwater, and land became arable again. In 1984 the government paved Mexico 19 from San Pedro (out of La Paz) and Cabo San Lucas, leading the way to an economy built on tourism and permanent expat residents.

SIGHTS
◖ Historic District

A stroll along streets near the historic town plaza reveals hundred-year-old homes made of brick and some adobe, many of them now owned by outsiders and carefully restored in an array of pastel colors. Oversized windows and doors framed by decorative pilasters (rectangular supports that look like flat columns) are a signature design, borrowed from the classic revival style of architecture. The present-day Café Santa Fé on Calle Centenario, facing the plaza, is one of the largest adobe structures left standing in town. The facades on the surrounding streets are likely to look more homogenous in coming years, as a uniform appearance is one of the contingencies of funding made available through the Pueblo Mágico program. Check *El Calendario* (www.elcalendariotodossantos.com) for the timing of the annual historic home tour, when owners open their doors to visitors.

Centro Cultural Profesor Nestor Agúndez Martínez

To immerse yourself in Todos Santos's past, visit the Centro Cultural (Juárez at Obregón, 8 A.M.–5 P.M. Mon.–Fri., 9 A.M.–1 P.M. Sat.–Sun., free admission), which occupies a large brick building on Calle Juárez that once served as the town's schoolhouse and was named for a local high school teacher who passed away in 2009. Several exhibits inside cover the anthropology, ethnography, and history of the area, including a few examples

of modern art and handicrafts. Murals in the lobby depict scenes from Baja's history. They were painted in 1933 as a public works project during the administration of President Álvaro Obregón. Among the highlights are arrowheads, pottery, and other artifacts as well as photos of important figures in the town's history, local sugar mills, and silver mines at El Triunfo.

Los Pinos Park

This small park on Colegio Militar between Zaragoza and Degollado across from the Aguila Bus Terminal has become a pleasant gathering place since the addition of a large, modern play structure for kids. Buy a treat from the snack bar or a *paleta* from up the street and relax while the little ones climb to their heart's content.

BEACHES

Just about every dirt road heading west from Todos Santos ends at the beach. But few of them are paved or signed, which means you

'nside the Todos Santos cultural center

TODOS SANTOS DETAIL

OBREGÓN

CENTENARIO

JUAREZ

BANORTE

CENTRO CULTURAL ★

★ PALAPA SOCIETY & LIBRARY

MANGOS

BOUTIQUE SANTA MARIA

CAFFÉ TODOS SANTOS

JOYERÍA BRILANTI

GALERÍA DE TODOS SANTOS & MICHAEL'S AT THE GALLERY

TODOS SANTOS INN/LA COPA & LANDI'S

BENITO ORTEGA

TRE GALLINE

TOPETE

★ LA ARCA   GUAYCURA HOTEL & SPA

EL PERICO AZUL

MANOS MEXICANOS

GALERÍA LA CORONELA

LEGASPI

FONDA EL ZAGUÁN

HEARTSEASE

GOT BAJA?

HIDALGO

EL TECOLOTE BOOKS/ TZINTZUNTZAN

TACOS CHILAKOS

BOYITACOS

POLICE

CAFÉLIX

CITY HALL

HISTORIC DISTRICT

TEATRO MÁRQUEZ DE LEÓN

CAFÉ SANTA FÉ

LA SIEMPRE VIVA

MÁRQUEZ DE LEÓN

LA IGUANA, AGUA Y SOL/ARTESANÍAS EL CARDÓN

TRES HERMANOS

IGLESIA NUESTRA SEÑORA DEL PILAR

SCALE NOT AVAILABLE

© AVALON TRAVEL

THE WEST CAPE

may be in for an adventure when you try to find a particular spot along the coast. Ask for directions before you set out and remember that routes often shift a little with each successive season of rain—and with ongoing road construction. With the exception of Los Cerritos near El Pescadero and sometimes Playa Las Palmas/San Pedrito, beaches near Todos Santos are not swimmable because of strong currents, heavy surf, and rocky bottoms. (The exception may be in summer, when the swell subsides for long periods of time.) Plan to sunbathe, fish, stroll the beach, or surf, but save the splashing around for the pool.

Punta Lobos and Puerto Algodones

Starting south of town, local fishing boats launch out of Punta Lobos, marked by a rocky point and sea lion colony on the south side of a sandy cove. The *pangas* return to shore around 3 P.M.; watch the captains time the waves so that they can safely run the boats onto the beach. You can often buy fresh catch directly from the *pangueros*. If you walk north along the beach, past the lighthouse, you'll reach **Playa Las Pocitas** and **Playa La Cachora**.

The signed access road to Punta Lobos leaves Mexico 19 about two kilometers south of Todos Santos at Km. 54. As you near the beach, you'll see the ruins of an old turtle cannery. To walk to Punta Lobos from town (20–30 minutes each way), follow Calle Pedrajo southwest one long block to a wide dirt road. Turn left and follow this road until you can see the lighthouse on your right; take the next dirt road west to Punta Lobos.

Between Punta Lobos and Playa San Pedrito, an old port bound by cliffs was used in the early 20th century to ship fresh produce, sugarcane, and canned fish. Climb (carefully) out to the old pier or to the summit above it for some of the most memorable views. You can swim here, but pay attention to currents and tides.

The access road to this secluded bay is rough and steep in parts. Turn off Mexico 19 toward Punta Lobos and turn left when you pass the cannery ruins (before the beach). You probably won't be able to make it all the way to the port. Alternatively, leave your car at Punta Lobos; it will take about an hour to get there by foot.

Local outfitters, including Todos Santos Eco Adventures and La Sirena Eco-Adventures, sometimes lead cliff walks here if you prefer to have a guide.

◖ La Poza

Bird-watchers rejoice in this freshwater lagoon located west of the *huerta* and south of La Cachora road—and just beyond the tide line. With dunes in front and palms behind, La Poza provides ideal habitat for a long list of birds, including pelicans, herons, egrets, gulls, frigate birds, ibis, ducks, cormorants, sandpipers, and stilts. The beach in front of the lagoon is called Playa Las Pocitas, and it meets Playa La Cachora to the north, where La Cachora road meets the coast.

A word of warning: The lagoon appears to be shallow but is in fact very deep. Most of the time it is separated from the ocean by a high sand dune; however, the dune occasionally breaks in large swells, and when this happens, a trickle of water out of the lagoon can turn into a towering wall of water almost instantly. Unsuspecting visitors have drowned in these situations. Stay back from the water's edge and monitor the wave patterns at all times.

To reach the beaches and the lagoon from downtown, start on Calle Topete near the Galería de Todos Santos and follow it north, down a small hill and around to the west, across the orchard. Turn left at the first sand road, which comes immediately before a low rock wall. If you start going uphill and pass La Esquina restaurant on your left, you've gone too far. La Cachora road heads west to the beach, passing a few homes and an inn or two along the way.

A steep and rocky path also skirts to La Poza to the south. Turn southwest off Degollado (Mexico 19) onto Calle Olachea or Calle Carrillo and follow the blue and white signs to Posada La Poza. Park along the road (not in the spots that are reserved for guests of the inn) and walk to the end of the road, where the short trail begins.

Playa La Pastora

If you skip the turnoff to La Cachora and drive past the rock wall up the small hill, you'll find yourself in the *otro lado* (other side) of Todos Santos, with yet more beaches at the end of unnamed dirt roads and a few housing developments in various states of completion. Follow this coastal road about 5.6 kilometers farther northwest to a wide arroyo that leads to a sandy beach. Resist the urge to drive all the way up onto the sand to check the surf from your car. Chances are you will get stuck. The break is a right point in a northwest swell and occasionally also a beach break in a south swell.

North to Punta Márquez and Punta Conejo

If you're up for some serious off-road exploration, continue north along the coastal road. After Playa La Pastora, the road veers east and reaches a T, from which you can turn right to get back to Mexico 19 or turn left to continue northwest more or less parallel to the coast. At Rancho los Inocentes (57 km from La Pastora), you can once again head inland (straight) to rejoin Mexico 1 north of La Paz (29 km from Rancho los Inocentes) or turn left to stay on the coast. This road eventually reaches Punta Márquez (24 km north of Rancho el Tomate) and Punta Conejo (18 km north of Punta Márquez), two well-known points for surfing. This entire stretch of the Pacific coast is lined with sandy beaches and, in winter, surfable breaks on a succession of reefs and points. You can camp anywhere along the shore—just be sure to bring all your supplies, as the nearest commercial outposts are a long drive away.

SPORTS AND RECREATION
Fishing

Since it lacks a marina or protected harbor (other than the abandoned pier at Puerto Algodones), Todos Santos does not have much of a charter fishing business. However, if you speak Spanish, you can talk to the *pangueros* to arrange a day of sportfishing. Prices average about US$30 per hour, usually with a three-hour minimum. Alternatively, contact Todos Santos Eco Adventures (Cerro La Poza, Guaycura, tel. 612/145-0780, www.tosea.net, US$175 for 2 nights, US$275 per boat per day) or La Sirena Eco-Adventures (Olachea off Degollado, tel. 612/145-0353, www.lasirenakayaksurf.com, US$250 for five hours) to arrange guided trips. With accommodations and sportfishing services in Todos Santos and La Paz, **Iguana de los Mangos** (tel. 624/114-1351, www.bajasurtodossantos.com, US$250 per day) launches a *panga* from Punta Lobos.

Playas San Pedrito (Palm Beach), San Pedro, and Los Cerritos are among the easiest (and safest) places for surf-casting from shore. Experienced locals also head to La Pastora and points north. The catch from shore includes sierra (mackerel), cabrilla (sea bass), *pargo* (snapper), and robalo (snook).

Ferretería Oasis de Todos Santos (Rangel at Zaragoza, tel. 612/145-0754, 8 A.M.–3 P.M. and 4–7 P.M. Mon.–Fri., 8 A.M.–4 P.M. Sat.) carries some fishing supplies. You can buy live bait from the local fishermen at Punta Lobos.

Whale-Watching

Whale-watching from Todos Santos is from a distance, compared to the up-close encounters you can have in the birthing lagoons farther north. But an afternoon spent watching juvenile gray whales breach and slap their tales offshore while you sip margaritas on a rooftop deck makes for great entertainment nonetheless. December–April are the best months for catching the whales on their journey up the coast.

Pangueros at Punta Lobos may be willing to take passengers out to see the whales for about US$30 an hour; book at the beach or through any of the hotels in town.

La Sirena Eco-Adventures (Olachea off Degollado, tel. 612/145-0353, www.lasirenakayaksurf.com) leads whale-watching trips (US$49 pp for three hours). **Todos Santos Eco Adventures** (Cerro La Poza, Guaycura, tel. 612/145-0780, www.tosea.net) also includes whale-watching as part of its multiday trips. **Iguana de los Mangos** (tel. 624/114-1351, www.bajasurtodossantos.com, US$150 per day) is another option.

Surfing and Kayaking

Winter months are best for surfing the Todos Santos area, when the local breaks catch the strong northwest swell. In summer the action moves south to the Los Cabos Corridor between Cabo San Lucas and San José del Cabo or to lesser-known spots around the lower East Cape.

Contact Mario Becerril, owner of Mario Surf School (tel. 612/142-6156, www.mariosurfshop.com) for lessons, rentals, and ding repair. He is a highly reputable instructor, with several other instructors on staff, all of whom have experience with the local breaks.

La Sirena Eco-Adventures (Olachea btw

Villarino/Verduzco, tel. 612/145-0353, U.S. tel. 213/265-9943, www.lasirenakayaksurf.com) rents surfing equipment and supplies, offers surfing instruction (US$60/hour), and leads kayak tours (US$60) to the old port. **Iguana de los Mangos** (tel. 624/114-1351, www.bajasurtodossantos.com, US$150 per day) also leads kayak trips.

Hiking

You can arrange guided day or overnight hikes into the Sierra de la Laguna through **Todos Santos Eco Adventures** (Cerro La Poza, Guaycura, tel. 612/145-0780, www.tosea.net, US$175 for two nights) or **La Sirena Eco-Adventures** (Olachea btw Villarino/Verduzco, tel. 612/145-0353, U.S. tel. 213/265-9943, www.lasirenakayaksurf.com, US$200 for one night and US$300 for three nights).

Yoga and Spa Services

Hatha and Ashtanga yoga classes meet several times a week at La Arca building on Topete (Hatha at 8 A.M. Mon., Wed., Fri., Ashtanga at 9 A.M. Tues., Thurs, Sat., US$6 per class) and at the Hotelito (road to Playa La Cachora, tel. 612/145-0099, www.thehotelito.com) at 9 A.M. Tuesday and Thursday mornings. In the same location, **El Dharma de Todos Santos** (tel. 612/145-0676, www.eldharma.com) holds dharma talks and *vipassana* meditation classes 10–11:30 A.M. Sundays.

Tai chi chuan classes take place at the Centro Cultural 3–4:30 P.M. on Wednesdays October–June for around US$6.

Casa Bentley offers massage treatments (US$50 for 30 minutes) and yoga instructions for group of three or more. Book ahead at the Casa Bentley website (www.casabentleybaja.com). The **Guaycura Aena Spa** (Lesaspi at Topete, tel. 612/175-0800, www.guaycura.com) offers massage and body treatments (US$90–100) and a steam room.

Aloha Massage (tel. 612/119-7045) owner Diane Moore will come to your Todos Santos *casita* to provide massage, Reiki, and reflexology services as well as yoga instruction and spa treatments.

Organized Tours

Todos Santos Eco Adventures (Cerro La Poza, Guaycura, tel. 612/145-0780, www.tosea.net) leads half-day outings to nearby waterfalls, cliff walks, and visits to observe mountain potters at work in nearby San Vicente and La Candelaria for US$55 as well as overnight trips to the Sierra Laguna, fishing trips (US$275 per boat for up to six hrs.), and horseback riding (US$100 per trip). A 90-minute walking tour of historic sites in Todos Santos is US$15 per person.

La Sirena Eco-Adventures (Olachea btw Verduzco/Villarino, tel. 612/145-0353, www. lasirenakayaksurf.com) leads similar trips, including whale-watching (US$35 pp for two hours), fishing (US$50/hour), and waterfall hikes (US$40 pp).

SHOPPING

Todos Santos has a growing collection of boutiques that are fun to browse if you want to return home with gifts or something special for yourself. The quality is generally high, but note that most of the inventory in these stores comes from the mainland, not from Baja. Most of the shopping centers around the historic district near the plaza. Upscale shops and galleries line the narrow side streets off Calle Topete, near the Todos Santos Inn. More affordable souvenir shops can be found along Calles Hidalgo and Márquez de León.

Home Furnishings, Gifts, and Jewelry

In business since 1994, **Fénix de Todos Santos** (Juárez at Hidalgo, tel. 612/145-0808, 10 A.M.–5 P.M. Mon.–Sat.) has a selection of handblown glass, Talavera pottery, *equipal* pigskin furniture, and decorative tinware.

Emporio Hotel California (Juárez btw Morelos/Márquez de León, tel. 612/145-0217, 10 A.M.–7 P.M. daily) has a variety of apparel, jewelry, ceramics, coffee-table books, posters, and other gifts on display in a large storefront adjoining the hotel.

Mangos Folk Art (Centenario btw Topete/Obregón, tel. 612/145-0451, 10 A.M.–5 P.M. Tues.–Sat.) specializes in folk art from mainland Mexico, woodcarvings, and Guatemalan textiles.

Also on Centenario at Topete, **Manos Mexicanas** (tel. 612/145-0538, 10 A.M.–5 P.M. Mon.–Sat.) has arts and crafts from Guadalajara and Michoacan on the mainland, plus ceramics created by local artist Rubén Gutiérrez.

Joyería Brilanti (Centenario 24 btw Topete/Obregón, tel./fax 612/145-0799, www. brilanti.com, 10 A.M.–5 P.M. Mon.–Sat.) has a distinctive history as one of the earliest silver designers from Taxco on the mainland. Today the business is run by the son of the original founder, Ana Brilanti, who counted First Lady Eleanor Roosevelt among her distinguished customers. In addition to a beautiful selection of silver pieces, the gallery has sculptures and paintings for sale.

The smell of lavender wafts out of **Heartsease,** where Canadian Gwenn McDonald (Juárez at Hidalgo, heartsease@ mts.net, 10 A.M.–5 P.M. Mon.–Sat.) makes natural soap and skincare products. This is the place to get moisturizer for your face when the desert climate starts to take its toll. Gwen also makes a natural bug repellent that's safe for kids. Call in advance to book a Swedish or Shiatsu massage or Reiki and foot reflexology (US$60 for one hour).

New in 2010, **GotBaja** (Juárez at Hidalgo, www.gotbajamaps.com, 9 A.M.–8 P.M. daily) publishes handy, free tourist maps for Todos Santos, La Paz, and the East Cape. The store sells souvenir T-shirts (including kids' sizes), mugs, stickers, magnets, key chains, and the like.

Manos Mexicanos (Topete at Centenario, tel. 612/145-0538) carries pottery and other crafts made by artist Rubén Gutiérrez as well as other locally made goods such as Desert Soaps (www.desertsoaps.com) from the East Cape.

Clothing

Boutique Santa Maria (tel. 612/145-0009, 9 A.M.–6:30 P.M. daily), located across from the Centro Cultural on Juárez, carries casual cotton apparel made on the mainland in Guadalajara. There are styles for men, women, and kids.

Arts and Crafts

For less expensive souvenirs, several vendors usually are set up near the plaza, though their names change frequently. **Bazar Agua y Sol** (tel. 612/145-0537) has jewelry, sculptures, pottery, and paintings. Credit cards are accepted here.

Pintoresco (Colegio Militar at Zaragoza, tel. 612/145-0222, cell tel. 612/158-8457, 10 A.M.–7 P.M. Mon.–Sat.) is divided into two locales in the same shopping gallery: The first features more tourist-oriented crafts from various parts of Mexico, including textiles, jewelry, and decorations; the second is next door and features fine art, all of Mexican origin. The gallery is at Local #5 in the shopping gallery on Colegio Militar at the corner of Zaragoza.

Books

El Tecolote Books/Libros (Juárez and Hidalgo, tel. 612/145-0295, fax 612/145-0288, janethowwey@yahoo.com, 10 A.M.–4:30 P.M. Mon.–Sat., 11:30 A.M.–3:30 P.M. Sun.) is a book lover's shop—the kind of place that makes you want to run an independent bookstore in your retirement. The owner, Janet, stocks the shelves with a mix of foreign and Mexican periodicals, new and used paperback fiction, and hardcover design and coffee-table books, plus maps and a good section of Baja-related titles. It's no Borders or Barnes & Noble, but whether you want to read Tom Clancy or Graham Greene, chances are you'll find something you like at this shop. Bilingual children's books make a nice gift for kids. You can also buy books on tape and rent or buy movies. Besides the books, the store carries some art supplies. Note: Janet stays open seven days a week from Thanksgiving until the crowds dwindle in spring. After that, she reduces to five days a week for the duration of the low season.

Artist Studios and Galleries

The art scene in Todos Santos has come of age in recent years, with more than a dozen galleries representing internationally known artists from the United States and Mexico. Although the founder of the town's artist colony, Charles Stewart, passed away in 2011, he is remembered fondly and the community continues to grow.

In a new location next to the Centro Cultural, **Galería de Todos Santos** (Juárez, tel. 612/145-0500, www.galeriadetodossantos.com, 11 A.M.–4 P.M. Mon.–Sat.), established in 1994, is one of the few in town representing both local and foreign artists and, accordingly, diverse styles. Among those represented here are owner Michael Cope himself, celebrated local artist Erick Ochoa, and the whimsical stylings of Jennifer Power.

Jill Logan creates the original oils and mixed media works featured in the **Galería Logan** (tel. 612/145-0151, www.jilllogan.com, 11 A.M.–4 P.M. Mon.–Sat., by appointment Sun.). Logan has an extensive education in fine art, and her work has been exhibited across the United States as well as in Mexico.

La Paz native Ezra Katz, known for murals and etchings featured in a number of Cabo San Lucas restaurants and hotels, has opened **Galería Indigo** (Juárez at Hidalgo, tel. 612/137-3473, 10 A.M.–5 P.M. Mon.–Sat. or by appt.), featuring John Comer, Lindy Duncan, Lesley Rich, and others in addition to his own artwork.

Galería/Studio de N. E. Hayles (Cuauhtémoc, tel./fax 612/145-0183, www.ne-hayles.com, 11 A.M.–4 P.M. Mon.–Sat.) displays unique paper-tile mosaics, multimedia art, and tables fashioned by artist-owner Nanette E. Hayles. **Galería Wall** (Hidalgo and Colegio Militar, a few feet away from Café Brown, tel. 612/145-0527, www.catherinewallart.com, 11 A.M.–4 P.M. Mon.–Sat.) shows Mexican-themed original oils by artist Catherine Wall.

Gabo Galería (Márquez de León, btw Juárez/Colegio Militar, tel. 612/145-0514, gaboartist@hotmail.com, 10 A.M.–4 P.M. Mon.–Sat.) features paintings by Gabo, who was born in Mexico, studied in Europe, and settled in La Paz in 1978. In the years since, he has played a major role in the art scene in La Paz and Todos Santos. His works are known for their bright colors and humorous style.

Tours of his studio are by appointment only, while the gallery keeps regular hours.

ENTERTAINMENT AND EVENTS
Bars
Todos Santos has a number of options for grabbing a few drinks and enjoying the company of your hosts or fellow travelers, but places shut down around "Baja midnight," or 10 P.M., so if you want to carry on later than that, you'll need to move the party back to your own place.

In the historic Todos Santos Inn, **La Copa Bar** (Legaspi 33, tel. 612/145-0040, 3–11 P.M. daily) is a classy venue with romantic appeal. The entrance is on Calle Topete.

The bar in the Hotel California's uniquely decorated **La Coronela** (Juárez btw Morelos/Márquez de León, tel. 612/145-0525), frequented by local expats as well as the hotel's guests, is a fun place to have a few drinks. Stop in for live music on Saturday evenings.

On Thursday, Friday, or Saturday night, head over to **Mario's Bar** (Calle La Cachora, tel. 612/145-0099, 5–10 P.M. Thurs.–Sat.) at the Hotelito for cocktails, wine, sushi, *satay,* and Indian curry, served by the town's best-known surf instructor.

Theater
The restored **Teatro Márquez de León** (Legaspi at Márquez de León, no tel.) hosts music and dance performances, often during the annual October town fiesta. Before the La Paz city theater was built, Todos Santos had the only true theater in the state.

Festivals and Events
Fiesta Todos Santos takes place in October each year, around the feast day of the Virgen del Pilar (October 12). This four-day extravaganza begins on the second Saturday of the month and involves dances, sports competitions, horse races, theater performances, and amusement-park rides. Most of these events center around the town plaza.

The Christmas holidays are especially festive in Todos Santos, where for 12 days beginning

Enjoy a glass of fine wine at La Copa Bar.

on the **Día de Guadalupe** (December 12), local residents hold nightly candlelight processions to the Iglesia Nuestra Señora del Pilar. The season culminates in a midnight Mass worship service on **Christmas Eve.**

In late January or early February, the government-funded **Todos Santos Art Festival** takes place with sculptures, paintings, ceramics, and other visual works by local artists. Performing arts groups also arrive from out of town to participate in the event. Then in early March, the **Todos Santos Latin Film Festival** comes to town.

Also once a year, usually in February or March, historic homes in Todos Santos open to the public. Check *El Calendario* (www.todossantos-baja.com) for more information.

ACCOMMODATIONS

Overnight guests in Todos Santos can choose from a variety of luxury and modest hotels, bed-and-breakfasts, and private vacation rentals. As more visitors arrive each year, new properties are opening, old ones are renovating, and others are just raising prices without making significant improvements. Many properties are now up for sale, and if water and sewer rights are worked out, several large resorts may be coming to the area in the not-too-distant future.

The principal complaint that many first-time visitors express is frustration with the noise that comes with staying in a non-resort town. From the rumble of 18-wheelers to the persistent dog-barking and chicken-clucking, Todos Santos can feel like a town that doesn't sleep. In general, places closer to the beach are quieter (though not silent, and farther from town). Before you book, ask your host what to expect at night. Locations near La Poza and El Otro Lado (north side of town) mean a longish walk to town but more convenient beach access.

There are three accommodations in town with "Todos Santos" in their name: The Hacienda Todos Los Santos is located in the palm grove at the end of Avenida Juárez; the Todos Santos Inn is on Calle Topete, with its own wine bar; and the Hacienda Inn Todos Santos is north of town. Details for each are given in this section.

Hotels, Inns, and Bed-and-Breakfasts
UNDER US$50
Large, clean rooms are centrally located at **Motel Guluarte** (Juárez and Morello, tel. 612/145-0006, US$35). This place is well known among budget travelers. On-site laundry is a plus.

US$50-100
The former Hotel Misión del Pilar got a fresh coat of paint inside and out in 2006 and opened under new ownership as the **【 Maria Bonita Hotel** (Militar at Hidalgo, tel. 612/145-0850, mariabonitahotel@prodigy.net.mx, US$40–55). The office and 12 guestrooms are all on the second floor, above the popular Café Brown. Though rooms are plai⌐ ⌐e clean off-white walls, new curtains and bedspreads, and comfortable mattresses make for a pleasant stay. Small but clean bathrooms have shower stalls with glass doors and hot water aplenty. A great value, this hotel is a wise choice for budget travelers who need a place to crash for the night. Rates include tax.

At **Bed and Breakfast Las Casitas** (Rangel btw Obregón/Hidalgo, tel./fax 612/145-0255, www.lascasitasbandb.com, US$60–100), Canadian artist Wendy Faith has lovingly restored four *chiname* adobe cottages and one four-person suite over the last decade. Set among lush landscaping, rooms are small, with low ceilings, one bed, and brightly colored walls and ceilings. Accommodations here are basic but artsy, with hand-painted murals in some rooms and the artist's own glasswork in others. Breakfast includes the bed-and-breakfast's own blend of coffee. An authentic *palo de arco casita* houses the owner's studio.

To get to the **Hotel Santa Rosa** (Olochea btw Verduzco/Villarino, tel. 612/145-0394, www.hotelsantarosa.com.mx, US$70), go three blocks south of the Pemex station on Calle Degollado, turn right on Calle Olachea, and go two blocks. There are eight rooms with kitchenettes and queen beds, plus a well-maintained pool, hot tub, and enclosed parking. The hotel offers a 5 percent discount for weeklong stays, 10 percent off for two weeks, and 33 percent off for a monthlong reservation. Wi-Fi available.

In the Las Tunas area two kilometers north of town, **Iguana de los Mangos** (cell tel. 612/119-7880, www.bajasurtodossantos.com, US$90) is a newer studio *casita* that sleeps two adults and up to two children. Special touches include fluffy towels and luxury bed linens, plus a rooftop terrace, hammock, BBQ, and daily breakfast. It's about a 10-minute walk to the water's edge.

US$100-150

Set among towering palm, mango, and banana trees, **Jardín de Pilar** (Pilar btw Topete/Hidalgo, tel. 612/145-0386, www.jardinde-pilar.com, US$105) has two beautifully appointed *casitas* for rent. Details include colorful high-end linens and bamboo accents, as well as wireless Internet and swimming pool.

On the road to Playa La Cachora, the **Hotelito** (tel. 612/145-0099, www.thehotelito.com, US$125–135) is a boutique-style inn with four cottages that blend a modern Mexican and European style. For recreation, the inn has a small swimming pool and morning yoga classes twice a week. Rates include breakfast. On all but the hottest days you can comfortably walk about a half mile to the beach or into town.

Much loved for its location, sparkling pool, and friendly service, **(Hacienda Todos Los Santos** (Juárez, tel. 612/145-0547, www.tsha-cienda.com) has three *casitas* and four suites, each with its own unique personality. All have air-conditioning, private terraces, and spacious bathrooms. Casa Santa Luz (US$190) has a queen-size bed, TV/VCR, and fireplace. Casa del Palmar (US$165) is a studio suite with multiple terraces, king-size bed, and TV/VCR. Casita del Encanto (US$125) is a studio suite complete with two patios, queen-size bed, and seating area. Casa de los Santos has one room (US$125) and three suites (US$165–225),

and the whole house rents for US$850 a night. The upstairs suites have great views of the surrounding farmland. Amenities on the property include Wi-Fi, swimming pool, and lush gardens for strolling. Walk to town or the beach.

Centrally located in the historic district, **Casa Bentley** (Calle Pilar 99 at Hidalgo, tel. 612/145 0276, www.casabentley.com, US$90–170) offers five contemporary guest suites in three houses—one is a restored adobe structure and the other two are modern stone construction. Guests enjoy air-conditioning, luxury linens, and use of a heated swimming pool. Access to an outdoor kitchen is provided with some units and available by special arrangement for the others.

US$150-250

On the road to La Pastora, the **Hacienda Inn Todos Santos** (tel./fax 612/145-0193, US$110–140 with continental breakfast) is about two kilometers from the center of town. The inn has a swimming pool and restaurant with a bar. All 14 rooms and suites have air-conditioning, cable TV, and comfy bathrobes. Turn right at the El Sol II grocery store to find the inn.

A stay at the elegant **(Todos Santos Inn** (Legaspi 33 at Topete, tel./fax 612/145-0040, www.todossantosinn.com, US$125–225) takes visitors back to the town's sugarcane era in the 19th century. Housed in a restored brick building, the inn is beautifully designed and appointed with high ceilings, antique furnishings, and tile floors. Amenities include private terraces, ceiling fans, and air-conditioning. Guests enjoy use of a small pool and the on-site La Copa Bar. Spanish-language instruction is available, either separately or as a package with accommodations (10 hrs. for US$200).

Last renovated in 2003, two-story **Hotel California** (Juárez btw Morelos/Márquez de León, tel. 612/145-0525, www.hotelcalifor-niabaja.com, US$110–190) has eight suites, a small swimming pool, and courtyard garden. It also has its own restaurant, **La Coronela,** and a gift shop called **Emporio Hotel California.**

(Posada La Poza (tel. 612/145-0400, www.lapoza.com, US$195–460) blends the relaxed pace of life in Baja with a Swiss sensibility for quality and efficiency. Hosts Jörg and Libusche Wiesendanger opened the hotel in 2002. Guests stay in one of four garden suites (and these days, the garden is as lush as can be), two junior suites with private hot tubs, or the master suite. Suites here come with views of the lagoon and ocean beyond, plus air-conditioning, a CD player, and Swiss bed linens. Guestrooms and common areas also feature Libusche's oil and acrylic paintings. You can splash around in a large saltwater swimming pool, soak in the saltwater 10-person whirlpool tub, enjoy the small beach area right in front of the inn, watch for whales from the deck, or borrow a bicycle for a ride into town. And when you've had your fill of the great outdoors, you might give yourself an aromatherapy treatment in the on-site sweat lodge, which is filled with heated lava rocks topped with eucalyptus leaves, rosemary, or other herbs. Internet access is available. Rates include continental breakfast, and **El Gusto!** restaurant serves hearty Mexican and international dishes like pork loin, rib eye, and lobster. The road to La Poza is well marked: Turn southwest off Degollado (Mexico 19) onto Calle Olachea or Calle Carrillo and follow the blue and white signs.

OVER US$250

In a restored two-story dormitory on Calle Topete, **Guaycura Hotel** (Lesagpi at Topete, tel. 612/145-0800, US$350) offers 14 luxury guestrooms, three of which have ocean views. Guests can lounge by the small rooftop pool in the morning, take a stroll around town or head to the beach midday, and return for spa treatments in the afternoon.

Guesthouses and Vacation Rentals

Several Todos Santos community websites list vacation rentals in the area. They include www.baja.com, www.bajawesternonion.com, www.todossantos.cc, and www.todosantos-guide.com. Vacation Rental by Owner (www.vrbo.com) also has a few West Cape listings. Here are a few of the most popular options in this category:

© NIKKI GOTH ITOI

The Guaycura Hotel occupies a restored brick building in the historic district of Todos Santos.

US$50-100

Over the last decade, a fun-loving retired couple from Italy has built six guest *casitas* on their Las Brisas area property, collectively known as **La Supercionfola** and located on the West side of Camino a Las Tunas. Each *casita* has a clear view of the ocean and dunes before it, and the sand is a five-minute walk from your door. Simple yet elegant designs are beautifully constructed with separate private kitchens and sculpted concrete counters. Two units have two bedrooms each, two are one-bedroom *casitas,* and one is a studio. All but the studio have private kitchens. Though in a somewhat developed area, the landscaping makes the setting feel secluded and completely private. The location is about 10 minutes from town—ideal for independent travelers. Contact manager Emy Festa, who also manages the Gemma Inn in La Paz (tel. 612/123-5508, cell tel. 612/168-7937, info@gemmagroup.it) for details. Longer term stays are preferred, and the rates are US$55/night or US$300/week for the studio (two-night min.), US$500/week for the one-bedroom *casitas,* and US$700/week for the two bedroom *casitas.* Inquire about discounted monthly and half-year rates.

The **Garden Casita** (Olachea and Mutualismo, tel./fax 612/145-0129, www. todossantos-baja.com/gardencasita.htm, US$300 week) is a unique redbrick guesthouse with a *palapa* roof. The *casita* has a living area, separate bedroom, and patio with enclosed courtyard. Wireless high-speed Internet is included, and the long-term rates include weekly maid service.

In roughly the same neighborhood, **Las Flores Posada** (formerly Jane's Place, Pedrajo and Villarino, tel. 612/145-0216, www.todossantosguide.com/vacationrentals/lasfloresposada.htm, US$65–95) has four cozy but well-worn *casitas* on an acre of property centered around a courtyard with a fountain. There are three studio bungalows, each with private bath and kitchen and a main bungalow with two bedrooms, kitchen, and living room.

Named for the sugarcane mill ruins that adjoin the property, **Hotel Posada del Molino** (Rangel and Progreso, tel. 612/145-0233, www.posadadelmolino.com, US$90–110) has four air-conditioned studios next to a swimming pool. Each studio has a queen-size bed, wireless Internet, satellite TV, and fully equipped kitchenettes. Breakfast at the on-site Pura Vida café makes a nice way to start the day.

Situated in a residential neighborhood off Calle Degollado, midway between downtown and the beach and next to the Hotel Santa Rosa, **La Sirena Eco-Adventures** (Calle Olachea btw Villarino/Verduzco, tel. 612/145-0353, U.S. tel. 213/265-9943, www.lasirenakayaksurf.com) rents two one-bedroom, private-bath houses inside a gated property called Casitas La Paloma (US$60–65). An additional suite rents for US$500 per week with discounts for multiweek stays. Wi-Fi available. This property is a convenient walk from the bus station.

US$100-150

At **Los Colibrís** (Cerro La Poza, Calle Guaycura, tel. 612/145-0780, www.loscolibris.

com, US$115/night, US$700/week), the friendly proprietors of Todos Santos Eco Adventures, Sergio and Bryan Jáuregui, offer two rental homes and two *casitas* on their hillside property, with stunning ocean views overlooking the freshwater estuary and beach beyond. Tiled baths have rain showers and sculpted concrete countertops. Lampposts made of decorative tree trunks, colorful linens, and hummingbird feeders are few of the special touches. Units have ceiling fans, some with air-conditioning, well-equipped kitchens, bottled water, and iPod docking stations for music. Outdoor space is limited, given the steep incline of the property, but the addition of a small infinty pool and hot tub on a stone terrace give the illusion of more space.

On the road leading to Playa la Cachora, **Las Puertas** (tel./fax 612/145-0373, www.alaspuertas.com, US$135–175) offers a large two-bedroom guesthouse, a one-bedroom guesthouse, and a suite with ocean views. All the structures are nicely furnished, private, and built in classic Baja style with *palapa* roofs and adobe walls. The oceanview suite is the newest addition and has the nicest furnishings, a fireplace, and exceptional views. Daily maid service is included.

US$150-250

Below the main property, **Casa Colina** (tel. 612/145-0780, www.casacolina-ts.com, US$195/night, US$1,095/week)is a two-story, two-bedroom home with a little more space and a private driveway. Large picture windows in the bedrooms and kitchen open to ocean views, while balconies on both bedrooms face the mountains. Each bedroom has a king-size bed with luxury linens, ceiling fan, and its own bath. The casa also has a fully equipped kitchen.

Villas La Mar (Cerrada Guaycura 26, tel. 612/145-0116, www.hotelvillaslamar.com, US$185) rents several newly constructed villas built against a hillside on the south side of La Poza. From Degollado, follow the signs toward Posada La Poza and Los Colibris.

About 2.5 miles north of town in the La

Tunas area, **Las Casitas Cal y Canto** (www. calycanto.com, US$150–200) consists of three newly constructed two-story homes on a five-acre property on the east side of the road. Design accents include Saltillo floors, Talavera tiles, outdoor showers, and mesquite furniture. Swing in a hammock on the patio or walk 10 minutes to the beach. In winter proximity to the break at La Pastora, two miles away, is a plus for surfers. Together, the *casitas* can accommodate a group of 18 people.

Camping and RV Parks

El Litro RV Park has only five short-term camping sites, since it is nearly full of permanent residents. RV sites are in a large dirt lot surrounded by palm trees, south of Mexico 19 at the end of Calle Olachea. Full hookups cost US$15 a night or US$250 a month, including hot showers, clean bathrooms, and laundry facilities. The park also has 30 tent camping sites (US$8 per night). The beach is a 15-minute walk. The owners can store your rig for US$40 a month.

The beaches north of town offer good camping but no facilities. The farther north you go, the more remote and secluded it gets.

FOOD

With the wide variety of cuisines at just about every price point, you'll be hard-pressed to go hungry in Todos Santos.

Contemporary Mexican

On the back patio of a beautifully restored adobe house, **Los Adobes** (Hidalgo btw Juárez/ Colegio Militar, tel. 612/145-0203, www.losadobesdetodossantos.com, 11:30 A.M.–9 P.M. Mon.–Sat., mains US$15–22) prepares gourmet Mexican cuisine with prices to match. The menu includes grilled fish entrées, chicken mole, and steak fajitas.

El Gusto! at Posada la Poza on Playa La Cachora (tel. 612/145-0453, 11:30 A.M.–4 P.M. and 6–9 P.M. Fri.–Wed.) is the only beachfront restaurant in Todos Santos. A tapas menu is available on the Whale Terrace. The menu changes based on what organic produce is

AGUAS FRESCAS

Ladled out of large glass jars, refreshing *aguas frescas* are made of still water infused with fresh fruit and sweetened with sugar. Popular flavors include *fresa* (strawberry), *jamaica* (hibiscus flower), *melón* (cantelope), and *sandía* (watermelon). Although technically not an *agua fresca*, *horchata*, rice milk flavored with cinnamon and sugar, is often served alongside the fruit drinks. Look for *aguas frescas* at taquerias, *licuados* stands, and Mexican restaurants up and down the Baja Peninsula.

available, but there is usually a wide variety of seafood and meat choices. El Gusto! is a popular spot for sunset margaritas.

Traditional Mexican

Inside the Todos Santos Inn, **Landi's** (tel. 612/145-0020, 9 A.M.–9 P.M. Mon.–Sat., dinner mains US$8–15) offers traditional Mexican and some fusion dishes such as fettucine al tequila to please the gringo palate. Live music plays on Thursdays. Known for lightly battered chiles rellenos smothered in sautéed tomatoes and onions, **Miguel's** (Degollado and Rangel, 8 A.M.–9 P.M. daily, mains US$6–10) also serves enchiladas, burritos, and cheeseburgers. A dozen tables are arranged on a sand floor under a *palapa* roof. The owner has opened a second restaurant at Playa Los Cerritos.

You'll be hard-pressed to find anything on the menu over US$7 at **Restaurant la Ramada** (Militar and Obregón, no tel., 9 A.M.–9 P.M. Mon.–Sat., mains US$3–8). This local spot serves tacos, tostadas, and the like in a clean kitchen with friendly service; it's open for breakfast, lunch, and dinner.

For casual dining (plastic tables under a *palapa* roof), **Ataxcon** (Militar at Hidalgo, tel. 612/176-1275, 8 A.M.–7 P.M. Mon.–Sat.) serves traditional Mexican dishes of the state of Guerrero on the mainland at reasonable prices.

THE WEST CAPE

Seafood

The friendly ◖ **Mariscos Mi Costa** (Colegio Militar at Ocampo, no tel., 10 A.M.–8 P.M. daily, mains US$8–15) is a simple seafood restaurant with a raked sand floor. Its *sopa de mariscos* and *camarón al ajo* continue to impress.

Located a few doors down from the Tecalote bookstore, ◖ **Fonda El Zaguán** (Juárez btw Topete/Hidalgo, tel. 612/127-0398, noon–9 P.M. Mon.–Sat., US$6–15) is an open-air restaurant that does seafood right. Fish takes the center stage in its ceviche dish, unlike at many other places that serve it. Choose basil, poblano, or peanut sauce for your fish filet. If *robalo* (snook) is available, get the fish tacos or order it as a filet. The margaritas are strong, and the sangria is refreshing on a hot afternoon. Specials are usually written on a chalkboard out front.

Restaurant las Fuentes (Degollado and Colegio Militar, tel. 612/145-0257, 7:30 A.M.–9:30 P.M. Tues.–Sun., mains from US$6) is a large open-air restaurant that has benefited from the rerouting of truck traffic away from the downtown area. The house special, *pescado empapelado,* is fish baked in paper with tomatoes and mild chilies.

At a busy intersection near the Pemex, **La Casita** (Degollado at Militar, tel. 612/145-0192, http://lacasitatapasandwinebar.com/default.aspx, tapas for US$8–13) emphasizes organic produce and fresh seafood, served as small plates. Coconut shrimp and tequila jalapeño sea bass are among the most memorable dishes. Its wine bar is stocked with some of the best Baja labels at reasonable prices as well as others from around the world. Red table linens and candlelight create an intimate atmosphere, but the persistent din of traffic right outside makes it a safe place to bring the kids, too.

Asian and International

Hotel California on Calle Juárez boasts the atmospheric **La Coronela** restaurant/bar (Juárez btw Morelos/Márquez de León, tel. 612/145-0525, 7 A.M.–1 A.M. daily, dinner mains US$8–20). Prepared by a Belgian chef, the international menu has some creative dishes, such as almond-crusted Pacific oyster tacos and yellowtail in an opal basil/ginger/coconut sauce. Visa and MasterCard are accepted.

Across from the Pemex, **Ana San Sushi Bar** (Degollado at Militar, tel. 612/137-9856, 1–9 P.M. Mon.–Sat.) prepares sushi, sashimi, soups, and salads.

Suki's (Hidalgo btw Rangel/Cuauhtémoc, no tel., 5–9 P.M. Tues.–Sat.) prepares a moderately priced menu of pan-Asian cuisine, with pad Thai, teriyaki, and Korean specialties.

When resident expats want to dine out on the town, they head to **Michael's at the Gallery** (Juárez at Topete, tel. 612/145-0500, dinner Thurs.–Sat., reservations recommended) to enjoy creative Asian cuisine in an open-air sculpture garden.

Italian

With a 20-year track record for excellence, **Café Santa Fé** (Centenario 4, tel./fax 612/145-0340, noon–9 P.M. Wed.–Mon., mains US$20 and up) is this town's best-known and highest-ranked restaurant. It offers a broad menu of high-end Italian fare, including wood-fired pizzas, ravioli, fish *crudo,* and fresh pasta. Given its international acclaim, you will pay U.S. prices here.

At ◖ **Tre Galline** (Topete and Juárez, tel. 612/145-0274, noon–10 P.M. Mon.–Sat., mains US$15–20), Angelo and Magda Dal Bon serve delicious northern Italian fare in a less formal atmosphere and at more reasonable prices. Starters may include homemade rolls, eggplant Parmesan, and a celery soup with smoked trout. Main dishes range from homemade pasta to a daily fresh catch, and organic roasted chicken. Magda's cakes and imported espresso complete the meal. This is where local Italian families come to celebrate special occasions. In the morning hours, Angelo and Magda also run Caffe Todos Santos.

Buena Vida (Hidalgo at Militar, cell tel. 612/348-8178, noon–3 P.M. and dinner from 5 P.M. Mon.–Fri., dinner from 5 P.M. Sat.–Sun.) offers a dinner menu of pizzas (US$10), salads, and wines. **Il Giardino** (Degollado btw

Olochea/Carrillo, tel. 612/145-0199, 5–10 P.M. Tues.–Sat. and 2–10 P.M. Sun.), serving wood-fired thin-crust pizza (US$18) and other casual Italian fare.

Antojitos and Fast Food

Tres Hermanos on Márquez de León between Juárez and Militar (8 A.M.–2 P.M. daily) is among the best taco stands in town. Try the clam tacos for something different. Local Mexican residents praise **Barajas Tacos** (8 A.M.–11 P.M. Wed.–Mon.), on Degollado (Mexico 19) toward the south edge of town, for serving authentic carnitas and *tacos de pescado y camarones* during the day and *tacos de carne asada* and *papas rellenas* at night.

Next to Caféllix, **Boyitacos** (Juárez at Hidalgo, tacos US$1–2, mains US$5–8) prepares tasty papas rellenas—baked potatoes layered with butter, cream, mushrooms, corn, and choice of meat or *mixtos* with cheese. Plastic tables are arranged under a *palapa* roof with a ceiling fan. Order drinks from the fully stocked bar and watch the traffic roll by on Calle Juárez.

El Pastorcito (Degollado at Carrillo, mains US$3–7) wins hands-down for the best *pastor* around, served traditional-style with raw onions and cilantro. This is where the mariachi bands from Los Cabos stop to eat their lunch. Meals begin with a tray of four fresh salsas. If pork isn't your thing, try the tacos *de pollo,* carne, or chorizo. Look for an outdoor grill and patio with red and blue plastic tables on the east side of Degollado, at the speed bumps and across from the turn to La Poza.

Cafés

Attention to detail and a love of improvisation set **Café Brown** (Hidalgo and Colegio Militar, tel. 612/145-0813, 8 A.M. A.M.–8 P.M. Wed.–Sun., mains US$4–9) apart from your average small-town café. Enjoy a limited menu of home-style cooking made from quality ingredients (Sonora beef, breads from a bakery in La Paz) while you check your email on the fastest wireless connection in town (US$2/hr.). Friendly and attentive service sets the

The best tacos *al pastor* in Baja are at El Pastorcito.

tone; good music completes the experience. Art that doesn't have permanent gallery space often finds a home here. And from informal cooking classes and independent films to percussion instruction and salsa dancing, owners Iker and his wife love to throw a good party. Iker also offers cooking classes around town. Look for Café Brown in the back of the María Bonita Hotel (formerly Hotel Misión del Pilar) complex.

Next to Boyitacos, **Caféllix** (Juárez near Hidalgo, tel. 612/145-0568, 8 A.M.–10 P.M. daily, mains US$4–6) makes good coffee, bagels, hot breakfasts, smoothies, and more. The Wi-Fi is free and reliable.

The smell of homemade bread and mini donuts wafts out of **Caffé Todos Santos** (Centenario 33, tel. 612/145-0300, 7 A.M.–2 P.M. Mon., 7 A.M.–9 P.M. Tues.–Sun., mains US$6–12) in the morning. This is the place to get your espresso fix, with fresh pastries, waffles, and omelets to boot.

Five minutes north of town on the way to La Pastora, **La Esquina** (Topete at Horizonte,

THE WEST CAPE

© NIKKI GOTH ITOI

tel. 612/145-0851, www.laesquinats.com, 7 A.M.–7 P.M. Mon.–Sat., mains US$3–6) offers strong coffee, build-your-own sandwiches with three different kinds of homemade bread, excellent soup of the day, and a huge variety of fresh fruit juices and smoothies as well as a great selection of loose and bagged teas. There's free wireless—and they do occasional movie screenings in the evenings as well as hosting eco-café nights, featuring discussions on local ecological issues. Pick up your own bag of organic coffee beans from Chiapas. Drop by on Wednesday mornings for a farmers market 9 A.M.–noon.

If all you need is a cup of coffee, look for **Café Combate** (Juárez, Mexico 19, no tel., hours vary) on the way to La Paz.

Next to Buena Vida Pizza, **Pastelería La Espiguita** (Hidalgo at Militar, tel. 612/145-0878, laespiguita@yahoo.com, hours vary) makes a long list of *licuados* and pastries to go with the drinks.

Groceries

Basic food supplies line the shelves of several markets in town, including **Mercadito Guluarte** (next to Hotel Guluarte), **Tienda Disconsa** (Colegio Militar), **Super Mercado Hermanos González** (Pedrajo), and **Supermercado El Sol** (Degollado, open till 10 P.M. nightly). A second El Sol is on the road to Playa La Pastora one block west of Hacienda Inn Todos Santos.

La Siempre Viva (Juárez and Márquez de León, open from 7 A.M.) sells meats, cheeses, produce, and honey from local farms and ranches. It usually opens an hour or two earlier than the competition, and it carries some household goods and ranch supplies in addition to groceries.

The government-subsidized **ISSSTE Tienda** (Juárez btw Zaragoza/Morelos) offers an ever-changing selection of inexpensive groceries and holds a fairly well-stocked pharmacy.

Panadería Todos Santos (Rangel and Ocampo, 2–8 P.M. or until sold out Mon.–Sat.) sells a full lineup of Mexican breads, including *bolillos* and *pan dulce*—all baked in a wood-fired oven. The bakery occupies an unsigned two-story brick building at the north end of Calle Rangel near Ocampo. Bread lovers enjoy it, as there aren't many places like this one around.

You can buy fresh *tortillas de maíz* for about US$1 per kilo at the **Super Tortillería de Todos Santos** (Colegio Militar btw Morelos/ Márquez de León). Head to Punta Lobos to buy fresh seafood directly from the *pangueros*. Closer to town, **Pescadería Todos Santos** (Degollado btw Cuauhtémoc/Carrillo, hours vary) carries a sampling of the local catch. **Bodega Lizarraga**, at Colegio Militar and Obregón, has the biggest selection of fruits and vegetables in town, and it's without question the cleanest.

Homemade ice cream awaits at **Paletería la Paloma** (8 A.M.–9 P.M. daily), on Colegio Militar next to Hotel Maria Bonita, along with icy fresh fruit *paletas* (popsicles). Pushcart vendors sometimes sell *paletas* around town. **Nevería Rocco** (Hidalgo btw Centenario/ Juárez), a small shop in a pink house, sells Carnation ice cream and *paletas*.

When the tacos and beer catch up with you, head to **Pura Vida** (tel. 612/169-2095, www.posadadelmolino.com, 8 A.M.–5 P.M. Wed.–Mon., mains US$4–8) for healthier fare. Located inside the Hotel Posada del Molino, this tiny store stocks local organic eggs, soy milk, Sprouted brand breads and tortillas, Brown Cow yogurt, desert honey, herbal teas, and a limited selection of Asian foods. Order a smoothie or panini and enjoy the patio setting.

La Esquina Farmers Market takes place 9 A.M.–noon Wednesday mornings. Vendors sell organic produce, artisan cheeses, tamales, handicrafts, and more. On Saturdays a similar market tales place at La Cañada del Diablo.

For a bottle of top-quality, made-in-Baja wine, browse the shelves at **La Bodega de Todos Santos** (Hidalgo btw Juárez/Militar, tel. 612/152-0181, 11 A.M.–7 P.M. Tues.–Sat.), where Mac and Alexandra, distributors of boutique Baja California (Norte) wines to local restaurants, now sell directly to the public as well. The shop carries wines from Bodega

Barón Balch'é, Mogor Badan, Viñas Pijoan, Vinisterra, Victor Torres Alegre y Familia, and others. Inside the shop, you can view a map and photos of the wine country and ask the owners about this relatively undiscovered grape-growing region. Prices are reasonable, starting at about US$15 per bottle. On Mondays 5–8 P.M., Mac and Alexandra pour tastings and wines by the glass, with local cheeses and tapas from local restaurants. Pick up a bottle of olive oil cultivated in the Valle de Guadalupe while you're there.

INFORMATION AND SERVICES
Tourist Assistance

Todos Santos does not have an official tourist office, but most businesses in town are usually able to answer visitors' questions. El Tecolote Libros is usually a good place to start. If you speak Spanish and want information on the sierra backcountry, go to La Siempre Viva, which is where the ranchers often go to stock up on supplies.

The monthly *El Calendario de Todos Santos* (www.elcalendariodetodossantos.com) publishes current events listings and short articles on local culture; it's distributed free at various locations around town.

Medical and Emergency Services

For police, fire, and Red Cross services, call tel. 612/145-0445. The Centro de Salud (tel. 612/145-0095, open 24/7 for emergencies) is located at the corner of Calle Juárez and Degollado. **Farmacia Guadalupe** (Juárez, tel. 612/145-0300) fills prescriptions 24/7. Another option is **Farmacia Genericos y Similares** (Hidalgo at Militar, no tel.), in the Hotel Maria Bonita complex.

Money

You can withdraw dollars or pesos from the ATMs in town. **Banorte** (Juárez at Obregón, no tel., 9 A.M.–4 P.M. Mon.–Fri.) will cash travelers checks or exchange dollars (passport required). **Bancomer** (no tel.), at Juárez and Zaragoza, is another option.

Post and Telephone

The post office in Todos Santos has moved to the outskirts of town at Villarino between Olochea and Piacentini. It's supposed to be open 8 A.M.–1 P.M. and 3–5 P.M., but the hours tend to be erratic, since the manager is often out delivering mail.

Long-distance phone calls can be made from several Ladatel phones around town, including one on Hidalgo, near Tecolote Books. **El Centro de Mensajes Todos Santos (The Message Center),** in the lobby of Hotel California (Juárez btw Morelos/Márquez de León, tel. 612/145-0525, fax 612/145-0288, messagecenter1@yahoo.com, 8 A.M.–3 P.M. Mon.–Fri., 8 A.M.–2 P.M. Sat.) offers long-distance service at reasonable rates. The office also provides fax, DHL, mail forwarding, travel, and answering services.

For mobile phone needs, there are Telcel stores on Militar at Zaragoza, on Militar at Hidalgo, and on Degollado next to the Pemex.

Internet Access

Many Todos Santos guesthouses and hotels now have wireless Internet service. In addition, **Café Brown** (Hidalgo and Colegio Militar, tel. 612/145-0813, 8 A.M.–8 P.M. Wed.–Sun.), in the Hotel María Bonita complex, has high-speed access on its own PC or via a wireless connection. Cafénix and La Esquina are also good options for free Wi-Fi on the go.

Laundry

The *lavandería* (tel. 612/145-0006, 7:30 A.M.–7:30 P.M. daily), on Juárez in the Hotel Guluarte, provides laundry service for about US$4 per load, or less if you do it yourself. **Neptune's Laundry** on Colegio Militar between Morelos and Zaragoza is a larger, but full-service-only, operation.

Gas

There is a **Pemex** station in town located at the intersection of Militar and Degollado (Mexico 19) and one at Km. 50–51 on the way north to La Paz. Count your change carefully at either one.

THE WEST CAPE

Language Courses

Guillermo Bueron (cell tel. 612/161-4165, g_bueron@yahoo.com) teaches Spanish-, English-, and French-language classes at the Centro Cultural (Juárez at Topete) using the Berlitz approach. He offers group and individual classes at all levels. Classes take place at 9 A.M. Monday–Friday. Check the Todos Santos Inn website (www.todossantosinn.com) for weeklong packages that include two hours of language instruction per day, plus accommodations. Casa Bentley (www.casabentley.com) also arranges on-site classes with Guillermo for its guests.

Hardware and Auto Parts

Ferre Todos Santos (Zaragoza at Rangel, tel. 612/145-0565, 8 A.M.–2 P.M. and 3–6:30 P.M. Mon.–Sat.) has employees who speak English and stocks a decent selection of hardware goods. **Ferreteria Oasis de Todos Santos** (Rangel at Zaragoza, tel. 612/145-0754, 8 A.M.–3 P.M. and 4–7 P.M. Mon.–Fri., 8 A.M.–4 P.M. Sat.) has fishing supplies as well as plumbing and electrical parts.

Across from Neptune's laundry, well-stocked **Autopartes de la Rosa** (Militar btw Morelos/Zaragoza), 10 A.M.–6 P.M. Mon–Sat.) can help with a variety of automotive needs.

Volunteer Opportunities

Todos Santos has a few well-organized non-profit organizations working toward the betterment of the community that accept temporary volunteers—as well as a wide variety of donations, from sheets and pillows to toys and books for children. Those traveling with some extra time and/or the desire to integrate themselves into the community might like to hook up with some of those organizations and leave the place a little better than they found it.

The Palapa Society of Todos Santos, A.C. (Obregón 15, tel. 612/145-0299, www.palapasociety.org), founded in 2003, is a multicultural nonprofit Mexican Civil Association that provides programs, events, and activities for children in the area—as well as medical services, educational scholarships, English-language instruction, and environmental education. Visitors can get involved by mentoring a child in English for a day, assisting local artists in mural-painting workshops, or visiting the Todos Santos bilingual library. Proceeds from some of the town's events, such as the February Historic Home Tour, benefit this organization and its programs.

For the environmentally inclined, **Tortugueros Las Playitas A.C.** (www.todostorutgueros.org) seeks volunteers for its sea turtle conservation work November through April. This is a great way for kids and adults to get involved in an initiative that affects visitors and residents alike.

For an organized trip that includes some volunteering, check the VolunTourism page on the Todos Santos Eco Adventures site (www.tosea.net/AV04.htm). For more ideas, stop by the **Centro Cultural** (no tel.) on Calle Juárez at Topete.

BACKGROUND

The Land

GEOLOGY

The Baja Peninsula separated from mainland Mexico and opened up the Sea of Cortez some 5–10 million years ago in the Cenozoic Age, as the result of a gradual shifting of land masses called plates. The process, called plate tectonics, began as far back as the Mesozoic Age (63–230 million years ago), when the North American and Pacific Plates began to collide, pushing up mountains from Alaska to the tip of Baja. As the collision took place, the thicker North American Plate rode over the thinner Pacific Plate, forming a new landmass prone to volcanic activity along volatile faults such as the San Andreas, which runs through the middle of the Sea of Cortez. Over a period of tens of millions of years, the Pacific Plate drifted northward, tearing Baja from the mainland of Mexico. About five millions years ago, Baja pulled far enough away from the mainland to open up the Sea of Cortez. Many of the islands we see today were formed during the last ice age, when low-lying valleys filled with water, leaving only the highest points along the coast exposed.

Baja continues to drift northward today as part of the Pacific Plate, and geologists predict it will eventually become an island, proving the early Spanish explorers right.

GEOGRAPHY

The lower California peninsula stretches 1,300 kilometers (806 mi) from top to bottom. It begins at Tijuana at the border with the United States and extends 193 kilometers (120 mi) east to Mexicali and south to the cape at San Lucas below the Tropic of Cancer. Baja lies 250 kilometers (155 mi) west of mainland Mexico at its greatest distance. In between is the Golfo de California (Gulf of California), more commonly known as the Mar de Cortés (Sea of Cortez). On the west coast of the peninsula is the Pacific Ocean. At its narrowest point, between Bahía de La Paz and the Pacific Ocean, the peninsula measures just 45 kilometers (28 mi) across.

Numerous mountain ranges (23 to be exact) run the length of the interior, from northwest to southeast, with the highest peak, Picacho del Diablo, rising more than 3,000 meters (10,000 ft.). The longest and highest ranges include the **Sierra de Juárez** and **Sierra de San Pedro Mártir** in the north, the **Sierra de la Giganta** in the central peninsula, and the **Sierra de la Laguna** in the south.

At the foot of the sierras are vast desert areas comprising about 65 percent of the peninsula. The San Felipe Desert covers much of northeastern Baja, while the Gulf Coast Desert extends from Bahía de Los Angeles to San José del Cabo in the south. The Vizcaíno Desert, in the west-central part of the peninsula, is Baja's largest desert area and has been designated a protected Biosphere Reserve by the United Nations. South of this area, the Magdalena Plains (Llano Magdalena) border Bahía Magdalena, the largest bay on either side of the peninsula. Together, these two desert areas are often called the Desierto Central.

In addition to these extremes, the peninsula features coastal wetlands, sandy beaches, more than 100 islands (most of them located along the Gulf coast), and deep canyons filled with palms.

The Sea Of Cortez

The Mar de Cortés (Sea of Cortez) was originally named for the legendary Spanish explorer, Hernán Cortés, in the 16th century, and was sometimes also called the Mar Vermejo (Vermillion Sea) on early maps—a name that referred to the massive schools of pelagic red crabs that float on the water's surface in the spring. The Mexican government changed the official name to the Golfo de California (Gulf of California) in the early 20th century. Both names are used on maps today.

The sea is 669 miles long, extending from the mouth of the Colorado River to the cape at San Lucas. The northern section of the sea is shallow, the result of silt deposits from the river. Tidal fluctuations are extreme, as much as six meters near San Felipe.

Around the Midriff Islands near Bahía de los Angeles, the sea gets deeper and colder, and strong currents bring more nutrients, which sustain a phenomenal diversity of life—more than 900 species of marine vertebrates and more than 2,000 invertebrates. It's an environment that Jacques Cousteau once called the aquarium of the world.

South of La Paz, the gulf becomes more like an ocean, with deep trenches, submarine canyons, and towering seamounts.

The Sea of Cortez meets the Pacific Ocean below the tip of the Baja Peninsula, offshore from the rocky point known as Finisterra (Land's End).

ENVIRONMENTAL ISSUES

Many books, articles, and websites are now dedicated to the communication of Baja's environmental challenges. Travelers should understand that the rapid growth of tourism and real estate development, especially in the Los Cabos area, has strained fragile ecosystems up and down the peninsula. Coastal development threatens the mangrove habitat on the Mogote Peninsula near La Paz and the Estero San José. The delicate coral reef offshore from Cabo Pulmo could deteriorate rapidly if the water gets polluted from ongoing beachfront development. Even the pristine islands offshore from La Paz are showing signs of stress from the increase in camping and organized trips.

ECOTOURISM

In recent years, the number of low-impact activities and accommodations throughout the peninsula has increased, giving travelers a way to experience Baja without wreaking havoc on its fragile desert and marine ecosystems. From Bahía de los Angeles to Loreto to Cabo Pulmo, you'll find solar-powered *casitas*, organic produce, self-sufficient resorts, and proprietors who put the environment first. Bird-watching near San Ignacio, whale-watching in Bahía Magdalena, and sea turtle conservation efforts at Bahía de los Angeles and around Los Cabos are just a few of the ways to get involved.

On both sides of the peninsula, endangered sea turtles face poaching and loss of habitat for laying eggs. Commercial fishing has taken a toll on other species as well, with prized billfish reportedly now much smaller in size than in the early years of Baja's fishing camps. Desperate to make ends meet, poachers take illegal reef fish, flying mobula rays, lobster, and desert pronghorn. At the same time, aggressive international corporations negotiate with the Mexican government for licenses to use harmful longline fishing techniques in the Sea of Cortez, which destroy all manner of marine life. Conservationists are routinely called to help rescue whales, whale sharks, and dolphins from these nets.

In the long term, the scarcity of freshwater and ability of municipalities to keep up with water and sewage treatment needs pose another concern. Communities from Los Cabos to La Paz have banded together to fight the potential of open-pit gold-mining in the Sierra de la Laguna, which could contaminate drinking water with arsenic.

On the bright side, gray whales have made a remarkable comeback, and reefs are showing signs of recovery as local groups team up

with the government to provide education and training so that fishermen can earn a living as ecotour guides instead of poaching.

Residents and visitors, both Mexican and foreign, are getting involved to help conserve the environment for years to come. For example, Grupo Tortuguero (www.grupotortuguero.org) runs a turtle conservation program in Baja, and Pro Peninsula (www.propeninsula.org) publishes an informative website and quarterly newsletter about Baja's environmental concerns.

Comunidad y Biodiversidad A.C. (COBI, www.cobi.org.mx) is a Mexican non-governmental organization (NGO) that promotes marine conservation throughout Baja California Sur. Another NGO, Rare Conservation (www.rareconservation.org), uses grassroots methods to promote sustainable fishing within marine parks in the Gulf of California.

CLIMATE

The most important feature of Baja's climate for most travelers is its abundance of warm, sunny, dry days. In fact, your chances of enjoying a winter beach vacation without rain are higher here than in Hawaii or Florida. (Wind is another matter, however.) Across the entire peninsula, the climate ranges from Mediterranean to desert to tropical. In general, the mountains are cooler than the coast, the Pacific coast is cooler than the Gulf coast in summer (but can be warmer than the Gulf coast in winter), and the northern part of the peninsula is cooler than the southern part. But within these guidelines are numerous microclimates, caused by the interplay of mountains, bays, currents, fog, and winds.

In summer and fall, tropical storms called *chubascos* can bring rain and high winds for a few hours to a few days at a time. Hurricanes are less common, but they do occur every few years. The most recent one to strike Baja was Hurricane John in 2006, which made landfall at Cabo Pulmo, bringing heavy rains and 150-mph winds all the way to Mulegé and Santa Rosalía.

Flora

According to botanist estimates, the unique ecosystems of the Baja Peninsula and its islands support more than 4,000 varieties of plants. For an introduction to about 550 of them, consult the *Baja California Plant Field Guide*, by Norman C. Roberts. Here are some of the highlights:

CACTI

Scientists have identified 120 species of cactus here, and the majority of them live only on this peninsula or its offshore islands. Many of them flower after summer and fall rains, painting the desert in splashes of bright color for a few weeks of the year. One of the most common cacti in Baja is the *cardón (Pachycereus pringlei)*, the tallest of them all, which is especially prevalent in the Valle de los Gigantes (Valley of the Giants) south of San Felipe. They can grow to heights of 18 meters (60 ft.) and weights of 12 tons (not counting the roots), and they live for hundreds of years.

© NIKKI GOTH ITOI

a cholla cactus on the East Cape

Less common but also unique to Baja, the *biznaga (Ferocactus)*, or barrel cactus, lives only on a few islands in the Sea of Cortez. It has red-tinged spines and blooms yellow and red flowers in the spring.

The indigenous Pericú treasured the *pitahaya dulce*, or organ pipe cactus, for its watermelon-like fruit. During the late summer and early fall harvest, the Pericú ate the abundant fruit until they fell asleep, waking only when they were ready to eat some more. The species lives south of the Sierra de San Borja in Central Baja and on a few islands in the Sea of Cortez. A related species, *pitahaya agria* (galloping cactus) has a less sweet but still edible fruit.

Multiple kinds of cholla and nopal (prickly pear), both part of the *Opuntia* species, grow throughout the region. The nopal is an edible cactus, common on menus up and down the peninsula.

AGAVES

Nineteen types of agave are found in Baja, including several varieties of yucca. Agaves are pollinated most commonly by bats and flower only after several years. Many of them are edible. The tree yucca, or *datilillo* (little date), looks a lot like a date palm and thrives on the west side of the Vizcaíno Desert, among other places. You can eat its fruit and flowers, boil its roots to soften soap or leather, and weave the leaves into sandals, baskets, or mats. Maguey, or century plant, flowers only once in its lifetime, sending up a tall, slender stalk after maturation. It was another major source of food and fiber for the indigenous people that inhabited the peninsula.

FOUQUIERIACEAE

The most striking plant in this family of succulents is easily the most distinctive in all of Baja. Indeed, the tall and lanky *cirio* (candle) or Boojum tree looks like an upside-down carrot—something right out of a Dr. Seuss

desert flowers, East Cape

book. Almost as tall as the *cardón,* it grows about three centimeters a year and lives for hundreds of years. In order to see this unusual plant, you have to venture into central Baja. It only grows between the southern end of the Sierra de San Pedro Mártir and the Sierra Tres Vírgenes and on Isla Angel de la Guarda, near Bahía de los Angeles. If you're driving the Transpeninsular Highway south, your first glimpse of the species comes as you enter the desert below El Rosario.

Also part of the same family, the *ocotillo* and *palo adán* (Adam's tree) are found throughout the peninsula and often used to make fences.

TREES
Palms

A universal symbol of the tropics around the globe, palm trees are used as landscaping in warm climates all over North America. But there is something spectacular about seeing them grow in the wild, especially when they are clinging to the walls of a deep canyon high in the sierras. Seven varieties live in the Baja California wilderness. Besides providing shade and an overall tropical aesthetic, they are used to make woven baskets, thatched roofs, and construction materials such as roof beams or rails for fences.

The endemic blue fan palm (also called the Mexican blue palm, and in Spanish *palma ceniza* or *palma azul*) has bluish-colored leaves and grows from the canyons and arroyos of the Sierra de Juárez in the north to San Ignacio in the south, reaching heights of 24 meters (79 ft.).

The smallest palm found in Baja is the *tlaco* palm (also called the *palma palmia* and the *palma colorado*). It's found south of Loreto. The tallest palm in Baja, also with fan-shaped leaves, is the Mexican fan palm (Baja California fan palm, skyduster, or *palma blanca*). It tops out at 27–30 meters (90–100 ft.).

Spanish Jesuit missionaries brought the feather-leaf date palm to Baja, and it continues to thrive near Loreto, Comondú, Mulegé,

San Ignacio, and San José del Cabo. And the coconut palm *(cocotera),* the only other feather-leaf palm in Baja, grows south of Mulegé.

Elephant Tree

Part of the sumac family of trees that emit a milky sap, the *Pachycormus discolor* (*copalquín* or *torote blanco* in Spanish) has a gnarled trunk and branches covered in a gray-white outer layer that peels off, exposing a smooth blue-green inner bark. It's most common in the Desierto Central. This tree is often confused with *Bursera odorata* (*pachycormus,* also called *torote blanco* in Spanish), a member of the torchwood family, which has a yellow inner bark and grows south of Bahía Concepción.

Conifers

An unexpected delight when exploring the interior of the peninsula is the wide variety of conifers that grow in the high sierras. Cypress, cedar, juniper, white fir, and lodgepole pine are just a few examples. The Tecate cypress grows on the western slopes of the Sierra de Juárez and north to Orange County in Alta California, while the San Pedro Mártir cypress lives on the eastern escarpment of the Sierra de San Pedro Mártir. Cedros Island in the Pacific Ocean has its own endemic conifer, the Cedros Island pine, as does Isla Guadalupe, with the Guadalupe Island pine.

Ironwood

If you browse any of Baja's arts and crafts markets, you'll often see shelves filled with animals carved out of wood. The raw material for these crafts comes from the ironwood tree (*palo fierro* or *tesota* in Spanish). A hard, hot-burning wood, it has been logged extensively

on the peninsula and is no longer as common as it once was.

Mimosas

Mimosas are a subfamily of the pea family *(Leguminosae),* all of which have linear seed-pods and double rows of tiny leaves. Within this subfamily, mesquite and acacia occur throughout the peninsula. Baja's indigenous people had many uses for mesquite wood, from construction materials to herbal remedies, and the traditions are carried on today by those who live in the most rural parts of the peninsula.

When it blooms in the spring, the small white blossoms of the *palo blanco* tree are a sight to behold. The Sierra de la Giganta, near Loreto, is one of the best places to find it.

Wild Figs

Even figs grow wild in Baja. Called *zalates,* they tend to prefer the rocky areas of Southern Baja, below La Paz.

HERBS

A number of herbs used in cooking and alternative medicine thrive in the hot, dry Baja climate. For example, white sage is found on the rocky hillsides in Northern Baja. Another type of sage, the rare chia, grows only in the desert areas of Baja, Sonora, and the southwestern United States. But the herb most commonly associated with Baja California is damiana *(Turnera diffusa),* consumed either as a tea or in a liqueur and believed to be a powerful aphrodisiac. When you see a Baja margarita on the menu, it usually contains damiana liqueur instead of triple sec. This shrub prefers the rocky areas of Southern Baja, near the capes.

Fauna

LAND MAMMALS

Baja's marine and animal life is just as diverse as its plant life. More than 100 mammals inhabit the peninsula, two dozen of which are considered endemic. The extreme terrain and climate has made for some interesting adaptations. Among the list of carnivores that live in the wilderness are coyotes, mountain lions, foxes, bobcats, and raccoons. Mule deer live below 1,500 meters (5,000 ft.), while fewer white-tailed deer live in the higher elevations.

Desert bighorn sheep *(borrego cimarrón)* have yet to recover from excessive big-game hunting of the early 20th century. And the endangered peninsular pronghorn *(berrendo)* survives only in the protected preserve of the Vizcaíno Desert. Also on the endangered species list is the endemic black jackrabbit.

GRAY WHALES

Before it was overhunted by Dutch, British, and American whalers in the 19th century, the gray whale inhabited the Atlantic Ocean, Baltic Sea, and North Sea, as well as the Pacific Ocean. Today it lives only in the Pacific. The object of many organized trips to Baja, gray whales migrate around 19,300 kilometers (12,000 mi) a year from the Arctic Circle, where they feed, to the shallow lagoons on the west side of Baja California, where they give birth to their calves. Adults measure 10–15 meters (35–50 ft.) long and weigh 20–40 tons. Their skin is almost black at birth, but the growth and scarring of barnacles over the years makes them look more gray than black.

There are three lagoons along the central Pacific coast of Baja where visitors can observe the gray whales up close: Laguna Ojo de Liebre near Guerrero Negro, Laguna San Ignacio, and Bahía Magdalena.

OTHER MARINE MAMMALS

Besides the social gray whale, Baja's Pacific and Gulf waters host two dozen species of whales and dolphins, including the endangered vaquita

© NIKKI GOTH ITOI

a mother and baby burro on the road to the East Cape

dolphin, which once thrived in the northern Sea of Cortez near San Felipe.

The elephant seal and Guadalupe fur seal have made a recent comeback on Isla Guadalupe and nearby islands, where they were hunted nearly to the point of extinction in the 19th century. More common California sea lions, or *lobos marinas,* live on and around several islands in the Sea of Cortez, including Isla Ángel de la Guarda near Bahía de los Angeles and Isla Espíritu Santo near La Paz.

FISH

Marine biologists have labeled the Sea of Cortez the richest body of water in the world. Diverse marine environments along both sides of the Baja Peninsula support thousands of species of fish. There are sailfish and marlin (collectively called billfish); corvinas and croaker, including the protected totuava; yellowtail, amberjack, pompanos, and roosterfish; dorado (mahimahi), wahoo, and bluefin, albacore, and yellowfin tuna, which can grow to sizes exceeding 180 kilograms (400 lbs.); various types of sea bass, including *garropa* (grouper) and cabrilla; flounder and halibut; snappers (*pargo,* including the red snapper, which is called *huachinango* in Spanish). More than 60 types of sharks live here, among them the hammerhead, thresher, bonito (mako), bull, whitetip, sand, blue, blacktip, and whale shark—the world's largest fish at 18 meters (59 ft.) and 3,600 kilograms (almost four tons).

Eagle rays, guitarfish, stingrays, and other rays often rest on the sandy bottom of the sea, offshore from the southern part of the peninsula. Divers and snorkelers are sometimes lucky enough to see the Pacific manta ray glide by. With a wingspan of up to seven meters (23 ft.), it can weigh nearly two tons.

The Humboldt squid is another unusual deepwater creature. It grows to 4.5 meters (15 ft.) long and weigh up to 150 kilograms (330 lbs.).

Barracuda are found in both the Pacific and the Sea of Cortez. And in Southern Baja, the flying fish puts on a good show as it leaps out of the water offshore.

Abundant shellfish, including clams, oysters, mussels, scallops, and shrimp, and spiny lobster, are found all along the coast.

BIRDS

With this great variety of plant and fish life comes an equally fantastic bird population. Ornithologists have identified at least 300 species, but unfortunately no one has published a Baja-specific field guide to date, though several Mexican bird guides include the species found on the peninsula and its islands.

Baja California Sur Birds (BCS Birds, www.bcsbirds.com) is dedicated to raising awareness of the area's potential as a world-class birdwatching destination. The BCS Birds website is designed as a reference for naturalists and birders who wish to identify what they have seen here and who wish to learn what species are regularly observed in Baja California Sur.

Coastal Birds

The Midriff Islands in particular provide habitat for many rare and endangered species, and the Mexican government protects 49 of these islands as wildlife preserves. Well known among birders, Isla San Pedro Mártir has the blue-footed booby as well as the brown booby and masked booby. Tiny Isla de Raza is another popular birding destination.

Brown pelicans are common in Baja but gone from the coastal islands of California and the U.S. shores of the Gulf of Mexico. Other noteworthy birds include the frigate, fisher eagle, cormorant, egret, gull, heron, loon, osprey, plover, sandpiper, and tern.

Boaters sometimes see pelagic birds such as the albatross, black-legged kittiwake, red phalarope, shearwater, surf scoter, south polar skua, storm petrel, black tern, and red-billed tropic bird.

Freshwater Birds

The inland ponds, springs, lakes, streams, and marshes of Baja support two species of bittern, the American coot, two species of duck, the snow goose, the northern harrier, six species of heron, the white-faced ibis, the common moorhen, two species of rail, five species of sandpiper, the lesser scaup, the shoveler, the common snipe, the sora, the roseate spoonbill, the wood stork, three species of teal, the northern waterthrush, and the American wigeon.

Birds of the Sierra

The golden eagle, western flycatcher, lesser goldfinch, black-headed grosbeak, red-tailed hawk, pheasant, yellow-eyed junco, white-breasted nuthatch, mountain plover, acorn woodpecker, and canyon wren live in the peaks and valleys of the sierras, along with two species of hummingbird, four species of vireo, and eight species of warbler.

Desert Birds

Falcons, flycatchers, hawks, hummingbirds, owls, sparrows, and thrashers live in the hot, dry desert environment, along with the American kestrel, merlin, greater roadrunner, vernon, turkey vulture, ladder-backed wood-pecker, and cactus wren.

The largest bird in North America is the endangered California condor *(Gymnogyps californianus),* which weighs up to 11 kilograms (24 lbs.), with a wingspan of nearly 3.6 meters (12 ft.). A group of U.S. and Mexican scientists plans to release captive-bred condors in Baja's Sierra de San Pedro Mártir in hopes that the more limited human presence will permit the bird to survive in the wild.

REPTILES AND AMPHIBIANS

Thirty types of lizards live on the Baja Peninsula, including the large chuckwalla, which inhabits several islands in the Sea of Cortez and can grow to one meter (3 ft.) long. The desert iguana and the endemic coast-horned lizard are also noteworthy species. With lots of color photos, *Amphibians and Reptiles of Baja California,* by Ron McPeak can help you identify the many frogs, toads, salamanders, snakes, and lizards of the peninsula.

Turtles

Five sea turtles live in Baja waters: the leatherback, green, hawksbill, western ridley, and loggerhead, which swims 10,460 kilometers (6,500 mi) between the island of Kyushu in Japan and the Sea of Cortez. All these turtles

© NIKKI GOTH ITOI

Turtle protection signs are posted along Bahía de la Ventana, near La Paz.

> ## SAVE A SEA TURTLE
>
> One of the most magical experiences of a Baja adventure is watching a group of baby turtles hatch and make their way from nest to sea. A dedicated group of volunteers in Todos Santos is doing its part to protect the turtles and their habitat from the threat of encroaching development. **Tortugueros Las Playitas A.C.** (tel. 612/145-0353, U.S. tel 213/265-9943, www.todostortugueros. org) seeks volunteers for its sea turtle conservation work November through April. Travelers and residents from the United States, Canada, Mexico, and Europe have participated in these conservation efforts over the last few years, assisting in the rescue of thousands of sea turtle eggs from three species: leatherback, black, and olive ridley. Nests are incubated in a greenhouse due to the low sand temperatures during the winter and spring in Todos Santos. This is the only sea turtle nest incubation greenhouse in Baja. Visit www.todostortugueros.org to get involved.

are endangered, and it's illegal to hunt any of them or collect their eggs, but enforcing the law has been a challenge.

Many organizations are involved in turtle conservation efforts in Baja. One of the largest is Grupo Tortuguero (www.grupoturtuguero. org), which holds its annual meeting in late January–early February in Loreto. A who's who of Baja influencers usually attends.

Snakes

There are 35 species of snakes *(serpientes)* in Baja, about half of which are poisonous, although they rarely come into contact with people.

Nonvenomous kinds *(culebra)* include the western blind snake, rosy boa, Baja California rat snake, spotted leaf-nosed snake, western patch-nosed snake, bull snake, coachwhip, king snake, Baja sand snake, and California lyre snake.

Among the poisonous types *(víbora)* are

the yellow-bellied sea snake, which resembles a floating stick in the water, and 18 species of rattlesnake (*serpiente de cascabel* or *cascabel*), including the common Baja California rattler, red diamondback, and western diamondback, which is the largest and most dangerous of Baja's snakes and lives in the canyons of the northern sierras.

The only rattler that's endemic to Baja California is the rattleless rattlesnake *(Crotalus catalinensis)*, which lives only on Isla Santa Catalina in the Sea of Cortez.

History

PRE-CORTESIAN HISTORY

The Asians who crossed the Bering Strait land bridge beginning around 50,000 B.C. most likely migrated as far south as the Baja Peninsula, but relatively little archeology has been done to test the theory. About 7,000 years ago, a group called the San Diegito moved south into Northern Baja and lived near the peninsula's freshwater sources. Next came the Yumanos, around 2,500 years ago, who painted much of the peninsula's rock art—the only aspect of the culture that survives today. Yumano tribes included the Cucapá, Tipai, Paipai (or Pa'ipai), Kumyai, and Kiliwa.

Historians believe that the indigenous people who lived in Central and Southern Baja at the time of the Spanish conquest were more primitive than the Yumanos, who engaged in more advanced hunting, fishing, and cultivation. But it is difficult to know for sure because the missionary histories—the only documentation available—were written with a strong bias against the indigenous people, whom they sought to convert. According to the missionaries, the Cochimís inhabited the central peninsula and Comondú, while Guaycuras (consisting of the Pericú, Huchiti, and Guaicura tribes) lived in Southern Baja near the capes.

THE SPANISH CONQUEST

Following its conquest of Mexico and Central America in the early 16th century, Spain turned its attention farther west. Early explorers believed the Baja Peninsula was an island and that the present-day Sea of Cortez was a northwest passage to the Atlantic. Legendary

SEBASTIÁN VIZCAÍNO EXPEDITIONS

—— Expedition of 1596
······· Expedition of 1602–03

Monterey

San Diego

PACIFIC OCEAN

Mazatlán

Cabo San Lucas

Navidad

Acapulco

0   300 mi
0   300 km

© AVALON TRAVEL

conquistador Hernán Cortés directed four voyages into the Sea of Cortez beginning in 1532. In 1534 the first Europeans set food on the peninsula, landing at La Paz, but most were promptly killed by the indigenous inhabitants. A few survivors returned to the mainland with stories of rich pearl-oyster beds on a big island.

Cortés himself landed in the Bahía de La Paz in 1535, but he failed to establish a permanent colony. He sponsored a fourth voyage in 1539, led by Captain Francisco de Ulloa, who explored the entire perimeter of the Gulf of California and then continued north along the Pacific coast, as far as Isla Cedros. Ulloa is credited with naming the Mar de Cortés.

Cortés returned to Spain in 1541 and was replaced by a Portuguese explorer named Juan Rodríguez Cabrillo, whose expedition explored the Pacific coast, as far north as Oregon.

Manila Galleons

When the Portuguese conquered the Philippines, they quickly established a trade route from Manila to the New World, following the Japanese Current across the Pacific Ocean. The ships that made this arduous journey were called the Manila galleons; in order to make it safely to Asia, their crews needed a place to stop for freshwater and a protected harbor to hide their treasure from enterprising pirates like the famous Sir Francis Drake. Baja's fate as a target for European colonization was sealed.

As English and Dutch privateers began to raid Spanish ships with increasing frequency and success, the Spanish got more serious about settling Baja. Sebastián Vizcaíno landed in Bahía de La Paz in 1596, encountered friendly indigenous inhabitants, and named the place La Paz. From there, he traveled north along the Gulf coast and then returned to mainland Mexico. He returned in 1602 and sailed around the cape and up the Pacific coast to Mendocino, California, renaming the islands, bays, and points along the way. But the Spanish would not prevail in Baja for another 80 years.

The next expedition, led by Admiral Isidor Atondo y Antillón and Jesuit Padre Eusebio Francisco Kino, landed first at La Paz and later at San Bruno to the north, where they established a mission that lasted less than two years. Lack of food and freshwater forced the colonists to head home to the mainland.

THE MISSION ERA
The Jesuits (1697-1767)

Padre Juan María Salvatierra established Antigua California's first permanent Spanish mission in 1697. He landed in San Bruno but promptly found a more reliable source of freshwater 24 kilometers (15 mi) south of the original mission, and proceeded to establish the mission that would become "the mother of all California missions," Nuestra Señora de Loreto. Historians estimate the indigenous population at about 50,000 at the time of Salvatierra's arrival.

Over the next 70 years, the Jesuits established 22 settlements and supporting *visitas* (visiting missions), creating a mission trail south to the cape at San José and north to Cataviña in the Desierto Central. The missionaries introduced the indigenous people to the "civilized" Spanish way of life and offered food and water in exchange for labor. The indigenous people planted crops, dug waterways, and built churches. But they did not always welcome the missionary efforts to change their

© NIKKI GOTH ITOI

Baja's first permanent Jesuit mission, founded in 1697

MISSIONS
(1697-1856)

FRANCISCAN
DOMINICAN
JESUIT

ways, particularly when it came to the decree against polygamy.

Uprisings were a frequent occurrence during the missionary period. The Pericú rebellion of 1734 caused extensive damage, destroying four missions in the southern part of the peninsula and killing two of the padres. Through the rest of the 18th century, the indigenous population decreased rapidly due to epidemics of European-borne diseases such as smallpox and measles. By 1748 more than 80 percent of the population estimated at Salvatierra's arrival had perished. With no one left alive to convert, the missions began to close. By 1767 only one member of the entire Huchiti branch of the Guaycura nation had survived.

In the wake of disease and death, the missionaries pressed northward, always seeking more "neophytes" for their religious activities.

On June 15, 1767, King Charles III of Spain issued the Jesuit Expulsion Decree, requiring the 16 missionaries left in Antigua California to return to the mainland, where they were shipped back to Europe and imprisoned or exiled. Historical accounts of the reason for the expulsion differ. One theory says the Jesuits were accused of stealing the hidden treasures of Antigua California from the crown; others believe the Jesuits were punished for speaking out against government corruption. In any case, they were replaced immediately by the Franciscan Order.

The Franciscans and Dominicans

Fourteen Franciscan padres landed in Loreto in 1768, including Padre Junípero Serra, who carried the mission torch north to Alta California. The Franciscans established one mission in Northern Baja, San Fernando Velicatá, before crossing into the present-day U.S. state of California to establish a mission at San Diego and a new mission trail that would extend as far north as Sonoma.

With his attention on Alta California, Serra transferred the Baja missions to the Dominican Order in 1772, and the first of nine Dominican missions (and one *visita*) was established at El Rosario in 1774, which became the official boundary between Alta and Baja California in 1777. In 1776 Monterey replaced Loreto as the capital of the two Californias.

By 1800 only 5,000 indigenous people survived on the peninsula, and the Spanish government could no longer justify support of the missions.

THE 19TH CENTURY

Mexico's revolt against the Spanish crown began on September 16, 1810, a date celebrated annually as Día de la Independencia, or Mexican Independence Day, in a climate of social and economic instability. In an attempt to regain control over the powerful Catholic Church, the Spanish government had seized all church funds, which left the local economy in turmoil. Padre Miguel Hidalgo y Costilla issued the call for independence from the mainland city of Dolores, Guanajuato. It would take more than a decade, but Mexico would finally emerge independent from Spain in 1821. According to the Plan de Iguala treaty, the Catholic Church would remain the dominant force in Mexico, a constitutional monarchy would rule, and mestizos and Mexican-born Spaniards would gain equal rights under the new regime. Former viceroy Agustín de Iturbide became emperor of the new republic but only for two years. In its first 30 years of independence, Mexico would weather 50 changes in government.

In 1830 the capital of Baja California moved from Loreto to La Paz following a severe hurricane, and in 1834 the last Dominican mission in Baja was established at Guadalupe, northeast of Ensenada.

The Mexican-American War

In 1833 Antonio López de Santa Anna, a powerful general who had enforced the expulsion of Spain's troops from Mexico, seized power, revoked the Constitution of 1824, and set in motion the chain of events that would lead to independence for Texas, war with the United States, and the loss of vast territories in the north.

The United States declared war on Mexico in 1846, following a series of skirmishes over the border with the newly established U.S. state of Texas. In Baja, Mexican and U.S. forces confronted each other at Santo Tomás, Mulegé, La Paz, and San José del Cabo. Mexico City surrendered to the United States in March 1847, and the two countries signed the Treaty of Guadalupe Hidalgo in 1848, in which Mexico conceded the Rio Grande area of Texas as well as part of New Mexico and all of Alta California in exchange for US$25 million and the cancellation of all Mexican debt. The treaty moved the border between Baja California and Alta California from El Rosario to Tijuana, establishing a new international border zone.

In 1849 many Baja California residents left the peninsula to pan for gold in the California gold rush. As Baja's population dwindled, it became a land of bandits, pirates, outlaws, and misfits.

The latter part of the 19th century brought more turbulence for Mexico. In 1853 Mexico sold Arizona and southern New Mexico to the United States for US$10 million, and American military "freebooter" William Walker invaded La Paz with 45 mercenaries and declared himself president of the Republic of Lower California. The Americans fled when he heard that Mexican troops were en route to La Paz. Walker was tried and acquitted in the United States for violating neutrality laws, but he was subsequently executed for a similar attempt in Nicaragua two years later.

The War of Reform

The Mexican people overthrew General Santa Anna in 1855, and he was replaced by a Zapotec lawyer named Benito Juárez. In 1858 a civil war called the War of Reform broke out on the mainland, with the wealth of the church at the root of the conflict. The liberals, led by Juárez, drafted a new constitution to limit the powers of the church, while the opposition seized control of Mexico City. The liberals declared victory in 1861, and Juárez became president.

The French invaded Mexico the following year, after Mexico failed to pay its debts to France. Napoleon III captured Puebla and then Mexico City, where he placed Austrian Ferdinand Maximilian as emperor of Mexico. The United States pressured France to withdraw, Maximilian was executed by a Juarista firing squad, and Juárez resumed control of the nation in 1867.

The end of the decade brought a series of reforms to strengthen the Mexican economy and its educational system. Juárez died in 1872 and his political opponent Porfirio Díaz took over, continuing the program of reform but with a much more authoritarian approach. Díaz ran the country for nearly three decades, and during this time, he improved its transportation and education systems, but at the expense of political freedom.

Foreign Investment

Díaz promoted aggressive foreign investment in Baja, selling large tracts of land to U.S. and European corporations. The peninsula's gold- and silver-mining era began in 1878, with the arrival of the American Progreso Mining Company. In 1883 the International Company of Mexico, a joint venture among U.S., British, and Mexican investors, bought the rights to develop more than seven million hectares (18 million acres) of land south of Tijuana. The British would build a pier and flour mill near San Quintín, but colonization efforts would end without success. A French mining company named Boleo & Cie commenced mining operations and built the town of Santa Rosalía beginning in 1885. In 1889 the discovery of gold near Ensenada triggered a rush to Santa Clara.

The Territory of Baja California was divided into two districts, north and south, at the 28th parallel, in 1885.

THE 20TH CENTURY
The Mexican Revolution

Several decades of political oppression under Díaz and an ever-widening gap between rich and poor sowed the seeds for a full-scale revolution. The country's underrepresented workers and peasants—led by liberal Francisco Madero and aided by a bandit named Pancho Villa and a peasant named Emiliano Zapata—rose up against Díaz. The rebels prevailed, but through the course of the conflict, they divided into factions, one of which, the Magonistas, took control of Tijuana in 1911. Madero was executed in 1913.

Following several more years of instability, revolutionary Venustiano Carranza became president and drafted the Constitution of 1917, which returned lands to the peasants as cooperatively owned *ejidos*. Three years later, supporters of Carranza's political opponent, Álvaro Obregón, overthrew Carranza.

Obregón stayed in office four years and initiated more educational reforms. Plutarco Elías Calles, who succeeded him in 1924, redistributed three million hectares (7.5 million acres) of land and helped establish the National Revolutionary Party (PNR), a regime that would maintain a tight grip on the country for the next 70 years.

U.S. Prohibition

Northern Baja began to develop a tourism-driven economy around the time of the U.S. Prohibition, in 1920. With alcoholic beverages illegal north of the border, U.S. residents flocked to Tijuana and Mexicali to drink and gamble in newly opened casino resorts. Flush with cash, the cities began to invest in manufacturing and agricultural infrastructure. Building of the Transpeninsular Highway began in 1927. The repeal of Prohibition in 1933 caused a deep recession just a few years later.

Nationalist Reforms and World War II

In 1938 PNR candidate Lázaro Cárdenas, a mestizo, became president of Mexico and enacted far-reaching social reforms. He redistributed 18.6 million hectares (46 million acres) to the *ejidos* and established Petróleos Mexicanos (Pemex), as a government-owned oil monopoly. Foreign investors fled the country as a result. Under Cárdenas, the PNR became the Partido Revolucionario Institucional

(PRI), which would control the Mexican government until 2000.

In 1942 the United States allowed Mexican citizens to work north of the border for short periods of time under the Bracero Program, which stayed in place until 1962 and contributed to rapid urban development along the international border.

Statehood

Following World War II, Mexico enjoyed steady growth in its manufacturing and agricultural sectors. Northern Baja became Mexico's 29th state in 1952, with a population of 80,000 (the minimum required for statehood). Southern Baja remained a sparsely populated territory of isolated ranches and fishing settlements. A small number of Mexicans from the mainland visited La Paz to shop in the duty-free zone. But commerce by land was difficult because it took 10 days to drive the rough road from Tijuana to La Paz. A paved highway was needed to link the prosperous border zone with the rest of the peninsula. Construction of the 1,700-kilometer (1,054-mi) Transpenisular Highway (Mexico 1) was completed in 1974, opening the door to greater commerce and tourism. Baja California Sur became Mexico's 30th state less than one year later. In 1975 the government decided to invest in tourism infrastructure along the corridor between San José del Cabo and Cabo San Lucas, setting the stage for the destination resort we know today as Los Cabos.

Baja California (Norte) and Baja California Sur are socially more progressive than the majority of mainland states. In 1989 BCN elected a National Action Party candidate as governor, becoming the first state in the nation to vote in an opposition party to the PRI. For its part, BCS voted in a leftist coalition party consisting of the PRD (Partido Revolucionario Democrático, or Democratic Revolutionary Party) and the PT (Partido Trabajadores, or Workers Party). These victories represented major milestones in Mexican politics, long notorious for election fraud and corruption.

From Devaluation to Democracy

Mexico experienced another period of instability under President Ernesto Zedilo when the North American Free Trade Agreement (NAFTA) took effect in 1994. Indigenous uprisings in Chiapas on the mainland, the assassination of PRI presidential candidate Luis Donaldo Colosio in Tijuana, and the exposing of systemic corruption at the highest level of government scared investors out of the country, triggering a currency crisis and severe recession in early 1995.

But in the final years of the century, a grassroots movement succeeded in gradually and peacefully transforming the country into an open, multiparty democracy. In July 2000 the Mexican people elected the first non-PRI candidate in 70 years to the presidency, Vicente Fox of the National Action Party. *Opening Mexico: The Making of a Democracy,* written by *New York Times* reporters Julia Preston and Samuel Dillon, chronicles this period of change in an engaging, narrative format.

With its close ties to the U.S. economy, Baja California emerged from the currency crisis stronger in many ways than the mainland. But it faces grave challenges today in the form of organized crime, human trafficking, and corruption among law enforcement officials.

In July 2006 Felipe Calderón (PAN) was elected president of Mexico in a contentious election by a margin of only 0.56 percent over López Obrador (PRD). Amidst allegations of voting irregularities by the losing party, the initial election results were challenged. The ghosts of Mexico's past civil unrest hung in the air during the months it took to confirm the initial results.

During his term, Calderón took on the drug cartels and corruption at the city level. The Tijuana city police force had its guns confiscated and officers temporarily armed themselves with slingshots. Narco-violence raged on at press time, although it was confined to the border region and a few mainland states.

Government and Economy

GOVERNMENT
Political Boundaries
The 28th parallel divides the Baja California peninsula into two states, Baja California (BC) north of the parallel and Baja California Sur (BCS) to the south. The northern state is sometimes called Baja California (Norte) or BCN to distinguish the state from the entire peninsula.

Mexicali is the capital of Baja California (Norte), and the state consists of five *municipios* that are similar to U.S. counties: Tijuana, Rosarito, Ensenada, Mexicali, and Tecate. The state shares an international northern border with the United States.

Baja California Sur also consists of five *municipios:* La Paz, Los Cabos, Mulegé, Loreto, and Comondú. La Paz is the state capital.

Political System
The 31 United Mexican States form a representative democracy, which functions according to a constitution that was ratified in 1917. There are three branches: executive, legislative, and judicial. Presidents serve for six-year terms with no reelection. The legislature consists of two houses, the Senate and the Chamber of Deputies. States and municipalities (counties) have some independence, but each one must follow a republican form of government based on a congressional system.

Three parties dominate Mexican politics today: the National Action Party (PAN), the Party of the Democratic Revolution (PRD), and Institutional Revolutionary Party (PRI), which was the single reigning party through most of the 20th century.

The present governor of BCN is José Guadalupe Osuna Millán (PAN), an economist and former representative in the federal Chamber of Deputies. He took office in 2007. In February 2011 Baja California Sur elected a new governor, Marcos Covarrubias, from President Felipe Calderón's National Action Party (PAN). The election ended 12 years of rule by the leftist PRD. The former ruling party, PRI, won local elections in La Paz and Loreto, while the PRD was victorious in Mulegé and Los Cabos.

ECONOMY
Tourism, commercial fishing, large-scale agriculture, and manufacturing in the border zone drive the economy of the Baja Peninsula. The mining of salt and other minerals plays a lesser role in the state of BCS. Organic agriculture is on the rise, with peppers, tomatoes, mangoes, basil, asparagus, and oranges among the crops that are being grown without the use of pesticides.

In the border region, hundreds of maquiladoras produce airplanes, electronics, automobiles, and medical devices. This part of the Baja economy is inseparably tied to that of the County of San Diego in the United States. People on both sides of the border regularly cross to the other side to work, shop, and travel.

Income and Employment
People who live in Baja are well-off compared to the majority of their fellow citizens on the mainland. Per-capita income in both states ranks higher than the national average, while unemployment is the lowest in the country. Workers employed by the in-bond plants earn higher wages than at comparable jobs elsewhere in the country, though the pay is far less than what their U.S. counterparts would make on the other side of the border.

Recent Economic Conditions
President Calderón has spent his term fighting the drug cartels and ridding the government of corrupt officials at every level. Immigration, corruption, and narco-terrorism continue to pose grave challenges to the Mexican economy. Some see these problems as isolated border issues, and they say that the increase in violence is a sign that the strategy to prevent the flow of illegal drugs is working. Others believe the entire country could be on the brink of collapse if it doesn't stop the violence soon.

People and Culture

The people of Baja California are a diverse mix of farmers, anglers, laborers, entrepreneurs, students, and professionals. Some belong to families that have lived on the peninsula for generations; others arrived more recently from mainland Mexico, the United States, Canada, or Europe. But regardless of their line of work and heritage, Baja's residents tend to share a common outlook on life: Somewhere along the line, they decided to search for—and found—a better way of life, albeit one that requires resourcefulness. Mainland Mexicans tend to regard Baja California in the same way that Americans view Hawaii or Alaska—as a faraway place that captures the imagination.

AMERINDIANS OF BAJA CALIFORNIA

© AVALON TRAVEL

POPULATION

The current population of the Baja Peninsula is between three and four million people, most of whom reside above the 28th parallel in Baja California (Norte). More than half the population lives in Mexicali or Tijuana. The rest of the peninsula is sparsely populated, with an average density of less than one person per 26 square kilometer (one person per 10 sq mi).

Mexico's population growth rate is estimated at 1.1 percent per annum for 2011. The average for Baja California is probably somewhat higher than the national average because of immigration. Baja California Sur is Mexico's least-populated state.

ORIGINS

When the Spanish missionary period began in 1697, historians estimate the indigenous population of Baja was about 50,000. Less than 100 years later, only 20 percent of the population survived. Today very few people of the central and northern Cochimí and Yumano tribes live in the valleys and sierras of Northern Baja.

True *bajacalifornianos* are a multicultural lot, with a much more diverse heritage than Mexican people from the mainland. Many are a mix of the Spanish and Indian cultures, but others descend from British, French, German, Dutch, Chinese, Russian, and other roots.

In addition to the families that have been in Baja since the early days of colonization, the peninsula has attracted a sizable population of U.S. and Canadian retirees as well as increasing numbers of younger professionals from Mexico City and groups of migrant workers from Oaxaca.

RELIGION

The Spanish missionaries first introduced Catholicism to Baja California, and it remains the dominant religion today. Like the rest of Mexico, Baja's Catholics celebrate Our Lady of

BAJA FESTIVALS AND EVENTS

In addition to celebrating Mexico's national holidays as well as the major Catholic religious holidays, every town in Baja that is named after a Catholic saint holds an annual fiesta on the feast day of its namesake. Add to this seasonal festivals that celebrate lobster, gray whales, wine, etc., and you stand a pretty good chance of happening upon an event of one sort or another on your trip. Here are some of the highlights:

JANUARY

- **New Year's Day,** January 1, is a national holiday.

- **Día de los Santos Reyes** (Day of the King-Saints), January 6, is a Catholic religious holiday, the conclusion of Las Posadas.

FEBRUARY

- **Constitution Day,** February 5, is a national holiday.

- **Carnaval** takes place in late February or early March before Lent. La Paz and Ensenada put on the biggest celebrations in Baja.

- **Flag Day,** February 24, is a national holiday.

- The **Festival Internacional de Ballena Grís** takes place in Puerto López Mateos.

MARCH

- The **Birthday of Benito Juárez,** March 21, is a national holiday.

- **Spring Break** is not a Mexican festival, but a time when U.S. college students invade Rosarito, Ensenada, San Felipe, and Cabo San Lucas to party.

APRIL

- **Semana Santa** (Holy Week) takes place during the week leading up to Easter. After Christmas, it's the most important holiday of the year for Mexicans, and a time when many popular resorts are likely to fill up with visitors from the mainland.

- The **Rosarito-Ensenada 50-Mile Bicycle Ride** takes place on a Saturday in April and attracts thousands of cyclists. It is sponsored by **Bicycling West** (P.O. Box 9441, San Diego, CA, 92169-0441, U.S. tel. 858/483-8777, www.rosaritoensenada.com).

- **The Newport-Ensenada Yacht Race,** one of the largest international yachting regattas in the world, takes place on the last weekend in April (U.S. tel. 949/644-1023, www.nosa.org).

MAY

- **International Workers' Day,** May 1, is a national holiday.

- **Cinco de Mayo,** May 5, honors the defeat of the French at the mainland city of Puebla, in 1862.

JUNE

- **Día de la Marina** (Navy Day), June 1, is a national holiday, celebrated most enthusiastically in San Felipe and La Playita near San José del Cabo.

SEPTEMBER

- **Día de Nuestra Señora de Loreto,** September 8, is a special day in Loreto, when the community honors the founding of the first Spanish mission in the Californias.

- **Fiesta Patria de la Independencia** (Mexican Independence Day), September 16, is also called Diez y Seis, referring to the date. This is Mexico's celebration of independence from Spain, which dates back to 1821. Mexicali and La Paz put on fireworks, parades, *charreadas*, music, and folk-dance performances.

- The **Rosarito-Ensenada 50-Mile Bicycle Ride** is held again on the last Saturday in September.

OCTOBER

- **Día de la Raza,** October 12, commemorates the arrival of Christopher Columbus in the New World and the subsequent founding of the Mexican race.

NOVEMBER

- **Día de los Muertos** (Day of the Dead), November 1-2, is Mexico's third-most important holiday after Christmas and Easter. It is similar to the European All Saints Day.

- The **Baja 1000** off-road race takes place during the second or third week of November between Ensenada and La Paz. On alternate years, the course is shorter and limited to Northern Baja only. The event is sponsored by SCORE International (U.S. tel. 818/225-8402, www.score-international.com).

- The **Anniversary of the 1910 Revolution,** November 20, is a national holiday.

DECEMBER

- The Virgen of Guadalupe, also called Our Lady of Guadalupe, is one of the most important religious and cultural symbols in Mexico. The feast day for this patron saint, **Día de Nuestra Señora de Guadalupe,** takes place on December 12.

- **Las Posadas,** December 16–January 6, are nightly candlelight processions to local nativity scenes.

- **Día de la Navidad** (Christmas Day), December 25, is the most important holiday period in Mexico, as well as the United States. Resorts book well in advance around this time, and rates go up accordingly.

Guadalupe as an icon of the Virgin Mary on December 12. Baja has fewer churches per capita than the mainland, so in order to accommodate demand for worship services, some churches *(iglesias)* hold a dozen or more masses a day.

LANGUAGE

Latin-American Spanish is the primary language spoken in Baja California. People who work in the tourism industry tend to speak at least some English, especially in the larger cities, but a little Spanish goes a long way in day-to-day interactions with the local residents. Learning and using the basic greetings and a few essential phrases will show respect and build trust with the people you meet, which will likely result in a better overall travel experience.

ESSENTIALS

Getting There

BY AIR

Baja California has several international airports with direct connections to cities in the western United States. By far the busiest of these is the Los Cabos International Airport (SJD), with flights originating in Atlanta, Chicago, Dallas, Denver, Houston, Los Angeles, New York, Oakland, Phoenix, San Diego, San Francisco, and San Jose. You can also get to Los Cabos via connections on the mainland. La Paz (LAP) and Loreto (LOR) offer limited direct connections to the United States but also have flights to and from the mainland. Alaska Airlines is the only U.S. carrier that has offered direct service consistently from the United States to these airports in recent years. American, United, and Delta have offered on-again, off-again connections. Virgin America introduced direct service from San Francisco to SJD at competitive prices in 2010.

Flying out of Tijuana International Airport (TIJ) is an economical way to get to Southern Baja. A new discount carrier called Volaris offers luxury bus service from downtown San Diego to the Tijuana airport and competitively priced flights on new planes to La Paz. Volaris and Southwest have announced a partnership to coordinate service to popular destinations in Mexico, but they have yet to provide a date for extending the partnership to Baja.

© PAUL ITOI

Aereo Servicio Guerrero (tel. 615/157-0137, toll-free Mex. tel. 800/823-3153, www.aereo-serviciosguerrero.com.mx) operates flights to and from Isla Cedros four times a week (Mon., Wed., Thurs., Fri.). The flight time is about 30 minutes, and a one-way ticket runs US$65; the airline office, next to the police station on Boulevard Zapata, is open 9 A.M.–4 P.M. Monday–Saturday. The company also does charters upon request and flies to other destinations within Mexico.

Guerrero Negro's airfield is located north of town near the state line. Look for the turnoff between Km. 125 and 126.

General Aviation

Pilots can fly their own aircraft over the border to remote destinations all over the peninsula. The majority of landing fields in Baja are unattended dirt strips. The process for crossing the border is straightforward and well documented, but allow a few weeks for the paperwork from the Federal Communications Commission and U.S. Customs and Border Protection to arrive in the mail after you submit your applications and fees. Contact **Bush Pilots International** (formerly Baja Bush Pilots) (U.S. tel. 480/730-3250, www.bajabushpilots.com) and the **Aircraft Owners and Pilots Association** (toll-free U.S. tel. 800/872-2672, www.aopa.org) for up-to-date information about destinations, entry requirements, insurance policies, airport fees, runway conditions, and fuel availability.

BY BUS
To Tijuana

Greyhound Bus Lines (U.S. tel. 619/515-1100, www.greyhound.com) offers frequent service from San Diego (120 W. Broadway) to Tijuana (both the downtown bus terminal and the Central de Autobuses (for southbound connections). Fares are US$14–19 one-way to the Tijuana airport and US$13–19 to downtown Tijuana. You can also take Greyhound from Los Angeles (1716 E. 7th St., U.S. tel. 213/629-8401, US$23–31 one-way to downtown TJ),

which is a four-hour trip. There's no extra charge for boxed bikes.

The easiest way to get from downtown San Diego to the border is the **Blue Line Trolley** (U.S. tel. 619/685-4900, www.sdcommute.com, US$2.25), which connects the Old Town Transit Center with the San Ysidro Transit Center (about an hour-long ride). Trolleys depart every 15 minutes (U.S. tel. 619/685-4900 for general info or U.S. tel. 619/233-3004 for schedule and stops, 5 A.M.–1 A.M. daily, "night owl" service 2–5 A.M. Sat.). You can bring your bike along.

The most economical bus from downtown San Diego to the border at San Ysidro is city bus 932 (U.S. tel. 619/685-4900, www.sdcommute.com, US$2.25), with daily departures every half hour, 6 A.M.–11 P.M. every day. The trip takes about 80 minutes one-way.

Once you've reached the border, **Mexicoach** buses (tel. 664/685-1470, U.S. tel. 619/428-9517, US$5) leave every 30 minutes 8 A.M.–9 P.M. for the Terminal Turística Tijuana (Av. Revolución btw Calles 6/7).

To Mexicali and Calexico

Greyhound (toll-free Mex. tel. 800/710-8819, www.greyhound.com.mx) and its Mexican partner Crucero offer daily bus service from Los Angeles (US$36–48) and San Ysidro (US$25–34) to Calexico. A short walk from the station gets you through the border gateway and into downtown Mexicali.

Buses to and from Mainland Mexico

Transportes Norte de Sonora (TNS, Tijuana tel. 664/688-1979) and **Autotransportes Estrellas del Pacífico** (www.estrellablanca.com.mx) run long-distance express connections to Mexicali (Calzada Independencia 1244, Col. Centro Cívico, tel. 686/557-2450), Tecate (Juárez 321, Zona Centro, tel. 665/654-2343), Tijuana (Lázaro Cárdenas at Río Alamar s/n, Col. La Mesa, tel. 664/621-2982), and Ensenada (Calle 11 at Riverol, Zona Centro, tel. 646/178-6677) from various mainland destinations.

Green Tortoise

Budget travelers who like the idea of exploring Baja with an organized group might consider Green Tortoise (U.S. tel. 415/956-7500 or 800/867-8647, www.greentortoise.com). It offers nine-day (from US$720) and 15-day (US$1,050) trips to Baja November–April that begin in San Francisco (pickups in L.A. and San Diego are possible) and go as far south as Cabo Pulmo. Prices include transportation, accommodations (on the bus), food, guided hikes, and side trips to the beach.

BY CAR
Driving into Baja

It's easy to drive yourself across the border for a Baja adventure. There are several places to cross. The busiest is San Ysidro/Tijuana, and the quietest is Tecate. You don't need a permit for your vehicle unless you plan to continue on to the mainland. You do need a validated tourist permit (US$25–30) if you plan to go south of Maneadero or stay longer than 72 hours anywhere on the peninsula.

Mexican Auto Insurance

There is a lot of confusion and misinformation in travel circles about why and how to insure your vehicle when driving in Mexico. Whether you are driving your own vehicle into Mexico, renting a car to drive over the border, or renting within Mexico, read this section carefully:

Before driving into Baja, all drivers should arrange for Mexican vehicle insurance. Why? Mexican law requires drivers to have proof of financial liability (a minimum of US$50,000 worth) for any property damage or bodily injury they cause to other parties in an accident. Unless you have a bond with a Mexican bank or cash in hand at the time of an accident, the only practical way to comply with the law is to purchase an insurance policy underwritten by a Mexican company. Without it, a minor traffic accident can turn into a nightmare, involving jail time and steep financial penalties. *No matter what your own insurance company may tell you, Mexican authorities do not recognize foreign insurance policies for private vehicles in Mexico.*

DRIVING DISTANCES

Distances from Tijuana, along the Trans-peninsular Highway, using the Tijuana-Ensenada toll road:

Ensenada	109 km (68 mi)
San Quintín	301 km (187 mi)
El Rosario	359 km (226 mi)
Cataviña	481 km (298 mi)
Punta Prieta	599 km (371 mi)
Bahía de los Angeles	654 km (405 mi)
Guerrero Negro	714 km (443 mi)
San Ignacio	856 km (531 mi)
Santa Rosalía	928 km (575 mi)
Mulegé	990 km (614 mi)
Loreto	1,125 km (698 mi)
Ciudad Constitución	1,268 km (786 mi)
La Paz	1,483 km (919 mi)
Cabo San Lucas	1,704 km (1,056 mi)

If you are planning to drive your own vehicle, you can purchase short-term insurance—as little as one day's worth—from one of 20 or so online vendors of Mexican Tourist Auto Insurance. Simply request a quote, complete an application, pay by credit card, and print a certificate from home before you leave for your trip. (You can purchase a policy in advance and set it to begin on the day you plan to cross the border.) Policy terms and quality of service vary significantly, so be sure you are dealing with a reputable broker before you buy. A good way to tell is to call and speak to a live person and then complete the process online.

MEXICAN AUTO INSURANCE POLICY CHECKLIST

Consider the following criteria before buying Mexican insurance for your private vehicle:

- Look for a U.S.-based claims office.

- Deductibles should be clearly stated, typically a minimum of $500 or 2 percent of the value of the vehicle.

- The better policies include legal coverage, roadside assistance, plane tickets home if your car cannot be driven, and medical evacuation.

- Some premium policies include extra coverage for uninsured drivers.

- Policies with a "combined single limit" (CSL) for bodily and property damage are preferred over "split limits," which are less flexible.

- The policy should allow you to handle repairs in the United States or Canada.

- The policy should clearly state an hourly labor rate high enough to cover the cost of repairs in the United States (the US$15/hour standard in Mexico will not be sufficient).

- Keep one copy of your policy in the glove-box and another in your wallet (in case the car is stolen).

- Call your claims number when you cross into Mexico to verify that it works.

- If you have a claim, report it before you leave Mexico within the time limit specified in your policy; some companies will not honor the policy once you have left the country.

- Claims adjusters can reach most parts of Baja within two hours.

- Driving on the beach is considered a non-conventional road: If you get stuck and the tide comes in and floods your car, it's probably not going to be covered.

- Any roads that require four-wheel drive are probably not covered.

When shopping online:

- Websites should display an insurance license logo.

- Check that the site is secure before you transmit personal data.

- When in doubt, call the vendor to verify services.

If you're not the plan-ahead type or you prefer to speak in person, you can stop in at several agencies found in nearly every border town between the Pacific Ocean and the Gulf of Mexico. Again, read the terms carefully before paying.

The first decision you'll need to make is between a liability-only policy (to comply with the law) or full coverage (to protect your vehicle). Liability-only policies typically cover third-party liability from a minimum of US$50,000, up to US$300,000, plus legal expenses (levels range widely from US$500 to US$30,000), medical payments for you and your passengers (US$2,000–5,000 per person; US$19,000–25,000 per accident), and some form of roadside assistance. Higher-end policies may include medical evacuation and a flight home if your car is stolen or not drivable. Standard deductibles begin at US$500 and scale to 2–10 percent of the value of the vehicle, or a flat US$5,000 for motorcycles.

Full coverage adds physical damage and theft coverage to the list. Since the cost of upgrading from liability-only to full coverage amounts to a few dollars more per day, it usually makes sense to add the theft coverage and enjoy the peace of mind. Theft coverage typically carries a higher deductible than just liability.

In business since 2001, Santa Cruz, California–based **Adventure Mexican Insurance** (U.S. tel. 831/477-0599 or 800/485-4075, www.mexadventure.com) provides daily, monthly, and annual Mexican auto insurance to individual travelers as well as travel organizations. The company's website clearly explains Mexican insurance options and allows you to compare various policies from its three underwriters; well armed with information, you can then purchase online in a matter of minutes. For a long weekend trip to Baja, you'll pay around US$30 for liability only and US$40 for full coverage (both at the minimum liability level of US$50,000). Full coverage monthly rates range US$200–350, depending on the value of the vehicle. Its policies cover repairs in the United States and include a bundled travel assistance package for medical evacuation of up to four passengers and plane tickets home if your vehicle is not drivable. Call toll-free for detailed information about insuring an RV, trailer, or other special circumstances. Short-term policies cover travel in all of Mexico, but for long-term policies, customers have the option of a regional North West policy covering Baja as well as the mainland states of Sonora, Chihuahua, and Sinaloa at a reduced rate.

Several travel clubs offer discounted rates to members: For example, **Discover Baja Travel Club** (3264 Governor Dr., San Diego, tel. 619/275-4225, toll-free U.S. tel. 800/727-2252, www.discoverbaja.com, 9 A.M.–5 P.M. Mon.–Fri., 10 A.M.–1 P.M. Sun.) offers liability insurance for only US$83 per year and full coverage starting at US$152. AAA members can purchase Mexican auto insurance through the travel club website (www.aaa.com) or by phone.

If you forget to purchase insurance before you leave or prefer to purchase your policy in person, try **Instant Mexico Insurance Services** (223 Via de San Ysidro, U.S. tel. 619/428-4714, or 800/345-4701, www.instant-mex-auto-insur.com, 24 hrs. daily) at the last exit before the San Ysidro/Tijuana border crossing. You can also purchase tourist cards, fishing permits, maps, guidebooks, and other Baja requisites here.

Once you've purchased a policy, make several copies of it and put the originals in a safe place, separate from the copies. You should also carry a copy of the first page—the "declaration" or "renewal of declaration" sheet—of your home country insurance policy, since Mexican law requires drivers to enter the country with at least six months' worth of insurance in their home country.

Temporary Vehicle Import Permits

If you plan to head to the mainland from Baja (via ferry from Southern Baja or via land in Northern Baja), you'll need to obtain a temporary vehicle import permit from a Mexican customs office at any of the border crossings or in La Paz at the ferry terminal. Bring a valid state registration for the vehicle (or similar document certifying legal ownership), driver's license, and major credit card (not debit card) issued outside Mexico.

If you are leasing or renting the vehicle, you'll also have to present the contract you've signed that allows you to bring the vehicle into Mexico. If you are borrowing the vehicle, you'll need a notarized letter from the owner giving you permission to take the vehicle to Mexico.

Once Mexican customs officials have approved your documents, you'll be directed to pay by credit card (issued to the name of the driver of the vehicle) at an adjoining Banjercito office (US$20). (If you don't have a credit card, you'll have to post a bond (1–2 percent of the vehicle's blue-book value) issued by an authorized Mexican bond company, a time-consuming and expensive procedure.

Permits are valid for the same period of time shown on your tourist card or visa. You can drive back and forth across the border—at any crossing—as many times as you wish during the this time; however, you need to cancel the permit at the completion of your trip or the government will presume that you've permanently imported your vehicle (illegally) in Mexico and forbid you from obtaining another temporary vehicle import permit, should you need one for a future trip. Mexico has implemented a computerized vehicle permit tracking system, so you do not need to return the permit at the same place as you checked it in. You do, however, need to stop at the Banjercito office on the Mexican side of the border before leaving the country. Mexican border officials will scan your permit before you leave the country and give you a receipt for revoking the permit. For more information on this process, call toll-free U.S. tel. 800/922-8228.

BY FERRY FROM MAINLAND MEXICO

If you are on the Pacific coast of the mainland and want to get to Baja, you can take a modern passenger or car ferry service from Mazatlán or Topolobampo/Los Mochis to La Paz or from Guaymas to Santa Rosalía. Routes and schedules change periodically, so double-check the current service offerings a week or so before you want to cross. At last check, **Baja Ferries** (Pichilinque Terminal, tel. 612/123-0208, U.S. tel. 915/833-3107, downtown La Paz office: Allende 1025 at Rubio, tel. 612/123-6600 or 800/122-1414, www.bajaferries.com, 8 A.M.–5 P.M. daily) was running two routes: La Paz–Topolobampo (6 hrs., US$65 per seat) and La Paz–Mazatlán (12 hrs., Tues.–Sun. once daily, US$74 per seat). Cabins (US$64) and cars (US$86–203) cost extra. Baja Ferries has another ticket office at the Mega grocery store in San José del Cabo (Mexico 1 at the traffic circle). If you're starting from Topolobampo, the local number is 668/862-1003.

Transportación Marítima de California (TMC) (La Paz office tel. 800/744-5050, Mazatlán office tel. 800/700-0433, www.ferrytmc.com) also runs a car ferry between La Paz and Mazatlán (15.5 hrs.). A car and driver cost US$167; RVs up to 10 meters (about 33 ft.) cost US$650.

Getting Around

Most Baja visitors navigate the peninsula by car—either their own vehicle or a rented one. If you stay at a large resort and don't want to venture far from it, you may be able to rely on shuttles and taxis to get around. Other ways to get around include domestic flights, such as from Tijuana to La Paz or Los Cabos, as well as intercity and municipal buses.

BY BUS
Intercity Bus Service

Several companies offer connections between Northern and Southern Baja towns. It takes about 30 hours to complete the journey from Tijuana to Cabo San Lucas by bus with **Autotransportes Aguila** (tel. 612/122-4270, www.autotransportesaguila.com, US$148) or **Autotransportes de Baja California** (ABC, tel. 800/025-0220, www.transportes-abc.com, US$142). Many travelers divide the trip into two parts by stopping overnight in La Paz.

Transportes Norte de Sonora (TNS, tel. 664/688-1979) operates buses in Northern Baja, connecting Tijuana, Ensenada, Tecate, and Mexicali with the mainland state of Sonora.

Buses are modern, comfortable, and usually air-conditioned for longer trips. Schedules vary (this is not Switzerland), and prices are reasonable. You don't usually need reservations (stop by the day before just in case), and in many cases, it's not possible to make them.

The Spanish word for ticket is *boleto*. Fares are usually posted on the wall inside the depot.

Municipal Buses

Tijuana, Ensenada, Mexicali, San Quintín, La Paz, and San José del Cabo have city bus systems that cost a dollar or two per trip (pesos only). The route or destination (a street name or district) usually is posted on the front of the bus.

BY TAXI

Taxis wait at the larger hotels and designated taxi stands in most of the larger towns along the peninsula. There are no meters; you pay a set fare based on the distance you are traveling.

© NIKKI GOTH ITOI

Municipal buses transport citizens around town in San José del Cabo.

Ask around for the going rate to your destination and negotiate the fare with the driver before you hop in. Even the smaller towns often have a few taxis for hire near the town plaza or bus terminal.

Larger cities with their own bus systems (Tijuana, Rosarito, Ensenada, and Mexicali) also have *taxis de ruta* (route taxis), which follow a set route, like a bus, but stop wherever someone flags them down or a passenger asks to get off. These taxi services use large American station wagons that hold up to 12 passengers. Fares tend to be marginally higher than comparable bus fare.

BY CAR

Driving the Transpeninsular Highway and the few other paved routes in Baja is fairly straightforward. Road conditions can vary, though—with potholes, speed bumps *(topes),* livestock, construction, rock slides, and other unexpected obstacles possible around every bend. In Southern Baja, road crews have been busy building bridges over arroyos that flood in the rainy season. Watch for *Desviación* signs and slow down. There may or may not be a worker

flagging vehicles to stop, and workers take few precautions to protect themselves from oncoming traffic. Drive carefully through any construction zones. Among the greatest challenges are the deep *vados,* dry river beds that fill with water after heavy rains; the narrow width of the road, and the fact that it has no shoulder in many places; and the 18-wheelers that barrel along at high speeds, often passing cars on blind turns.

Other than the four-lane toll roads between Tijuana and Ensenada, Tijiana and Mexicali, La Paz and Todos Santos, and San José del Cabo and Cabo San Lucas, these highways are two-lane roads. Several dirt roads have been recently paved, connecting inland communities such as San Javier, near Loreto, and Los Planes, near La Paz, to the Transpeninsular Highway. But aside from those developments, all other roads in Baja are gravel, dirt, or sand.

Off-Highway Travel

The condition of Baja's unpaved roads varies widely, from smooth graded paths to heavy washboard, soft sand, and steep grades with frequent washouts. Good road maps categorize dirt roads to give you an idea of what to expect, but it's best to ask about current road conditions before embarking on an off-highway excursion.

Travelers who aren't intending to venture into the backcountry often get stuck in the sand the moment they pull off the coastal road to check the surf or park at the beach. Carry a shovel for digging yourself out, plus something to put under the wheels to provide traction, like a piece of wood or ribbed plastic. It also helps to let some of the air out of your tires, but bring a compressor for pumping the tires back up.

Driving Precautions

Common sense and a few additional precautions will get you safely from one town to the next in Baja. Wherever you go, plan the driving so that you are not on the road at night. The biggest danger after dark is animals—cows, burros, and dogs, which appear in the road

ROADTRIPPER'S CAR KIT

Automotive fuel and supplies are much easier to come by these days than in the past, especially if you stick to paved Mexico 1; however, extra supplies for your vehicle can save precious time and money, should things go awry. Here's what to pack:

- air filters
- battery cables
- brake, clutch, steering, and transmission fluids
- eight-meter tow rope
- emergency flares
- fan belts
- fire extinguisher

- fuel filters
- fuses
- lug wrench and jack
- one five-gallon water container
- one or two five-gallon gas cans
- radiator hoses
- spare tire
- spark plugs
- tire gauge
- tube-repair kit (if appropriate)
- 12-volt air compressor
- water filters

more frequently than you'd think. Other concerns include local vehicles without headlights, brake lights, or tail lights; drivers under the influence of alcohol; and the lack of lighting or reflectors on most of these roads.

Follow the speed limits, even though the locals often drive much faster (they know the road, you don't). Taking it slow gives you a little extra time to react in an emergency situation and also reduces the chance that you'll inadvertently commit a traffic offense. Plus, it's a better way to enjoy the scenery.

Note that *topes* and *vados* are not always marked, so pay attention and be ready to slow down immediately upon spotting them. We've seen cars take particularly bad speed bumps at full speed and launch themselves in the air to reveal the undercarriage of the vehicle. Measure the depth of water in any *vado* before driving through.

Highway Signs

Highway signs in Baja are usually self-explanatory, with symbols or pictures are well as words. Some of the more useful road signs include:

- *Curva Peligrosa* (Dangerous Curve)
- *Despacio* (Slow)
- *Zona de Vados* (Dip Zone)
- *Desviación* (Detour)
- *No Tire Basura* (Don't Throw Trash)
- *Conserve Su Derecha* (Keep to the Right)
- *Conceda Cambio de Luces* (Dim Your Lights)
- *No Rebase* (No Passing)
- *No Hay Paso* (Road Closed)

Kilometer Markers

Baja's major highways feature kilometer markers that count up or down between cities, depending on which direction you are heading. People often use these markers when measuring distances and giving directions (e.g., "Turn off at Km. 171."). In Baja California (Norte), the markers start at zero (Km. 0) in Tijuana and ascend heading south. Starting at the state line with Baja California Sur, the markers descend as you continue south, beginning with Km. 220 in Guerrero Negro.

Traffic Offenses

In the larger cities, it can be difficult to navigate busy streets and unfamiliar intersections; foreign motorists do get pulled over for running hard-to-see (or nonexistent) stop signs and other legitimate (though understandable) violations. The best way to prevent this kind of incident is to drive slowly and assume you must stop at every urban intersection, whether you see a sign or not.

If you're stopped, respond kindly and respectfully and you may be let go without a ticket. If the officer persists, you'll need to proceed to the nearest police station to pay the fine. If the officer asks you to pay on the spot, you're being targeted for *la mordida,* a minor bribe.

In Baja these incidents tend to happen in Tijuana, Rosarito, Ensenada, and La Paz. If it happens, you should insist on going to the nearest station to pay the fine, and when you pay, ask for a receipt. The charges may well be dropped at this point.

Something many drivers don't know that could invite trouble with the police is that in Mexico, it's illegal to display any foreign national flag except over an embassy or consulate—this includes small flags flying from the antenna of your vehicle.

Fuel

Motorists fill their tanks in Mexico at government-owned Pemex stations, which are common in the larger towns and less prevalent as you get into the more remote parts of the peninsula. Barrel gas is sometimes available in rural settlements. You can choose among regular unleaded fuel (*magna sin,* octane rating 87), a.k.a. *verde* (green); a high-test unleaded (premium, octane rating 89), a.k.a. *roja* (red); and diesel. Rates are the same from station to station (but exchange rates offered may vary if you pay in dollars). At press time, a gallon of *verde* in Baja was US$2.47 and for *roja* US$2.92. The price should always be marked in pesos on the pump.

Most Pemex stations are full-serve (though Los Cabos now has the first self-serve station on the peninsula), and a visit begins with two

questions: How much and what type of gas do you want? *"Lleno con premium (roja)/magna (verde), por favor"* is the usual answer. Leave a small tip (up to US$1) for window washing or other extra services.

Mexico's Pemex attendants are notorious for inflating prices or adjusting exchange rates to their advantage. Follow these steps to prevent corruption at the pump.

- Check to make sure the pump is zeroed before the attendant starts pumping your gas.
- Get out of your vehicle to watch the pumping procedures.
- Carry a handheld calculator to check currency conversions.
- When paying in large bills, tell the attendant what denomination you are handing him and make sure he acknowledges the amount; then count your change carefully. A common scam happens when you hand over a 500-peso bill, expecting change, and the attendant comes back to say you only gave him a 50.

Cash is the only way to pay for gas in Mexico. Some stations near the border and in the Los Cabos Corridor will accept U.S. dollars, but they are notorious for offering below market exchange rates. At press time, many were following the old 10:1 rule, while the exchange rate was closer to 12:1.

Parts and Repairs

Just about every town has a *llantera* (tire repair). Experienced mechanics are harder, but not impossible, to come by. Try any of the larger towns and cities. For those used to the systematic process of a large U.S. auto shop, the Baja approach might seem haphazard, but they do seem to get the job done most of the time. For extensive driving in remote areas, bring your own spare parts.

Roadside Assistance

If you have a breakdown while traveling in Mexico, chances are one of the **Angeles Verdes** (Green Angels) will come to the rescue.

Sponsored by the Secretaría de Turismo, these green trucks patrol the highways in Baja twice a day and offer roadside assistance to anyone with car troubles. The service is free, but tips are appreciated. Trucks are equipped with first-aid kits, shortwave radios, fuel, and spare parts. Drivers can do minor repairs for the cost of the parts and/or provide towing for distances up to 24 kilometers (15 mi). If they can't solve your vehicle's problem or tow it to a mechanic, they'll arrange for other assistance. They can also radio for emergency medical assistance if necessary. Visit www.sectur.gob.mx/wb2/sectur/sect_9454_rutas_carreteras to see a map of the roads that are patrolled by the Green Angels.

Military Checkpoints

When driving the Transpeninsular Highway, you'll encounter numerous military checkpoints *(puestos de control),* or roadblocks at which uniformed officials search vehicles for drugs and firearms. Although the concept is foreign to many U.S. and Canadian residents, the soldiers are courteous (and often just curious about your travels) and it rarely takes more than a few minutes. If you have any concerns about a search, discreetly record information such as badge numbers, names, or license numbers, and file a report with the Mexican Attorney General for Tourist Protection.

Recreational Vehicles

Baja has long been popular with RV travelers because it offers so many beautiful and accessible places to camp; however, driving a big rig along the narrow and winding stretches of Mexico 1 can be a white-knuckle experience for first-timers. One way to learn the ropes is to join an organized caravan, which leads a group of RVers along a set itinerary down the peninsula and back. These trips cost around US$100 a day, not including meals and fuel.

Car Rental

You can rent cars in Tijuana, Rosarito, Mexicali, Ensenada, Loreto, La Paz, Los Barriles, Todos Santos, San José del Cabo, and Cabo San Lucas. In general, larger cities offer the least-expensive rentals. Most of the international chains offer economy/compact cars for around US$30–45 a day with unlimited miles or US$60–75 for an SUV or Jeep. Rates in La Paz are slightly lower than in Los Cabos. Mexican liability insurance costs an additional US$25 a day with these companies, and deductibles are often high (US$1,000 and up). It pays to shop around. Book ahead online or comparison shop when you arrive.

Online discount car rental services, such as Hotwire (www.hotwire.com), offer substantially lower rates than the major brands by selling excess inventory for their partner companies. Rentals through Hotwire come from names like Avis, Hertz, or Budget, but you won't know which company until you agree to purchase the rental. The other difference is that you prepay for the rental at the time of reservation, so you won't be able to change your mind once you get to Baja. Prepaying is a risky strategy in Baja because the rental car companies frequently overbook and they tend to give cars on a first-come, first-serve basis regardless of whether you have a reservation or have prepaid for the vehicle. The agency will do its best to get you a car, but it could be a full 24 hours later than the date you reserved.

Independent agencies are another option, sometimes at lower cost but often with per-kilometer charges in addition to the daily rate.

Rentals out of San Diego are sometimes a bit cheaper, but most agencies that allow their cars into Mexico won't allow them any farther south than Guerrero Negro. Some only allow travel 40 kilometers (25 mi) into Baja. If you drive beyond these limits, you won't be covered. They often add mandatory collision damage waivers to the cost as well. If you're planning to rent in San Diego, note that even though Avis and other companies allow you to drive across the border, Hotwire's contracts with its partners stipulate no cross-border travel. Go directly to the rental car provider if you want to rent from San Diego.

California Baja Rent-A-Car (9245 Jamacha Blvd., Spring Valley, CA 91977, U.S. tel.

CAR RENTALS

ACE Rent a Car (tel. 624/146-1839, www.acerentacar.com)

• Los Cabos International Airport (SJD)

Advantage (tel. 624/143-0466 or 624/146-5500):

• Cabo San Lucas

• Los Cabos International Airport (SJD)

Alamo (tel. 800/849-8001, www.alamorentacar.com.mx):

• Los Cabos International Airport (SJD)

• San José del Cabo

Avis (tel. 624/146-0201, U.S. tel. 800/331-2112, www.avis.com):

• Cabo San Lucas (three locations: Ave. Lázaro Cárdenas, Hotel Pueblo Bonito Rosé, and Pueblo Bonito Pacifica)

• Los Cabos International Airport (SJD)

• La Paz (downtown at Paseo Obregón)

• La Paz International Airport (LAP)

• Tijuana (downtown in the Zona Río)

• Tijuana International Airport (TIJ)

Budget (tel. 624/146-5333, U.S. tel. 800/527-0700, www.budget.com):

• Los Cabos Corridor (Marquis Hotel)

• Los Cabos International Airport (SJD)

• Loreto International Airport (LOR)

• Mexicali International Airport (MXL)

• San José del Cabo (Crowne Plaza)

• Tijuana International Airport (TIJ)

• Todos Santos (Marquez de Leon 4)

Dollar Rent A Car (tel. 624/105-8410, U.S. tel. 866/434-2266, www.dollar.com or www.dollarloscabos.com):

• Cabo San Lucas (four locations: downtown at Blvd. Marina, and at Club Cascadas, Hotel Finisterra, and Hotel Meliá Cabo Real)

• Los Cabos Corridor (Hotel Fiesta Americana)

• La Paz International Airport (LAP)

• La Paz/Pichilingue (La Concha Hotel)

• Mexicali downtown (Blvd. Benito Juárez)

• San José del Cabo (two locations: downtown at Blvd. Castro and at the Presidente InterContinental)

• Tijuana downtown (Zona Río)

Europcar (tel. 612/124-7011, U.S. tel. 877/940-6900, www.europcar.com):

• La Paz (downtown at Obregón)

• La Paz International Airport (LAP)

• Loreto (downtown)

• Loreto International Airport (LOR)

• Los Cabos International Airport (SJD)

Hertz (tel. 624/146-1803, U.S. tel. 800/821-1727, www.hertz.com) with locations in:

• Cabo San Lucas (Ave. Lázaro Cárdenas 6)

• Ensenada (downtown at Ave. Alvarrado 143)

• La Paz (downtown at Obregón 2130-D)

• La Paz International Airport (LAP)

• La Paz/Pichilingue (Marina Costa Baja, Km 61, Carr. a Pichilingue)

• Loreto (downtown on Calle Romanita)

• Loreto International Airport (LOR, Km 5, Mexico 1)

• Los Cabos Corridor (Westin Los Cabos)

• Los Cabos International Airport (SJD)

• Mexicali (two locations downtown: Blvd. Benito Juárez and at Hotel Araiza Inn)

- Mexicali International Airport (MXL)

- Tijuana (four locations downtown: Camino Real, in the Zona Río 9575, and at Grand Hotel and Hotel Pueblo Amigo)

- Tijuana International Airport (TIJ)

National (tel. 624/142-2424, U.S. tel. 877/567-3572, www.nationalcar.com):

- Cabo San Lucas (two locations: Ave. Lázaro Cárdenas and at the Riu Palace)

- Los Cabos Corridor (four locations: Hilton Los Cabos, Hotel Casa del Mar, One&Only Palmilla, and at the Sheraton Hacienda del Mar)

- Los Cabos International Airport (SJD)

- La Paz International Airport (LAP)

- La Paz (downtown at Obregón)

- Los Barriles (20 de Noviembre)

- San José del Cabo (Posada Real Los Cabos)

- Tijuana (Ave. Nezuhuatcoyotl 1640)

- Tijuana International Airport (TIJ)

Payless Car Rental (tel. 624/105-8411, www.paylesscarrental.com):

- Cabo San Lucas (two locations: ME by Melia Cabo, in Cabo San Lucas, and Melia Cabo Real, along the Los Cabos Corridor)

- La Paz International Airport (LAP)

- Los Cabos Corridor (two locations: Dreams Los Cabos and at the Westin Resort)

- San Felipe

- San José del Cabo (two locations: downtown at Blvd. Mijares and Nissan and at the Crowne Plaza Hotel)

- Tijuana International Airport (TIJ)

619/470-7368 or 888/470-7368, www.cabaja.com) specializes in vehicle rentals for driving the Baja Peninsula. Internet discount rates start at about US$50 a day plus US$0.35 per mile beyond 100 miles per day for a subcompact. A Wrangler rents for US$110 a day plus US$0.35 per mile (100 free miles per day), while a Suburban costs US$130 daily plus US$0.39 per mile (100 free miles per day). Mexican insurance is included in these discounted rates. Dropoffs in Cabo San Lucas can be arranged for an extra charge. Optional accessories include satellite phones, Sirius satellite radio, and coolers. Note: This agency is located about 20 minutes from the San Diego airport and did not have a shuttle at press time, so customers need to take a US$40–45 cab to the pickup location.

Insuring Your Rental Car

The Mexican proof of financial responsibility law applies to drivers of rental cars in Mexico, except in this case, you don't get to choose a specific policy—rather, you agree to pay an additional US$25–40 per day for whatever coverage the rental car company provides. The exact amount depends on the size of the rental car and how far into Baja you drive it (if you rent from San Diego). Terms and coverage limits vary among the various agencies, and they don't make it easy to see the fine print before you arrive at the counter. To learn about the policy before you agree to rent the car, call the local office for the company you are considering. Read the contract carefully at the rental car counter, and be sure you understand the terms. If you drive farther than the contract permits, fail to report an accident within the time specified, or violate other clauses, your coverage may be nullified.

Avis (U.S. tel. 619/688-5000 or 800/852-4617) allows renters to drive inside the Free Trade Zone area, which is up to 40 kilometers (25 mi) from the U.S. border. **Hertz** (U.S. tel. 619/767-5700) allows customers to drive a rental car from the San Diego airport location only into Baja. Mexican insurance costs US$25 a day for an economy- to regular-size car, US$35 a day for a premium car or minivan, up to 40 kilometers (25 mi) south into Mexico (which won't get you very far); and US$35–40 a day for travel between 41–400 kilometers (26–250 mi) south of the border. Coverage limits are US$25,000 for collision, US$25,000 for theft, US$50,000 for liability; legal and medical are not specified.

Deductibles at Thrifty were as high as US$2,500 at last check.

BY MOTORCYCLE

The open roads of Baja have captured the imagination of many a motorcyclist. The **Adventure Rider Motorcycle Forum** (www.advrider.com) has some of the best motorcycle trip reports around.

Motorcycle mechanics are even harder to come by in Baja than auto mechanics, so you'll need to be self-sufficient in handling equipment problems. Midday travel may be impossible in some parts of the peninsula due to intolerably high temperatures. Factor this into your trip planning.

Chris Haines Motorcycle Adventure (P.O. Box 966, Trabuco Canyon, CA 92678, toll-free U.S. tel. 866/262-8635, www.bajaoffroadtours.com) operates four-day rides from Ensenada to Mike's Sky Ranch for US$2,100 and seven-day rides from Ensenada to Cabo San Lucas for US$4,550, including equipment and road support. Custom itineraries are also possible.

BY BICYCLE

It's not unusual to meet cyclists riding their way down the Transpeninsular Highway, often as part of longer coastal journeys from Alaska all the way to Panama. While we understand the attraction of this epic cycling tour, we believe the dangers of riding along the highway have been downplayed for too long. In the early days of the paved road, when traffic was lighter, cycling may have been a safer option, but today motorists, RVers, and truckers drive at faster speeds and in greater numbers. The

problem is the width of the road. When two 18-wheelers approach from opposite directions, they pass with inches of pavement between them. If the driver must choose between colliding with an oncoming truck or pushing a cyclist off the road, the cyclist is inevitably going to lose out. Shoulders and guardrails are nonexistent on many of the most dangerous stretches of road.

If your dream is to ride your bike the length of Baja, consider an off-road route à la the Baja 1000. This way, you can enjoy more of the coastal and mountain scenery and avoid putting yourself in danger on the highway.

Some of the best trail riding in Baja awaits in the Parque Nacional Constitución de 1857, close to the international border. The Cataviña Boulder Field in the Desierto Central also has some good off-road riding. In Southern Baja, the Camino Rural Costero between San José del Cabo and Cabo Pulmo is a fantastic route along the coast, as is the dirt road between Los Barriles and Bahía de los Muertos.

Equipment and Repairs

Many cyclists have never completed an overnight bike trip before planning a ride through Baja. Though the larger towns in Baja all have bicycle repair shops, here are some of the basics you'll need before starting your trip:

- Camping gear
- Helmet
- Rearview mirror
- Locking cable
- Removable handlebar bag for valuables
- Four one-liter bottles of water per day (puncture resistant)
- Heavy-duty tires (including one spare) and, preferably, slime tubes (2–3 spares)
- Tire gauge
- Complete tire repair kit
- Basic first-aid kit, including duct tape and moleskin
- Spare parts and tools to work on them

Bicycle Transportation

Bikes are permitted on the **Blue Line Trolley** (U.S. tel. 619/233-3004), and they may be checked as luggage (if boxed) for no additional cost on **Mexicoach** and **Greyhound** buses.

Guided Bicycle Trips

Pedaling South (U.S. tel. 707/942-4450 or 800/398-6200, www.tourbaja.com), offers a number of multiday mountain biking tours: Sierra Ridge Ride (nine days, US$1,195) and Sierra Giganta (eight days, US$995). Combo sea kayak/mountain bike trips are also available. If you bring your own bike, Pedaling South deducts US$95 from the tour rates. Included in the price are accommodations, ground transport, meals on tour days, camping gear, tents, guides, tracking vehicles, and first aid.

Visas and Officialdom

ENTRY REGULATIONS
Passports and Tourist Permits

Under the Western Hemisphere Travel Initiative, as of January 2007, anyone traveling by air between the United States, Canada, Mexico, Central and South America, the Caribbean, and Bermuda (including infants) is required to present a valid passport. The same applies to anyone traveling by land or sea as of January 2008.

Citizens of the United States or Canada (or of 42 other designated countries in Europe and Latin America, plus Singapore) who are visiting Mexico as tourists do not need a visa. They must, however, obtain validated tourist cards, called *formas migratorias turistas,* or FMTs, available at any Mexican consulate or Mexican tourist office, on flights to Mexico and at any border crossing. The tourist card is valid for 180 days and must be used within 90 days of issue. It expires when you exit the country. If you are planning to enter and leave Mexico more than once during your trip, you can ask for a multiple-entry tourist card, which is available at Mexican consulates.

To validate the tourist card, you need to present proof of citizenship to a Mexican immigration officer, either at the border or in the airport. Acceptable documentation includes a birth certificate (or certified copy), voter's registration card, certificate of naturalization, or passport. Your driver's license won't suffice.

In 1999 the Mexican government instituted a tourist fee (currently around US$25), which is factored into your airfare if you fly but must be paid separately at a bank in Mexico if you cross the border by land or sea. The immigration office you visit will direct you to the nearest bank. Once you've paid, you'll get a receipt, which you can bring back to the immigration office in exchange for validation of the tourist card. If you do not plan to travel south of Ensenada or San Felipe, you are not required to pay this fee.

Tourist Visas

Tourists from countries other than the 45 countries referenced earlier must obtain visas before arriving in Mexico. Apply in person at a Mexican consulate and expect about a two-week turnaround. The Mexican Consulate General in San Diego can often issue same-day tourist visas. Required documentation includes a valid passport, valid U.S. visa for multiple entries, form I-94, proof of economic solvency (such as an international credit card), and a round-trip air ticket to Mexico. The visa fee costs about US$40.

Foreign visitors who are legal permanent residents of the United States do not need visas to visit Mexico for tourism. You can get a validated tourist card by presenting your passport and U.S. residence card at the airport or border control.

Pets

Dogs and cats may be brought into Mexico with proof of current vaccinations and a **health certificate** issued within 72 hours before entry into Mexico and signed by a registered veterinarian.

BORDER CROSSINGS

Baja California's international border with the U.S. has six official crossings:

- San Ysidro/Tijuana (24 hrs daily)
- Otay Mesa (24 hrs daily)
- Tecate (5 A.M.–11 P.M. daily)
- Calexico East (6 A.M.–midnight daily)
- West/Mexicali (24 hrs daily)
- Los Algodones (6 A.M.–10 P.M. daily)

Tijuana is the largest and busiest of the bunch, with waits up to two hours, but even the less-crowded ones have lines during morning and afternoon commute hours and on weekends. The pedestrian crossing is a great way to avoid the lines. Public and chartered buses are also allowed to jump to the front of the lines.

Mexican Consulate in San Diego

San Diego's Mexican Consulate General (1549 India St., San Diego, CA 92101, U.S. tel. 619/231-8414, www.consulmexsd.org, 8 A.M.–1:30 P.M. Mon.–Fri.) is 30–45 minutes by car from the Tijuana border crossing. The office can help with visas, immigration problems, special-import permits, and questions concerning Mexican customs regulations.

CUSTOMS
Entering Mexico

Mexico allows tourists to enter the country with personal items that they will use during their trip and additional merchandise worth less than US$75 per person if arriving by land or US$300 if arriving by air. There are official limits for the number of electronic devices (2 cameras, 2 mobile phones, 1 laptop), musical instruments (2), liters of liquor (3), cartons of cigarettes (20), fishing rods (4), and other recreational sports equipment you may bring. For the most part, as long as it doesn't look like you are sneaking in items that you intend to sell or bringing bags of professional equipment for business instead of tourism, you'll be able to enter without declaring anything. In addition, you may carry up to US$10,000

in cash without paying a duty. Do not under any circumstances attempt to bring firearms without a permit (issued for hunting only) or illegal substances. For the latest information in Spanish, visit www.aduanas.sat.gob.mx.

Returning to the United States

The process of returning to the United States almost always takes longer than leaving. U.S. customs officials may ask to search your luggage, and they'll ask a few routine questions. Sometimes they also use dogs to inspect luggage and/or vehicles for illegal substances and undocumented immigrants.

Many items made in Mexico may be imported duty-free. Adults may bring only one liter (33.8 fluid ounces) of alcohol and 200 cigarettes (or 100 cigars) per person. Remember that it is illegal to import Cuban cigars into the United States. You can bring US$400 worth of purchases within any 31-day period without declaring the goods.

Here is a list of prohibited items. Regulations change occasionally, so check with a U.S. consulate before crossing or visit www.cbp.gov for the latest information:

- oranges
- grapefruits
- mangoes
- avocados
- potatoes
- straw
- hay
- unprocessed cotton
- sugarcane
- any plants in soil (including houseplants)
- wild and domesticated birds (including poultry, unless cooked)
- pork or pork products
- raw eggs (cooked eggs are okay)

Returning to Canada

Duty-free items for travelers returning to Canada include 200 cigarettes (or 50 cigars or

200 grams of tobacco) and one bottle (1.1 liters) of liquor or wine, 24 cans or bottles (355 ml) of beer or ale, and gifts up to C$60 per gift (other than alcohol or tobacco). Exemptions run C$50–750, depending on how long you've been outside the country. To obtain the maximum exemption of C$750, you must travel outside Canada for at least one week.

LEGAL MATTERS
The Mexican legal system differs from the U.S. system in several ways. It does not provide for trials by jury; rather, a judge decides the fate of the accused. The Mexican system also does not provide the writ of habeas corpus, although it does stipulate that you must be charged within 72 hours of incarceration or set free. Arrested foreigners rarely are granted bail, so once you are in jail, it can be very difficult to get out. You do have the right to notify your consulate if you are detained. You can also contact the local state tourism offices for help in emergencies.

Sports and Recreation

Travelers to Baja California pursue a long list of recreational activities in water and on land. Most of these can be pursued independently or as part of an organized trip. Here is a summary of the highlights; specific routes and outfitters are covered in the respective destination chapters.

HIKING AND BACKPACKING
Hiking in Baja can range from desert walks to high-sierra summits. You might spend half a day on trails in the coastal hills or a full week in the backcountry. It all depends on your experience level, preferred wilderness environment, and amount of time you have. Some of the top places to hike in Baja include the two national parks in the north (Parque Nacional Sierra San Pedro Mártir and Parque Nacional Constitución de 1857), the desert trails near Cataviña in the Desierto Central, and the Sierra de la Laguna in Southern Baja. Facilities are minimal in all these places, so hikers should expect primitive camping and plan to be self-sufficient.

Trails, if they exist, are often not well marked, so bring the appropriate topo maps for the area you plan to hike. **Mexico Maps** (U.S. tel. 805/687-1011, www.mexicomaps.com) offers GPS maps and digital maps for some areas as well as printed topo maps.

The **Instituto Nacional de Estadística,** **Geografía e Informática** (INEGI, www.inegi.gob.mx)—with offices in La Paz (Plaza Cuatro Molinos, Calle Altamirano 2790, Col. Centro, tel. 612/123-1545 or 612/122-4146), Mexicali (Calzada Independencia 1086, Centro Cívico, tel. 686/557-5883 or 686/556-0995), and Tijuana (Av. Via Rapida Oriente 9306, Zona Río, tel. 664/979-7900 or -7909)—sells topo maps at a much lower cost.

What to Bring
Protective footwear and plenty of water (2–5 liters per person per day, depending on the season) are the two most important items for any Baja hike. Bring layers of clothing for overnight trips in the sierras. Pack a first-aid kit with an elastic bandage for sprains, snakebite treatment, and pair of tweezers for removing thorns and cactus spines. Other essentials include a flashlight, compass, waterproof matches, knife, extra batteries, rain gear, and signal device (mirror or whistle). Consider a telescoping fishing rod with light tackle if you are hiking near the shore. Don't count on mountain springs to resupply your water. Purify any water you use from these sources.

Camping Tips
Avoid setting up your tent under the shade of a coconut palm or in arroyos. Open fires are permitted most remote places in Baja, but keep

them small. Dried ocotillo and cactus skeletons burn well. Follow basic low-impact camping guidelines: Pack out all trash, including cigarette butts. Bury human waste 15 centimeters (six inches) down, and don't use soap in streams or springs.

FISHING

Baja's tourism industry was largely built by the will and frontier spirit of the traveling anglers. Baja offers an unparalleled variety of species and fishing styles. Whether it's blue-water billfishing, fly-fishing for roosterfish, or spearing wahoo, the fisheries of Baja still have more fish and fewer crowds than just about anywhere other than Alaska. If you plan to freelance your way through fishing in Baja, pick up a copy of the longtime bible of Baja fishing, *Baja Catch,* or the newer *Angler's Guide to Trailer-Boating.*

There are endless ways to fish in Baja, but if you have never fished here before, one of the best ways to get started is to hire a *panga* for the morning. Prices vary depending on location and season, but the captain should have extensive knowledge of the hotspots as well as where the bite was on in the days leading up to your trip.

If you decide to fish while on a trip, you can buy a surf-casting rod and some tackle and fish from shore without a license. Corvina, sierra mackerel, and snapper can all be caught in the surf.

If you are targeting trophy billfish, you will want to visit the Los Cabos or East Cape region of Southern Baja. Loreto, Los Barriles, San José del Cabo, Cabo San Lucas, and La Paz all host numerous sportfishing fleets for hire.

Seasons

The ebb and flow of the various fish populations in Baja are difficult to generalize in a simple calendar. The *Angler's Guide to Baja California* has a calendar for each of 10 fishing zones, but you should always check with the locals before getting your heart set on a certain species. As a rule of thumb, April–October offer the warmest water and the greatest variety

of fish, but there are year-round species, including yellowtail and rockfish.

Tackle

A good selection of high-quality tackle is increasingly available in the larger Baja fishing towns, but you are better off assembling your gear before your trip, since supplies can still vary. Given the variety of species, there is no single ideal Baja rod. Since airlines currently allow up to four rods as "personal gear," consider packing two trolling rods with 60-pound test, one shore rod with 25-pound monofilament, and a light six-foot rod for bait fishing. Remember that you are only allowed to fish with one rod at a time.

Licenses and Regulations

It's worth noting up front that even if you have fished for years in Baja without ever hearing anyone mention a fishing license, the times have changed. There have been numerous reports of poles and coolers of fish being confiscated at the airport from travelers without a license. The best practice today is to obtain a Mexican fishing license before going on your trip and to keep it until you get back home.

A fishing license is required for anyone over 16 years old fishing from a boat. Anyone on a boat that is equipped for fishing (whether or not you intend to fish) is required to have a license, but as of January 2008, a boat permit is no longer required. Single-day fishing licenses are often sold at marinas and sometimes by the fishing guide. At last check, a one-day license was US$9, US$22 for a week, US$34 for a month, and US$45 for the year.

The easiest way to obtain your license is through the mail before you leave for your trip. You can send in your request to the **Mexico Department of Fisheries (PESCA)** (2550 Fifth Ave., Suite 101, San Diego, CA 92103-6622, U.S. tel. 619/233-4324). You can also buy one at the Mexican insurance companies near the border, from some outfitters, or in some tackle shops in Baja.

For the most recent fishing regulations for Mexico and an online license request form, check www.conapescasandiego.org before going on your trip. The daily limit is 10 fish per person, including no more than 5 of any one species. Some species have lower limits, but they also count toward the 10-fish limit: The big game species—including marlin, sailfish, and swordfish—are limited to one per day, and it should be noted that most anglers release these fish unless it's obvious the fish will not survive. Dorado, roosterfish, halibut, shad, and tarpon are limited to two fish per day per person.

You can only have 30 fish in possession on a multiday fishing trip, and you cannot filet the fish while you are on the boat.

The same limits apply to spearfishing. Spearfishing is limited to free diving, so tanks and hookahs are strictly off-limits. Gas-powered spear guns and powerheads are also prohibited.

Although the harvesting of any species of shellfish by a noncitizen of Mexico is officially prohibited, very few people would consider it a citable offense if a tourist were to dig up a few clams. That does not apply to abalone or lobsters.

Taking live fish for your tank at home is also strictly prohibited, and you shouldn't try to sell anything you catch.

U.S. Customs and State of California Regulations
Keep your Mexican fishing license or the receipt if you've purchased seafood. U.S. regulations mirror the Mexican bag limits, but make sure to keep the species of the fish the filet comes from identifiable by leaving the skin on. For more information, contact the California Department of Fish and Game (1416 9th St., Sacramento, CA 95814, U.S. tel. 916/445-0411, www.dfg.ca.gov).

HUNTING
Upland hunting for pheasant, dove, and several species of quail draws hunters, primarily from Southern California and Arizona. Duck hunting near San Quintín was once popular, but now it's viewed primarily as a brandt hunting area. The seasons are similar to those in the United States, starting in October and extending into February for some species. Most hunters head toward Mexicali, Ensenada, and San Quintín.

Guns and ammunition are highly regulated in Mexico. Getting caught with either without the proper paperwork will involve serious consequences, including jail time and fines. The fee for having the outfitter register your gun for the season is typically over US$350, so almost all outfitters rent guns for a daily fee. The quality of available guns varies, but make sure to inspect the barrel of any rental gun for kinks and obstructions. Also make a point to ask about the choke installed on the gun and if alternate chokes are available. A hunting license and game tags are also required.

Recent changes to the regulations require that any noncitizen hunter be accompanied by a licensed hunting guide while in the field. Most outfitters employ "bird boys" to act as blockers and retrieve the game. To bring your dog with you, make sure you have up-to-date vaccination records and a health certificate from your veterinarian, issued within 72 hours of your departure. Many outfitters discourage or prohibit dogs, since there are risks associated with snakes, cacti, and burrs. If you do decide to bring your dog, make sure to have a full-field first-aid kit.

Questions to ask your outfitter include:

- What type of species are available in the region and during that part of the season?
- Are dogs or bird boys used?
- What is the type of terrain and what will the weather typically be like during that time of year?
- What does the package include? Lodging, license, guide fee, gun rental, bird tags, bird cleaning, shells, meals, drinks, transportation?
- What is a typical day like (e.g., start time, finish time)?
- What type of guns are available, and how old are they?
- If you are left-handed, it can't hurt to ask if

there are any left-handed or straight-stocked guns.

Keep in mind that there is no hunter safety course requirement to obtain a license in Mexico, so you may be paired with an inexperienced hunter. If you are uncomfortable with the situation, speak up and request to hunt with a private guide instead.

BOATING

Popular since the 1950s, recreational boating remains one of the most pleasurable ways to experience Baja's marine environments. Some people cruise all the way down from California, following the path of John Muir; but the vast majority haul their boats down the peninsula via Mexico 1 and launch from one of Baja's many well-developed marinas. The Sea of Cortez offers safer conditions and more protected places to anchor than the exposed Pacific coast, which gets pounded with big swells and high winds. Types of recreational boats suitable for use in Baja vary from lightweight cartoppers and inflatables to large trailered boats and multimillion-dollar mega-yachts.

Nautical Charts and Tide Tables

Charlie's Charts: The Western Coast of Mexico (Including Baja) is a compilation of all U.S. nautical charts from San Diego to Guatemala, updated with anchorages, boat ramps, hazards, and fishing and diving spots. The 11th edition is available in many U.S. marine supply stores and from the company's website (www.charliescharts.com).

Other options include waterproof, tear-resistant, double-sided plastic charts published by **Fish-n-Map** (U.S. tel. 303/421-5994, www. fishnmap.com, US$8 per sheet) and **Gerry Cruising Charts** (U.S. tel. 520/394-2393, US$32–55). Gerry Cruising Charts also has tide tables for the Pacific and Gulf coasts.

Port Check-Ins

Several Baja towns have port captain's offices, where you must check in upon arrival by boat. These include Ensenada, Guerrero Negro, Bahía Magdalena (San Carlos), Cabo San Lucas, San José del Cabo, La Paz, Puerto Escondido, Loreto, Mulegé, Santa Rosalía, Bahía de los Ángeles, and San Felipe. You don't need to check out each time, except when leaving your port of origin.

Fuel, Parts, and Repairs

Several full-service marinas are open year-round in Ensenada, Cabo San Lucas, San José del Cabo, La Paz, Puerto Escondido (south of Loreto), and Santa Rosalía. Bring extra fuel containers in case you need to ask for fuel at a boatyard or fish camp when a marina is not in range.

Marine supplies and places for repairs are hard to come by in Baja. Ensenada, Cabo San Lucas, and La Paz are your best bets. Bring plenty of spare parts.

The owner of Baja Coast SeaFaris has compiled a thorough list of FAQs for novice and experienced sailors that covers topics related to cruising in Baja at www.bajaseafaris.com/cruise.html.

SEA KAYAKING

Kayaking expeditions in the Sea of Cortez have become increasingly popular as more visitors look for ecofriendly ways to travel the peninsula and more marine preserves come under government protection from commercial exploitation. Paddlers can get to remote coastal and island beaches that are inaccessible to larger boats or those traveling by land. There are appropriate destinations for all abilities, from Bahía Concepción for beginners to the Loreto/La Paz route for advanced kayakers. (The Gulf Current makes north-to-south itineraries the most logical approach.)

Kayaking on the Pacific side requires more experience. Punta Banda, south of Ensenada, is popular with San Diego residents. Bahía Magdalena in Southern Baja draws a crowd of paddlers in winter for whale-watching, but you shouldn't venture out into the bay during the season without a guide.

Organized Kayak Trips

Paddling South (U.S. tel. 707/942-4550 or 800/398-6200, www.tourbaja.com) leads multiday trips out of Loreto. **Baja Expeditions** (U.S. tel. 858/581-3311 or 800/843-6967, www.bajaex.com) offers kayaking trips to Bahía Magdalena, Isla Espíritu Santo, near La Paz, and from Loreto to La Paz. **Sea Trek** (U.S. tel. 415/488-1000, www.seatrekkayak.com, US$995/7 days) is another well-established outfitter.

KITEBOARDING AND WINDSURFING

November–March is the season for kiteboarding and windsurfing in Baja. The two main destinations for these sports are Los Barriles, on the East Cape, and Bahía de la Ventana, southeast of La Paz. Which one you choose depends on your level of experience and what kind of post-recreation scene you prefer. La Ventana generally provides more consistent conditions and a safe place for beginners to learn, with rustic accommodations (camping or *casitas*) in a more remote setting. The stronger winds at Los Barriles appeal to advanced kiters and sailors. Los Barriles also is more developed as a tourist town, with a broader mix of accommodations and restaurants. You can take lessons and rent gear at either destination.

SURFING

At even the most remote spots in Baja, the chances you're the first one to surf a break are low, but with an empty lineup and not a building in sight, you can get the full surf-pioneer experience within a few hours of the California border.

The variety of surf experiences you can have in Baja runs the entire spectrum. You can ride your first wave on a longboard with the Pescadero Surf Camp or you can win US$50,000 for charging down an 18-meter (60-ft.) face at Islas Todos Santos. The saturated breaks along the northern beaches from Rosarito to Ensenada can feel like extensions of the localized and aggro scene in Southern California. Those willing the walk to the next point or drive a little farther can quickly fall off the known surf map and find their own mecca. Perhaps the biggest threats to Baja

surfing aren't the fleets of Honda Elements or the longboarders poaching waves on the outside but the accelerating development along the coastline and the drive to close off beach access along both sides of the peninsula.

There are more than 75 named breaks along the Pacific coast, across the corridor between Cabo San Lucas and San José del Cabo, and up the lower East Cape. Some, of course, are more accessible than others. Which region you choose depends on the time of year, your surfing ability, and how much time you have. Some of the top surfing destinations in Baja include the coast near Ensenada, Islas Todos Santos, Scorpion Bay, and the beaches near Todos Santos and El Pescadero on the West Cape.

There are more than 25 known point, reef, and beach breaks around the cape alone. Stop by the **Costa Azul Surf Shop** along the Corridor at Playa Costa Azul or in Todos Santos for a map with descriptions of the breaks or buy a copy of the incredibly detailed *Surfer's Guide to Baja California,* by Mike Parise.

Water temperatures on the Pacific side are only slightly warmer than in Southern California until you get south of Bahía Tortuga. In fact, at Punta Banda near Ensenada, the water is actually colder than in San Diego, due to the proximity of the California Current, which causes an upwelling of colder waters from below. You'll need several millimeters of neoprene to be comfortable in temperatures that range from as high as 21°C (70°F) in the early fall to the 10–11°C (low 50s°F) in the spring. The southern Pacific coast warms to highs of 24°C (about 75°F) in the fall and drops to 15–20°C (in the 60s°F) in the spring. The Corridor gets even warmer, with temperatures often exceeding 26°C (80°F). A shortie-style wetsuit works well in these warmer waters.

Equipment

Experienced surfers bring as many boards as possible for their Baja expedition, plus wax and a patch kit for repairing dings. A cooler and first-aid kit will come in handy as well. Surf shops in Ensenada and San José del Cabo and at Playa

Los Cerritos in El Pescadero, near Todos Santos, sell boards, apparel, and accessories.

Airlines have made it more expensive these days to fly with your quiver; but a few allow surfboards for free. Check the going rate before you choose a carrier. Renting a board sounds pretty good when checking it costs US$100 each way. For longer trips, buying and reselling a board while you're there is another option.

Organized Trips

Baja Surf Adventures (BSA, toll-free U.S. tel. 800/428-7873, www.bajasurfadventures. com) runs a surf camp in Northern Baja that welcomes novice-to-advanced surfers. Other surf camps are located in El Pescadero (West Cape) and Bahía Magdalena.

SCUBA DIVING AND SNORKELING

Baja California offers several different types of marine environments for underwater exploration. The northern Pacific coast features a number of islands surrounded by rock reefs, seamounts, and kelp forests. The water here is cold (wear lots of neoprene or, preferably, a dry suit), visibility is often limited, and conditions favor advanced divers. But for those who make the trip, the marine life is fantastically unusual and diverse, and the spearfishing is excellent. La Bufadora and the Islas Coronado and Todos Santos are the top dive destinations in this region.

At the other end of the spectrum, the southern Sea of Cortez along the East Cape offers tropical conditions for diving and snorkeling, with drift diving over a living coral reef, sea lion colonies, dozens of islands, secluded coves, and white-sand beaches. A few sunken ships have formed artificial reefs over the years. The most popular dive destinations in Central/Southern Baja are Loreto, La Paz, and the Los Cabos Corridor. Water temperature ranges 20–30°C

(from the high 60s to the 80s°F), and visibility often exceeds 30 meters (100 ft.). July–October is the best time to go.

Baja's only dive shops are located in Ensenada, Mulegé, Loreto, La Paz, Buena Vista (East Cape), Cabo Pulmo (East Cape), San José del Cabo, and Cabo San Lucas. Most of these shops offer guided dive and snorkel tours, rental gear, and lessons. Note: When diving in the protected marine parks near Cabo Pulmo, Loreto, and Cabo San Lucas, diving with a guide is required by law. For this reason, the shops in Cabo Pulmo do not offer airfills to independent divers.

The *Solmar V* (www.solmarv.com, tel. 866/591-4906) and the *Nautilus Explorer* (www.nautilusexplorer.com, tel. 888/434-8322) both offer liveaboard diving, to the Socorro Islands, Guadalupe Island, and Sea of Cortez, among other trips.

Scuba gear is hard to buy in Baja, even in the resort areas. Bring your own or plan to rent. On that note, it's a good idea to bring your own spare parts kit and safety equipment, even when diving with a guide. You don't want to sit out a dive when your mask strap breaks or the O-ring on your tank blows. Likewise, a safety sausage, whistle, and dive knife are must-have accessories.

Recompression Chambers

Cabo San Lucas (**Buceo Medico Mexicano,** Plaza Marina, tel. 624/143-3666, cabo@ sssnetwork.com), La Paz (**Baja Diving and Service,** tel. 612/122-7010, www.clubcantamar.com), and Playas de Tijuana (**Centro Hosp. Internacional Pacífico,** CHIP, tel. 664/685-2566) have the only recompression chambers on the peninsula. In San Diego, head to the **Hyperbaric Medicine Center** at the University of California Medical Center in San Diego (U.S. tel. 619/543-6222, 7:30 A.M.–4:30 P.M. Mon.–Fri. and for emergencies).

Accommodations and Camping

First-time Baja travelers faces some tough choices when it comes to deciding where to sleep. Remote or central? Luxury or rustic? Mexican or foreign-owned? These are just some of the considerations. Self-sufficient travelers can camp for free most of the way down the peninsula and back, or step it up a notch and camp at designated campgrounds, which offer varying levels of service and facilities. If you want a roof over your head, there are budget motels, rental condos, boutique inns, and large international chain hotels. You can spend US$10 or US$1,000 per night, depending on your means and the level of comfort you seek.

RATES

Prices range from US$30 per night at the low end to US$200 and up for an upscale room and US$1,000 or more for a luxury resort experience. In most towns you can find something basic for under US$50 a night. Rates may drop considerably midweek versus weekend and in the low season (winter for Northern Baja, summer for Southern Baja). Many of the larger hotels add 12 percent tax and 10 percent service charge to the rate. Prices given in this book reflect double-occupancy, high-season (but not holiday) rates. Discounts are often available for longer stays.

MAKING RESERVATIONS

People who book their accommodations in advance almost always pay more than those who book in person when they arrive. It takes more time to shop around, but the reward is often lower prices and the opportunity to inspect a room before you commit. (Website photos can be deceiving.) It's also difficult to get deposits back from the smaller inns and motels if you pay upfront and then your plans change.

If you are planning a short trip to a popular resort in the peak season, you may not have the flexibility to wait and see what's available. In this case, it makes sense to shop around online

and go with a name you trust. When visiting hotels in person, don't be afraid to ask to see more than one room. Mexican hotel managers have a curious tendency to offer less-desirable rooms first, even if the cost is the same and the rest of the rooms are empty.

HOTELS AND MOTELS

Hotels and motels come in every shape and size in Baja, from 10-room family-owned establishments with basic but clean rooms to sprawling corporate complexes with hundreds of rooms and long lists of amenities. Rooms often are arranged around a central courtyard for added privacy and security. Most towns have at least one option with secure parking (gated and/or monitored by a security guard). Multistory properties may not have elevators, so consider the ground floor if you have a lot of luggage to transport to the room.

BOUTIQUE HOTELS

A growing number of higher-end places in Baja offer a distinctive and more intimate lodging experience in restored historic buildings and/or striking natural settings with exquisitely appointed guest rooms. They include La Villa del Valle in the Northern Baja wine country; Casa Natalie in Ensenada; Clementine's Inn in Mulegé; Posada de las Flores in Punta Chivato, Loreto, and La Paz; Posada la Poza in Todos Santos; La Alianza in El Pescadero; Casa Bella in Cabo San Lucas; and Casa Natalia in San José del Cabo.

FULL-SERVICE RESORTS

Many Baja hotels, motels, and campgrounds call themselves resorts, but in this book, we reserve the term for the large, full-service establishments that pamper guests with gourmet meals, spa treatments, golf clubs, fitness programs, infinity pools, swim-up bars, and the like. Meals are often but not always included. Rates for this type of accommodations vary from around US$200 a night at the Wyndham

BAJA'S BOUTIQUE HOTELS

Once confined to the Los Cabos area of the peninsula, boutique hotels are popping up from Ensenada to El Pescadero. Here are some of the highlights:

- **La Villa del Valle** (Valle de Guadalupe): Tuscan-style accommodations atop a hill on 70 acres with sweeping views of surrounding vineyards, orchards, and gardens.

- **Casa Natalie** (Ensenada): Five suites and three newer rooms, all furnished to a level rarely seen in Baja. The ideal home base for a weekend of wine-tasting in the Guadalupe Valley.

- **Clementine's Inn** (Mulegé): The most comfortable beds in Baja in a moderate price range. The owners made a speedy recovery after the flood of September 2006 and bought all new beds, linens, appliances, and artwork for their guest accommodations.

- **Posada de las Flores** (Punta Chivato, Loreto, La Paz): Among the most charming properties found in Baja. Rustic Mexican furniture and tile are used throughout, and all-marble bathrooms feature large bathtubs and extra-thick towels.

- **Posada La Poza** (Todos Santos): Enjoy the relaxed pace of life in Baja with a Swiss sensibility for quality and efficiency.

- **La Alianza** (El Pescadero): Marble floors, robes, Egyptian cotton sheets, and fluffy towels in a five-room property near San Pedrito point.

- **Casa Natalia** (San José del Cabo): A contemporary European-style boutique hotel with rooms set around a small pool and individually decorated with authentic artwork from San Miguel de Allende, Oaxaca, and Puebla.

Cabo San Lucas to more than US$1,500 a night at the exclusive One&Only Palmilla on the Los Cabos Corridor.

BED-AND-BREAKFASTS

For a more personal stay—often at a good value, too—consider one of Baja's many bed-and-breakfast inns, where you'll likely meet the owner(s) and learn a bit about the surrounding community. Cabo San Lucas, La Paz, San José del Cabo, Todos Santos, Loreto, Mulegé, and San Ignacio all have bed-and-breakfasts at varying price points.

VACATION RENTALS

Independent travelers planning a stay of a week or more who like the flexibility of preparing some of their own meals tend to prefer vacation rentals over the hotel experience. Whether you are stretching a budget or need to accommodate the needs of small children, the convenience of a kitchen makes it easy to avoid pricier restaurant fare, especially in the larger towns. Rental condos and villas are often foreign-owned and easy to find online via sites like Vacation Rental by Owner (www.vrbo.com) and Craigslist (www.craigslist.com). They often are part of vacation communities with many of the same amenities as a midsize hotel, such as fitness centers, swimming pools, maid service, and restaurants. The tradeoff is that vacation rentals are managed by individual owners, so it can be hard to know in advance what kind of service you'll get, especially if there are maintenance issues or other problems when you arrive.

CAMPING AND RV PARKS

There are hundreds of places to camp in Baja, ranging from isolated fish camps and high-sierra campsites to fancy big-rig RV parks. Fees range from around US$5 for a place to set up a tent to US$30 or more for RV spots with full hookups and access to recreational facilities. Many of these campgrounds feature some of the best views anywhere on the peninsula. Best of all, you don't need four-wheel drive to get there.

Food and Drink

Fresh seafood, hearty ranch-style foods, organic produce, and the fusion of culinary influences from around the world are some of the delights of eating your way through Baja California.

FOOD SAFETY

First-time Baja travelers tend to share two concerns about the food in Mexico: Will I get sick from the food? and Can I drink the water?

The answer to the first is, most likely not, but the dreaded *turista* does happen. Here's how to avoid overtaxing your system: Go easy at first—lots of heavy, spicy foods combined with alcoholic drinks and desert heat are a recipe for digestive trouble. If you're prone to food illness or especially worried about getting it, avoid street food, raw fruits and vegetables (except the ones you wash and peel yourself), and fresh salsas—at least until your stomach has had a few meals to adjust. (Many of these foods are fine to eat, but if there's going to be trouble, they are a likely source.) Some people swear by Pepto-Bismol tablets as preventative medicine.

If you do get a case of the runs, drink lots of purified water and revert to a diet of bland foods. The symptoms usually go away within a few days. Unfortunately, this can also be the duration of your visit.

As for the water, it's not recommended. Use purified water to brush your teeth and rinse fruits and vegetables before consuming them. Most tourist-oriented restaurants and hotels use only purified water and ice in their kitchens. When buying *licuados* (Mexican-style smoothies), *aguas frescas,* and drinks with ice from street stands, try to do your own inspection first. Many, but not all, use purified water, but asking whether they use *agua purificada* will most likely elicit an affirmative, whether or not it's true. Some hotels and vacation

© NIKKI GOTH ITOI

chilies for sale in Todos Santos

homes are equipped with water filtration systems; most just provide bottled water.

For extended stays, economical 20-liter (approx. five-gallon) plastic jugs called *garafónes* are sold in most Baja towns. They cost about US$6 for the first container, which includes a deposit on the jug, and then US$2 for each refill.

WHERE TO EAT

Travelers generally have many choices at mealtimes in Baja, although in more remote areas or off-peak seasons, you may have to settle for any place that's open. Restaurants vary from traditional Mexican establishments that seat a dozen patrons in plastic chairs around metal tables on a raked sand floor to culinary destinations that offer creative dishes in a white-linen and candlelight setting. You could make your way down the peninsula searching for the best *taquería* in every town. Or plan an itinerary around the top five or ten chefs that are defining contemporary Baja California cuisine. Serious foodies find some of the most exciting options in Tijuana (La Diferencia), Ensenada and the Valle de Guadalupe wine country (Laja), La Paz (Tres Vírgenes), San José del Cabo (Don Emiliano), and Cabo San Lucas (Nick-San Sushi).

To find the best *taquería* in any given town, stroll near the plaza in the evening and look for the longest line. Locals eat tacos for the evening meal *(cena),* not for lunch *(comida).* Casual places may be called *loncherías,* cafés, *cenadurías,* or restaurants. Most will serve a variety of Mexican *antojitos,* such as tacos, burritos, enchiladas, quesadillas, tamales, *flautas,* and the like, plus main dishes emphasizing meat and/or seafood. Some offer *comida corrida,* affordable multicourse meals for a fixed price of US$5–7. In more remote places, restaurants serve whatever they happen to have on hand.

Aside from these eateries, one of the real pleasures of traveling around Baja is the chance to shop in local markets and create your own meals using the variety of fresh ingredients on hand, including tortillas, shellfish and seafood, chiles, avocado, mango, cheese, limes, and more.

BAJA'S GOURMET RESTAURANTS

Gourmet restaurants are no longer just in Los Cabos. You'll now find gourmet eats in towns such as Tijuana, Ensenada, and La Paz. Here are some of the highlights:

- **La Diferencia** (Tijuana): Seasonally available *chile en nogada* or duck with a hibiscus flower-based sauce stand out on an all-around excellent menu. Attentive service and a contemporary setting make the meal.

- **El Taco de Huitzilopochtli** (Ensenada): No other restaurant in the area serves more authentic Central Mexican food.

- **Restaurant Laja** (Valle de Guadalupe): The brainchild of former Four Seasons chef Jair Téllez prepares farm-fresh cuisine on par with California's celebrated Chez Panisse and French Laundry restaurants.

- **Nick-San Restaurant** (Cabo San Lucas): The best food in Cabo San Lucas, period.

- **Don Emiliano** (San José del Cabo): A member of the Slow Food movement and run by Margarita C. de Salinas, a well-known chef from Mexico City.

- **Las Tres Vírgenes** (La Paz): Local expats call it the best meal they've had in La Paz.

WHAT TO EAT

Centuries ago, Spanish, Asian, French, and indigenous foods met in Mexico to form a distinctive—if varied—cuisine. Far removed from the culinary traditions of such mainland states as Oaxaca Puebla, Veracruz, and Yucatán, Baja California was known only for its fish tacos, until the turn of the 21st century, when celebrated chefs from the mainland and overseas began bringing their talents to the Los Cabos Corridor, La Paz, and the Valle de Guadalupe wine Country. The Baja

California cuisine that is emerging today blends fresh seafood from the coast with ranchero staples from the interior and organic produce from the fertile valleys in between. The flavors are fresh and unique, reflecting influences from around the world.

Antojitos

The majority of menus in Baja feature a long list of *antojitos* ("little whims"), or traditional Mexican fast-food fare such as tacos, *tortas* (sandwiches), *flautas* (stuffed and fried corn tortilla roll), chile rellenos (stuffed, breaded, and fried poblano peppers), enchiladas, and quesadillas.

When ordered as main dishes, these items typically come with rice and beans on the side.

Meats

Beef appears in many forms on Baja menus, including as steak *(bistec),* carne asada (in tacos), and hamburgers *(hamburguesas).* Chicken *(pollo)* and pork *(puerco)* are the next most common meats. Worth seeking out in Rosarito, La Paz, or San José del Cabo, carnitas (sold by the kilo) is a slow-braised pork dish originally from the mainland state of Michoacán.

Seafood

A trip to Baja isn't complete without a sampling of fresh fish and shellfish. Order the *pescado del día* and enjoy the fresh catch of the day, which may be mahimahi *(dorado),* sea bass *(corvina),* or red snapper *(pargo).* Huachinango is a whole red snapper cooked over an open flame. Mackerel (sierra) is commonly used in ceviche (raw fish "cooked" in lime juice). Puerto Nuevo, between Rosarito and Ensenada, is the self-proclaimed lobster capital of the region, although these days, most of its lobsters come from Southern Baja. Oysters, shrimp, scallops, and clams also make their way onto many seafood menus.

But the simplest and tastiest seafood delight in Baja is the fish taco—small filets of white fish breaded and fried, topped with shredded green cabbage, raw onion, fresh cilantro, and a squeeze of fresh lime and then wrapped in a

---

A CULINARY GUIDE TO BAJA

For those who like to travel from one meal to the next, Baja presents a lot more than Tecate beer and fresh fish tacos (although both of these are must-taste delights). Use the list below as a culinary guide to the peninsula.

1. Ceviche – many different styles; often served as a seafood cocktail in a martini glass with red sauce
2. California lobster platters – in Puerto Nuevo, Baja's lobster capital
3. Fish tacos – made everywhere, but especially tasty at the Mercado de Mariscos in Ensenada
4. Mexicali Chinese – Cantonese cuisine with a Mexican twist
5. The best *bolillos* – at El Mejor Pan in Tecate
6. Freshly made tortillas – corn *(maiz)* or flour *(harina),* buy them hot off the press at any *tortillería* for about US$1 per dozen
7. Abalone sausage – from Isla Cedros
8. Clamato cocktail – a meal in a cup that is nothing like its American counterpart
9. Award-winning red wines – made in the Valle de Guadalupe
10. *Alta cocina mexicana* – served at upscale restaurants in San José del Cabo, La Paz, and Tijuana

---

tortilla and devoured. The variations are infinite, but the result is always delicious.

Fruits and Vegetables

Given the dry climate, Baja does not have the same variety and abundance of fresh produce as mainland Mexico. In fact, most of what you'll find in the larger grocery stores is imported from the mainland. However, in Southern Baja, a handful of boutique growers are farming organic produce and supplying it to local restaurants. The Saturday farmers market in San José del Cabo is a good place to buy from these growers.

True vegetarian cuisine is difficult but not impossible to find; you'll often find a restaurant or two, plus a few natural foods stores, in the larger cities.

Salsas and Condiments

Many restaurants in Baja distinguish themselves by the variety and presentation of condiments that accompany their meals. Trays of ceramic dishes containing half a dozen salsas, plus guacamole and *crema* (thinned sour cream) are common. Most places make their own original salsa recipes, with varying levels of spiciness, so no two will taste alike.

Beverages

Soft drinks like Coca-Cola tend to taste better in Mexico because they contain cane sugar instead of high-fructose corn syrup, which is what is used in the U.S. versions, and the beer in Mexico is a bit stronger than in the United States. Tecate in the north and Pacífico in the south are the local beers of choice. When you've had enough cerveza and tequila, try some of the local nonalcoholic treats: Refreshing *agua de jamaica* (hibiscus) is an iced-tea-like drink served from large glass jars; other flavors of *agua fresca* include strawberry *(fresa),* watermelon *(sandia),* and lime *(limón).* A *limonada natural* is freshly squeezed lime juice mixed with sparkling water and a simple syrup.

If you're particular about coffee, you may want to bring your own; the larger towns have decent coffeehouse chains with beans from Chiapas on the mainland, but the stuff you get in ordinary hotels and restaurants is pretty weak; oftentimes it's instant.

BUYING GROCERIES

If you're traveling on a tight budget or you have dietary restrictions, preparing your own food will be easier and more economical. You can shop at large supermarkets, smaller *abarrotes* stores, or municipal markets called *mercados.* You'll find a mix of familiar international brands as well as local Mexican foods, which generally cost less. For the most interesting, authentic, and cost-effective food-shopping experience, seek out the *mercados,* which typically have a butcher, fish market, and several produce stands.

Conduct and Customs

TIME AND APPOINTMENTS

Whether you are waiting for your meal to arrive at a restaurant or waiting to board a ferry to the mainland, it helps to know that things happen at a slower pace in Baja than you may be used to at home. Dubbed the "*mañana* attitude" (as in, everything gets done tomorrow), this flexibility with time is deeply rooted in the Mexican culture. But it doesn't mean that everyone you meet in Baja will be late to scheduled events or that you should show up two hours late for a scheduled tour. Many businesspeople in Baja know that foreign visitors expect a more punctual approach and will be there on time. If you come with patience and an understanding of the culture, you'll have a better time when the day doesn't go exactly as planned.

YES OR NO?

A related cultural difference between Mexico and the United States is the tendency to avoid answering in the negative to any direct question. This practice can cause confusion for visitors in a variety of situations. For example, when confirming a reservation, you might ask, "Are we confirmed on this flight?" The answer may be "*Sí,*" even if there is a problem with the reservation. You won't know until you show up at the airport.

Likewise, if you invite someone to a social engagement, the person may accept, even if they are not able to come, because it is better to accept and not show up than to decline the invitation at the outset.

To avoid getting a false no, try to avoid

asking yes/no questions or rephrase the question, giving the person the opportunity to answer in the affirmative ("Do we need to do anything else to confirm our reservation?").

SIESTA

Many small businesses close for a few hours in the middle of the day, between 2 and 4 P.M., when the owners eat lunch and take care of personal business or relax. The trade-off is they often stay open much later at night than their U.S. counterparts (until 7–8 P.M.).

Hours tend to vary day by day as well. Banks and post offices, which follow regularly scheduled hours, are the exception.

DRESS

Many of the larger tourist centers in Baja are used to seeing visitors strolling around town in their swimsuits, sarongs, and flip-flops, but this doesn't mean that anything goes. Outside of Rosarito, Cabo San Lucas, and San Felipe, beachwear should be confined to the beach. If you visit any church or chapel, even for a quick look, you should wear close-toed shoes and long-sleeve shirts and remove your hat.

Tips for Travelers

OPPORTUNITIES FOR STUDY AND EMPLOYMENT

Two primary areas of professional study in Baja California draw students from around the world: sociology and marine biology.

Students of social sciences enroll in the Universidad Autónoma de Baja California (www.uabc.mx) to study the emerging border culture in Tijuana. UABC has campuses in Tijuana, Tecate, and Mexicali.

Marine biologists study at the Universidad Autónoma de Baja Calfornia Sur (www.uabcs.mx).

You may find opportunities for internships with international conservation organizations or with outfitters that run kayak, scuba diving, and other trips. Or you can enroll in a Spanish-language school.

ACCESS FOR TRAVELERS WITH DISABILITIES

Baja can be a difficult place to travel independently if you have mobility needs. Sidewalks are uneven with many sudden drop-offs, and older buildings often do not have elevators or ramps; however, many of the larger resorts do provide wheelchair access, and we are starting to see an occasional Pemex station (San Ignacio), campground (Baja Expeditions at Laguna San Ignacio), vacation rental (Coco

Cabañas de Loreto), and other facilities built to accommodate travelers with disabilities. Mobility International USA (www.miusa.org) has extensive information and advice for planning and enjoying overseas travel.

TRAVELING WITH CHILDREN

Baja is without question a family-friendly destination. People are warm and inviting toward children, and there are many suitable activities for kids of all ages. With the exception of a few adult-only resorts, most accommodations are happy to have families as their guests, and the bed configurations can usually be adjusted to work for families that want to share a room or suite.

Parents and guardians should take extra precaution to supervise young children. Beaches and swimming pools typically do not have lifeguards. Keep a close eye on kids near the water at all times. From scorpions to cactus thorns in the desert to uneven sidewalks and unmarked construction areas in towns, there are hazards you may not be used to at home. Bring a first-aid kit to treat minor wounds and insect bites and over-the-counter medicines or home remedies in case of illness. Protective clothing such as long-sleeve shirts and pants that can be worn in hot weather will help prevent sunburn, scrapes, and insect bites. Sunhats and

WHAT TO TAKE

Seasoned Baja travelers pride themselves on the detailed nature of their packing lists. Spreadsheets with multiple tabs for each kind of gear are not unheard of. These are some of the items you should consider:

Gadgets: A camera is a must-have for any trip to Baja. A GPS, laptop, cell phone, and portable music player may also come in handy while on the road, but the more electronics you pack, the heavier your bags will be, and the more you'll have to keep track of your belongings. Even if you don't plan to camp, a headlamp is useful in remote places where there are no streetlights for getting around at night.

Toiletries and First Aid: You can buy just about anything you need in major cities and larger towns, but bring any favorite specialty items from home, just in case. Tums and Pepto-Bismol come in handy when you OD on the hot sauce. Bug repellent and anti-itch

lotion help prevent and soothe insect bites. Hand sanitizer is always a good idea.

Shoes, Clothes, and Accessories: Bring sturdy footwear for walks and hikes, and Tevas or other water-friendly footwear for the beach. A sunhat, sunglasses, and sunscreen are essential. Layers come in handy. Also pack your reading material of choice – English-language books and magazines are hard to find and more expensive in Baja.

Sports Equipment: Consider the size of your vehicle when packing up the sports closet. Camping equipment, fishing rods, scuba gear, and surfboards take up lots of room. Bring straps for securing gear on the roof and repair kits for fixing dings and leaks. Renting equipment is an option in the more developed towns. Even out-of-the-way places sometimes have kayaks and scuba gear available for rent.

---

sunscreen are essential packing items. You may also want plenty of hand sanitizer to wash up after trips to public restrooms and before eating meals on the go. Remind children not to drink the tap water.

For infants, bring a mosquito netting that can cover your stroller, backpack, or travel crib. A backpack is more convenient than a stroller, unless you are staying at one resort. You can buy infant formula, diapers, toys, and most other baby supplies (including the U.S. brands) at the larger supermarkets in Baja, including Mega and Soriana. These stores also have pharmacies in case you need prescription medication. And they are well stocked with toys, art supplies, and beach gear for older children.

If you venture away from the busiest tourist centers, you may find yourself far from a full-service hospital in case of an emergency. Before leaving home, find the location and contact information for the nearest medical clinics along your itinerary. Bring contact information for your doctor at home, and if you are worried about access to medical

care, consider purchasing emergency evacuation insurance from **Aeromedevac** (toll-free Mex. tel. 800/832-5087, U.S. tel. 619/284-7910, toll-free U.S. tel. 800/462-0911, www. aeromedevac.com), **Air Evac Services, Inc.** (U.S. tel. 602/244-9327, toll-free U.S. tel. 800/321-9522, www.airevac.com), **Advanced Aeromedical Air Ambulance Service** (toll-free U.S. tel. 800/346-3556, www.aeromedic. com), and SkyMed (toll-free Mex. tel. 866/805-9624, toll-free U.S. tel. 800/475-9633, www. skymed.com).

WOMEN TRAVELING ALONE

Women traveling alone who have some prior experience with overseas travel need not think twice about planning a relaxing resort vacation to the Los Cabos Corridor. Transportation to or from the airport can be arranged ahead of time, and you can plan a wide range of group activities through your hotel.

There are a few more factors to consider if you want to venture into the more remote areas of the peninsula. Driving long distances solo is not recommended unless you speak Spanish and are self-sufficient in automotive trouble-shooting. Rental cars frequently have maintenance problems, and you may be far from a mechanic when trouble arises. If you travel by bus, you will often have long walks or cab rides from the highway to the beach. It's also riskier and hard to enjoy the many outdoor activities without a travel companion for safety. Consider booking an organized trip through an outfitter if the cost is not prohibitive, or try to meet up with other solo travelers once you arrive. Enrolling in a Spanish-language school is another way to find meet fellow travelers.

SENIOR TRAVELERS

With an appropriate sense of adventure, travelers of any age can enjoy the outdoor recreation and desert/tropical charm that Baja has to offer. In fact, older travelers are one of the largest groups of visitors to the destination each year. At the start of every winter, flocks of snowbirds with empty nests arrive by plane, boat, and RV to enjoy the desert/tropical environment. Some return home to the United States, Canada, or Europe after the winter season; others choose to make Baja their new permanent residence. Travelers aged 50 and up will find friendly gringo communities in Los Cabos, Los Barriles, Cabo Pulmo, Todos Santos, La Paz, Loreto, Mulegé, and many other coastal towns and campgrounds.

GAY AND LESBIAN TRAVELERS

Gay and lesbian travelers should feel comfortable traveling throughout the Baja Peninsula. **Alyson Adventures** (U.S. tel. 800/825-9766, www.alysonadventures.com) is a leader in adventure travel for gay men, lesbians, and "open-minded friends and family who enjoy tours with a gay flair." In recent years, it has offered a guided kayak trip to Baja, but it did not have a trip on its calendar at press time due to reduced demand for travel to the region. It's still worth a call to ask about information and advice for planning your own trip.

The more international and cosmopolitan regions of Tijuana, La Paz, and Los Cabos will have more options for accommodations, entertainment, and nightlife. The expat community in bohemian Todos Santos also welcomes GLBT travelers. Consult the Purple Roofs GLBT Travel Directory (www.purleroofs.com) for a current listing of accommodations in Mexico that give an especially warm welcome to gay and lesbian travelers. Here are a few examples:

- Loreto: Sukasa Bungalows
- La Paz: Casa Tuscany and Hotel Mediterrané
- Los Cabos: Casa Contenta
- Todos Santos: Todos Santos Inn

Health and Safety

A trip to Baja California exposes travelers to relatively few health risks compared to mainland Mexico. Driving and recreational activities pose the greatest danger, which you can minimize through common-sense precautions.

SUNBURN AND DEHYDRATION

Most people worry about drinking the water in Baja, but the most common afflictions are sunburn and dehydration. Get used to carrying a bottle of water and sunscreen at all times.

Most visitors aren't used to the intensity of the tropical sun in Baja. Use sun protection in all its forms, even if you aren't prone to sunburn. Even mild sunburn can sap your energy and make sleeping and showering painful.

Hats, sunglasses, light long-sleeve shirts, and sunscreen are essential. Apply sunblock of at least SPF 25 to any skin exposed to the sun—especially the face and neck region as well as the scalp if it is exposed. Bring sunblock with you and reapply it after swimming or perspiring.

PAY ATTENTION AT THE PUMP

These days, refueling at the Pemex can be the most unpleasant part of a Baja Peninsula road trip. Corruption at the pump seems to be on the rise in these hard economic times, and motorists need to stay alert in order to prevent fraud.

On a recent road trip, 9 out of 10 attendants attempted one kind of scam or another. One attendant tried the familiar trick of shortchanging the driver by 100 pesos when giving back change for a 500 peso bill. Another attempted to convince us that we had given him a 50-peso bill when we knew for a fact that it was a 500-peso bill. And there was the convenient miscalculation of the exchange rate when we paid in dollars and received change in pesos.

But the most blatant example happened at a station near the Los Cabos International Airport in December 2010. We were on a roll catching Pemex scams in the making and felt especially on guard by this point in the trip. The pump was on the passenger side of the car, and I was the designated Pump Watcher for this Pemex adventure. I was prepared to pay exact change in pesos. I saw the pump register 180 pesos worth of fuel and knew the

tank was almost full. Just as the pump was about to switch off, a second attendant came over to the driver side and said to my husband, "Excuse me, you will pay in cash?"

That was a strange question because you have to pay cash for fuel in Mexico. Suspecting foul play, I whipped my head back around to see the final reading on the pump. Sure enough the dial now showed 283 pesos. The two attendants had staged the distraction so they could add 100 pesos to the cost. We had caught them in the act, and they knew it. I said firmly in Spanish, *"Ciento ochenta y tres,"* paid the correct amount, and we drove off, incredulous.

I can only imagine how often this trick works on visiting motorists. Follow these guidelines and you'll avoid losing money at the Pemex: Take your time when refueling. Get out of the car and watch the pump closely. Pay in pesos and count your change before you go. Use a calculator if necessary to check your math. When paying in large bills, tell the attendant what denomination you are handing over and make sure he or she acknowledges the amount; then count your change carefully.

Familiarize yourself with the signs of heat exhaustion and heat stroke. The symptoms include flushed face, excessive perspiration and then the inability to perspire, headache, and dizziness. If you suspect heat exhaustion, the first priority is to get the victim in the shade and cool him with a wet towel and rehydrate him. Heat stroke can be fatal, so if the symptoms persist, get to a doctor.

MOTION SICKNESS

Some say the best views of Baja are found from the gently rocking bow of a *panga*. Unfortunately, that rocking can cause many people to get seasick. If you haven't been on a small boat, it's better to assume that you are one of the 60 percent of people who will experience motion sickness on a rocking boat, even if you've never been carsick.

Preventing seasickness seems to be more art than science, since a drug that works for one person might not work for the next. The main side effect of motion-sickness medications is drowsiness. There are over-the-counter drugs such as Dramamine, Bonine, Meclizine, and Marezine; prescription drugs include Antivert, Phenergan, and Transderm Scopolamine. Transderm Scopolamine, popular with boaters, is a dime-sized patch worn behind the ear for 72 hours. The most important thing is to take the medication well before boarding the boat. These drugs do not work after you have begun to feel sick.

Yawning and drowsiness are the earliest signs of seasickness. Try to stay alert, stand or sit as close to the center of the boat as possible, and get a view of the horizon. Some people swear that lying down and closing their eyes is the best remedy, while others guarantee that will cause the condition to get worse. Stay in the fresh air and avoid exhaust fumes if at all possible.

BITES AND STINGS
Mosquitoes and *Jejenes*

Mosquitoes and *jejenes* (gnats or no-see-ums) can pose a minor or major nuisance, depending on the time of year you travel (times of rain and little wind are the worst), where you go (oasis towns like San Ignacio and Mulegé are the worst), and how susceptible you are to insect bites. Malaria is not a concern, however. Use liberal amounts of insect repellent and wear lightweight clothes that cover your arms and legs. Bring Caladryl or another brand of calamine lotion to relieve itching.

Scorpions

Scorpions are common throughout the peninsula, especially in thatched-roof shelters and buildings. The sting is rarely dangerous, but it can be painful. Check showers and avoid walking around barefoot or sticking your bare hand in damp, dark, warm places. Shake out your shoes and always check bedding in the desert before climbing in. If you do get stung, lie down to avoid spreading the venom. Use ice packs to prevent swelling. Seek medical attention for small children (under 13 kg/30 lbs.). Ultraviolet flashlights can be a fun way to find scorpions at night. When this black light shines on a scorpion, the insect turns fluorescent yellow.

Poisonous Sea Creatures

Jellyfish, Portuguese man-of-war, cone shells, stingrays (in sandy areas), sea urchins (in rocky areas), and fish with poisonous spines present a potential danger when swimming, snorkeling, or diving. Look before you leap, and you'll be able to avoid most of these marine creatures. Scan the surface for jellies before hopping off the dive boat, wear a Lycra dive skin and water shoes even in warm water, and learn to do the stingray shuffle when entering the water to send any rays resting in the sand scurrying away.

If you do get stung, don't scratch the area with your hands, since you'll spread the poison wherever you touch next. Seek immediate medical attention for any allergic reactions.

MEDICAL ASSISTANCE

You can find knowledgeable medical practitioners in just about every sizable town on the peninsula. Facilities range from hospitals (in Tijuana, Mexicali, Ensenada, Guerrero Negro, Ciudad Constitución, San José del Cabo, and La Paz) to Red Cross stations and private and public clinics. There are public IMSS clinics or Red Cross (Cruz Roja, tel. 066) stations in nearly every other town.

Emergency Evacuation

Several companies offer emergency evacuation services from Baja via land or sea, but read the fine print before you buy a policy. Providers include **Aeromedevac** (toll-free Mex. tel. 800/832-5087, U.S. tel. 619/284-7910, toll-free U.S. tel. 800/462-0911, www.aeromedevac.com), **Air Evac Services, Inc.** (U.S. tel. 602/244-9327 or 800/321-9522, www.airevac.com), **Advanced Aeromedical Air Ambulance Service** (toll-free U.S. tel. 800/346-3556, www.aeromedic.com), and SkyMed (toll-free Mex. tel. 866/805-9624, toll-free U.S. tel. 800/475-9633, www.skymed.com).

SAFETY

Outside of the border zone, Baja California is a relatively crime-free place; even in Tijuana, where drug-related violence has gripped the city of late, the statistics are lower than comparable figures for many U.S. cities. Tourists are rarely, if ever, the targets in these incidences, though it is possible to get caught in the crossfire.

Precautions

Common sense and keeping a low profile are the best ways to prevent being the victim of crime. Leave valuables at home, and safely stow the ones you must bring. Experts disagree on the relative safety of using in-room

IS BAJA SAFE?

If you've read any of the news headlines coming out of Mexico in the past year, you have to wonder, Is it safe to visit Baja right now? It's a fair question that's difficult to answer. Here's the context:

When he took office in December 2006, President Felipe Calderón vowed to crack down on the country's drug traffickers and refused to negotiate with the cartels. While necessary and admirable, the policy has led to a dramatic increase in violence and corruption throughout the border region. Warring cartels are battling each other for power and testing the government in an unprecedented stand-off that was ongoing as of June 2011. The facts alone are gruesome enough, but when the U.S. media begins to sensationalize them, it can be difficult to uncover the truth.

Visitors need to remember that tourists are not the target in this fight, although they certainly can get caught in the crossfire. The kidnappings and shootouts have taken place primarily in the northern and eastern parts of Tijuana, which are not places tourists frequent. And statistically, Tijuana is safer than several U.S. cities, based on the number of homicides per capita.

That said, there is another, likely related trend playing out: The entire northwestern Baja California region has experienced a rise in armed robberies of a more professional nature than the petty theft that might have occurred in the past. From surfers and RVers to veteran Baja 1000 participants, foreigners have been pulled over, held at gunpoint, and robbed of their possessions. The victims represent a tiny percentage of all the visitors who make their way through Baja, but it's enough of a shift to give cause for concern.

Those who are studying the problem believe the trend is connected with rising drug use within some Baja communities. In the past, drugs flowed through the peninsula but were too expensive for most residents to buy. That apparently has begun to change, and the result is troubling.

For every local and traveler who tells you it's business as usual in Baja, there are others who counter with a well-intentioned warning to take precautions. We can't rule one way or the other, but we do advocate a few basic guidelines that have always applied to travel in this part of the world: Drive only during daylight hours, travel in groups whenever possible, and keep a low profile at all times.

hotel safes; in theory, anyone can call the number on the box to get the combination and remove your money. We prefer a strategy of hiding money and electronics in unlikely places, such as hard-to-find luggage compartments or simply the dustiest place in the room. When out and about, keep your belongings close to you, especially in busy tourist areas, to avoid tempting a pickpocket. Use the locks on your hotel room and vehicle, but don't leave any valuables in clear view. Call the **SECTUR** (State Secretary of Tourism) hotline (tel. 555/250-0123 or 800/903-9200) for emergencies of all kinds.

Information and Services

MONEY

Currency

The Mexican currency is called the **peso,** which is abbreviated as MXN and uses the same symbol ($) as the U.S. dollar. It's printed in denominations of Mex$20, Mex$50, Mex$100, Mex$200, and Mex$500. There are also 5, 10, 20, and 50 centavo coins and Mex$1, Mex$2, Mex$5, Mex$10, Mex$20, and Mex$100 coins. If you see the abbreviation *m.n.* next to a price, it stands for *moneda nacional* (national money), which is another term for pesos.

Dollars vs. Pesos

U.S. currency is accepted in many places on the peninsula, but you may not always get the current market exchange rate. It's better to bring an ATM card and withdraw pesos from a Mexican bank when you arrive. You can also use a major credit card at many businesses in the larger towns and cities.

If you need to exchange currency, banks offer the best rates but have limited hours (in the mornings only).

Tipping

Tips of 10–15 percent are the norm at restaurants, unless a service charge appears on the bill. Tip bellhops about US$2, maids US$2–5/day, and Pemex attendants US$1 if they wash your windows or check your oil.

BUSINESS HOURS

Standard business hours for small businesses in Baja are 9 A.M.–2 P.M. and 4 or 5 P.M. until 7 or 8 P.M. Monday–Friday. Many open on Saturday as well. Government offices are generally open 8:30 A.M.–3:30 P.M., although hours do vary day to day.

CHANGING CURRENCY EXCHANGE RATES

For a number of years, the ratio between the Mexican Peso (MXN) and the U.S. dollar (USD) hovered near 10:1, making it easy to do the math when reading prices in local currency and paying in foreign denominations. Recently, however, turbulence in global markets has pushed the dollar up in value versus the peso (to approximately 12:1 at press time), which means a hotel room priced at MXN 900 a night should cost US$62 instead of US$90 – a significant savings.

But there's a catch: Many businesses in Baja have begun pricing their goods and services in dollars instead of pesos. This has made for some rather steep hikes. Others keep their prices in pesos, but if you pay in dollars, they offer only the old 10:1 conversion. Pemex stations in particular are known for this practice.

There are several steps travelers can take to navigate the more complicated and volatile currency exchange environment:

• Take your time when negotiating prices and making purchases, and be sure you understand the real price of any item or service before you commit.

• Only spend money at places that you believe are charging a fair price relative to the market; if you think it's over-priced, then go elsewhere.

• Carry a calculator for computing exchange rates on the fly.

• Carry some of both currencies to avoid situations in which a merchant might offer a below-market exchange rate.

• Remember that many business owners in Baja are dependent on revenue from tourism to make ends meet, and they are feeling the effects of the global recession just the same as you.

Banks are usually open 8:30 A.M.–3 P.M. Monday–Friday, but the foreign exchange service usually closes around noon.

TOURIST INFORMATION

Mexico's national Secretaría de Turismo (SECTUR) has an office in La Paz that distributes free brochures, maps, hotel and restaurant lists, and information on local activities (Km. 5–6, Mexico 1 or Abasolo, tel. 612/124-0100, toll-free Mex. tel. 800/903-9200, toll-free U.S. tel. 800/482-9832, www.sectur.gob.mx). It's located outside town on the way to the airport and the Fidepaz marina.

SECTUR maintains the Mexican Tourism Board (www.visitmexico.com) offices in the United States and other countries to market the country's tourist destinations.

Travel Clubs

A few Baja-specific travel clubs offer information, services, and discounts to members. For example, **Discover Baja Travel Club** (3089 Clairemont Dr., San Diego, CA 92117, U.S. tel. 619/275-1836 or 800/727-2252, www.discoverbaja.com, US$39/yr.) has a conveniently located San Diego office, which many members visit for the latest information before entering Baja.

MAPS

The best road map currently available for the Baja Peninsula is the **Baja Almanac** for US$24.95 (www.baja-almanac.com). Our copy was the talk of the plane on a recent flight to Loreto.

National Geographic **Baja North and Baja South Baja Adventure Travel Map** (www.natgeomaps.com, US$19.95) are printed on waterproof, tear-resistant paper and feature insets of the larger cities, with most of the popular dive, fishing, sailing, and surfing locations identified. We used these maps for much of the research for the last edition and found them to be a significant improvement over previously published maps by AAA and ITM.

Guia Roji (www.guiaroji.com.mx), the largest map publisher in Mexico, publishes city maps

BAJA MIDNIGHT

Outside of Cabo San Lucas and La Paz, Baja is not a late-night kind of place. In most of its sleepy coastal communities, early to bed, early to rise is the mantra. Full days of water sports, beachcombing, and sunset cocktails, combined with a dependence on the sun for electricity, mean most places shut down soon after dark. When you hear a local refer to Baja Midnight, they usually mean 10 P.M., or as early as 9 P.M. in winter.

(scale 1:20,000) for Tijuana (2007, US$11.95) and La Paz (hasn't been updated since 2004), plus state maps for Baja California Sur (scale 1:350,000) and Baja California (Norte) (scale 1:1,000,000). The complete *2008–09 Mexico Tourist Road Atlas* (English edition, paperback, US$38.95) is invaluable for extended trips that include the mainland.

Topographical Maps

For serious off-road exploration, topographic maps are essential. Order them before your trip, unless you're going to be in the La Paz area, where the **Instituto Nacional de Estadística Geografía e Informática** (INEGI, in Plaza Cuatro Molinos at Altamirano 2790, Col. Centro, tel. 612/123-1545 or 612/122-4146, www.inegi.gob.mx) sells them.

WEIGHTS AND MEASURES

Mexico uses the metric system for measuring weights, volumes, temperature, and distances. Driving directions are given in kilometers (1 km is 0.6 mi), meat is bought by the kilo (1 kg is 2.2 lbs.), temperature is measured in degrees Celsius (27°C is 80°F), and Pemex stations sell gas by the liter (1 liter is 0.26 gallons).

In this book, distances are given in kilometers. Most other measurements are given in the metric system, except for boat lengths and fishing-line tests, which are given in feet and pounds in Baja.

Time

Baja California (Norte) follows Pacific time, whereas Baja California Sur follows Mountain time. Don't forget to adjust your clocks when you cross the state line. Daylight saving time takes effect in both states from the first Sunday in April to the last Sunday in October.

Electricity

Mexico uses the same electrical system as the United States and Canada: 110 volts, 60 cycles, and alternating current (AC). U.S.-style outlets work with appliances that have standard double-bladed plugs. This means you can recharge your electronics without bringing an adapter.

Communications and Media

TELEPHONE SERVICES

You can make local calls from public phones in most towns for just a few pesos. It's almost always more expensive to make local phone calls from your hotel, which adds a surcharge. The larger cities also have public TelMex offices. Private telephone services, often available at Internet cafés and office/business centers, are another place to make calls. Yellow Ladatel pay phones accept TelMex phone cards for local or long-distance calls. You can buy these cards in many grocery stores, pharmacies, bus depots, and airports in 20-, 30-, 50-, and 100-peso denominations. These days, using Skype or another Internet phone service is much cheaper and easier than navigating the public phone system.

Area Codes and Local Numbers

Phone numbers in Mexico follow the same format as U.S. numbers, with a three-digit area code (except for Mexico City, which is 55/) followed by a seven-digit local number. The difference is that numbers are not hyphenated according to any standard format. In this book, we've adopted the U.S. convention of a slash after the area code and a dash between the middle three and last four digits. Prior to 2001, numbers followed an older format, which some businesses still use.

To dial long-distance within Mexico, use 01 before the area code. Calling cards from Sprint, AT&T, MCI, Bell Canada, and British Telecom can also be used. Each has its own access code (usually toll-free) in Mexico for direct dialing. To reach toll-free 800 numbers in Mexico, dial 01 first.

Mobile Phones

Most of the Baja Peninsula now enjoys reliable mobile phone access through two competing companies: Telcel and Movistar. Telcel has better coverage and lower rates. For extended stays in Baja, during which you plan to make a number of local calls, buying a low-cost GSM phone and prepaid cards can make sense. Using it to call the United States, however, will cost a fortune, unless you are an AT&T customer in the United States.

Two U.S. carriers offer North America plans that include calling to and from Mexico and the United States: AT&T charges US$4.99 a month and US$0.59 per minute, or no monthly fee and US$0.99 per minute, for roaming in Mexico. There are plans that offer data services for smartphones, such as BlackBerries and iPhones, that start at US$25 a month and US$5 per MB transferred. If you travel with your phone, make sure to disable the features on your phone that automatically check email and download data or you may find yourself with a sky-high roaming bill. SMS messages cost US$0.50 to send; receiving them is free. Picture or video messages cost US$1.30 to send via SMS. You can activate the international service over the phone, but you need to call before you leave the country.

Verizon (www.verizonwireless.com/international) partners with Movistar to offer North America calling for US$60 a month for 450 minutes, and US$0.45 per minute after the monthly allowance. International roaming on a standard U.S. plan through Verizon costs US$0.99 per minute. Remember to call

Verizon before you leave the United States to check if international roaming is activated on your phone. SMS charges are US$0.50 for each message sent and US$0.05 for each one received.

In 2007 rates for calling a Mexican cell phone from the United States jumped to US$0.17 cents a minute due to changes in the Mexican government's regulation of the telephone industry. Also, a caller-pays policy began in 2006. When calling a Mexican cell phone number from the United States, it's now necessary to add a 1 after the country code: 52 1 612/xxx-xxxx. Within Mexico, you need to add 044 before the area code: 044 612/xxx-xxxx.

International Calls

To dial an international number from Mexico to the United States or Canada via TelMex, dial 001 and then the area code and number. Rates are about US$0.25 per minute. For international calls to other countries, dial 00 followed by the country code, area code, and number. To make an operator-assisted call, dial 09 before the country code.

Internet Phones

In areas with reliable high-speed Internet access, voice-over-IP (VoIP) calling is quickly replacing the need for satellite phones and Ladatel cards. Skype (www.skype.com) and Gizmo VoIP (www.gizmovoip.com) are two of the many service providers out there. Rates are about US$0.01–0.03 per minute, plus an account setup fee of around US$10. Some companies include a free U.S. number for family and friends back home to dial while you are on the road.

Long Distance the Old-Fashioned Way

If you don't have access to the Internet, you can dial access numbers to reach operators from AT&T, MCI, or Sprint for calling-card or credit-card calls. Beware the no-name phone companies that try to get you to call the United States collect or via credit card. They are notorious for overcharging, and some have forged

partnerships with hotels that get a cut when guests use their inflated services.

Satellite Phone

For the many areas of Baja where there are no regular telephone lines, no radio phones, no Internet, and no cellular phone service, the only solution is satellite phone—assuming you *have* to stay in phone contact at all times. **California Baja Rent-a-Car** (9245 Jamacha Blvd., Spring Valley, CA 91977, U.S. tel. 619/470-7368 or 888/470-7368, www.cabaja.com) rents GPS-satellite phones, as does **Discover Baja Travel Club** (3089 Clairemont Dr., San Diego, CA 92117, U.S. tel. 619/275-1836 or 800/727-2252, www.discoverbaja.com).

EMAIL AND INTERNET ACCESS

To the surprise of many first-time visitors, high-speed Internet access is almost ubiquitous in Baja these days. Hundreds of miles of fiber-optic cable were buried alongside the Transpeninsular Highway in 2002–2003, replacing the need for slow dial-up connections in most towns and connecting Baja residents and visitors to computers and websites around the world.

Reliability is another matter, however. Even the most well-equipped business centers have trouble keeping their connections up 24/7. If all you need to do is check your email now and then, this won't be a problem. But if you intend to run business processes remotely while on the road, it may be difficult to find a good setup.

Five-star resorts, espresso bars, marinas, and RV parks all have set wireless antennas for guests who travel with their own laptop or other Internet-enabled devices. Some charge extra by the hour or day; others throw it in for the price of a latte. In the larger condo complexes, you may be able to find an open (unsecured) Wi-Fi network to use. And for those traveling sans computer, there are dozens of Internet cafés in hotels, real estate offices, and business centers with desktop machines, as well as printers, copiers, and scanners for imaging needs.

Rates vary widely, from free with a food or beverage purchase to US$8 an hour at one of the hotels in San José del Cabo.

In more remote areas of the peninsula, some residents and RV owners have costly satellite Internet service through providers like HughesNet (formerly Direcway) and Starband.

POSTAL SERVICES

The Mexican postal service, **Correos de México** (www.correosdemexico.gob.mx), is slower than you're used to at home, though letters and postcards do arrive eventually (usually within 10 days).

Most towns in Baja have a *correo* (post office), where you can receive general-delivery mail. Correspondents should address letters in your name (capitalize the last name), followed by a/c Poste Restante, Correo Central, the town name, the state (BC or BCS), and the country (Mexico). For example, Nikki Goth ITOI, a/c Poste Restante, Correo Central, Loreto, Baja California Sur, Mexico. Mail sent this way is usually held up to 30 days. If you know the postal code for the town or city, add it after the state name.

Many visitors who are seasonal Baja residents forward their mail to a hotel or RV park. You can rent a post office box at the larger post offices, but the application process may take several weeks. Some of the larger towns also have private mail companies that rent boxes to visitors.

The Mexican post office offers express service (domestic and international) called Mexpost. UPS, Airborne Express, DHL, FedEx, and other courier services operate in some of the larger cities.

MEDIA

A few English-language newspapers are published regularly in Baja, but they tend toward tourism marketing. For real news, you'll need to read Spanish or visit the Internet. In Southern Baja, the *Gringo Gazette* (www.gringogazette.co) has a long and colorful history of covering local news and issues from the expat perspective. *El Calendario de Todos Santos* (www.todossantos-baja.com/elcalendariotodossantos.htm) covers the West Cape. In Northern Baja the *Baja Times* (www.bajatimes.com) is a free biweekly, also published online.

In tourist hotels, you may be able to find day-old copies of the *San Diego Union-Tribune, Los Angeles Times,* or *USA Today.*

RESOURCES

Glossary

abarrotes groceries

aduana customs service

alta cocina mexicana Mexican food prepared in a "high cuisine," or gourmet, style

antojitos literally "little whims," quick Mexican dishes like tacos and enchiladas

aparejo burro saddle

bahía bay

basura trash or rubbish; a sign saying *No Tire Basura* means Don't Throw Trash

BCD buoyancy compensation device

BCN the state of Baja California (Norte)

BCS the state of Baja California Sur

boca literally "mouth," a geographic term describing a break in a barrier island or peninsula where sea meets lagoon

calle street

callejón alley or lane

cañon canyon

cardón *Pachycereus pringlei,* the world's tallest cactus

casa de huéspedes guesthouse

cerro mountain peak

cerveza beer

charreada Mexican-style rodeo

charro/charra horseman/horsewoman

colectivo van or taxi that picks up several passengers at a time for a standard per-person fare, much like a bus

correo post office

corrida de toros "running of the bulls" or bullfight

COTP captain of the port, *capitanía del puerto* in Spanish

curandero traditional healer

Diconsa Distribuidora Conasupo, S.A., a government-subsidized food distributor

efectivo cash payment

ejido collectively owned agricultural lands

ensenada cove or small bay

Fonatur Fondo Nacional de Fomento del Turismo (National Foundation for Tourism Development)

Gral. abbreviation for General (rank)

hostería hostelry, inn

IMSS Instituto Mexicano del Seguro Social (Mexican Social Security Institute)

INAH Instituto Nacional de Antropología e Historia (National Institute of Anthropology and History)

indios Mexicans of predominantly Amerindian descent; **indígenas** indigenous people (**indígenes** is the less common, but more politically correct, term)

INEGI Instituto Nacional de Estadística, Geografía e Informática (National Institute of Statistics, Geography, and Information)

ISSSTE Instituto de Seguridad y Servicios Sociales para Trabajadores del Estado (Security and Social Services Institute for Government Workers)

laguna lagoon, lake, or bay

llano plains

lleno full

malecón waterfront promenade

maquiladora or maquila a "twin-bond" or "in-plant" manufacturing enterprise where foreign components may be imported and assembled, then exported to a foreign country, free of customs duties in each direction

mariscos literally "shellfish," but often used as a generic term for seafood

mercado market

mochila knapsack or backpack
mochilero backpacker
nopalitos strips of cooked or pickled prickly-pear cactus
PADI Professional Association of Dive Instructors
palacio municipal literally "municipal palace," equivalent to city or county hall in the United States
palapa thatched, umbrella-like shade shelter or roof
PAN Partido Acción Nacional
panadería bakery
panga aluminum skiff used for fishing and diving in Baja
panguero captain of a *panga*
parrada bus stop
Pemex Petroleos Mexicanos (Mexican Petroleum)
pensión boardinghouse
playa beach
plazuela smaller plaza
PRD Partido Revolucionario Democrático
pre-Cortesian a reference to Mexican history before the arrival of Spanish conquistador Hernán Cortés, i.e., before 1518; other terms with the same meaning include pre-Columbian (before Columbus's arrival) and pre-Hispanic (before the arrival of the Spanish)

PRI Partido Revolucionario Institucional
punta point
ramal branch road
rancheria a collection of small ranching households, most often inhabited by *indios*
ranchito small ranch
SECTUR Secretaría de Turismo (Secretariat of Tourism)
SEDESOL Secretaría de Desarrollo Social (Secretariat of Social Development)
SEMARNAT Secretaría de Medio Ambiente y Recursos Naturales (Secretariat of the Environment and Natural Resources)
tienda store
tinaja pool or spring
topes speed bumps
ultramarinos minimarket/delicatessen

ABBREVIATIONS
Av. Avenida
Blvd. Boulevard
Calz. Calzada
Col. Colonia (neighborhood)
Fracc. Fraccionamiento
nte. *norte* (north)
ote. *oriente* (east)
pte. *poniente* (west)
s/n *sin número* ("without number," used for street addresses without building numbers)

Spanish Phrasebook

Your Mexico adventure will be more fun if you use a little Spanish. Mexican folks, although they may smile at your funny accent, will appreciate your halting efforts to break the ice and transform yourself from a foreigner to a potential friend.

Spanish commonly uses 30 letters – the familiar English 26, plus four straightforward additions: ch, ll, ñ, and rr, which are explained in "Consonants," below.

PRONUNCIATION
Once you learn them, Spanish pronunciation rules – in contrast to English – don't change. Spanish vow~ ; generally sound softer than in English. (Note: The capitalized syllables below receive stronger accents.)

Vowels
a like ah, as in "hah": *agua* AH-gooah (water), *pan* PAHN (bread), and *casa* CAH-sah (house)
e like ay, as in "may:" *mesa* MAY-sah (table), *tela* TAY-lah (cloth), and *de* DAY (of, from)
i like ee, as in "need": *diez* dee-AYZ (ten), *comida* ko-MEE-dah (meal), and *fin* FEEN (end)
o like oh, as in "go": *peso* PAY-soh (weight), *ocho* OH-choh (eight), and *poco* POH-koh (a bit)

u like oo, as in "cool": *uno* OO-noh (one), *cuarto* KOOAHR-toh (room), and *usted* oos-TAYD (you); when it follows a "q" the **u** is silent; when it follows an "h" or has an umlaut, it's pronounced like "w"

Consonants

b, d, f, k, l, m, n, p, q, s,
t, v, w, x, y, z, and ch
pronounced almost as in English; **h** occurs, but is silent – not pronounced at all.

c like k as in "keep": *cuarto* KOOAR-toh (room), Tepic tay-PEEK (capital of Nayarit state); when it precedes "e" or "i," pronounce **c** like s, as in "sit": *cerveza* sayr-VAY-sah (beer), *encima* ayn-SEE-mah (atop).

g like g as in "gift" when it precedes "a," "o," "u," or a consonant: *gato* GAH-toh (cat), *hago* AH-goh (I do, make); otherwise, pronounce **g** like h as in "hat": *giro* HEE-roh (money order), *gente* HAYN-tay (people)

j like h, as in "has": *Jueves* HOOAY-vays (Thursday), *mejor* may-HOR (better)

ll like y, as in "yes": *toalla* toh-AH-yah (towel), *ellos* AY-yohs (they, them)

ñ like ny, as in "canyon": *año* AH-nyo (year), *señor* SAY-nyor (Mr., sir)

r is lightly trilled, with tongue at the roof of your mouth like a very light English d, as in "ready": *pero* PAY-doh (but), *tres* TDAYS (three), *cuatro* KOOAH-tdoh (four).

rr like a Spanish r, but with much more emphasis and trill. Let your tongue flap. Practice with *burro* (donkey), *carretera* (highway), and Carrillo (proper name), then really let go with *ferrocarril* (railroad).

Note: The single small but common exception to all of the above is the pronunciation of Spanish **y** when it's being used as the Spanish word for "and," as in "Ron y Kathy." In such case, pronounce it like the English ee, as in "keep": Ron "ee" Kathy (Ron and Kathy).

Accent

The rule for accent, the relative stress given to syllables within a given word, is straightforward. If a word ends in a vowel, an n, or an s, accent the next-to-last syllable; if not, accent the last syllable.

Pronounce *gracias* GRAH-seeahs (thank you), *orden* OHR-dayn (order), and *carretera* kah-ray-TAY-rah (highway) with stress on the next-to-last syllable.

Otherwise, accent the last syllable: *venir* vay-NEER (to come), *ferrocarril* fay-roh-cah-REEL (railroad), and *edad* ay-DAHD (age).

Exceptions to the accent rule are always marked with an accent sign: (á, é, í, ó, or ú), such as *teléfono* tay-LAY-foh-noh (telephone), *jabón* hah-BON (soap), and *rápido* RAH-pee-doh (rapid).

BASIC AND COURTEOUS EXPRESSIONS

Most Spanish-speaking people consider formalities important. Whenever approaching anyone for information or some other reason, do not forget the appropriate salutation – good morning, good evening, etc. Standing alone, the greeting *hola* (hello) can sound brusque.

Hello. *Hola.*
Good morning. *Buenos días.*
Good afternoon. *Buenas tardes.*
Good evening. *Buenas noches.*
How are you? *¿Cómo está usted?*
Very well, thank you. *Muy bien, gracias.*
Okay; good. *Bien.*
Not okay; bad. *Mal or feo.*
So-so. *Más o menos.*
And you? *¿Y usted?*
Thank you. *Gracias.*
Thank you very much. *Muchas gracias.*
You're very kind. *Muy amable.*
You're welcome. *De nada.*
Goodbye. *Adios.*
See you later. *Hasta luego.*
please *por favor*
yes *sí*
no *no*
I don't know. *No sé.*
Just a moment, please. *Momentito, por favor.*
Excuse me. *Disculpe or Con permiso.*
I'm sorry. *Lo siento.*
Pleased to meet you. *Mucho gusto.*
How do you say . . . in Spanish? *¿Cómo se dice . . . en español?*
What is your name? *¿Cómo se llama usted?*

Do you speak English? *¿Habla usted inglés?*
Is English spoken here? (Does anyone here speak English?) *¿Se habla inglés?*
I don't speak Spanish well. *No hablo bien el español.*
I don't understand. *No entiendo.*
How do you say . . . in Spanish? *¿Cómo se dice . . . en español?*
My name is . . . *Me llamo . . .*
Would you like . . . *¿Quisiera usted . . .*
Let's go to . . . *Vamos a . . .*

TERMS OF ADDRESS

When in doubt, use the formal *usted* (you) as a form of address.

I *yo*
you (formal) *usted*
you (familiar) *tú*
he/him *él*
she/her *ella*
we/us *nosotros*
you (plural) *ustedes*
they/them *ellos* (all males or mixed gender); *ellas* (all females)
Mr., sir *señor*
Mrs., madam *señora*
miss, young lady *señorita*
wife *esposa*
husband *esposo*
friend *amigo* (male); *amiga* (female)
sweetheart *novio* (male); *novia* (female)
son; daughter *hijo; hija*
brother; sister *hermano; hermana*
father; mother *padre; madre*
grandfather; grandmother *abuelo; abuela*

TRANSPORTATION

Where is . . . ? *¿Dónde está . . . ?*
How far is it to . . . ? *¿A cuánto está . . . ?*
from . . . to . . . *de . . . a . . .*
How many blocks? *¿Cuántas cuadras?*
Where (Which) is the way to . . . ? *¿Dónde está el camino a . . . ?*
the bus station *la terminal de autobuses*
the bus stop *la parada de autobuses*
Where is this bus going? *¿Adónde va este autobús?*
the taxi stand *la parada de taxis*

the train station *la estación de ferrocarril*
the boat *el barco*
the launch *lancha; tiburonera*
the dock *el muelle*
the airport *el aeropuerto*
I'd like a ticket to . . . *Quisiera un boleto a . . .*
first (second) class *primera (segunda) clase*
roundtrip *ida y vuelta*
reservation *reservación*
baggage *equipaje*
Stop here, please. *Pare aquí, por favor.*
the entrance *la entrada*
the exit *la salida*
the ticket office *la oficina de boletos*
(very) near; far *(muy) cerca; lejos*
to; toward *a*
by; through *por*
from *de*
the right *la derecha*
the left *la izquierda*
straight ahead *derecho; directo*
in front *en frente*
beside *al lado*
behind *atrás*
the corner *la esquina*
the stoplight *la semáforo*
a turn *una vuelta*
right here *aquí*
somewhere around here *por acá*
right there *allí*
somewhere around there *por allá*
road *el camino*
street; boulevard *calle; bulevar*
block *la cuadra*
highway *carretera*
kilometer *kilómetro*
bridge; toll *puente; cuota*
address *dirección*
north; south *norte; sur*
east; west *oriente (este); poniente (oeste)*

ACCOMMODATIONS

hotel *hotel*
Is there a room? *¿Hay cuarto?*
May I (may we) see it? *¿Puedo (podemos) verlo?*
What is the rate? *¿Cuál es el precio?*
Is that your best rate? *¿Es su mejor precio?*

...mething cheaper? ¿Hay algo
...ómico?

a single room un cuarto sencillo
a double room un cuarto doble
double bed cama matrimonial
twin beds camas gemelas
with private bath con baño privado
hot water agua caliente
shower ducha
towels toallas
soap jabón
toilet paper papel higiénico
blanket frazada; manta
sheets sábanas
air-conditioned aire acondicionado
fan abanico; ventilador
key llave
manager gerente

FOOD

I'm hungry Tengo hambre.
I'm thirsty. Tengo sed.
menu carta; menú
order orden
glass vaso
fork tenedor
knife cuchillo
spoon cuchara
napkin servilleta
soft drink refresco
coffee café
tea té
drinking water agua pura; agua potable
bottled carbonated water agua mineral
bottled uncarbonated water agua sin gas
beer cerveza
wine vino
milk leche
juice jugo
cream crema
sugar azúcar
cheese queso
snack antojo; botana
breakfast desayuno
lunch almuerzo
daily lunch special comida corrida (or el
  menú del día depending on region)

dinner comida (often eaten in late afternoon);
  cena (a late-night snack)
the check la cuenta
eggs huevos
bread pan
salad ensalada
fruit fruta
mango mango
watermelon sandía
papaya papaya
banana plátano
apple manzana
orange naranja
lime limón
fish pescado
shellfish mariscos
shrimp camarones
meat (without) (sin) carne
chicken pollo
pork puerco
beef; steak res; bistec
bacon; ham tocino; jamón
fried frito
roasted asada
barbecue; barbecued barbacoa; al carbón

SHOPPING

money dinero
money-exchange bureau casa de cambio
I would like to exchange traveler's
  checks. Quisiera cambiar cheques de
  viajero.
What is the exchange rate? ¿Cuál es el tipo
  de cambio?
How much is the commission? ¿Cuánto es
  la comisión?
Do you accept credit cards? ¿Aceptan
  tarjetas de crédito?
money order giro
How much does it cost? ¿Cuánto cuesta?
What is your final price? ¿Cuál es su último
  precio?
expensive caro
cheap barato; económico
more más
less menos
a little un poco
too much demasiado

HEALTH

Help me please. *Ayúdeme por favor.*
I am ill. *Estoy enfermo.*
Call a doctor. *Llame un doctor.*
Take me to . . . *Lléveme a . . .*
hospital *hospital; sanatorio*
drugstore *farmacia*
pain *dolor*
fever *fiebre*
headache *dolor de cabeza*
stomach ache *dolor de estómago*
burn *quemadura*
cramp *calambre*
nausea *náusea*
vomiting *vomitar*
medicine *medicina*
antibiotic *antibiótico*
pill; tablet *pastilla*
aspirin *aspirina*
ointment; cream *pomada; crema*
bandage *venda*
cotton *algodón*
sanitary napkins *use brand name, e.g., Kotex*
birth control pills *pastillas anticonceptivas; píldora*
contraceptive foam *espuma anticonceptiva*
condoms *preservativos; condones*
toothbrush *cepillo dental*
dental floss *hilo dental*
toothpaste *crema dental*
dentist *dentista*
toothache *dolor de muelas*

POST OFFICE AND COMMUNICATIONS

long-distance telephone *teléfono larga distancia*
I would like to call . . . *Quisiera llamar a . . .*
collect *por cobrar*
station to station *a quien contesta*
person to person *persona a persona*
credit card *tarjeta de crédito*
post office *correo*
general delivery *lista de correo*
letter *carta*
stamp *estampilla, timbre*
postcard *tarjeta*
aerogram *aerograma*

air mail *correo aereo*
registered *registrado*
money order *giro*
package; box *paquete; caja*
string; tape *cuerda; cinta*

AT THE BORDER

border *frontera*
customs *aduana*
immigration *migración*
tourist card *tarjeta de turista*
inspection *inspección; revisión*
passport *pasaporte*
profession *profesión*
marital status *estado civil*
single *soltero*
married; divorced *casado; divorciado*
widowed *viuda/o*
insurance *seguros*
title *título*
driver's license *licencia de manejar*

AT THE GAS STATION

gas station *gasolinera*
gasoline *gasolina*
unleaded *sin plomo*
full, please *lleno, por favor*
tire *llanta*
tire repair shop *vulcanizadora; llantera*
air *aire*
water *agua*
oil (change) *aceite (cambio)*
grease *grasa*
My...doesn't work. *Mi...no sirve.*
battery *batería*
radiator *radiador*
alternator *alternador*
generator *generador*
tow truck *grúa*
repair shop *taller mecánico*
tune-up *afinación*
auto parts store *refaccionería*

VERBS

Verbs are the key to getting along in Spanish. They employ mostly predictable forms and come in three classes, which end in *ar, er,* and *ir,* respectively:

to buy *comprar*
I buy, you (he, she, it) buys *compro, compra*
we buy, you (they) buy *compramos, compran*
to eat *comer*
I eat, you (he, she, it) eats *como, come*
we eat, you (they) eat *comemos, comen*
to climb *subir*
I climb, you (he, she, it) climbs *subo, sube*
we climb, you (they) climb *subimos, suben*

Here are more (with irregularities indicated):
to do or make *hacer* (regular except for *hago*, I do or make)
to go *ir* (very irregular: *voy, va, vamos, van*)
to go (walk) *andar*
to love *amar*
to work *trabajar*
to want *desear, querer*
to need *necesitar*
to read *leer*
to write *escribir*
to repair *reparar*
to stop *parar*
to get off (the bus) *bajar*
to arrive *llegar*
to stay (remain) *quedar*
to stay (lodge) *hospedar*
to leave *salir* (regular except for *salgo*, I leave)
to look at *mirar*
to look for *buscar*
to give *dar* (regular except for *doy*, I give)
to carry *llevar*
to have *tener* (irregular but important: *tengo, tiene, tenemos, tienen*)
to come *venir* (similarly irregular: *vengo, viene, venimos, vienen*)

Spanish has two forms of "to be":

to be *estar* (regular except for *estoy*, I am)
to be *ser* (very irregular: *soy, es, somos, son*)

Use *estar* when speaking of location or a temporary state of being: "I am at home." *"Estoy en casa."* "I'm sick." *"Estoy enfermo."* Use *ser* for a permanent state of being: "I am a doctor." *"Soy doctora."*

NUMBERS
zero *cero*
one *uno*
two *dos*
three *tres*
four *cuatro*
five *cinco*
six *seis*
seven *siete*
eight *ocho*
nine *nueve*
10 *diez*
11 *once*
12 *doce*
13 *trece*
14 *catorce*
15 *quince*
16 *dieciseis*
17 *diecisiete*
18 *dieciocho*
19 *diecinueve*
20 *veinte*
21 *veinte y uno* or *veintiuno*
30 *treinta*
40 *cuarenta*
50 *cincuenta*
60 *sesenta*
70 *setenta*
80 *ochenta*
90 *noventa*
100 *ciento*
101 *ciento y uno* or *cientiuno*
200 *doscientos*
500 *quinientos*
1,000 *mil*
10,000 *diez mil*
100,000 *cien mil*
1,000,000 *millón*
one half *medio*
one third *un tercio*
one fourth *un cuarto*

TIME
What time is it? *¿Qué hora es?*
It's one o'clock. *Es la una.*
It's three in the afternoon. *Son las tres de la tarde.*
It's 4 A.M. *Son las cuatro de la mañana.*

six-thirty *seis y media*
a quarter till eleven *un cuarto para las once*
a quarter past five *las cinco y cuarto*
an hour *una hora*

DAYS AND MONTHS

Monday *lunes*
Tuesday *martes*
Wednesday *miércoles*
Thursday *jueves*
Friday *viernes*
Saturday *sábado*
Sunday *domingo*
today *hoy*
tomorrow *mañana*
yesterday *ayer*
January *enero*
February *febrero*

March *marzo*
April *abril*
May *mayo*
June *junio*
July *julio*
August *agosto*
September *septiembre*
October *octubre*
November *noviembre*
December *diciembre*
a week *una semana*
a month *un mes*
after *después*
before *antes*

(Courtesy of Bruce Whipperman, author of *Moon Pacific Mexico*.)

Suggested Reading

TRAVELOGUES

Amey, Ralph L. *Wines of Baja California: Touring and Tasting Mexico's Undiscovered Treasures.* San Francisco: Wine Appreciation Guild, 2003. A compilation of historical information and winery profiles covering the Valle de Guadalupe and other regions in Northern Baja.

Berger, Bruce. *Almost an Island: Travels in Baja California.* Tucson: University of Arizona Press, 1998. Berger, a pianist, poet, desert aficionado, and keen observer of human behavior, surveys Baja's social landscape, with a special focus on La Paz.

Mackintosh, Graham. *Into a Desert Place.* New York: W. W. Norton & Co., 1995. One of the most widely read accounts of a gringo discovering Baja for the first time. With no wilderness experience, Graham decides to walk the entire coastline of Baja California.

Mayo, C. M. *Miraculous Air: Journey of a Thousand Miles through Baja California, the Other Mexico.* Minneapolis: Milkweed Editions, 2007. Poignant, contemporary memoir by a fiction writer originally from the United States who is now a Spanish/English translator and editor living in Mexico City.

Miller, Max. *Land Where Time Stands Still.* Gleed Press, 2007 (paperback). A classic 1940s travelogue that recounts the author's trip from San Diego to Cabo San Lucas.

Salvadori, Clement. *Motorcycle Journeys Through California and Baja,* 2nd ed. North Conway, NH: Whitehorse Press, 2007. A well-known motorcycling journalist advises kindred spirits on the best way ride the Baja Peninsula.

Steinbeck, John. *The Log from the Sea of Cortez.* New York: Penguin USA, Viking, 1951. This classic armchair-travel read tells of Steinbeck's journey with marine biologist Ed Ricketts from Monterey, California, down the Pacific coast, around the tip of Baja, and up the Sea of Cortez.

HISTORY AND CULTURE

Crosby, Harry. *Antigua California: Mission and Colony on the Peninsular Frontier, 1697–1768.* Albuquerque: University of New Mexico Press, 1994. A well-written academic account of the Jesuit mission era in Baja California, from planning through expulsion.

Niemann, Greg. *Baja Legends.* San Diego: Sunbelt Publications, 2002. A light read that bring the ghosts of Baja past alive, one town at a time.

NATURAL HISTORY AND FIELD GUIDES

Case, T. J., and M. L. Cody, eds. *A New Island Biogeography in the Sea of Cortez,* 2nd ed. New York: Oxford University Press, 2002. An interesting read if you want to learn more about conservation efforts in the Sea of Cortez.

Edwards, Ernest Preston. *The Birds of Mexico and Adjacent Areas.* Austin: University of Texas Press, 1998. This field guide may come in handy but is not Baja-specific, and birders find it frustrating that birds of the same species are illustrated on different color plates.

Gotshall, Daniel W. *Sea of Cortez Marine Animals: A Guide to the Common Fishes and Invertebrates Baja California to Panama.* Gig Harbor, WA: Sea Challengers, 1998. A good reference guide for divers, sailors, and snorkelers.

McPeak, Ron. *Amphibians and Reptiles of Baja California,* Gig Harbor, WA: Sea Challengers, 2000. This is the book to get if you want to identify the many frogs, toads, salamanders, snakes, and lizards of the peninsula. It includes lots of color photos.

Peterson, R. T., and E. L. Chaliff. *A Field Guide to Mexican Birds.* Boston: Houghton Mifflin Co., 1999. The closest thing to a Baja-specific bird-watching guide lacks Spanish names for the birds.

Roberts, Norman C. *Baja California Plant Field Guide.* La Jolla, CA: Natural History Publishing Co., 1989. The must-have field guide to Baja's desert and sierra flora.

CONSERVATION

Dedina, Serge. *Saving the Gray Whale: People, Politics, and Conservation in Baja California* Tucson: University of Arizona Press, 2000. The author describes the natural history and life cycles of gray whale, its habitat, and the human ecology of Scammon's Lagoon and San Ignacio Lagoon in Baja California.

Dedina, Serge. *Wild Sea: Eco-Wars and Surf Stories from the Coast of the Califorias,* Tucson: University of Arizona Press, 2011. The author is an environmental activist who lives in Imperial Beach, California, near the Tijuana border, and has played a key role in fighting major industrial development along the California and Baja coastlines.

Nabhan, Gary Paul. *Gathering the Desert,* Tucson: University of Arizona Press, 1986. A 200-page guide to the history and uses of 12 Sonoran Desert plants, organized into a collection of scholarly essays.

Peterson, Brenda, and Linda Hogan. *Sightings: The Gray Whales' Mysterious Journey,* National Geographic, 2003. A nature writer and a native American poet teamed up to tell the story of the gray whale through the eyes of researchers, fishermen, and coastal communities whose past and future are tied to the endangered mammal.

Russel, Dick. *Eye of the Whale: Epic Passage from Baja to Siberia,* New York: Simon & Schuster, 2001. This popular account of threats to the gray whale's habitat along the Pacific coast centers around the thwarted effort by a Japanese corporation to build a salt plant in the gray-whale breeding ground.

SPORTS AND RECREATION

Breeding, Shawn, and Heather Bansmer. *Sea of Cortez: A Cruiser's Guidebook,* Kirkland, WA: Blue Latitude Press, 2009. Spiral-bound guide with detailed information for boaters, such as nautical mileage tables and charts.

Eckardt, Dave. *The Guide to Baja Sea Kayaking: The Sea of Cortez and Magdalena Bay.* Paddle Publishing, 2008. The newest resource for kayakers covers San Felipe to Los Cabos and all the islands in between, plus Bahía Magdalena on the Pacific coast. Includes GPS coordinates and color maps.

Kelly, Neil, and Gene Kira. *The Baja Catch: A Fishing, Travel & Remote Camping Manual for Baja California,* 3rd ed. Valley Center, CA: Apples and Oranges, 1997. The undisputed bible of Baja fishing has a lot of information on camping as well.

Lehman, Charles. *Desert Survival Hand-book,* rev. ed. Phoenix: Primer Publishers, 1998. Practical information for surviving in the desert—essential for any serious Baja exploration.

Parise, Mike. *The Surfer's Guide to Baja.* Surf-Press Publishing, 2007. A must-have resource for Baja-bound surfers, the guide includes detailed directions to more than 75 breaks along the peninsula, plus maps and wave height charts.

Williams, Jack. *Baja Boater's Guide, Vols. I and II.* Sausalito, CA: H. J. Williams Publications, 2001 (Vol. I, 3rd ed.) and 2003 (Vol. II, 4th ed.). These ambitious guides, one each on the Pacific Ocean and the Sea of Cortez, contain useful aerial photos and sketch maps of Baja's continental islands and coastline.

REAL ESTATE AND LIVING ABROAD

Luboff, Ken. *Living Abroad in Mexico.* Berkeley, CA: Avalon Travel, 2005. This resource gives advice and tips for Americans thinking of moving from the United States to Mexico.

Peyton, Dennis John. *How to Buy Real Estate in Mexico.* San Diego: Law Mexico Publishing, 2006. If you've decided you want a place of your own in Baja, read this book first. It will answer many of your questions, saving time and minimizing frustration in the process.

COOKBOOKS

Hazard, Ann. *Cooking with Baja Magic Dos.* El Cajon, CA: Sunbelt Publications, 2005. A collection of updated recipes drawn from conversations with restaurant owners and other Baja characters, plus the author's own experience of living in La Bufadora and Buena Vista.

Schneider, Deborah M. *Baja! Cooking on the Edge,* Emmaus, PA: Rodale, 2006. More than 250 colorful pages of recipes, stories, and photos. Learn to make clams in tequila butter or homemade *paletas.* Well-written anecdotes share the history of Baja foods and the author's culinary experience in Baja.

Szekely, Deborah, and Schneider, Deborah M. *Cooking with the Seasons with Rancho La Puerta,* New York: Harry N. Abrams, Inc., 2008. Try preparing your own spa food using these secret recipes from "The Ranch."

MEMOIR

Smith, Jack. *God and Mr. Gomez,* Santa Barbara: Capra Press, 1997. A lightly told memoir of the author's adventure in buying land and building a home in Santa Tomás on the Pacific coast of Baja California (Norte).

FICTION

Reveles, Daniel. *Enchiladas, Rice, and Beans: Tales from Tecate, a Baja border town where miracles happen every day in ordinary lives....* New York: Ballantine Books, 1994. These laugh-out-loud novellas poke fun at the cultural differences between ranching families living in Tecate and the gringos from the Other Side. Reveles has written three more collections since the original, equally as entertaining: *Salsa and Chips* (1997), *Tequila, Lemon and Salt* (2004), and *Guacamole Dip* (2007).

Internet Resources

The Internet remains an invaluable resource for Baja-bound travelers. Even out-of-the-way establishments often have at least a basic website with directions and current pricing. The most technologically savvy ones use the Google Earth application to show visitors exactly where they are located. Some are experimenting with mobile applications and other communication tools. When it comes to directory-type sites, you need to be careful what you read. The vast majority of these sites are advertising engines with unedited and out-of-date information. Here is a short list of some of the most useful all-Baja sites:

Baja Books and Maps
www.bajabooksandmaps.com
Online bookstore with a comprehensive collection of Baja-related titles. This company is also the sole distributor of Baja-related titles to English-language bookstores throughout Southern Baja.

Baja Bound
www.bajabound.com
One of many businesses that offers Mexican auto insurance policies for travelers driving their own vehicles to Baja. Lots of related travel information, too.

Baja.com
www.baja.com
Destination community site with vacation rental listings and regional guides, mainly for Southern Baja.

BajaInsider.com
www.bajainsider.com
Comprehensive online publication for visitors and residents with news, weather, and commentary.

Baja Nomad
www.bajanomad.com
An interactive forum with extremely active participants, many of them veteran Baja travelers and local business owners. If you have the time to read through all the threads, you'll find a wealth of information about border crossings, road conditions, restaurant and hotel reviews, and more. If it's not on Baja Nomad, it probably hasn't happened yet.

Baja Times
www.bajatimes.com
Online version of the biweekly English-language newspaper serving tourists and residents of the main Northern Baja communities with news, real estate, and travel information.

Border Wait Times
http://apps.cbp.gov/bwt
Real-time border crossing times from the U.S. Customs and Border Protection. Scroll down to find the list of Mexican Border Ports of Entry.

Bush Pilots International
www.bajabushpilots.com
A must-read for pilots interested in flying a private aircraft to Baja. It costs US$50 a year to access the forums, which might be worth it even if you're not a pilot.

Instituto Nacional de Antropología e Historia (INAH)
www.inah.gob.mx
INAH is the government institution responsible for protection of Baja's cultural sights, including the historic Jesuit missions and ancient cave paintings. It runs museums in La Paz and Loreto and issues visitor permits for trips to the cave paintings and other protected areas.

Instituto Nacional de Estadística, Geografía e Informática (INEGI)
www.inegi.gob.mx
INEGI is a Mexican government agency that publishes statistics on population and economics for the entire country as well as topographical maps. It also has an interactive map of Mexico, including Baja California. Spanish only.

iWindsurf.com and iKitesurf.com
www.iwindsurf.com and www.ikite-surf.com
Daily Baja wind forecast and reports for windsurfers, plus a whole range of consumer weather delivery services, from the parent company WeatherFlow.

Los Cabos Guide
www.loscabosguide.com
Relatively up-to-date, advertiser-driven listings of hospitality and tourism businesses in the Los Cabos area, with some coverage of the East Cape and Todos Santos. Useful restaurant reviews and hotel listings. Fairly comprehensive.

Mexico Fishing News
www.mexfish.com
Weekly fishing report that covers the entire peninsula with conditions, regulations, catches, and photos.

Olsen Currency Converter
www.xe.com/ucc
This online tool for currency conversions comes in handy now that the dollar-to-peso exchange rate is no longer an easy 1:10 ratio.

Sunbelt Publications
www.sunbeltpub.com
This book publisher specializing in upper and lower California has an online catalog of its Baja titles.

U.S. Embassy
http://mexico.usembassy.gov
Visit the U.S. Embassy in Mexico City online, with information on services for U.S. citizens, plus current State Department travel warnings.

Index

A

Abreojos (Punta Abreojos): 150
accommodations: 445-446; all-inclusive
    resorts 323; Cabo San Lucas 357-365; *see
    also specific place*
agriculture: Mexicali 104; San Javier 203; San
    Juán de los Planes 260; Santiago 293; San
    Vicente 89; Valle de Santo Tomás 88
aguas frescas: 399
Agua Verde: 204
air travel: 424
all-inclusive resorts: 323, 445
aquariums: 220
archaeological sights: Cañon de Guadalupe 62,
    112; Central Desert 137; Misión San Fernando
    Velicatá 128; Museo de las Californias 34;
    Museo Regional de Antropología e Historia
    219; Sierra de Guadalupe 174; Sierra de San
    Francisco 159-160; *see also* cave paintings
Arroyo San Bartolo: 262, 293
art galleries: Cabo San Lucas 356; Galería
    Bahía 149; Galería de Arte Carlos Olochea
    220; Galería de la Ciudad (Ensenada) 66;
    GaleríAH 84; Historic Art District (San José
    del Cabo) 312; La Paz 236; San José del
    Cabo 318
arts and crafts: Cabo San Lucas 28, 355;
    Curtiduría Miraflores (Miraflores Tannery)
    297; desert soaps 271; El Triunfo 291;
    Ensenada 72-73; Guerrero Negro 144;
    Historic Art District (San José del Cabo)
    312; La Candelaria 377; La Paz 237; Loreto
    193; Mercado de Artesanías (Rosarito) 48;
    Mexicali 107; Museo Kumiai 55; Rancho Pilar
    378; San Felipe 118; San José del Cabo 21,
    318; Tecate 57; Tijuana 37; Todos Santos 24,
    392, 393, 395
Art Walk (San José del Cabo): 26, 317
ATV tours: 270, 352, 377, 378
auto insurance: 427, 435
auto parts: 404

B

backpacking: general discussion 439-440;
    Sierra de Juárez 112; Sierra de la Laguna
    295, 299; Sierra de San Francisco 159-160;
    Sierra de San Pedro Mártir 92-94
Bahía Asunción: 148
Bahía Concepción: 13, 17, 20, 138-140, 171, 176-180
Bahía Coyote: 176
Bahía de La Paz: 18, 220
Bahía de las Palmas: 264-280
Bahía de la Ventana: 19, 212, 252-259
Bahía de los Angeles: 13, 20, 130-136
Bahía de los Frailes: 286-287
Bahía de los Muertos: 260
Bahía de los Sueños: 260
Bahía de San Quintín: 12, 95-98
Bahía Magdalena: 13, 20, 23, 184, 206-210
Bahía Pulmo: 281
Bahía San Francisquito: 132
Bahía San Gabriel: 224
Bahía San Juanico (Scorpion Bay): 180, 181
Bahía San Luis Gonzaga: 13, 101, 123
Bahía San Rafael: 147
Bahía Santa Inés: 175
Bahía Santa María: 96
Bahía Santa Teresa: 146
Bahías Chileno and Santa María: 302, 333
Bahía Tortugas: 151
Banco Gorda: 262, 289
Bar Eclipse: 25, 194
Barón Balch'é: 25, 84
baseball: 35, 107
beach camping: Bahía San Luis Gonzaga 123;
    Bahía Santa Teresa 146; Bahía Tortugas 151;
    El Camino Rural Costero 280; Isla Angel
    de la Guarda 131; island 20; La Jolla 80;
    Puertecitos 123; Puerto Santo Tomás 87;
    Punta Arena 176; Punta Bufeo 123; Punta
    Chivato 176; Punta San Jacinto 90; San
    Antonio del Mar 89; San Felipe area 123;
    San Lucas Cove 167; Vizcaíno Peninsula 147;
    whale camps 162-163
beaches: Bahía Concepción 176-180; Bahía
    Pulmo 281-283; Bahía Santa Inés 175;
    Cabo San Lucas 344-346; Corridor, the
    333; El Cardonal 266; Ensenada Blanca
    204; Estero Beach 79; Estero Percebú 122;
    Half Moon Bay 88; Isla Cedros 152; Isla
    Partida 224; La Fonda 51; La Paz 14, 220-
    222; Mogote Peninsula 222; Playa Don
    Miguelito 144; Playa El Rincón 281; Playa
    Los Cerritos 378; Playa San Felipe 116;
    Playas de Tijuana 35; Rosarito Beach 46;
    San José del Cabo 313, 314; San Quintín
    96; sunset walks on 27; Todos Santos
    388-390; West Cape 377-380; *see also
    specific place*

bed-and-breakfasts: 177-178, 242, 288, 363-364, 382, 395-397, 446
beer: 54
biking: general discussion 436; La Paz 233-234; Los Barriles 270; Rosarito 48
bird-watching: Bahía de los Angeles 133; Bahía Magdalena 207; Estero de Coyote 151; Guerrero Negro 144; Islas Los Coronados 45; La Poza 389; Playa El Sombrerito 170; Tecate 56
boating: general discussion 442; Bahía de los Angeles 133; Cabo San Lucas 351; cruises 13, 70, 346, 351; Ensenada 69; La Paz 231-233; Loreto 190, 191; San Felipe 117; San Quintín 96; Tommy Bahama Newport-Ensenada Race 71
border crossings: 42, 110, 438
Boulevard Mijares: 19, 26, 304, 309
boutique hotels: 446
Buena Vista: 266, 274, 279
business hours: 457
bus travel: 425, 429
Buzzard's Bar and Grill: 26, 329

C

Cabo Falso: 377
Cabo Pulmo: 19, 21, 22, 262, 281
Cabo San Lucas: 14, 19, 22, 24; accommodations 357-365; beaches 344-346; entertainment and events 353-355; food/restaurants 365-370; information and services 371-372; map 342-343; outdoor recreation 346-353; shopping 355-356
Cabo Villas: 28, 361
Cabo Wabo: 28, 365
cacti: 122, 313, 408
Café Santa Fe: 27, 400
Caffé Milano: 27, 244
Calexico: 100
camping: 446; see also specific place
Canal de las Ballenas: 126, 131
Cañon de Guadalupe: 13, 62, 101, 112
Cañon de la Zorra: 23, 262, 296
Capella Pedregal: 27, 363
Carnaval: 71, 118, 166, 212, 235
car travel: 426-429, 430
Casa Bella: 27, 359
Casa Natalia: 27, 321
Cataviña: 13, 17, 128
cave paintings: Bahía de la Ventana 256; Central Desert 129; El Cardonal 266; El Diablito (Little Devil) 62, 114; La Trinidad 175; Museo de Sitio El Vallecito 62; San Borjitas

175; Sierra de Guadalupe 169; Sierra de San Francisco 156, 159-160
Chateau Camou: 25, 84
children's activities: Acuario de Las Californias 220; Bosque de la Ciudad 106; Centro Interactivo Sol del Niño 106; Los Pinos Park 388; Tijuana Fair 37
children, traveling with: 451
Chinesca: 13, 106
cigars: 356
Ciudad Constitución: 18, 204
clambakes: 194
clam digging: 96
climate: 14, 407
clothing: 451
cloud forests: 297
Comondú: 139, 180
conservation, environmental: 407
consulates, Mexican: 438
cooking classes: 256
coral reefs: 14, 22, 283
Corona Hotel: 24, 74
Corridor, the: 332-340
crafts: see arts and crafts
crime: 455
cruises: Bahía Concepción 13; Cabo San Lucas 346, 351; Ensenada 70
Cucapá (People of the River): 103
Cueva de las Flechas: 159-160
Cueva del Ratón: 159-160
Cueva Pintada: 159-160
culture: 421-423
customs, immigration and: 438, 441
customs, social: 450-451

D

dance clubs: 36; see also specific place
Danzante: 20, 191
Del Borracho Saloon and Grill: 26, 201
disabilities, travelers with: 451
diving: general discussion 444; Bahía Concepción 17, 176; Bahía de la Ventana 252, 254-255; Bahía de los Angeles 133; Bahía de los Frailes 286-287; Bahía Pulmo 281; Bahías Chileno and Santa María 334; Banco Gorda 289; Buena Vista 270; Cabo San Lucas 28, 347-350; costs 228, 349; Ensenada 70; Isla Cerralvo 259-260; Isla Espíritu Santo 224; Isla Partida 224; Isla San Marcos 168; Islas Los Coronados 45; Islas San Benito 153; La Bufadora 80; La Paz 227-230; Loreto 191; Los Islotes 225; Mulegé 170; Puerto Santo Tomás 87; Pulmo

reef 283; Roca Pelicano 345; San José del Cabo 26, 315; tips 22
Dominican missions: 416
Don Emiliano: 26, 27, 325
Dreams Los Cabos Suites Golf Resort & Spa: 27, 336
drinks: general discussion 447-450; *aguas frescas* 399; Cabo Wabo 365; *michelada* 135
driving tips: 296, 426-429
drugs, illegal: 30, 46, 456

E

East Cape: 14,18, 261-289
economy: 420
ecotourism: 407
Edith's: 28, 354
El Ángel Azul: 27, 242
El Arco: 19, 344
El Bajo: 22, 225, 227
El Camino Rural Costero: 280-289
El Cardonal: 266, 272, 277
El Chilar: 26, 325
electricity: 459
El Nido: 24, 49
El Pescadero: 19, 378, 379
El Rey del Taco: 25
El Rosario: 12, 17, 20, 99
El Sargento: 19, 252
El Sauzal: 20, 52
El Squid Roe: 28, 354
El Triunfo: 18, 23, 262, 291
email: 460
emergencies: 455
employment: 420, 451
Ensenada: 12, 16, 24, 44, 65-79
Ensenada Blanca: 204
environmental issues: general discussion 406-407; Bahía Magdalena conservation 206; desert pronghorn endangerment 149; gray whale conservation 142; Leave No Trace 224; Los Cabos mine 291; Mogote Peninsula 222; NOM-029 226; overfishing 114; Sea of Cortez 282
Esperanza Resort: 27, 338
Estero Beach: 79
Estero San José: 27, 302, 312
estuaries: 79, 204, 312
exchange rates: 457

F

fauna: 148, 411-414
ferries: 429

festivals: 50, 57, 71, 84, 107, 166, 208, 236, 337, 394, 422
film festivals: 395
Finisterra (Land's End): 302, 344
fish: 200, 411
fishing: general discussion 440-441; abalone 151; environmental issues 114; Loreto Dorado International Fishing Tournament 194; Reserva de la Biósfera Desierto de Vizcaíno 149; shore fishing 269; spearfishing 254-255; *see also specific place*
flora: general discussion 408-410; desert 128, 291-292
food: general discussion 447-450; ceviche recipe 124; common dishes 449; egg dishes 75; Feria Internacional del Pescado y el Marisco 71; J. D. Hussong Baja International Chili Cookoff & Salsa Contest 71; Muestra Gastronómica 107; romantic dining 27; seafood 50; *see also specific place*
Franciscan missions: 128, 416
French Riviera: 26, 328

G

gardens: Cactimundo Botanical Gardens 313; La Paz 219; Parque Hidalgo 53; Santuario de Cactus 291-292
gas station scams: 454
gay travelers: 453
gear, automotive: 431
gear, personal: 452
geography: 406
geology: 106, 405
Giggling Marlin: 28, 353
golf: Cabo San Lucas 353; Gran Sueños 260; Loreto 192; Los Cabos Corridor 334-335; San Felipe 117; San José del Cabo 315; Tijuana 36
government: 420
gratuities: 457
gray whales: 13, 141, 160-163, 411
groceries: 450; *see also specific place*
Guadalupe Valley: 81-86
Guerrero Negro: 13, 16, 17, 20, 138-147

H

hazards, driving: 430
health: 453-456
Hemingway's: 28, 354
hiking: general discussion 439-440; Bahía de la Ventana 256; Bahía de los Angeles 131; Cañon de la Zorra 296; Isla Espíritu

Santo 224; Isla Partida 224; La Paz 234; Parque Nacional Sierra San Pedro Mártir 92; Rancho La Puerta 56; San Ignacio 156; Sierra de Juárez 61, 112; Sierra de la Laguna 14, 298-299, 380; Sierra de San Pedro Mártir 94; Tecate 56; Todos Santos 391; Valle de los Gigantes 122; Volcán las Tres Virgenes 160; see also backpacking
Historic Art District (San José del Cabo): 302, 312
Historic District, Todos Santos: 387
history: 414-419; see also specific place
horseback riding: Boca de Las Palmas 288; Cabo San Lucas 352; La Paz 234; Rancho La Venta 293; San José del Cabo 26
hotels: 445; see also accommodations, specific place
hot springs: Cabo Pulmo 284; Cañon de Guadalupe 62, 112; Puertecitos 123; San Borja 136; Santiago 296; Tecate 56
hunting: 441
Hurricane Jimena: 206
Hurricane John: 261
Hussong's Cantina: 24, 70

I

Ibarra's Pottery: 27, 237
immigration documents: 15, 77, 110, 249, 437
INAH: 175
income: 420
indigenous culture: history of 414; Museo Campo Alaska 62, 114; Museo de Historia de Ensenada 66; Museo de Naturaleza y Cultura 130; Tecate Cultural Center 55
insurance, auto: 427, 435
Internet services: 460
Isla Angel de la Guarda: 131
Isla Carmen: 20, 190-191
Isla Catalana: 190
Isla Cedros: 152
Isla Cerralvo: 19, 259-260
Isla Coronado: 190
Isla Espíritu Santo: 14, 18, 20, 22, 23, 212, 222
Isla Guapa: 171
Isla Natividad: 153
island hopping: 224; itinerary 20
Isla Partida: 224
Isla Requesón: 171
Isla San Marcos: 168
Isla Santispac: 171
Islas del Golfo de California: 131
Islas Encantadas: 123

Islas Los Coronados: 45
Islas San Benito: 153
Islas Santa Inés: 171
itineraries: 12, 16-28

JKL

Jesuit missions: 18, 415-416
jewelry: 28, 318
Joyería Albert: 28, 355
kayaking: see sea kayaking
kiteboarding: general discussion 443; Bahía Concepción 176-180; Bahía de la Ventana 252-254; Bahía de los Angeles 130, 133; Bahía Magdalena 209; Loreto 191; Los Barriles 268
La Bocana: 87, 151
La Bufadora: 16, 64, 80
La Candelaria: 374, 377
La Capilla Sportfishing and Eco Tours: 269
La Casa de Doña Lupe: 84
La Casa Vieja: 84
La Chinesca: 101, 106
La Esquina de Bodegas: 25, 73
La Fonda: 28, 51
Laguna Hanson: 62, 114
Laguna Ojo de Liebre: 17, 139, 141
Laguna Salada: 61, 112
Laguna San Ignacio: 17, 139, 160
La Laguna: 299
Land's End: 19, 22, 27
language: 423
language schools: 77, 248, 256
La Panga Antigua: 26, 325
La Paz: 211-251; accommodations 238-243; diving 22; entertainment 235-236; food 243-247; highlights 212; history 214-215; islands 222-225; itineraries for visiting 14, 18, 20, 23; kayaking 20; maps 213, 216, 218-219; recreation 225-234; services 248-249; shopping 236-238; sights 217-220; transportation 249-251
La Picazón: 25, 199
La Playita: 26, 313
La Poza: 374, 389
La Purísima: 139, 180
La Realeña: 292
La Ribera: 266, 275, 279
La Rumorosa: 62, 113
Las Aquilas (The Eagles): 107
Las Cabañas de Loreto: 25, 196
Las Cañadas Campamento: 87
Las Cruces: 221

Las Gardenias: 28, 365
Las Tinajitas: 137
Las Tres Vírgenes: 27, 243
Las Ventanas al Paraíso: 27, 338
La Trinidad: 175
La Ventana: 19, 252
La Villa del Valle: 25, 85
Leave No Trace: 224
legal system: 439
lesbian travelers: 453
lighthouses: 186, 377, 389
long weekends: 24-28
Loreto: 13, 17, 20, 25, 183-203
Loreto Bay National Marine Park: 25, 186
Los Barriles: 19, 23, 262, 266, 272, 277
Los Cabos: 14, 301-372; accommodations 306-307; Cabo San Lucas 340-372; Corridor, the 332-340; highlights 302; history 303-305; itineraries 21-24; maps 304, 305; San José del Cabo 309-332; transportation 307-308; weather 15
Los Cabos Corridor: 19, 332-340
Los Islotes: 22, 225

M

malecón (Ensenada): 12, 69
malecón (La Paz): 14, 23, 212, 217
malecón (Loreto): 184, 189
malecón (San Felipe): 101, 116
Mama's Royal Café: 28, 369
Maneadero: 20, 87
Mango Deck: 27, 362
marina, Cabo San Lucas: 341, 351
Marina Mercado: 28, 355
marina, San José del Cabo: 309
Mariscos Mazatlán II: 26, 326
Maro's Shrimp House: 28, 367
Marquis Los Cabos: 27, 338
media: 461
Mercado de Mariscos: 25, 74
Mexicali: 12, 45, 100, 103-112
Mexicali 500: 107
Mexican-American War: 417
Mexican Revolution: 418
military checkpoints: 433
mining: abandoned mines 131; Guerrero Negro area 13; Isla San Marcos 168; onyx 128; Santa Rosalía 164, 165; Sierra de la Laguna 289, 291
missions: history of 415-416; Misión de Santiago El Apóstol Aiñiní 295; Misión El Descanso 50; Misión Nuestra Señora de

Guadalupe de Huasinapi 169; Misión Nuestra Señora de Guadalupe del Norte 81; Misión Nuestra Señora de Loreto Conchó 184, 187; Misión Nuestra Señora del Pilar de la Paz Airapí 214; Misíon Nuestra Señora del Rosario De Viñadaco 99; Misión Nuestra Señor San Ignacio de Kadakaamán 139, 155-156; Misión San Fernando Velicatá 126, 128; Misión San Francisco Borja de Adác 136; Misión San Francisco Xavier de Viggé-Biaundó 203; Misión San José del Cabo Añuiti 309; Misión San Luis Gonzaga Chiriyaqui 206; Misión San Miguel Arcángel de la Frontera 51; Misión San Pedro Mártir de Verona 93; Misión Santa Catalina Virgen y Mártir 86; Misión Santa María de los Angeles 129; Misión Santa Rosa de las Palmas 387; Misión Santa Rosalía de Mulegé 169; Misión Santo Domingo de la Frontera 91; Misíon Santo Tomás de Aquino 88; Misión San Vicente Ferrer 89; Museo de Historia de Ensenada 66; Museo de los Misiónes 187
Mocambo de Los Cabos: 28, 366
Mogote Peninsula: 222
money: 457
Montevideo: 137
Monte Xanic: 25, 84
Morgan's Restaurant and Cellar: 26, 317
motels: 445; *see also specific place*
motorcycling: 436
mountain biking: 233-234; *see also* biking
Mulegé: 17, 20, 169-176
Museo Regional de Antropología e Historia: 23, 212, 219

NOP

nightlife: "Baja Midnight" 458; Cabo San Lucas 353-354; Ensenada 70; Loreto 194; Mexicali 107; Rosarito 48; San Felipe 116, 117; San José del Cabo 317; Tijuana 36
Nikki Beach: 27, 370
Nowhere Bar: 28, 353
off-road races: Gran Carrera de Tecate 57; Mexicali 500 107; SCORE Tecate Baja 500 57, 71; SCORE Tecate Baja 1000 71, 236; Tecate SCORE San Felipe 250 118
off-road vehicle use: ATV tours 270, 352, 377, 378; Cabo San Lucas 352; Parque Nacional Constitución de 1857 86; Sierra de Juárez 112; tips for 430
One&Only Palmilla: 334, 339
onyx mining: 128

opals, fire: 27
packing tips: 452
Palacio Municipal (Loreto): 189
Palacio Municipal (San José del Cabo): 309
Palapas Ventana: 254, 256
Palmira: 220
panga fishing: 347; *see also specific place*
Papas and Beer: 24, 71
passports: 15, 437
Patagonia: 24, 368
pearls, La Paz: 214
Pelican Rock: 28, 345, 348
performing arts: Casa de la Cultura 312; Centro
    Cultural Tijuana 34, 37; La Unidad Cultural
    Profesor Jesús Castro Agúndez 220; Todos
    Santos 394
pets: 437
phone numbers: Cabo San Lucas 371; La Paz
    249; San José del Cabo 330; Tijuana 42
phone services: 459-460
Pichilingue Peninsula: 14, 23, 219, 220
planning tips: 12-15
plants: 408-410
Playa Agave Azul: 380
Playa Balandra: 220
Playa Buenaventura: 178
Playa Chileno: 19, 26, 333
Playa Costa Azul: 26, 27, 314
Playa Coyote: 178
Playa del Amor: 19, 24, 28, 302, 345
Playa Destiny: 123
Playa Don Miguelito: 144
Playa El Bledito (Tequila Cove): 333
Playa El Burro: 178
Playa El Coyote: 221
Playa El Médano (Dune Beach): 27, 28, 344,
    360
Playa El Requesón: 179
Playa El Rincón: 281
Playa El Sombrerito: 139, 170
Playa El Tecolote: 18, 23, 212, 221
Playa El Tesoro: 220
Playa Escondida: 123, 178
Playa La Cachora: 389
Playa La Pastora: 20, 24, 390
Playa La Sirenita: 282
Playa Las Pocitas: 27, 389
Playa Las Viudas (Widows Beach): 333
Playa Los Arbolitos: 282
Playa Los Cerritos: 19, 24, 374, 378
Playa Los Cocos: 178
Playa Migriño: 377

Playa Palmilla: 27, 333
Playa Pichilingue: 220
Playa Punta Colorada: 220
Playa San Pedrito (Playa Las Palmas): 374, 380
Playa San Pedro: 380
Playa Santa María: 16, 19, 26
Playa Santispac: 139, 177
Playas de Tijuana: 35
Playa Solmar: 27, 346
Plaza Amelia Wilkes: 341
Plaza Cívica: 69
Plaza Constitución: 219
Plaza Río Tijuana: 34
Plaza Salvatierra: 189
Plaza Teniente José Antonio Mijares: 302, 309
police corruption: 46
politics: 420
Popotla: 50
population: 421
Posada de las Flores: 27, 176, 446
postal services: 461
Puebla Cedros: 152
Pueblo Bonito Pacifica: 27, 363
Pueblo La Playa: 313
Puerta Vieja: 26, 340
Puertecitos: 13, 122, 123
Puerto Algodones: 389
Puerto Cancún: 208
Puerto Chale: 208
Puerto Escondido: 189
Puerto López Mateos: 208, 210
Puerto Los Cabos: 313
Puerto Nuevo: 25, 50
Puerto Paraíso: 28, 356
Puerto Paraíso Mall: 341
Puerto San Carlos: 18, 208, 209, 210
Puerto San Isidro: 88
Puerto Santo Tomás: 87
Punta Abreojos: 150
Punta Arena: 176
Punta Arenas de la Ventana: 260
Punta Banda: 20, 79
Punta Bufeo: 123
Punta Chivato: 176
Punta Colorada: 266-268, 275
Punta Conejo: 390
Punta Eugenia: 152
Punta Final: 123
Punta Gorda: 289
Punta Lobos: 20, 389
Punta Márquez: 209, 390
Punta Perico: 260

Punta Pescadero: 264, 272, 277
Punta Prieta: 152
Punta San Jacinto: 90

QR

Quadman: 270
Rancho Ecológico Sol de Mayo: 297
Rancho El Carricalito: 204
Rancho La Puerta: 56, 58-59
Rancho La Trinidad: 175
Rancho La Venta: 293
Rancho Meling: 94
Rancho Percebú: 122
Rancho Pescadero: 378
Rancho Piedras Blancas: 146
Rancho Pilar: 378, 380
Real del Mar: 35
real estate: 276
recompression: 444
recreational vehicles: 433
religion: 421
rental cars: 433-435
resorts, all-inclusive: 323, 445
Restaurant Laja: 25, 85
restaurants: 448; see also food, specific place
roadside assistance: 432
road trip itinerary: 16-20
rock art: see archaeological sights
rock climbing: Cañon de Guadalupe 62, 112;
    Tajo 61; Tecate 56
romance: 27
Rosarito: 12, 24, 31, 45-50
Rupestres: 62, 112, 114, 122
Ruta del Vino: 25, 64, 81-85
RV parks: 446; see also specific place

S

safety: 453-456
San Antonio: 19, 292
San Bartolo: 19, 293
San Borja: 126, 136
sand dunes: 144, 204, 377
sand falls: 22, 348
San Felipe: 13, 112, 114-124
San Francisquito: 146
San Ignacio: 17, 20, 155-163
San Isidro: 180
San Javier: 13, 18, 26, 184, 203
San José del Cabo: 14, 19, 21, 26, 287, 309-332
San Marcos: 168
San Miguel: 52
San Quintín: 16, 20, 95-98
Santa Agueda: 169

Santa Inés: 175
Santa Rosalía: 17, 163-169
Santa Rosalillita: 136
Santiago: 293-297
Santiago Town Plaza: 262, 295
Santuario de Cactus: 291
San Vicente: 89
scams, gas station: 454
scooter rentals: 79
scuba diving: see diving
sea creatures, poisonous: 455
sea kayaking: general discussion 442-443;
    Agua Verde 204; Bahía Concepción 176,
    180; Bahía de los Angeles 130, 133; Bahía
    Pulmo 281; Cabo San Lucas 28, 351; island
    hopping itineraries 20; kayak fishing 270;
    La Paz 230-231; Loreto 190; Los Islotes 225;
    Mogote Peninsula 222; Mulegé 171; Playa del
    Amor 345; Pulmo Bay 283; Todos Santos
    391
sea lions: Canal de las Ballenas 131; Finisterra
    (Land's End) 345; Isla Angel de la Guarda
    131; Islas Los Coronados 45; Islas San Benito
    153; Islas Santa Inés 171; La Paz 22; Los
    Islotes 225; Punta Lobos 389
Sea of Cortez: general discussion 14, 19;
    environmental issues 282; geography 406;
    watersports 130; weather 15
sea turtles: 126, 131, 256, 377, 413
senior travelers: 453
Sergio's Sportfishing Center: 25, 69
Shell Island: 122
shopping: see arts and crafts; specific place
Sierra de Guadalupe: 168
Sierra de Juárez: 61, 86, 112
Sierra de la Laguna: 14, 289-300, 380
Sierra de San Francisco: 156
Sierra de San Francisco rock art: 139, 159-160
Sierra de San Pedro Mártir: 92-94
siesta: 451
1697: 25, 199
skating: 381
skydiving: 353
snorkeling: general discussion 13, 444; Bahía
    Concepción 17, 176; Bahía de la Ventana
    254-255; Bahía de los Frailes 286-287;
    Bahía Pulmo 281; Bahías Chileno and Santa
    María 333; Cabo Pulmo 21; Cabo San Lucas
    28; costs 228, 349; El Caimancito 220; El
    Cardonal 266; Isla Espíritu Santo 224; Isla
    San Marcos 168; La Paz 227-230; Los Islotes
    225; Mulegé 170; Playa Balandra 220; Playa
    Las Viudas (Widows Beach) 333; Playa

Palmilla 333; Pulmo reef 283; Punta Chivato 176; Punta Perico 260; Punta Pescadero 264-265; Roca Pelicano 345; San José del Cabo 315
soccer: 36, 55
Spanish conquest: 214, 414
spas: Bahía de la Ventana 256; Cabo San Lucas 353; Ensenada 70; La Paz 234; Las Rocas Resort and Spa 50; Loreto 193; Los Barriles 271; Los Cabos Corridor 335; Rancho La Puerta 56; recommended 27; Rosarito 47; San José del Cabo 316; Todos Santos 391; West Cape 381
sportfishing: *see* fishing
sports: 35; *see also specific place*
spring break: 118
stand-up paddling: 255
study abroad: 451
Sunset da Mona Lisa: 26, 339
surfing: general discussion 443; Bahía Magdalena 209; Bahía San Juanico (Scorpion Bay) 180, 181; Bahía Santa Rosalillita 137; Bahía Tortugas 151; Cabo San Lucas 351; East Cape 269; El Sauzal 52; Ensenada 70; Isla Natividad 153; La Fonda 51; Los Cabos Corridor 333; Mexican Surf Fiesta 71; Open Doors break 153; Playa Costa Azul 314; Playa Los Cerritos 379; Playa San Pedrito (Playa Las Palmas) 380; Playa San Pedro 380; Puerto San Isidro 88; Punta Abreojos 150; Punta Gorda 289; Punta Prieta 152; Punta San Jacinto 90-91; Punta Santa Rosalillita 137; Rosarito 47; San Antonio del Mar 89; San José del Cabo 26, 315; San Miguel 52; San Quintín 96; Santo Tomás 87; Todos Santos 391; West Cape 381
swimming: Bahías Chileno and Santa María 333; Cabo San Lucas 344; Cañon de la Zorra 297; Playa Costa Azul 314; Playa El Tecolote 221; Playa Las Viudas (Widows Beach) 333; Playa Los Cerritos 379; Playa Palmilla 333; Playa Punta Colorada 220; Playa San Pedrito (Playa Las Palmas) 380; Tecate 56; Unidad Deportiva CREA 36; Villa del Faro 287; West Cape 381; *see also specific place*

T
Tailhunter Bar & FUBAR Cantina: 23, 235
Taxco: 28, 355
taxis: 429
Tecate: 12, 16, 20, 31, 45, 52-62
telephone services: 459-460
temperatures: 14

tequila: 37
Tequila Restaurant: 26, 325
theft: 455
Theory Café: 28, 369
Tijuana: 12, 20, 24, 29-45
time: 458, 459
timeshares, Cabo San Lucas: 358-359
tipping: 457
Todos Santos: 14, 19, 23, 28, 385-404
Tomas Spangler gallery: 28, 356
tourism: 215
tourist documents: 437
tourist information: 458
tours: ATV 270; costs 193; Laguna San Ignacio 162-163; La Paz recreational 234; Loreto 193; Mulegé 171; San Ignacio 156; San José del Cabo 316; Sierra de la Laguna 380; Sierra de San Pedro Mártir 94; snorkeling 350; Tijuana 36; Todos Santos 392; Volcán las Tres Virgenes 160; wine country 84; *see also specific place*
transportation: 15, 424-437
travel clubs: 458
Tropicana Bar and Grill: 26, 326

UV
UNESCO sites: 147, 190, 282, 291
vacation rentals: 446
Valle de Guadalupe: 81-86
Valle del Guadalupe Wine Country: 61
Valle de los Cirios: 126, 128
Valle de los Gigantes: 13, 101, 122
Valle de Santo Tomás: 64, 88
vegetation: 408-410
vehicle permits: 428
veterinarians: 331
Villa del Faro: 287
Villa del Palmar Loreto: 204
Villa Jesus María: 137
Villa Montefiori: 84
Viña de Liceaga: 81
violence: 46
Vizcaíno Peninsula: 147-154
Volcán las Tres Virgenes: 160

WXYZ
Wall, The: 13, 137
waterfalls: Arroyo San Bartolo 293; Cañon de Guadalupe 62, 112; Cañon de la Zorra 296; Santiago 296; Sierra de la Laguna 14; Sierra de San Pedro Mártir 94
water slides: 56
weather: 14

weddings, destination: 337
West Cape: 14, 19, 373-385
Westin Los Cabos: 27, 337
whale sharks: 131
whale-watching: Bahía Magdalena 23, 184, 206-208; Cabo San Lucas 352; Canal de las Ballenas 131; Ensenada 70; Festival de Ballena Gris (Gray Whale Festival) 208; Guerrero Negro 141-143; Laguna San Ignacio 160-163; La Paz 230; Puerto San Carlos 18, 208; Todos Santos 391; Vizcaíno Peninsula 147
wildlife viewing: Canal de las Ballenas 131; Reserva de la Biósfera Desierto de Vizcaíno 148; Roca Pelicano 345; sea turtles 131, 256, 377, 413; *see also* sea lions; whale-watching
windsurfing: general discussion 443; Bahía de la Ventana 252-254; Bahía de los Angeles 130, 133; Bahía Magdalena 209; Loreto 191; Los Barriles 268; Punta Abreojos 150; Punta Arena 176; Punta Santa Rosalillita 137
wine/wineries: Bodegas de Santo Tomás 69, 88; Cabo San Lucas 356; Ensenada 76-77; Fiesta de la Vendimia Bajacaliforniana 71; history of 83; Ruta del Vino 81-85; tours 84; wine schools 84
women travelers: 452
yoga: 316, 353, 381, 391
Yumano tribes: 103
zoos: 106

List of Maps

Front color maps
Northern Baja: 2-3
Central Baja: 4-5
Southern Baja: 6-7

Discover Baja
chapter divisions map: 13
Best of Baja Road Trip: 17

Tijuana, Rosarito, and Tecate
Tijuana, Rosarito, and Tecate: 31
Tijuana: 33
Avenida Revolución: 35
Rosarito: 46
Tecate: 53

Ensenada to El Rosario
Ensenada to El Rosario: 65
Ensenada: 67
Downtown Ensenada: 68
Valle de Guadalupe and the Ruta del Vino: 82
Parque Nacional Sierra San Pedro Mártir: 92
Valle and Bahía de San Quintín: 95

Mexicali to San Felipe
Mexicali to San Felipe: 102
Mexicali: 104-105
San Felipe: 115

Desierto Central to Bahía de los Angeles
Desierto Central to Bahía de los Angeles: 127
Bahía de los Angeles: 131
Bahía de los Angeles and Vicinity: 132

Guerrero Negro to Bahía Concepción
Guerrero Negro to Bahía Concepción: 140
Guerrero Negro: 141
Isla Cedros: 153
Isla Natividad: 154
San Ignacio: 156
Santa Rosalía: 164
Isla San Marcos: 168
Mulegé: 170
Bahía Concepción: 177
Bahía Coyote: 179

Loreto and Bahía Magdalena
Loreto and Bahía Magdalena: 185
Loreto and Vicinity: 186
Loreto: 188
Bahía Magdalena: 207
Puerto San Carlos: 208

La Paz and Vicinity
La Paz and Vicinity: 213
La Paz: 216
Downtown La Paz: 218-219
Beaches and Islands near La Paz: 221
Isla Espíritu Santo, Isla Partida, and Los Islotes: 223
La Ventana and El Sargento: 253
Bahía de La Ventana: 254

The East Cape and the Sierra de la Laguna
The East Cape and the Sierra de la Laguna: 263
Bahía de las Palmas and Vicinity: 265
Los Barriles: 267
El Camino Rural Costero: 281
Sierra de la Laguna and Vicinity: 290
Santiago to Miraflores: 294
Sierra de la Laguna Hiking Trails: 298

Los Cabos
Los Cabos: 304-305
San José del Cabo: 310-311
Pueblo La Playa: 313
Cabo San Lucas: 342-343

The West Cape and Todos Santos
The West Cape and Todos Santos: 375
Cabo Falso to Playa Migriño: 377
El Pescadero and Vicinity: 379
Todos Santos: 386
Todos Santos Detail: 389

Background
Sebastián Vizcaíno Expeditions: 414
Missions (1697-1856): 416
Amerindians of Baja California: 421

Acknowledgments

This edition of *Moon Baja* was written while watching the downwinder parade at Bahía La Ventana; hiking trails at sunrise at Rancho La Puerta (then sneaking donuts in Tecate); snorkeling with whale sharks in the Bay of La Paz and touching gray whales in a Pacific lagoon; eating *aguachile* with the Baja Expeditions camp staff; reconnecting with old friends in Todos Santos; enjoying panoramic views and a moonlight spa at Los Colibris; finding scorpions at night with black lights; enduring an arctic freeze in Loreto; slurping oysters on the half-shell moments after they were harvested from the sea; surfing on Christmas morning, then eating fresh-caught corvina for Christmas dinner; celebrating the New Year with friends in Los Frailes; tasting made-in-Baja Baron Balch'é; trying (unsuccessfully) to find a beach in Baja Sur where a four-year-old could dig for clams; and serving our kids *papas rellenas* and *horchata* many meals in a row.

Special thanks to these Baja aficionados for their insight and hospitality: Pablo, Carmel, and Lucas in Los Frailes; the Hatler family and Anna at Palapas Ventana; Jim Tolbert in San José del Cabo; Allessandra and Enrico, Sergio and Bryan in Todos Santos; Emily Evans, José Sanchez, and the Baja Expeditions staff; Aida Alibegovic at Rancho La Puerta; Beto and Jeannine Perez, Adriana Torres, and Ana Gloria Benziger in Loreto.

My dear friends Deborah Claymon and Susan Harper were enthusiastic travel companions who adapted well to the breakneck pace of guidebook research and reminded me what it's like to experience Baja for the first time. My husband Paul Itoi offered endless hours of support, both on the road and back at home. Avalon Travel's Leah Gordon, Albert Angulo, and Domini Dragoone worked their magic once again. Thank you to all who helped to shape to this edition.

www.moon.com

DESTINATIONS | ACTIVITIES | BLOGS | MAPS | BOOKS

MOON.COM is ready to help plan your next trip! Filled with fresh trip ideas and strategies, author interviews, informative travel blogs, a detailed map library, and descriptions of all the Moon guidebooks, Moon.com is all you need to get out and explore the world—or even places in your own backyard. While at Moon.com, sign up for our monthly e-newsletter for updates on new releases, travel tips, and expert advice from our on-the-go Moon authors. As always, when you travel with Moon, expect an experience that is uncommon and truly unique.

KEEP UP WITH MOON ON FACEBOOK AND TWITTER
JOIN THE MOON PHOTO GROUP ON FLICKR

MAP SYMBOLS

▦	Expressway	◖	Highlight	✗	Airfield	⚲	Golf Course
	Primary Road	○	City/Town	✈	Airport	🅿	Parking Area
	Secondary Road	◉	State Capital	▲	Mountain	🔺	Archaeological Site
- - - - -	Unpaved Road	⊛	National Capital	✛	Unique Natural Feature	♠	Church
- - - - -	Trail	★	Point of Interest			⛽	Gas Station
⋯⋯⋯	Ferry	•	Accommodation	🐟	Waterfall	◌	Glacier
▭▭▭	Railroad	▾	Restaurant/Bar	♠	Park		Mangrove
	Pedestrian Walkway	▪	Other Location	▣	Trailhead		Reef
▥	Stairs	⋀	Campground	✗	Skiing Area		Swamp

CONVERSION TABLES

$°C = (°F - 32) / 1.8$
$°F = (°C \times 1.8) + 32$
1 inch = 2.54 centimeters (cm)
1 foot = 0.304 meters (m)
1 yard = 0.914 meters
1 mile = 1.6093 kilometers (km)
1 km = 0.6214 miles
1 fathom = 1.8288 m
1 chain = 20.1168 m
1 furlong = 201.168 m
1 acre = 0.4047 hectares
1 sq km = 100 hectares
1 sq mile = 2.59 square km
1 ounce = 28.35 grams
1 pound = 0.4536 kilograms
1 short ton = 0.90718 metric ton
1 short ton = 2,000 pounds
1 long ton = 1.016 metric tons
1 long ton = 2,240 pounds
1 metric ton = 1,000 kilograms
1 quart = 0.94635 liters
1 US gallon = 3.7854 liters
1 Imperial gallon = 4.5459 liters
1 nautical mile = 1.852 km

MOON BAJA

Avalon Travel
a member of the Perseus Books Group
1700 Fourth Street
Berkeley, CA 94710, USA
www.moon.com

Editor: Leah Gordon
Series Manager: Kathryn Ettinger
Copy Editor: Jade Chan
Graphics Coordinator: Sean Bellows
Production Coordinator: Domini Dragoone
Cover Designer: Domini Dragoone
Map Editor: Albert Angulo
Cartographers: Kaitlin Jaffe, Chris Hendrick
Indexer: Rachel Kuhn

ISBN: 978-1-59880-889-6
ISSN: 1098-6685

Printing History
1st Edition – 1992
9th Edition – October 2011
5 4 3 2 1

Front cover photo: Inside the tube of a backlit breaking wave, San José del Cabo, © Mark A. Johnson/Getty Images

Title page photo: © Nikki Goth Itoi

Front color photos: pg. 8, 9 (center), 10, 11 (top and bottom left), 18 (bottom), 19, 21, 22, 24, 26, & 28 © Nikki Goth Itoi; pg. 9 (left), 11 (bottom right), & 23 © Paul Itoi; pg. 9 (right), 12, & 15 © Neil Kraft; pg. 14 © Carmel Tsabar; pg. 16 Courtesy of www.discoverbajacalifornia.com; pg. 18 (top) Courtesy of Gemma Inn; pg. 25 Courtesy of Las Cabañas de Loreto.

Printed in Canada by Friesens

KEEPING CURRENT

If you have a favorite gem you'd like to see included in the next edition, or see anything that needs updating, clarification, or correction, please drop us a line. Send your comments via email to feedback@moon.com, or use the address above.